Negro Heritage Library

NEGRO HERITAGE LIBRARY

VOLUME I

The

American Negro

Reference Book

Edited by JOHN P. DAVIS

EDUCATIONAL HERITAGE, INC., YONKERS

Chicago — New York — Philadelphia — Los Angeles — San Francisco

The American Negro Reference Book
edited by John P. Davis

© 1966 by Prentice-Hall, Inc., Englewood Cliffs, N. J.

Negro Heritage Library editions published by
arrangement with Prentice-Hall, Inc., Publishers

Copyright © 1966 by Educational Heritage, Inc.
Library of Congress Catalogue Card No. 66-25013

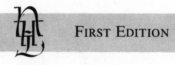 FIRST EDITION

Designed by Harold Franklin

Printed in the United States of América
by American Book-Stratford Press—New York

A NOTE FROM THE PUBLISHERS

THE NEGRO HERITAGE LIBRARY is Educational Heritage's response to a major historical, social and psychological necessity of our times. There is little question that the Negro has emerged as the dominant figure on the American scene today, and yet he remains a stranger to most white Americans and often to himself as well.

Too many Americans, Negro and white, have scant knowledge of the fact that the Negro has a proud heritage of notable achievement. This ignorance—and euphemisms serve no valid purpose here—is easily explained. The standard texts on the history of America and the Western world, the very sources from which we have drawn our knowledge of Man and Society, have consistently excluded the Negro's contribution. I submit that this omission has been a significant factor in the perpetuation of white prejudice and the distortion of Negro self-esteem. An honest reckoning of the Negro's contribution to the building of our society is long overdue.

Accordingly, we have set ourselves the combined tasks of:

strengthening the Negro's confidence and assurance
that he *has* historical roots deep
within the soil of Western civilization, and

restoring to History those missing pages whose absence
has crippled America's ability to understand the Negro,
hence retarding fulfillment of the American ideal of equal justice
to all men, regardless of race, creed, color or national origin.

This can only be done by a truthful and accurate recounting of the Negro's remarkable story. It is our hope that the content of these volumes will serve this high purpose.

Table of Contents

Preface

The purpose of *The American Negro Reference Book* is to bring together in a single volume a reliable summary of current information on the main aspects of Negro life in America, and to present this information in sufficient historical depth to provide the reader with a true perspective. In the footnotes to the text and following most of the chapters are bibliographical references to help the student go more deeply into subjects covered here. At the same time, a full index with numerous cross-references makes possible the use of this book as a convenient spot reference tool to specific questions about the American Negro.

It is hoped that *The American Negro Reference Book* will have many uses. The book as a whole is designed to give the persevering reader a fully-dimensioned picture of the Negro within the context of past and present American Society. Certain chapters read together furnish the student of social sciences or the humanities a rounded discussion of the Negro in these fields. For example, the chapters on "The Negro Population in the United States" (Taeuber and Taeuber), "Patterns of Employment of Negro Men and Women (Ginzberg and Hiestand), and, "The Negro in the National Economy" (Brimmer) form a unit which provides an analysis of the socioeconomic characteristics of the Negro. Or reading the chapters "The Negro and American Music" (George), "Blues, Jazz and the Negro" (Jones), "The Negro in Fine Arts" (Brown), "The Negro and American Entertainment" (Hughes), and, "The Negro Contribution to American Letters" (Bontemps) will give anyone interested in American culture fresh insights into the Negro contribution of this culture. A look at the Table of Contents will soon suggest other useful groupings of the material.

There are books within the book which hold special interest. Dr. John Hope Franklin's "Brief History of the Negro in the United States" is one example. New York State Senator Constance Baker Motley's "The Legal Status of the Negro in the United States" is almost by itself a handbook on civil rights. Other chapters cover in some depth many facets of the Negro experience in the United States.

Changes in the status of the Negro in the United States have occurred and are occurring with such rapidity and over so wide a range that it is impossible to speak with scientific finality about any significant feature of Negro life in America. All the reader may fairly hope to find here is an historical appraisal (brought up to date) of the directions in which Negroes are moving in American society; with possibly here and there a reasoned prediction as to future trends. Rather than weakness, this is, perhaps the book's greatest strength. For in charting the trend of advantages and disadvantages facing the Negro in his search for full citizenship rights, it may well be providing the reader with the most meaningful benchmark that can be found to measure social progress.

Twenty-four scholars have contributed twenty-two articles which make up the main body of material in this book. A list of these contributors and their scholarly interests will be found on page ix. Each of the contributions has been read by one or more review consultants who, while not responsible for the final text presented here, have made valuable criticisms of the material. In listing their names below we make public acknowledgment of our sincere thanks:

Dr. Morroe Berger, professor of sociology, Princeton University; Mr. Arna Bontemps, head librarian, Fisk University; Dr. Lewis A. Coser, professor of sociology, Brandeis University; Dr. W. Allison Davis, professor of education, University of Chicago; Mrs. Dina Epstein, scholar in the field of musical Americana; Mr. James C. Evans, counselor, Office of the Assistant Secretary of Defense; Judge William H. Hastie, United States Circuit Court of Appeals; Dr. Dale Hiestand, assistant professor of economics, Graduate

*Negro Heritage Library Editor's Note: In order that the Negro Heritage Library Edition of *The American Negro Reference Book* would conform to the format established for other volumes in the series, we have added illustrations and bound the work in two volumes. However, the chapters follow their original sequence and the text has not been altered.

School of Business, Columbia University; Dr. Hylan G. Lewis, director of the Child-Rearing Study, Health and Welfare Council of the District of Columbia; Dr. Vernon McKay, professor of African Studies, Advanced School of International Studies, Johns Hopkins University; Professor Charles Page, Head of the Department of Sociology and Anthropology, Princeton University; Dr. Ira DeA Reid, professor of sociology, Haverford College; Dr. Gregory P. Stone, associate professor of psychology, University of Minnesota; Mr. Robert L. Teague, correspondent on the news staff of the National Broadcasting Company, formerly sports writer on *The New York Times*; Dr. Charles H. Thompson, professor of education, Howard University; Dr. Glenn W. Trimble, Home Missions Research Department, National Council of the Churches of Christ in the USA; Dr. Caroline F. Ware, member of the President's Commission on the Status of Women; Dr. Lauris B. Whitman, executive director, Bureau of Research and Survey, National Council of the Churches of Christ in the USA; Dr. Vincent H. Whitney, chairman, Department of Sociology, University of Pennsylvania, and, representative for Asia, Demographic Division, The Population Council; and, Mr. Hale Woodruff, professor of art education, New York University.

Since this book is sponsored by the Phelps-Stokes Fund it will not be amiss to add a brief word about the sponsor. The Fund was created in 1911 through a bequest in the will of Miss Caroline Phelps Stokes. From its beginning it has sought to stimulate objective study of the American Negro, to aid and encourage the publications which will be of value to an understanding of the Negro at home and abroad. The Fund gave financial assistance to the late Dr. Monroe N. Work for the publication of his monumental *Bibliography of the Negro* (1928). It sponsored exploratory work of the late Dr. W. E. B. DuBois and Dr. Guy B. Johnson of the University of North Carolina which led to the publication of *Encyclopedia of the Negro—Preparatory Volume* (1945). The Fund has sought—especially in this period of profound social change in the life of the Negro in the United States—to encourage a broad program of American Negro studies. The present volume is evidence of the Fund's continued commitment to this goal. We hope to see *The American Negro Reference Book* become the first volume in *The American Negro Reference Shelf*, containing a whole array of timely books by scholars of proven merit. We hope—in time—to see evolve from these monographs an *Encyclopedia of the American Negro*.

The Phelps-Stokes Fund is deeply indebted to a foundation for a generous grant which has made possible its work in this field. The Fund for the Advancement of Education made monies available to "explore the need for and feasibility of a handbook/or encyclopedia on the American Negro." With this help a survey was made of the need of public libraries for current materials on the Negro; and conferences were held at which a number of experts gave wise counsel in the development of the project. To The Fund for the Advancement of Education the Phelps-Stokes Fund wishes publicly to express its thanks.

Finally, the editor would exercise his prerogative of acknowledging his own debts. Sincere thanks are most certainly due the Trustees and Officers of the Fund for their confidence in the project; and warm appreciation must be extended to the entire staff of the Fund for the day-to-day encouragement and cooperation it has given the editor during the preparation of this book. A special debt of gratitude is owing to the Chairman of the Board of Trustees, Mr. I. N. P. Stokes; to the President of the Fund, Dr. Frederick D. Patterson; and, to Trustees, Dr. Ralph J. Bunche and Dr. Carroll V. Newsom. From the beginning they have seen the great need for and high purpose of this book and have unstintingly shared their time and wisdom to see it through.

The Editor

List of Tables

Chapter 3/
The Negro in American Agriculture

Chapter 4/
Employment Patterns of Negro Men and Women

Chapter 5/
The Negro in the National Economy

VOLUME I

The

American Negro

Reference Book

chapter 1

John Hope Franklin

A Brief History

of the Negro

in the United States

John Hope Franklin. Professor of American History, University of Chicago, Chicago, Illinois. Formerly Chairman of the Department of History, Brooklyn College, Brooklyn, New York; and William Pitt Professor of American History and Institutions, Cambridge University, England. Author of *From Slavery to Freedom, The Militant South, Reconstruction After the Civil War, Emancipation Proclamation* and other books.

NEW WORLD ADVENTURE

Negro Pioneers in the New World

It is significant that the first Negroes in the New World were not from Africa but from Europe. Their involvement in the European exploration of the New World in the fifteenth and sixteenth centuries is an important commentary on the connections that had developed between Europe and Africa by that time. As early as the fourteenth century, if not earlier, Europeans had begun to bring Africans into Europe. As the Spanish and Portuguese made contacts with the coast of Africa, going as far as the Gulf of Guinea, they began to appreciate the possibility of using Africans as an important source of labor for European ports, businesses and homes. Thus, they took Africans to Europe and made servants of them, justifying this invasion of human rights by declaring that Africans would have the opportunity to cast off their heathenism and become Christians.

It was not long before Europeans were selling Negro servants in their home markets, as well as other African imports. Soon the slave trade came to be accepted as an important part of European commerce. Spanish and Portuguese traders appreciated the economic advantages afforded by the African slave trade; and by the time Portugal's remarkable Prince Henry died in 1460 the trade in black men had become more than a passing fancy. Europeans were becoming accustomed to having Negroes do their work; and already they were looking into the possibility of using them in other ways. It was only natural, therefore, that as Europeans turned their eyes toward the New World they would enlist the services of the Africans to help further the cause of Christianity as well as to aid in their plans for domination of the New World.

There was never a time in the Europeans' exploration and exploitation of the New World when they were without the services of some black Europeans. The claim that Pedro Alonso Niño of Columbus' crew was a Negro has never been disproved; and if he was indeed a Negro he performed more than yeoman service for the Admiral of the Ocean Sea. In 1501 Spain lifted her ban on the taking of Negroes to the New World, and after that time Negroes almost invariably accompanied Spanish explorers and settlers. There were at least thirty Negroes with Balboa when he discovered the Pacific Ocean in 1513. When Hernando Cortes conquered Mexico in 1519 he had several Negroes with him, one of whom planted and harvested the first wheat crop in the New World. Alvarado, the intrepid explorer of Equatorial South America, had two hundred Negroes with him when he arrived at Quito; and in his Peruvian expedition Pizarro took several Negroes along. Indeed, they were the ones who took their leader into the cathedral after he was murdered.

When the Spanish and Portuguese explorers moved into what is now the United States, Negroes were with them. They accompanied Narváez on his expedition in 1527 and were with Cabeza de Vaca in the exploration of the Southwest. Perhaps the outstanding Negro explorer was Estevanico, Little Stephen, who went deep into the interior of the Southwest. When he encountered hostile Indians, he insisted that he was the emissary of white men; but they killed him, believing him to be an imposter. Even so, he had paved the way for the conquest of the Southwest by the Spaniards.

The French also had their Negro servants when they undertook their explorations of the New World. In the Canadian expeditions, Negroes were with the Jesuit missionaries. As the French opened up the Mississippi Valley in the seventeenth century, Negroes assisted in the settlement of the region. At the places that were later to be known as St. Louis and New Orleans, French Negroes helped plant the flag of France and establish the culture that was to make an indelible mark on the interior of the United States.

Exploitation of the rich natural resources of the New World was the primary aim of the Europeans. For this they needed an abundance of labor. Soon it became obvious that Indians would not do. The great susceptibility of Indians to the diseases of the Europeans, their firm commitment to a much simpler economic system, and their determination to escape the wrath and inhumanity of the Europeans ruled them out as a permanent and satisfactory source of labor. Europeans not only wanted more tractable servants, but they also wanted them in greater quantities than the Indians could provide. They used Indians to the extent possible, but they soon turned to other possible sources.

Europeans did not at first regard Negroes as the solution. They first considered the poorer Europeans. In the first half of the seventeenth century, these landless, penniless whites were brought over in considerable numbers. Some were voluntary indentured servants, others were prisoners working out their fines, and still other powerless Europeans, especially the English, were kidnaped and sold into servitude. As Eric Williams has indicated in his *Capitalism and Slavery*, the horrors that the poor whites of Europe experiencd were as great as any experienced by any group in the later years of the African slave trade.

The English gradually came to realize that white servants would not do, either. Whites tended to become restive, and when they ran away it was extremely difficult to identify them as servants bound to a particular master. Some of them, conscious of their rights as Englishmen, began to sue their masters for illegal detention. Even if these white servants worked well, their terms of service were not indefinite; and the task of recruiting new white workers was at best irksome. Englishmen soon came to realize that Negroes presented few of the difficulties they were encountering with whites. Negroes could be purchased outright, and their years of servitude would be for life, making them cheaper in the long run. Since they came from a pagan land, moreover, with no exposure to the principles of Christian brotherhood, they could be subjected to the most rigid discipline with impunity. And the masters could rationalize that they were giving Negroes advantages of Christianity to which they would not be exposed otherwise. More and more, this appeared to Europeans to be the solution; and finally they embraced it with enthusiasm.

The Beginnings of the Slave Trade

In 1517 the great Spanish bishop, Bartolomé de Las Casas, took a step that greatly encouraged the establishment of slavery in the New World. He had noticed with apparent horror the wholesale destruction of the Indians by the Spaniards in the effort to force them to work. Convinced that the Indians could never become good slaves and hoping, at any rate, to make good Christians out of them, he persuaded Charles V to encourage immigration to the New World by permitting Spaniards to import twelve slaves each. This step may be regarded as the formal opening of the slave trade to the New World. In subsequent years an increasing number of Africans was imported into the Spanish colonies, at times by Dutch traders, at other times by Portuguese, French or English. Soon the trade had become a huge, profitable enterprise. By 1540 the annual importation of Negro slaves into the West Indies had reached ten thousand.

The trade continued, and by the seventeenth and eighteenth centuries it was largely in the hands of Dutch, French and English companies. In 1621 the Dutch West India Company was organized with a monopoly both of the African trade and of trade with the Dutch colonies in the New World. This company then challenged the right of the Portuguese to trade on the coast of Africa, and by the middle of the century it had gained a substantial foothold there. Perhaps the English would have challenged the Dutch, but they were preoccupied with civil wars at home. Soon the Dutch slavers were visiting the ports of almost all the American colonies, and were even engaged in trade with the French and Spanish colonies.

The trade was so profitable that the English were not content to see the Dutch reap all the benefits. The Dutch wars with France and England, moreover, generally weakened the position of the leading slave trading power, giving the English an opportunity to make a bid for at least a portion of the rich trade. Although the French would make a rather feeble effort to enter the picture, they were never a match for the English who seemed to be in the ascendancy in this area as well as in others.

English interest in Africa and the slave trade was by no means new when she made a bid for leadership in the second half of the seventeenth century. Before the end of the reign of Henry VII in 1509 traders from Britain were establishing connections along the Guinea coast and at other important points in Africa. England contented herself by trading in gold, ivory and spices until 1562, when Captain John Hawkins broke the Portuguese monopoly in Africa and the Spanish monopoly in the New World by taking slaves from Portuguese Africa to Spanish America. It thus became easy for James I in 1618 to grant a charter to the Company of Adventurers of London, trading into parts of Africa which had control over the West Coast trade. In 1631 Charles I granted a group of traders a 31-year monopoly of the trade in Guinea, Benin and Angola. This became the pattern by which the English claimed a large share of the African trade in human flesh.

Competition for the slave trade was keen not only among nations but also among trading companies within countries. In England, for example, many individuals and organizations, including the powerful East India Company, were interested in the African slave trade. As the demand for slaves in the New World increased and as conditions in Europe remained unsettled, it seemed that any group might have a chance to reap some benefits from the slave trade. The restoration in England brought with it a semblance of stability as well as renewed activity in Africa. In 1672 the King chartered the Royal African Company, which held a monopoly for a decade, and which dominated the slave trade for another fifty years. It assumed the responsibility for driving the Dutch and the French out of

West Africa, and its efforts were crowned with considerable success. It held sway until 1731 when, with its margin of profits in the slave trade dwindling, it began to devote its attention to ivory and gold dust.

What the Royal African Company failed to do in driving the other European powers from Africa, the English succeeded in doing in the eighteenth century. In a series of wars the English had defeated the Dutch, thus dealing a powerful blow to Dutch prestige in Africa. Then the English defeated the French, thereby securing in 1713 the exclusive right to carry slaves to the Spanish colonies. With a strengthened navy and almost unlimited resources England could now undertake to provide not only her own colonies with slaves but those of the other European nations as well. As English hegemony in the New World became secure, the slave trade provided an important source of strength and wealth.

Slave Trading as Big Business

In the eighteenth century the African slave trade became an important economic institution; and since the English dominated it, their slave-trading practices became standard. Slavers left European ports laden with goods to be used in the trade: cotton textiles, brass, pewter, beads, gunpowder, whiskey, brandy and rum. They proceeded to the trading posts maintained by the company or the country, where the factors in charge maintained contacts with key Africans. The factors secured permission from the chief who was plied with gifts, to trade on his domain. From this point on it was not too difficult to round up some Africans—slaves of the chiefs or captives in war —to be sold. The price varied, of course, depending on the age and condition of the slave, the period of trading and the location of the post.

It was not at all unusual for a slaver to make calls at a number of posts before a full complement of slaves was secured for the voyage to the New World. On occasion it was necessary for a slaver to call at four or five posts before securing a sufficient number of slaves. Once that was done, the captain of the slaver had to make certain that he had sufficient provisions to make the crossing to America. Foodstuffs, water and medicines were indispensable to a successful voyage. If any room was left, spices and ivory were regarded as certain to bring revenue which the captain might not even have to report to the company that had engaged him.

Perhaps the most poignant aspect of the transaction was the resistance that the slaves put up to their forced sale and incarceration on the floating prison. Fierce wars broke out between tribes when the members of one sought to capture members of another for the purpose of selling them to traders. Even after the slaves were sold and chained, it was necessary to guard them heavily lest they make a futile attempt to escape and injure or kill themselves in the process. One trader remarked that the Negroes were "so wilful and loth to leave their own country that they have often leap'd out of the canoes, boat and ship, into the sea, and kept under water till they were drowned." They preferred a watery grave or to be devoured by sharks to enslavement in some faraway land.

Mankind has experienced few tortures as ghoulish and uncivilized as the transportation of slaves from Africa to the New World, known as the "Middle Passage." The men were chained two by two, the right wrist and ankle of one to the left wrist and ankle of another. They were then sent to the hold or to the "house" that the sailors had built on deck. On some ships the women and children were allowed to wander about almost anywhere by day, the women being regarded as fair prey for the sailors; but at night they were sent to rooms other than those occupied by the men. There were two schools of thought among captains of slavers regarding the loading of slaves. The "loose packers" believed that by giving the slaves a bit more room and better food, they reduced the mortality and could get a better price for healthier slaves in the New World. The "tight packers" argued that although the loss of life might be greater if they started out with larger numbers, they were likely to arrive with more and thereby get a larger profit from the cargo.

Regardless of the point of view of the captains, most ships transported many more Negroes than could be adequately accommodated; and this is undoubtedly responsible for the high incidence of disease and death during the Middle Passage. Usually they were packed in so close that they had no room even to sit upright during the entire voyage. In some instances they were packed close together like books on a shelf. Remarking on a situation such as this, one contemporary said, "The poor creatures, thus cramped, are likewise in irons for the most part which makes it difficult for them to turn or move or attempt to rise or to lie down without hurting themselves or each other. Every morning, perhaps, more instances than one are found of the living and the dead fastened together."

Because of the enormous profits made by some slavers the "tight loaders" gained the ascendancy. Despite the death from a variety of maladies, it was not unusual for a ship carrying 250 slaves to net as much as £7,000 on one voyage. Profits of 100 percent were not uncommon for Liverpool merchants. As a result there emerged in England and, to a lesser extent, on the Continent a class of wealthy men whose new position was firmly based on the trade in men. They gained not only economic power but also political influence and were in a position to resist for many years the efforts of the humanitarians to control the slave trade and, ultimately, to put a stop to it.

There is no way of knowing how many Negroes were taken in Africa and sent on to slavery in the New World. In the period between 1783 and 1793 Liverpool traders alone were responsible for sending out some 300,000 slaves, while in the following decade they were certainly responsible for as many if not more. It has been estimated that 2,750,000 were sent in the seventeenth century, 7 million in the eighteenth, and 4 million in the nineteenth. Millions died en route, and millions who arrived were permanently disabled. Millions arrived and were sold into slavery. Whatever the total number, whether ten or fifteen millions or more, it is a remarkable commentary on the profitableness of the trade as well as on the brutality and ruthlessness of the Europeans who were willing to enjoy the luxury and wealth afforded by such an operation.

Early Slave Practices

African slavery thus solved the labor problem for Europeans in the New World. The seventeenth century, which witnessed the coming of age of the slave trade, also witnessed the rapid growth of colonial enterprise in the New World. In the Caribbean, where the European foothold was strongest, one sees the evolution of the institution of slavery as the vehicle for the development of the earliest major economic enterprise on this side of the Atlantic.

Negroes were first used on the tobacco plantations of the Caribbean islands. As the European tobacco market became glutted, the Caribbean planters turned to sugar and other staples for their money crops. As sugar became a major crop, the importation of Negroes into the Caribbean began in earnest. In 1640 there were only a few hundred Negroes in Barbados. By 1645, after the new sugar plantations had proved themselves, there were six thousand slaves there. By the middle of the century the Negro population had increased to twenty thousand. A similar growth in the slave population could be seen on the other Caribbean islands. Indeed, the importation of slaves accelerated to such a degree that by the end of the century, when the demand for slaves on the islands was declining, the importation not only continued but, in some cases, increased.

There were few humanizing influences on the institution of slavery in the West Indies in the seventeenth century. The slaves were "black gold," as their labor produced the profits that made the islands the favorite colonies of the European powers. Many of the landlords were in London or some other European city; and their only interest was in the profits that were increasing annually. The islands were not places of residence, but merely sources of wealth; and the slaves were not human beings, but merely factors in production. Overseers and plantation managers were expected to perform any tasks that increased profits, and this included getting work out of slaves by whatever method seemed necessary. Slaves who offered resistance were to be "broken in," and this meant flogging or any other form of torture that would get results.

Since the Negro population tended to exceed that of the whites, the laws governing the conduct of Negroes were designed to provide a maximum of security for the whites as well as to make the Negroes effective workers. Slaves had few if any rights in the English colonies, while in the French colonies, though they were recognized as persons with souls, conditions were scarcely better. But the laws did not succeed in creating a tractable, docile slave population. There were uprisings in Jamaica, Barbados, Saint Domingue and elsewhere. Groups of Negroes organized themselves into Maroons and defied the whites to attempt to subjugate them. On occasion, therefore, it became necessary for the whites in the Caribbean to resort to the force of arms to keep the Negro slaves in line.

By the end of the seventeenth century the Caribbean was no longer the principal source of wealth of Europe in the New World. Already the Portuguese had Brazil as their main New World colony, while the Spaniards had numerous important colonies in North and South America. The British were turning their attention more and more to their colonies that extended from the Carolinas to Massachusetts; and they were concentrating their attention on the mainland. They began to import slaves from Africa to the mainland and to send many of them from the islands to the mainland. Soon the European powers expected to increase their profits many times over by utilizing the experience they gained in the island colonies to establish a much more elaborate system of plantation slavery in Virginia, the Carolinas and similar mainland colonies than had ever existed in the islands. If there was disappointment over the decline in Jamaica, there was hope for unlimited expansion in Maryland. More and better slaves would make the difference.

COLONIAL SLAVERY

Virginia's Leadership

The twenty Negroes who were put ashore at Jamestown in 1619 by the captain of a Dutch frigate were not slaves in a legal sense. And, at the time, the Virginians seemed not to appreciate the far-reaching significance of the introduction of Negroes into the fledgling colony. These were simply more of the indentured servants; they happened to have been black. They were listed as servants in the census counts of 1623 and 1624; and as late as 1651 some Negroes whose period of service had expired were being assigned land in much the same way as it was being done for whites who had completed their indenture. During its first half-century of existence Virginia had many Negro indentured servants; and the records reveal increasing numbers of free Negroes.

Only after Virginia had failed to satisfy her labor needs with Indians and indentured servants did she give serious thought to the "perpetual servitude" of Negroes. She began to see what her neighbors in the Caribbean had already seen, that Negroes could not easily escape without being identified, that they could be disciplined, even punished, with impunity since they were not Christians, and that the supply seemed inexhaustible. Black labor was precisely what Virginia needed in order to speed up the clearing of the forests and the cultivation of larger and better tobacco crops. All that was missing was the legislative approval of a practice in which many Virginians were already involved.

The actual statutory recognition of slavery in Virginia came in 1661. The status of Negroes already there was not affected if they had completed their indenture and were free. Indeed, the recognition was almost casual and was first indicated in a law directed at white servants: "That in case any English servant shall run away in company with any negroes who are incapable of making satisfaction by addition of time . . . that the English so running away . . . shall serve for the time of said negroes absence as they are to do for their owne. . . ." In the following year Virginia took another step toward slavery by indicating in her laws that children born in the colony would be held bond or free according to the condition of the mother. Some mitigation to the recognition of slavery was intended by the law of 1667 that provided that slaves could be baptized as Christians. In order to protect the institution of slavery, however, the law continued, "the conferring of baptisme doth not alter the condition of the person as to his bondage or freedome." Thus, "diverse masters, freed from this doubt, may more carefully endeavour the propagation of christianity."

At first the Negro population of the colony grew quite slowly. In 1625 there were only twenty-three Negroes there; and as late as the middle of the century scarcely three hundred could be counted. With the chartering of the Royal African Company in 1672 the shipment of slaves into the colony was accelerated. By the end of the century they were being brought in at the rate of more than one thousand per year. It was in the eighteenth century that the Negro population grew at what some Virginians began to view as an alarming rate. In 1708 there were 12,000 Negroes and 18,000 whites. By 1756 there were 120,156 Negroes and 173,316 whites. By that time Negroes outnumbered the whites in many Virginia communities.

Although Virginians greatly appreciated the importance of Negro slave labor in the development of the colony, they soon became apprehensive about such large numbers of Negroes living among the whites. Already whites and Negroes were mixing, and a mulatto population was emerging. There were, moreover, the persistent rumors of conspiracies of rebellion; and many whites feared for their lives. Those who were apprehensive took the lead in attempting to control the importation of slaves, but the commercial interests fought off these attempts with all the resources at their command. For the time being they were successful.

But the fears of insurrection were not groundless. Within two years after the first statutory recognition of slavery, the Negroes of Virginia were showing clear signs of dissatisfaction and had begun to plot rebellion against their masters. In 1687 a group of slaves in the Northern Neck planned an uprising during a funeral, but it was discovered before it could be carried out. Rumors continued, and plots of varying sizes were uncovered. Where there were no plots there was general disobedience and lawlessness. By 1694 the Virginia slaves had become so ungovernable that Governor Andros complained that there was insufficient enforcement of the code which, by that time, had become elaborate enough to cover most activities and relationships of slaves.

The Virginia slave code, borrowing heavily from practices in the Caribbean and serving as a model for other mainland codes, was comprehensive. No slave was permitted to leave the plantation without the written permission of his master. Slaves wandering about without such permits were to be taken up and returned to their masters. Slaves found guilty of murder or rape were to be hanged. For major offenses, such as robbing a house or a store, a slave was to receive sixty lashes and be placed in the pillory where his ears were to be severed from his head. For petty offenses, such as insolence and associating with whites or free Negroes, they were to be whipped, maimed or branded. The docility of which masters boasted was thus achieved through the enactment of an all-inclusive code containing provisions for punishment designed to "break" the most irascible "blacks" in the colony. With the sheriffs, the courts and even the slaveless whites on their side, the masters should have experienced no difficulty in maintaining peace among their slaves.

Slavery in Maryland

While slavery in Maryland was not recognized by law until 1663, the first Negroes introduced into the colony were sold into slavery immediately. As early as 1638 there was reference to slavery in some discussions in the legislature; and in 1641 the governor himself owned a number of slaves. The colonists had no difficulty, therefore, in turning their attention to the problem of the status of Negroes and concluding that legislation was necessary to fix their status as slaves. The law of 1663 was rather drastic. It undertook to reduce all Negroes in the colony to slavery even though some were already free, and it sought to impose the status of slaves on all Negroes to be born in the colony regardless of the status of their mothers. It was not until 1681 that the law was brought in line with established practices by declaring that Negro children of white mothers and children born of free Negro mothers would be free.

The slave population of Maryland was slow to increase, not because of any disinclination on the part of the colonists to own slaves, but because they were not in ample supply during the early years of the colony. This is the principal reason why, during the restoration period, laws were enacted to encourage and facilitate the importation of slaves. In 1671 the legislature declared that the conversion of slaves to Christianity would not affect their status. Masters now felt that they could import African heathens, convert them to Christianity and thus justify the act of holding them in slavery. By the end of the century the importation of slaves was increasing steadily. In 1708 the governor reported that six or seven hundred had been imported during the preceding ten months. By 1750 there were 40,000 Negroes as compared with 100,000 whites.

As in Virginia, the Negroes of Maryland early showed resentment against their status as slaves. In several instances white masters died at the hands of their slaves; and there was more than one case of a Negro cook poisoning her owner. In 1742 seven Negroes were executed for the murder of their master. Others were convicted for committing acts of sabotage such as arson, stealing of property and the brutal treatment of livestock.

The increase in the Negro population and the whites' fear for their own safety led to the enactment of stringent laws covering the conduct and activities of Negroes. In 1659 came the laws relating to the return and treatment of fugitive slaves. Soon there were laws forbidding slaves to deal in stolen goods and liquor, and laws providing for the punishment of free Negroes and slaves found guilty of murder, arson, larceny, association with whites, insolence and going about without permission. Punishment ranged from death to branding and whipping. Enforcement was rigorous, but clemency was not rare. There were numerous examples of intervention on the behalf of accused slaves by masters who, while approving the strict enforcement of the law, would want "on just this occasion" a bit of leniency.

The Carolinas and Georgia

It was a foregone conclusion that slaves would be introduced into the Carolinas as soon as was feasible. After all, four of the proprietors of the colony were members of the Royal Africa Company and fully appreciated the profits that could come from the slave trade. By 1680, moreover, the example of Virginia and Maryland led them to believe that Carolina could become a prosperous colony with plantation slavery as one of the important foundations. Perhaps John Locke had these things in mind when, in his *Fundamental Constitutions*, he wrote, "every freeman of Carolina shall have absolute power and authority over his negro slaves, of what opinion

or religion soever." This sanctioned slavery and protected it against any possible destruction that might have come through the conversion of slaves to Christianity.

Negroes were in the Carolina colony virtually from the beginning. This was undoubtedly the result of the deliberate encouragement of the importation of slaves by the proprietors themselves. In 1663 they offered to the original settlers twenty acres for every Negro man slave and ten acres for every Negro woman slave brought into the colony in the first year. Somewhat smaller incentives were offered for the importation of slaves in subsequent years. Perhaps such legislation had the desired results, for twenty years after the original settlements, the Negro population in the Carolinas was equal to that of the white. By 1715 the Negroes led the whites with 10,500 to 6,250. In 1724 there were three times as many Negroes as whites, and the growth of the Negro population was to continue for decades to come.

As in the other colonies the growth of the Negro population led to the enactment of legislation looking to its control. As early as 1686 the Carolina colony forbade Negroes to engage in any kind of trade; and it enjoined them from leaving their masters' plantation without written authorization. In 1722 white justices were authorized to search Negroes for guns, swords "and other offensive weapons" and to take them unless the Negro could produce a permit less than one month old authorizing him to carry such a weapon. Patrols were given authority to search Negroes and to whip those deemed to be dangerous to peace and good order. Punishments for offenses by slaves were summary and severe.

The Carolinians had not established their controls too soon; for as early as 1711 there were rumors that the Negroes were getting out of hand. In 1720 several slaves were burned alive and others were banished because of implication in a revolt near Charleston. In subsequent years there were other revolts or rumors of revolts. In 1739 the well-known Cato conspiracy twenty miles west of Charleston threw the countryside into a state of terror. After slaves killed two guards in a warehouse and secured arms, they went on a full-scale drive to destroy slavery in that area. Soon, the uprising was put down, but not before thirty whites and forty-four Negroes had lost their lives. Later in the century there were other uprisings, and the general state of affairs led to a full-scale revision of the slave code. Before the Revolution, South Carolina, then divided from North Carolina, had enacted one of the most stringent sets of laws governing slaves to be found in the New World.

Georgia was the only important New World colony established by England in the eighteenth century. In several significant ways it was different from the others: it was to grant no free land titles, permit the use of no alcoholic beverages and to allow no slavery. From the time of its establishment in 1733, however, each of these proscriptions was subjected to enormous pressure on the part of the settlers themselves. One by one they fell. It was in 1750 that the third petition of the colonists brought about the repeal of the hated prohibition against Negroes. From that point on the Negro population grew, and slavery flourished. By 1760 there were six thousand whites and three thousand Negroes. In the last estimate before the War for Independence, in 1773, the white population had increased to eighteen thousand, while the Negro population numbered some fifteen thousand.

Georgia adopted her slave code in 1755, and much of it was taken from the South Carolina code. It reflected South Carolina's experience rather than Georgia's. For example, the interdiction against more than seven Negroes being out together without a white chaperon was taken from the general fear of South Carolina against Negro uprisings. Between Saturday evening and Monday morning, not even those slaves who were authorized to possess firearms were permitted to carry them on their person. Under no conditions were Negroes to be taught to read and write.

If the slaves of colonial Georgia did not erupt into rebellion, they resisted their enslavement by running away into Florida as well as by sabotage. Strangely enough, Georgia displayed a relative indifference to insurrection by subjecting her slaves to service in the militia. Perhaps the service which Spanish Florida rendered as a place of escape for the more discontented Negroes made possible the paradoxical practice of using Negroes as Georgia militiamen in the colonial period.

The Middle Colonies

Although the Dutch were primarily interested in the slave trade and made great profits from transporting them to various colonies, they did not neglect their own New World settlements. There were large plantations in New Netherland, particularly in the valley of the Hudson River, and by 1638 many of them were cultivated largely with the labor of Negro slaves. The institution of slavery as practiced by the Dutch in the New World was relatively mild, with slaves receiving fairly human treatment and many considerations as to their personal rights. The Dutch slave code was not elaborate, and manumission was not an uncommon reward for long or meritorious service. Although the demand for slaves always exceeded the supply, the number imported by the Dutch never reached such proportions as to cause serious apprehension or difficulty during the period of their domination.

The character of the institution of slavery changed the moment the English took over New Netherland in 1664. The Royal African Company promoted slavery in New York as it did in other colonies. In the year following the takeover, the colonial assembly recognized the existence of slavery where persons had willingly sold themselves into bondage; and in the statute of 1684 slavery was recognized as a legitimate institution in the province of New York. As a result the Negro population of New York grew. In 1698 there were only 2,170 Negroes in a total population of 18,067, while in 1723 the census listed 6,171 slaves. By 1771 the Negro population had increased to 19,883 in a total population of 168,007.

The slave code of New York became refined early in the eighteenth century. In 1706 a law was enacted stating that baptism of a slave did not provide grounds for the slave's claim to freedom. A further significant provision was that a slave was at no time a competent witness in a case involving a freeman. In 1715 the legislature enacted a law providing that any slaves caught traveling forty miles above Albany, presumably bound for Canada, were to be executed upon the oath of two credible witnesses. Meanwhile, New York City was enacting ordinances for the better control of slaves. In 1710 the city forbade Negroes from appearing "in the streets after nightfall without a lantern with a lighted candle in it."

The concentration of an increasing number of slaves in the city of New York brought with it increased dangers to the white population. Negroes defied authority and disobeyed the laws. In 1712 the ungovernable temper of New York Negroes flared up into a fully organized insurrection, in which twenty-three slaves armed with guns and knives met in an orchard and set fire to a slaveholder's house. In the melee that followed nine whites were killed and six were injured. In the ensuing trial of the accused Negroes twenty-one were found guilty and executed. Later, in 1741, rumor of an even larger insurrection occurred. After a series of fires, the rumor spread that Negroes and poor whites were conspiring to destroy law and order in the city and seize control. After the city offered generous rewards for the apprehension of the conspirators, almost two hundred whites and Negroes were arrested and prosecuted. At least one hundred Negroes were convicted, of whom eighteen were hanged, thirteen burned alive, and seventy banished. Four white people, including two women, were hanged. There were no more serious outbursts during the colonial period, and by the time of the Revolution New York had begun to recognize the moral and economic undesirability of holding men in bondage.

South of New York, the colonies of New Jersey, Pennsylvania and Delaware each in their own ways subscribed to the institution of slavery. After the English came to dominate New Jersey, they encouraged slavery in every way. Soon, the Negro population there was growing steadily: 2,581 in 1726, 3,981 in 1738, and 4,606 in 1745 out of a population of 61,000. In Pennsylvania the growth was not so rapid, due largely to the opposition to slavery by the members of the Society of Friends. In 1688 the Germantown Quakers issued their celebrated protest, and in 1693 George Keith remonstrated Pennsylvanians for holding men in perpetual bondage. But in 1685 no less a person than William Penn himself had expressed the view that Negro slaves were better than white servants; and this had the effect of greatly encouraging slavery in some quarters. In 1721 the Negro population of Pennsylvania was estimated as being between 2,500 and 5,000. Thirty years later there were about 11,000 in the colony. In 1790 there were 10,274 Negroes, of whom 3,737 were slaves and 6,537 were free. Meanwhile, as early as 1636 slavery existed on the right bank of the Delaware. Since Delaware was a part of Pennsylvania down to 1703 the laws of the latter colony applied to Delaware. After that date Delaware was on its own, and the slave population increased at a somewhat more rapid rate than that of Pennsylvania. As this occurred, Delaware drifted away from her mother colony and became more and more identified in interests with her Southern neighbors.

Slavery was never really successful in the Middle Colonies. Their predominantly commercial economy, supplemented by subsistence agriculture, did not encourage any large-scale employment of slave labor; and many of the slaves that cleared through the New York and Pennsylvania ports were later sent into the Southern colonies. Even where there were extensive agricultural enterprises, there was no desire for slaves; for the Dutch, Swedes and Germans cultivated their farms with such meticulous care that they were not inclined to use slaves. Many of them, moreover, had moral scruples against using slaves at all. The Quakers, with their respect for Negroes as human beings, and others like them contributed as much to the failure of slavery as the economic practices that were antithetical to the institution. Thus, many in the Middle Colonies welcomed the arguments against slavery that became more pronounced during the Revolutionary period.

The Negro in Colonial New England

Although New England's primary interest in slavery was in the trade, Negroes were early introduced into Massachusetts and Connecticut. In 1638 a Salem ship unloaded several Negroes in Boston, and in the following year there were Negroes in Hartford. Before a decade had passed Negroes were used in the construction of houses and forts in New Haven and New Hampshire. By the middle of the century the refugees who founded Rhode Island were employing Negroes to help establish that colony. While the status of these early New England Negroes was rather uncertain, it gradually became clear in all New England colonies that slavery was a legitimate institution. In 1641, for example, Massachusetts cautioned that only those slaves could be brought in who were taken in wars or had willingly sold themselves or were sold to the traders by someone else.

Whether slaves landing in New England were to be settled there or shipped to other colonies, they became important to the commercial life of the New England colonies. New England slave traders competed in the trade, although they were at a serious disadvantage with the powerful European trading companies. After England secured a monopoly of the slave trade to the New World in 1713 she welcomed New England merchants into the trade, for there was enough for more traders than England could herself provide. In the first half of the eighteenth century the New England traders thrived. Boston, Salem, Providence and New London bustled with activity as outgoing ships were loaded with rum, fish and dairy products, and as Negroes, molasses and sugar were unloaded from the incoming ships. Down to the War for Independence the slave trade was vital to the economic life of New England and, indeed, the very heart of the highly profitable triangular trade.

The Negro population in New England grew slowly. In 1700, when the total population of the entire region was approximately 90,000, there were only 1,000 Negroes there. In the eighteenth century the growth was more rapid. Massachusetts led with 2,000 Negroes in 1715 and 5,249 by 1776. Connecticut was second, with 1,500 Negroes in 1715 and 3,587 by 1756. The largest percentage of Negroes was to be found in Rhode Island where in 1774 there were 3,761 Negroes to 54,435 whites. The number in New Hampshire remained negligible all during the colonial period.

New England slavery needed little legal recognition for its growth and development. When the codes emerged late in the seventeenth century slavery had already become well established. In 1670 Massachusetts enacted a law providing that the children of slaves could be sold into bondage, and ten years later it began to enact measures restricting the movement of Negroes. In 1660 Connecticut barred Negroes from military service, and thirty years later it restrained Negroes from going beyond the limits of the town without a pass. The restrictions against the education of slaves were not as great as in other regions, and frequently Negroes learned to read and write with no difficulty.

Since the number of slaves remained relatively small throughout the colonial period, there was no great fear of insurrections in New England as in some other colonies. Nevertheless, many slaves indicated their dislike of the institution by running away. Others attacked their masters and even murdered them. Still others plotted to rebel. In 1658 some Negroes and Indians in Hartford decided to make a bid for their freedom by destroying several houses of their masters. In the eighteenth century there were several conspiracies to rebel in Boston and other Massachusetts towns. The situation became so serious in Boston in 1723 that the selectmen found it necessary to take precautionary measures by forbidding slaves to be on the streets at night and refrain from "idling or lurking together."

The Negro in New England was rather unique in colonial America. He was not subjected to the harsh codes or the severe treatment that his fellows received in the colonies to the south. But it is possible to exaggerate the humanitarian aspects of their treatment. Masters in New England held a firm hand on the institution and gave little consideration to the small minority that argued for the freedom of the slaves. Although the New Englander took his religion seriously, he did not permit it to interfere with his appreciation of the profits of slavery and the slave trade. At the same time, he did not glut his home market with slaves and increase the number to the point where he would be fearful for the safety of himself and his family. There seemed to be the characteristic Yankee shrewdness in the New Englander's assessment of the importance of slavery to his economic and social life.

NEGROES AND THE RIGHTS OF MAN

Slavery and the American Revolution

By the middle of the eighteenth century slavery had become a very important part of the evolving economic order in colonial America. There had been some reservations registered by certain individuals and groups, of course. The Quakers had questioned the right of one man to hold another in perpetual bondage. Some colonists greatly objected to the indefinite expansion of the slave system lest the slaves themselves engulf the whites in a blood bath of resentment and revenge. Some Christians persisted, moreover, in their belief that there was a fundamental contradiction between the principles of Christian brotherhood, on the one hand, and the enslavement of one's brother—whether he be Christian or heathen—on the other. None of these reservations prevailed, however; and the colonists, preoccupied with critical problems of a social and economic nature, either tolerated slavery as unavoidable or embraced it with enthusiasm as indispensable.

When England revised her colonial policy at the end of the French and Indian War in 1763, she ushered in a new approach on the part of the colonists to the problem of slavery. If the colonists were to object to the new, stringent policies imposed by England, they felt also compelled—for the sake of consistency—to say something against the holding of slaves, which was, after all, a similar form of oppression. John Woolman, the New Jersey Quaker, and Anthony Benezet, the Philadelphia Huguenot, had already begun their antislavery activities even before the controversy between England and her colonies flared into the open. But when England imposed new laws on the colonists, such as the Sugar Act of 1764 and the Stamp Act of the following year, the colonists began to think of their dual roles as oppressed and oppressor. Soon the leaders were denouncing not only England's new imperial policy but slavery and the slave trade as well.

It was almost natural for the colonists to see a connection between the problem of slavery and what they regarded as their oppression by England. When James Otis penned his eloquent protest on the *Rights of the British Colonies* he affirmed the Negro's inalienable right to freedom. "Does it follow that it is right to enslave a man because he is black?" Otis asked. He and a respectable number of colonists began to insist on freedom for all as well as political independence from England. Negroes themselves sensed the dilemma of their masters and began to press for their own freedom. Addressing the Massachusetts General Court in 1774, several of them said, "we have in common with all other men a natural right to our freedoms without Being depriv'd of them by our fellow men as we are a freeborn Pepel and have never forfeited this Blessing by any compact or agreement whatever."

For the time being the General Court could not be moved to act. But neither the members of the General Court nor the other citizens of Massachusetts could soon forget the incident a few years earlier in which, according to the Negro historian, George Washington Williams, a Negro became the "first to pour out his blood as a precious libation on the altar of a people's rights." The presence of British soldiers in Boston in 1770 excited the indignation of the people, and many wondered what could be done about it. On the fifth of March, a crowd of colonists began to taunt a group of British soldiers under the command of Captain Thomas Preston. When one of the soldiers received a blow from the unruly mob, the soldiers began to fire. One of the patriots, a mulatto named Crispus Attucks, "whose looks was enough to terrify any person . . . had hardiness enough to fall in upon them, and with one hand took hold of a bayonet, and with the other knocked the man down." But Attucks had been fatally struck, and with his fall the first blood of the struggle against England had been shed. The colonists were shaken by the realization that their fight for freedom had been waged by one who was not as free as they.

In the years that followed the Boston Massacre, as the incident was called, the colonists almost always spoke out against slavery and British colonial policy at the same time. In 1774 Abigail Adams wrote to her husband John, "It always appeared a most iniquitous scheme to me to fight ourselves for what we are daily robbing and plundering from those who have as good a right to freedom as we have." Their feeling of inconsistency was reflected in the act of the Continental Congress that provided that after December 1, 1775, no slaves would be imported into the colonies. One would have assumed that the colonists' stand against slavery and the slave trade would become unequivocal and irrevocable.

The real test of the colonists' regard for slavery came in their reaction to the Declaration of Independence submitted to the Continental Congress by Thomas Jefferson. Most of the draft was acceptable, but one of the arraignments against the King was not. In part it declared that the King had "waged cruel war against human nature itself, violating the most sacred rights of life and liberty in the persons of a distant people who never offended him, captivating and carrying them into slavery in another hemisphere, or to incur miserable death in their transportation thither." Such acts were described as piratical warfare, and they were vigorously denounced by the Declaration. This charge was described by John Adams as the "vehement phillipic against Negro slavery." But it was unacceptable to the Southern delegation at the Continental Congress, and it was stricken from the final draft of the Declaration. In thus declining to accuse the King of perpetuating slavery and the slave trade and making certain that these practices would survive independence, the colonists contented themselves with engaging in what one critic called "glittering generalities." Thus, the status of the Negro was connected all too vaguely with the philosophy of freedom for all men.

There was no uniform policy among the several colonies on the use of Negroes as soldiers when hostilities broke out in April, 1775. In Massachusetts slaves as well as free Negroes fought in the battle of Bunker Hill. Peter Salem, who had been a slave in Framingham, won the plaudits of his fellows when he shot down the British Major Pitcairn. Another, Salem Poor, a soldier in a largely white company, distinguished himself by behaving "like an experienced officer as well as an excellent soldier." There were other Negroes who, like Poor and Salem, fought bravely at Bunker Hill: Caesar Brown of Westford, who was killed in action; Titus Coburn and Alexander Ames of Andover; and Prince Hall, later an abolitionist and leader of the Masons.

The performance of Negroes at this early stage of the revolutionary struggle did not settle their status as soldiers in the War for Independence. Shortly after George Washington took command of the Continental Army in 1775 an order was issued to recruiting officers instructing them not to enlist "any deserted from the ministerial army, nor any stroller, negro or vagabond, or person suspected of being an enemy of the liberty of America nor any under eighteen years of age." In October of that year Washington's council of war agreed unanimously to reject all slaves and, by a large majority, to reject Negroes altogether. This remained the policy until the end of the year.

It was British policy that forced the Americans to change their position with regard to enlisting Negroes in the Continental Army. When Lord Dunmore, the governor of Virginia, invited Negroes into the British army in November, 1775, General Washington seemed to begin to realize that he had made an error in turning down Negro volunteers. Later in the year he learned that Negroes, slave and free, were rallying to the British flag. Wherever the British armies went they attracted many Negroes with their promise of freedom to those who would serve. On December 31 Washington reversed his policy and, with the approval of Congress, ordered the enlistment of free Negroes. In the ensuing months the policy was liberalized further, so that before the end of the war Negroes, slave and free, were being permitted to enlist in all states with the exception of Georgia and South Carolina.

Of the 300,000 men who saw service in the cause of American independence, some 5,000 were Negroes. They served in the Navy as well as the Army; some volunteered, while others were substituted for whites. Most of them served in outfits that were predominantly white, but there were a few predominantly Negro fighting units, such as the two companies in Massachusetts, one in Connecticut, and one in Rhode Island. They saw action all over the country: at Lexington, Concord, Ticonderoga, Bunker Hill, Trenton, Princeton, Brandywine, Saratoga, Savannah, Eutaw Springs and Yorktown. Most of them remain anonymous, as far as military exploits are concerned. Indeed, Benjamin Quarles points out in his *The Negro in the American Revolution* that many Negroes who enlisted were enrolled without specific names. They were "A Negro Man," or "Negro by Name" or "A Negro name not known."

Some Negroes distinguished themselves by the service that they rendered. Two of them, Prince Whipple and Oliver Cromwell, were with Washington when he crossed the Delaware on Christmas Day, 1776. Lemuel Haynes, who was later to have a career as a minister to white congregations, joined the expedition to Ticonderoga to stop the inroads of Burgoyne's northern army. The victory of Anthony Wayne at Stony Point in 1779 was made possible by the spying of a Negro soldier named Pompey. At the siege of Savannah in 1779 more than five-hundred Negroes from Haiti were with the French forces that helped save the day. Among them and perhaps the youngest was Henri Christophe, "who one day would become King of Haiti, but was then a bootblack and messboy, not yet out of his teens."

The First Antislavery Movement

Early in the seventeenth century colonists here and there began to speak out against slavery. It was not until the revolutionary period, however, that a full-scale, organized opposition to the institution of slavery emerged. In a sense it was nurtured by the same sentiments that fostered the movement for independence. In Rhode Island the Reverend Samuel Hopkins made a house-to-house canvass urging masters to liberate their slaves. In Pennsylvania Anthony Benezet, who has been called "the foremost antislavery propagandist of his day," was writing and speaking against the practice that was "repugnant to humanity" and "inconsistent with the Bible." He joined with others, like Benjamin Rush, in organizing The Society for the Relief of Free Negroes Unlawfully Held in Bondage. This and other organizations with similar purposes reflected the social implications of the revolutionary philosophy. In 1785 the New York Society for Promoting the Manumission of Slaves was organized with John Jay as president. In Delaware a similar society was set up in 1788; and by 1792 there were antislavery societies in every state from Massachusetts to Virginia.

Negroes themselves took heart from the efforts of the whites as well as from the congenial climate produced by arguments for the rights of man. In 1777 a group of Massachusetts Negroes asked for a law against slavery, declaring that a life of slavery was "far worse than Nonexistence." Two years later a group of nineteen Negroes in New Hampshire asked the state to enact a law whereby they might regain their liberty, "and that the name of slave may not more be heard in a land gloriously contending for the sweets of freedom." Throughout the country individual Negroes

and groups of Negroes were seeking legislation that would bring an end to slavery.

States soon began to respond to the pressure. As early as 1777 the Massachusetts legislature considered a bill for "preventing the practice of holding persons in Slavery"; but it postponed action. In 1780, however, the new Massachusetts constitution stated that "all men are born free and equal," and this was the beginning of the end of slavery in that state. New Hampshire legislators debated the question of abolishing slavery in 1780, but postponed action to a "more convenient opportunity." While some states equivocated Pennsylvania took decisive action. On March 1, 1780, it passed a law providing that when children of slaves reached twenty-eight years of age, they would be free. Manumission acts were passed in New York in 1785 and in New Jersey in 1786, although effective legislation was not achieved in those states until 1799 and 1804 respectively. Finally, Congress indicated its interest in the antislavery movement by enacting a law providing that in the Northwest Territory neither slavery nor involuntary servitude should exist.

Slavery and the Constitution

The antislavery leaders experienced only limited success during and after the War for Independence. Resistance to the abolition of slavery hardened in the Southern states, where much capital was invested in slaves and where, during the postwar years, a new economic importance was being attached to slavery. Nowhere was the resistance to abolition reflected better than in the convention that wrote a new Constitution for the United States in 1787. In the debates over representation in Congress, the question arose as to how the slaves should be counted. Most of the Northern delegates regarded slaves as property and therefore not deserving of representation. Southerners were loud in their demands that slaves be counted as people, in which case the slave states would gain in the number of members they would have in Congress. Despite the objection on the part of some antislavery delegates to recognizing slavery in the Constitution, the compromise finally agreed upon permitted states to count slaves as three-fifths of other persons.

By 1787 several states, including such slave states as Virginia, North Carolina and Georgia, had taken action to prevent the importation of slaves. The opponents to the slave trade hoped that the convention would put an end to the trade in all parts of the United States. When the matter came before the convention, it was debated with such vehemence that some feared a disruption of the entire proceedings. One Southerner said that his own state, South Carolina, could never accept a constitution that prohibited the slave trade. After much acrimonious debate the members agreed on a compromise that provided that the slave trade "shall not be prohibited by the Congress prior to the Year one thousand eight hundred and eight, but a Tax or duty may be imposed on such importation, not exceeding ten dollars for each Person."

Runaway slaves had always been a problem in the colonies; and it is significant, but not surprising, that there was almost no opposition to the proposal that states give up fugitive slaves to their owners. When Roger Sherman of Connecticut declared that he saw "no more propriety in the public seizing and surrendering a slave or servant, than a horse," he found little support, even among his New England colleagues. Thus, the provision was written into the Constitution calling for the rendition of fugitive slaves "upon Claim of the Party to whom such Service or Labour may be due." In these several ways the new Constitution not only recognized the institution of slavery but offered the resources of the government of the United States in its protection and support. To the extent that it did it made it more difficult to carry out the sentiments regarding the rights of man that had been set forth in the Declaration of Independence.

Negroes in the New Nation

When the new Constitution went into effect, there were approximately three-quarters of a million Negroes in the United States. Almost 90 percent of them were slaves in the South Atlantic states, while some 60,000 free Negroes were scattered all over the country. The Negro population was essentially rural. Here and there one found a slight concentration in the cities: New York City with 3,252, Philadelphia with 1,630 and Baltimore with 1,578. Nowhere was the Negro population dying out; indeed, there were signs of significant increase, especially in the slave states. In the North the only significant development was the increase in the number of free Negroes. By 1790 all of Boston's 761 Negroes were free.

Nor was the American Negro altogether anonymous, even at this early date. There was, for example, Phillis, the personal maid of Mrs. Susannah Wheatley of Boston. She early displayed an interest in writing poetry; and in 1770 her first poem, "On the Death of Reverend George Whitefield," appeared. Three years later she published a collection of her verse, *Poems on Various Subjects, Religious and Moral.* During the war she composed a tribute to "His Excellency General Washington," which the general acknowledged by declaring that the poem was "striking proof of your great poetical talents." Then there was Paul Cuffee, the Massachusetts Negro who built and sailed his own ships. He owned a 69-ton schooner, the *Ranger,* two brigs and several smaller vessels. When settlers refused to do so, he built a school in Westport, Massachusetts, and gave it to the community. He also helped build a meeting house for the Society of Friends, to which he belonged. In 1780 he presented a petition to the Massachusetts legislature asking to be relieved from paying taxes since he and the Negroes who joined him in signing the petition had "no voice or influence in the election of those who tax us." As businessman, philanthropist and petitioner he won recognition among his fellow citizens in Massachusetts.

Perhaps the most significant of the Negroes in the new nation was Benjamin Banneker, mathematician, astronomer and political philosopher. In 1791 this Maryland free Negro published his first almanac, a worthy yearly undertaking that lasted until 1802. Thomas Jefferson, to whom Banneker sent a copy of his first almanac, was greatly impressed and told Banneker that it was a work that justified the Negro's resentment against the claims that he was intellectually inferior. At the suggestion of his friends, George Ellicott and Thomas Jefferson, Banneker was appointed by Washington to serve with the commission to define the boundary and lay out the new Capital—the District of Columbia.

There were also several Negro religious leaders who became well known for their initiative and courage in the early days of the new nation. George

Liele founded a Baptist church in Savannah in 1779 before quitting the United States and settling in Jamaica. In Philadelphia Richard Allen founded the African Methodist Episcopal Church after he was thrown out of the St. George Church because he refused to accept segregation. Soon branches of Allen's church sprang up in Baltimore, Wilmington and various Pennsylvania and New Jersey towns. Able colleagues such as Absolom Jones, Daniel Coker and Morris Brown helped to promote this branch of Methodism among Negroes in the South as well as the North. In New York in 1796 Negroes, under the leadership of Peter Williams, James Varick and Christopher Rush withdrew from the John Street Methodist Church and organized the African Methodist Episcopal Zion Church. Before the beginning of the nineteenth century Negro Baptist and Methodist churches had been established in all the states of the Union.

If there were no outstanding Negro leaders in the field of education, it did not prevent a movement for the education of Negroes from getting under way. In 1798 a separate school for Negro children was established by a white teacher in the home of Primus Hall, a prominent Boston Negro. In 1800 the Negroes of Boston asked the city to establish a school for Negroes, but the request was not granted. Not until 1820 did the city open the first school for Negro children. The first school for Negroes in New York City was established in 1787 by the Manumission Society. By 1820 the school had more than five hundred children. New Jersey began educating her Negro children in 1777. Soon there were schools in several New Jersey towns. Philadelphia, which began Negro education in 1787, had seven schools for Negroes before the end of the century. In the other states the beginnings were not as auspicious and the task was more difficult, but even in Virginia and the Carolinas schools for Negroes were founded. The insurrection of 1800 in Richmond frightened many slaveholders who feared that Negroes were reading incendiary literature. From that point on it became increasingly difficult to establish and maintain schools for Negroes in the slave states.

AMERICAN NEGRO SLAVERY

Growth of an Institution

By the beginning of the nineteenth century there were unmistakable signs of profound economic and social change taking place in the United States. The commercial activities of the new nation were expanding; and there were those who already were beginning to think in terms of promoting industrial development similar to that which was occurring in England and on the Continent. Beyond the areas of settlement, rich new land was beckoning settlers who could plant staple crops and enjoy the freedom offered on the frontier. In 1803 the United States purchased the vast Louisiana Territory, and although it would be many years before the entire area would be settled, Americans and European immigrants were rapidly moving beyond the mountains. The greater portion of the people who moved from the Atlantic seaboard were committed to the institution of slavery, and if they had any slaves they took them along. Not even the War of 1812, in which several thousand Negroes fought, halted the march of Americans and slavery into the new West.

When peace came in 1815 the movement to the West accelerated. The men of the South and West, the most enthusiastic supporters of the war, now felt that they had a right to move on to better lands. Into the Gulf region went large numbers of settlers to clear the rich lands and cultivate extensive crops of cotton and sugar. Louisiana had already become a state in 1812; Mississippi and Alabama became states in 1817 and 1819 respectively. By 1820 the Gulf region had about 200,000 inhabitants, and twenty years later there were almost a million people there. The increase of the white population, coupled with the tremendous growth of the Negro population, largely slaves, is essentially the story of the emergence of the cotton kingdom.

The rise of the cotton kingdom was America's response to the growing demand for cotton brought on by the industrial revolution in England. The system of producing cotton textiles was undergoing revolutionary changes; and with the invention of spinning and weaving machinery the manufacturing process was so cheapened that the demand for cotton goods was greatly stimulated. The demand for cotton fiber to feed the newly developed machinery seemed insatiable, and the cotton farmers of the United States undertook to satisfy this demand. Already, they had made two significant steps in that direction. First, they put into use a type of cotton, the short-staple variety, that could be grown almost anywhere in the South. Secondly, they made greater use of the cotton gin that had been developed by the Connecticut schoolteacher, Eli Whitney. Within a few years the South was on its way toward making the economic transition that these new developments induced.

As the planters expanded their operations, the need for additional labor became urgent. By now they were committed to Negro slavery, but the supply of slaves was not abundant. The African slave trade had officially closed in 1808, but even after that date American capital, American ships, and American sailors were carrying on an extensive slave trade between Africa and the New World. The long, unprotected coast, a sure market for their wares, and the prospect of huge profits were enough to tempt many Americans. W. E. B. Du Bois, in his *The Suppression of the African Slave Trade*, asserts that thousands of slaves were smuggled into the country each year from the time of the closing of the trade down to the outbreak of the Civil War. It was the domestic slave trade, however, that constituted the principal means by which farmers of the cotton kingdom secured the slaves that they needed.

Even before 1800 the domestic slave trade in Maryland and Virginia was well developed. As tobacco cultivation tended to decline and as the farmers of the upper South proceeded to diversify their economic activity, they discovered that there was a ready market for the surplus of slaves they had on hand. Slave-trading firms like Woolfolk, Saunders and Overly of Maryland and Franklin and Armfield of Virginia did a lively business in purchasing slaves in the upper South and selling them "down the river" to planters in Mississippi and Louisiana who desperately needed them. Traders made individual deals with planters or attended auctions of estates and sales by the sheriff of bankrupt estates. At times planters sold incorrigible slaves—habitual runaways or those who refused to work—and the traders in turn sold them to unsuspecting planters in some faraway community. Baltimore, Washington, Richmond, Norfolk and Charleston were principal trading centers in the older states; while Montgomery, Memphis, and New Orleans were the outstanding markets in the newer areas.

The domestic slave trade involved some of the most sordid practices that were developed in the sordid business of slavery. Slave families were ruthlessly divided, with mothers being frequently sold away from their children or vice versa. In his journal William Reynolds, an itinerant merchant, recorded this account of the sale of twenty-three slaves at auction in Memphis: "One yellow woman was sold who had two children. She begged and implored her new master . . . to buy her children, but it had no effect. . . . She then begged him to buy her little girl, about five years old, but all to no purpose." In the states of the upper South owners encouraged the breeding of slaves in order to increase profits. As early as 1796 a South Carolina slaveholder declared that the fifty slaves he was offering for sale were purchased for stock and breeding. In 1832 Thomas R. Dew admitted that Virginia was a "Negro-raising state" and that she was able to export six thousand slaves per year because of breeding. Moncure Conway of Fredericksburg, Virginia, boldly asserted that the "chief pecuniary resource in the border states is the breeding of slaves. . . ."

Because of the foreign slave trade, the illicit foreign slave trade after 1808, slave breeding, the normal excess of births over deaths among slaves, and a booming domestic slave trade, the Negro population grew steadily in the first half of the nineteenth century. In 1790 there were 604,000 slaves. By 1808, when the foreign slave trade officially closed, there were about one million. In 1830 there were 2,156,900; and by 1860 the number had increased to 3,953,760. In 1860 Virginia continued to lead in numbers with 549,000, followed by Georgia with 465,000 and Alabama and Mississippi with approximately 435,000 each. The most significant increase was in the states of the cotton kingdom—Georgia, Alabama, Tennessee, Mississippi, Arkansas, Louisiana and Texas—where by 1860 there were approximately two million slaves, more than half the Negro population.

There were 384,000 owners of slaves in 1860; and this means that since the white population of the South numbered around eight million, fully three-fourths of the whites had neither slaves nor any immediate economic interest in the institution of slavery. Most of the slaveowners had only a few slaves: 200,000 owners had five slaves or less, while 338,000 owners, or 88 percent, held less than twenty. Nevertheless, the institution came to dominate the political and economic thinking of the entire South. The vast majority of the staple crops was produced on those relatively few plantations employing large numbers of slaves (2,000 planters had more than 100 slaves each in 1860), thus giving such owners an influence all out of proportion to their numbers. Even those who had no slaves hoped that some day they would; and they took on the habits and patterns of thought of the slaveholders. Too, in the context of a slave society in which all slaves were black people, the color of the whites became a badge of superiority in which *all* whites took pride.

Slaves were a special kind of property, not quite like houses or beasts of burden, but not quite like people, within the meaning of the law. They required, therefore, a special set of laws designed to protect the owners of such property and to protect the whites against any dangers that might arise from the presence of so much slave property. These codes began to develop in the seventeenth century, and long before the Civil War they were fully refined. From time to time it was necessary to modify them and they differed from state to state; but in important particulars they were quite similar. Since they were designed to achieve due subordination of the slaves, they were frankly repressive; and the white planters and legislators made no apologies for them.

A slave had no standing in the courts. He could not be a party to a suit at law; and he could not offer legal testimony except against another slave or a free Negro. Since he had no legal responsibility, his oath was not binding. Thus, he could not make a contract, and his marriage was therefore not legal. His children were not legitimate. The ownership of property by slaves was generally forbidden, although some states permitted them to possess certain types of property. There was no legal basis for even this concession. A slave could not strike a white person, even in self-defense; but the killing of a slave, however malicious, was rarely regarded as murder. The rape of a female slave was a misdemeanor because it involved trespassing on the property of another person. Slaves could not leave the plantation without the permission of their master; and any white person encountering a slave who was away from the plantation without permission could take him up and turn him over to the public officials. Slaves could not possess firearms and, in Mississippi, they could not beat drums or blow horns. Laws generally forbade the hiring out of slaves by themselves, but many owners ignored this proscription.

Slaves could not purchase or sell goods or visit the homes of whites or free Negroes. They were never to assemble unless a white person was present; and they were never to receive, possess or transmit any incendiary literature calculated to incite insurrections. They were not to be taught to read or write or cipher; and any white person or free Negro found guilty of violating this law was to be subjected to severe punishment of fine or imprisonment or both. Slaves guilty of petty offenses were to be punished by whipping, but the more serious offenses drew severe punishments, such as branding, imprisonment or death. Arson, rape of a white woman and conspiracy to rebel, for example, were capital crimes in all the slaveholding states. Since slaves were always regarded with suspicion and since they could not testify against a white person who accused them, many of them were found guilty of crimes they did not commit and against which they were unable to defend themselves.

Despite the elaborateness of the slave codes and the machinery of enforcement. there were numerous infractions that went unpunished altogether. When times were quiet the laws were disregarded; the slaves could get away with a great deal. But when there were rumors of revolts among the slaves, the white community became apprehensive and tended to enforce the codes with unusual zeal. Slave owners, moreover, were not inclined under ordinary circumstances to give much attention to the slave codes where their own slaves were concerned. The planter conceived of himself as the source of law and justice, and he preferred to take all matters involving his own slaves into his own hands and mete out justice in his own way. He was certain that he could handle his own slaves, if only something could be done about those on the neighboring plantation! Such an attitude was not conducive to the uniform, effective enforcement of the slave codes.

Slaves at Work

A great deal has been written about the institution of slavery as "a matrimonial bureau," and "a chapel of ease" and the like. All too often the planter is described as a patrician who, as a great humanitarian and Christian, maintained his establishment largely as a civilizing institution. Such descriptions hardly square with the facts. Slavery was essentially an economic institution; the primary concern of the slaveowner was to get work out of his slaves. And the work was largely agricultural. In his study of urban slavery Richard Wade has pointed out that only some 400,000 slaves lived in towns and cities in 1850 and that slavery in the urban areas was largely unsuccessful. Of the 3,200,000 slaves in the United States in 1850 approximately 2,800,000 worked on farms and plantations. Some 1,800,000 of these were on cotton plantations, while the remainder worked in tobacco, sugar and rice fields. Where there were few slaves on the agricultural unit, as was the case in a vast majority of instances, the slaves and their owners worked together in the fields and were compelled to engage in a variety of tasks. On the larger plantations, where organization and the division of labor were elaborate, there was extensive supervision by the owner or his overseer or both. In such instances there might be two distinct groups of slaves, the field hands and the house servants.

The cultivation of a crop was a most demanding activity; and the entire future of both slaves and owners depended on the success with which this was carried out. It was generally believed that one Negro was required for the successful cultivation of three acres of cotton. The planting, cultivation and picking of the cotton required little skill, but a great deal of time. Men, women and children could be used and, indeed, they all were used. Other duties included clearing new land, burning underbrush, rolling logs, splitting rails, carrying water, mending fences, spreading fertilizer and breaking the soil. Small wonder that many slaves worked not merely from sunrise to sunset, but frequently long after dark.

On some plantations slaves were assigned tasks for each day, and when they had completed their tasks they were through for the day. Much more common was the gang system, in which gangs of slaves were taken to the field and put to work under supervision. Where there was not watchful supervision little was likely to be accomplished. Negro slaves felt no compulsion to extend themselves, since their benefits were more or less the same, regardless of effort, except on the few plantations where systems of bounties and rewards were developed. Masters complained much about the idleness and laziness of slaves. If slaves felt overworked they frequently feigned illness or simply walked off for a day or two, or perhaps forever. The constant evasion of work was one reason why planters always felt the need for more slaves in order to increase productivity.

In order to get work out of slaves the lash was frequently used. There was the general belief, born of a naïve defense of the institution of slavery, that Negroes were a childlike race and should be punished just as children were punished. The excessive use of the lash was one of the most flagrant abuses of the institution of slavery. As Thomas Jefferson pointed out in his *Notes on Virginia,* the whole master-slave relationship was "a perpetual exercise of the most boisterous passions, the most unremitting despotism on the one part; and degrading submission on the other. . . ." The dominion over the slave that the master enjoyed all too frequently brought out the worst in the master and stimulated a brutality in treatment that seemed to be inherent in the relationship. Excessively cruel treatment at the hands of the planter or the overseer, together with his natural aversion to enslavement, explain the tendency of slaves to run away or, worse still, to revolt against their masters.

An Ignoble Existence

Except for the house servants who had special advantages and opportunities, it may be said that slaves generally merely subsisted. Many planters were so preoccupied with growing staple crops that they gave little attention to growing foodstuffs for their slaves. Many plantations were compelled to purchase food and other supplies for the slaves and for the planting family. Few Mississippi planters raised enough food for their needs and were compelled to purchase large quantities from the outside. The meal and meat, infrequently supplemented by potatoes, peas and syrup, was not a particularly exciting fare. Some slaves had their own gardens and chickens, but there was always the possibility of incurring the disfavor of the owner by spending too much time in this pursuit. It would be too much to suppose that slaves always resisted the temptation to take food from the owner's larder if the opportunity presented itself. As far as clothing was concerned, no more was provided than was absolutely necessary. Housing was especially poor and uncomfortable. When Frederick L. Olmsted toured the South he was shocked to see such small, dilapidated cabins on some of the plantations he visited.

Generally, slaves had no time that they could call their own. They might expect, however, to be free from work on Saturday afternoons and Sundays. But there was little in the way of enjoyment or satisfaction during the moments or hours they were off the job. Plantations were isolated, and slaves were not free to go and come at will. There was not much to do, even during the free periods, unless the plantation were large enough to have enough slaves to provide some social diversions of their own. At Christmastime and on a few other holidays, the rules of the plantation were relaxed, additional food was provided and slaves were permitted to dance and sing. Some were permitted to hunt and fish on special occasions. But there was little to relieve their existence of the depressed drabness that seemed to be inevitable.

As long as the proper precautions were taken there was little opposition to some form of religious activity among the slaves. After the Nat Turner revolt of 1831, some states banned Negro preachers and required slaves to attend the churches of their masters. Generally, however, Negro congre-

gations flourished in the towns and on certain plantations, supported by several neighboring planters. Toward the end of the slave period Negro churches were generally frowned upon; and planters were encouraged to permit religious services for slaves only when some responsible white person was present. If this was not possible, slaves were expected to worship in white churches. The earliest examples of the segregation of Negroes are to be found in the practices of the white churches. In one instance the white congregation constructed a partition several feet high to separate the masters from the slaves.

Even if the slave had some social life and even if he was permitted to attend church regularly, he could never escape the fact that he was a slave and that his movements as well as his other activities were almost always under careful surveillance. This created a restiveness among some and a sense of despair among others. If a slave found it possible to be indifferent to the ignoble existence to which fate consigned him, it was because he possessed a remarkable capacity for accommodation or he was totally ignorant of the depth of his degraded position.

The prevailing notion a century ago was that the slave was docile, tractable and happy; and this view is held in some quarters even today. Advocates of the institution of slavery defended it on these grounds, and they pointed to the conduct of many slaves to support their contention. Slaves developed many techniques to mislead the owner regarding their real feeling. In the process of adjustment they learned how to escape work as well as punishment, and they were not above obsequiousness and meekness when it served their purposes. These actions do not reveal the real feelings of the slaves about the institution of which they were the unwilling victims. For, as old as the institution of slavery was, human beings had not, even by the nineteenth century, brought themselves to the point where they could be subjected to it without resistance and protest. Resistance to slavery has been found wherever slavery has existed, and Negro slavery in the United States was no exception. There are numerous examples of kindness and understanding on the part of the owner as well as docility and tractability on the part of the slave; but this can hardly be regarded as typical of a system based on the exploitation of one group by another.

Slaves reacted to their status in various ways. Some sang songs and expressed the hope that their burdens would be relieved in the next world. As long as they were in this world, they attempted to make the most of an unwelcome situation by loafing on the job, feigning illness in the fields and on the auction block and engaging in sabotage. Slaves would destroy farming tools, drive animals with a cruelty that suggested revenge, and when possible damage the crops, burn forests and homes and destroy their master's property in other ways. Self-mutilation and suicide were popular forms of resistance to slavery. Slaves would cut off their toes and hands in order to render themselves ineffective as workers. Or they would do violence to the master class. Poisoning was always feared, and with reason. As early as 1761 the *Charleston Gazette* remarked that the Negroes had "begun the hellish act of poisoning." On occasion slaves murdered their masters by stabbing, shooting and choking.

Running away began the first year that slavery was established in the New World and continued down to emancipation. There was Federal and state legislation to assist in the recovery of runaway slaves, but many of them escaped forever. Long before the Underground Railroad became an efficient operation under the abolitionists, slaves were running away: men, women and children, singly, in pairs, in groups. Some disguised themselves; others, armed with counterfeit passes, claimed that they were free. If they were apprehended, they would do it again. One woman in North Carolina fled from her master's plantation no less than sixteen times. While there is no way of even approximating the number of runaways, it is obvious that it was one of the most effective means of resisting slavery. Neither the Fugitive Act of 1793 nor that of 1850 could put an end to it.

Revolting against the whites was the most desperate form of resistance to slavery. To Negroes, it was "carrying the fight to the enemy." To the whites, it was a mad, sinister act of desperate savages, who had no appreciation for the benign influences of slavery. There were numerous revolts, large and small. And there were numerous rumors of revolts. Whether they were real or fancied, any suggestion of them threw the white community into a paroxysm of fear and led it to adopt desperate measures to prevent a blood bath. In 1800 a thousand slaves, led by Gabriel Prosser, attempted to march on Richmond and destroy the town and their masters. A violent storm and betrayal by two slave informers brought a tragic end to the attempt. In 1822 the slaves and free Negroes of Charleston planned a revolt, under the leadership of Denmark Vesy. The word leaked out, and it was aborted. In 1831 the Negroes of Southampton County, Virginia, under Nat Turner, were almost successful in their bid for freedom through revolt. They began by killing Turner's master and his family and several other white families. Within the first day some sixty whites had been killed, and the revolt was spreading rapidly when the main body of Negro revolutionaries were met and overpowered by state and Federal troops. More than a hundred slaves were killed immediately, and within a few weeks Turner himself was captured and executed. Right down to the Civil War slaves demonstrated their violent antipathy to slavery by attempting to rise against it, but their successes were few indeed.

Free Negroes, South and North

In 1790 there were some 59,000 Negroes in the United States who were not slaves, a considerable increase over the twenty black indentured servants who landed in Jamestown in 1619. By 1830 there were 319,000; and by 1860 there were 488,000, of whom 44 percent lived in the South and 46 percent in the North. Some had been set free by their masters. Others had purchased their freedom. Some were born of free mothers, white and Negro. Others had run away and made good their bid for freedom. In the South the existence of a large number of free Negroes proved to be a source of constant embarrassment to the slaveholders, since their existence undermined the very foundation on which slavery was built. Southerners carried on a campaign of vilification against free Negroes and undertook a program of legislation designed to keep the free Negro in his place.

A free Negro's existence, even in the North, was precarious. A white person could claim, however fraudulently, that the free Negro was his slave; and the heavy burden of proof that he was not rested on the accused. There was the danger, moreover, of his being kidnaped, as often happened. In the South the chances of being reduced to servitude or slavery by court decree was also great. All Southern states required free Negroes to have passes and certificates of freedom. Some states, such as Virginia, Tennessee, Georgia and Florida, required registration; some others compelled free Negroes to have white guardians.

The controls which the state and community exercised over free Negroes increased year by year. In no Southern state could a free Negro move about as he wished, and in some Northern communities it was dangerous to try. Some states forbade free Negroes to possess or carry firearms without a license. By 1835 the right of assembly had been taken away from almost all Negroes in the South, and their contact with others was, by law, kept to a minimum. Many proscriptions interfered with their making a living. In 1805 Maryland prohibited free Negroes from selling corn, wheat or tobacco without a license. In 1831 North Carolina required all Negro traders and peddlers to be licensed, while most states required free Negroes to work and their means of support had to be visible.

In the nineteenth century Negroes steadily lost their various citizenship rights. In 1800 they voted almost everywhere. By 1835 they could vote in no Southern state, while Pennsylvania and Indiana confined the franchise to whites in 1838 and 1851 respectively. Seldom did they enjoy protection at the hands of the state or local government. In cities such as Pittsburgh, Philadelphia and New York they were attacked with impunity by mobs, their homes and churches destroyed, and they were run out of the community. It was this kind of treatment, North and South, that caused Fanny Kemble to say, "They are not slaves indeed, but they are pariahs, debarred from every fellowship save with their own despised race. . . . All hands are extended to thrust them out, all fingers point at their dusky skin, all tongues have learned to turn the very name of their race into an insult and a reproach."

In the face of all this, however, there were free Negroes who not only survived but did rather well. They were engaged in numerous occupations, and some of them accumulated considerable wealth. Individual cases of affluence are numerous. They extend from the wealthy Thomy Lafon, who accumulated an estate in New Orleans of more than a half-million dollars, to James Forten, the Philadelphia sailmaker who had a fortune of more than one hundred thousand dollars. Schools for Negro children increased in the North during the nineteenth century; and in some communities, such as Boston and New Bedford after 1855, they were permitted to attend school with the whites. In the South, where teaching of free Negroes was generally outlawed after 1830, many of them received private instruction. There are examples, moreover, of free Negroes going to the North, to Canada and to Europe for an education during the antebellum period. Some Northern free Negroes were attending colleges and universities. Bowdoin was the first college to graduate a Negro when John Russwurm received his degree there in 1826. After that time Oberlin, Harvard and other institutions received free Negroes.

Negroes were becoming articulate and expressed their views in a variety of media. They held conventions, beginning in 1831, and in their resolutions and petitions they indicated their feelings and aspirations. They published newspapers, *Freedom's Journal*, the *North Star* and the *Anglo-African*. They wrote books: Frederick Douglass and a host of former slaves wrote autobiographies; J. W. C. Pennington wrote a history of the Negro people; George Moses Horton published a book of verse, and William Wells Brown published numerous works, including a novel.

Perhaps the most important work performed by free Negroes was the general assistance they gave to the antislavery movement as it increased in intensity after 1830. Negroes were among the most enthusiastic supporters of William Lloyd Garrison when he began to publish his *Liberator* in 1831. Many joined the American Antislavery Society and the regional and state societies when they were organized. Frederick Douglass was merely the best known of a larger number of writers and speakers in the antislavery cause. Others were Charles Remond, Charles B. Ray, Henry Highland Garnet, David Ruggles, Sarah Remond, Frances Harper, Sojourner Truth and Harriet Tubman. In their militant bitterness the Negro abolitionists equaled and sometimes surpassed their white colleagues. Perhaps not even Garrison reached the intensity of feeling against slavery that David Walker, a Boston Negro, reached in his *Appeal in Four Articles*. Many Negro leaders, moreover, counseled violence if no other approach against slavery was successful. In 1854 the Negro convention adopted a resolution that represented the views of an increasing number of Negroes. In part it declared that "those who, without crime, are outlawed by any government can owe no allegiance to its enactments. . . . We advise all oppressed to adopt the motto, 'Liberty or Death.'" This was five years before John Brown attacked Harper's Ferry.

CIVIL WAR AND RECONSTRUCTION

The Evolution of Federal Policy

The unequivocal stand that white and Negro abolitionists took against slavery in the 1850's made compromise difficult, if not impossible, from their point of view. The vigorous defense of slavery by white Southerners as best for the country and best for the Negro, ruled out any possibility of concessions on their part. The impasse was not relieved by the position of the leading political parties: the Southern Democrats held that the election to the Presidency of a "Black Republican" such as Abraham Lincoln was wholly unacceptable to them and they would prefer secession to abolitionist rule. The Republicans would not concede that slavery should be permitted in the territories, and while they would permit slavery to continue where it existed, they were determined to pursue a policy of containment. When Lincoln was elected the Southern leaders concluded that secession was their only recourse. When Lincoln decided that the secessionists were not entitled to all the Federal forts, post offices and other properties in the South, the war broke out.

When Lincoln issued a call for 75,000 volunteers in April, 1861, Negroes rushed forward to offer their services. Frederick Douglass expressed the sentiments of many Negroes when he said, "Standing outside the pale of American humanity, denied citizenship, unable to call the land of my birth my country . . . and longing for the end of the bondage of my people, I was ready for any political upheaval which should bring about a change in the existing condition of things." Indeed, as the Negro historian, Joseph T. Wilson, recalled, "at the sound of the tocsin at the North, Negro waiter, cook, barber, bootblack, groom, porter and laborer stood ready at the enlisting office." In many parts of the country—Boston, Providence, Philadelphia, Cleveland, Battle Creek—Negroes organized themselves into military corps and offered their services. In every instance their services were declined. The Secretary of War was curt and firm: "this Department has no intention to call into the service of the Government any colored soldiers."

Negroes were critical of the Government for rejecting them, and so were many whites. Horace Greeley, after the fiasco at Bull Run in the summer of 1861, was bitter in his denunciation as were some other antislavery editors. But the Lincoln government wanted to be careful not to convey the impression that the war was one for freedom. There were many Northerners, including some soldiers, who feared that it would become one. "We don't want to fight side and side with the nigger," said a young soldier from New York; "We think we are too superior a race for that." But if Negroes could not fight, they would help in other ways. Many Southern Negroes offered to help the Confederacy, which also rejected their services as soldiers. Northern Negroes offered money, goods and their support of the Union in other ways. They served as cooks, teamsters, hospital attendants and body servants.

At some point early in the war, perhaps in the first year, Negroes even in the South began to believe that their freedom was connected with the war. As they did, they not only took a greater interest in the war but also did whatever they could to promote a Union victory. Slaves, who had vowed to help their masters in any way that they could, now began to leave the plantations and join the Union lines, if they were close enough. Loyalty, about which masters boasted, became the exception rather than the rule, according to Bell Irvin Wiley in his *Southern Negroes, 1861–1865*. When the slaves of Georgetown, South Carolina, sang "We'll fight for liberty" in 1861 they were thrown in jail. By the second year of the war, slaves were leaving the plantations in such large numbers that the whites became apprehensive not only because of the loss of labor but also because they feared uprisings and acts of revenge.

President Lincoln was under severe pressure from a powerful sector in Congress not only to permit Negroes to enlist as soldiers but also to issue a proclamation setting all Negroes free. Charles Sumner, United States Senator from Massachusetts, was one of the leaders urging such a policy upon the President. But the President was adamant. He feared, he said, that if Negroes were set free and given arms, thousands of white soldiers from the border states would lay down their arms. In his newspaper Frederick Douglass urged a policy of emancipation, declaring that the "Union cause would never prosper till the war assumed an Antislavery attitude, and the Negro was enlisted on the loyal side." But the President would not be moved.

Union generals were moving, however, much to the embarrassment of the President. In May, 1861, the daring, flamboyant Benjamin Butler, in command at Fort Monroe, refused to give up three slaves and, in effect, had set them free as contrabands of war to be employed by the Union forces there. In August, 1861, General John C. Frémont proclaimed martial law in Missouri and declared as free the slaves who had been confiscated from persons resisting the authority of the United States. Lincoln ordered Fremont to show leniency as to martial law and to modify the emancipation order to conform to existing law. In March, 1862, General David Hunter, in command of the Department of the South, began to issue certificates of emancipation to all slaves who had been employed by the Confederacy. In the following month he declared slaves free throughout the Department of the South. This was too much for Lincoln. On May 19 he countermanded the Hunter proclamation, making it clear that neither Hunter nor any other commander had been authorized to emancipate the slaves.

Even the Congress was moving. In August, 1861, it passed the first Confiscation Act, providing that when slaves were engaged in hostile military service, the owners' claims to the labor of such slaves were forfeited. In April, 1862, Congress abolished slavery in the District of Columbia, and in the following June it abolished slavery in the territories. Congress took its boldest step toward emancipation when it passed the Second Confiscation Act in July, 1862. The act provided that if anyone committed treason, his slaves were free. It further provided that the slaves of all persons supporting rebellion should be "forever free of their servitude, and not again held as slaves." Perhaps now it was time for the President to act.

While Lincoln was unequivocally opposed to slavery, he firmly believed that Negroes and whites could not live together side by side once Negroes were free. He therefore looked toward the colonization of Negroes outside the United States—in Africa or in the Caribbean area. He attempted to enlist the support of Negroes as well as influential members of Congress in his colonization schemes, but he was totally unsuccessful. The President also believed that there would be less controversy over emancipation if the owners of slaves were compensated for their losses. It was at his insistence that Congress wrote into the act setting slaves free in the District of Columbia a provision for the compensation of their owners. But he was unable to persuade any considerable number of the wisdom of such a policy.

Early in the second year of his administration Lincoln decided that he should emancipate the slaves. It was not only just and right, he was later to say; it was also good policy that would hasten the end of the war. In the late spring of 1862 he began to draft a proclamation setting the slaves free. After the Second Confiscation Act was passed, he rewrote his draft and read it to a meeting of the Cabinet on July 22, 1862. Some members did not like it at all, while others thought that he should wait until a propitious moment to issue it. He decided to wait. Meanwhile, he was attacked by numerous persons for not issuing such a proclamation. Five days after the Battle of Antietam, he issued the preliminary Emancipation Proclamation, declaring that slaves in states still in rebellion on January 1, 1863, would be set free.

Reaction to the Proclamation was mixed. The President's critics said that it was an act of desperation calculated to incite the slaves against their masters. His supporters greeted the Proclamation with enthusiasm. Even the abolitionists, while not entirely satisfied, regarded it as a good beginning. When the President issued the final Emancipation Proclamation on January 1, 1863, he named the states and portions of states where it was applicable. He also invited Negroes to enlist in the armed service of the United States "to garrison forts, positions, stations, and other places, and to man vessels of all sorts in said service." As he put his signature to the Proclamation, the President said, "I never, in my life, felt more certain that I was doing right than I do in signing this paper." There was rejoicing throughout the Union. Union policy had evolved.

Negroes Fighting for Freedom and Union

Even before Lincoln issued the Emancipation Proclamation, the War Department had authorized the enlistment of Negroes in the Department of the South, "not exceeding five thousand"; and Ben Butler in Louisiana and Jim Lane in Kansas were receiving Negroes in the Army. Early in 1863 the enlistment of Negroes accelerated. In the North leading Negroes like Frederick Douglass acted as recruiting agents, while in the South white soldiers were assigned to the task of enlisting slaves. Rallies were held at which speakers urged Negroes to enlist; and in Boston, New York, and Philadelphia they went to the recruiting stations in large numbers. By the end of the war more than 186,000 Negroes had enrolled in the Union Army. From the seceded states came 93,000; from the border slave states, 40,000; and from the free states, approximately 53,000. It is possible that the total figure was larger, for some contemporaries insisted that many mulattoes served in white outfits without being designated as Negroes.

While some whites declined to command the men serving in the group designated as "United States Colored Troops," others were pleased to do so. Among them were outstanding leaders such as Colonel Thomas Wentworth Higginson, of the First South Carolina Volunteers; Colonel Robert Gould Shaw, of the Fifty-Fourth Massachusetts Regiment, and General N. P. Banks, of the First and Third Louisiana Native Guards. There were several outstanding Negro officers: Captain P. B. S. Pinchback and Major F. E. Dumas of Louisiana; Major Martin Delany and Captain O. S. B. Wall of the One Hundred and Fourth Regiment; hospital surgeons such as Charles B. Purvis and John Rapier, and chaplains such as Henry M. Turner and James Underdue. At the beginning there was discrimination in pay, and the Negro soldiers were bitter in their denunciation of the practice. Finally, in 1864 they were successful in their drive to secure equal pay.

Negroes saw action in every theater of operation. They were at Milliken's Bend in Louisiana, Olustee in Florida, Vicksburg in Mississippi and at the siege of Savannah. They took part in the reduction of Petersburg and were at the surrender at Appomattox Court House. Many of them were cited for gallantry. Four men of the Massachusetts Fifty-Fourth earned the Gilmore Medal for their heroism in the assault on Fort Wagner, in which their commanding officer, Colonel Shaw, lost his life. George Washington Williams, in his *History of the Negro Troops in the Rebellion*, says that Negroes saw action in more than 250 skirmishes and that the "roll of honor is luminous with the names of Negro soldiers who, by deeds of personal valor, won the applause of the commanding general and the Congress of the United States."

Negroes served in other ways. They organized raiding parties, went through Confederate lines to destroy fortifications and supplies, built fortifications and supplies, built fortifications along the coasts and up the rivers, and served as spies and scouts. Some women, such as Harriet Tubman, spied for the Union army.

More than 38,000 Negroes lost their lives in the war, their rate of mortality being about 40 percent greater than that of the white soldiers. It would be difficult for later critics to say that Negroes did not fight for their freedom but had it handed to them, just as it was unrealistic for white soldiers to object to fighting on the grounds that they were not anxious to risk their lives to set idle Negroes free.

If the end of the war marked a victory for the theory of the indestructibility of the Union, it was a signal victory for the cause of freedom. The end of the war brought to a close a period of enslavement that had lasted for some two hundred and fifty years. The desire for freedom had been kept alive through the centuries by those Negroes who demonstrated by their conduct that freedom and the right to it transcended racial lines. The victory was won, in part, by their struggles through the centuries as well as by their services in the final battles.

An Uncertain Peace

As the war progressed Lincoln made many plans. One of them had to do with the settlement of the problems of war once the hostilities ceased. In his Proclamation of Amnesty and Reconstruction, in December, 1863, he spelled out these plans. The spirit was one of leniency. Only a few of the leaders of the Confederacy were not to be restored to the full enjoyment of their rights as citizens, and when 10 percent of the 1860 electorate had taken the oath of allegiance, the government of a given state would be restored. This meant, of course, that the government would be exclusively white. But Lincoln also had plans for Negroes. He hoped that they would be given the franchise; and in 1864 he suggested to the governor of Louisiana that at least Negroes of education and property should be permitted to vote. He also hoped, through the Freedmen's Bureau and otherwise, that adequate educational opportunities for Negroes would be provided. On more than one occasion toward the end of the war, he indicated that Negroes should receive the same treatment as other citizens.

The former Confederate states that were restored by Lincoln and, after April, 1865, by Johnson were dominated by former Confederate leaders. They had no intention of extending any semblance of equality to their former slaves. Indeed, they had little enthusiasm for the Thirteenth Amendment that was being ratified during the summer and fall of 1865. It is not surprising, therefore, that as these governments formulated new policies they were controlled by the view that the Negro was inferior and should be kept subordinate. The new black codes, passed by the Southern legislatures in 1865 and 1866, gave expression to this view. Negroes could now own and dispose of property, could make contracts and enter into marriage and were competent witnesses in cases involving Negroes. The vagrancy laws, authorizing the arrest of Negroes with no visible means of support, were a thinly disguised plan to exploit the services of the Negro working force. Some states forbade Negroes to purchase farm land, while others enacted curfew laws for Negroes, forbade the possession of liquor and firearms by Negroes and outlawed acts of insolence by Negroes. No South-

ern state made any provision for the education of Negroes at the time that schools for whites were being established.

When Congress met in December, 1865, it was greeted with the news of the black codes and of the domination of the Southern state legislatures by former Confederates. Congress refused to seat members from those states, and many members began to talk openly of the necessity of punishing traitors. Early in the following year the Joint Committee that had been set up by Congress recommended the continuation of the policy of keeping Southern members out and the enactment of legislation designed to protect freedmen.

One piece of legislation growing out of these recommendations was the Civil Rights Act of 1866 that guaranteed the rights of all citizens regardless of race. Another was the extension of the Freedmen's Bureau, which was vetoed by the President but finally passed over his veto. A third was the passage of a resolution that incorporated in it the provisions of the Civil Rights Act and that became in 1868 the Fourteenth Amendment. News from the South put Congress in an even more uncompromising mood. The Freedmen's Bureau was helping destitute whites as well as Negroes and was making provisions for schools for Negroes where the whites had neglected them; but it was being bitterly opposed in virtually every Southern community. White Northern teachers who had been engaged by the Bureau or by religious groups to teach Negroes were not only ostracized by the whites but were, in some cases, run out of the community. Negroes, moreover, were being subjected to numerous forms of intimidation and terror. In their conventions in 1865 and 1866 the Negroes passed resolutions asking the President and Congress for protection. In the spring and summer of 1866 race riots in Memphis and New Orleans confirmed the worst fears of the Northerners. A reign of terror was sweeping the South. Something would have to be done.

It was in March, 1867, that Congress took over from the President the task of Reconstruction. It reimposed military rule on the South, disfranchised all former Confederates who had voluntarily taken up arms against the United States, called for new governments based on the suffrage of all loyal men, regardless of race, and required the ratification of the Fourteenth Amendment as a condition for readmission to the Union. No provisions were made for the economic rehabilitation of the former slaves, no "forty acres and a mule" that some had believed they would receive. Political power was in the hands of the Northern whites who had taken up residence in the South, Southern whites who could take the oath that they had not voluntarily fought against the United States, and the Negroes. Economic power, however, remained in the hands of the former Confederates who, now, were sitting on the sidelines, ready to attack and oppose everything that the new political leaders sought to establish.

In the constitutional conventions called to write new organic laws for the former Confederate states, Negroes were in the majority in only one of them, South Carolina. In Louisiana the forty-nine Negro delegates were equal in number to the whites. In some states, such as Georgia, Alabama and North Carolina, the native whites outnumbered the Negroes. In states such as Texas and Arkansas, the number of Negroes in the conventions was small. Even so, the conventions were ridiculed as "Ethiopian minstrelsy" and "Ham radicalism." Much more was said about how the delegates looked than about what the delegates did.

The conventions gave the South the best constitutions it had ever had. The new documents forbade any race or color distinctions in their suffrage provisions. They provided for free common school systems; but only in South Carolina and Louisiana were integrated schools attempted. The right to travel, to a proper trial and to the fair administration of justice were provided for. They eased the burdens of the debtors, but did not provide for the confiscation and redistribution of the land. In each state the black codes were either repealed outright or superseded by new laws. By the summer of 1868 all states, except Virginia, Texas and Mississippi, had been readmitted to the Union and their representatives in Congress seated. By 1870 all states were back in the Union.

The period that followed has been described as one of Negro rule. But Negroes were not in control of the state governments at any time anywhere in the South. They held public office and, at times, played important parts in public life. Only in South Carolina did they ever have a numerical majority in the lower house of the legislature. From the outset, whites controlled the upper house. At all times the governor was white. There were other leaders: Negroes were lieutenant governors in 1870 and 1872. From 1868 to 1872 Francis Cardozo was secretary of state and from 1872 to 1876 he was state treasurer. The situation was not so favorable for Negroes anywhere else in the South. In Mississippi of seven state officers, only one, that of secretary of state, was filled by a colored man, until 1873 when colored men were elected to three of the seven offices. In some states, very few Negroes held positions of prominence.

The Negroes who stood out were those of education and experience. Cardozo of South Carolina had been educated at the University of Glasgow and in London. Hiram Revels, elected to the United States Senate from Mississippi, had been educated in a seminary in Ohio and at Knox College in Illinois. James T. Rapier, Negro member of Congress from Alabama, had been sent by his white father to school in Canada. Jonathan J. Wright had been educated in Pennsylvania and was a member of the Pennsylvania bar before he migrated to South Carolina, where he became a member of the state supreme court. Some, however, were self-made, like Robert Smalls who had won fame during the Civil War by piloting the Confederate ship, the *Planter,* out of Charleston harbor and delivering it to Union officials. He was later to sit in Congress. Or, like John R. Lynch, speaker of the house in Mississippi and later a member of Congress, who sat outside the window of a white school and learned everything the white students were being taught.

Sixteen Negroes served in Congress between 1869 and 1880. Two of them, Hiram Revels and Blanche K. Bruce, represented Mississippi in the Senate. South Carolina sent six Negroes to the House of Representatives, the largest number from a single state; but they were not all in the House at the same time. Alabama sent three, while Georgia, Florida, Mississippi, North Carolina and Louisiana sent one each. Their responsible conduct moved James G. Blaine, their contemporary, to observe, "The colored men who took their seats in both Senate and House did not appear ignorant or helpless. They were as a rule studious, earnest, ambitious men, whose public conduct . . . would be honorable to any race."

It cannot be said that the Reconstruction governments or that the Negro leaders were more corrupt than their contemporaries in other parts of the country. There was graft in connection with railroad construction, printing contracts, public works and the like. Wherever there was corruption, it was marked by the participation of all segments of society: former Confederates as well as Northern Whites and Negroes. Corruption was bisectional, bipartisan and biracial.

If no race or party had a monopoly on public immorality, it can be said that no group was the sole keeper of the public conscience. In the South, however, the groups that opposed Reconstruction insisted that they were. They insisted that "Negro rule" had brought on evils and sufferings and must be destroyed. This view is what stimulated the growth of the Ku Klux Klan and similar groups after 1867. Rumor had it that the Union League, which had been organized during the war, was teaching Negroes not only to be faithful to the Republican Party but also to regard themselves as the equals of whites in every respect. The Klan began to assail the league as the enemy of the South. It began to attack white and Negro members, destroy their property, and whip and sometimes murder them. Politically minded Negroes and so-called Negro militia units were the special objects of attack by Klansmen. Despite the fact that very few troops had ever been in the South after the Civil War, the Klan used any and all armed Negroes as an excuse to attack Negroes generally. Murders, lynchings and drownings were the hazards facing Negroes and whites who played any part in the reconstruction of the South.

Reconstruction had no chance in the South because it did not provide for even a semblance of economic security and independence on the part of the Negroes. Negro voters were still at the mercy, for a livelihood, of those who were bitterly opposed to their exercising the franchise. It is remarkable that Negroes were able to gain any economic security, but some of them did. By 1866 the freedmen in Florida had secured homesteads covering 160,000 acres of land; and by 1874 the Negroes of Georgia owned more than 350,000 acres. Those with some skills, moreover, such as tailors, caulkers, blacksmiths and cabinetmakers, were able to secure employment. But the vast majority of Negroes had neither the means nor the skills to achieve economic stability. Most of them were employed by their former masters who could merely threaten them with starvation if they persisted in exercising the franchise. Meanwhile, Northern financiers and industrialists were gradually moving in to establish economic control over the South. Negroes were excluded altogether from the new opportunities; and they could hold their old jobs only if they obeyed the command of their employers to stay out of politics. The economic stranglehold that the whites held over Negroes was enough to put an end to Reconstruction.

Indeed, Reconstruction was over in some places almost before it began. If one measures the time from the readmission of the reconstructed states to the time of Democratic victories, one is impressed with how short the period was. While these periods varied from state to state, they were less than a decade, except in Florida, South Carolina and Louisiana. Even during the time it existed, Reconstruction was not very radical. Segregated schools and laws against intermarriage persisted. There was no confiscation and redistribution of the land. The military occupation was brief and ineffective, and Negroes did not dominate any governments. The Fourteenth Amendment was, on the whole, a dead letter; and the Fifteenth Amendment was not enforced by the Federal Government. In the end, the Negro was only slightly better off than he had been when the war came in 1861.

EARLY STRUGGLES FOR CITIZENSHIP

Loss of Civil Rights

When chattel slavery was abolished in 1865, some interested observers made the direst predictions about the future of the freedmen. They entertained serious doubts about the Negro's capacity to survive as a free man. Ignoring the incredible suffering that made little distinction among the races at the end of the war, these observers saw in the destitution and disease among Negroes a portent of their complete extinction. An eminent white Southerner, Dr. C. K. Marshall of Mississippi, was quite certain about this when he said in 1866, "In all probability New Year's Day, on the morning of the first of January, 1920, the colored population in the South will scarcely be counted." While most Americans were uncertain about the future of the Negro in the United States, they were not nearly as pessimistic regarding numbers as Dr. Marshall. Most of them seemed to agree that the American Negro would at least survive; and many entertained the hope that he could be utilized, if not exploited, in the advancement of American civilization. The Negro not only survived, but demonstrated a remarkable capacity to thrive even in an atmosphere where his freedom was continually compromised. When the war came in 1861 there were approximately 4,441,830 Negroes in the United States, of whom 3,953,000 were slaves. By 1900 the Negro population had virtually doubled.

While the problem of survival was early solved once and for all, the problem of the status of the Negro was a continuing one, long after the end of Reconstruction. Toward the end of Reconstruction, as the collapse of the enforcement of Federal laws deprived Negroes of their opportunity to vote, their enjoyment of other rights was also being challenged. Congress made one last effort to protect them. In May, 1870, Senator Charles Sumner introduced the most far-reaching civil rights bill that was to be considered by Congress until 1964. The bill provided for equal rights in railroads, steamboats, public conveyances, hotels, licensed theaters, houses of public entertainment, common schools, all institutions of learning authorized by law, churches, cemetery associations and juries in Federal and state courts. For a time the bill had a rocky and uncertain fate. When it finally became law in 1875, it declared that the United States should "mete out equal and exact justice to all, of whatever nativity, race, color, or persuasion, religious or political." From the beginning the climate in the country was not favorable to the enforcement of the act, which had already been "watered down" by the deletion of the provision to desegregate the schools. During its eight years of life the act provided little protection for Negroes because of the rather general failure to enforce it.

That the act would ultimately be tested in the courts was a foregone conclusion; and its unhappy fate was almost as certain. Of the incidents involved in the cases that came to the Supreme Court under the Civil Rights Act, one involved the use of a parlor car by a Negro in Tennessee; another involved the denial of hotel accommodations for Negroes in one Northern state; others involved the use of public facilities in Missouri, California, Kentucky and New York. In the decision of the Court, Mr. Justice Bradley, speaking for the majority, held the relevant provisions of the act unconstitutional. Congress could enact legislation to meet the exigency of state action adverse to the rights of citizens as secured by the Fourteenth Amendment, he said. But Congress could not properly "cover the whole domain of rights appertaining to life, liberty, and property, defining them and providing for their vindication."

Under the Fourteenth Amendment, as interpreted by the Court, there could be no significant advancement of the Negro toward full citizenship. Negroes were generally discouraged by the decision, and they recalled that the Court had not been a source of strength, as far as they were concerned. The Dred Scott decision in 1857 had declared that Negroes were not citizens. The decisions in the Reese and Cruikshank cases in 1876 indicated that the Congress could not enact legislation to protect the rights guaranteed in the Fifteenth Amendment. Now, in the Civil Rights Cases the Fourteenth Amendment was rendered ineffective. Small wonder that Negroes saw it as reversing the trend and moving the Negroes back toward slavery. T. T. Allain, a Negro leader in Louisiana, said that the decision showed that whites of the North and South had allied "to leave the Negro to fend for himself." T. Thomas Fortune, the Negro editor and essayist, said that Negroes felt that they had been "baptized in ice water." John Mercer Langston who, in 1889, would become the only Negro ever elected to Congress from Virginia, called the decision "a stab in the back."

The attitudes of vast numbers of the country's influential white people had as much to do with defining the status of the Negro as anything that the Supreme Court or any other branch of the Federal Government was doing. The dark cloud of assumed racial differences became more ominous than ever; and it bespoke a new, more frightening conclusion that many Americans had reached: that racial differences were normal and natural and the American Negro was a classic example of the hopeless inferiority of a whole race of people. It was the Darwinian mood that sustained the belief in Anglo-Saxon superiority and obsessed many American thinkers in the last quarter of the nineteenth century. Whites were in a dominant position because they were the superior race; they were the fittest. Primitives such as Negroes were in an arrested stage of childhood or adolescence and could never gain the full stature of manhood. Distinguished white scholars argued that it was absurd to attempt to change the natural order of things. As early as 1876 William G. Sumner advocated the restoration of "home rule" in the South because Reconstruction had attempted the impossible in trying to reverse the natural course of things in which superior whites ruled over inferior blacks.

The leading and most respected literary journals of the country reflected the view that the Negro was inferior and did not possess rights which should be protected by government. In the last two decades of the nineteenth century such journals as *Harper's*, *Scribners*, and the *Atlantic Monthly* strained their own ample ingenuity by portraying the Negro in the most unfavorable light. In an exhaustive study of the period, *The Negro in American Life and Thought*, Rayford W. Logan has shown that every possible insulting term was used by these journals in reference to Negroes. They were made to appear ludicrous by the bestowal of absurd titles on them. Invariably they were described as ugly. In articles, stories, anecdotes, poems and cartoons, Negroes were made to appear superstitious, dull, stupid, imitative, ignorant, happy-go-lucky, improvident, lazy, immoral and criminal. Southern writers were doing the same thing. In his *The*

Leopard's Spots: A Romance of the White Man's Burden and in other works, Thomas Dixon, Jr., described in vivid terms the "base" character of the Negro. This, he argued, justified almost any degradation the Negro received at the hands of his white superiors.

It followed that if Negroes were as undesirable and unfit for civilization as the writers, North and South, claimed, they were not fit associates for white people and should be segregated. There had been some segregation, both in law and in practice before and during Reconstruction. But, as C. Vann Woodward has pointed out in *The Strange Career of Jim Crow*, it was not nearly so extensive as was once believed. There were many instances of unsegregated relations between Negroes and whites. The major Protestant churches were divided as between North and South even before the war; but within the South there were few if any separate white and Negro Protestant churches. From their beginnings after the Civil War, the public schools of the South were, with few exceptions, segregated. The armed services were segregated during the Civil War and remained so during the following years. The first state segregation statutes were those of Mississippi and Florida in 1865. The Tennessee law of 1881, sometimes referred to as the first jim crow law, directed railroad companies to provide separate cars or portions of cars for first-class Negro passengers, instead of relegating them to second-class accommodations, as had been the custom.

In the ensuing twenty years, the separation of Negroes and whites on public carriers and almost everywhere else became a favorite preoccupation of some Southern legislators, although opposition on the part of some articulate whites, such as George W. Cable, continued until the end of the century. By 1892 six southern states had joined Tennessee in segregating Negroes on public carriers—Texas, Louisiana, Alabama, Arkansas, Georgia, and Kentucky. In some states there was substantial opposition on the part of Negroes and their white supporters. In Louisiana a Negro representative declared that the segregation law would humiliate Negroes and "make them appear before the world as a treacherous and dangerous class of people." In Arkansas a Negro member of the House sought to ridicule the segregation bill's supporters by insisting that if whites did not want to associate with Negroes, there should be laws to divide the streets and sidewalks so that Negroes could go on one side and white people on the other. He would like "to see an end put to all intercourse between white and colored people by day, and especially by night."

As the pattern of segregation took shape in some states, pressure for various forms of segregation mounted in other states. South Carolina passed a law segregating Negroes and whites on railroads in 1898. North Carolina and Virginia enacted similar legislation in 1899 and 1900 respectively. When Oklahoma entered the union in 1907 every conceivable form of segregation had already been provided for. Segregation was spreading to other activities related to transportation. In 1888 the railroad commission of Mississippi was authorized to designate separate waiting rooms for Negroes and whites. By 1893 the railroad companies, on their own initiative, were doing the same thing in South Carolina. By 1907 segregation had been enacted into law in all Southern states on street cars, penitentiaries, county jails, convict camps, institutions for the blind and deaf, hospitals for the insane and other institutions.

While the Southern states were in the process of enacting laws to separate the races, the Supreme Court, in the decision of *Plessy* v *Ferguson,* gave them all the encouragement they needed. In 1890 Louisiana had enacted a law providing that "all railway companies carrying passengers in their coaches in this state, shall provide separate but equal accommodations for the white and colored races." When Plessy, who was as white as any person in New Orleans but who was known to have Negro blood, boarded a coach reserved for whites, he was ordered to the colored coach. When he refused to do so, he was arrested and charged with violating the law. Plessy argued that the Louisiana statute was in conflict with the Thirteenth Amendment abolishing slavery and the Fourteenth Amendment, which prohibits certain restrictive legislation on the part of the states. The Supreme Court did not agree. Speaking for the Court, Mr. Justice Bradley interpreted the statute as intending to enforce "absolute equality of the two races before the law" while recognizing fundamental distinctions between them. Thus, the doctrine of "separate but equal" became the law of the land and gave moral as well as legal support to those who were busily engaged in enacting segregation statutes.

Meanwhile, the Southern states had undertaken to disfranchise Negroes in order to make certain that they would not have the political strength to resist the move to make permanent their status as second-class citizens. Advocates of disfranchisement had to be certain that they did not contravene the Fifteenth Amendment or offend illiterate poor whites. As early as 1886 sentiment in Mississippi, where a majority of the population were Negroes, was strong for constitutional revision. A convention met in 1890 for the primary purpose of disfranchising the Negro. A suffrage amendment was written which imposed a poll tax of two dollars, excluded voters convicted of bribery, burglary, theft, arson, perjury, murder and bigamy, and also barred all who could not read any section of the state constitution, or understand it when read, or give a reasonable interpretation of it. Before the convention Negroes from forty counties met and protested to President Harrison their impending disfranchisement. The President did nothing; and since the new constitution was never submitted for ratification but simply put into effect, its opponents had no change of working to defeat it.

South Carolina followed Mississippi by disfranchising Negroes in 1895. Ben Tillman, who had initiated the campaign for disfranchisement, left the United States Senate and returned to the convention in South Carolina to push through the desired revision of the constitution. The new clause called for two years' residence, a poll tax of one dollar, the ability to read and write the constitution or own property worth three hundred dollars, and the disqualification of convicts. Negro delegates bitterly denounced the move. In answer to Tillman's charge that Negroes had done nothing to demonstrate their capacity for government, Thomas E. Miller, a leading Negro in the state, replied that Negroes were largely responsible for the "laws relative to finance, the building of penal and charitable institutions and, greatest of all, the establishment of the public school system." The story was essentially the same in Louisiana where, in 1898, a new device, the "Grandfather Clause," was written into the constitution. This called for an addition to the permanent registration list the names of all males whose fathers or grandfathers were qualified to vote on January 1, 1867. At that time, of course, no Negroes in Louisiana were qualified to vote. Negroes, but not whites, therefore had to comply with the educational and property requirements. By 1910 the Negro had also been effectively disfranchised in Virginia, Georgia, North Carolina, Alabama and Oklahoma.

By the end of the nineteenth century the Negro had lost most of the civil rights that he had ever enjoyed, however fleetingly. He had been denied the use of public accommodations; he had been disfranchised; and the concept of "separate but equal" had given the whites an opportunity to reduce Negro schools to the lowest level of inadequacy. In South Carolina, where Negroes constituted 61 percent of the school population, they received 21 percent of the school funds. Already, separation seemed to be a guarantee not only of inequality in education but also of a permanently inferior status in American life.

Out of the Mainstream

The end of Reconstruction brought little improvement in the social and economic status of the Negro. While Southern whites were not willing to appropriate very much for the education of Negroes, they seemed less opposed than formerly to the support of Negro education by northern philanthropic and religious organizations. Meanwhile, many Negroes viewed education as their greatest single opportunity to escape the indignities and proscriptions of an oppressive white South. Negro parents sent their children to school in increasing numbers at great sacrifice to themselves; and while the schools were not excellent, they did provide the rudiments of an education. Religious groups such as the American Missionary Association and the Freedmen's Aid Society of the Methodist Church continued the work of the defunct Freedmen's Bureau. Philanthropic agencies such as the George Peabody Fund, the Anna T. Jeanes Fund and Rockefeller's General Education Board gave attention to special problems of Negro education such as teacher training and vocational education. Since many of the grants made by philanthropists were on the condition that local school boards and agencies would match their gift, they had the effect of stimulating a limited amount of local support for Negro education.

Negroes themselves were contributing substantially to the support of their own schools and colleges. At the Sixth Atlanta Conference for the Study of Negro Problems in 1901 it was reported that between 1870 and 1899 Negroes paid a total of $25 million in direct school taxes; while the indirect taxes they paid amounted to more than $45 million. Negroes had paid more than $15 million in tuition and fees to private institutions. The report concluded, "It is a conservative statement to say . . . that American Negroes have in a generation paid directly forty millions of dollars in hard-earned cash for educating their children." The institutions, meanwhile, had done much to sustain themselves. The Fisk Jubilee Singers had gone out in 1875 and had raised more than enough money to construct the first important building at the young university. Other institutions had sent out speakers, demonstrators, and others in the effort to gain support. Self-help became an important principle in the early days of Negro schools and colleges.

The results of the efforts of Negroes to secure an education were gratifying. In 1900 there were 28,560 Negro teachers and more than 1,500,000

Negro children in school. Thirty-four institutions for Negroes were giving collegiate training; and more Negroes were entering the institutions of higher education in the North. There were four state colleges for Negroes —in Virginia, Arkansas, Georgia and Delaware. By 1900 more than two thousand Negroes had graduated from institutions of higher learning, while more than seven hundred were in college at the time. As Negroes manifested an avid interest in education, there were some whites who questioned the wisdom of their securing an education to live in a society in which they were not in the main stream.

Even among Negroes there was no agreement as to the amount and type of education that Negroes should seek. Booker T. Washington, who founded the Tuskegee Institute in 1881, thought that Negroes could be most effective and would be acceptable in the Southern communities if they sought to provide many of the services and much of the produce that the white community needed. He emphasized the intelligent management of farms, ownership of land, proficiency in mechanics, domestic service and the professions. On numerous occasions, and especially in his celebrated speech at Atlanta in 1895, he assured the whites that the Negroes were their friends, that they did not seek social equality but merely an opportunity to serve. His advocacy of vocational education for Negroes was hailed by whites in the North and in the South. They came to regard him as the wisest and most reliable spokesman of his race.

Some Negroes, however, rejected him as their spokesman. Among them was W. E. B. Du Bois, a young Negro trained at Fisk, Harvard (where he received the degree of doctor of philosophy) and Berlin. In books, essays and addresses Du Bois criticized what he viewed as the narrow educational program of Washington which was too predominantly economic in its objectives. He accused Washington of preaching "a gospel of Work and Money to such an extent as apparently almost completely to overshadow the higher aims of life." Du Bois also criticized the manner in which Washington ignored or winked at the white South's denial of the Negro's civil rights. A policy of conciliation had resulted, he insisted, in the disfranchisement of the Negro and the enactment of discriminatory legislation of many kinds. Despite these criticisms of Washington, he remained the most important and, indeed, the most powerful Negro in the United States down to his death in 1915. It was during his ascendancy, however, that lynchings of Negroes reached a new high, Negroes were effectively disfranchised, and Negroes were systematically excluded from American industry and from American labor unions.

In 1880 some 75 percent of the Negroes in the United States were still in the former Confederate states and were primarily engaged in agricultural work. Most of them were without capital with which to purchase land and were compelled to engage in various forms of tenancy and sharecropping. As farm workers their incomes were meager. In 1902 farm laborers in South Carolina were receiving ten dollars per month, while those of New York were receiving twenty-six dollars per month. Some, however, accumulated enough capital to purchase farms. In 1890 Negroes owned 120,738 farms, while in 1910 they owned 218,972 farms, with the average size less than ten acres. Booker Washington, through the farmers' conferences at Tuskegee, sought to eliminate "the evils of the mortgage system, the one-room cabin, buying on credit" and the like; but it was a difficult task in the face of persistent hostility on the part of the white community.

As industry came to the South, the Negro, for the most part, was left out. The iron industry was growing in Tennessee and Alabama, cloth was being manufactured in the Carolinas, and the business of transporting manufactured goods to the Southern consumer was becoming a major economic activity. In 1891 some 196 industrial employers of the South were using only 7,395 Negroes, largely as menials. Ten years later the number had increased substantially, and some Negroes were employed in cotton seed oil mills, saw mills and furniture factories. By 1910 the Negro factory workers had increased to more than 350,000. Prejudice against the Negro worker and the refusal of numbers of whites, North and South, to work with Negroes served to exclude many Negroes from labor unions. Manufacturers thus had two excuses to justify their exclusion of Negroes from greater employment: they were temperamentally unfit, according to no less an authority than *The Manufacturer's Record,* and whites would not work with them.

But Negroes were, in some instances, contributing to the growing industrialization of the United States. Jan E. Matzeliger, a Negro from Dutch Guiana, invented the shoe-lasting machine, which was purchased by the United Shoe Machinery Company of Boston. In 1884 John P. Parker invented a "screw for tobacco presses" and through his own company made many presses. Elijah McCoy patented fifty different inventions relating principally to the automatic lubrication of machines. Granville Woods made significant contributions in the fields of electricity, steam boilers and automatic air brakes. Several of his inventions were assigned to the General Electric Company, the Westinghouse Air Brake Company and the American Bell Telephone Company.

Many Negroes concluded that since they were not in the mainstream of American economic life, they should organize and promote their own businesses. It was with this in mind that Booker Washington called a group of Negro businessmen together in 1900 in Boston and organized the National Negro Business League. Washington urged Negroes to enter a wide variety of business fields. Either in response to Washington's urging or because they already realized the importance of such moves, many Negroes organized their own businesses. They operated grocery and merchandise stores; they were restaurant operators, caterers, bakers, tailors, builders, and contractors. Some operated shirt factories, cotton mills, rubber stamp goods shops, lumber mills and carpet factories. They were also engaged in cooperative enterprises. Most of these businesses were not profitable and lasted only a short time. There were exceptions, however. Madam C. J. Walker founded a hair and skin preparation business and made a fortune. Negro banking and insurance companies in Richmond, Atlanta, Washington, Birmingham and Montgomery achieved both stability and respect.

These signs of progress and prosperity were not enough for many Negroes who remained dissatisfied with their lot in their communities. Their political and social degradation was not relieved by their economic condition; and some of them decided to leave the South for some other part of the country. In 1879 and 1880 thousands of Negroes left the lower South and took up residence in the North and West, and the movement continued for the next several decades. While they met hostile labor unions and rejection by industrialists in the North, they continued to believe that their opportunities were greater elsewhere than in the South. Neither a Congressional investigation nor promises by Southern whites of good treatment and high wages could dissuade them. They were in search of the mainstream of American life that seemed more and more like a will-o'-the-wisp.

The Negro World

Whites in the South and in the North maintained a discreet distance from Negroes and welcomed them into no area of their social activities. Negroes were compelled to work out their own means of survival in a hostile world, and this involved creating institutions and activities that, in turn, created a Negro world. One of the mainstays in the process of providing group cohesion and rendering self-help was the Negro church. Seeing that they were not welcome among the white Baptists, Negroes in 1880 organized the National Baptist Convention. Soon the National Baptist Publishing House began to circulate Sunday School and other religious literature among Negroes. The older denominations among Negroes, African Methodists and Colored Methodists, continued their activities; and in the cities the churches did many things to assist Negroes to adjust to their new environment. In New York, Detroit, Chicago, St. Louis and other cities the Negro churches established employment bureaus, maintained schools of domestic training, and organized various clubs for boys and girls. In Atlanta, Dr. H. H. Proctor's Congregational church organized a day nursery, kindergarten, gymnasium, and school of music; while in Springfield, Massachusetts, Dr. W. N. DeBerry led his Congregational members in the establishment of a home for working girls and a welfare league for women.

Fraternal organizations, with auxiliary activities such as insurance and burial societies, became numerous during the period. The Knights of Pythias and the Knights of Tabor competed for membership among Negro men. Others, such as the Independent Order of St. Luke and the Order of True Reformers, were open to men and women. Out of some of these organizations came the founders of important insurance companies. S. W. Rutherford left the True Reformers and organized the National Benefit Life Insurance Company of Washington, D.C. In Durham, North Carolina, John Merrick, who had been a True Reformer, joined several others to establish the North Carolina Mutual Life Insurance Company. These and similar businesses grew into important social and economic institutions, providing a variety of benefits for the Negro community.

As Negroes became better educated and more articulate they began to write extensively; and most of their writings dealt with their being Negroes in a white world. Frederick Douglass and Booker Washington wrote their autobiographies. Henry O. Flipper wrote of his experiences as a Negro cadet at West Point. In the effort to refute the arguments of some whites that Negroes had contributed nothing to American civilization, several writers published histories of the Negro in the United States. In 1883 George Washington Williams published his *History of the Negro Race in America* in two volumes. Soon there were histories by E. A. Johnson, W. H. Crogman, and Booker Washington. In 1896 W. E. B. Du Bois brought out his *Suppression of the African Slave Trade*, which became the first work in the Harvard Historical Studies. Negroes were also writing about "the Negro problem" as is evidenced in T. T. Fortune's *Black and White* in 1884 and *The Negro in Politics* in 1885. Meanwhile, Charles W. Chesnutt rose to prominence as a novelist with such works as *The House Behind the Cedars, The Marrow of Tradition* and *The Conjure Woman.* Perhaps no Negro writer of the period had a greater impact than Paul Laurence Dunbar, whose poems won the critical acclaim of such a person as William Dean Howells. Dunbar's *Lyrics of a Lowly Life* and *Oak and Ivy* were widely read at the turn of the century.

Negro newspaper editors remained preoccupied in this period, as they had earlier, with the problem of fighting for a larger place for Negroes in American life. Magazines like the *Southern Workman,* published at Hampton Institute, and the *A.M.E. Review* begun in 1884 were concerned primarily with educational, literary and religious matters. In 1900 there were three daily newspapers—in Norfolk, Kansas City and Washington—and 150 weekly newspapers. Some were widely read and provoked considerable discussion. In Boston, George Forbes and Monroe Trotter were publishing the *Guardian,* which led the fight against Booker Washington. In the nation's capital, the *Washington Bee* was vigorous and outspoken and the *New York Age,* edited by T. Thomas Fortune, was outstanding.

Nothing suggests the extent to which the Negro was still out of the mainstream of American life more than the attention given to the Negro problem by conferences and conventions by whites and by Negroes. At the Lake Mohonk Conference on the Negro Question white citizens in 1890 discussed the educational and economic problems affecting Negroes. The Hampton Conference, conducted in part by Negroes, dealt with similar problems, as did the Capon Springs Conference. There were, moreover, the Tuskegee Conferences conducted by Booker Washington and the Atlanta University Conferences on the Negro Problem conducted by W. E. B. Du Bois. Out of some of them, such as the Atlanta Conferences, came significant published studies. Out of all of them came much talk. Out of none of them came any effective solutions of the many problems that beset American Negroes at the turn of the century.

NEW PATTERNS OF RACIAL ADJUSTMENT

Urban Problems

Writing shortly after the beginning of the twentieth century, W. E. B. Du Bois said that the problem of that century would be the problem of the color line. It was the experience of the closing years of the nineteenth century that prompted Du Bois to make the observation. It was not merely the Supreme Court decision in the Plessy case, or the riot in Wilmington, North Carolina, or the increase in the number of lynchings each year. It was also the employment of the total political and legal apparatus of many of the states for the purpose of making full citizenship for Negroes impossible. It was the meek acquiescence of the Federal Government in the South's so-called "legal" disfranchisement of Negroes through state constitutional amendments that were as transparent as they were specious. It was the use of law enforcement officers to sanction the denial of the rights of Negroes. It was the perfection of the machinery of segregation and discrimination in many parts of the country. It was the determination to frustrate those Negroes, who, like so many other Americans, believed that their major problems could be solved in the cities to which they flocked in ever increasing numbers.

The trickle of Negroes northward, that began in the late eighteen seventies, was almost a steady stream by 1900. The stimulus was not only the depressing conditions of the South but also the opportunities that Negroes thought they would have in the North. Agents of Northern employment offices or Northern factory owners went to Southern farms as well as Southern towns to lure Negro workers to the North. As long as the agents could evade hostile local police or other authorities their task was not very difficult. Thousands of Carolina and Georgia Negroes migrated to the industrial Northeast. Similar groups from the South Central states—Alabama, Mississippi, Louisiana—went to Ohio, Indiana, Michigan and Illinois cities. Those who did not dare venture so far went to Atlanta, New Orleans, Louisville, and other thriving Southern cities.

By 1900 only 27.7 percent of the Negro population was urban, but this represented a significant increase over the figure in 1860, when approximately 16 percent of the nation's Negroes were living in cities. In 1900 there were seventy-two cities with more than five thousand Negroes, while six cities—Philadelphia, New York, Baltimore, Washington, Memphis and New Orleans—each had more than fifty thousand. There were several cities of moderate size, all in the South, where Negroes outnumbered the whites. Among them were Charleston, Savannah, Jacksonville, Montgomery, Shreveport, Baton Rouge and Vicksburg.

As the Negro urban population grew, its problems multiplied. There was no longer the stultifying control by the Southern plantation owner, and the opportunities for education were somewhat improved. But labor unions were as hostile to Negroes as they were to other newly arrived groups. Most of them excluded Negroes from membership; and when Negroes accepted employment to break a strike, labor leaders accused Negroes of betraying the principles of trade unionism. Likewise, Negroes arriving in the city fresh from the country discovered that all but a few sections of the city were closed to them for housing. And when they crowded into the few areas that were open to them, where housing was frequently already substandard and falling apart, they were accused of destroying property values and running down the neighborhood. It was this attitude that led to the passing of the first housing segregation law in Louisville, Kentucky, in 1912. The law provided that city blocks containing a majority of whites were designated as white blocks; and those with a majority of Negroes were Negro blocks. No Negroes could move into the white blocks, and vice versa. Other cities, including Baltimore, Richmond and Atlanta, followed Louisville's lead; and Negro ghettoes, sanctioned by law, became well established in many parts of the country.

One of the most characteristic manifestations of the problem of Negro assimilation in the urban community at the beginning of the century was the race riot. Lynchings and burnings were rural fare; but rioting, on an even larger scale than occurred in Philadelphia and New York before the

Civil War, became the typical expression of resentment of the urban Negro in the twentieth century. While there were outbreaks in numerous small Southern towns in the first decade of the century, the Atlanta riot of 1906 was the largest Southern disturbance of the period. For months the city had been lashed into a fury of race hatred by loose talk and by the movement to disfranchise Negroes. In September Atlanta newspapers told of four successive but entirely unsubstantiated assaults on white women by Negroes. The country people, in town on the last Saturday of the month, joined the urban element in creating an outraged, panic-stricken mob. Whites began to attack every Negro they saw. Many innocent persons were beaten, others were dragged from vehicles. For several days rioting continued; factories were closed and all transportation stopped. Many Negroes were killed, and there was a general destruction of Negro property. When it was all over, the whites confessed their shame and condemned the rioters. But a scar remained on Negro-white relationships in the fastest-growing city of the South.

Rioting in Northern cities was about as prevalent as in the South. Springfield, Ohio, had two riots within a few years—in 1904 and 1906. The Northern riot that shook the entire country occurred in Springfield, Illinois, in August, 1908. A white woman claimed that she had been dragged from her bed and raped by a Negro, who was then arrested and jailed. Before a special grand jury the woman admitted that she had been severely beaten by a white man whose identity she refused to disclose and that the Negro had no connection whatever with the incident. By this time, however, feeling was running high. Mobs gathered, raided stores, secured guns and other weapons, and began to destroy Negro businesses and drive Negroes from their homes. Before order was restored by more than five thousand militiamen, two Negroes had been lynched, four white men killed and more than seventy persons injured.

Thus, in the early decades of the twentieth century Negroes found scant acceptance in the American urban community. They were unable to make good their claim to equal treatment in the labor market; and in the laissez-faire atmosphere that prevailed, the Government declined to come to their rescue. Indeed, in 1894 Congress had repealed much of the Civil Rights Act of 1866 that could have been invoked for the protection of Negroes. Theodore Roosevelt, who had become President in 1901 and on whom many Negroes had pinned their hopes, had proved a great disappointment. He talked a great deal about justice, but did little for the Negro aside from inviting Booker T. Washington to dine at the White House. Negroes had already come to the conclusion that Harold Laski was to reach much later: that Roosevelt had great "verbal audacity" but this was accompanied "by a relative caution in action." Negroes were suffering numerous political disabilities and enormous personal indignities, including living in ghettoes; and they were lucky to escape with their lives from the violent attacks of white mobs. What little relief Negroes got came from organized groups of whites and Negroes who could no longer tolerate the conditions that prevailed.

The tragic events of the early years of the century caused many Negroes to lose faith in government at every level. They no longer felt that any whites could be trusted to act in their behalf. As one Negro put it, "In the degree that the southern people stand by in silence and see the Negro

stripped of his civil and political rights by a band of unscrupulous men
. . . they compromise their own civil and political freedom. . . . If by
a mere technicality one class of citizens can be deprived of their rights
and immunities . . . what is to prevent any other class from sharing the
same fate?" It was at this point that some Negroes began to think in terms
of an action program capable of formulating specific plans to secure full
citizenship for all Americans, black and white. Soon, groups as far apart
as the New England Suffrage League and the Georgia Equal Rights
League had resolved to press for equal rights for Negroes.

New Organizational Efforts

The most articulate spokesman in this new drive for full citizenship
was W. E. B. Du Bois who in 1905 called a conference of Negro leaders to
meet in Niagara Falls, Canada, to formulate a program. After discussing
their numerous problems, they drew up a "Declaration of Principles," which
stated, among other things, that "We believe that Negroes should protest
emphatically and continually against the curtailment of their political
rights. We believe in manhood suffrage; we believe that no man is so good,
intelligent or wealthy as to be entrusted wholly with the welfare of his
neighbor." The group demanded equal economic opportunity, equal education, a fair administration of justice, and an end to segregation. For the
next three years members of the group, now calling itself "The Niagara
Movement," met and renewed its protests against injustice. By 1908 the
group had won the respect and support of large numbers of Negroes,
including the Equal Suffrage League, the National Association of Colored
Women's Clubs and college and high school students. And it had begun
litigation to knock out some of the jim crow laws of the Southern states.
By that time, however, several of its leading members had become involved in another movement which was soon to eclipse the Niagara
Movement.

The Springfield riot of 1908 plunged Negroes to the bottom of despair
and shocked the sensibilities of many whites. In a widely read article,
"Race War in the North," William English Walling deplored the conduct of
the white people of Springfield and called on the responsible whites of
the country to make amends. In 1909, in response to Walling's call, a
small group met and formulated plans for an organization to fight for the
rights of Negroes. In May, 1910, there came into existence the National
Association for the Advancement of Colored People. It was composed of
prominent whites, as well as distinguished Negroes; and it pledged itself
to work for the abolition of all forced segregation, equal education for
Negro and white children and the enforcement of the Fourteenth and
Fifteenth Amendments. Moorefield Storey of Boston was the first president,
and Du Bois became the director of publicity and research and editor of
the house organ, *The Crisis*.

In its first year of existence the NAACP launched a program to widen
industrial opportunities for Negroes, to seek greater police protection for
Negroes in the South, and to carry on a crusade against lynching and
lawlessness. Instrumental in carrying out this program were *The Crisis*
and the Legal Redress Committee, of which a New York lawyer, Arthur
B. Spingarn, was chairman. White and Negro attorneys worked closely

with Spingarn, and within a short time plans were made to test the constitutionality of state laws and state constitutions discriminating against Negroes. Spingarn's committee reasoned that if the Supreme Court was hostile of efforts of Congress to implement civil rights—as was inferred from the decision in the Civil Rights cases of 1883—perhaps it could be persuaded to frown upon the efforts of states to eliminate the Negro from consideration as a citizen.

The NAACP contended that the Negro's best opportunity to protect his rights lay in his exercise of the franchise. It was fitting, therefore, that the organization's first efforts would be against franchise restrictions. In 1910 it began its attack on the Grandfather Clause of the Oklahoma state constitution. It assailed that provision which stated that "no person who was, on January 1, 1866, or who was at any time prior thereto, entitled to vote under any form of government . . . and no lineal descendant of such person shall be denied the right to register and vote because of his inability to read and write" any section of the state constitution. In 1915 the United States Supreme Court, in its decision in *Guinn* vs. *United States,* pronounced as unconstitutional the suffrage provision of the Oklahoma constitution. "We seek in vain" Chief Justice White declared, "for any ground which would sustain any other interpretation but that the provision . . . adopted . . . to make [those conditions] the basis of the right to suffrage conferred in direct and positive disregard of the Fifteenth Amendment." In another NAACP case two years later, *Buchanan* vs. *Warley,* the Supreme Court outlawed the city ordinances requiring Negroes and whites to live in separate blocks in the city.

Fair administration of justice was one of the most serious obstacles to the Negro's enjoyment of full citizenship. The NAACP was determined to put an end to the abuse of the Negroes' rights in the courts; and it found ample opportunity to launch its crusade in Elaine, Arkansas. During a riot that followed, when a group of white men fired on an assemblage of Negroes in a church, one white man was killed. For several days after, Negroes were hunted down and killed like animals. In the melee, another white man was killed, for which crime several Negroes were arrested and charged with murder. The Negroes were tried in the midst of a surging, unruly mob. Thy had no opportunity to consult with counsel, and witnesses were not called. The trial lasted forty-five minutes; the jury deliberated less than five. The verdict was murder in the first degree. When the NAACP took the case to the Supreme Court on the ground that the defendants had been denied due process of law, the Court agreed. Justice Holmes was appalled by the flagrant denial of the rights of the five defendants; and the decision of the state court was reversed and a new trial ordered.

The NAACP also sought to meet, head on, the violence against Negroes that was increasing almost everywhere. It organized a parade in New York City to protest the terror against the Negro community that characterized the riot of East St. Louis, Illinois, in 1917. Two years later it held a national conference on lynching, at which the chief speaker was Charles Evans Hughes. Shortly thereafter, it was engrossed in a campaign to secure the passage of a Federal law against lynching. In 1921 a Missouri representative, L. C. Dyer, introduced such a bill in the lower house of

Congress, and it passed by a vote of 230–119. When it reached the floor of the Senate the Southern senators succeeded in organizing a filibuster that ultimately prevented a vote on the measure.

Economic opportunities for Negroes were even less certain, if such was possible, than their enjoyment of their civil rights. Their situation as farm employees and sharecroppers was deteriorating; and in the new Southern industries exclusion or discrimination continued. Even as they migrated to the cities, their problems were, in some instances, aggravated. Employment opportunities were fewer than the number of people moving to urban areas; and Negroes found great difficulty in securing anything except the more onerous and less attractive jobs, if they were lucky enough to secure anything at all. They continued to live around the "ragged edge of industry" with organized labor evincing a pronounced feeling of hostility. Only the Cigarmakers' International Union and the United Mine Workers of America seemed to welcome Negroes, although some other unions had Negro members. Negro women more easily found employment than men, as maids and household servants; and the more certain employment of women had the effect of attracting a larger number of women than men to the cities. The implications of this for family disorganization, juvenile delinquency and other problems were considerable.

Although the NAACP included in its program a plan to widen industrial opportunities of Negroes, it had neither the time nor the resources to do much in this area. More and more it concentrated on securing civil rights for Negroes. The need for organized effort in the economic and social spheres was especially urgent. In 1905 two organizations were established in New York looking toward the solution of the major economic and housing problems among Negroes. They were the Committee for Improving Industrial Conditions of Negroes in New York City and the National League for the Protection of Colored Women. Soon, they began to work together; and in 1911 they organized the National League on Urban Conditions, commonly known as the National Urban League. The new organization undertook to open new opportunities for Negroes in industry and to assist newly arrived Negroes in their problems of adjustment in the cities. Branches were opened in many of the larger cities, with programs for meeting the migrants, directing them to jobs and lodgings and offering information on how to live in the city. It did an effective job in bringing the employer and employee together and easing the difficulties of mutual adjustment.

There were numerous other efforts on the national and local levels to assist Negroes with their problems. The Young Men's Christian Association and the Young Women's Christian Association began to organize Negro branches and provide recreational as well as religious opportunities in the Negro community. Civic clubs among Negro men and women took on special projects designed to raise the level of aspiration among Negroes. Some of them fostered civic pride by encouraging home improvement, while others grappled with the more serious problems of crime and juvenile delinquency. In some Northern communities Negro political groups were already attempting to capitalize on the concentration of Negroes and elect Negroes to local offices.

Negroes had never been wholly politically inactive, despite the concerted efforts of the Southern whites and some of their Northern white friends to make them so. During the Roosevelt and Taft administrations, they made themselves felt in some sectors of the Republican Party; but their disillusionment deepened when neither Roosevelt nor Taft did much to help them secure their civil rights. In 1912 they were willing to turn to any group that promised some hope. To some Negroes, Woodrow Wilson seemed to provide some hope when he said, during his campaign, that he wished to see "justice done to the colored people in every matter; and not mere grudging justice, but justice executed with liberality and cordial good feeling." Shortly after Wilson's inauguration, it became clear to most Negroes that they could not rely on Wilson or his party for support in their efforts. Soon, segregation was reintroduced in the nation's capital and in the offices of the Federal government.

The experience of Negroes during World War I pointed up the painful fact that nowhere, not even in the armed services of the United States, did Negroes enjoy full citizenship. Under the Selective Service legislation 2,290,525 Negroes registered and 367,000 of them were called into the service. But everywhere there was discrimination. In the newly organized Air Force, Negroes were rejected altogether. In the United States Navy they were used only as menials; and in all other branches of the service they were segregated. The war was well under way before the War Department begrudgingly made some arrangements for the training of Negro officers at Fort Des Moines, Iowa. Few if any communities were pleased to have Negroes in training camps near them, and there were numerous incidents of clashes between Negro soldiers and white civilians. Negro soldiers complained, moreover, that they were constantly subjected to insults at the hands of their white officers.

Overseas, the situation was not much better. Negro combat troops were placed in various divisions of the French Army, and they were naturally faced with numerous problems of adjustment. They were taunted by the Germans who reminded them that they were fighting for the benefit of "Wall Street robbers" and others and not for their own freedom. Meanwhile, the French soldiers and citizens were warned by white Army officials from the United States not to treat Negro soldiers as equals. Despite all this, Negroes fought loyally and gallantly. Hundreds of them received the Croix de Guerre and other citations by the French Army, but none of them received the Medal of Honor from the United States.

During the war Negroes rushed to Northern industrial communities in the hope of finding employment in war-time industries. Upwards of 300,000 Negroes left the South and settled in the North and West in the war decade. Consequently, the urban problems became more acute than ever. In 1916 the National Urban League held a Conference on Migration and issued recommendations and advice to employers and migrants. But the hostility directed against Negroes was a clear indication that they were not welcome. The riot in East St. Louis, Illinois, in which forty Negroes lost their lives in 1917, was merely the worst of a series of racial clashes arising from the resentment of whites to the presence of Negro workers. Even so, many Negroes secured the best jobs they ever had. They were engaged in the manufacture of ammunition and iron and steel products. They were in the meat packing industries, and large numbers found employment in the new automobile industry. They were in the coal mines, on the railroads, and in the shipbuilding yards.

Some articulate Negroes despaired over the treatment that Negroes were receiving. For their article, "Pro-Germanism among Negroes," in which they severely criticized the policy of the United States, the editors of *The Messenger*, A. Phillip Randolph and Chandler Owen, were sentenced to jail for two and a half years and their second-class mailing privileges revoked. They did not serve their sentences, however. More influential among Negroes, however, was the editorial in July, 1918, by W. E. B. Du Bois, entitled "Close Ranks." In it, he said, "Let us not hesitate. Let us, while this war lasts, forget our special grievances and close our ranks shoulder to shoulder with our white citizens and the allied nations that are fighting for democracy."

The Reaction

Talk of democracy during the war had raised the hopes of most Negroes, and they were optimistic about the future. But their hopes were soon dashed by the events that followed the war. Already, the Ku Klux Klan had been revived and had adopted a broad program "for uniting native-born white Christians for concerted action in the preservation of American institutions and the supremacy of the white race." Within ten months, shortly after the close of the war, the Klan made more than two hundred public appearances in twenty-seven states. Soon, the Klan and other anti-Negro groups were terrorizing the Negro population in a variety of ways. Returning Negro soldiers discovered that neither they nor their fellows had won a semblance of equality or decent treatment for themselves. More than seventy Negroes were lynched during the first year of the post-war period. Ten Negro soldiers, several still in their uniforms, were lynched. Mississippi and Georgia mobs murdered three returned Negro soldiers each. Fourteen Negroes were burned publicly; and eleven of them were burned alive. In despair a Negro editor in South Carolina cried out, "There is scarcely a day passes that newspapers don't tell about a Negro soldier lynched in his uniform. Why do they lynch Negroes anyhow? With a white judge, a white jury, white public sentiment, white officers of the law, it is just as impossible for a Negro accused of crime or even suspected of crime to escape the white man's vengeance or his justice as it would be for a fawn to escape that wanders accidentally into a den of hungry lions."

With the summer of 1919 came the riots, twenty-five of them, North and South. In Longview, Texas, a Negro school principal was flogged on the streets, and several leading Negro citizens were run out of town. In Washington, D.C., mobs, consisting primarily of white sailors, soldiers and marines, ran amuck through the streets for three days, killing several Negroes and injuring scores of others. In Chicago, when a Negro attempted to swim in a part of Lake Michigan that whites had reserved for themselves, a riot began that lasted for thirteen days. Thirty-eight persons were killed —fifteen whites and twenty-three Negroes—and more than five hundred were injured. More than a thousand families, largely Negroes, were home-less due to the burnings and general destruction of property.

The racial strife of the post-war years indicated that the Negro was will-ing to fight and die for himself as well as for democracy in Europe. It was no longer a case of one race intimidating another into submission. Now it was war in the full sense of the word, and Negroes were as determined to win at home as they had been in Europe. And even if they could not win in an obviously one-sided struggle, they sought to make a good show-ing. They loudly protested against what they termed injustices and op-pressions. But soon, they realized that protests were not enough; not even fighting back was enough. Intelligent planning and action were needed. The following years would be characterized by their efforts to do precisely that.

THE RESTORATION OF SELF-RESPECT

The New Negro

The migration of Negroes from their ancestral homes on the plantations to urban America that began during the war placed the destiny of the Negro into his own hands more than ever before. And the forces that touched off this wave of migration gave way to other factors in the years following the war that continued to stimulate the migration of Negroes down to the present day. The urban North was becoming increasingly attractive, while the South, even as it became industrialized, gave every indication that it had no intention of revising its views regarding the inferior position in which the Negro should be kept. In 1910 no city in the United States had as many as 100,000 Negroes. By 1920 there were six such cities; and by 1940 there were eleven: New York, Chicago, Philadel-phia, Detroit, Washington, Baltimore, New Orleans, Memphis, Birming-ham, St. Louis, and Atlanta. Meanwhile, scores of thousands of Negroes were moving into urban communities where, up to that time, the Negro population had been negligible if, indeed, it existed at all.

This extensive urbanization of the Negro had a profound effect upon his status and, especially, on the way he viewed himself. He developed a sense of responsibility and a self-confidence that he had not previously known. During the war he learned from no less a person than his President of the promise of freedom, and on the battlefield he served his country. He began to see the discrepancies between the promise of freedom and his experiences in his own country. He became defiant, bitter and impatient. In company with his fellows, who were congregating in the cities in large numbers, he was no longer afraid as he had been on the Southern plantation. And he was more than willing to speak out against his injustices. It was not the timorous, docile Negro of the past who said, "The next time white folks pick on colored folks, something's going to drop—dead white folks."

The Negro was achieving, moreover, a degree and kind of articulation that made it possible for him to state his feelings clearly and forthrightly.

Despite his intense feelings of hate and hurt, he possessed sufficient restraint, if not objectivity, to use his materials artistically, but no less effectively. He was sufficiently in touch with the main currents of American literary development to adapt the accepted forms to his own materials and, therefore, gain a wider acceptance. The result was the emergence of a remarkable crop of Negro writers who made up what was later called the "Harlem Renaissance." Through poetry, prose and song they cried out against social and economic injustices. They protested against segregation and lynching; and they demanded better conditions of work. And in their demands they were almost unanimous in their efforts to secure justice in the framework of the existing economic and political structure.

There was a sense of satisfaction among Negroes as they insisted that they were on the right side of the country's professed ideals. As Alain Locke said in his volume, *The New Negro*, published in 1925, "The Negro mind reaches out as yet to nothing but American wants, American ideas. But this forced attempt to build his Americanism on race values is a unique social experiment, and its ultimate success is impossible except through the fullest sharing of American culture and institutions. . . . We realize that we cannot be undone without America's undoing. It is within the gamut of this attitude that the thinking Negro faces America, but with variations of mood that are, if anything, more significant than the attitude itself." Articulate Negroes sensed the moral advantage that they possessed, and they used it in every way possible.

The number of Negroes who now came forth in the nineteen-twenties to write about the plight of their race was itself an indication of the intellectual achievement so many of them had made. Du Bois continued his creative writings, bringing out several novels, two volumes of poems and essays, and other works. James Weldon Johnson, who had published his *Autobiography of an Ex-Colored Man* in 1912 and in the following year his poem "Fifty Years," commemorating the anniversary of the Emancipation Proclamation, was even more prolific in the years following the war. His Book of *American Negro Poetry* and his own volume of folk poems, *God's Trombones*, placed him in the mainstream of American writers. Claude McKay, regarded by many as the leading poet of the Harlem Renaissance, was also one of the most caustic in his strictures of American life. His *Harlem Shadows* and *Home to Harlem* intensively examined the Negro ghetto in poem and prose. Countée Cullen published his first volume of poems, *Color*, in 1925, when he was only twenty-two years old. In succeeding works such as *The Ballad of the Brown Girl* and *Copper Sun* he demonstrated his capacity for imagination as well as critical insight into the problems that beset the American Negro. There were others: Jean Toomer, whose *Cane* displayed a rare talent; Langston Hughes, whose most significant work belonged to a later period; Jessie Fauset, who captured the problems of the middle-class Negro to a remarkable degree, and Walter White, whose studies of lynching did much to dramatize American mob violence. These and a dozen others gave ample evidence that the new Negro was not only deeply sensitive but extremely articulate.

There were other even more dramatic manifestations of the New Negro, orthodox and unorthodox. The NAACP was not only carrying on its campaign against lynching, under the leadership of James Weldon Johnson and Walter White, but it was also attempting to break the practice of Southern states of excluding Negroes from Democratic primaries. It succeeded, in the case of *Nixon* vs. *Herndon* (1927), in having the Supreme Court of the United States declare null and void a Texas statute which excluded Negroes from the Democratic primaries in the state. When the Texas legislature enacted a law giving the executive committee of the party the authority to fix the qualifications for party membership, the association, in *Nixon* vs. *Condon* (1932), succeeded in having the law nullified by arguing that the statute had set up a party committee and made it a state agency with certain powers and duties. It suffered a setback, however, in 1935, when, in *Grovey* vs. *Townsend,* the Court refused to interfere with the exclusion of Negroes from the Democratic primaries when such an exclusion had been effected by a resolution of the state convention of the party. It was not until 1944 that the NAACP recovered its lost ground when, in *Smith* vs. *Allwright,* the Court decided that the exclusion of Negroes from the Democratic primary was a clear violation of the Fifteenth Amendment. Although these decisions were to prove insufficient to destroy the resistance to Negroes voting in the South, they were important steps toward the enjoyment of political participation.

The concentration of Negroes in urban centers in the North had much to do with another manifestation of the New Negro, namely, political regeneration. As early as 1915 a Negro, Oscar DePriest, was elected alderman from the densely populated South Side of Chicago. In 1917 the Negroes of New York sent E. A. Johnson to the state assembly. In the years following they became more aware of their political strength and took advantage of it. By 1928 some Negroes began to turn from the Republican Party to support Alfred E. Smith, a Democrat, for the Presidency because they thought he would do more for them than Herbert Hoover, the Republican candidate. In the same year they sent Oscar DePriest to Congress, the first Negro to serve there since 1901. And in 1930 they used their political influence to block the confirmation of John J. Parker for the Supreme Court, because they regarded him as an enemy of Negroes. By the time that Franklin D. Roosevelt ran for President in 1932 on the Democratic ticket, Negroes were in a position to use their political strength to force greater consideration on the part of the major parties.

The New Negro became more militant in the economic sphere. In 1929 the National Negro Business League, more certain than ever that white businesses and labor unions were passing the Negro by, organized the Colored Merchants Association, which undertook to establish stores and to purchase their wares cooperatively. Shortly thereafter a "Jobs-for-Negroes" movement began in earnest in St. Louis, where the Urban League led a boycott against a white-owned chain store whose trade was almost exclusively Negro but employed no Negroes. The movement spread to Pittsburgh, Chicago, Cleveland and other midwestern cities, and many Negroes found employment because of the pressure brought on white employers in Negro sections. Even during the depression such movements continued. In New York City the Reverend John H. Johnson organized in 1933 the Citizens' League for Fair Play and attempted to persuade white merchants to employ Negro clerks. When their first efforts failed they resorted to picketing the stores and appealing to Negroes with the motto, "Don't Buy Where You Can't Work." The campaign resulted in the employment of hundreds of Negroes in the white stores of Harlem and in such public utilities as the telephone, electric and bus companies.

There were some Negroes, bitter, defiant and frustrated, who believed that practical programs to achieve equality were impossible. The strain and stress of living in hostile urban communities left them completely disillusioned and willing to accept more drastic solutions to their problems. That is why so many of them embraced the Universal Negro Improvement Association, organized by Marcus Garvey during the war. Garvey insisted that the Negro had no future in the United States, and he declared that the only hope for American Negroes was to flee America and return to Africa to build up a country of their own. "Wake up Ethiopia!" he cried out; "Wake up Africa! Let us work toward one glorious end of a free, redeemed and mighty nation. Let Africa be a bright star among the constellation of nations." To inculcate a sense of self-esteem among Negroes Garvey exalted everything black. He insisted that black stood for strength and beauty, not inferiority.

The Garvey Movement grew rapidly. He claimed that he had six million followers in 1923. That was a wild exaggeration, of course; but even his severest critics conceded that he had perhaps a half-million members, which was more than the NAACP had at any time during this period. His Universal African Legion, Black Eagle Flying Corps, Black Star Steamship Line, and his numerous orders of African nobility captured the imagination of many American Negroes. His many projects came to naught, but not before they had given many frustrated Negroes a sense of hope and dignity that had long been denied them. It was the first and only real mass movement that Negroes had embraced; and its momentary success is a testimony of the extent to which Negroes entertained doubts about ever gaining first-class citizenship in the country of their birth.

Perhaps even more bizarre was the movement led by George Baker, commonly known as "Father Divine," who promised his followers a veritable heaven on earth. Beginning with a small group on Long Island in 1919, this remarkable leader built up a following within the next two decades that amused some observers and perplexed others. Although his followers deserted their churches and began to call their leader "God," it was as much a social movement as a religious development. By 1930 Father Divine was holding open house and feeding thousands in buildings that came to be known as "heavens." In many Eastern cities and in some Midwestern communities Father Divine had large followings. It became interracial as early as 1926, and within a few years it had attracted a considerable number of white members, some of whom were wealthy. That such a movement flourished at all suggests a variety of social ills as well as a great deal of frustration among whites as well as Negroes.

The New Deal

Despite the growing political sophistication of the American Negro, it is doubtful that a majority of them turned away from the Republican Party and supported Franklin D. Roosevelt, when he was elected to the Presidency in 1932. But he was not long in office before he gained a large following among Negroes and other minority groups. He was the first President to appoint Italo-Americans and Negroes to the Federal bench. He frequently received Negro visitors, and it was widely reported that he listened to suggestions and advice from certain powerful Negro politicians. Mrs. Roosevelt, moreover, was active in a variety of social programs that involved the improvement of disadvantaged groups, including Negroes. On several occasions, during his first year in office, the President denounced lynching and mob violence. His Secretary of the Interior, Harold L. Ickes, had been president of the Chicago branch of the NAACP, thus becoming the first Cabinet officer to have been so intimately associated with the struggle for Negro rights. The President appointed Negroes as "advisers" in several executive departments; and it was assumed that they were in a position to state the case for the economic and political equality of Negroes. In some sectors of the Federal government the racial segregation that had been established by the last Democratic President was abolished by Roosevelt.

While there was no civil rights legislation during the period of the New Deal, the relief and recovery legislation helped to improve, to a limited extent, conditions among Negroes as well as the rest of the population. Under such agencies as the Agricultural Adjustment Administration, the Rural Electrification Administration and local production credit associations, Negroes received benefits, though not in proportion to their numbers and needs. They were substantially aided by the Farm Security Administration, which insisted that there be no discrimination between white and Negro farmers. The Civilian Conservation Corps and the National Youth Administration provided employment for thousands of young Negroes. By 1939 more than one million Negroes owed their living to employment under the Works Progress Administration. Even some of the writers, actors and musicians who got their start during the period of the Harlem Renaissance found an opportunity to continue their creative work under the WPA. There was much discrimination against Negroes, particularly in the local administration of New Deal agencies in the South and in some places in the North. However, the old patterns of discrimination that had existed for decades were weakened to some extent during the New Deal period.

The New Deal was particularly favorable to labor, but not necessarily to Negro labor. The Wagner Act of 1935 gave permanency and strength to the National Labor Relations Board, which enjoyed wide powers in handling labor disputes and in settling strikes. It was labor's "bill of rights," but it did not break the barriers by which Negroes were excluded from the unions. The Fair Labor Standards Act of 1938 established the principle of a minimum and a maximum work week. Better than a million Negroes were affected by the act, but several millions were not. The act meant little to Negroes if they were unable to secure employment in those industries covered by it. There were few unions like the United Mine Workers which brought together in one union all the workers of the industry and which, since its organization in 1890, had encouraged the organization and participation of Negro workers. Most of the principal unions in the American Federation of Labor either barred Negroes or accepted their membership only on a segregated basis.

It was the so-called industrial bloc in the American Federation of Labor that gave the Negro his first real opportonity in organized labor. Led by John L. Lewis of the United Mine Workers, the bloc organized the Congress of Industrial Organizations and left the Federation. Soon, the C.I.O. was organizing the mass production industries; and the Amalgamated Clothing Workers, the International Ladies Garment Workers and the Steel Workers gave Negro members something resembling equal opportunity to participate in the affairs of the unions. The C.I.O. became active in the political sphere and sought equal opportunities for Negroes through its Committee to Abolish Racial Discrimination and its Political Action Committee. Meanwhile, the Brotherhood of Sleeping Car Porters, under the leadership of A. Philip Randolph, successfully pressed for better working conditions for its members and proved that Negroes, when given the opportunity, could adhere to the principles of organized labor.

The Negroes' patience, in waiting for justice through the courts and for equity at the hands of government leaders—including those of the New Deal—was wearing thin. They had to fight for their rights, many began to insist. As one Negro wrote to President Roosevelt's Attorney General, "It strikes us that the time is just about at hand when we must cast aside our Bible, stop offering so many solemn addresses to the Supreme Being and fight for our rights. . . . We would prefer death in lieu of remaining here on earth and have our manhood trampled upon." Such views were provoked by the persistence of the denial of the rights of Negroes, even when so much was being said about the protection and support of the disadvantaged elements of the American population. Consequently, Negroes sought to mobilize their intellectual and political resources for the purpose of pressing for their rights. Even as they supported Roosevelt in 1936 and 1940 they made it clear that they reserved the right to give their support to the political organizations that were most sensitive to their needs. In organizations such as the Joint Committee on National Recovery, the National Negro Congress and the Southern Negro Youth Congress they came together and formulated plans for pressing ever more vigorously for full citizenship. Even if these groups accomplished little, they developed approaches and techniques that were to be most valuable in the decades ahead.

The New Negro Community

The inability of the Negro to become a part of the mainstream of American life in the urban community did much to disillusion him further as well as make more permanent his separate institutions. The almost universal difficulty in securing adequate housing, discrimination in employment, and the absence of equity in the administration of justice contributed significantly to family disorganization among Negroes. At the same time, as E. Franklin Frazier pointed out in his *The Negro in the United States*, there has been an improvement in the stability of the Negro urban family in recent years. With the growth of the Negro middle class and the improvement of educational opportunities the Negro family as well as other institutions reflected a capacity to provide some strength and stability for the Negro community.

The practice of forcing Negroes into ghettoes and of barring them from participation in the life of the white community helped to create new forces for the perpetuation of the Negro's world. In a nation dedicated to the idea of the essential equality of mankind and in which there is a general commitment to the fusion of races and cultures, the existence of a separate Negro community constitutes one of the truly remarkable social anomalies of the twentieth century. This situation has created innumerable problems of a political, social and economic nature that have confounded both Negroes and whites who have sought solutions to them.

The most powerful institution in the Negro's world is the church. More and more, as he found himself rejected by the white churches and by the white community generally, the Negro turned to the church for self-expression, recognition and leadership. Nothing in his world was so completely his own as the church, whether it was one of the more common branches like the Baptists or Methodists or one of the more exotic institutions like the Apostolic Overcoming Holy Church of God or the Kodesh Church of Immanuel. The Negro church stimulated pride and preserved the self-respect of many who had been humiliated in their efforts to adjust themselves in American life. By the middle of the twentieth century thirty-four all-Negro denominations claimed a membership of more than five million Negroes, more than 35,000 churches, and property valued at $200 million. By that time one could see the first signs indicating a move to reintegrate American religious institutions. Roman Catholics insisted that they could never countenance segregation in the churches, while even the Methodists began to take steps to unite the Negro and white branches.

In the new Negro community the press played an increasingly important part. The white press of the South ignored the Negro community except to publicize crimes allegedly committed by Negroes, while the white press of the North paid scant attention to the activities of Negroes. The Negro press became the medium for the dissemination of information among Negroes and a powerful voice in expressing the aspirations of Negroes. It was during World War I that the Negro press became powerful and prosperous. It encouraged Negroes to move to industrial centers in search for work; it urged support of the war; but it also led the fight for the complete integration of Negroes in American life. Newspapers such as the *Baltimore Afro-American*, the *Chicago Defender*, the *Norfolk Journal and Guide* and the *Pittsburgh Courier* made rapid strides both in circulation and influence. In later decades the number of Negro newspapers, primarily weeklies, increased enormously, while weekly and monthly periodicals such as *Jet* and *Ebony* provided brief, pictorial summaries of Negro life in modern America.

The free, separate Negro community provided a great stimulation for the rise of Negroes in the professions. The Negro world needed teachers, clergy, physicians, dentists, pharmacists, nurses, attorneys, social workers, recreation leaders, morticians and many others to minister to its needs. They constitute the most highly trained group in the Negro community and are the basis for the rise of the Negro middle class. Preoccupied as they necessarily have been with their own training and service and the maintenance of high standards, they have not always been as aggressive in the advocacy of full citizenship for all. They have been compelled to organize their own associations for their protection and mutual assistance, but it would not be accurate to suggest that they have altogether neglected the important role of leadership in the Negro community. There are numerous examples of Negro attorneys and physicians and members of the clergy serving as officials in civil rights organizations, for they would be the first to realize that segregation and discrimination are, in the last analysis, as oppressive to them as to the least advantaged member of their race.

The education of Negroes remained a separate enterprise, for the most

part. Almost nowhere did Negroes enjoy equal educational opportunities, although the white community was scrupulously careful in seeing to it that such opportunities remain separate. In the South separate schools were maintained by law. In the North they were maintained by the Negro ghetto. In the South the disparity between the money spent on the education of white children and that spent for the education of Negro children prevailed throughout the first half of the twentieth century. As late as 1935–36 the current expenditures per Negro pupil in ten Southern states averaged $13.09, while such expenditures per white pupil averaged $37.87. While precise figures for ghetto schools in the North cannot be obtained, even a most cursory observation of buildings, equipment and facilities indicate considerable disparity.

It is not possible to measure precisely the effects that separate and unequal education have had on both white and Negro populations in the areas where it has been maintained. Separate schools have been one of the strongest supports of the concept of white supremacy in the South. They have, moreover, contributed to the perpetuation of a leadership devoted not only to separate education but to the maintenance of economic and political inequalities between the white and Negro populations of the South. In the face of these difficulties, however, the number of Negro schools, colleges and universities increased, while the Negro student population virtually exploded in the years following World War I.

Even out of the confused pattern of education for Negroes there emerged a body of highly trained men and women who may be regarded as scholars by any criteria. While almost all of them, until quite recent years, received their graduate and professional training in Northern and European universities, many of them were products of separate schools on the lower levels and even of Negro colleges. There was, of course, the usual complement of Negro clergy, teachers, physicians and attorneys; but to these were added, in more recent years, an increasing number of scholars in various scientific fields, history, sociology, political science and the humanities. Negro scholars became increasingly articulate, contributing articles to learned journals and publishing numerous books. Many of them devoted much of their talents and energies to studying and describing the place of the Negro in American life. The Association for the Study of Negro Life and History, founded in 1916 by Carter G. Woodson, went so far as to promote the works of Negro scholars and, indeed, of white scholars who were concerned with reassessing the role of the Negro in American history. Its *Journal of Negro History* soon became a respected periodical in the most scholarly circles, while the *Journal of Negro Education,* published at Howard University, and *Phylon, A Journal of Race and Culture,* published at Atlanta University, joined in the vigorous efforts of Negro scholars and their friends to restore the American Negro to a place of respect in the larger community.

GLOBAL WAR AND THE AFTERMATH

Fighting for the Four Freedoms

Negroes were among the first Americans to advocate intervention against the aggression of the fascist powers. As early as 1935 they were bitterly protesting the invasion of Ethiopia by Italy. In many communities funds were raised for the defense of the African kingdom. In New York the International Council of Friends of Ethiopia was organized, and one of its founders, Willis N. Huggins, pleaded before the League of Nations for support of Ethiopia. The *Pittsburgh Courier* sent a reporter, J. A. Rogers, to cover the war; and upon his return he published *The Real Facts About Ethiopia* and lectured to many Negro and white groups. As they witnessed the rape of Ethiopia by Italian fascists and the slaughter of Jews by German Nazis, Negroes reached the conclusion that racism in Europe was inimical to their best interests.

When Europe was plunged into war in September, 1939, the armed services of the United States were in a low state of preparedness. The Army in 1940 contained some 230,000 enlisted men and officers, of whom less than 5,000 were Negroes. Only the four Negro units in the standing army, the 24th and 25th Infantries and the 9th and 10th Cavalries, were up to their full strength. Some other Negro units were activated: quartermaster regiments, antiaircraft battalions, corps of engineers and some others. But Negroes generally had had little interest in the armed services in the years between the wars; and few were, therefore, ready to participate in the first stages of building up a large fighting force.

Under the Selective Service Act of 1940 more than three million Negro men registered for service in the armed forces of their country. In the first year of the operation of the act, while hope remained that the United States could stay out of the war, only 2,069 Negroes were drafted. In the following year more than 100,000 entered the service, while in 1942 approximately 370,000 Negroes joined the armed forces. In September, 1944, when the Army was at its peak, there were 700,000 Negroes in that branch of the service alone. Approximately 165,000 served in the Navy, 5,000 in the Coast Guard, and 17,000 in the Marine Corps. The total number of Negroes in the several branches of the armed services during World War II was in the neighborhood of one million men and women.

At the beginning of the war the armed services were generally segregated, and there was considerable discrimination. But the Negro had a much greater opportunity to serve his country than in any previous war. Negroes were in the infantry, coast and field artillery, cavalry, tank battalions, transportation units, signal corps, engineer corps, medical corps and many other branches where they had previously served. When the Women's Auxiliary Corps was organized, Negroes were received; and before the end of the war more than four thousand Negro women had enlisted. In 1940 the War Department announced that Negroes would be trained as aviation pilots at Tuskegee, Alabama. Some Negroes violently objected to the segregation of Negroes in the Air Force, but others looked upon the acceptance of Negroes as candidates as officer-pilots as a step forward. Late in 1941 the 99th Pursuit Squadron was ready for organization into a fighting unit, and other groups of

Negro fighter pilots were undergoing training. Approximately six hundred Negro pilots had received their wings before the end of the war.

In June, 1940, there were four thousand Negroes in the Navy, and most of them served as messmen. Since World War I Negroes had no opportunity either to learn the many trades provided in naval training or to become combat seamen. In April, 1942, the Secretary of the Navy announced that the Navy would accept the enlistment of Negroes for general service and as noncommissioned officers. Soon, a program for the training of Negroes as officers was launched, and Negro women were permitted to enlist in the Waves. At the same time it was announced that Negroes would be received in the Marine Corps, a break with tradition that was as old as the Corps itself. In the Army, meanwhile, a policy had been laid down of training Negro and white officer candidates in the same schools. Despite considerable resistance on the part of some white officers of the regular Army, Negroes received their commissions and through pressures brought by William H. Hastie, the Civilian Aide to the Secretary of War, and others, they received advanced training that made them eligible for promotion.

Approximately a half-million Negroes saw service overseas during World War II. Most of them were in separate outfits, more frequently than not, commanded by white officers. They served in port battalions, truck companies and other units of the transportation corps. After D-Day in 1944, more than fifty thousand Negro engineers erected camps, tents, and buildings, cleared debris, rebuilt cities and performed other important services. Twenty-two Negro combat units participated in the ground operations in the European theater. Negro fighter squadrons participated in the air operations over Italy, Rumania and Austria. In January, 1945, the War Department announced that Negro troops would be integrated with white troops in an experimental unit to fight on German soil. Negroes everywhere were elated over the news of the experiment and were delighted to learn that the mixed units were a success. Meanwhile, Negro troops were becoming more active in the war in the Pacific and the Orient. Negro combat units saw action against the Japanese in the New Georgia Islands, the Solomons, the Philippines and elsewhere, while Negro engineers worked on the building of the Ledo Road and various military installations.

The problem of maintaining high morale among Negroes in the service was a most difficult one. White officers and white civilians subjected Negroes to numerous indignities and humiliations. In Durham, North Carolina, a white bus driver was found not guilty of murder after he left his bus in July, 1944, and killed a Negro soldier with whom he had argued on the bus. In the South Negro soldiers were refused food in places where German prisoners of war were eating and enjoying American hospitality. In Kentucky three Negro WACS were beaten by civilian police when the women did not move promptly from the white waiting room in a railroad station, when asked to do so. In South Carolina a white policeman gouged out a Negro soldier's eyes in an altercation. On military posts the situation was scarcely better. At many camps Negro soldiers were forced to wait until white soldiers had boarded the buses and, if any room was left, they could ride. When the War Department issued an order in 1944 forbidding racial segregation in recreational and transportation facilities at all Army stations, the *Montgomery Advertiser* said, "Army orders, even armies, even bayonets cannot force impossible and unnatural social relations upon us."

If whites were resisting moves toward the equal treatment of Negro soldiers, Negro newspapers and Negro leaders were constantly protesting against all forms of segregation and discrimination. They protested the practice of the Red Cross of separating Negro and white blood in the banks that had been established for the relief of wounded servicemen. They were quick to point out that there would, perhaps, have been no blood banks without the work of a Negro, Dr. Charles Drew. They also criticized the USO when that organization banned Ruth Benedict's *The Races of Mankind* in its clubs. While Negroes were willing to serve their country in war as well as in peace, most of them insisted that the Four Freedoms and the other noble sentiments expressed in the war aims should be practiced at home as well as abroad. The *Pittsburgh Courier* launched a vigorous Double V campaign: Victory at home as well as abroad.

Problems of Employment

As the United States began to put itself on a war footing, Negroes wondered where they would fit in as far as defense and war industries were concerned. They found untold difficulties in securing employment. The first benefits they derived from the boom in defense industries were in securing the jobs deserted by whites who were attracted by higher wages to plants making weapons of war. The Federal Government made several gestures to discourage discrimination. The Office of Education declared that in the expenditure of funds in the defense training program there should be no discrimination based on race, creed or color. In August, 1940, the National Defense Advisory Committee issued a statement against the refusal to hire Negroes in defense plants. These actions brought few satisfactory results, and discrimination continued. Negroes saw wages skyrocket in plants holding huge defense contracts, and they saw few signs that the rigid anti-Negro policy in industry was undergoing any change. All too typical of industry was the statement by a West Coast aviation factory which said, "We will receive applications from both white and colored workers. However, the Negro will be considered only as janitors and in other similar capacities. Regardless of their training as aircraft workers, we will not employ them."

Such positions as these were indications to Negro leaders that they should develop a program for drastic action. In January, 1941, A. Philip Randolph, president of the Brotherhood of Sleeping Car Porters, advanced the idea of fifty to one hundred thousand Negroes marching on Washington and demanding that their government do something to insure the employment of Negroes in defense industry. The idea was received with enthusiasm by many Negroes, while Federal officials viewed the prospect as most regrettable. Soon, a full-scale March on Washington Movement had developed; and it was supported by the heads of all the major Negro organizations. The President sought to head off the movement by speaking out against discrimination; but Negroes felt that he was not doing enough. Mrs. Roosevelt and Mayor LaGuardia of New York attempted to persuade the Negro leaders to abandon the idea of the march, insisting that it would do more harm than good. The President himself appealed to Randolph and his colleagues to call off the March, but Randolph remained adamant.

In late June, 1941, Negroes all over the United States—thousands, if not a hundred thousand—were making preparations to entrain for Washington to be ready to march to the Capitol and White House on July First. Governmental officials became more desperate. Finally, after several conferences, the President said that if Randolph would call off the march, he would issue an order prohibiting discrimination in employment in defense industries. Randolph agreed, and on June 25, 1941, the President issued his famous Executive Order 8802, saying, "There shall be no discrimination in the employment of workers in defense industries or Government because of race, creed, color, or national origin. . . . And it is the duty of employers and labor organizations . . . to provide for the full and equitable participation of all workers in defense industries, without discrimination because of race, creed, color, or national origin. . . ." Later a Fair Employment Practices Committee was established; and this was the beginning of the involvement of the Federal Government in programs to improve the economic status of Negroes. Undoubtedly, many employers persisted in their discriminatory practices, but the even lukewarm commitment of the Federal Government to fair employment created a generally improved climate in which Negroes could seek employment.

In another way, however, the climate was deteriorating. The migration of large numbers of Negroes to the North and West raised anew the difficult question of how Negroes and whites could live together peacefully in communities where the patterns of race relations were not clearly defined. Within the five-year period between 1940 and 1945 the Negro population of Los Angeles County increased from 75,000 to 150,000. Negroes were also moving in large numbers to Oakland, Detroit, Cleveland, Chicago and other industrial centers. The lack of housing, the presence of race-baiters and demagogues, the problem of organizing the newly arrived workers and the impotence of the local government created an ideal atmosphere in which racial violence could break out.

Consequently, as Negroes and whites were fighting the Germans, Italians and Japanese abroad, they were fighting each other at home. In June, 1943, the most serious race riot of the war period broke out in Detroit. Months of race tension were climaxed on June 20 when a fist fight occurred between a Negro and a white man. Soon, several hundred persons were involved, and Negroes and whites were fighting in various parts of the city. Nothing effective was done to bring order out of chaos until President Roosevelt declared a state of emergency and sent six thousand troops to patrol the city. After thirty hours of rioting, twenty-five Negroes and nine whites had been killed, and property valued at several hundred thousand dollars had been destroyed. There were other racial clashes on a smaller scale, in New York, Los Angeles, Chicago and several Southern cities. No city wanted to become another Detroit, however, and numerous efforts were made after the summer of 1954 to prevent the recurrence of such a tragedy.

Post-War Breakthrough

Shortly after Harry S. Truman took office, upon the death of President Roosevelt in April, 1945, it became clear that the new President would be an active exponent of a greater enjoyment of equality for Negroes. In an address to the annual meeting of NAACP in 1947, he said, "As Americans we believe that every man should be free to live his life as he wishes. He should be limited only by his responsibility to his fellow countrymen. If this freedom is to be more than a dream, each man must be guaranteed equality of opportunity. The only limit to an American's achievement should be his ability, his industry and his character." Already, the President had taken steps to provide this equality of opportunity. Late in 1946 he created the President's Committee on Civil Rights "to inquire into and determine whether and in what respect current law enforcement measures and the authority and means possessed by federal, state, and local governments may be strengthened and improved to safeguard the civil rights of the people." After surveying every aspect of American life involved in the problem of civil rights, the committee published its report under the title, *To Secure These Rights*. It made comprehensive and far-reaching recommendations calling for concrete measures to improve the administration of justice, protect the exercise of the franchise and the elimination of segregation in American life. In the same year the President appointed another interracial committee to look into the problem of higher education. In their report the committee recommended not only the elimination of inequalities in educational opportunities but the abandonment of all forms of discrimination in higher education.

The integration in the armed services that had been inaugurated in the closing years of World War II was accelerated by President Truman. In 1948 he appointed a committee to study the problem, and its report, *Freedom to Serve*, was a blueprint of the steps by which integration was to be achieved. In Korea, in 1950, there were new opportunities to test military integration under battlefield conditions. Between May and August, 1951, integration in the Korean forces jumped from 9 percent to 30 percent of troops in the field. A special Army report declared that the integration of Negroes had resulted in an overall gain for the army. At long last American Negroes had become a vital and integral part of the manpower pool of the nation.

In February, 1948, President Truman sent to Congress a special message on civil rights, the first such message that any President had ever sent. He called for the establishment of a permanent Commission on Civil Rights, Federal legislation against lynching, the establishment of a permanent Fair Employment Practices Committee, the prohibition of discrimination in interstate transportation facilities and the strengthening of existing civil rights statutes. Congress did nothing to implement the demands of the President or the recommendations of his several commissions. But the stand taken by the President was a new one for American Presidents. After Truman, no President could turn his back on this important problem.

While Congress paid little attention to the matter of civil rights, the Supreme Court was willing to take cognizance of them in a variety of cases. Indeed, there was scarcely an area of American life in which the rights of citizens were jeopardized that escaped the Court's attention in the years following World War II. In 1946, in a case coming up from Virginia, *Morgan* vs. *Virginia*, the Court held unconstitutional a Virginia law that segregated passengers traveling across state lines. In 1948 the Court held that racially restrictive covenants in the conveyance of real property could not be enforced in the courts. The decision in this case, *Shelley* vs. *Kraemer*, was the first significant assault on segregation and discrimination in housing since the ordinance requiring whites and Negroes to live in separate blocks was outlawed in 1917. In 1950 the Court, which in 1938 had already required states to provide Negroes with professional training if it was provided for whites, held that such facilities not only must be equal but must, indeed, be the same facilities. To many white Southerners, this was a frightening departure from the "separate but equal" doctrine laid down in the Plessy case in 1896. It seemed clear that in time the Court would open all public institutions of higher education to Negroes. Many whites hoped that the Court would not desegregate primary and secondary schools.

In the hope that the Court would not disturb separate schools at the lower levels, the Southern states made a desperate effort to equalize Negro primary and secondary schools. In the late Forties and early Fifties, they spent millions of dollars for the improvement of segregated Negro schools. The more they spent the more they seemed to convince themselves that this was the best, indeed, the only solution to the problem of segregated education in the South.

The assault on segregated schools was the part of a larger drive to eliminate segregation in the United States. It could be seen in the emergence of new groups that joined with the older ones to challenge segregation laws and practices. In the midwest the American Council on Race Relations was active. In the North the Anti-Defamation League, the American Jewish Congress, the CIO Committee to Abolish Racial Discrimination, the National Lawyers Guild, the American Veterans' Committee, the Workers Defense League represented a wide variety of interests working for the elimination of segregation. In the South the Southern Conference for Human Welfare and the Southern Regional Council began to take action. In Washington the National Committee on Segregation in the Nation's Capital was working. In 1948 it described Washington, D.C., as the "capital of white supremacy," and called for the elimination of all practices of segregation and discrimination. Early in 1949 the Washington hotels began to accept Negro guests. Soon, some theaters and motion picture houses took steps to desegregate. In 1953 the Supreme Court, invoking a law that had been passed in 1873, declared that restaurants in Washington could not refuse to serve "well-behaved and respectable persons."

The move to desegregate Washington schools was a part of the move to desegregate schools in other parts of the country. Taking cognizance of the efforts of many Southern states to make their segregated schools equal as far as facilities were concerned, the NAACP and its supporters began to argue that segregated education, regardless of equal facilities, was *per se* unconstitutional. They set forth this position in the five cases arising in Kansas, South Carolina, Virginia, Delaware and the District of Columbia. Numerous organizations entered briefs in behalf of the position of the Negroes. The Attorney General of the United States asked the Court to strike down the doctrine of "separate but equal." Racial discrimination, he said, furnishes "grist for the communist propaganda mills, and it raises doubt even among friendly nations as to the intensity of our devotion to the democratic faith." The decision of the Court on May 17, 1954, was the most significant breakthrough of the twentieth century. It was unequivocal in outlawing segregation in public schools. Speaking for a unanimous court, Chief Justice Warren said, "Separate educational facilities are inherently unequal." There was no doubt, therefore, that Negro children who were segregated in public schools had been deprived of the equal protection of the laws guaranteed by the Fourteenth Amendment. The implications of the decision were highly significant and they would not be fully appreciated for many years to come.

There were those, however, who understood, from their own vantage point, what the decision meant. A Richmond editor denounced the Court as "that inept fraternity of politicians and professors" who had "repudiated the Constitution and spat upon the Tenth Amendment." More than a hundred Southern members of Congress issued a manifesto saying, "The unwarranted decision of the Supreme Court . . . is now bearing the fruit always produced when men substitute naked power for established law. We regard the decision as a clear abuse of judicial power." But one white editor in Knoxville, Tennessee, said, "No citizen, fitted by character and intelligence to sit as a justice of the Supreme Court, and sworn to uphold the Constitution . . . could have decided this question other than the way it was decided." A group of leading Negro educators said simply, "It was the right and moral thing to do."

TOWARD ONE AMERICA

An Improved Climate

Many factors and forces were operating to create a better climate for Negroes in the years following World War II. The assumption by the United States of a position of leadership in world affairs made the country particularly vulnerable regarding the position of the Negro in the United States. As one of the chief builders of the United Nations and as the host country to the new international organization, it became increasingly embarrassing to speak out against the denial of human rights in far away lands and be forced to admit that there were flagrant denials of those same rights in many parts of the United States. Other nations, including Russia, India, France and the Philippines, entertained serious doubts about the sincerity of America's professions regarding the rights of all peoples. The United States became sensitive to the discrepancies in its own human relations and sought to make amends by appointing Negroes to the delegations to the United Nations and to commissions dealing with international problems. Such moves, however, did not cover up the housing and employment problems that Negroes experienced and that even the casual visitor could see; nor did it obscure the numerous practices of segregation and discrimination that were mentioned all too frequently in the Russian press.

The emergence of independent states in Africa added to America's distress, in a sense. Beginning with Ghana in 1957, one African state after another gained its independence, and as they did so they inadvertently contributed toward the changing of the racial climate in the United States. Psychologically, the Negroes of the United States immediately identified with the new African nations and pointed with pride to the accomplishments of their brothers. They also reminded white Americans that Negro states in Africa were "living proof" of the Negro's ability to assume responsibilities at the highest level; and this "living proof" stimulated the Negroes of the United States to press a bit harder for their own rights. Equally important was the presence in the United States of an increasing number of African representatives to the United States and ambassadors to the United States and their staffs. In the "cold war" competition with Russia, it was most important that the African nations be won by the United States; and it was most difficult for the United States to accomplish this feat in the face of insults and indignities heaped upon African diplomats by white Americans. It became a major concern of the United States, therefore, not only to treat the Africans with dignity and respect but also to assure them that such treatment should be accorded Americans of dark skins. As this problem came to be a major concern of the President of the United States and the Secretary of State, they used their power and prestige to seek to correct some of the racial practices in the United States. And in so doing, they contributed to the improvement of the racial climate.

The extensive urbanization of the American Negro during and after World War II greatly contributed to the improvement of the political climate as far as the Negro was concerned. Between 1940 and 1960 the Negro population outside the old Confederacy increased two and one-fourth times, from nearly four million to more than nine million, representing 48 percent of the total Negro population. Most of this growth outside the South has been in the central cities of the twelve largest metropolitan areas of the United States: New York, Los Angeles, Chicago, Philadelphia, Detroit, San Francisco-Oakland, Boston, Pittsburgh, St. Louis, Washington, Cleveland and Baltimore. These twelve areas now hold 31 percent of all the Negroes in the United States; and these areas and other areas where the Negro population is concentrated are where the Negro wields the greatest amount of political influence.

Ironically, one of the very significant results of herding Negroes into urban ghettoes in the North has been the enormous increase in their political power. Negroes sit in law-making bodies in every Northern state where the Negro population is concentrated in the large cities. They serve as state and municipal judges, city commissioners, corporation counsels and in a variety of other important elective and appointive public offices. Negroes have been elected to the school boards of Atlanta and Houston, to the state senate in Georgia, and to the councils of several Southern cities. They have won state-wide elections, as, for example, the election of Edward Brooke to be attorney general of Massachusetts, Otis Smith to be auditor general of Michigan and Gerald Lamb to be state treasurer in Connecticut. Five of the great metropolitan areas of the North—New York, Chicago, Philadelphia, Detroit, and Los Angeles—have Negroes in Congress: Adam C. Powell, William L. Dawson, Robert N. C. Nix, Charles C. Diggs, Jr., John L. Conyers, Jr. and Augustus F. Hawkins.

The growing political strength of the Negro and the improved climate are reflected in a notable way in the appointment of Negroes to important positions by the Chief Executive of the Federal Government. It began with the appointment of William H. Hastie to the United States Court of Appeal for the Third Circuit. It was continued by President Eisenhower in his appointment of J. Ernest Wilkins as Assistant Secretary of Labor, Scovel Richardson as Chairman of the United States Parole Board and later to the United States Customs Court, E. Frederic Morrow to the White House Staff and Clifton Wharton as Ambassador to Rumania. President Kennedy made numerous appointments of Negroes to important posts: Robert Weaver as Administrator of the Housing and Home Finance Agency, Clifton Wharton as Ambassador to Norway, Carl Rowan as Ambassador to Finland, Thurgood Marshall to the United States Circuit Court, James B. Parsons, Wade McCree and A. Leon Higginbotham to the United States District Court, Merl McCurdy and Cecil F. Poole as United States Attorneys and John B. Duncan as a member of the District of Columbia Board of Commissioners. In his first year in office President Johnson appointed Carl Rowan to be Director of the United States Information Agency Andrew F. Brimmer, Assistant Secretary of Commerce and Mrs. Frankie Freeman as a member of the United States Commission on Civil Rights.

There were numerous other manifestations of an improved racial climate in the United States. Both political parties, for example, came out for strong civil rights planks in their platforms in 1960. In 1964 the Republican Party was equivocal on the issue, but the Democrats strengthened their pro-Civil Rights position. In every section of the country, even in the South, white citizens are becoming active in the civil rights struggle; and religious bodies —Protestant, Catholic, and Jewish—have become more active in behalf of equality than they ever have been before. Numerous local and national groups that heretofore had excluded Negroes from membership have, in the last decade, opened their doors to all qualified persons. In most litigations involving civil rights in recent years, numerous groups—law school professors, religious organizations, civic groups, and educational societies— have presented briefs as friends of the court asking that segregation laws and discrimination practices be outlawed.

The manner in which Negroes entered areas of American life that had always been closed to them was a measure of the improved climate in the years following World War II. When Jackie Robinson entered organized baseball in 1947 as a member of the Brooklyn Dodgers, it created a sensation. Within a few years virtually all the baseball teams in the two major leagues had Negroes, and the signing of an additional Negro team member was no longer even newsworthy. Despite the long tradition of Negro singers performing creditably on the concert stage, the announcement that Marian Anderson, one of the world's greatest contraltos, would have a small part in a production at the Metropolitan Opera Association was sensational news. Within five years Negroes were singing leading roles, and in 1961 Leontyne Price sang the title role on opening night. For many years Negroes played only stereotype roles as clowns and servants in motion pictures and on the legitimate stage. In recent years actors and actresses such as Sidney Poitier, Ossie Davis, Ruby Dee and Diahann Carroll were accepted on the basis of their skills and talents rather than their color. When Negro professors are appointed to predominantly white colleges and universities, it no longer surprises anyone. Thus, the air was clearing; and the climate was much improved by 1965.

A Brief History of the Negro in the United States   95

The Involvement of Government

The involvement of government at every level in the movement to improve the condition and status of Negroes in the United States has been one of the most significant developments of the post-war period. Many of the states of the North and West had civil rights statutes dating back to the period before World War I, but many of them were universally disregarded. In the nineteen-fifties, there was a significant move to revive and enforce such statutes and, in many cases, to strengthen them. By 1964 twenty-one states had enacted enforceable fair employment practice laws. New York took the lead in 1945, and the number of such states had increased to eight by 1950. In 1955 three states— Michigan, Minnesota and Pennsylvania—enacted fair employment practice laws; and in each succeeding year new states passed such legislation. By 1965 nineteen states and fifty-five cities had barred discrimination in some aspect of housing. Eleven states, the Virgin Islands and three cities adopted fair housing laws which apply to privately financed as well as governmentally aided housing. Meanwhile, many volunteer fair housing groups have been organized in many sections of the country.

The courts, especially the Federal judiciary, continued to support the general principle of equality. In 1955, one year following the Supreme Court's decision in the school segregation cases, the Court remanded the cases to the courts of origin and indicated that it expected the courts to require that the states make a prompt and reasonable start toward full compliance with the decision of May, 1954. From that point on, the district and circuit courts have had the responsibility of examining the compliance measures of the several states. In numerous cases the judges of the lower Federal courts have carried out the decision of the Supreme Court by refusing to countenance techniques and devices developed by the several states to render ineffective the historic Supreme Court decision. The decision, moreover, sped up action in other areas. Even after the Morgan decision in 1946, there had been numerous efforts to segregate Negroes in interstate transportation as well as travel within the state. After hearing a variety of cases on the subject over the years, the Supreme Court seemed exasperated in 1962 when it stated in *Bailey* vs. *Patterson*, "We have settled beyond question that no state may require segregation of interstate or intrastate transportation facilities. . . . The question is no longer open; it is foreclosed as a litigable issue." The Court also upheld the argument advanced by Negro litigants that tax-supported public institutions, including parks, golf links and swimming pools, could not be segregated. In 1964 it ruled unconstitutional the separate but equal provision of the Hill-Burton Act which provides federal funds for hospital construction.

Even the Congress reacted favorably to the winds of change that were sweeping over the United States in midcentury. In 1957 it passed a civil rights act, the first such legislation since 1875. Among other things the act created a Civil Rights Commission as a continuing agency concerned with the enforcement of civil rights and enlarged and strengthened the Civil Rights Section of the Department of Justice. Furthermore, it authorized the Department of Justice to institute injunction proceedings against persons conspiring to deprive citizens of their rights. The act was certainly not revolutionary as many Southern members of Congress claimed; nor was it merely a sham, as Senator Wayne Morse of Oregon claimed. It focused attention on the Government's responsibility in the area of civil rights in a way never done before. The Negroes of Tuskegee now had a national agency to which they could relate the manner in which they had been gerrymandered out of the city limits and denied the right to vote. Negroes in Louisiana could now tell of acts of violence and intimidation against them if they attempted to vote. And the reports of the Civil Rights Commission would constitute a significant body of information to be used in the protection of civil rights in the future.

Having broken its silence in 1957 after so many years, Congress in 1960 took another step by enacting additional civil rights legislation. Opposition had not been stilled; and only after one of the longest and bitterest debates in the nation's history did the rather mild bill become law. The law singled out for punishment any person or persons defacing or damaging synagogues, churches or other buildings. All election officials were required to keep registration and other records for twenty-two months and make them available, upon request, to the Attorney General or his representatives. If a court found a pattern or practice of denial of the right to vote by reason of race or color, any Negro within the affected area would be entitled to vote upon proof of qualification. Court-appointed referees could receive applications, take evidence and report the findings to the court. The Attorney General hailed the new law as having "historic significance" by making it clear "that all branches of the Federal Government firmly support the proposition that the Fourteenth and Fifteenth Amendments to the Constitution are not to be considered mere promises but must become realities for all citizens in all areas of the country." No dramatic changes stemmed from the laws of 1957 and 1960, but the Civil Rights Commission gathered very important information on the status of the rights of citizens and there was soon a groundswell of interest in and support for a strong Civil Rights Act.

The executive branch of the Federal Government was, in recent years, even more active than the other branches in promoting equality in American life. The work begun by Truman and continued by Eisenhower was carried forward with vigor by Presidents Kennedy and Johnson. During the campaign, candidate Kennedy indicated that he fully appreciated the significance of the civil rights struggle. When the civil rights leader, Dr. Martin Luther King, was in jail in Georgia, Kennedy called Mrs. King, expressed his sympathy, and offered to do whatever he could to help. Although many factors contributed to the Kennedy victory in the closest Presidential contest in years, there can be no doubt that one telephone call swung thousands of votes to Kennedy in states that otherwise would have been in doubt. Once in office he would have every opportunity to demonstrate what he contended during the campaign, that the office of the President of the United States was "a place of moral leadership."

It appeared for a time that the new President would not provide the kind of leadership in this area that many hoped for and others expected and still others feared. He took the position that no additional legislation was needed except, perhaps, to protect voting rights. At the same time, however, he and his brother, the Attorney General, worked quietly with Southern railroads and Southern municipal governments in a largely successful effort to eliminate segregation in interstate transportation facilities. In September, 1961, he issued a personal plea for the ending of segregation and discrimination in restaurants and other places of public service. President Kennedy took the initiative in promoting fair employment by creating the President's Committee on Equal Employment Opportunity, with Vice President Lyndon B. Johnson as Chairman. At that time he said, "I have dedicated my Administration to the cause of equal opportunity in employment by the government or its contractors. The Vice President, the Secretary of Labor and the other members of this committee share my dedication." For the next three years the committee took steps to eliminate discrimination in employment in government and private enterprise.

Meanwhile, the Kennedy administration, through the Department of Justice, the Federal Bureau of Investigation, and the several Executive Offices sought to implement the stated commitment of the administration to equality. The Department of Justice participated in numerous litigations for the protection of civil rights. The Federal Bureau of Investigation not only looked into numerous complaints regarding discrimination and the denial of civil rights, but in the interest of a better administration of justice conducted numerous schools and institutes for law-enforcement officers. In November, 1962, the President signed the long-awaited order prohibiting discrimination in federally assisted housing. During the campaign, two years earlier, he had taunted President Eisenhower by saying that he could have done that "with the stroke of a pen." When asked why he waited so long, he replied that he had always intended to issue the order at the right time, and the right time had come.

The President was not slow to act in emergencies, however. In September, 1962, when the state of Mississippi, in defiance of a court order, attempted to prevent the enrollment of James Meredith at the University of Mississippi, the President acted promptly by sending Federal troops as President Eisenhower had done in Little Rock, to protect Meredith in the exercise of his rights. When the Birmingham demonstrations were at their height in April, 1963, he sent three thousand Federal troops to protect the rights of Negroes. When it appeared that the governor of Alabama, in June, 1963, would prevent the enrollment of three Negroes at the University of Alabama, the President ordered Federal officials to the University to assist in enforcing the court order to admit the Negro students. He then addressed the American people and warned them that there was "a rising tide of discontent that threatens the public safety"; and he declared that "the events in Birmingham and elsewhere have so increased the cries for equality that no city or state or legislative body can prudently choose to ignore them."

The Civil Rights Revolution

One of the most significant chapters in the recent history of American Negroes has been the development of new techniques to achieve old goals. Within the past decade, many people—white and Negro—began to consider the possibility of taking matters into their own hands by direct action. They had seen violent direct action in the emergence of the white citizens councils and the revival of the Ku Klux Klan to fight, with every means at their disposal, the enforcement of desegregation decisions. Perhaps, some

Negroes began to believe, that they might accelerate the rights through nonviolent direct action. In 1956, a year before the passage of the Civil Rights Act, the Negroes of Montgomery, Alabama, began to boycott the bus lines of the city to protest white driver's abuse of Mrs. Rosa Parks, who had refused to move to the back of the bus with other Negro passengers. They now wanted to obtain a more satisfactory seating practice on the buses and to secure the employment of Negro drivers on buses serving predominantly Negro sections of the city.

As Negroes proceeded with their boycott, the white community was outraged. Some ninety Negroes were indicted under a 1921 antiunion law forbidding conspiracy to obstruct the operation of a business. Their leader, the Reverend Dr. Martin Luther King, Jr., was the first to be tried. He was found guilty. Immediately he served notice of appeal, while the bus company frantically sought to settle the problem before it became bankrupt. The Montgomery Negroes finally won their battle; and the effective weapon of boycott gained in popularity as Negroes of Tallahassee, Atlanta and Nashville successfully tested the practice of picketing and boycotting as civil rights weapons.

Soon, other organizations committed themselves to direct, nonviolent action. Within the next few years numerous groups, most of them interracial, became active. Among them were the Congress of Racial Equality, the Southern Christian Leadership Conference, and the Student Non-Violent Coordinating Committee. In addition, there were other groups giving aid and comfort to those involved in direct action. Among them were the NAACP, the National Urban League, the Southern Regional Council, numerous religious groups and labor and civic organizations.

On February 1, 1960, four students from the Negro Agricultural and Technical College of Greensboro, North Carolina, entered a variety store, made several purchases, and sat down at the lunch counter and ordered coffee. They were refused service because they were Negroes; and they remained in their seats until the store closed. This was the beginning of the sit-in movement, the second phase of the civil rights revolution, which spread rapidly through the South and to some places in the North. In the spring and summer of 1960 thousands of young people, white and Negro, participated in similar peaceful forms of protest against segregation and discrimination. They sat in white libraries, waded into white beaches and slept in the lobbies of white motels. Many of them were arrested for trespassing, disorderly conduct and disobeying officers who ordered them off the premises.

A Southern journalist labeled the sit-ins "the South's new time bomb," and observed that young Negroes were infused with a new determination to risk violence to acquire some of the rights they believed were due them. When Negro students were criticized for their actions, they placed a full-page advertisement in the white *Atlanta Constitution*, in which they said, "We do not intend to wait placidly for those rights which are already legally and morally ours to be meted out to us one at a time." Negro students and their white colleagues were on the march to secure their rights. As a result, literally hundreds of lunch counters across the South began to serve Negroes, and other facilities began to open up. When their efforts were not successful, they boycotted white businesses or engaged in "selective purchasing," thus bringing to bear another effective weapon to secure their rights.

In May, 1961, an even more dramatic attack on segregation and discrimination than sit-ins was undertaken by the Congress of Racial Equality. It sent "Freedom Riders" through the South to test segregation laws and practices in interstate transportation. In Alabama the interracial team was attacked at Anniston and Birmingham. Although the Attorney General was obviously a bit annoyed by the aggressiveness of these unorthodox fighters for civil rights, he ordered the Federal Bureau of Investigation to look into the matter and made it clear that the Freedom Riders would be protected. In the summer of 1961 the jails of Jackson, Mississippi, and other Southern communities were virtually filled with Freedom Riders who had been arrested for the alleged violation of some law. The Federal Government maintained an active interest in these proceedings, sent some four hundred United States marshals to Alabama to restore order and secured an injunction to prohibit any attempt to stop, by force, the Freedom Riders from continuing their test of bus station segregation.

At about the same time the Negroes of Albany, Georgia, began to demonstrate their plight by marching through the streets and holding large mass meetings. Hundreds were arrested, and the officials of the city were adamant in their refusal to discuss the situation with Negro leaders. In the two years that followed, marching, picketing and public demonstrations were taken up by Negroes in Atlanta, Danville, Virginia, Cambridge, Maryland, and many other communities. In March, 1963, for example, the Negroes of Leflore County, Mississippi, began to march in order to dramatize a voter registration drive sponsored by the Student Non-Violent Coordinating Committee. In April, 1963, Dr. King inaugurated the forty days of marching in Birmingham, Alabama, during which time more than 2,500 Negroes were arrested. The Birmingham marches inspired scores of others, North and South; and some were attended by violence and rioting. They were the occasion, moreover, for the focusing of attention on the Black Muslims, who used the marches to point out one of the basic tenets of their position: that the United States will never grant equality to Negroes. Negroes, therefore, should reject any semblance of cooperation and turn their attention to the development of their own culture as well as their own political and economic institutions. While the movement is not large in numbers, its popularity is considerable, even among those who reject its program.

In the year of the centennial of the Emancipation Proclamation the civil rights revolution reached its peak. The numerous successful demonstrations and marches suggested to the leadership that one massive march on Washington might dramatize to the nation and to the world the importance of solving the problem of the status of the Negro in the United States once and for all. Soon, plans were made to carry out the march on August 28, 1963. All of the major Negro organizations joined in formulating the plans, and they were joined by scores of other organizations, white and Negro. A wide-eyed world watched as a quarter of a million Negroes and whites converged on Washington from all over the United States, by every conceivable mode of transportation and under every conceivable auspice.

Washington had never seen such a day as this. The businesses in the downtown area closed, not out of respect to the marchers but because of the fear of rioting and looting. Most of the Federal employees took the day off, some to participate in the march, others to get as far from the center of things as possible. Before the impressive memorial to Abraham Lincoln the civil rights leaders spoke: Whitney Young, Roy Wilkins, Martin Luther King. From his jail cell in Louisiana, James Farmer, Director of the Congress of Racial Equality, sent a message. Mahalia Jackson sang. Ministers, movie stars, radio commentators, college students, thousands of organizations and ordinary citizens participated. The President of the United States cordially received the leaders, while others called on their Representatives and Senators. The nation looked on via television, and the entire world would later see in the newspapers and on the newsreels the most remarkable testimony in behalf of the equality of mankind ever made in this or any other country. One important figure was absent. Fifty-odd years earlier he had assumed the leadership in the fight for equality. On the eve of the march, W. E. B. Du Bois, now a citizen of Ghana, had passed away in Accra.

In June, before the march, President Kennedy had asked Congress to enact laws that would provide a legal guarantee to all citizens of equal access to the services and facilities of hotels, restaurants, places of amusement and other public establishments in interstate commerce; authorize the Attorney General to start school desegregation suits when he is requested by someone unable to do so; broad Federal action to stop discrimination in Federal jobs and activities financed wholly or in part with Federal funds; create a Community Relations Service to act as a mediation agency in communities with racial tensions; make it clear "that the Federal Government is not required to furnish any kind of financial assistance to any program or activity in which racial discrimination occurs."

The President's message of June 19, 1963, is not only a historic document, a veritable landmark in the history of the drive for equality. It is also the best summary available of the unfinished business of democracy. He deplored the fact that Negroes did not have equal access to public accommodations and facilities. "No one has been barred on account of his race from fighting or dying for America—there are no 'white' and 'colored' signs on the foxholes and graveyards of battle. Surely, in 1963, one hundred years after emancipation, it should not be necessary for any American citizen to demonstrate in the streets for the opportunity to stop at a hotel, or to eat at a lunch counter in the very department store in which he is shopping, or to enter a motion picture house, on the same terms as any other customer." With regard to segregated schools, he said, "Many Negro children entering segregated grade schools at the time of the Supreme Court decision in 1954 will enter segregated high schools this year, having suffered a loss which can never be regained. Indeed, discrimination in education is one basic cause of the other inequities and hardships inflicted upon our Negro citizens."

Those who marched on Washington in August, 1963, were doing what they could to emphasize the importance of enacting the legislation the President had called for. More than that, they were expressing their continuing faith in the efficacy of democratic institutions in righting the wrong of centuries and of giving themselves a new lease on life through a process of self-purification. But those who marched were under no illusions and were not blindly optimistic. As soon as they returned to their respective homes, they continued their fight. In Chicago they urged the end of *de facto* segregation in the schools in a boycott which kept 250,000 Negro children out of classes. In New York they did the same. In Birmingham they called for some tangible indication of good faith on the part of the city administration. In Placquemine Parish, Louisiana, they called for obedience of the law regarding the rights of citizens to register and vote.

The Civil Rights Act of 1964

When President Kennedy was assassinated on November 22, 1963, many civil rights leaders as well as ordinary citizens thought that the cause of civil rights had suffered a permanent setback; and many were disconsolate. The manner, however, in which the new President, Lyndon B. Johnson, counseled with Negro leaders, the numerous instances during his early days in office in which he pledged himself to fight for equality, and his unequivocal stand in favor of a strong civil rights bill without crippling amendments were a source of some considerable satisfaction. With the Senate Majority Whip, Hubert H. Humphrey, in charge of the bill and with strong bipartisan support, Congress proceeded to enact the strongest civil rights bill that had ever been passed. The very process of enactment was historic, in that a majority of the members of both parties supported the bill, thereby making it possible for the Senate to invoke cloture and cut off the bitter-end marathon filibuster conducted by a bloc of Southern Senators.

It was a great day of rejoicing, therefore, when President Johnson signed the new civil rights bill, on July 2, 1964, in the presence of Congressional and civil rights leaders. The chances for the enforcement of the bill were substantially increased when several prominent Southern Senators who had fought its passage called for Southerners to obey the new law. The appointment of Leroy Collins, former governor of Florida, as the first director of the Community Relations Service, was widely hailed as an auspicious beginning in the effort to gain acceptance of the law, despite the fact that one prominent Southerner called him a "renegade Confederate." There was vigorous opposition in some quarters, of course, but the prompt declaration by a Federal district court that the bill was constitutional and the refusal of Supreme Court Justice Black to suspend its enforcement contributed to the decrease of opposition. Consequently, Negroes began to eat in restaurants and register in hotels in many parts of the South where hitherto they had not found it possible to secure service.

Perhaps it was the general improvement of the climate of race relations that brought about other desegregation steps in the months following the enactment of the civil rights bill of 1964. The summer had witnessed some ugly manifestations of racial unrest, as rioting erupted in New York City, Philadelphia, Chicago and several New Jersey cities. But civil rights leaders were quick to point out that these were not civil rights riots but the angry outbursts of poverty-stricken, jobless people living under intolerable conditions in the city slums. There had also been numerous incidents of violence in the South—the mysterious murder of three civil rights workers in Mississippi and the brutal slaying in Georgia of a Negro educator returning from reserve officer training to his home in Washington. But the process of desegregation continued. Segregated public facilities in many parts of the country bowed to the new law, and the pace of school desegregation increased noticeably. In Orangeburg, South Carolina, Negro children attended desegregated schools for the first time in September, 1964. In the same month, other Southern schools were desegregated, notably some for the first time anywhere in Mississippi as well as in Americus, Georgia, and

St. Helena Parish, Louisiana.

The issue of civil rights became an important matter in the presidential campaign of 1964. While the bill had received generous bipartisan support in Congress, the man who became the Republican nominee for the Presidency, Senator Barry Goldwater, had voted against the bill on the ground that he regarded certain parts of it as unconstitutional. This gained for him strong support in many parts of the South, but it alienated virtually all Negroes—even those who had been lifelong Republicans—from the Republican nominee. If the votes of the so-called white backlash—those opposed to the Negro's vigorous drive for equality—drifted to the Republican party, there were those of what President Johnson and his supporters called the frontlash—supporters of civil rights—who joined the Democratic ranks. Nearly six million Negro voters gave their overwhelming support to the election of the Johnson-Humphrey ticket in November 1964.

The Civil Rights movement was greatly strengthened when, in an early test case, the Supreme Court upheld the Act of 1964. The world spotlight was again thrown on the movement when Martin Luther King was awarded the 1964 Nobel peace prize for his leadership. Shortly thereafter, King and other leaders stepped up their voter registration campaign in Marion and Selma, Alabama. The coordination of all federal civil rights activities by the new Vice President, Hubert H. Humphrey, was a source of some encouragement to Negroes.

Thus, Negroes faced their second century of emancipation not only with a new President whose stand on civil rights, housing, and poverty they generally supported, but also with a new civil rights law that many regarded as an indication that at long last the government of the United States was on their side. Perhaps the second century, some of them thought, would not be as difficult as the first.

BIBLIOGRAPHY

Bennett, Lerone, *Before the Mayflower,* Chicago, Johnson Publishing Company, 1964.

Butcher, Margaret J., *The Negro in American Culture,* New York: Alfred A. Knopf, Inc., 1956.

Franklin, John Hope, *From Slavery to Freedom, A History of American Negroes,* New York, Alfred A. Knopf, Inc., 1956.

Frazier, E. Franklin, *The Negro in the United States,* New York, The Macmillan Co., 1957.

Hill, Herbert, *Soon One Morning, New Writing of American Negroes,* New York, Alfred A. Knopf, Inc., 1963.

Logan, Rayford W., *The Negro in American Life and Thought,* New York, Dial, 1954.

Meier, August, *Negro Thought in America,* Ann Arbor, University of Michigan, 1963.

Myrdal, Gunnar, *American Dilemma,* New York, Harper & Row, 1963.

Rose, Arnold, *Assuring Freedom to the Free,* Wayne State University, 1964.

Redding, Saunders, *Lonesome Road,* New York, Doubleday & Co., Inc., 1958.

U.S. Commission on Civil Rights, *Freedom to the Free,* Washington, D.C., Government Printing Office, 1963.

Woodson, Carter G. and Wesley, Charles H., *The Negro in Our History,* Washington, D.C., Associated publishers, 1961.

(News Voice International, photo by Ed Bagwell)

Karl E. Taeuber
and Alma F. Taeuber

chapter **2**

The Negro Population
in the United States

Alma F. Taeuber.   Research Associate, Department of Sociology, University of Wisconsin, Madison, Wisconsin. Coauthor (with Karl E. Taeuber) of *Negroes in Cities: Residential Segregation and Neighborhood Change* (Aldine Press, 1965).

Karl E. Taeuber.   Professor of Sociology, University of Wisconsin, Madison, Wisconsin. Coauthor (with Alma F. Taeuber) of "The Negro as an Immigrant Group" and "The Changing Charactor of Negro Migration" (*American Journal of Sociology*, January 1964 and January 1965); author of "Negro Residential Segregation: Trends and Measurements" (*Social Problems*, Summer 1964).

FIGURE 1—Regions and Geographic Divisions of the United States

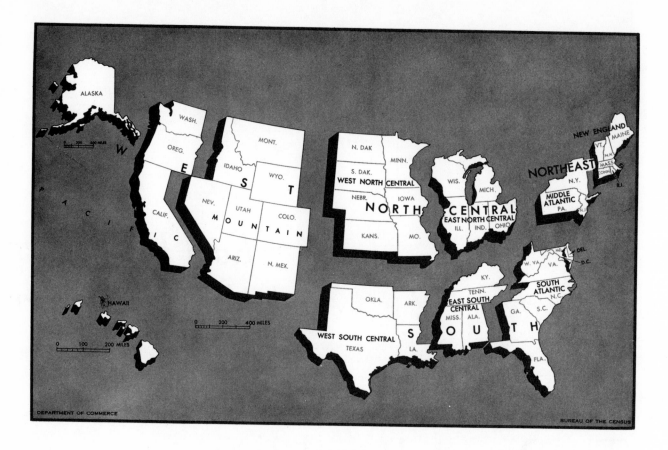

Both Negroes and whites originally came to North America as immigrants, and the history of their settlement is only a few hundred years old. Most of the white immigrants came in search of an increased measure of freedom and enlarged opportunity. Most of the Negro immigrants came after losing their freedom, in the bondage of others. As the years went by, both groups expanded in number, and participated in the settling of a continent and the creation of a gigantic urban and industrial nation out of a small number of agricultural · colonies. In this chapter, many of the ensuing social transformations are traced with the aid of population statistics from a long series of national censuses.

Data from the censuses tell a story of increasing numbers of Negroes and whites, of expanding Negro settlement in the South, and then in the cities of the North and West. Other data tell of the characteristics of Negroes today, their social and economic status, their housing, the rates at which they give birth and the rates at which they die. The charts and tables that tell this story are, like pictures, worth thousands of words. The reader who examines the charts and tables will find far more information than can be conveyed in the text, and will be able to form his own conclusions.

A few words of introduction to census data may help the reader of this chapter and several later chapters. The category "Negro" as used in census publications is a peculiar one. It is arbitrarily designed for simple application and does not convey any biological, anthropological or legal meanings.

A person who appears to be or claims to be white is so listed. Everyone else is regarded as nonwhite and classified according to "race" as Negro, Indian, Japanese, Chinese, etc. Taking a census is a massive operation, and it is not possible to make finer distinctions. The color-race classification used by the census is merely a rough estimate of the person's social identity in his local community.

In this volume, attention is centered on the Negro population. Sometimes, however, data will be presented for nonwhites. In 1960, Negroes made up 92 percent of all nonwhites in the country. Except for a few areas (mainly in the West) containing large numbers of Indians, Orientals or other non-whites, figures for nonwhites may be regarded for practical purposes as referring to Negroes.

Many people attribute too much accuracy to statistical data. It is important to realize that a census is taken by tens of thousands of enumerators, administrators and other personnel, and many errors are possible. Although the 1960 census reported a total Negro population of 18,871,831, nobody would claim that the last few digits are precise. Furthermore, it is not important whether they are, since to know that there were in 1960 about 19 million Negroes is quite accurate enough for almost any purpose. The data presented are not perfectly accurate, but they are more accurate than anybody's guess.

There are many ways of dividing the country into North, South and West. Census data are usually presented for four geographic regions, or nine geographic divisions, portrayed in Figure 1. In this chapter, "the South" refers to all those states in the three southern divisions; the "West" refers to those states in the Mountain and Pacific divisions; and "the North" refers to all other states. The term "conterminous United States" refers to the first forty-eight states, excluding Alaska and Hawaii.

GROWTH AND DISTRIBUTION OF NEGRO POPULATION

The history of Negro population is one of gradual obliteration of the slave heritage of southern rural residence and depressed social and economic status. In the decades since Emancipation, the Negro population has been approaching a pattern of distribution and of social characteristics increasingly like that of the white population. At the time of our first national census in 1790, the total population of the new nation was about four million, 3.2 million whites and 757,000 Negroes. Nearly all of the Negroes were slaves, and nearly all lived in the South. On the eve of the Civil War the situation of the Negro population was not greatly different. In 1860, there were about 4.4 million Negroes in the United States—more than the total national population at the time of the first census. Nearly 90 percent were slaves and more than 90 percent still lived in the South. In the one hundred years since Emancipation, however, there have been dramatic changes. The Negro population increased to 19 million in 1960, of whom 7.5 million lived outside the South and 14 million lived in cities.

The Spread of Slavery

Many of the current features of Negro population distribution are the product of patterns laid down before the Revolutionary War and the formation of the United States. The southern colonies developed as suppliers of agricultural commodities to Britain, and plantation agriculture proved to be an efficient means of exploiting some of the rich resources of the region.

The first ship bringing Negroes to the colonies reportedly arrived in Virginia in 1619. From this beginning, an agricultural system utilizing slave labor was gradually developed and expanded. Slaves were used in the raising of tobacco in Virginia and Maryland before 1700, and spread into South Carolina and Georgia with rice cultivation after 1700. Cotton was not a big crop until later, but once under way in South Carolina and Georgia, it spread rapidly. The invention of the cotton gin in 1793 led to an increase in the efficiency of slave labor. With the depletion of much of the land in the eastern portions of the South, there was a westward expansion of cotton and tobacco cultivation, and of slavery. The maps in Figure 2 reveal very clearly this westward movement as well as the heavy concentrations of Negro slaves in selected agricultural areas of the South, and their virtual absence from other areas—particularly the Appalachians and the Ozarks.

The slave trade flourished well into the nineteenth century, despite its legal abolition in 1808. It is estimated that about 400,000 slaves were imported between 1619 and 1808, and another 270,000 entered illegally after 1808 to meet the continuing demand for agricultural labor.

For Negro slaves, there was always some possibility, however slight, for a change in status from slave to free. Because of the constitutional provision that slaves counted only three-fifths as much as free persons in determining congressional representation, the 1790 census and subsequent censuses to 1860 counted the number of Negroes who were slave and the number who were free. Although manumission became increasingly difficult as various Southern states enacted legislation discouraging it, the free Negro population grew, being added to by births occurring to free Negroes, by legal abolition of slavery in Northern states and by the escape of slaves into freedom. In 1790, about 8 percent of Negroes were free and the other 92 percent were slaves. In 1830, about 14 percent of all Negroes were free, but during the decades before the Civil War the growth of the free Negro population slowed and by 1860 this percentage had slipped back to 11.

The slave population was very heavily concentrated in the South. In fact, slavery outside the South after 1830 was found almost exclusively in Missouri. Free Negroes, on the other hand, were more equally divided between North and South, with about 40 percent living in the North. At a time when only a small portion of the white population and an even smaller portion of the slave population lived in cities, many free Negroes found that large cities offered greater freedom and wider opportunities for earning a living. Sizable free Negro colonies appeared in several cities of the South —Baltimore, Washington, New Orleans, Charleston, Richmond and Petersburg. In the North, Negro population (virtually all free) was concentrated in Boston, New York, Chicago, Cincinnati and Philadelphia. Despite discrimination and restrictive legislation, free Negroes in cities held a variety

FIGURE 2—Geographic Distribution of Slave Population, 1790, 1800, 1830 and 1860

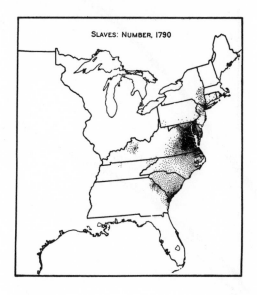

Each dot represents 200 slaves

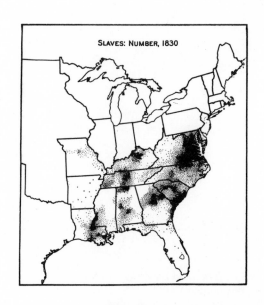

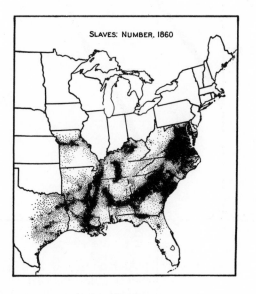

SOURCE: E. Franklin Frazier, *The Negro in the United States* (New York: The
Macmillan Company, 1957), Maps II, III, IV, and V.

FIGURE 3—Population of the United States by Race, 1650–1960

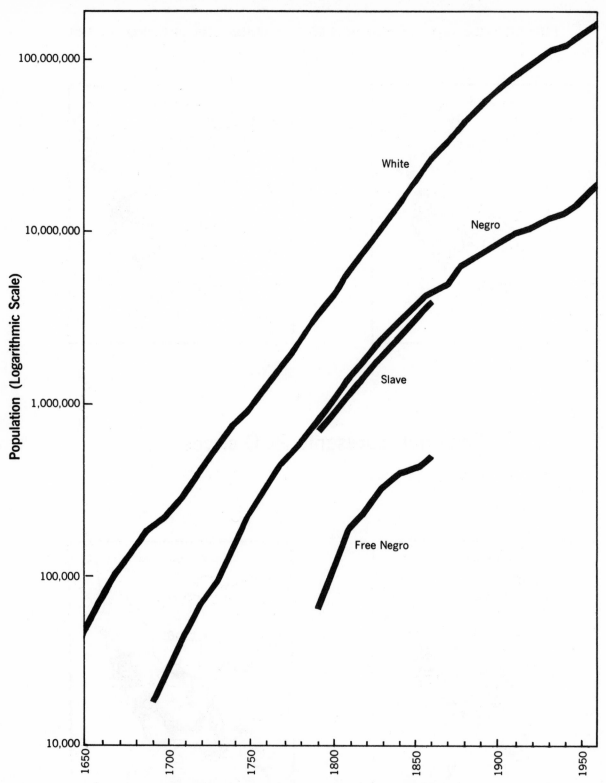

SOURCE: 1650–1950 from U. S. Bureau of the Census, *Historical Statistics of the United States, Colonial Times to 1957* (Washington, D.C.: U.S. Government Printing Office, 1963), Series Z 1–19 and Series A 95–122; 1960 from U.S. Bureau of the Census, *U.S. Census of Population: 1960, General Population Characteristics, U.S. Summary,* Final Report PC (1)–1B (Washington, D.C.: U.S. Government Printing Office, 1961), Table 44.

of skilled jobs and in many cases owned property and voted. In general, however, the economic circumstances of free Negroes were precarious, whether in large cities or rural areas.

Growth of White and Negro Population

The population of the colonies in 1650 included an estimated 1,600 Negroes and 48,768 whites. During the next three centuries, both groups grew rapidly, although their periods of rapid and slow growth did not always coincide. By 1960, there were in the United States 18.9 million Negroes and 158.8 million whites. The patterns of growth from 1650 to 1960 are portrayed in Figure 3.

The relative proportions of Negroes and whites in the population have varied considerably throughout our history. This is shown in Figure 4. During the colonial period, there was little new immigration of Europeans, but continued importation of slaves. Negro population grew at a faster rate than white population, and the percentage of Negroes in the total rose from 1.3 percent in 1630 to a peak of 21.4 percent in 1770. During the next fifty years, both Negroes and whites gained population mainly by natural increase, the excess of births over deaths, and the percentage of Negroes remained close to 20.

Since the Civil War, the Negro population has increased very little due to immigration. The white population, however, embarked upon a period of very rapid growth as the great period of migration from Europe began. Millions of immigrants were added to a high rate of natural increase. The percentage of Negroes declined, reaching a low point of 9.7 in 1930. With restrictive legislation choking off the flow of immigrants from Europe in the early 1920's, both white and Negro populations in recent decades have grown mainly by natural increase. During these decades, Negroes have been increasing at a slightly faster rate, and their share in the population has been increasing slowly. By 1960, Negroes constituted 10.6 percent of the United States population, and this figure may increase slowly in the years to come. Nonetheless, Negroes will continue to comprise a smaller percentage of the population than at the time of the founding of the country.

Regional Distribution

Although many free Negroes and a small share of the slave population lived in the North, the overwhelming bulk of Negro population until recently was concentrated in the South. At every census from 1790 to 1900, at least 90 percent of the Negro population of the United States lived in the South (Figure 5). In 1910, 89 percent of Negroes still lived in the South, but the percentage fell in succeeding decades, to 85 percent in 1920, 77 percent in 1940 and 60 percent in 1960. The reverse pattern, of course, is apparent for Northern and Western states. Prior to 1900, states outside the South never contained more than 10 percent of the Negro population, but by 1920 they contained 15 percent, by 1940, 23 percent, and by 1960, 40 percent.

It is clear that the last few decades have been a time of great migrations for Negroes. Millions of Negroes made the long journey from South to

FIGURE 4—Percent Negro of Total Population in the United States, 1630–1960

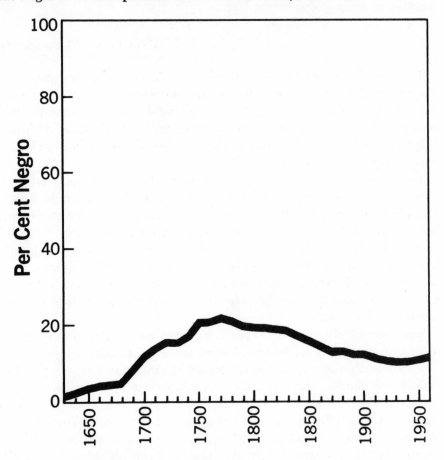

SOURCE: Donald J. Bogue, *The Population of the United States* (New York: The Free Press of Glencoe, 1959), Table 7–2; U.S. Bureau of the Census, *Historical Statistics of the United States, Colonial Times to 1957* (Washington, D.C.: U.S. Government Printing Office, 1963), Series Z 1–19; and U.S. Bureau of the Census, *U.S. Census of Population: 1960, General Population Characteristics, U.S. Summary,* Final Report PC(1)–1B (Washington, D.C.: U.S. Government Printing Office, 1961), Table 44.

North or West. After a century of relative stability in the regional distribution of Negro population, amazingly rapid and profound changes have taken place within the last fifty years.

For nearly fifty years before 1910, however, Negroes had the freedom to move. The freedom to move was granted with Emancipation, and there are many reports of newly freed slaves testing their freedom by moving to another farm, village, county or state. During the decades following the Civil War, there was a continued westward settlement within the South carrying increasing numbers of Negroes as well as whites into new agricultural lands in Louisiana and Texas. Within the North there was also westward movement into Ohio, Michigan, and Illinois, with a few Negroes accompanying the many whites settling these states. Yet there was very little movement of Negroes from South to North for fifty years after Emancipation. During the war and its aftermath, thousands of Negroes migrated to Washington, D.C. and even further north, but hundreds of thousands of Negroes remained near where they had lived as slaves.

The explanation for the stability of Negro population in the decades following Emancipation must lie in the failure of Emancipation to bring with it any organized programs to provide Negroes with new means of earning a livelihood. Many plans were considered, and some tried on a small scale, but for a variety of reasons the Reconstruction programs never included any major effort to alter the economic circumstances of Negroes. Colonization abroad was discussed then as in later times, but never undertaken on a large scale. Utilization of Negroes in the expanding industrial cities of the North was ruled out by prejudice, lack of effort and the continuing availability of millions of European immigrants. Major governmental programs would have been necessary to provide large quantities of land for Negro agricultural settlement either on new farm lands in the North and West or by facilitating Negro land ownership in the South.

FIGURE 5—Percent Distribution by Region for Negroes, 1790–1960

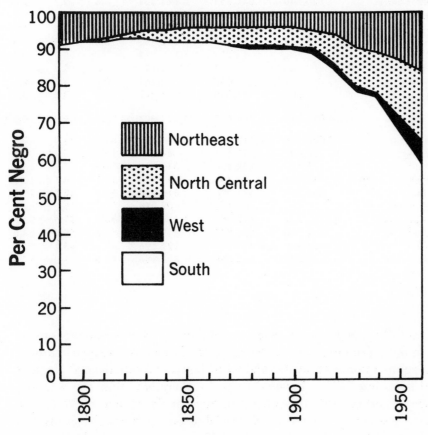

SOURCE: 1960 from U.S. Bureau of the Census, *U.S. Census of Population: 1960, General Population Characteristics, U.S. Summary*, Final Report PC(1)–1B (Washington, D.C.: U.S. Government Printing Office, 1961), Table 57; 1790–1950 from U.S. Bureau of the Census, *Historical Statistics of the United States, Colonial Times to 1957* (Washington, D.C.: U.S. Government Printing Office, 1963), Series A 95–122.

TABLE I—Negro Population and Percent Negro by States, 1860, 1910 and 1960

State	Negro Population			Percent Negro		
	1860	1910	1960	1860	1910	1960
NORTH	340,240	1,027,674	6,474,536	1.7	1.8	6.7
New England	24,711	66,306	243,363	0.8	1.0	2.3
Maine	1,327	1,363	3,318	0.2	0.2	0.3
New Hampshire	494	564	1,903	0.2	0.1	0.3
Vermont	709	1,621	519	0.2	0.5	0.1
Massachusetts	9,602	38,055	111,842	0.8	1.1	2.2
Rhode Island	3,952	9,529	18,332	2.3	1.8	2.1
Connecticut	8,627	15,174	107,449	1.9	1.4	4.2
Middle Atlantic	131,290	417,870	2,785,136	1.8	2.2	8.2
New York	49,005	134,191	1,417,511	1.3	1.5	8.4
New Jersey	25,336	89,760	514,875	3.8	3.5	8.5
Pennsylvania	56,949	193,919	852,750	2.0	2.5	7.5
East North Central	63,699	300,836	2,884,969	0.9	1.6	8.0
Ohio	36,673	111,452	786,097	1.6	2.3	8.1
Indiana	11,428	60,320	269,275	0.9	2.2	5.8
Illinois	7,628	109,049	1,037,470	0.5	1.9	10.3
Michigan	6,799	17,115	717,581	0.9	0.6	9.2
Wisconsin	1,171	2,900	74,546	0.2	0.1	1.9
West North Central	120,540	242,662	561,068	5.6	2.1	3.6
Minnesota	259	7,084	22,263	0.2	0.3	0.7
Iowa	1,069	14,973	25,354	0.2	0.7	0.9
Missouri	118,503	157,452	390,853	10.0	4.8	9.0
North Dakota	—a	617	777	—a	0.1	0.1
South Dakota	—a	817	1,114	—a	0.1	0.2
Nebraska	82	7,689	29,262	0.3	0.6	2.1
Kansas	627	54,030	91,445	0.6	3.2	4.2
SOUTH	4,097,111	8,749,427	11,311,607	36.8	29.8	20.6
South Atlantic	2,058,198	4,112,488	5,844,565	38.4	33.7	22.5
Delaware	21,627	31,181	60,688	19.3	15.4	13.6
Maryland	171,131	232,250	518,410	24.9	17.9	16.7
District of Columbia	14,316	94,446	411,737	19.1	28.5	53.9
Virginia	548,907	671,096	816,258	34.4	32.6	20.6
West Virginia	—	64,173	89,378	—	5.3	4.8
North Carolina	361,522	697,843	1,116,021	36.4	31.6	24.5
South Carolina	412,320	835,843	829,291	58.6	55.2	34.8
Georgia	465,698	1,176,987	1,122,596	44.1	45.1	28.5
Florida	62,677	308,669	880,186	44.6	41.0	17.8

Neither did the newly freed Negroes find many new economic opportunities in Southern cities, where they had to eke out an existence earning wages in competition with whites and with skilled and experienced Negroes who had been free before Emancipation. Furthermore, after the war, the high price of cotton eased the process of Southern economic recovery and encouraged the continued use of Negro labor on white-owned farms and plantations, under new forms of tenancy. One result was a high degree of stability in Negro population distribution.

No one of the major regions of the country is homogeneous, and there are wide differences within each region in the distribution of Negro population. During the last century, for example, the movement of Negroes from South to North has meant a decline in the percentage of Negroes in the

State	Negro Population			Percent Negro		
	1860	1910	1960	1860	1910	1960
East South Central	**1,394,360**	**2,652,513**	**2,698,839**	**34.7**	**31.5**	**22.4**
Kentucky	236,167	261,656	215,949	20.4	11.4	7.1
Tennessee	283,019	473,088	586,876	25.5	21.7	16.5
Alabama	437,770	908,282	980,271	45.4	42.5	30.0
Mississippi	437,404	1,009,487	915,743	55.3	56.2	42.0
West South Central	**644,553**	**1,984,426**	**2,768,203**	**36.9**	**22.6**	**16.3**
Arkansas	111,259	442,891	388,787	25.6	28.1	21.8
Louisiana	350,373	713,874	1,039,207	49.5	43.1	31.9
Oklahoma	—	137,612	153,084	—	8.3	6.6
Texas	182,921	690,049	1,187,125	30.3	17.7	12.4
WEST	**4,479**	**50,662**	**1,085,688**	**0.7**	**0.7**	**3.9**
Mountain	**235**	**21,467**	**123,242**	**0.1**	**0.8**	**1.8**
Montana	—	1,834	1,467	—	0.5	0.2
Idaho	—	651	1,502	—	0.2	0.2
Wyoming	—	2,235	2,183	—	1.5	0.7
Colorado	46	11,453	39,992	0.1	1.4	2.3
New Mexico	85	1,628	17,063	0.1	0.5	1.8
Arizona	—	2,009	43,403	—	1.0	3.3
Utah	59	1,144	4,148	0.2	0.3	0.5
Nevada	45	513	13,484	0.7	0.6	4.7
Pacific	**4,244**	**29,195**	**962,446**	**1.0**	**0.7**	**4.5**
Washington	30	6,058	48,738	0.3	0.5	1.7
Oregon	128	1,492	18,133	0.2	0.2	1.0
California	4,086	21,645	883,861	1.1	0.9	5.6
Alaska	—	—	6,771	—	—	3.0
Hawaii	—	—	4,943	—	—	0.8
U.S. TOTAL	**4,441,830**	**9,827,763**	**18,871,831**	**14.1**	**10.7**	**10.5**

[a] Dakota Territory.

SOURCE: 1860 and 1910 from U.S. Bureau of the Census, *Negroes in the United States, 1920–32* (Washington, D.C.: U.S. Government Printing Office, 1935), Chapter II, Table 12 and Chapter III, Table 4; 1960 from U.S. Bureau of the Census, *U.S. Census of Population: 1960, General Population Characteristics, U.S. Summary,* Final Report PC(1)–1B (Washington, D.C.: U.S. Government Printing Office, 1961), Table 56.

population of the South. Whereas in 1860 Negroes comprised 37 percent of the total, in 1960 they comprised 21 percent. In Kentucky, however, the change was from 20 to 7 percent, while in Mississippi it was from 55 to 42 percent. Full data on the Negro population in each state in 1860, 1910 and 1960, and the percentage of Negroes at each date, are given in Table I. Differences between states in their response to school desegregation and many other aspects of race relations can be traced in part to differences in population such as those found between Kentucky and Mississippi.

Similar arguments about variation in Negro population distribution can be applied to states. Southern states with high percentages of Negroes may have some counties where Negroes form a vast majority of the population, and others where they make up only a small percentage. Similarly, those states with small percentages of Negroes may nonetheless have some counties with large concentrations of Negro population. In 1880, there was a belt of about 300 mainly contiguous counties in the rich argricultural area of the central South in which Negroes constituted more than half of the population. The number of "black belt" counties has been steadily declining, numbering 264 counties in 1910 and 138 in 1960. Several Southern states (Delaware, Kentucky, Maryland, Oklahoma and West Virginia) have no counties in which Negroes are in the majority. Such counties are still found in the remaining Southern states, particularly Georgia (34), Mississippi (29), Virginia (15), and South Carolina (15). Washington, D.C., is the only large city in the country in which Negroes outnumber whites; in 1960 Negroes comprised 53.9 percent of the population of the capital city. Space does not permit a full presentation of data for small areas. Readers are urged to consult the census volumes for their states to obtain specific information on such local variations.

PATTERNS OF MIGRATION, 1870–1960

If the early history of Negro population is linked with the development of southern agriculture, its current history is part and parcel of the history of the entire nation. Millions of Negroes have left the South to seek new opportunities in the cities of the North, and to join with whites in the ever-increasing migrations to the West. The volume of these movements during some decades has been nearly unbelievable, especially when it is recognized that the movement often involves radical transformations in the way of life of the Negro migrant.

The Evidence of Migration

A population in a given area can grow through an excess of births over deaths (natural increase) or by an excess of in-migrants over out-migrants (net migration). In the absence of migration, population growth occurs within a fairly narrow set of biological limits. The Negro population of the U.S. has rarely increased by more than 25 percent in a single decade. Thus, the extremely rapid increases in Northern Negro population in the last fifty years are the product of large-scale population movement. Had these migrations not occurred, the Negro population would still be 90 percent Southern.

During the first fifty years after Emancipation, the relative stability in residential distribution was broken only by some movement to new agricultural areas in the western portion of the South. Although the movement of whites to cities in North and South was already gaining momentum, the rural Southern character of the Negro population remained substantially intact. In the decades since 1910, Negro migrations, rural-to-urban and North-to-South, have been proceeding at a rapid pace, at times at an incredible pace, completely altering the patterns of distribution which would have resulted in the absence of migration.

From 1870 to 1910 the Negro rural population of Georgia increased steadily from 500,000 to 952,000, but despite a continuing excess of births over deaths, this population diminished to 478,000 in 1960. The same pattern is true of Negro rural population in many other states. At the same time, the Negro urban population of New York State, which numbered 118,000 in 1910, has multiplied tenfold in the past fifty years, numbering more than one million in 1960. In fact, in 1960 for the first time, a Northern state, New York, had a larger Negro population than any southern state.

That continuing massive migrations of Negroes have been taking place in the past half-century is obvious from these facts of population redistribution. Unfortunately, direct information is lacking on the numbers involved, the characteristics of migrants, the paths they follow and the forces that impel them to leave their homes for new places and opportunities. In the United States, anyone can move from one part of the country to another without notifying the government and without any records being kept. Data on migration come indirectly. The fact of out-migration, for instance, becomes apparent when the census counts fewer Negroes in Mississippi in 1960 than in 1950, and records a doubling of the Negro population of California in the same period.

Immigration from abroad is evident from the decennial census questions on place of birth. Negroes, however, are overwhelmingly a native population. Since the days of the slave trade, there has been only a tiny stream of Negro immigration. At no time during this century have foreign-born Negroes comprised as much as one percent of the total Negro population. In 1900, the census recorded only 20,000 Negroes as born abroad. During the next fifty years, this number increased, primarily as a result of immigration from the West Indies. In 1950, of a total of 114,000 foreign-born Negroes, 67,000 or three-fifths were from the West Indies. Over half of all foreign-born Negroes lived in the New York metropolitan area. Similarly detailed data are not available for 1960, but the total number of foreign-born Negroes was up only slightly, to 125,000.

Migration from South to North, 1910 to 1960

The general patterns of Negro migration during each decade from 1910 to 1960 can be seen from the data in Table 2. This table presents, for geographic divisions and selected states, the estimated net population gain or loss from migration. Northward movement of Negroes was large between 1910 and 1920, and increased to even larger numbers in the next decade. During the depression decade, migration into the North continued at a much diminished pace. The volume of migration picked up during the war decade of 1940–50, and reached the highest levels ever recorded during 1950–60. The movement of Negroes to the West, which has been gaining momentum since 1940, has been mainly to California.

Negro migration out of the South was greater during 1920–30 than 1910–20, but fell off during the depression decade. During the 1940's and 1950's, net out-migration of Negroes from the South assumed record proportions. Between 1950 and 1960, the South lost nearly 1.5 million Negroes by migration, while the North gained more than one million and the West nearly 400,000.

TABLE II —Estimated Net Intercensal Migration of Negroes, for Geographic Divisions and Selected States, by Decade, 1910–1960

Area	1950–60 ᵃ	1940–50	1930–40	1920–30	1910–20
Geographic Division					
New England	70,000	24,900	5,200	7,400	12,000
Middle Atlantic	472,000	386,800	165,700	341,500	170,100
East North Central	521,000	493,800	107,700	323,700	200,400
West North Central	37,000	35,000	20,100	40,300	43,700
Mountain and Pacific	385,000	304,300	49,000	36,100	28,400
South Atlantic	−542,000	−424,100	−175,200	−508,700	−161,900
East South Central	−620,000	−484,600	−122,500	−180,100	−246,300
West South Central	−295,000	−336,000	− 49,800	− 60,200	− 46,200
Selected States					
Pennsylvania	77,000	89,600	20,300	101,700	82,500
New York	282,000	243,600	135,900	172,800	63,100
Illinois	189,000	179,800	49,400	119,300	69,800
Michigan	127,000	163,300	28,000	86,100	38,700
Ohio	133,000	106,700	20,700	90,700	69,400
California	354,000	258,900	41,200	36,400	16,100
District of Columbia	54,000	61,200	47,500	16,000	18,300
Florida	101,000	7,200	49,900	54,200	3,200
Virginia	− 70,000	− 30,600	− 36,900	−117,200	− 27,200
North Carolina	−207,000	−127,300	− 60,000	− 15,700	− 28,900
South Carolina	−218,000	−159,000	− 94,400	−204,300	− 74,500
Georgia	−204,000	−191,200	− 90,300	−260,000	− 74,700
Alabama	−224,000	−165,400	− 63,800	− 80,700	− 70,800
Mississippi	−323,000	−258,200	− 58,200	− 68,800	−129,600
Arkansas	−150,000	−116,100	− 33,300	− 46,300	− 1,000
Louisiana	− 92,000	−113,800	− 8,400	− 25,500	− 51,200
Texas	− 27,000	− 67,200	4,900	9,700	5,200

Note: A minus sign indicates net out-migration; no sign indicates net in-migration.

ᵃ Figures for 1950–60 refer to non-whites and were estimated by a different procedure from that used for the 1910–50 estimates.

SOURCE: U.S. Bureau of the Census, *Historical Statistics of the United States, Colonial Times to 1957* (Washington, D.C.: U.S. Government Printing Office, 1963), Series C 25–73; and U.S. Bureau of the Census, *Current Population Reports,* Series P-25, No. 247, Table 4.

Causes of Migration

There is still no scholarly agreement on the precise causes of these massive movements of population. Their timing, however, provides some insight into the factors involved. The major northward migration of Southern Negroes appears to have started about 1915 and to have continued at a high rate during most of the next ten years. In discussing causes of migration, it is helpful to distinguish between those causes of dissatisfaction in the local community which "push" people out, and those attractions at the place of destination which "pull" people in.

Among the push factors it might be thought that discrimination, segregation and injustice would be the most important. However much these factors contributed to a general willingness to move, there is no evidence that they were any worse during 1915–25 than in preceding years. This is not to deny that many of the Negroes leaving the South before 1915 as well as later did so out of a sense of personal mistreatment. But the causes of the change in volume of out-migration must include certain precipitating factors not present in earlier periods, such as the severe devastation of Southern agriculture caused by the combination of the boll weevil and a series of bad crop years. Conditions had often been depressed, but the devastation and depth of the agricultural depression in many counties were greater than ever before. Out-migration increased greatly from many of the hardest hit counties.

A change in pull factors inducing migration is also clearly evident about the time of the rapid increase in Negro northward migration. With the onset of war in Europe, immigration of Europeans to the United States, which had been bringing more than a million persons a year to Northern industrial cities, was cut off. The war, even before direct U.S. involvement, brought new demands upon Northern manufacturing industries. Industry, which had been providing hundreds of thousands of jobs each year for new immigrants, now had this labor supply cut off during a period of great demand for labor. Despite widespread prejudice and concern about the "suitability" of Negroes as industrial laborers, many firms not only found that Negroes were suitable, but sent out labor recruiters to the South to encourage Negroes to come North. Many Negroes who made the move encouraged friends and relatives to join them, and the move became easier for those with someone at the other end to help them find a place to live and a job. After the First World War, immigration from Europe resumed, only to be cut back permanently by restrictive legislation in the early 1920's. The Negro then retained a position in the Northern industrial scheme.

Migration Rates and Their Social Impact

The impact of migration on both the community where the migrants originate and the community which is their destination can be better appreciated if the number of migrants is related to the number of people left behind or the number already at the destination. When expressed in this way, the Negro migrations imply tremendous upheavals in both Northern and Southern communities. For instance, between 1910 and 1920, the state of Alabama lost one-tenth of its Negro population by out-migration. Between 1940 and 1950, Mississippi lost over one-fourth of its Negroes by out-migration. Without the continual replenishment of population by natural increase, these states would by now have few Negroes left.

Migration is a highly selective process. Young adults are usually much more eager to give up the old for the new than are those with families, homes, and secure attachments to customary ways of earning a living. The Negro migrations are no exception to this rule, for they have always drawn most heavily from those in the young adult ages. Some of the migration rates shown in Table III for young Negro males are almost beyond belief. Consider Negro males in Georgia who were between the ages of fifteen and thirty-four in 1920. Out-migrants among this group during the 1920–30 decade numbered forty-five out of every one hundred average population in Georgia. Similarly, between 1940 and 1950, Mississippi lost nearly one-half of its young Negro adults by out-migration, principally to Northern states. The impact of migration on the Negro population in some Northern states was also large. In 1920, 1930 and 1950, from one-third to one-half or more of the young adult Negroes in such states as Michigan, Illinois and

New York were persons who moved there within the preceding ten years.

Dramatic as some of these figures are, they are understatements. They refer to net migration, the balance of in- over out-migration or out- over in-migration. Not all Negroes who move from one state to another go from South to North. Many who have been in the North move back to the South. Many others move from one Southern state to another or from one Northern state to another. Thus, in-migration and out-migration are both heavy, and the figures shown in the tables indicate the extent to which one movement predominates over the other. But gross movement is always higher, usually much higher, than net movement.

The impact of migration is also understated by using states as units. During the First World War, there are stories of special trains taking away virtually the entire young adult population of a small Southern community at one time, and many entire families. Similarly, the dramatic impact of Negro migration on New York City's Harlem or Chicago's South Side is somewhat obscured when data are presented for entire states.

The social costs of these migrations are extraordinarily difficult to calculate. High rates of natural increase among rural Southern Negroes have not led to a piling up of Negro population in depressed agricultural areas. Rather, the continuing migrations sketched above have transferred much of the increase in Negro population from the South to the North. To an extent, this out-migration helps alleviate economic problems, for in its absence the South would have been confronted with the need to provide jobs and housing for a great many additional Negroes. Out-migration, however, is not an unmitigated blessing. The South's investment in food, clothing, housing and schooling required to raise children from birth to an age when they are ready to begin productive employment is lost when these youths migrate. Hundreds of thousands go North to add to the productive labor force there rather than in the region which raised and educated them. The remaining Southern rural Negroes are a population with many dependent children and old folks, but with depleted numbers of young and middle-aged adults to support them. The effects of these migrations on Northern cities are similarly complex. A rapid rate of in-migration not only permits a rapid expansion in the productive labor force, but also augments housing shortages, accelerates overcrowding, complicates the task of providing suitable jobs for all those seeking work, and adds to the need for city social and welfare services.

As economic opportunities outside of agriculture increase in the South, and as the number of rural and village Negroes decreases, it seems unlikely that the volume of net out-migration from the South will continue at the same high levels as in the recent past. Whether it does or not, the impact of Negro in-migration on Northern cities cannot again attain its former dimensions. As the Negro population increases in the North, a given number of new in-migrants forms a smaller percentage of the population already there. In the past, migration has accounted for a high proportion of Negro population increase in most Northern and Western cities. The share of population growth attributable to natural increase, however, has been moving rapidly upward and is already the major source of growth in many cities.

Despite the high rates of Negro migration from South to North during the past half-century, just under one-half of the nonwhite residents of the North and West were born in the South. There were even 146,000 Northern-born nonwhites living in the South in 1960. Many Northern Negroes have never been in the South. Currently a high proportion of these Northern-born Negroes are children, but there are already many in the adult ages, and this number is increasing rapidly. If these children are inadequately trained and educated, the North and not the South must bear the responsibility.

Residential Mobility and Short-Distance Moving

Mobility is a prominent feature of an urban industrial society. People in the United States are frequent movers, and Negroes are no exception. They move from one community to another or from one house or apartment to another with high frequency. In March, 1961, the Bureau of the Census asked a large sample of the population where they were living one year earlier. Of nonwhites, 23 percent were in a different house, compared to 20 percent for whites. Every year, about one of every five families, white and Negro, shifts residence. No wonder that the 1960 census reported that only 11 percent of nonwhites and 14 percent of whites had lived in their present housing unit since 1940.

Sociologists sometimes split residential mobility into "migration," referring to moves involving a change of community, and "local movement," referring to moves within a single community. The Bureau of the Census makes a similar distinction by referring to persons moving from one county to another as "migrants," and to persons whose move is entirely within a county as "local movers." Most of the one-fifth of people who move each year are "local movers" rather than "migrants." In 1960–61, for nonwhites, 18.4 percent of the mobile population were local movers and 4.3 percent were intercounty migrants. Of the migrants, roughly one-half moved to a different county within the same state, and one-half moved to a different state. The Bureau of the Census has been collecting similar data each year since 1948, and although the specific percentages vary from year to year,

TABLE III—Net Intercensal Migration for Negro Males Age 15–34 at Beginning of Decade, by Decades for Selected States, 1870–1950

Intercensal Period	Southern States			Northern States		
	Alabama	Georgia	Mississippi	Illinois	Michigan	New York
1870–80	−20.9	−4.6	4.0	37.1	12.5	23.9
1880–90	−8.8	2.9	−4.1	28.7	—	32.1
1890–00	−12.5	−7.6	−2.6	53.9	10.5	55.2
1900–10	−10.1	−5.0	−5.5	33.3	25.0	44.4
1910–20	−22.1	−16.7	−23.3	67.4	138.4	53.6
1920–30	−21.3	−44.7	−14.2	65.5	88.4	79.3
1930–40	−11.7	−13.5	−9.8	14.5	19.0	29.8
1940–50	−32.3	−30.9	−47.0	59.0	81.5	54.3

Note: A minus sign indicates net out-migration; no sign indicates net in-migration.

SOURCE: Everett S. Lee, Ann Ratner Miller, Carol P. Brainerd, and Richard A. Easterlin, *Population Redistribution and Economic Growth, United States, 1870–1950, I. Methodological Considerations and Reference Tables* (Philadelphia: The American Philosophical Society, 1957), Table P–1.

A Country Boy (Standard Oil of N. J. Photo)

the general pattern has been remarkably constant for both whites and non-whites. Each year about one in five persons moves, with about two-thirds of movers shifting residence within a county and the remaining one-third migrating to a different county.

It is misleading to view "local moving" as being without social consequences. A move from one neighborhood to another can entail as many changes in the lives of a family as a move from one city to another. The consequences for urban planning are likewise just as important for the short move as for the long. When one-fourth, one-third, or even more (as is true of many apartment areas) of the population has lived for less than a year in a neighborhood, how much sense of community identification can there be? Under such circumstances, can there be effective local participation in planning, as envisioned by many planners and written into Federal urban renewal law? An urban industrial society, however, is a changing one, and it could not function in the absence of residential mobility. Not only is the freedom to move necessary for the adjustment of people to changing situations and changing opportunities, but it is a basic liberty of Negroes and whites alike.

URBANIZATION OF THE NEGRO POPULATION, 1910–1960

One simple piece of information from the 1960 census summarizes the profound change in the status of the Negro population that has been taking place during the past half-century. In 1960, Negroes were more urbanized than whites. Of the nonwhite population, 73 percent lived in cities, as compared to 70 percent of the white population. Not only has the movement of Negroes from South to North been a movement to cities, but within the South itself Negroes have been moving from rural areas to cities. Civil rights struggles in Birmingham and Little Rock, Atlanta and Norfolk share headlines with those in Chicago, Detroit and New York. Although there are still hundreds of thousands of Negroes living in poverty in the rural South, the picture of the typical American Negro as a Southern sharecropper is a long outdated stereotype.

Urbanization before 1910

The United States began as a rural nation, with most of its people dependent on agriculture for their livelihood. Her rise to world power, however, depended not only on her bountiful agriculture, but also on her becoming an urbanized industrialized nation. Cities have always played an important part in national life. Boston, New York, Philadelphia, Charleston and other cities were already centers of commerce, trade, politics and culture in the eighteenth century. Even the largest cities of those days, however, would be considered small by today's standards. It was not until the nineteenth century that American cities, paced by New York, increased by leaps and bounds to truly large size. The urbanization of America was accelerated after the Civil War by rapid industrial growth and the laying out of the nationwide rail transportation network. Already by 1910 most of the large cities of today had reached large size. Yet in 1910 fewer than 50 percent of Americans lived in cities. The movement of people to cities has continued at a rapid pace ever since.

Negro participation in the urbanization of America was slight during the early stages. The concentration of free Negroes in cities has been discussed above, but their numbers were never large relative to the total population of the cities in which they lived. Within the South, Negro slaves were utilized in greatest numbers in agriculture, and they lived in rural areas and villages. Rural settlement, however, was also characteristic of the white population. The small Southern urban population included its proportionate share of Negro population.

From 1860 to 1910 the movement of Negroes from the South to Northern cities was very slight. Within the South, what Negro migration occurred was primarily in response to changing opportunities in agriculture, particularly the westward movement of cotton. As of 1910, just over one-fourth of Negroes and just under one-half of whites in the United States lived in cities. These national figures mask considerable regional variation. Within the South, Negroes and whites were equally urbanized, with about one-fifth living in cities. Within the North and West, Negroes, with 77 percent in cities, were much more urbanized than whites. These patterns are portrayed in Figure 6. In 1910, nearly all Negroes lived in the South. Despite the high percentages shown as "urban" among Northern Negroes, the numbers involved were small and the national average reflected primarily the pattern in the South. For whites, however, the national percentage urban was an average of the high figure in the North and West, and the low figure in the South.

Urbanization since 1910

During the fifty years from 1910 to 1960, urbanization has proceeded rapidly among both whites and Negroes in every region. Within regions, however, the differences between whites and Negroes have remained much as they were fifty years ago. In the South, despite a period of particularly rapid urbanization since 1940, Negroes and whites have maintained nearly identical proportions in cities. In 1960, 58 percent of Southern Negroes and 59 percent of Southern whites lived in cities. In the North and West, Negroes continue to be more highly urbanized than whites. In 1960, the percentages living in cities were, in the North, 96 for Negroes and 73 for whites, and in the West, 93 for Negroes and 78 for whites.

On a national basis, there has been a convergence between whites and Negroes in percentage urban. This is portrayed in the graph for "Total" in Figure 6. Note that this graph differs from each of the regional graphs. Within each region, the differences between Negroes and whites in urbanization (or lack of differences in the South) have remained about the same for the last fifty years. Yet when all regions are grouped together into the total United States, the picture is one of the percentage urban among Negroes catching up to and surpassing the figure for whites. This peculiar difference between urbanization when viewed within regions and urbaniza-

FIGURE 6–Percent Urban by Race and Region, 1900–1960

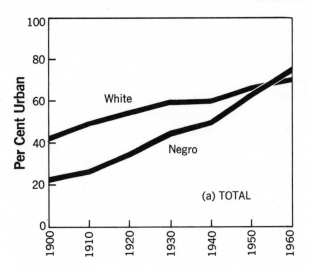

(a) TOTAL

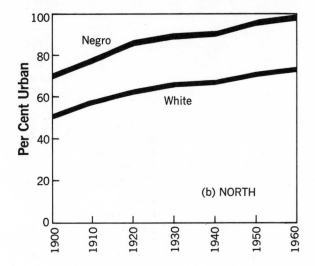

(b) NORTH

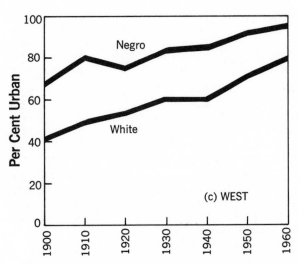

(c) WEST

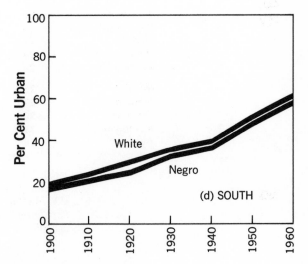

(d) SOUTH

Note: Definition of "urban" not fully comparable throughout this period.

SOURCE: 1960 from U.S. Bureau of the Census, *U.S. Census of Population: 1960, General Population Characteristics, U.S. Summary,* Final Report PC(1)–1B (Washington, D.C.: U.S. Government Printing Office, 1961), Table 51; 1950 from U.S. Bureau of the Census, *U.S. Census of Population: 1950,* Vol. II, *Characteristics of the Population,* Part 1, U.S. Summary (Washington, D.C.: U.S. Government Printing Office, 1953) Table 145; 1940 from U.S. Bureau of the Census, *Sixteenth Census of the U.S.: 1940, Population,* Vol. II, *Characteristics of the Population,* Part 1, Table 21 and *Characteristics of the Nonwhite Population by Race,* Table 3 (Washington, D.C.: U.S. Government Printing Office, 1943); 1930 from U.S. Bureau of the Census, *Sixteenth Census of the U.S.: 1940, Population,* Vol. II, *Characteristics of the Population,* Parts 1-7 (Washington, D.C.: U.S. Government Printing Office, 1943), Table 5 for each state; and 1900–1920 from U.S. Bureau of the Census, *Fourteenth Census of the U.S. Taken in the Year 1920,* Vol. II, *Population* (Washington, D.C.: Government Printing Office, 1922), Table 20, p. 79.

TABLE IV—The Twenty-Five Leading Cities in Negro Population, 1910 and 1960

City	1910 Negro Population (000)	Percent Negro	City	1960 Negro Population (000)	Percent Negro
Washington	94	28.5	New York	1,088	14.0
New York	92	1.9	Chicago	813	22.9
New Orleans	89	26.3	Philadelphia	529	26.4
Baltimore	85	15.2	Detroit	482	28.9
Philadelphia	84	5.5	Washington	412	53.9
Memphis	52	40.0	Los Angeles	335	13.5
Birmingham	52	39.4	Baltimore	326	34.7
Atlanta	52	33.5	Cleveland	251	28.6
Richmond	47	36.6	New Orleans	236	37.2
Chicago	44	2.0	Houston	215	22.9
St. Louis	44	6.4	St. Louis	214	28.6
Louisville	41	18.1	Atlanta	186	38.3
Nashville	37	33.1	Memphis	184	37.0
Savannah	33	51.1	Newark	138	34.1
Charleston	31	52.8	Birmingham	135	39.6
Jacksonville	29	50.8	Dallas	129	19.0
Pittsburgh	26	4.8	Cincinnati	109	21.6
Norfolk	25	37.1	Pittsburgh	101	16.7
Houston	24	30.4	Indianapolis	94	20.6
Kansas City	24	9.5	Richmond	92	41.8
Mobile	23	44.2	Oakland	84	22.8
Indianapolis	22	9.3	Kansas City	83	17.5
Cincinnati	20	5.4	Jacksonville	83	41.1
Montgomery	19	50.7	Norfolk	79	25.8
Augusta	18	44.7	Columbus	77	16.4

SOURCE: 1910 data: U.S. Bureau of the Census, *Negro Population 1790–1915* (Washington: Government Printing Office, 1918), p. 93; 1960 data: U.S. Bureau of the Census, *U.S. Census of Population: 1960, General Population Characteristics* (Washington, D.C.: U.S. Government Printing Office, 1961), Table 21 for states.

tion when viewed for the total United States results from the massive shift of Negro population from South to North during this half-century. Negroes in the South have always been as urbanized as whites in the South, but they have been much less urbanized than Negroes in the North and West. As hundreds of thousands of Negroes have moved from the South to the North and West, they have taken on the urban residential distribution of Negroes in the North and West. In 1910, the percentage urban for Negroes for the total United States was very close to the percentage for the South alone, since 89 percent of Negroes in the United States lived in the South. In 1960, 60 percent of Negroes lived in the South and the percentage urban for the total United States is in between the figure for the South and the figure for the North and West.

In 1910, there were fewer than one million Negroes living in cities in the North and West. In 1960, there were more than one million Negroes in New York City alone, and more than seven million in cities throughout the North and West. Fifty years ago, there were a few Northern cities with large Negro populations, but most urban Negroes lived in Southern cities. The twenty-five cities with the largest Negro populations in 1910 and 1960 are listed in Table IV.

In 1910, no single city had as many as 100,000 Negro residents, as compared with a 1960 total of eighteen cities with more than 100,000 Negro residents. In 1910, there were eight Northern and no Western cities on the list. In none of these Northern cities did Negroes comprise as much as 10 percent of the population because the cities were so large. There were few large cities in the South, and even though Negroes often comprised 30, 40 or 50 percent of the population, few southern cities had as many as 20,000 Negro residents.

The rapid urbanization of the Negro population since 1910, and particularly the pronounced movement to Northern and Western cities, is evident in the changes in the list of the twenty-five leading cities in Negro population between 1910 and 1960. New York, Chicago, Philadelphia, and Detroit lead the 1960 list, and Los Angeles and Cleveland also appear in the top ten. Fourteen of the twenty-five cities are in the North or West. In all of these cities, Negroes comprised more than 10 percent of the population. In contrast to fifty years earlier when Negroes were but a very small segment of most Northern and Western cities, in several cities Negroes now comprise one-fourth to one-third of the population.

Sources of Urban Population Growth

Migration from the South to Northern cities and within the South from rural areas to cities has been taking place at a rapid rate during much of the last fifty years. Migration, however, is not the only source of growth of urban Negro population. The excess of births over deaths contributes to population growth even in the absence of migration. In the previous section it was demonstrated that migrants tend to be young adults of both sexes. Migration thus brings to cities large numbers of young couples and young persons about to form families. As compared to a population with a larger share of older persons, a city population heavily augmented by migration contains many couples in the childbearing ages. Birth rates are therefore high, and in the absence of a large older population, death rates are low. The difference between high birth rates and low death rates is a high rate of natural increase. Urban Negro populations, therefore, are increasing rapidly not only because of in-migration, but also because of natural increase.

The large volume of natural increase augmenting the growth of urban Negro populations is undercutting still another aspect of the old stereotypical picture of Negroes as Southern sharecroppers. In a more up-to-date version of this stereotype, Northern urban Negroes are pictured as recent migrants from the rural South, lacking in knowledge of the manners and niceties of city living. However, more than half of Northern Negroes are Northern-born. Of the migrants from the South, many come from Southern cities rather than rural areas. For instance, of nonwhite males aged 45–64 living in large metropolitan areas, nearly two-thirds have lived in the same city for at least twenty years. While there undoubtedly are some Negro migrants to Northern cities who have difficulties adjusting to urban living, their share in the total northern Negro population must be small.

NEGROES IN METROPOLITAN AREAS

As the urbanization of the United States has progressed, the society has increasingly come to be organized around the large cities. The sphere of influence of a large city extends far beyond its boundaries. A very large city such as New York has economic and cultural ties with every part of the country and with much of the world. Other cities do not have such an extensive range of influence, but there is at least a high degree of interdependence between each large city and its surrounding area. The political boundaries of large cities have not expanded to encompass the entire population that is socially and economically integrated with the city. The entire suburban area of a large city, together with much of the close-in rural area, can be considered together with the central city as comprising a single metropolitan area.

Consideration of the changing distribution of Negro population, thus, is incomplete without an indication of the position of Negroes in the metropolitan system of the country. To permit analysis of metropolitanization, the Federal Government has recognized, for statistical purposes, a number of "Standard Metropolitan Statistical Areas" (SMSA's). Each SMSA consists of at least one city of fifty thousand inhabitants or more, together with the county (or counties) in which the city is located, and as many contiguous counties as are essentially metropolitan in character and socially and economically integrated with the central city. The metropolitan area concept is quite distinct from the concept of urban population. Cities are politically incorporated units. A metropolitan area includes at least one large city, a number of nearby large and small cities, and considerable rural population, both farm and nonfarm.

Both Negro and white population movement has been largely to the cities and suburbs of metropolitan areas. Cities outside of metropolitan areas have not participated to the same degree in the urbanization of the population. The increasing concentration of Negroes and whites in metropolitan areas over the period 1900 to 1960 is shown in Table V. In 1900, 44 percent of whites and 27 percent of Negroes lived in metropolitan areas, whereas by 1960 the figure was 63 percent for whites and 65 percent for Negroes. (In this section, all data for metropolitan areas refer to the 212 SMSA's as delineated for the 1960 census.)

TABLE V—Percent Residing in SMSA's by Race and Region, 1900–1960*

Race and Year	Conterminous United States	Region		
		North	West	South
NEGRO				
1960	64.7	92.8	92.8	45.9
1950	55.6	91.5	91.1	38.7
1940	45.4	88.7	86.0	32.5
1930	42.0	87.1	83.3	29.8
1920	33.9	81.7	68.4	25.7
1910	28.7	72.5	72.5	23.3
1900	26.6	66.1	66.7	22.1
WHITE				
1960	62.8	67.1	71.6	48.7
1950	59.5	65.8	67.1	41.9
1940	56.2	64.2	62.4	35.2
1930	55.7	63.9	61.4	33.2
1920	51.4	60.0	52.2	29.1
1910	47.7	55.5	50.6	26.0
1900	44.0	50.9	47.0	23.9

* SMSA's as defined in 1960.

SOURCE: Compiled from data in U.S. Bureau of the Census, *Historical Statistics of the United States, Colonial Times to 1957* (Washington, D.C.: U.S. Government Printing Office, 1960), Table A 95–122; U.S. Bureau of the Census, *U.S. Census of Population: 1960, General Population Characteristics, United States Summary,* Final Report PC(1)–1B (Washington, D.C.: U.S. Government Printing Office, 1961), Table 56; and U.S. Bureau of the Census, *U.S. Census of Population: 1960, Selected Area Reports, Standard Metropolitan Statistical Areas,* Final Report PC(3)–1D (Washington, D.C.: U.S. Government Printing Office, 1963), Table 1.

TABLE VI—Percent Distribution of Population by Size of SMSA, Race, and Region, 1960

Size of SMSA	Region and Race							
	Conterminous United States		North		West		South	
	White	Negro	White	Negro	White	Negro	White	Negro
3,000,000 or more	27.8	31.3	35.9	24.5	24.5	46.7	—	—
1,000,000–3,000,000	26.5	26.8	27.1	55.6	33.7	30.7	26.2	28.9
500,000–1,000,000	16.7	16.5	11.4	9.4	22.9	12.7	26.3	25.4
250,000–500,000	14.5	11.3	12.8	5.6	11.4	6.2	21.8	18.9
100,000–250,000	12.9	13.1	11.6	4.7	6.2	3.5	22.5	24.6
Less than 100,000	1.6	1.0	1.2	0.2	1.3	0.2	3.2	2.2
TOTAL	100.0	100.0	100.0	100.0	100.0	100.0	100.0	100.0

SOURCE: Compiled from U.S. Bureau of the Census, *U.S. Census of Population: 1960,* Vol. I, *Characteristics of the Population* (Washington, D.C.: U.S. Government Printing Office, 1963), Table 21 for each state.

Regional Trends in Metropolitanization

Because the population movements to urban areas have been principally to urban places within metropolitan areas, regional differences in the patterns for Negroes and whites resemble those already noted for urbanization. In the South, both Negroes and whites have participated about equally in metropolitan concentration, with just under one-fourth of each group in metropolitan areas in 1900 and just under one-half in 1960. In the North and West, Negroes have always been more concentrated than whites in metropolitan areas. In 1960, over 90 percent of Negroes in these regions were metropolitan, as compared to about 70 percent of whites.

A large proportion of metropolitan population lives in the very large metropolitan areas—in 1960, 54 percent of metropolitan whites and 58 percent of metropolitan Negroes were in areas of over 1,000,000 total population (Table VI). Regional differences are again evident. Large metropolitan areas are principally located in the North and West, and Negroes moving North have been particularly attracted to these centers. In 1960, 80 percent of metropolitan Negroes in the North lived in areas of this size. In the South, however, metropolitan Negroes and whites are similarly distributed among areas of each size.

The concentration of Negro population in a few locations, particularly in the North and West, is even greater than indicated by the figures for all metropolitan areas combined. One of every fifteen Negroes in the country lives in the New York metropolitan area. Ten metropolitan areas in the North, each with more than 100,000 Negro residents, together contain 70 percent of all Northern Negroes (Table VII). Two metropolitan areas in the West contain 65 percent of that region's Negro population. There are thirteen metropolitan areas in the South with more than 100,000 Negro residents, and together they contain one-fourth of the region's Negro population.

TABLE VII—List of SMSA's with 100,000 or More Negroes in 1960, by Region

Region and SMSA	Negro Population	Region and SMSA	Negro Population
NORTH	**4,525,234**	**SOUTH**	**2,811,082**
Chicago	889,961	Atlanta	230,737
Cincinnati	127,713	Baltimore	378,333
Cleveland	257,258	Birmingham	219,482
Detroit	558,792	Dallas	155,081
Kansas City	117,210	Houston	246,118
Newark	223,210	Jacksonville	105,624
New York	1,224,590	Memphis	227,180
Philadelphia	670,939	Miami	137,492
Pittsburgh	160,845	Mobile	100,933
St. Louis	294,716	New Orleans	267,303
		Norfolk-Portsmouth	150,442
WEST	**701,540**	Richmond	107,240
		Washington	485,117
Los Angeles-Long Beach	464,112		
San Francisco-Oakland	237,428		

Regional differences in the course of metropolitanization of Negroes have many causes. In the South, Negroes were an integral part of the initial settlement of the region and have always been distributed similarly to the white population. Both races are now responding in similar fashion to the social and economic forces which are producing a metropolitan society. In the South, both races started as predominantly rural and the process of urbanization since 1900 has been gradually erasing their common rural heritage. In the North and West, on the other hand, Negroes represent a new group, similar in this respect to the immigrants of the past, being superimposed upon established settlement patterns.

Negro Migration to Metropolitan Areas, 1955–60

The large Negro population in metropolitan areas has been achieved by the migration of thousands of Negroes in search of a share in the economic benefits accruing from industrialization. Lack of data, however, has prohibited careful documentation of the character of these migrations. The best detailed migration data for the United States refer to the two periods 1935–40 and 1955–60, and are based upon responses to a census question on place of residence five years earlier.

Much of what we know about the early movement is based upon fragmentary sources and the reports of observers. Most of this literature is in agreement that Negro in-migrants to cities were of lower social and economic status than the resident Negro population and, as a result, considerable friction was generated between the two groups and between them and whites. Increased racial tensions were blamed upon the heavy influx of Negroes of low socio-economic status. Considerable evidence also exists that the newcomers were a higher status segment of the Southern Negro population from which they were drawn. Several studies have shown with regard to educational levels that the better-educated Negroes in the South were the ones who tended to migrate, but because their educational level was below that of Negroes already residing in cities, the net effect of the movement was to dampen the educational level of the Negro population both at place of origin and place of destination.

As the Negro population in metropolitan areas has grown, movement of Negroes between metropolitan areas has been added to the earlier rural-to-urban movement. This intermetropolitan movement is an increasingly important component of total Negro migration. Among nonwhite in-migrants to Northern metropolitan areas between 1955 and 1960, about one-half, on the average, came from other metropolitan areas (Table VIII). The figure is about one-third among nonwhite migrants to Southern metropolitan areas. Once resident in a metropolitan area, Negroes are much more likely to move to other metropolitan areas than back to the rural areas and small towns of the South. Clearly, in a society which is overwhelmingly metropolitan, the predominant movement is intermetropolitan rather than rural-to-urban. Most Negro newcomers, particularly to Northern metropolitan areas, have had considerable experience with metropolitan living.

It is possible to trace the origins of in-migrants and the destinations of out-migrants in somewhat more detail. Table IX presents the distribution by region of origin of nonwhite in-migrants to twenty-five metropolitan areas with large Negro populations. Nonwhite migrants to metropolitan

TABLE VIII—Metropolitan Origin of Nonwhite In-Migrants and Metropolitan Destination of Nonwhite Out-Migrants for Selected SMSA's, 1955–60

SMSA	Percent of In-Migrants from Other SMSA's	Percent of Out-Migrants Going to Other SMSA's
NORTH		
Chicago	44.0	66.3
Cincinnati	58.9	71.1
Cleveland	56.2	70.5
Detroit	56.6	73.7
Kansas City	45.2	72.6
Newark	48.0	61.5
New York	48.8	65.6
Philadelphia	53.7	69.8
Pittsburgh	57.9	72.7
St. Louis	41.1	71.6
WEST		
Los Angeles-Long Beach	71.6	77.7
San Francisco-Oakland	68.3	75.4
SOUTH		
Atlanta	29.4	57.7
Baltimore	43.7	64.0
Birmingham	34.4	75.4
Dallas	34.1	67.8
Houston	34.2	61.9
Jacksonville	37.8	56.5
Memphis	19.5	71.9
Miami	32.4	57.1
Mobile	30.4	59.7
New Orleans	28.5	65.4
Norfolk-Portsmouth	45.4	64.1
Richmond	33.2	58.2
Washington	47.2	67.2

SOURCE: U.S. Bureau of the Census, *U.S. Census of Population: 1960, Subject Reports, Mobility for Metropolitan Areas*, Final Report PC(2)–2C (Washington, D.C.: U.S. Government Printing Office, 1963), Tables 1 and 5.

areas in the Northeast (Newark, New York, Philadelphia and Pittsburgh) are drawn primarily from the Atlantic Seaboard states. Metropolitan areas in the North Central region (St. Louis, Detroit, Cleveland, Cincinnati and Chicago) receive substantial shares of their nonwhite in-migrants from the states of the middle South (the East South Central division). Los Angeles-Long Beach and San Francisco-Oakland draw from the states along the western edge of the South (the West South Central division) and the North Central region. For metropolitan areas of the South, the major source of in-migration is the nonmetropolitan areas of their own or neighboring states.

Corresponding information on the destinations of out-migrants is presented in Table X. Less than one-third of the nonwhites leaving Northern metropolitan areas moved to the South, while one-third to one-half of those leaving most Southern areas moved to the North or West. Most of the nonwhites leaving Southern SMSA's stayed within the South, the overwhelming majority of them going to nonmetropolitan areas of the same or nearby states.

TABLE IX—Percent Distribution of Nonwhite In-Migrants to Selected SMSA's by Region of Origin, 1955–60

SMSA	Total			Region or Division of Origin				
		Same State	North-east	North Central	West	South Atlantic	East South Central	West South Central
NORTH								
Chicago	100.0	5.3	3.5	18.1	4.4	8.2	46.2	14.3
Cincinnati	100.0	17.2*	7.0	17.9	3.5	20.4	32.4	1.6
Cleveland	100.0	11.1	10.8	14.6	2.6	22.6	34.2	4.1
Detroit	100.0	8.3	6.5	16.9	3.9	21.0	33.8	9.6
Kansas City	100.0	13.3*	4.5	18.9	8.3	3.3	15.4	36.3
Newark	100.0	17.0	16.7	3.8	1.4	55.9	4.3	0.9
New York	100.0	2.5	11.4	6.6	2.9	67.0	7.3	2.3
Philadelphia	100.0	7.8*	17.2	6.0	2.7	59.9	4.0	2.4
Pittsburgh	100.0	17.0	10.1	20.4	3.4	34.3	11.1	2.7
St. Louis	100.0	10.2*	3.1	21.4	5.0	4.3	36.5	19.5
WEST								
Los Angeles-Long Beach	100.0	13.9	6.5	19.7	15.5	5.3	11.5	27.6
San Francisco-Oakland	100.0	23.4	5.1	14.0	16.2	7.1	7.6	26.6
SOUTH								
Atlanta	100.0	62.2	5.4	6.9	1.8	9.1	12.4	2.2
Baltimore	100.0	8.8	13.1	4.2	2.6	66.5	3.1	1.7
Birmingham	100.0	65.7	4.7	13.9	1.8	7.5	5.5	0.9
Dallas	100.0	68.1	0.6	4.2	6.4	1.3	2.5	16.9
Houston	100.0	58.7	1.5	2.8	5.8	2.2	3.3	25.7
Jacksonville	100.0	27.3	8.5	4.1	2.8	49.7	5.1	2.5
Memphis	100.0	18.4	1.7	11.8	1.7	2.6	51.6	12.2
Miami	100.0	21.5	7.5	4.2	0.9	50.8	13.5	1.6
Mobile	100.0	64.0	4.7	6.5	3.2	4.5	14.2	2.9
New Orleans	100.0	39.7	2.8	4.6	4.5	4.8	37.4	6.2
Norfolk-Portsmouth	100.0	20.5	15.1	7.1	2.7	47.3	3.9	3.4
Richmond	100.0	58.6	8.6	0.9	0.7	29.2	1.7	0.3
Washington	100.0	6.8*	13.6	7.6	3.5	60.8	4.6	3.1

* Since SMSA crosses state boundaries, "same state" refers to in-migrants to that portion of the SMSA lying in a given state from the remainder of that state.

SOURCE: U.S. Bureau of the Census, *Mobility for Metropolitan Areas, op. cit.,* and U.S. Bureau of the Census, *U.S. Census of Population: 1960, Subject Reports, Mobility for States and State Economic Areas,* Final Report PC(2)–2B (Washington, D.C.: U.S. Government Printing Office, 1963), Table 34.

These data reveal the existence of a large circulation of nonwhite population between metropolitan areas within each region, from Southern to Northern and Western areas, and a smaller movement in the reverse direction. The movement from nonmetropolitan to metropolitan areas occurs principally in the South, and is accompanied by a sizable reverse movement. Each of these "streams" of nonwhite migrants tends to consist of persons with different socio-economic characteristics.

Data on the relative frequency of high school graduates and white collar workers in the several migrant groups are presented in Tables XI and XII for a few of the largest metropolitan areas. The intermetropolitan migrants,

TABLE X—Percent Distribution of Nonwhite Out-Migrants from Selected SMSA's by Region of Destination, 1955–60

SMSA	Total	Same State	North-east	North Central	West	South Atlantic	East South Central	West South Central
NORTH								
Chicago	100.0	10.4	7.0	29.7	24.0	8.1	12.2	8.6
Cincinnati	100.0	30.3*	11.5	15.5	14.9	11.7	12.6	3.5
Cleveland	100.0	26.2	13.7	15.2	16.2	12.8	11.9	4.0
Detroit	100.0	16.5	10.0	25.8	17.6	13.9	10.0	6.2
Kansas City	100.0	12.1*	3.4	23.8	39.0	5.1	2.8	13.8
Newark	100.0	33.9	22.6	5.1	7.5	26.8	1.7	2.4
New York	100.0	13.2	29.0	8.1	12.0	30.9	3.2	3.6
Philadelphia	100.0	14.3*	27.0	7.2	10.0	34.3	3.4	3.8
Pittsburgh	100.0	18.4	18.1	25.6	10.4	19.8	4.4	3.3
St. Louis	100.0	16.9*	6.6	30.2	25.2	5.0	8.9	7.2
WEST								
Los Angeles-Long Beach	100.0	45.3	5.0	11.2	16.4	5.1	2.3	14.7
San Francisco-Oakland	100.0	56.0	5.6	6.9	14.9	4.2	1.4	11.0
SOUTH								
Atlanta	100.0	34.2	14.7	16.9	7.3	16.1	8.1	2.7
Baltimore	100.0	18.6	28.8	5.8	7.1	34.3	2.7	2.7
Birmingham	100.0	24.7	13.3	30.9	12.5	11.6	4.6	2.4
Dallas	100.0	47.7	2.5	7.2	33.6	2.5	1.1	5.4
Houston	100.0	45.1	2.3	5.1	30.3	3.5	2.2	11.5
Jacksonville	100.0	38.4	22.3	4.2	7.3	22.0	3.7	2.1
Memphis	100.0	9.5	6.7	41.7	17.5	4.9	11.2	8.5
Miami	100.0	40.9	19.3	6.3	4.4	21.1	5.5	2.5
Mobile	100.0	32.6	9.9	14.5	16.1	12.7	8.4	5.8
New Orleans	100.0	29.9	5.5	12.8	31.2	5.4	9.1	6.1
Norfolk-Portsmouth	100.0	22.4	30.3	4.7	8.0	30.8	2.1	1.7
Richmond	100.0	36.8	27.8	3.3	4.6	23.8	2.2	1.5
Washington	100.0	5.9*	25.3	10.1	12.2	39.0	3.4	4.1

* Since SMSA crosses state boundaries, "same state" refers to out-migrants from that portion of the SMSA lying in a given state to remainder of that state.

SOURCE: U.S. Bureau of the Census, U.S. *Census of Population: 1960, Subject Reports, Mobility for States and State Economic Areas,* Final Report PC(2)–2B (Washington, D.C.: U.S. Government Printing Office, 1963), Table 36.

TABLE XI—Percent of Nonwhites Over 25 Completing Four or More Years of High School, by Migration Status 1955–1960, for Selected SMSA's

| SMSA | Total Population | In-Migrants | | | Out-Migrants | | |
		Total	From Other SMSA	From Non-met Area	Total	To Other SMSA	To Non-met Area
NORTH							
Chicago	29.0	32.2	39.5	24.5	41.3	47.8	27.5
Cleveland	28.1	37.5	40.1	33.0	34.4	38.2	23.3
Detroit	26.5	37.3	41.4	30.3	31.8	33.3	26.6
New York	31.2	37.4	42.0	31.2	40.6	45.7	28.5
Philadelphia	23.6	36.1	41.0	29.0	39.4	43.0	29.9
St. Louis	23.7	31.2	42.0	21.3	36.2	40.7	24.3
SOUTH							
Atlanta	21.0	25.4	33.5	20.7	31.4	37.6	23.3
Baltimore	19.7	32.2	39.7	25.7	35.8	39.2	28.7
Birmingham	19.1	20.4	29.4	14.4	30.4	33.6	21.4
Memphis	14.6	16.0	32.9	10.9	23.3	27.6	13.6
New Orleans	15.0	22.0	35.0	14.9	30.6	35.7	21.3
Washington	33.5	45.7	54.3	36.6	45.5	50.0	34.8

SOURCE: U.S. Bureau of the Census, *U.S. Census of Population: 1960, Subject Reports, Mobility for Metropolitan Areas,* Final Report PC(2)–2C (Washington, D.C.: U.S. Government Printing Office, 1963), Tables 4 and 5.

those moving from one metropolitan area to another, are of unusually high educational and occupational status. By contrast, in-migrants from non-metropolitan areas as well as out-migrants to nonmetropolitan areas are of much lower socio-economic status.

The net effect of migration on the educational and occupational status of the resident nonwhite population during 1955 to 1960 was, in most areas, to retard improvement slightly. This effect is the product of both the number and characteristics of the movers during the 1955–60 period. Very likely a high status intermetropolitan stream of migration always existed, but its relative importance has increased substantially in recent years owing to the rapid urbanization of the Negro population. It is only the in-migrants of nonmetropolitan origin who even partially resemble the stereotype of the poorly educated and economically depressed migrant. With continuing metropolitanization, it seems reasonable that this component will decline and the intermetropolitan component increase in relative importance. The general educational and occupational levels of migrants should continue to improve.

As the character of the Negro population has changed from a disadvantaged rural population to a largely metropolitan population of rising socioeconomic position, its patterns of migration have begun to manifest the same responses to economic pushes and pulls as are found in the white population. Although Negro in-migrants in the past generally were of somewhat lower socioeconomic status than the resident Negro population, this is no longer an adequate description of current patterns of Negro

TABLE XII—Percent of Nonwhite Employed Males Engaged in White
Collar Occupations, by Migration Status 1955–60, for Selected
SMSA's

SMSA	Total Population	In-Migrants			Out-Migrants		
		Total	From Other SMSA	From Non-met Area	Total	To Other SMSA	To Non-met Area
NORTH							
Chicago	14.8	21.2	28.7	15.1	30.2	34.2	17.0
Cleveland	16.4	17.9	22.0	13.2	24.2	24.4	23.4
Detroit	14.9	24.7	31.3	15.1	18.4	19.0	15.8
New York	27.1	25.5	32.3	18.6	31.7	32.5	28.7
Philadelphia	18.4	21.3	28.6	14.0	26.6	27.6	23.0
St. Louis	17.1	21.0	28.4	14.7	25.8	28.2	17.3
SOUTH							
Atlanta	12.3	14.7	25.1	11.1	25.7	28.5	21.2
Baltimore	16.3	22.7	36.1	13.9	21.5	24.4	14.4
Birmingham	8.6	9.7	14.1	7.4	17.6	17.9	16.3
Memphis	11.3	14.0	24.3	11.6	18.0	18.3	17.1
New Orleans	12.8	10.9	20.7	7.1	24.9	24.9	25.0
Washington	28.2	29.3	40.0	21.1	37.6	42.2	24.3

Note: "White collar" includes professional, manager, clerical and sales occupations.

SOURCE: U.S. Bureau of the Census, *U.S. Census of Population: 1960, Subject Reports, Mobility for Metropolitan Areas,* Final Report PC(2)–2C (Washington, D.C.: U.S. Government Printing Office, 1963), Tables 4 and 6.

migration. There is a large and increasingly important high status inter-metropolitan movement in the over-all migration of the Negro population.

The redistribution of Negro population from the rural South to northern cities appears to be an indirect process. Few Negroes move directly from southern farms to Chicago or New York. Negro farmers, croppers, or farm laborers are more likely to move to a nearby southern city. Later they or their children may move to one of the northern cities. Such "stage migra-tion" may encompass a number of moves, from farm to village to town to city to metropolis. Some migrants, indeed, do skip all or most of the inter-vening stages. Others move only one or two stages, and still others, few in number, move in the reverse direction, from North back to South, or from large place to small. The exchange of migrants between regions and types of place is an incredibly complex process. If the data presented here help demolish old stereotypes of migrants, they should show also that there is no such thing as the "typical" migrant.

Negroes in Suburbs

A metropolitan area can conveniently be divided into two parts—the central city (or cities) which gives it its name, and the surrounding sub-urban "ring." The extent of suburbanization can then be measured by the percentage of a metropolitan area's population which resides in the sub-urban ring. Using this measure, it is easy to document that Negroes and whites have not shared equally in the movement to the suburbs. Although whites and Negroes are about equally concentrated in metropolitan areas, within metropolitan areas Negroes are confined to the central cities to a much greater extent than are whites (Table XIII). In all metropolitan areas combined, about half of the whites live in the suburban ring as compared to only 20 percent of Negroes. This underrepresentation of Negroes in suburban areas obtains within each region.

From 1900 to 1960, the concentration of metropolitan Negroes in central cities increased, in contrast to the suburbanization trend among the white population (Table XIV). As a result, the racial composition of cities and suburban rings has been altered. If the Negro and white populations of cities (or rings) changed at the same rate, then Negroes would remain a constant percentage of the total city or ring population. To the extent that the percent Negro in the city or ring increases, this indicates that the Negro population is growing at a faster rate than the white population. Similarly, a decline in the percent Negro in an area indicates that the white population is growing at a faster rate than the Negro population. In the North and West, both suburban rings and central cities have in-

TABLE XIII—Metropolitan Distribution by Race and Region, 1960

Metropolitan Residence	Population (000)		Percent Distribution	
	White	Negro	White	Negro
CONTERMINOUS U.S.	**158,455**	**18,860**	**100.0**	**100.0**
Inside SMSA's	99,509	12,202	62.8	64.7
In Central City	47,575	9,704	30.0	51.5
In Ring	51,934	2,498	32.8	13.2
Outside SMSA's	58,946	6,658	37.2	35.3
NORTH	**89,525**	**6,475**	**100.0**	**100.0**
Inside SMSA's	60,102	6,010	67.1	92.8
In Central City	28,617	5,105	32.0	78.8
In Ring	31,485	905	35.2	14.0
Outside SMSA's	29,423	465	32.9	7.2
WEST	**25,453**	**1,074**	**100.0**	**100.0**
Inside SMSA's	18,220	997	71.6	92.8
In Central City	7,841	723	30.8	67.3
In Ring	10,379	274	40.8	25.5
Outside SMSA's	7,233	77	28.4	7.2
SOUTH	**43,477**	**11,312**	**100.0**	**100.0**
Inside SMSA's	21,187	5,194	48.7	45.9
In Central City	11,116	3,875	25.6	34.3
In Ring	10,071	1,319	23.2	11.7
Outside SMSA's	22,290	6,118	51.3	54.1

SOURCE: U.S. Bureau of the Census, *Historical Statistics of the United States, Colonial Times to 1957* (Washington, D.C.: U.S. Government Printing Office, 1960), Table A 95–122; U.S. Bureau of the Census, *U.S. Census of Population: 1960, General Population Characteristics, United States Summary,* Final Report PC(1)–1B (Washington, D.C.: U.S. Government Printing Office, 1961), Table 56; and U.S. Bureau of the Census, *U.S. Census of Population: 1960, Selected Area Reports, Standard Metropolitan Statistical Areas,* Final Report PC(3)–1D (Washington, D.C.: U.S. Government Printing Office, 1963), Table 1.

creased in percent Negro during 1900–60, indicating that the Negro population in both components of metropolitan areas was increasing more rapidly than the corresponding white population (Table XV). The percent Negro in cities, however, rose to much higher levels than in rings. In Southern metropolitan areas, on the other hand, the percent Negro in the rings has declined rapidly, while the color composition of the cities has remained about the same.

Recent gains in the Negro population residing in some suburban rings, although small, have been hailed by some as the beginnings of large-scale suburbanward movement of Negroes. Such a forecast may well be correct, but a closer look at actual trends to date prompts a more cautious view. Not all parts of the suburban ring conform to the suburbia of the Sunday supplements. For illustrative purposes, consider the Chicago metropolitan area. The Negro population outside Chicago city increased from 44,000 to 78,000 between 1950 and 1960. More than half of the 34,000 increase went to neighborhoods in such industrial suburbs as Evanston, Joliet, North Chicago, and similar places listed in Table XVI. These suburbs already had Negro communities in residentially segregated neighborhoods in 1950, and the addition of Negro population to these areas did not represent an opening up of suburbs in general to Negro residents. An additional one-fourth of the increased Negro population in Chicago's suburban ring is accounted for by the addition of Negro population to existing or newly created "Negro suburbs," entire communities or separate sections of com-

TABLE XIV—Percent of SMSA Population Residing in Central City by Race and Region, 1900–1960*

Race and Year	Conterminous United States	Region		
		North	West	South
NEGRO				
1960	79.5	84.9	72.5	74.6
1950	77.2	83.5	69.9	72.0
1940	74.6	81.1	78.3	69.5
1930	72.8	79.8	79.8	67.3
1920	67.2	78.0	83.8	61.1
1910	60.4	72.1	81.7	55.7
1900	54.5	68.6	80.3	49.5
WHITE				
1960	47.8	47.6	43.0	52.5
1950	56.6	58.1	49.6	57.3
1940	61.6	62.5	57.7	60.6
1930	63.9	64.4	61.5	63.6
1920	65.9	66.8	66.8	61.0
1910	64.9	66.4	65.3	56.0
1900	62.8	64.7	62.3	51.8

* SMSA's as defined in 1960.

SOURCE: U.S. Bureau of the Census, *U.S. Census of Population: 1960, Selected Area Reports, Standard Metropolitan Statistical Areas*, Final Report PC(3)–1D (Washington, D.C.: U.S. Government Printing Office, 1963), Table 1.

Residence and Year	Conterminous United States	Region		
		North	West	South
TOTAL SMSA				
1960	10.8	9.1	5.1	19.6
1950	9.4	6.9	3.9	20.4
1940	8.0	5.0	1.7	22.4
1930	7.5	4.4	1.4	22.9
1920	6.8	3.1	1.1	24.6
1910	6.7	2.4	1.1	27.4
1900	7.4	2.4	1.0	30.7
CENTRAL CITY				
1960	16.8	15.1	8.2	25.8
1950	12.4	9.6	5.4	24.3
1940	9.6	6.4	2.3	24.8
1930	8.4	5.5	1.8	23.9
1920	6.9	3.6	1.5	24.6
1910	6.3	2.6	1.3	27.5
1900	6.5	2.5	1.3	29.6
RING				
1960	4.6	2.8	2.5	11.6
1950	5.2	2.8	2.4	14.3
1940	5.5	2.6	0.9	18.2
1930	5.7	2.6	0.7	21.0
1920	6.5	2.1	0.5	24.5
1910	7.5	2.0	0.5	27.4
1900	8.9	2.1	0.5	31.7

* SMSA's as defined in 1960.

SOURCE: U.S. Bureau of the Census, *U.S. Census of Population: 1960, Selected Area Reports, Standard Metropolitan Statistical Areas,* Final Report PC(3)–1D (Washington, D.C.: U.S. Government Printing Office, 1963), Table 1.

munities developed expressly for the purpose of providing new suburban housing for Negroes. There are several such developments in Cook County just southwest of Chicago. The net gain of Negro population in all the rest of the suburban area surrounding Chicago was less than 6,000 in the entire decade.

Moderate increases in the number of Negroes have produced large percentage increases in Negro suburban population elsewhere than in Chicago. There is little evidence, as yet, that much of this suburbanization is different from the expansion of Negro residential areas within the central cities, except that it is taking place outside the city limits. Clearly little of it represents the development of integrated residential patterns.

Urban Residential Segregation

Within the central cities of our large metropolitan areas dwell a high proportion of the nation's Negroes. Not only are these Negroes virtually

TABLE XVI—Negro Population in 1950 and 1960 of Selected Chicago Suburbs

Suburb	Negro Population		Change 1950–60	Percent Negro, 1960
	1960	1950		
INDUSTRIAL SUBURBS				
Aurora	2,227	1,151	1,076	3.5
Chicago Heights	6,529	4,109	2,420	19.0
Elgin	1,595	768	827	3.2
Evanston	9,126	6,994	2,132	11.5
Harvey	1,986	1,010	976	6.8
Joliet	4,638	1,950	2,688	6.9
Maywood	5,229	2,500	2,729	19.1
North Chicago	4,577	832	3,745	23.4
Waukegan	4,485	2,313	2,172	8.0
TOTAL			18,765	
"NEGRO SUBURBS"				
Dixmoor	1,855	554	1,301	60.3
East Chicago Heights	2,794	1,190	1,604	85.4
Markham	2,505	66	2,439	21.4
Phoenix	2,744	1,461	1,283	65.3
Robbins	7,410	4,729	2,681	98.7
TOTAL			9,308	
Total Ring of Chicago SMSA	77,517	43,640	33,877	2.9

Note: The designation of a suburb as "industrial" is based upon data for manufacturing establishments and employment and amount of commuting to Chicago to work, as described in the suburban histories of the Kitagawa and Taeuber volume cited below.

SOURCE: Evelyn M. Kitagawa and Karl E. Taeuber, *Local Community Fact Book Chicago Metropolitan Area 1960* (Chicago: Chicago Community Inventory, University of Chicago, 1963); U.S. Bureau of the Census, *U.S. Census of Population: 1960*, Vol. I, *Characteristics of the Population*, Part 15, Illinois (Washington, D.C.: U.S. Government Printing Office, 1963), Tables 21 and 22; and U.S. Bureau of the Census, *U.S. Census of Population: 1950*, Vol. II, *Characteristics of the Population*, Part 13, Illinois (Washington, D.C.: U.S. Government Printing Office, 1952), Tables 34 and 38.

absent from most of suburbia, but they are virtually absent from many residential neighborhoods within these cities. Individual city neighborhoods throughout the country tend to be occupied either by Negroes or by whites, with few areas of sustained racial intermixture on a residential basis. Civil rights struggles for open occupancy, against *de facto* school segregation and against a variety of other forms of segregation in parks, libraries and other public facilities have called attention to the prevalence of racial residential segregation in many cities. A recent study has documented the prevalence of residential segregation by examining data for individual city blocks from the 1940, 1950 and 1960 censuses. If race were not a factor in where a person lives, and whites and nonwhites had similar socio-economic characteristics, then every city block might be expected to have the same proportion of white and nonwhite residents as every other block. In fact, the data reveal very clearly that blocks tend to be occupied by whites or by nonwhites, with relatively few blocks having a high degree of intermixture. With these data it was possible to demonstrate that residential segregation is not characteristic only of Northern cities or only of Southern cities. Every city with a sizable Negro population displays a high degree of residential segregation, regardless of region or size, regardless of whether it is a manufacturing center, a trade center or a suburb. Sometimes groups protesting housing discrimination in a city contend that their city is the most segregated in the country. Examination of the census data indicates that this type of segregation is found in all American cities, and that no city can lay claim to being much more or much less segregated than any other.

HOUSING OF THE NEGRO POPULATION

Trends in Homeownership

Today more than 1.5 million Negro families are homeowners, and owners make up nearly 40 percent of Negro households. Despite this impressive achievement, Negroes still lag behind whites in homeownership, and in a variety of indicators of housing quality and amenities.

Trends in homeownership in the United States, pictured in Figure 7, tell a surprising story. From the earliest period for which reliable statistics are available, in 1890, until sometime after World War II, a minority of Americans were homeowners. For whites, the homeownership rate varied around 50 percent until 1940. It was only during the post-war period of economic prosperity, accompanied by high levels of accumulated savings, high rates of marriage and household formation and extensive governmental programs to facilitate homeownership, that the balance was finally tilted strongly in favor of ownership. In the two decades from 1940 to 1960 (and mainly in the fifteen years from 1945 to 1960) homeownership among whites climbed from 45 percent of households to 64 percent. The levels of homeownership among nonwhites have always been much lower than among whites, but the trend has been rather similar. From 1900 to 1940, the percent owners among nonwhites remained steady at 24–25, and then increased sharply to 38 percent in 1960.

For both Negroes and whites, the first thirty years of this century were a period of increasing income and wealth, which should have augmented homeownership. These years were also a time of rapid urbanization, however, and the move to cities inhibited the growth of ownership which otherwise would have occurred. Particularly prior to the days of mass automobile ownership and easy transportation over long distances, cities tended of necessity to be settled very densely. Under such circumstances, multiple-dwelling units predominated over single-family dwellings. In addition, millions of the immigrants from Europe and white and Negro migrants from rural America came to cities in search of economic opportunities.

FIGURE 7—Percent Owner-Occupied by Color: Conterminous United States 1890–1960

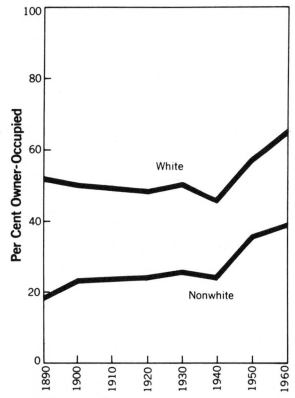

Note: Data for 1910 not available.

SOURCE: U.S. Bureau of the Census, *U.S. Census of Housing: 1960,* Vol. I, *States and Small Areas, United States Summary,* Final Report HC(1)–1 (Washington, D.C.: U.S. Government Printing Office, 1963), Table H.

Despite considerable improvement in the economic well-being of many of these migrants over their former circumstances, their incomes were not high in relation to the cost of urban housing.

The prevalence of homeownership varies greatly in different parts of the country, in different types of areas, in different cities and even in different parts of a single city. To a great extent these differences are determined when an area is first built up, for single-family detached dwellings are usually for purchase, and multiple-unit dwellings are for rent. Old units which were once owned may be converted into rental units, but the reverse seldom happens.

For nonwhites, in 1960, 30 percent of housing units in metropolitan areas of the North were owner-occupied. These nonwhites live chiefly in the old central portions of cities that were built up in the dense tenement pattern prevailing many decades ago. In the South this type of housing has always been less prevalent, and 39 percent of metropolitan nonwhites are owners. Outside of metropolitan areas in the South, the majority of nonwhites are also tenants in housing owned by others, but building codes are not as strict, inexpensive units are more common and 44 percent of the units are owner-occupied. For whites, the levels of ownership are much higher, but the variations tend to be similar. In Northern metropolitan areas, ownership is 60 percent, in Southern metropolitan areas 66 percent, and in the small towns and rural areas of the South 67 percent.

Housing Characteristics of Whites and Nonwhites

Whether they are renters or owners, the housing obtained by nonwhites is less adequate or less desirable in many respects when compared to housing obtained by whites. Evidence for this statement is presented in Table XVII. Nonwhite households are more likely to live in substandard housing, more likely to be overcrowded, less likely to be in new housing and less likely to have amenities such as air-conditioning or an automobile. Nonwhite households are even less likely to own television sets. Television is lacking in 28 percent of nonwhite units as compared to only 11 percent of white units.

The reported value of housing occupied by nonwhites tends to be less than that for housing occupied by whites. This pattern is particularly clear for owner-occupied housing. Within Northern metropolitan areas, half of the units owned by whites are valued at more than $14,200, and half for less. The corresponding median value for nonwhites is $9,400. Similar differences obtain in the South. In the South, rents paid by nonwhites are also lower than those paid by whites—the median rent is $53 monthly for nonwhites in metropolitan areas of the South, as compared to $73 for whites. In the Northern metropolitan areas, however, the difference is small—$73 for nonwhites and $77 for whites.

There is considerable controversy over the question of whether nonwhite housing is inferior because nonwhites pay less, or whether because of segregation and discrimination nonwhites get even less quality than they should for what they pay. One careful study of the situation in Chicago in 1956 came to the conclusion that for roughly equivalent housing, nonwhites had to pay about fifteen dollars a month more than whites.[1] To the extent that Negroes, by virtue of residential segregation, have access to only a limited amount of housing, despite rapidly increasing numbers, then the laws of supply and demand operate in Negro residential areas to raise housing prices in relation to housing quality. However, this is a controversial topic, and it is difficult to determine what conditions would be like in the absence of discrimination.

Regardless of the source of white-Negro housing differences—whether due to segregation and discrimination in housing, or whether it is traced back to segregation and discrimination in the means of earning a livelihood —Negroes usually pay a high proportion of their low incomes for their housing, whether good or bad. Nearly one-third of nonwhite renters, as compared to one-fifth of white renters, spends more than 35 percent of their annual income on rent (Table XVII). Interpretation of these figures can lead to very tricky problems in economic theory, but it is clear that the gap between Negroes and whites is much greater in income than in amounts actually spent on housing, and that the housing obtained by Negroes is much inferior to that obtained by whites.

TABLE XVII—Selected Characteristics of Housing Units by Color, Tenure, Region and Inside or Outside SMSA's, 1960

Color and Characteristic	Inside SMSA's				Outside SMSA's	
	North		South		South	
	Owner	Renter	Owner	Renter	Owner	Renter
Number of housing units (000)						
White	11,060.5	7,285.5	4,165.5	2,160.5	4,301.6	2,119.3
Nonwhite	510.8	1,182.8	517.5	813.6	628.2	796.3
Percent substandard						
White	3.6	13.5	5.5	14.7	26.4	41.1
Nonwhite	10.4	28.0	29.8	46.8	71.7	89.4
Percent overcrowded						
White	7.1	13.4	8.5	19.1	12.1	24.8
Nonwhite	14.6	31.8	22.8	42.4	29.4	52.3
Percent built 1950–60						
White	33.5	11.0	49.9	25.1	33.2	20.1
Nonwhite	10.6	8.2	26.7	18.8	23.2	12.9
Percent air-conditioned						
White	14.1	9.7	32.5	20.2	16.6	9.8
Nonwhite	7.1	2.9	9.2	3.3	3.1	1.3
Percent with automobile						
White	87.4	61.1	90.6	73.8	83.9	74.9
Nonwhite	68.3	35.8	64.0	36.4	53.7	39.8
Median value, gross rent						
White	$14,200	$77	$11,800	$73	$7,400	$53
Nonwhite	$ 9,400	$73	$ 6,900	$53	$5,000—	$30
Percent with gross rent 35% or more of income						
White	—	18.6	—	20.0	—	18.6
Nonwhite	—	32.6	—	33.5	—	29.6

Note: Substandard units include dilapidated units and all other units lacking some or all plumbing facilities. The measure of overcrowding relates the number of units with 1.01 or more persons per room to the number of multiple-person households.

SOURCE: U.S. Bureau of the Census, *U.S. Census of Housing: 1960, Metropolitan Housing*, Final Report HC(2)–1 through 10 (Washington, D.C.: U.S. Government Printing Office, 1963), Tables B–3, B–7, B–13, C–3, C–7, and C–13.

Sources of the Housing Supply

The number of nonwhite households has been increasing quite rapidly in recent decades, particularly within metropolitan areas. Yet only a small proportion of housing occupied by nonwhites is new. Obviously much of the additional housing required by increasing Negro population is obtained "hand-me-down" from whites. In connection with the 1960 census, a special investigation was made of these processes of change in the housing inventory. Understanding of the housing circumstances of Negroes and of the processes of neighborhood change occurring in cities throughout the country can be facilitated by studying the rather complex reports of this investigation.

What are the types of change which can affect the stock of housing and its racial composition? First, of course, is the addition of units by new construction. Additional units can also be obtained by converting one unit into two or more units by adding partitions and plumbing facilities. Garages, lofts and other nonresidential structures can be converted to residential use. Housing units may be lost through deliberate demolition for highways, urban renewal or other purposes, and through accidental demolition as by fire. Units can be merged together to create a single larger unit, and units can be converted to nonresidential use. During the 1950–59 period, the available stock of housing was affected by all of these types of change. Most of the housing inventory in 1959, however, had existed in 1950 and was retained through the decade. An additional complication arises when race of the occupant is considered, for although a housing

TABLE XVIII—Sources of 1959 Housing Inventory, by Color, Region and Inside or Outside SMSA's

Color and Source of 1959 Housing Inventory	U.S. Total		North	South	
	Inside SMSA's	Outside SMSA's	Inside SMSA's	Inside SMSA's	Outside SMSA's
Nonwhite-occupied dwelling units, 1959					
Total, in thousands	3,249.0	1,527.0	1,618.6	1,136.5	1,309.0
Percent	100.0	100.0	100.0	100.0	100.0
Same units, 1950–59	75.3	78.3	81.2	68.7	80.0
White-occupied, 1950	30.1	9.6	40.5	14.6	7.8
Nonwhite-occupied, 1950	36.7	52.7	32.9	44.8	56.1
New construction	13.4	15.7	6.4	19.7	14.4
Conversion	5.5	2.0	6.9	5.1	1.3
Other	5.8	4.0	5.5	6.5	4.3
White-occupied dwelling units, 1959					
Total, in thousands	29,711.4	18,468.0	18,138.8	5,946.3	7,060.4
Percent	100.0	100.0	100.0	100.0	100.0
Same units, 1950–59	66.1	71.6	71.0	58.0	68.8
White-occupied, 1950	58.7	60.3	64.2	49.1	56.0
Nonwhite-occupied, 1950	0.3	0.3	0.3	0.1	0.5
New construction	29.0	22.5	23.8	37.1	26.1
Conversion	2.6	2.2	3.0	2.5	1.7
Other	2.3	3.7	2.2	2.4	3.4

SOURCE: U.S. Bureau of the Census, *U.S. Census of Housing: 1960*, Vol. IV, *Components of Inventory Change*, Final Report HC(4), Part 1A, No. 1 (Washington, D.C.: U.S. Government Printing Office, 1962), Tables 1, 2, and 4.

unit may be the same in 1959 as in 1950, it may have been transferred from white to Negro occupancy or from Negro to white occupancy.

This scheme for accounting for what happens to housing during a decade is put to use in Table XVIII, where data from the 1959 National Housing Inventory are assembled to show the source of housing occupied by whites and nonwhites in 1959. To simplify the discussion, reference will be made mainly to the figures for all metropolitan housing in the United States.

In late 1959, there were about 3,249,000 dwelling units occupied by nonwhites in metropolitan areas. Three-fourths of these were "same units," units that existed in 1950, and were retained in use through 1959. Of same units, somewhat under one-half had been occupied by whites in 1950, and somewhat over half had then, as now, been occupied by nonwhites. (Some units which were vacant in 1950 or for which the color of the 1950 occupant could not be determined are not shown separately in the table.) One-fourth of nonwhite housing in 1959 remains to be accounted for. About 13 percent came from housing built during the decade, 5.5 percent came from conversion of one or more large units into two or more smaller ones, and 6 percent came from miscellaneous other sources.

Sources of metropolitan housing for white occupancy display a different pattern. New construction was much more important for whites, accounting for 29 percent of their housing in 1959. Only 5 percent came from conversion or miscellaneous sources combined. Two-thirds of the housing occupied by whites had existed in essentially the same form in 1950. In contrast to nonwhites, who obtained one-third of their housing from units formerly occupied by whites, only one out of every three hundred units occupied by whites was obtained from nonwhites.

The major regional variations in these patterns can be specified briefly for metropolitan housing. In the North, nonwhites obtained only 6 percent of their housing from new construction, and another 7 percent from conversion. More than 40 percent of their housing came from units occupied by whites ten years before. In the South, nonwhites obtained much more new housing (20 per cent) and there was much less transfer of dwellings from white to nonwhite occupancy.

One other piece of information from the National Housing Inventory may be noted. Nonwhites occupied a far higher proportion of units which were demolished during the decade than their share in the population would indicate. These demolitions included many due to highway construction and private redevelopment in addition to those undertaken for slum clearance and urban renewal. In their abstract technical way, these statistics help tell the story of thousands of urban Negroes forced to relocate, despite the difficulties encountered by Negroes in locating suitable housing.

SOCIAL, ECONOMIC AND HEALTH CHARACTERISTICS OF NEGROES

Negroes today are confronted with a wide variety of social problems, some of them the heritage of slavery, all of them a reflection of their current position in American society. At Emancipation, most Negroes were

TABLE XIX—Median Years of School Completed by Persons
25–29 Years Old, by Color and Sex, 1940–1962

Date	Male			Female		
	White	Nonwhite	Percentage, Nonwhite of White	White	Nonwhite	Percentage, Nonwhite of White
April, 1940	10.5	6.5	61.9	10.9	7.5	68.8
March, 1957	12.3	9.4	76.4	12.3	10.3	83.7
March, 1959	12.5	10.9	87.2	12.4	11.0	88.7
March, 1962	12.5	11.0	88.0	12.4	11.4	91.9
Increase, 1940–62	2.0	4.5		1.5	3.9	

SOURCE: 1962 from U.S. Bureau of the Census, "Educational Attainment: March 1962," *Current Population Reports*, Series P–20, No. 121, Tables 2 and 3; all other years from U.S. Department of Labor, *The Economic Status of Negroes in the United States*, Bulletin S–3, Revised 1962, Table 17.

illiterate, lived in the rural South, worked in agriculture (primarily as laborers) and received little cash income. Marriage was not a stable institution; large proportions of children were illegitimate and lived in families where a woman was the effective head. Sanitary conditions were often bad, medical and hygienic knowledge slight and death rates high. The history of the Negro since Emancipation has been one of absorption into a changing industrial society. For many of the characteristics which distinguished the position of the Negro from that of the white, the century since Emancipation has been one of gradual but not yet completed convergence of the races.

The topics touched upon in this section are especially difficult to discuss briefly. Several of them are subject to more extensive analysis in later chapters. Here the attempt is to emphasize the mutual interrelations, omitting some of the technical complexities and regional variations.

Educational Attainment

In 1870, about 80 percent of nonwhites were illiterate, and fifty years later the figure was down to 23 percent. Not until 1959 was illiteracy down to 7.5 percent, a level attained by whites seventy years earlier. Although Negroes have to a considerable degree caught up with whites in ensuring that their children receive at least a primary education, there is still a large lag at the higher educational levels.

Virtually all children between the ages of seven and thirteen, white and Negro, are enrolled in school. The percentage enrolled, however, falls off faster for nonwhites than for whites. At ages 14–17, the enrollment in the fall of 1962 was 87 percent for nonwhites, 93 per cent for whites. At ages 18–19, beyond the ages of compulsory attendance, the percentages dropped to 33 and 43 percent, respectively, and at ages 20–24, to 10 and 16 percent.

School attendance, of course, is not a valid measure of education actually received. There are substantial differences in the extent of age-grade retardation. For example, of 18–19 year-olds enrolled in school, 78 percent of the whites as compared to 50 percent of the nonwhites in 1962 were enrolled in college. Quality of education is more difficult to measure. If it is related to the educational attainment of teachers and the per capita expenditure on schooling, then nearly all Southern Negroes and the great bulk of Northern Negroes who attend predominantly Negro schools receive inferior education.

By age twenty-five most persons have completed their schooling. Examination of trends in the median years of school completed for whites and nonwhites in the 25–29 age group suggests convergence between the two groups during the last twenty-two years (Table XIX). While the figure for white males advanced from 10.5 school years in 1940 to 12.5 in 1962, the figure for nonwhites increased from 6.5 to 11.0. Nonwhites in the North and West report higher levels of education than do those in the South, while levels in the urban South greatly exceed those in the rural South. As Negroes have moved in large numbers from the rural South to the cities of all regions, they have improved their educational opportunities and attainment.

Educators have long recognized that a person's family background, even in a society which provides free public education, affects whether the child attends school and how far he progresses in school. A recent special survey by the Bureau of the Census revealed that college attendance is much more frequent among children of high school and college graduates than among children of parents with only a grade school education. Because of past differences between Negroes and whites, however, Negro children are much more likely than white children to come from those families which send few children on to college. Among families at each educational level, however, nonwhites were less likely to have children enrolled in college than whites. If a high percentage of Negro children fail to surmount this handicap, then they will become yet another generation of parents who are poorly educated, and whose children in turn are handicapped by lack of a family background encouraging educational attainment.

This vicious circle in educational attainment is difficult to break. Education takes place early in life, and is seldom continued after a person first leaves school. By the time a person reaches age twenty-five, therefore, he has reached the educational level which he will retain throughout the rest of his life. Persons who reach adulthood with low educational attainment must live out their life span before they can be replaced by persons with higher levels. Even if Negroes reaching ages 25–29 matched the educational achievements of whites, it would be more than a generation before educational levels in the total adult Negro population caught up with those in the white population.

Occupation and Income

The legacy of lower educational levels among the Negro population would be expected to be reflected in a concentration in the lower occupational levels. At each level of educational attainment, however, Negroes obtain a smaller proportion of upper level jobs than do whites with the same amount of education. Illustrative data are presented in Table XX for males aged 35–44 in 1960. For these men, the disparity between whites and nonwhites in occupational levels is greatest at the intermediate levels of education (where most of the population is found) and least at the lowest and highest levels of education. Apparently for persons with little formal education, few occupations are open, whether the person is white

TABLE XX—Percent Distribution of Major Occupation of Experienced Civilian Labor Force by Educational Attainment and Color for Males Aged 35–44 in Central Cities of Urbanized Areas, 1960

Years of School Completed and Color	Total *	Professional, Technical	Managers, Officials	Clerical	Sales Workers	Craftsmen, Foremen	Operatives	Service Workers	Laborers
Total									
White	100.0	13.3	13.9	8.7	8.4	23.5	21.0	6.2	5.0
Nonwhite	100.0	4.8	3.5	8.5	1.7	13.9	30.9	15.4	21.3
None									
White	100.0	1.2	4.0	2.3	2.1	18.9	29.7	13.2	28.6
Nonwhite	100.0	—	2.8	2.6	—	8.1	30.3	17.7	38.5
Elementary, 1–4 years									
White	100.0	0.8	3.5	2.6	2.6	23.0	36.2	11.5	19.8
Nonwhite	100.0	0.3	1.4	2.4	0.7	11.4	32.8	14.0	37.0
Elementary, 5–7 years									
White	100.0	1.0	4.9	3.9	2.8	28.3	37.7	8.4	13.0
Nonwhite	100.0	0.4	1.8	2.5	0.7	13.8	35.1	15.2	30.5
Elementary, 8 years									
White	100.0	1.2	6.3	5.5	3.9	29.0	36.7	7.8	9.6
Nonwhite	100.0	0.8	2.3	4.2	1.1	15.1	35.7	16.9	23.9
High School, 1–3 years									
White	100.0	2.8	9.6	8.1	6.2	30.3	29.6	7.5	5.9
Nonwhite	100.0	1.0	3.0	8.3	1.4	14.7	35.6	17.0	19.0
High School, 4 years									
White	100.0	7.6	16.0	12.2	10.7	26.8	17.2	6.7	2.8
Nonwhite	100.0	3.1	5.0	16.2	3.2	16.2	27.2	16.1	13.0
College, 1–3 years									
White	100.0	19.4	24.7	12.2	16.1	14.7	7.6	4.1	1.2
Nonwhite	100.0	11.1	7.7	21.9	3.3	14.5	19.4	14.3	7.8
College, 4+ years									
White	100.0	57.5	20.8	5.9	8.8	4.2	1.3	1.1	0.4
Nonwhite	100.0	58.4	9.4	13.9	2.6	3.9	4.5	5.4	1.9

* Occupation not reported excluded.

SOURCE: U.S. Bureau of the Census, *U.S. Census of Population: 1960, Subject Reports, Educational Attainment,* Final Report PC(2)–5B (Washington, D.C.: U.S. Government Printing Office, 1963), Table 8.

or nonwhite. At the college graduate level, nonwhites do fairly well in terms of broad occupational categories—perhaps because of the many outlets for professional employment within the Negro community as teachers, clergymen, doctors and lawyers serving a Negro clientele.

Some of the advancement in occupational status which has occurred for Negroes derives from an increase from 214,000 to over one million Negroes employed in Federal, state and local governments between 1940 and 1962. Much of the advancement in occupational levels, like that in educational levels, results from the migration of Negroes from areas with few economic opportunities to the rapidly growing metropolitan focal points of the expanding national economy.

The chief source of income for most Negro families is the wages received for their labor. With the twin disadvantages of lower educational attainment and lower occupational levels at each educational level, Negroes must be expected to fare much worse than whites in the amount of income they receive. Median family income for white families rose from $3,157 in 1947 to $6,237 in 1962, and for nonwhite families from $1,614 to $3,330. Throughout this post-war period the nonwhite figure remained about one-half of the figure for whites, and there was no discernible trend in the relationship. During the Second World War, the income of nonwhites increased faster than the income of whites, but changes in the post-war period have mainly been due to the regional migration of nonwhites from low-wage areas to high-wage areas. Nonwhite incomes are particularly low in the South, whereas in the North and West they receive as much as Southern whites, though still less than Northern and Western whites (Table XXI).

Basic to an individual's ability to get along in an industrial society is his training and education, which fit him for an occupation. A job, in turn, provides his principal source of income and largely determines the style of life he will be able to maintain for himself and his children. The preceding discussion shows that at several critical junctures in the life history of Negroes they are unable to keep pace with whites. In comparison with whites, Negroes complete less formal schooling, obtain poorer jobs than do whites with comparable levels of education, and apparently are rewarded by receiving lower earnings than do whites with similar educations and occupations. It was recently estimated that the average nonwhite with four years of college can expect to earn less over his lifetime than the average white who did not go beyond the eighth grade. The close relationships between education, occupation and income, however, suggest that reduction in discrimination might have a cumulative impact on the economic welfare of Negroes.

Family and Fertility

The Negro family under slavery was an unstable arrangement, for there was little security in the bond of marriage or parenthood. Fertility must have been high, for death rates were high and yet the Negro population increased by more than the number of slaves imported. There is evidence that at least since 1850, birth rates among Negroes have been higher than among whites. The historical trends, however, are difficult to document, and the statistical picture begins about 1920. Higher birth rates among Negroes since 1920 are apparent in Figure 8.

TABLE XXI—Median Total Money Income of Males 14 Years Old and Over, by Region and Color, 1960

Region	White	Nonwhite	Percentage, Nonwhite of White
U.S. Total	$4,297	$2,258	52.5
Northeast	$4,605	$3,513	76.3
North Central	$4,429	$3,359	75.8
South	$3,361•	$1,255	37.3
West	$5,043	$3,692	73.2

SOURCE: U.S. Bureau of the Census, "Income of Families and Persons in the United States: 1960," *Current Population Reports*, Series P–60, No. 37, Table 34.

Various aspects of population distribution and social structure are related to fertility patterns. Farm families and other rural families, for instance, tend to have more children than city families. Part of the high fertility among Negroes, then, can be attributed to their population concentration in the rural South. Since 1910, of course, Negroes have been leaving the rural South in great numbers and moving to cities where they have tended to display a lower rate of child-bearing. Whites were also moving from high fertility areas to low fertility areas, however, and the Negro-white difference persisted. In fact, during the 1920's and the first half of the 1930's, birth rates among both Negroes and whites fell rapidly, and both races rose sharply during World War II and the postwar "baby boom."

Since 1947, birth rates among Negroes and whites have followed divergent paths. White fertility diminished a bit after the peak during the baby boom, rose during the early 1950's, and has since entered a period of gradual decline. Negro fertility, by contrast, continued increasing after 1947 for another ten years. Only in the last few years have Negro birth rates reached a plateau, with some signs of a slight decline. Birth rates among Negroes are now far higher than among whites. Continuation of current rates of births and deaths for a generation would result in an increase in population of 60 percent for whites and 100 percent for Negroes. The dramatic fluctuations which have occurred in birth rates in recent decades, however, suggest how hazardous it would be to assume that birth rates among Negroes or whites will continue unchanged, and it would be equally hazardous to predict just what changes will take place.

Historically, Negroes in comparison with whites have had more childlessness among married couples, as well as a higher proportion of couples with large numbers of children. The net balance has been an average number of children per couple only slightly above the figure for whites. The childlessness among Negro couples, however, may often have been involuntary—venereal disease may well have placed a prominent role in Negro infertility. Since 1940, venereal disease has been largely brought under control, and many couples who might have remained childless due to disease are now able to bear children in the same numbers as other couples. The incidence of venereal disease is not known with high accuracy, but Figure 9 portrays the rapid decline in the rate of reported cases of syphilis during the post-war years. The figure also shows the resurgence in syphilis cases in the last few years which has alarmed public health personnel, although the rates are still far below levels obtaining in past decades.

In the post-war period, for both Negroes and whites, the proportion of women never marrying has declined, as has the proportion of married women remaining childless. Childbearing in the teens and early twenties has become much more prevalent. Both whites and Negroes appear to have developed a pattern of youthful marriage and early childbearing. These patterns probably reflect a high level of economic welfare and readily obtainable credit for home-buying and the purchase of other durable goods, as well as more permanent social changes. A better assessment can be made a few years from now, when it should be apparent whether the current plateaus in birth rates are the beginnings of a significant downturn, or whether fertility will continue at the high levels maintained throughout the post-war period.

Not all babies are born to mothers who are married. Illegitimacy is not uncommon in the United States, and has been increasing in recent years among both Negroes and whites. More than half of the nation's illegitimate

FIGURE 8—Births per 1,000 Females Aged 15–44 Years,[a] by Color, 1920–1961

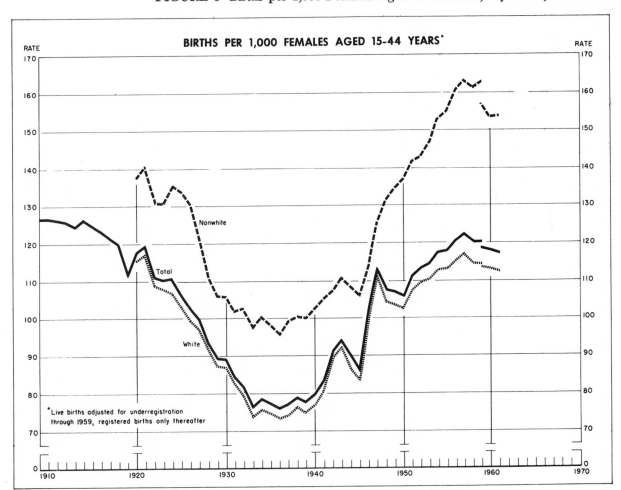

Note: Live births adjusted for underregistration through 1959; registered births, 1959-1961.

SOURCE: U.S. Department of Health, Education, and Welfare, *Health, Education, and Welfare Indicators*, March, 1963 (Washington, D.C.: U.S. Government Printing Office, 1963), p. xxvi.

**FIGURE 9—Primary and Secondary Syphilis Cases
per 100,000 Population, by Color, 1941–1962.**

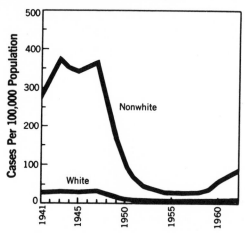

Note: Data not available for 1942 and 1946. Data include Alaska beginning with 1959 and
Hawaii beginning with 1960.

SOURCE: U.S. Department of Health, Education, and Welfare, *Health, Education, and Welfare Trends,* 1963 Edition (Washington, D.C.: U.S.
Government Printing Office, 1963), p. 18.

births occur to white mothers, but rates of illegitimacy are far higher
among Negroes (Figure 10). Many sociologists think Negro illegitimacy is
historically connected to conditions under slavery, when marriage was
unstable. The persistence of mother-centered families is facilitated by
social conditions which consign many Negro males to failure in their task
as breadwinners. Whatever the reasons, for both whites and Negroes,
illegitimacy is particularly prevalent among young girls, with just under
one-half of illegitimate births occurring to mothers under twenty years
of age.

Crude birth rates are sometimes poor measures of fertility. For instance,
in 1960 in Chicago birth rates among nonwhites were 37 per thousand
population, as compared to 21 per thousand among whites. These rates
are highly misleading. Nonwhites in Chicago include many who migrated
to the city in the past twenty years, and who are still young. Many
young white families, however, have moved to the suburbs, and white
birth rates in the city are low in part because of the high proportion
of older persons who are beyond the childbearing ages. If adjustments
are made for age differences and for the greater proportion of single
women among whites, the differences between the groups are considerably reduced. In fact, there is very little difference between whites
and nonwhites in Chicago in patterns of marital fertility. There is about
a 25 percent excess fertility of nonwhites, due to their high rates of illegitimacy.[2] Crude birth rates sometimes underlie assertions that Negroes are
breeding at extreme rates, or that there is a population problem among
U.S. Negroes comparable to that in many underdeveloped countries. Such
claims cannot be sustained if the facts are examined with due care.

Of the many factors affecting marriage and fertility, urban and rural
residence, levels of economic welfare and social status have traditionally

been important. During the period of rapidly declining fertility in the 1920's, fertility tended to be lower among those higher in economic and social status, while those with lower status bore children at higher rates. Now that knowledge of family planning has spread throughout society, and some degree of family limitation characterizes couples in all social and economic groups, the former differentials in fertility seem to have diminished, and even to have been partially reversed. A detailed analysis cannot be undertaken here but some of the recent patterns among Negroes can be indicated, if only to illustrate the complexity of reproductive behavior.

The illustrative data here refer to women who were aged 35–44 and living in urbanized areas at the time of the 1960 census. These women had largely completed their childbearing, much of which occurred during the late 1930's and the 1940's. Women of different ages in 1960 bore their children during different time periods, and the patterns for them might differ. In Table XXII, there are three columns of data for each race: percent ever married; percent childless of those ever married; and children per 1,000 ever-married women. In this group of women, nearly all were married at least once, 93 percent among both whites and nonwhites. Of those ever married, about 13 percent of white women, but 25 percent of nonwhite women, never bore any children. This high proportion of childlessness among nonwhite women reduces the fertility of the total group. Despite this, the number of children per 1,000 ever-married women was 2,515 for nonwhites, as compared to 2,352 for whites.

If women are classified according to their education, there is a distinct pattern among both whites and nonwhites of higher fertility among those with least education. Particularly striking is the low level of fertility among nonwhite women who are college graduates. About 12 percent of these women never married, and 27 percent of those who married remained childless (among this group it is obvious that disease was not the major cause). Among these nonwhite college graduates, children per 1,000 ever-

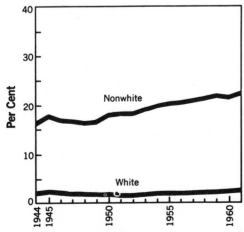

FIGURE 10—Percent of Total Live Births Illegitimate, by Color, 1944–1961

SOURCE: U.S. Department of Health, Education, and Welfare, *Health, Education, and Welfare Trends,* 1963 Edition (Washington, D.C.: U.S. Government Printing Office, 1963), p. 7.

married women numbered 1,649, as compared to 2,807 among nonwhite women with less than eight grades of school, and 2,235 among white women who are college graduates. At the highest educational levels, nonwhite fertility is less than white fertility.

Social scientists have been rather unsuccessful in their attempts to explain reproductive behavior. It is clear that among nonwhites, just as among whites, there are many different individuals, with many different characteristics. Their behavior in childbearing depends on their background, their education, their family status, the current occupation of husband and wife and similar social factors. Race is significant only as it involves the concentration of individuals with particular characteristics which are associated with high or low fertility.

Mortality and Health

Poverty and illness are intertwined in complicated ways. Sustained periods of illness may hamper a man in his efforts to earn a livelihood, and place a limit on his income. Sustained periods of low income, on the other hand, can lead to overcrowding, inadequate nutrition, a low level of preventive medical care and an increased incidence of ill health. That many Negroes in the United States are economically less well off than most whites has been demonstrated above. Nonwhites see physicians less often than do whites, make less use of hospitals, and have fewer of their hospital bills paid by insurance. That Negroes suffer from higher death rates should therefore not be surprising.

Perhaps the best single measure of the general level of health among a population is the expectation of life at birth. This figure summarizes the death rates prevailing among people of all ages during a given year. It indicates the average length of life a newborn child can expect, given the

TABLE XXII—Percent Ever Married, Percent Childless of Ever Married, and Number of Children Ever Born per 1,000 Ever-Married Women, for Women 35–44 Years Old, by Color and Educational Attainment, Urbanized Areas, 1960

Years of School Completed	Percent Ever Married		Percent Childless of Ever Married		Children Ever Born per 1,000 Ever-Married Women	
	White	Nonwhite	White	Nonwhite	White	Nonwhite
Total	92.8	92.8	13.0	24.5	2,352	2,515
Less than 8 years	92.0	92.1	13.6	25.1	2,869	2,807
8 years	93.9	93.5	13.6	25.6	2,444	2,621
High school, 1–3 years	95.1	93.8	11.5	23.0	2,417	2,663
High school, 4 years	93.4	93.2	13.2	23.8	2,244	2,219
College, 1–3 years	91.9	92.4	13.7	27.2	2,259	2,029
College, 4+ years	83.5	87.9	14.7	27.1	2,235	1,649

SOURCE: U.S. Bureau of the Census, U.S. Census of Population: 1960, Subject Reports, Women by Number of Children Ever Born, Final Report PC(2)-3A (Washington, D.C.: U.S. Government Printing Office, 1964), Tables 28 and 29.

FIGURE 11—Expectation of Life at Birth, by Color and Sex, 1900–1961

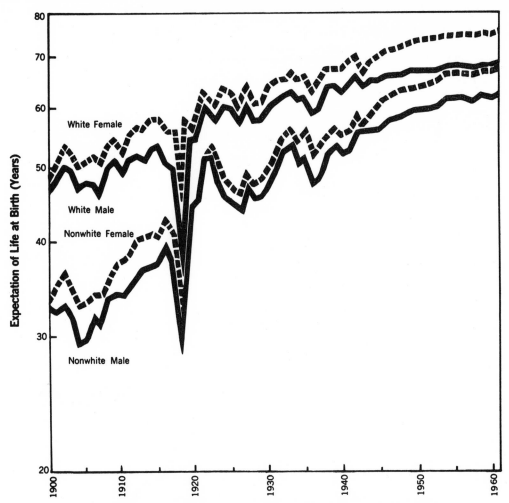

White Female

White Male

Nonwhite Female

Nonwhite Male

Note: Data include Alaska beginning with 1959 and Hawaii beginning with 1960. Data refer to the death registration area, which did not include the total United States, until 1933.

SOURCE: U.S. Bureau of the Census, *Historical Statistics of the United States, Colonial Times to 1957* (Washington, D.C.: U.S. Government Printing Office, 1950), Series B 92–100; and National Vital Statistics Division, *Vital Statistics of the United States, 1961*, Vol. II, Sec. 2, *Life Tables* Washington, D.C.: U.S. Government Printing Office, 1963).

current patterns of mortality. In 1900, white males in the United States had an expectation of life of 47 years, nonwhite males 32 years. In industrial societies the figures for women tend to be higher than those for men. Among females the white figure, 49 years, was nearly half again as large as the nonwhite figure, 34 years.

Death rates in the white population had already been falling for many decades prior to 1900, and continued to fall in succeeding years. The trend in expectation of life has been upward, with much annual fluctuation and a large interruption during the influenza epidemic of 1917–18 (Figure 11). The figures for nonwhites have followed somewhat the same path, but have shown an even sharper rate of increase. With improvements in

FIGURE 12–Infant Mortality Rate Per 1,000 Live Births, by Color, 1915–1960

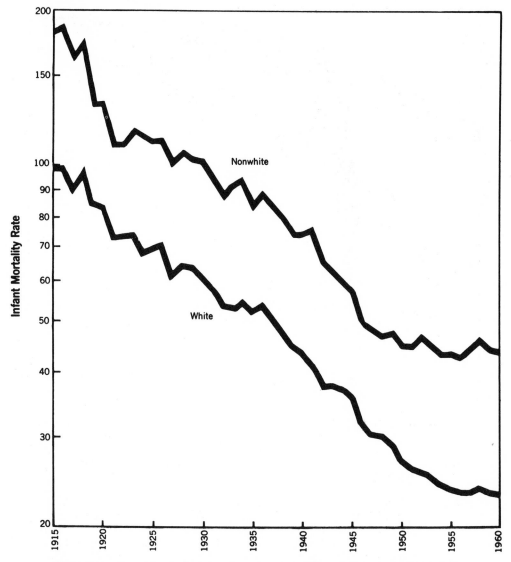

Note: Data refer to the death registration area, which did not include the total United States until 1933.

SOURCE: U.S. Bureau of the Census, *Historical Statistics of the United States, Colonial Times to 1957* (Washington, D.C.: U.S. Government Printing Office, 1960), Series B 101–112; and National Vital Statistics Division, *Vital Statistics of the United States, 1960*, Vol. II, Sec. 3, *Infant Mortality* (Washington, D.C.: U.S. Government Printing Office, 1963), Table 3–A.

levels of living, in hygienic knowledge and nutrition, in public health and general medical care, the gap between whites and nonwhites was considerably narrowed. In fact, by 1961 nonwhite females had nearly caught up with white males in expectation of life, 67.0 *vs.* 67.8 years.

Despite the remarkable trend toward convergence of white and nonwhite death rates, a gap still exists. In 1961, white babies had about seven more years of life to look forward to than did nonwhite babies. Many of the missing years of life for nonwhites are lost within the first year after birth. About 23 of every 1,000 white babies do not survive their first year. The figure is nearly twice as high for nonwhite babies, 43 per 1,000. Infant mortality rates, shown in Figure 12, have declined tremendously during this century, but during the last decade there has been a halt in the downward trend particularly for nonwhites and a widening of the differences between whites and nonwhites.

A recent study utilizing special tabulations for Chicago has assessed the impact of economic differentials between whites and nonwhites on their mortality differentials.[3] Using data for 1950, it was shown that virtually all of the differences between whites and nonwhites in death rates were attributable to their economic status differences. Within each color group, death rates were higher for those of lower status. If the death rates of the highest status group of whites are taken as a standard which could be achieved by the rest of the population, then one-fifth of the deaths among whites and one-half of the deaths among nonwhites were "excess" deaths that could have been avoided.

The Chicago study demonstrated that economic differentials in mortality were particularly large for the infectious diseases, and much less for the principal degenerative diseases, heart disease and cancer. The death rates for selected specific causes of death, presented in Table XXIII, indicate that white-nonwhite differences follow the same pattern. Nonwhite death rates from tuberculosis, influenza and pneumonia are more than double those for whites, while the excess of the nonwhite rates is less for the other principal disease categories.

TABLE XXIII—Age-Adjusted Death Rates per 100,000 Population for Selected Causes, by Color and Sex, United States, 1960

Cause of Death	White		Nonwhite		Percentage, Nonwhite of White	
	Male	Female	Male	Female	Male	Female
All Causes	917.7	555.0	1211.0	893.3	132.0	161.0
Major cardiovascular renal diseases	493.2	291.5	564.0	467.1	114.4	160.2
Malignant neoplasms	141.6	109.5	154.8	125.0	109.3	114.2
Accidents	70.6	25.4	101.1	36.1	143.2	142.1
Influenza and pneumonia	31.0	19.0	68.0	43.3	219.4	227.9
Diabetes mellitus	11.6	13.7	16.1	26.8	138.8	195.6
Cirrhosis of the liver	14.4	6.6	14.9	9.1	103.5	137.9
Tuberculosis, all forms	6.8	2.2	21.4	9.3	314.7	422.7

SOURCE: National Vital Statistics Division, *Vital Statistics of the United States, 1960*, Vol. II, Sec. 1, *Mortality Analysis and Summary* (Washington, D.C.: U.S. Government Printing Office, 1963), Table 1–J.

THE FUTURE NEGRO POPULATION

Forecasting the future is at best a tricky business, and the latest projections published by the U.S. Bureau of the Census show not one but four different estimates. According to these figures, the total population of the nation may increase from 192 million in mid-1964 to 248–276 million in 1985. If a major depression or war occurs, or some other factor produces radical changes in rates of birth, death or immigration, the actual figure in 1985 might well fall outside these limits.

The official projections do not include separate estimates for whites and Negroes. In 1960, Negroes constituted 10.6 percent of the total population. Since the rate of increase of Negro population has been greater than that of white population, it is likely that this percentage will slowly rise, to about 12 percent by 1985. The Negro population would then be about 30–33 million, as compared with 21 million in mid-1964. By extrapolation of recent trends in the distribution and composition of population, some reasonable guesses can be made about what changes to expect in where Negroes will be living and what their characteristics will be.

Changes in population distribution during past decades have already moved us beyond the position where problems of race relations can be regarded as regional, and the future will see a further spread of Negro population throughout the nation. The Negro population increase will probably accrue mainly to cities, and to cities in the North and West more than in the South. Well before 1985 a majority of the nation's Negro population may be living in Northern cities. Negroes may then comprise a majority or near-majority of the population in several large cities other than Washington, D.C., where they already outnumber whites. The Southern rural Negro population may continue to decrease in size, despite high fertility. Out-migrants from this population may be numerous, but they will be a diminishing share of all Negro migrants.

Large-scale migrations produce unusual age distributions in both the place of origin and of destination. Age distributions are further distorted by fluctuations in fertility rates. For example, many of the Negroes who moved to cities in the early 1940's were young adults in the childbearing ages. There would have been sharp increases in the number of Negro babies in these cities even without the post-war "baby boom." Barring major catastrophes, it is obvious that if more babies were born from 1946 to 1951 than from 1940 to 1945, more children will be reaching age 18 from 1964 to 1969 than from 1958 to 1963. In many cities, problems such as those of school dropouts and the provision of jobs for new entrants to the labor force are rapidly becoming more difficult, in large part because the number of people in the relevant ages is growing.

Anticipating changes in the age distribution of a population is relatively easy. Anticipating changes in socio-economic characteristics is more difficult. Educational advancement seems fairly certain to continue at a rapid pace, with high school graduation becoming increasingly common and college graduation more frequent. Just how rapidly improvements in educational background can be translated into rising occupational and income levels depends on the business cycle, actions of the Federal Government, and other quite unpredictable factors.

Social change is continuous, and with change comes a diminution in the importance of old social problems and a rise in the importance of new ones. For example, although the problems of the illiterate Negro sharecropper newly arrived in a Northern industrial city are perhaps more acute than ever, the number of such migrants is small and diminishing. In contrast, continued growth of urban Negro populations if combined with maintenance of a high degree of residential segregation can only aggravate the many problems already attributable to *de facto* segregation. How well these problems will be met we cannot predict. They can certainly be better met if the social transformations of the past fifty years are recognized, and continuing rapid changes during the coming years are anticipated.

NOTES

[1] Beverly Duncan and Philip M. Hauser, *Housing a Metropolis—Chicago* (New York: The Free Press of Glencoe, 1960).

[2] Evelyn M. Kitagawa and Philip M. Hauser, "Trends in Differential Fertility and Mortality in a Metropolis—Chicago," in Ernest W. Burgess and Donald J. Bogue (eds.), *Contributions to Urban Sociology* (Chicago: University of Chicago Press, 1964).

[3] *Ibid.*

BIBLIOGRAPHY

Bogue, Donald J., *The Population of the United States*, New York: The Press of Glencoe, 1959.

Davie, Maurice R., *Negroes in American Society*, New York: McGraw-Hill Book Co., 1949.

Frazier, E. Franklin, *The Negro in the United States*, rev. ed., New York: The Macmillan Co., 1957.

Hare, Nathaniel, "Changes in the Occupational Status of Negroes, 1930–1960: An Intracohort Analysis." Paper read before the annual meetings of the American Sociological Association, Los Angeles, 1963.

Journal of Negro Education, XXXII, No. 4 (Fall, 1963).

Kiser, Clyde V., "Fertility Trends and Differentials Among Nonwhites in the United States," *The Milbank Memorial Fund Quarterly*, XXXVI, No. 2 (April, 1958), 149–97.

Taeuber, Conrad and Taeuber, Irene B., *The Changing Population of the United States*, New York: John Wiley & Sons, 1958.

Taeuber, Irene B., "Migration, Mobility, and The Assimilation of the Negro," Population Reference Bureau, *Population Bulletin*, XIV, No. 7 (November, 1958), 125–51.

Taeuber, Karl E., "Negro Residential Segregation: Trends and Measurement," *Social Problems*, 12, No. 1 (Summer, 1964), 42–50.

U.S. Bureau of the Census, *Historical Statistics of the United States, Colonial Times to 1957*, Washington: U.S. Government Printing Office, 1960.

———. *Negroes in the United States 1920–32*, Washington: U.S. Government Printing Office, 1935.

———. *Negro Population 1790–1915*, Washington: Government Printing Office, 1918.

U.S. Department of Labor, "A Century of Change: Negroes in the U.S. Economy, 1860–1960," *Monthly Labor Review* (December, 1962), 1359–65.

———. *The Economic Situation of Negroes in the United States*, Bulletin S–3, revised, 1962.

———. "Economic Status of Nonwhite Workers, 1955–62," *Monthly Labor Review* (July, 1963), 1–9.

THE AMERICAN NEGRO FARMER

"...*The dominant trend in Negro affairs since the beginning of the Second World War has been the wholesale flight of people to the cities—the big cities—and the rising concern over the problems that face them there. In the tempo of urbanization, rural life is for many* declassé, *an unpleasant reminder of the miseries of the past that have been shaken off and exchanged for the hope of the metropolis. . . . Yet for all that the Negro rural population has dwindled and lost its place in the order of things, it still comprises nearly three-tenths of the total Negro population. Many of the problems that beset the Negro everywhere occur in their most severe, undiluted and least hopeful settings in the countryside, and to the extent that rural areas continue to be a seedbed for the cities, the problems of the rural minority continue to be the problems of all.*"

(All photographs in this section courtesy of the U. S. Department of Agriculture.)

chapter 3   *Calvin L. Beale*

The Negro

in American Agriculture

Calvin L. Beale.   Head, Farm Population Analysis Section, Economic Research Service, U.S. Department of Agriculture; formerly statistician with the Population Division, Bureau of the Census. Winner of the Superior Service Award of the Department of Agriculture for writings on the farm population. Co-author [with Donald J. Bogue], *Economic Areas of the United States* [Glencoe, Ill. The Free Press, 1961]; contributor to numerous government and social science bulletins and magazines.

"Not one single book, monograph, or article has been found which . . . adequately orients the current status of the Negro in American agriculture." This statement seems as true today as it was in 1946 when made by the compilers of a bibliography on the Negro in the United States.[1] In the reams of material written about the American Negro in the last few years there is little concerning the Negro farmer and farm hand.

Perhaps this should not be surprising, for the dominant trend in Negro affairs since the beginning of the Second World War has been the wholesale flight of people to the cities—the big cities—and the rising concern over the problems that face them there. In the tempo of urbanization, rural life is for many *declassé*, an unpleasant reminder of the miseries of the past that have been shaken off and exchanged for the hope of the metropolis. Nor is the study of a society in decline an attractive subject for most research workers. Yet for all that the Negro rural population has dwindled and lost its place in the order of things, it still comprises nearly three-tenths of the total Negro population. Many of the problems that beset the Negro everywhere occur in their most severe, undiluted and least hopeful settings in the countryside, and to the extent that rural areas continue to be a seedbed for the cities, the problems of the rural minority continue to be the problems of all.

Former Concentration of Negroes in Agriculture

Agriculture was the basic purpose of the importation of Negroes into the American colonies as slaves. Some were used as domestic servants and to a limited extent others were employed in industry in the South. But only in agriculture did their large-scale use develop. Free Negroes who moved North often settled in the cities, but their numbers were few compared with the farm workers still held as slaves.

Emancipation did not radically alter the dependence on agriculture. Comparatively few Negroes moved to the North, except from the border states, and these did not usually find themselves welcome. In the South, there was some initial rush to the towns, but urban work was scarce and cotton was still king.

An entirely new system of relations had to be worked out between the freed Negroes and their former owners. With rather rare exceptions, the freedmen were not provided land by the Federal Government and the land ownership of the planters was not broken. At first, efforts were made to hire the former slaves for wages. The result was not very successful. Cash was scarce for the average planter, the freedom-sensitive Negroes did not respond well to the demands of gang work any longer, and hiring made for an unreliable supply of workers. Soon a predominant system of renting developed in which a family was assigned to work a particular piece of land and receive a share of the crop as wages. This proved to be a more stable arrangement for all and guaranteed that a family would remain until the crop was in.

To finance this arrangement, a system of credit was created in which the tenants were "furnished" with supplies on which to live during the year by a merchant or by the planter (who was himself usually operating on credit). As security for the credit, the tenant mortgaged his share of the crop he was making and repaid his debts after the harvest.

In the absence of land reform and a program of Federal intervention, the system was probably the most practical available for getting the agriculture of the South on its feet again. But it provided many opportunities for abuse. The rates of interest charged the tenants were usually very high and the goods they received were often overpriced. Most of the Negroes were illiterate, and they were unable to detect sharp practices. At the end of a season they were essentially lucky if any cash were left after the bills were paid. Some of the most diligent and fortunate earned enough to buy a small farm of their own or to obtain tools and work animals and rent a farm for cash. For the majority, the share-tenant system seemed to encourage improvidence. The once-a-year payday led to unrealistic debts during the year and to quick dissipation of earnings in the fall. Share tenancy was not limited to Negroes. In the course of time, many small white farmers entered into similar arrangements. Their lot was not enviable either, but they were somewhat less likely to be victimized by the system.

In the same period when tenancy was becoming the prevailing way of life, the seeds of agricultural education for Negroes were first sown. There was much to do. Although many Negroes aspired for knowledge, it was professional training and classical subjects that attracted many. After years of servitude in the cotton fields, there was little incentive or felt need to learn to farm.

The beginning in the training of agricultural leaders came with the opening of Hampton Normal and Agricultural Institute at Hampton, Virginia, in 1868, under the auspices of the American Missionary Society.

A decade later Hampton had trained Booker T. Washington, whose ideas dominated Negro agricultural thinking for at least two generations thereafter. Washington established Tuskegee Institute in Alabama in 1881. Here in the years that followed he saw the need for demonstration work in the field, for scientific research at the Institute and for the organization of farmers. Tuskegee hired the man who was to become the foremost Negro scientist, George Washington Carver, in 1896, and sponsored the first Negro demonstration specialist, T.M. Campbell, in 1906. In the 1890's the Tuskegee Farmers Conference was created. This annual event had a South-wide influence in the shaping of programs and thought for Negro farm families, and similar conferences were developed by other states. Unfortunately it never became what perhaps was Washington's ultimate aim, an organized, economically effective organization of Negro farmers, and in time it lost its vitality.

The beginning of change

Twenty-five years after the Civil War, the census of 1890 showed that over 60 percent of all employed Negroes were farmers or farm laborers. In the south the figure was about 65 percent.

During the late nineteenth and early twentieth centuries, the position of the Negro in farming was not static, although the rapidity of chance in later years may make it appear so. A considerable westward movement took place as new lands were drained in the Mississippi Valley or cleared farther west. In certain older areas, the role of Negroes in farming declined, as final ruin came to rice farming along the South Atlantic States or as most Negro farmers gave up agriculture in the border ex-slave states, such as

TENANT FARMERS: "... *the traditional image of the Negro farmer has been that of the sharecropper. It is not surprising that this has been so, for from about World War I until 1950, half or more of all Negro farmers were landless tenants working for a share of the crops they produced. Others rented for cash, but until the end of World War II not more than one-fourth of Negro farmers owned their property....*"

166   THE NEGRO IN AMERICAN AGRICULTURE

Kentucky and Missouri. By and large, however, the increase in farmers in growing areas offset the losses elsewhere.

With the opening of the First World War, Negroes had a golden opportunity to enter industrial work in the North, first as foreign immigration was cut off and then as many white workers went into military service. This period is discussed elsewhere,* but suffice it to say that thousands of farm people moved out despite opposition from landlords and creditors. The lines of family communication with the North were soon established for the millions who have since followed.

In the same era, the menace of the boll weevil was reaching its climax. This beetle, which lays its eggs in cotton bolls and whose larvae consume the cotton, had entered southern Texas from Mexico in the 1890's. It gradually penetrated northeastward into the areas heavily settled by Negro farmers, and by 1921 had spread over the entire Cotton Belt. For a few years the boll weevil caused great panic as millions of acres of cotton were heavily damaged and production fell. Some of the sections most susceptible to damage were those with heavy slow-warming soils, such as in the Black Belt of Alabama, where the majority of farmers were Negroes. In these sections, cotton never regained its prominence, and thousands of Negroes emigrated as the landlords turned to livestock and dairying.

In the rolling Piedmont country of Georgia and South Carolina, severe erosion and soil depletion added to the problem and impelled other thousands to leave or look for industrial work. Thus, in general, the time between World War I and the depression was a time of troubles and receding activity in farming for Negroes in the old Cotton Belt. In less severely affected areas, means of limiting the damage by weevils were devised after a few years, and cotton expanded northward into safer areas. But the old pattern of Negro farming was never the same. Particularly affected were Negro owners, a number of whom lost their land or gave up farming. The developing opportunities in the fertile Delta country were mostly for tenants. Hundreds flocked in to work the large plantations on shares.

The Depression and the New Deal

It is difficult to say whether the great economic depression of the 1930's affected Negro farmers any worse than white farmers. It was nightmarish enough for both. With his already precarious financial position and limited possessions, perhaps the typical Negro had less room to fall.

The bottom dropped out of the cotton market. In many states the number of Negro farmers declined and the number of white tenants rose rapidly. In 1934 and later years the coming of the New Deal introduced an entirely new level of Federal Government activity in agriculture. In addition to widespread relief and welfare measures, the Government developed programs to provide cheap credit for farmers and to help them become land owners. Plantations heavily in debt were acquired by the Government, then subdivided and sold in family-farm sizes to former tenants. Writing of a Black Belt county in Alabama, Morton Rubin has said, "The number of Negroes who have become operators [owners] without the help of the

* See "The Negro Population in the United States" by Karl E. and Alma F. Taeuber in the preceding chapter.

federal government and its agencies is a small proportion of the total."[2]

At this time, too, the idea of farmers agreeing by majority vote to institute programs such as limitations of crop acreage in return for certain Federal price and other benefits was put into practice. It can be argued that these programs often worked to the ultimate disadvantage of the small farmer who found himself restricted to a very small allotment of acreage. But for many Negro farmers such programs offered an opportunity to do something that they had never been able to do before—vote.

WORLD WAR II TO THE PRESENT

Mechanization of Cotton

In the years just before Pearl Harbor the future character of cotton farming in the United States became discernible. In the northern part of the Mississippi Delta country instances occurred of scores of tenant people being "tractored off" the cotton plantations. Mules were replaced by tractors and families were displaced, to camp along the roadside until publicity and aroused public opinion induced some efforts to help them. But the tractor alone did not permit fully mechanized methods of cotton production. Indeed, in many respects the availability of tractor power created a frustrating situation for both landlord and tenant. The tractor was clearly preferable to the mule in preparation of land and planting. But no way had been found to mechanize the hand "chopping" operation (thinning and weeding) or the picking of cotton. Thus the planter continued to need large amounts of hand labor at certain times of the year but was not able to provide regular work for such laborers throughout the crop season.

In the same period the mechanical cotton picker was being developed and it was obviously only a matter of time before it would be perfected. The coming of the war rather effectively delayed the practical introduction of the picker, although in the drier cotton areas of Oklahoma and West Texas, where relatively few Negro farmers lived, efforts were made to harvest cotton during the war without hand picking.

After the war the mechanical harvesters began slowly but surely to replace hand picking and snapping, beginning first on the drier, flatter and larger farmlands in the western part of the Cotton Belt and working their way eastward as they were perfected. The machines can do the work of many hands, but they are rather expensive and require the creation of larger but fewer farms and fields to make their use economical. Thus they typically add one more competitive burden to the small-scale farm owner.

In the 1950's the final technical hurdle to complete elimination of hand field labor became possible through several developments in planting and weed control, especially the use of chemical and oil herbicides applied mechanically both before and after the cotton plants emerged from the ground. These methods are not perfect under all conditions, but under conditions of very heavy weed infestation they are even cheaper than laborers paid less than fifty cents an hour.

TABLE I—Percentage of cotton harvested by machine and by hand

Area	1962	1957	1950
United States			
Machine	70	32	8
Hand	30	68	92
California			
Machine	94	70	34
Hand	6	30	66
Texas and Oklahoma			
Machine	78	38	11
Hand	22	62	89
South, except Texas and Oklahoma			
Machine	55	11	1
Hand	45	89	99

SOURCE: Economic Research Service and Agricultural Marketing Service, U.S. Department of Agriculture.

As a result of the triple triumph of tractors, pickers and weed control, thousands of tenants—the majority of them Negroes—have been released who could not have been spared until all aspects of cotton cultivation were mechanized or chemicalized. Mechanical picking has advanced into the southeastern states, where much of the acreage once grown in the rolling Piedmont sections has been transferred with Government permission into the level Coastal Plain where more suitable field conditions can be created. The following table shows the progress of mechanical harvesting. From 8 percent of the crop in 1950, the proportion picked or snapped by machine rose to 32 percent in 1957 and 70 per cent in 1962 (see Table I). Further gains are continuing.

Another trend of equal importance for the Negro cotton farmer in the last generation has been the growth of cotton cultivation under irrigated conditions in the West. Until after World War I comparatively little cotton was grown in areas where there were few Negro farmers. However, it was found that with irrigation, bumper yields of cotton could be had in the High Plains of Texas, and in parts of California, Arizona and New Mexico. These Western farms did not inherit the Southern tenant system and often were developed by people with capital and zeal to operate under conditions of high labor productivity. The dry climate also gave certain advantages in harvesting. The Western cotton areas produced cotton at a lower price per bale than all but the most productive sections of the old Cotton Belt. Especially since World War II, the competition produced by the Western areas—in which few Negroes work except as hired hands—has helped to force many small independent Southern farms out of cotton and has hastened the tenant-displacing changes made by the plantations. The proportion of all cotton raised in Arizona, California and New Mexico and West Texas rose from 2 percent in 1919 to 34 percent in 1959.

The changes in methods and location of cotton cultivation, combined with the poverty of most Negro farmers, worked both to push Negroes out of farming and to make the attractions of city life irresistible. As a result the 482,000 nonwhite farmers growing cotton in the South in 1945 plummetted to 181,000 in 1959, a decline of 63 percent in slightly less than fifteen years. As noted in the discussion of the Negro as a hired farm worker, some of this loss was converted into an increase in hired hands, but most of it was not. The change was particularly acute in the Mississippi Delta lands where the large plantations were concentrated. Although the decline was greatest for tenants, it also affected the Negro owners.

Adding to the problem has been the steady erosion of the market for cotton, caused by competition from other fibers and increased production abroad. Marketing problems coupled with increased yields per acre have caused farmers to vote every year since 1954 to restrict the acreage planted. When a cut in acreage allotments occurred, as in 1955 and 1956, it was the Negro farmer with his predominantly tenant position who was most likely to find himself forced out altogether because there was simply not enough acreage to support as many tenants per landlord as before.

Diversification

As the cotton acreage in the South has declined since the mid-1920's, some of the land has been put to other agricultural uses and some has been taken out of farming altogether. Naturally the least productive and suitable lands have been the most likely to go out of cultivation. Many hundreds of thousands of acres of rolling land in the Piedmont country from North Carolina to Alabama have been put into timber. Vast acreages here and elsewhere have been turned into pastures or used to grow feed crops for cattle. Even in the fertile Delta sections a diversification into soybeans, grain and cattle has occurred.

The theme of diversification has been preached to Negro farmers just as it has been to white farmers. But the forms of agriculture resulting from diversification typically do not use a system of tenant operation and usually require more land than the average Negro owner-operator has or can obtain. In addition, in areas of the South where he has historically been concentrated in a few traditional field crops—cotton, tobacco, peanuts—the Negro farmer often finds himself unwelcome in other enterprises which might have been rather exclusively the white man's province. Such pressures vary widely from area to area and may range from completely prohibitive to nonexistent. But in many cases they are all too real. For example, the only feasible way to market some specialty crops may be through cooperatives and the Negro may find that the co-op will not handle his crops. In other instances the Negro farmer may be unable to obtain credit for any but his traditional enterprises, in some cases through nothing more malicious than a lack of confidence by lenders that he can succeed in other enterprises.[3]

The greatest single source of diversification for Southern farmers has been cattle raising. Since 1945 the number of Negro owner-operators who raise cattle for sale has been stable, despite the general decline in the total number of Negro-owned farms. But the average number of cattle and calves sold by Negro owners was only four animals per farm in 1959, representing the merest increase from three per farm in 1945. Thus, although there has been some gain in cattle raising, it has not been of a generally

VEGETABLE GARDEN: "... today the trend in agriculture is for farmers not to produce their own meat or milk or eggs, although the vegetable garden shows no sign of demise.... The ... emphasis that the Negro farmer puts on subsistence farming certainly offsets to some extent the money income difference between himself and the white farmers...."

significant nature. Furthermore, in 1959 the average value of cattle sold by Negro farmers was less than a hundred dollars per animal. Either because of a higher proportion of calves or lower quality of animals, this was one-fifth below the average for white farmers.

In crop production, an easy means of diversification has been to grow soybeans. The crop has had several advantages. It can be produced in many states under a wide range of conditions. The market for the beans in oleo-margarine, cooking oils and other uses has expanded rapidly, and the price has remained good. Furthermore, there are no restrictions on the acreage that a farmer may plant.

With these incentives the number of farmers growing the crop has increased in the South as elsewhere. Generally, soybeans are well adapted to those sections of the South where Negro farmers are located—in the Coastal Plain and the Mississippi Delta. Many Negro farmers grow soybeans as a supplement to their other crops, although the full number is not known.

The Increased Importance of Tobacco

During and after the First World War a trend developed in the habits of Western civilization that unquestionably intensified and prolonged the role of Negroes in American agriculture. This was the rise of cigarette smoking. Cigarettes were not new, but for whatever reasons—urbanization, the growing number of women smokers, a rise in personal income or the invention of cigarette-making machinery—the consumption of cigarettes soared. Much of the tobacco used was grown only in the South. The result was a steady expansion of tobacco farming throughout the Coastal Plain from North Carolina to northern Florida—predominantly in sections where many Negro farmers were already present.

The Negro farmer was well-suited to tobacco, which was grown strictly by hand and animal labor, making good use of the plentiful labor of large families. And tobacco was well-suited to the Negro farm owner, for it did not require much land. Between 1910 and 1945 the number of nonwhite Southern farmers who grew tobacco—both owners and tenants—rose from 42,000 to 91,000, in a period when the net change in cotton farmers was down. The increase in economic importance of tobacco was much greater than the mere change in number of farmers raising it. In 1910 hundreds of farmers in the Deep South were raising only small patches for home use, whereas almost all of the farms in the latter period were producing for sale.

The growth of the cigarette tobacco industry continued with little slackening until the middle 1950's. At that time, bumper yields, new methods of using less tobacco per cigarette, and a near halt in the growth of per capita consumption produced conditions that led to severe cutbacks in acreage allotments per farmer. A decline in number of farms raising tobacco has now set in, but not nearly so rapidly as with cotton. Thus tobacco has continued to increase in its relative importance to the Negro farmer.

The proportion of all Southern nonwhite farmers who grew any tobacco was less than 5 percent in 1910, but 14 percent in 1945 and 24 percent in 1959. In relation to cotton there was just one Negro farmer growing tobacco in 1910 for every sixteen growing cotton. Today there are fewer than three

Negro farmers producing cotton for every one growing tobacco.

In general, the Negro-operated farms growing tobacco (1) have been somewhat more likely to produce on a commercial scale than farms producing cotton; (2) have tended to yield a higher value of products sold; and (3) are somewhat more likely to be operated by owners than the cotton farms. Negroes have achieved a more important role in cigarette tobacco production than in any other commodity. They grow one-sixth of all cigarette tobacco, compared with one-tenth of cotton (1959). Of the principal cigarette type—flue-cured tobacco—Negro farmers account for one-fourth of the crop.

The greater persistence of tobacco than cotton is shifting the principal centers of Negro farming away from the Deep South over toward the Atlantic Coastal Plain. North Carolina, the leading tobacco state, is now second only to Mississippi in number of Negro farmers, and the total value of its Negro-operated farms—both owner and tenant—exceeds all other states.

THE POSITION OF NEGRO FARMERS TODAY

Number of Farms

At their peak in 1920, Negro farm operators numbered 926,000 (Table II) and comprised one-seventh of all farmers in the Nation. This number includes all tenant farmers, even though many of them exercised little or

TABLE II—Negro farm operators in the United States, 1900–1959

Area	1959	1950	1940	1930	1920	1900
United States	272,541	559,980	681,790	882,850	925,708	746,715
Northeast	596	1,002	1,432	1,021	1,469	1,761
North Central	4,259	6,700	7,466	10,083	7,911	12,255
South	267,008	551,469	672,214	870,936	915,595	732,362
West	678	809	678	812	735	337
Selected States						
Missouri	1,684	3,214	3,686	5,844	2,824	4,950
Maryland	2,132	3,595	4,049	5,264	6,208	5,842
Virginia	15,629	28,527	35,062	39,598	47,690	44,795
North Carolina	41,023	69,029	57,428	74,636	74,849	53,996
South Carolina	30,953	61,255	61,204	77,331	109,005	85,381
Georgia	20,163	50,352	59,127	86,787	130,176	82,822
Florida	3,664	7,473	9,731	11,010	12,954	13,521
Kentucky	3,327	4,882	5,546	9,104	12,624	11,227
Tennessee	15,018	24,044	27,972	35,123	38,181	33,883
Alabama	29,206	57,205	73,338	93,795	95,200	94,069
Mississippi	55,174	122,709	159,256	182,578	161,001	128,351
Arkansas	14,654	40,810	57,011	79,556	72,275	46,978
Louisiana	17,686	40,599	59,556	73,734	62,036	58,096
Oklahoma	2,633	5,910	8,987	15,172	13,403	6,353
Texas	15,432	34,389	52,648	85,940	78,597	65,472

SOURCE: 1959 Census of Agriculture, Volume II.

COTTON—TRADITIONAL FIELD CROP: *"In the fall of 1959, 56 percent of the commercial-size farms run by nonwhite farmers in the South were cotton farms. . . . The heavier Negro reliance on cotton was true throughout the South. In its most extreme form in Arkansas, 94 percent of all nonwhite commercial farmers were cotton specialists in 1959."*

no managerial functions and were essentially laborers paid with share of the crop. As a result of all the influences that have combined to lower the number of farms, only 273,000 Negro farmers were counted in the 1959 Census of Agriculture, a drop of 70 percent since 1920 and of 50 percent in less than ten years since 1950. In 1964, the number was not more than 180,000.

Currently (1965) about 3 percent of all employed Negro men work solely or primarily as farm operators. The comparable percentage for white men is 5 percent. An additional number of both races do some farming but spend most of their time at other jobs. About 8 percent of Negro men work as farm laborers. Thus direct work in agriculture is the sole or primary employment of about 11 percent, or one-ninth of the employed Negro male labor force. Including women, about 9 percent of all Negro workers are principally in agriculture compared with 6 percent of white workers.

Location of Farms

The great majority of Negro farmers are located in a huge sickle-shaped stretch of land that begins on the northeast in southern Maryland, sweeping southward through Virginia, the Carolinas and Georgia east of the Blue Ridge Mountains (Figures 1 and 2). The area curves through Georgia below the southern end of the mountains, across central Alabama, and in a northwestward direction through Mississippi, with the end in western Tennessee and eastern Arkansas. A handle can be thought of as extending across northern Louisiana, curving down into eastern Texas. There are very few Negro farmers in the mountain and plateau parts of the South, in the Florida peninsula or in the plains portions of Texas.

The densest concentrations are in the tobacco and cotton country of eastern North and South Carolina, and in the Cotton Belt for a distance roughly fifty miles north and seventy-five miles south of Memphis, Tennessee. In these areas, together with central Alabama, there are eighty-seven counties in which Negro farmers are still in the majority. Mississippi has had more Negro farmers than any other throughout this century—one-fifth of the national total in 1959. However, as a result of the rapid loss of cotton tenants now taking place in Mississippi, this distinction will probably go to North Carolina in the future.

Negro Farmers Outside the South

Little more than one percent of all Negro farmers live outside of the states where slavery existed at the time of the Civil War. It is the remarkable concentration in one region of the nation—the South—that so distinguishes the Negro's role in farming from his participation in other industries and that has such great influence on his prospects in farming.

In the post-revolutionary period of our history there was a scattering of Negro farmers in the Hudson Valley, in New Jersey and in southeastern Pennsylvania. These settlements were relics of the use of Negroes as slaves once attempted in the North or of the attraction of Negroes to Quaker communities, which usually had an active interest in the welfare of former slaves.

As the land north of the Ohio River was settled, where slavery was forbidden, some free Negroes and escaped slaves gradually moved in. Many were persons of mixed ancestry, some so much so that they formed distinct communities aloof from the general Negro population. A majority of the Negro settlers went to the hilly wooded country of southern Ohio and Indiana where farming was largely of a small-scale nature. Others, however, obtained better lands in the Corn Belt parts of these states and of southern Michigan and engaged in a more commercial type of agriculture.

Often the free Negro farmer was resented, and repressive laws were passed in some states that forbade any more to enter the state. The Civil War brought a number of refugees north, but after the war the Negro rural settlements began to decline despite ownership of land and an improved social climate. The farms were usually small, the land was often of below average quality and developing opportunities in the cities drained off the younger people.

West of the Mississippi, Negroes took very little part in the great homesteading movement after the Civil War. The one notable exception was in Kansas, where a number of communities of Negro farmers were founded in the so-called exoduster movement. But here again, almost no sooner had the settlements been founded than they began to decline. People accustomed to cotton farming with almost no managerial experience or capital found it very difficult to succeed as independent farmers in the plains.

In 1900, the North and West had 9,400 Negro-operated farms, with more than 1,000 each in Ohio, Indiana, Illinois and Kansas. By 1959, there were only 3,850 left. When the millions of rural Negroes who left the South in the twentieth century went North, they avoided like the plague the farm work they had been used to back home.

Today the largest number of Negro farmers in the North and West is in Michigan. The largest settlement is in Cass and Berrien Counties, Michigan, not far from South Bend, Indiana. This is perhaps the most persistent of the Northern areas developed by free Negroes in the generation before the Civil War. After a period of some decline as a commercial farming area, it has begun to grow again as a part-time farming and residential area. South of Chicago near Kankakee, Illinois, is another much more recent rural settlement. It consists largely of middle-aged and older families who combine a rural residence with off-farm sources of income.

In California, some Negroes worked in farming as hired hands many years ago. During the 1930's and early 1940's their number was greatly swelled by migrants fleeing the depression or, later, seeking defense work. A few have gone into agriculture on their own, so that by 1959 California with 443 farms operated by Negroes had become the third largest site of Negro farmers outside the South (after Michigan and Ohio). The farm families are somewhat scattered in California and no longer increasing, but the Negro farm community achieved a distinction recently when one of its young men was elected to head the state chapter of the Future Farmers of America.

The history of Negro farm communities outside of the South is often of

FIGURE 1—

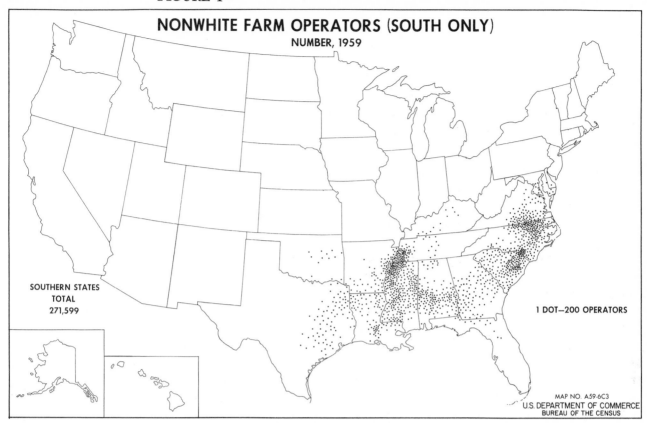

NONWHITE FARM OPERATORS (SOUTH ONLY)
NUMBER, 1959

SOUTHERN STATES
TOTAL
271,599

1 DOT—200 OPERATORS

MAP NO. A59-6C3
U.S. DEPARTMENT OF COMMERCE
BUREAU OF THE CENSUS

FIGURE 2—

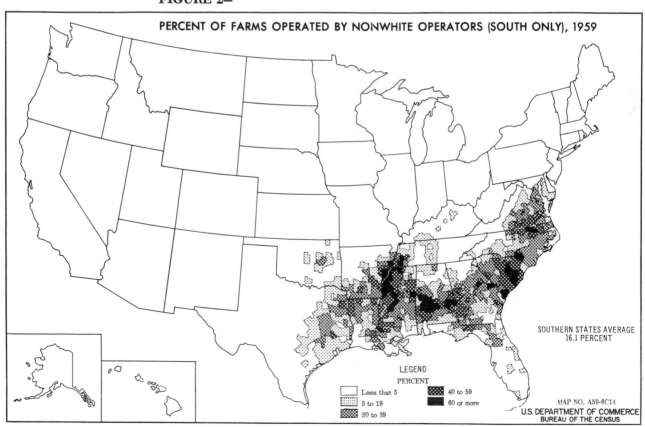

PERCENT OF FARMS OPERATED BY NONWHITE OPERATORS (SOUTH ONLY), 1959

SOUTHERN STATES AVERAGE
16.1 PERCENT

LEGEND
PERCENT

Less than 5   40 to 59
5 to 19   60 or more
20 to 39

MAP NO. A59-6C14
U.S. DEPARTMENT OF COMMERCE
BUREAU OF THE CENSUS

THE NEGRO IN AMERICAN AGRICULTURE   177

great interest. But with few exceptions these communities have been disintegrating in modern times. The people who have grown up in them have usually assimilated well the characteristics and aspirations of the local culture. But they are not staying in agriculture. Their stable Northern background and higher than average education have made it easier for them to succeed in the cities than for their Southern cousins, and it is to the cities that they are going. If those born to the land in the North and West seldom wish to make their future in farming, the reluctance of the Southern Negro to attempt to enter agriculture outside the South is understandable.

Tenure of Farming

In the twentieth century, the traditional image of the Negro farmer has been that of the sharecropper. It is not surprising that this has been so, for from about World War I until 1950, half or more of all Negro farmers were landless tenants working for a share of the crops they produced. Others rented for cash, but until the end of World War II not more than one-fourth of Negro farmers owned their property (mortgaged or un-mortgaged). Many white farmers were tenants also, but not in the same proportions as the Negroes. Even during the worst years of the 1930's, more than half of the Southern white farmers were owners. This difference has had a far-reaching effect on the ability of Negroes to survive and prosper in agriculture. Lacking land, the tenant has no defense against mechanization and may find himself displaced if the landlord decides to operate with more machinery and fewer men. He is usually the loser, too, when crop allotments are cut and there is less acreage to be divided among the tenants.

The number and proportion of Negro tenants has been greatly reduced in the last twenty years because of these and other reasons. Relatively few of them have become owners. From 1945 to 1959, a 70 percent loss of Negro tenants took place. Owners declined by 33 percent—a heavy loss in itself, but much less than that of tenants.

The most viable and progressive element among farmers in the post World War II period has been the part owners. These are men who own some land and rent additional land. The system has the advantage of enabling a man to expand his operations without tying up additional money in land. Instead, he may use his capital for machinery and then rent enough extra land to keep himself and his machines fully and profitably employed. Although the traditional view of the hierarchy of farmers has had the full owner at the top, the part owners as a class have larger operations and earn more money. Negro part owners were increasing in number as late as 1950, but have declined somewhat since then. Their relative importance has continued to grow, however, and they now account for a seventh of all Negro farmers.

Negro owners (full and part) numbered 127,000 and operated 8.7 million acres of land in 1959 (Table III). That is a little more than 13,000 square miles, an area about the size of Connecticut, Massachusetts and Rhode Island.

There are some counties (twenty in 1959) in which Negro farm owners outnumber white owners. About two-thirds of these counties are concentrated in the Black Belt of Alabama and the Coastal Plain of South Carolina.

RICE HARVEST: There are few rice farms in America. One of the largest is owned by this Negro farmer in Garwood, Texas.

TABLE III—Number, Acreage and Value of Farms Operated by Nonwhites in the South 1959, 1950 and 1920

Tenor of operator	Number of farms			Land in farms (Thou. acres)		
	1959	1950	1920	1959	1950	1920
Total	265,621	559,090	922,914	13,901	26,275	41,318
Full owners	89,749	141,482	178,558	5,577	8,391	11,950
Part owners	37,534	51,864	39,031	3,104	3,723	2,126
Managers	290	239	1,770	351	347	368
All tenants	138,048	365,505	703,555	4,869	13,815	26,874
Cash	14,855	39,562	100,275	784	2,097	4,011
Share cash	2,406	5,656	8,207	144	271	272
Crop share	31,714	95,461}	176,711	1,410	4,424}	7,815
Livestock share	946	1,736}		73	136}	
Croppers	73,387	198,057	333,713	1,880	5,540	10,141
Others and unknown	14,740	25,033	84,649	576	1,346	4,636

Average acres per farm			Average value of farms ($)		
1959	1950	1920	1959	1950	1920
52.3	47.0	44.8	6,240	2,792	2,414
62.1	59.3	66.9	6,255	3,062	2,561
82.7	71.8	54.5	9,436	4,165	2,421
1211.0	1451.1	207.9	107,072	43,661	12,166
35.3	37.8	38.2	5,284	2,464	2,352
52.8	53.0	40.0	4,299	2,021	2,016
60.0	47.9	33.1	8,297	3,532	3,668
44.5	46.3}	44.2	6,880	2,906}	2,765
77.1	78.5}		11,587	4,908}	
25.6	28.0	30.4	4,809	2,311	2,190
39.1	53.8	54.8	4,166	2,266	2,397

SOURCE: 1959 Census of Agriculture, Volume II.

In no case, however, do Negro farmers own the majority of the farmland in a county. The maximum relative land ownership occurs in Jefferson Davis County in southern Mississippi, where Negro owners operate 26 percent of all farmland.

Type of Farming

The peculiar concentration of Negro farmers in a few kinds of activities can be easily seen from census figures on the types of commercial farms (Table IV). In the fall of 1959, 56 percent of the commercial-size farms run by nonwhite farmers in the South were cotton farms (meaning that over half of their gross income came from the sale of cotton). Considering that Negroes were historically concentrated in the Cotton Belt, this percentage might not seem particularly high were it not for the much lower emphasis on cotton by Southern white farmers. The heavier Negro reliance on cotton was true throughout the South. In its most extreme form in Arkansas, 94 percent of all nonwhite commercial farmers were cotton specialists in 1959.

After cotton, tobacco culture is by far the most common type of farming for Negroes, being the principal product of 26 percent of nonwhite Southern commercial enterprises. Tobacco is especially important in North Carolina, where more than half of the nonwhite tobacco specialists operate.

The third most common commercial type for Negroes (6 percent of the total) is the general farm, on which no one product accounts for half of the total sales. Such a type sounds like the acme of stability and diversification—and often is larger than the cotton or tobacco specialty farms. In many cases, however, it simply represents farms on which small amounts of the traditional crops—cotton and tobacco—are of about equal importance or on which one or the other is supplemented with peanuts. A group which in the official statistics is called "other field crop" farms accounts for an additional 3 percent of the commercial farms and consists principally of peanut specialty farms in North Carolina and Georgia.

The four types cited—cotton, tobacco, general and other field crops—amount to 92 percent of all Southern nonwhite farms operated at the commercial level, as compared with 49 percent for Southern white farmers. The major significance of this fact is that the crops involved are allotted crops for which the acreage is restricted by law, that more often than not they are in surplus supply, and they are either stationary or contracting in acreage.

In contrast the nonwhite farmer has only minor representation in the sectors of agriculture that have been expanding in the South, such as livestock, dairy or poultry farming and truck crops. Throughout the South the agricultural colleges and other shapers of farming trends have long been preaching the theme of a "green revolution" to Southern farmers—

TABLE IV—Type of Commercial Farm by Value of Products sold in 1959, for Nonwhite-Operated Farms in the South

Type of farm	Total commercial	Value of products sold, 1959					
		$40,000 and over	$20,000 – $40,000	$10,000 – $20,000	$5,000 – $10,000	$2,500 – $5,000	Under $2,500
All types	154,298	197	520	2,663	20,230	51,862	78,826
Cash grain*	2,286	17	47	96	228	487	1,360
Tobacco*	40,670	—	80	891	9,831	17,942	11,921
Cotton*	87,074	66	193	839	6,828	26,839	52,139
Other field crops*	4,867	5	20	215	736	1,405	2,201
Poultry	448	52	36	85	80	80	115
Dairy	1,131	1	15	65	145	310	595
Livestock	6,618	9	36	72	319	970	5,222
General	9,596	11	48	339	1,868	3,498	3,832
Vegetable, fruit, nut and miscellaneous**	1,608	36	45	61	195	331	1,441

* Value of products sold not known for some farms.

** Distribution includes value of products sold for 501 grain, tobacco, cotton and other field crop farms.

SOURCE: 1959 Census of Agriculture, Volume I.

DIVERSIFICATION: *"The theme of diversification has been preached to Negro farmers just as it has been to white farmers.... [However, in 1959,] only 4 percent of nonwhite Southern farmers were livestock specialists (cattle, hogs, and sheep) and only an additional one percent were dairymen or poultrymen."*

that is, a conversion of lands to hay crops and improved pastures and the raising of more livestock. This movement clearly came of age in the 1950's, for the 1959 census revealed that the South as a region for the first time had more livestock farms than cotton farms. But for the Negro farmer it is almost as though such a change had never occurred. Only 4 percent of the nonwhite Southern farmers were livestock specialists (cattle, hogs, and sheep), and only an additional one percent were dairymen or poultrymen.

Nothing more sharply distinguishes white from nonwhite farmers in the South than the different degree of reliance on livestock. Ninety percent of the total value of products sold by nonwhite farmers in 1959 consisted of crops and only 10 percent of livestock and livestock products. On Southern white-operated farms, 52 percent of the total product value was from crops and 48 percent from livestock—almost an even balance.

Size of Farms

Perhaps the most widespread trend in American agriculture since the end of the depression has been the increase in the physical size of farms—in the number of acres of land per farm. The acreage needed to farm successfully differs widely from one part of the country to another—depending on the climate and the quality of land—and from one type of farming to another. In general, the greater the amount of labor per acre required to produce a commodity, the smaller the average amount of land in a family farm will be or need be. And the labor used per acre is roughly proportional to the money yielded. For example, tobacco requires heavy inputs of labor per acre and the average amount of land planted in tobacco per farm is small—only about three acres per farm in the South. However, the value of the crop may be more than a thousand dollars per acre. With cotton or peanuts typical production per acre might be one to two hundred dollars, depending on the region. But, with soybeans the best areas of the South would yield less than sixty dollars per acre on the average. Thus, the need for land varies with the crop. In livestock production, the acreage needed for pasture and to raise feeds is usually much larger for each dollar of product yielded than is true for cash crop farming.

The farms operated by Negroes have historically been small. With their limited capital, Negroes were lucky to acquire land at all, let alone buy a large place. If they were tenants, the usual rental included only as much cotton land as a family could work by hand and mule, plus a few acres to grow corn for the mule.

In 1935, at the time the modern trend toward larger farms was beginning, the average size of a Negro-operated farm in the South was 44 acres; white farmers averaged 131 acres. As the ability and necessity to have larger units grew, the size of white farms grew. This was not a result just of landlords displacing tenants and operating their land in fewer units without an overall increase in land holdings. All classes of white-operated farms became steadily larger, including tenant farms, and by 1959 the white average had nearly doubled, rising to 249 acres.

Among Negro farmers little of this trend is evident. Although hundreds of thousands of small tenant units have disappeared, the average size of all farms has gone up to only fifty-two acres, an increase of just eight

TABLE V —Economic Class of Nonwhite-Operated Farms in the South, by Tenure, 1959

Economic class*	Number of farms				Percentage distribution			
	Total**	Full owners	Part owners	All tenants	Total	Full owners	Part owners	All tenants
TOTAL	**265,336**	**89,754**	**37,534**	**138,048**	**100.0**	**100.0**	**100.0**	**100.0**
Commercial	**154,298**	**28,556**	**22,446**	**103,296**	**58.2**	**31.8**	**59.8**	**74.8**
$40,000 plus	197	50	105	42	.1	.1	.3	.0
$20,000–$40,000	520	109	197	214	.2	.1	.5	.2
$10,000–$20,000	2,663	294	921	1,448	1.0	.3	2.5	1.0
$ 2,500–$ 5,000	20,230	1,672	3,458	15,100	7.6	1.9	9.2	10.9
$ 5,000–$10,000	51,862	6,350	7,284	38,228	19.5	7.1	19.4	27.7
Under $2,500	78,826	20,081	10,481	48,264	29.7	22.4	27.9	35.0
Noncommercial	**111,038**	**61,198**	**15,088**	**34,752**	**41.8**	**68.2**	**40.2**	**25.2**
Part time †	67,065	32,475	10,091	24,499	25.3	36.2	26.9	17.7
Part retirement	43,973	28,723	4,997	10,253	16.6	32.0	13.3	7.4

* Dollar values refer to value of farm products sold from the farm in 1959. Part-time farms are those selling less than $2,500 of products a year whose operators are under age 65 and depend heavily on off-farm jobs or income. Part-retirement farms are those selling less than $2,500 of products a year whose operators are 65 years old or over.

** Total excludes 290 managers.

† Includes 1,000 noncommercial farmers of unknown age.

SOURCE: 1959 Census of Agriculture, Volume I.

acres since 1935. Nonwhite full owners average sixty-two acres and part owners eighty-three (Table III).

The limited size of land resources has been one of the factors retarding the ability or willingness of Negro farmers to diversify into more extensive types of farming such as grain and livestock. Typically the pasture land alone on a white livestock farm is larger than the entire acreage of a Negro-operated farm.

Economic Scale of Farming

Farms vary widely in the amount of business they do and it is necessary to consider this factor in judging the position of a group of farmers. The best available way to rank them is by the value of products sold from the farm. The Bureau of the Census classes as "commercial" farms those selling over $2,500 worth of products in a year, plus those selling a lower amount whose operators are not elderly and have little off-farm work. Under these rules 154,298 farms in the South operated by nonwhite farmers were termed commercial in 1959, amounting to about three-fifths of all nonwhite-operated farms. Of the others, 67,065 were classed as part-time, 43,973 as part-retirement farms whose operators were sixty-five years old or over (Table V).

The Department of Agriculture figures as a rule of thumb that a farmer must sell at least $10,000 of products annually if he expects to make a minimum net income of $2,500, and that he needs $2,500 of net income to maintain a minimum decent level of living. The gross sales needed for a net of $2,500 vary from one type of farming to another. For example, dairy and poultry farms typically have a high volume of sales and a low profit margin, whereas crop farms that are not turning over their capital as often usually have a higher profit margin. Because profit margins in agriculture have narrowed in recent years, the value of sales needed to return a given net income has risen steadily and will probably continue to do so. If $10,000 of sales is accepted as the minimum adequate scale of farming, then only 1.3 percent of all nonwhite farms in the South were of adequate size in 1959 (see Table V). By contrast, 14.1 of Southern white farmers had adequate sized units. If because of their concentration in annual cash crops it is suggested that nonwhite farmers might get by if they sell a minimum of $5,000, the proportion with adequate sized units is still only 9.0 percent, compared with 26.6 for white farmers. Since a majority of nonwhite farmers are still tenant farmers, it must be remembered that the landlord's share of the crop has to come out of the value sold.

The number of nonwhite farmers in the South who sold $10,000 or more of products in 1959 was 3,380. An additional 20,230 sold between $5,000 and $10,000 worth. At the lower extreme there were 130,688 commercial farmers whose gross receipts were less than $5,000. These figures indicate more clearly than any others how very small the number of Negroes is who have a real toehold in agriculture, and how large the proportion is who have little chance of making a decent living from farming alone without a radical change in their scale of operation. Among commercial farmers, the average value of products sold by all Southern nonwhite farmers was $3,029; the average for white commercial farmers was $10,396 (Table VI).

TABLE VI—Selected Characteristics of Southern Farms and Farmers, 1959

Characteristic	Nonwhite operators								White operators	
		Commercial								
						Tenants				
	Grand Total	Total	Full owners	Part owners	Cash	Crop share	Croppers	Noncom- mercial	Grand Total	Com- mercial Totals
Average farm size (acres)	52	56	82	104	64	47	27	47	249	382
Value of farm ($)	6,240	7,328	8,382	11,667	5,412	7,798	5,295	4,778	25,370	37,816
Value per acre ($)	122	134	107	115	85	166	192	104	111	107
Cropland harvested (acres)	20	26	23	41	28	28	21	10	51	85
Pasture, excl. woods (acres)	9	8	15	18	11	4	1	11	116	187
Have tractor (%)	22	26	37	51	26	27	11	16	61	75
Have hogs (%)	76	76	84	89	85	79	64	76	52	55
Have cattle (%)	50	45	68	66	67	47	22	58	75	75
Sold hogs (%)	25	24	36	43	29	23	12	27	29	35
Sold cattle (%)	23	18	35	33	26	14	6	30	61	64
Plant cotton (%)	68	—	—	—	—	—	—	—	24	—
Plant tobacco (%)	24	—	—	—	—	—	—	—	24	—
Corn per acre (bu.)	24	26	23	25	17	26	30	19	35	36
Value of products sold per farm ($):										
All products	2,055	3,029	2,130	3,725	1,916	3,281	3,196	700	6,068	10,396
Crops	1,840	2,777	1,652	3,168	1,711	3,168	3,123	537	3,272	5,688
Livestock (including dairy and poultry)	214	252	478	557	205	113	73	163	2,796	4,707
Average value sales per acre ($)	40	54	26	36	30	70	118	15	24	27
Operators having 100+ days off farm work (%)	21	4	4	7	3	3	4	55	35	17

SOURCE: 1959 Census of Agriculture, Volume II.

One of the most serious ultimate problems for the future of the Negro in agriculture is the low state of production by Negro farmers who own all or part of their land. With the steady decline of the tenant system of farming, the future of Negro farmers will be increasingly determined by the level of activity of the owner-operator. At present fully 60 percent of the Negro owners (full and part owners combined) are not even producing enough to be classed as commercial farmers. The part owners—who are the less numerous of the two owner groups—are usually commercial, but more than two-thirds of the full owners are not. In part the low production of the full owners is the result of age—many of them are too old to be active. But even among those under fifty-five years old, a majority fail to sell $2,500 worth of products.

In the light of the small size of most farms run by Negroes, one might logically expect that the farms would be fully utilized. However, the proportion of crop land that is idle or had crop failure is high. In 1959, one-fourth of all the crop land on the farms of Negro full owners was idle or had crop failure, compared with one-ninth on farms of white full owners, indicating the lower intensity of land use.

In addition, the proportion of land remaining in woods is high, amounting to about three-eighths of the total land acreage of commercial Negro owners. These woodlands are usually of low economic value in their present state, except for hunting and as a source of firewood to feed the archaic stoves that still serve as the means of cooking or heating on many farms.

In short, it is not surprising that with such small farms the Negro farmers remained concentrated in the production of intensive crops in which labor can be substituted for land. It is contrary to expectation, however, that their limited land resources are not used more fully. Generally the Negro farmer comes closer to operating his place in the old-time manner, using older methods and equipment and producing much for home use.

A generation ago the emphasis on food for home use would have gladdened the hearts of extension agents and others concerned for the rural Negro's welfare, for it was commonly observed that much of the debt of Negro tenants was for purchase of food that they would not or were not permitted to raise on their farms. But today the trend in agriculture is for farmers not to produce their own meat or milk or eggs, although the vegetable garden shows no sign of demise. Specialized production and marketing have commonly made it cheaper or safer or more convenient for the farmer to purchase most foods. The following figures clearly show that even commercial Negro farmers put much more emphasis on subsistence than do their white neighbors.

	Nonwhite	White
Percent of Southern commercial farmers who sold cattle, 1959	18	64
Percent who kept cattle but sold none	26	11
Percent who sold hogs, 1959	24	35
Percent who kept hogs but sold none	52	20

The majority of white Southern commercial farmers who keep cattle or hogs keep them for sale; the majority of Negro commercial farmers who have them keep them for home-produced meat. A similar pattern shows up

DIVERSIFICATION: " . . . *livestock specialists (hogs)* . . . "

for chickens and milk, although less pronounced. The additional emphasis that the Negro farmer puts on subsistence farming certainly offsets to some extent the money income difference between himself and white farmers, but it is unmistakably associated with a less advanced attitude toward farming as a business.

Productivity

In the last fifteen years, as profit margins have narrowed, farmers have attempted to maintain their income level by increasing the size of operation and raising the yields per acre. Production has been the key to survival.

The patterns of productivity per acre in the three crops that form the backbone of Negro agriculture—cotton, tobacco and peanuts—give some interesting insights into the competitive position of Negro farmers. The table below has been compiled for North Carolina where Negro farmers have been the most successful on the average and where all three crops are important. It shows the yields per acre for white and nonwhite commercial farmers in 1959—the latest and only year for which all data are available (Table VII).

Notice that the yields obtained by white full and part owners are substantially superior to those of nonwhite farmers for tobacco and peanuts and moderately so for cotton. On the other hand, among tenant farmers the yields of white farmers are only slightly higher than those of nonwhites.

Among the white farmers, owners (full or part) generally obtain somewhat better yields than do tenants. Applying conventional logic, this

TABLE VII—Yields per Acre of Specified Crops on Commercial Farms in North Carolina, by Color and Tenure of the Operator, 1959

Crop and color of operator	Total commercial	Tenure				
		Full owners	Part owners	Tenants		
				Total	Cash tenants	Croppers
Cotton (lbs.)						
White	440	450	443	433	435	434
Nonwhite	410	395	392	415	371	425
Peanuts (lbs.)						
White	1,578	1,566	1,632	1,529	1,180	1,535
Nonwhite	1,466	1,252	1,339	1,513	1,184	1,536
Tobacco (lbs.)						
White	1,490	1,543	1,489	1,466	1,410	1,468
Nonwhite	1,378	1,269	1,276	1,411	1,134	1,432
Soybeans (bu.)						
White	21.0	21.0	21.0	21.0	18.4	22.7
Nonwhite	20.2	17.5	18.2	22.0	17.3	22.2

SOURCE: 1959 Census of Agriculture, Volume I.

seems fitting, considering the higher ability and greater experience that one associates with those who have acquired farms compared with those who are landless.

But the conventional picture of the relationship between the tenure classes does not apply to nonwhite farmers. Among these men it is the tenants who show considerably greater yields of all three crops than do the owners. Furthermore within the tenant class, the croppers—who have been least successful in advancing towards farming independence, who have the least managerial ability, and bring nothing to their work except their labor—produce higher yields than the tenant groups who operate their own equipment.

The answer to the riddle is at least two-fold. First, Negro croppers typically occupy much of the best land owned by white landlords, compared with the poorer average quality of land that Negroes have been able to buy or to rent on a fixed rent or semi-independent basis. Secondly, the croppers' land is managed by the landlord, whereas the Negro owner or cash renter is his own boss.

The implication of the riddle is that the Negro owner-farmers—from whom most future Negro farmers will be drawn—do not compete well with white farmers in the same type of farming. To some extent economies of scale may operate. The Negro farm with its small typical size may be analogus to small family-run businesses in other industries competing with larger firms. But poorer land and smaller size considered, there seems also to be a residual factor of poorer average farming know-how and managerial performance.

The author recalls an interview with a Negro county extension agent in the best part of the North Carolina Coastal Plain. When the agent was asked about the farming practices of Negro owner-operators, he smiled a little wryly and said, "Sadly enough, the tenants are often the best farmers, and if I were going to take you to see a good Negro farmer I would probably show you a tenant." He attributed much of the difficulty to the fear of Negro owners of going into debt and to a lack of understanding on their part of the role of credit in modern farming. Many of the good tenant farmers might fail, he believed, if they assumed the burdens—real and psychological—of ownership.

As indicated under the discussion of diversification, many Southern farmers have added soybeans to their cash crops. In North Carolina, a leading producer, the proportion of farmers harvesting soybeans was the same for nonwhite commercial owners as for white (19 percent) in 1959. This equality of adoption of a profitable crop is superficial, however. The white owner-operators harvested twice as many acres of beans per farm and were obtaining about 15 percent more bushels per acre. Thus in newer crops as with the old, Negro farmers are handicapped by their smaller farms and by their lower productivity.

Facilities

Negro farmers, like all others, have moved into a completely different era from the days before the First World War when most power was supplied by hand or by animals, when it took all day to get to the county seat and back and when electrical or engine-driven equipment was unknown. The

DIVERSIFICATION: " . . . *one percent were dairymen or poultrymen.*"

extension of electricity to farms is now so nearly complete that the census of agriculture no longer bothers to inquire about it. True, Negro farmers were typically the last to obtain it, but today it is standard even in sub-standard houses.

The majority of Negro farmers (about two-thirds) also have acquired either an automobile or truck, giving them much more freedom of movement and choice in purchasing or selling. Still, the one-third with no automotive transportation is a much greater proportion than is common among farmers in general, and there are other facilities now conventional elsewhere that most Negro farmers do without.

For instance, only one out of every eight nonwhite operated farms has a telephone, compared with over half of the white farms. This is not just the result of so many Negro farmers being tenants. Even among commercial nonwhite farmers who own their places, just one-sixth have installed phones. Why should this be so? The statistics do not explain themselves. The answer seems to be a combination of lack of access to the telephone lines, lack of steady income to afford a phone and lack of strong desire for one—the persistence of older ways of doing business or communicating in which a phone does not figure.

Another facility of importance to a farmer is the paved or improved road. It improves his marketing ability and reduces his degree of isolation. But here as with other facilities, it is the Negro farmer who is more likely to find himself at a comparative disadvantage. The hard-surface or gravel road has come to the farms of a majority of Negro farmers, but not to the same degree as other farmers. In the South as a whole, 43 percent of all commercial scale nonwhite farmers were still located on a dirt or unimproved road in 1959, compared with 28 percent for commercial white farmers. The disparity was even greater for the noncommercial group.

Ironically enough, it is the least independent of the Negro farmers who are most likely to be on a good road. The croppers with minor exceptions work the farms of white landlords. Three-fifths of their farms are on improved roads, whereas only half of the full or part owners are so located. The least fortunate group in this respect is the cash tenant, nearly three-fifths of whom have to contend with dirt roads.

Again we wish the cold figures would tell us why, as well as whether. There certainly would seem to a correlation with the often repeated observation that as the last claimants to land Negro owners more often obtained poorer land away from the main-traveled roads. In the case of rented land, a landlord is more likely to rent poorer farms for a fixed rent (cash) than on a share basis. To these explanations, we must add the fact that Negro districts in the South have seldom received standard levels of public roads from the governing authorities. For thousands of Negro farmers a poor road is one more handicap they must carry in competition with other farmers. In a majority of instances the farmer whose place fronts on a dirt road is more than one mile from an improved road.

With few exceptions, modern types of farming require the use of a tractor for efficient operations. Particularly for farmers as heavily committed to field crops as Negro farmers are, the lack of a tractor connotes either a lack of capital or lack of incentive to advance beyond a low-income operation.

In examining the extent to which Negro farmers have acquired tractors, it would be somewhat misleading to focus on the overall frequency of tractors, for so many of the farmers are croppers. Although croppers by definition do not have their own machinery, they usually have the use of a tractor through the landlord. Limiting the comparison to commercial owners shows unmistakably, however, that even the elite group of Negro farmers is far behind the white in possession of tractors. Among full owners 38 percent of nonwhites had one or more tractors compared with 70 percent of the white farmers, and among part owners the percentages were 50 for nonwhites and 87 for white. Noncommercial Southern white farmers are more likely to have tractors than are commercial Negro full owners.

The corollary of these figures is the fact that the Negro farmer is more likely than the white farmer to be using a horse or mule. Nearly two-thirds of the nonwhite farmers, excluding croppers, had a horse or mule in 1959 as against 40 percent of white farmers. On tobacco farms the mule still has a useful place where rows are closely spaced, but the proportion of white farmers in the South who grow tobacco is the same as the proportion of Negro farmers who do, so tobacco farming is not the explanation for the overall differences.

CHARACTERISTICS OF FARMERS

Age

In each major tenure class—full owners, part owners and tenants—the average age of nonwhite southern farmers is older than that of white farmers. Yet the average age of all nonwhite southern farmers is younger than that of all white farmers. These two statements may appear to be contradictory, but the explanation is rather simple. Many young men who eventually own farms begin as tenants because they lack the money to buy land at an early stage of life. Thus, the average tenant farmer is younger than the average owner. Unless one inherits at an early date, ownership usually takes time. Since Negro farmers are abnormally concentrated in the tenant class, their overall average age (51.1 years) is a little lower than that of Southern white farmers (51.6). But the rapid decline in Negro operated farms has lowered the rate at which young Negro men enter farming, so that within each tenure group the Negro farmers tend to be older.

How much older? Not a great deal among commercial farmers—an average of a year older or less. But among noncommercial farmers, the average Negro owner or tenant is four to five years older than white farmers in the same tenure group. For example, noncommercial Negro full owners averaged 59.7 years of age in 1959; their white counterparts averaged 55.5. With many tenant farmers now being displaced or converted to hired workers, the average age of Negro operators is rising rapidly.

The most numerous group of farmers is that between the ages of 45 and 54. But among full owners the largest group consists of those 65 years old and over—more than one-third of all full owners. This high age level of owners explains in part the rather low level of productivity of Negro owned farms in general.

The position and prospect of the Negro as a farmer cannot be discussed without reference to the educational situation in the farm population. Even in the most progressive agricultural areas of the country the notion that a grade school training was sufficient for a farmer lingered for many years after it ceased to be valid.

For the Southern Negro farmer, several factors added to the traditionally conservative rural view of education to produce the lowest levels of schooling in the United States, outside of certain Indian tribes. These factors included the extended neglect of rural Negro school facilities, the closing of schools during peak farm work seasons for use of child labor, and the lack of educational incentive inherent in the sharecropper mode of life.

In 1960, the average years of schooling completed by the nonwhite farm population 25 years old and over was 5.7 years, compared with 8.9 years for the white farm population and 11.1 years for the total urban population. Only 7 percent of adult Negro farm residents have completed high school. Some gradual improvement is taking place, but the pace is so slow. The increase in high school graduates has gone only from 2 percent to 7 percent in 20 years. In this respect the Negro farm population is more than one generation behind white farm people, 14 percent of whom had a high school diploma in 1940.

More than 40 percent of the nonwhite farm people 25 years old and over did not complete as many as five years of school (compared with 8 percent of the white farm population). The situation is not much better for non-whites among the rural-nonfarm population, but is far better in the cities. Some of the problem in the Negro farm population is due to the siphoning off to the cities of those young people who do go through high school. Negro county extension agents are almost unanimous in saying that it is very difficult to interest rural high school students in farming. The good student usually associates the widespread poverty of the population from which he comes with agriculture, and sees the city as the avenue of opportunity.

But even among the young, the academic performance of children from Negro farm families is in a class totally apart from that of the general population. For example, in 1960 more than half (57 percent) of all Southern nonwhite farm boys aged fourteen and fifteen years old were retarded in school. That is to say, they had not reached the grades that are normal for persons of their age. The corresponding proportion for white farm boys that age was 26 percent in the South and only 11 percent in the North and West. Even more astonishing is the fact that of the nonwhite farm boys who were behind in school a substantial majority had fallen two or more years behind. In most instances retardation becomes a prelude to quitting school altogether—and three-fourths of all Negro farm boys do drop out before completing high school.

With such a small fraction of the Negro farm people having received a modern education, it is easy to understand how difficult it is to develop group leadership in that population, and how frequently it is possible for a semiliterate farmer to fail to understand the complexities of Government programs that affect his heavily controlled crops or to take full advantage of the services that the Government and the experiment stations can provide him.

Housing

Housing has been as much a perennial problem for the Negro population in the countryside as it is considered to be in the city. Rural housing has typically had two advantages over that in the city—it has often been provided "free" as part of a tenant farm or as part of a man's pay, and although families have often been very crowded in their own quarters, they have not usually had to share the same building with other families. On the other hand, the flush toilets, bathtubs, running water and central heating of most city slum housing were and still are amenities which the typical rural Negro has never had.

Farm housing for Negroes is often of inadequate original construction, frequently consisting of only one thickness of boards, without insulation, glassed windows or screens. Rooms are often small and usually number only from two to four for tenant families. Gradually much of the poorest housing has been abandoned as the number of farm people has decreased. In the 1940's and 1950's almost complete electrification occurred, even in the rudest shacks.

Today, aside from quality of the home, the greatest discrepancy in

TABLE VIII—Selected Family and Housing Characteristics, by Color and Residence for the South, 1950 and 1960

Characteristic	Urban		Rural nonfarm		Rural farm	
	1960	1950	1960	1950	1960	1950
Average number of persons per household						
White	3.19	3.30	3.49	3.67	3.62	4.06
Nonwhite	3.70	3.55	4.26	3.93	5.10	4.87
Percent 5–9 year old children in household not headed by parent						
White	4	7	5	6	7	8
Nonwhite	18	23	20	20	21	20
Percent of housing units not in sound condition						
White	2	6	7	15	7	19
Nonwhite	19	34	33	44	31	44
Percent of housing units having hot and cold piped water						
White	94	82	64	41	60	20
Nonwhite	58	27	16	5	10	2

SOURCE: 1950 and 1960 U.S. Censuses of Population and Housing.

Area, color and sex of worker	Number of workers	Farm work		
		Days worked	Wages earned	
			Per year	Per day
	Thou.	No.	Dol.	Dol.
United States				
Total	2,067	134	913	6.80
White	1,398	145	1,083	7.45
Male	1,162	159	1,232	7.75
Female	237	78	351	4.50
Nonwhite	669	111	556	5.00
Male	414	138	748	5.45
Female	255	68	243	3.60
South				
Total	1,127	122	689	5.65
White	574	136	917	6.75
Nonwhite	553	107	451	4.20

SOURCE: Advance Report on the Hired Farm Working Force of 1962, U.S.
Department of Agriculture, Table 5.

white and Negro rural housing or between rural and urban Negro housing
is in water supply. Most rural homes have a well or spring, but it is not as
easy to provide running water for the scattered population of the countryside as it is in the city. As a result, modern water facilities have lagged
behind electricity. In 1950, only one-fifth of the white farm families in the
South and two-fifths of the nonfarm white rural families had homes with
hot and cold running water. During the 1950's the white population made
great strides in modernizing its water supply, either through community
systems or individual pumps, so that by 1960 the majority of both the farm
and nonfarm white rural houses (over 60 percent) had installed heated
running water. On the other hand, only 2 percent of the Southern farm
Negro homes and 5 percent of other rural Negro homes had a modern
water supply in 1950. During the 1950's, a little progress was made as the
proportion with piped hot and cold water rose to 10 percent of the farm
homes and 16 percent of the nonfarm rural homes (Table VIII). However,
the improvement is so small compared to that of the white rural population
that the relative disparity between the adequacy of water supply of white
and Negro rural people actually widened in the decade.

The importance of hot and cold running water can hardly be overesti-
mated. It is the indispensable basis for adequate bathing facilities, for
sanitary indoor toilets and for modern kitchen equipment. There is no other
measure of level of living that continues to show such a disparity between
white and Negro rural people as water supply.

Despite the wholesale abandonment of much of the worst rural housing
in the South in recent years, the condition of the majority of homes of rural
Negroes remains "deteriorating" or "dilapidated," in Bureau of Census

THE TRACTOR, THE MODERN FARMER'S KEY TO ECONOMIC OPERATION: *"With few exceptions, modern types of farming require the use of a tractor for efficient operations. Particularly for farmers as heavily committed to field crops as Negro farmers are. . . ."*

terms. In 1960, 71 percent of all nonwhite farm homes were so described. These terms imply much more than mere shabbiness. A deteriorating house is one with defects of a nature that require more than a regular amount of repair, and that must be corrected if the house is to continue to provide safe and adequate shelter. A dilapidated house is one in such a poor state that it presently endangers the health, safety or well-being of the occupants. Thus, the great majority of all Negro farm housing is still far substandard. Rural nonfarm homes are in little better average condition. The problem is thus of a general rural character. Deterioration and dilapidation were characteristic of only 27 percent of all white farm homes—a serious enough condition in itself, but far better than the situation for Negroes.

Another useful measure of the adequacy of housing is the ratio of persons per room. In general, a dwelling unit is regarded as definitely overcrowded if there are more than 1.5 persons per room. In the case of nonwhite farm households, 30 percent had more than 1.5 persons per room in 1960. This was 10 times the relative frequency in white farm households (3 percent). Crowding has become somewhat worse in recent years.

One helpful approach to better rural housing has been developed in South Carolina, where a demonstration house for Negroes was built with the assistance of the General Education Board. Groups of women come to the house and live for a week, where they have the chance to enjoy and have training in the use of modern housing facilities. Such experience is often the stimulation to improvements in their own homes.

Two comparative aspects of Negro farm housing need emphasis. One is the fact that rural Negro housing is far inferior in quality to urban Negro housing. This can easily be lost sight of in the public and political attention being given to urban Negro housing problems. For example, although crowding in the homes and apartments of densely settled Negro districts in major cities is often stressed, only 11 percent of all urban dwellings inhabited by nonwhites contained more than 1.5 persons per room in 1960, compared with the 30 percent incidence of this condition in nonwhite farm homes. The proportion of urban nonwhite homes that were in sound condition (not deteriorating or dilapidated) was more than double that of nonwhite farm homes (62 percent vs. 29 percent).

The second point to be noted is that the adequacy and condition of farm tenant housing is usually much poorer than that of owner-occupied housing. Nonwhite farm tenant homes average one room less than owned homes, but typically have one more person per house. Thus the tenant families are much more likely to be overcrowded; 37 percent have more than 1.5 persons per room. (Half of all persons living in nonwhite farm tenant households live in households that have eight or more members.) Only 20 percent of nonwhite farm tenant homes are in sound condition; only 3 percent have bathrooms. Inasmuch as most tenant-occupied farm homes of nonwhites are received as a part of farm rental or as payment in kind for hired work, it is clear that this aspect of the total income of farm Negroes is just as low as the money income component.

There is a circular cause and effect to tenant housing that is difficult to break. It might be very costly in cash outlay for farm landlords to provide minimally decent housing of sound construction, ample space, and modern water, toilet and heating equipment. Yet the continued occupancy of present rural tenant housing undoubtedly has a severely limiting and conditioning effect on the lives of the children who grow up in it and of the adults who remain in it. Landlords, on the other hand, often complain that the tenants will not take care of the improvements that are made; that screens are soon broken out, etc. Probably the problems of rural Negro housing cannot successfully be attacked piecemeal and will not be solved until the whole structure of low education and underemployment of rural people is modified.

Hired Farm Workers

In one aspect of American agriculture the role of the Negro has increased somewhat rather than diminished. That aspect is doing farm work for cash wages. In many respects the sharecropper has been little different from a hired worker, because he usually contributes nothing to his operation except his labor. But technically the cropper has been an operator, for he is paid with a share of the crop rather than with money and is clearly attached to a particular farm for the season.

The hired farm wage laborer—black or white—is usually society's low man on the totem pole. He is typically at the bottom in income and in the respect accorded to him. Some of the reasons for the low standing of the occupation are not hard to find. The average wages paid to farm workers in the South were only seventy-eight cents an hour in 1963 without room and board. The frequency of unemployment is high, the average education of hired farm workers is lower than that of any other major occupation group, and except for inclusion in the Social Security system they are excluded from the basic protections that people in most other jobs take for granted. With few exceptions, farm workers are not covered by minimum wage and hour laws, not included in unemployment compensation insurance, not protected by workmen's disability compensation, and not guaranteed the right to bargain collectively with their employers. As a group they are the closest approximation that the United States has to a pariah occupational caste. Under these conditions it is extremely difficult to develop a career attitude towards hired farm work and to raise the status of the work.

Where does the Negro worker fit into this picture? Because of the low status of the job and the low degree of education expected, Negroes have always been heavily used in hired farm work wherever they have lived and have been a logical group to supply migratory workers to other parts of the Nation for seasonal farm work.

In 1961, one-fourth of all days of farm wage work in the United States was performed by Negroes. Today the hired Negro farm worker makes a greater labor contribution to supplying the nation's agricultural needs than does the Negro farmer. In the South, where Negro farmers comprise one-sixth of all farmers, Negro workers do fully half of all farm wage work.

In the North and West, the use of regular hired workers on farms has been declining almost everywhere. This is not true of Negroes in the South. The South has had mechanization just as the rest of the nation has, but landowners have often adjusted to it by abandoning the tenant method of working their land and substituting hired workers for tenants.

In April 1950 the South had 392,000 white hired farm workers and 298,000 nonwhite. Ten years later, in April, 1960, the white workers had declined to 308,000, while the nonwhites had increased to 311,000. For the first time nonwhites made up over half of the South's farm wage workers.

The switch from tenants to hired hands is nowhere more evident than in the Mississippi Delta country. Here in just five years' time, from the fall of 1954 to the fall of 1959, the number of tenant farmers (white and nonwhite) dropped by 60 percent (from 83,000 to 33,000). At the same time the number of regular hired workers on farms rose by 62 percent (from 24,000 to 39,000). The Delta is mostly cotton country. As the farm owners switched from hand chopping and hand picking by tenants to machine methods by wage hands, they have had to hire only about three new regular hands for each ten tenants displaced. Of course, many of the new wage hands are selected from former tenants—those who are good at mechanical work. The same type of trend has occurred at a slower rate in other cotton areas and in the tobacco and peanut belts.

When this type of mechanization arrives, the problems created are often severe for many people. Some men lose their work and many women and youths who worked in the fields at harvest time and other peak seasons find a much-needed source of income cut off. Yet the trend is inevitable. Hand methods of farming simply do not produce enough income to warrant continuing them when other ways are developed.

In the traditional "tenure ladder" the landless laborer was regarded as a more pitiable creature than the sharecropper. But interestingly enough this does not usually seem to be the case with the new Negro wage hand. Generally these former tenants who have survived the changeover seem to feel that they are better off. For one thing, there is a regular payday and less likelihood that a man will find himself badly in debt at season's end as tenants often do. Regular wage work is covered by Social Security, which gives some assurance for the future. And if a man can save some money and find off-farm work in slack farm seasons, he may even aspire to buy a house of his own, which as a furnished tenant he would not have done. To an increasing extent the hired workers are living away from the farm on which they work.

In 1962 there were 623,000 nonwhite households from which one or more persons did farm work for wages at some time during the year. More than 3,050,000 people lived in these households, indicating the large number of nonwhite people who have some financial dependence on farm wage work. In about half the cases the dependence was rather minor (less than twenty-five days of work by the household head and less than 150 days by all other family members).

A distinctive feature of nonwhite farm worker households is the abnormally high number of them that are headed by women. More than a fourth (26.5 percent) do not have a male head, compared with only 8.5 percent among white farm worker families. The occurrence of many families with a woman head is common in the urban and nonagricultural Negro population as well, but seldom is the difference between the white and nonwhite populations in this respect as great as it is among farm workers. Generally the women heads do not have farm work for as much as 150 days per year, and the income position of such families is often very low.

Several factors serve to concentrate the Negro hired farm worker in hand or stoop labor. Two-thirds of all nonwhite workers who did more than twenty-five days of farm wage work in 1961 worked only as hand or stoop laborers; only one-fourth operated or repaired trucks and machinery. Among white workers the situation is different, with the more skilled workers outnumbering the unskilled hand and stoop laborers. In part the nonwhite disadvantage results from their location in the South where hand work is more needed, and from the greater role of women, almost none of whom are used in machine jobs. Low education and lack of technical training are also factors.

The low average skill level of work performed seriously affects the income that nonwhite workers receive from farm wage work. This is not because hand laborers earn much less per day, but because they have fewer days of work. Male hand laborers actually earned as much per day ($6.40) as operators of self-propelled farm machines in 1961, but the hand workers averaged only ninety-three days of farm work in the year compared with two hundred for the machine operators. (See Table IX for selected statistics on hired farm workers.)

THE PROSPECT

Land—a Key Factor

In a preceding section the anomaly was mentioned that the Negro farmers who are landowners have poorer land on the average and work it less intensively than the Negro tenant farmers who do not control the land they work. Despite the apparent underuse of farms by many Negroes who have become owners, the possession of land is nevertheless a key to future participation by Negroes in American agriculture as operators.

Outright tenancy as a form of land occupancy is in full retreat, especially in the South. Until the end of World War II, Southern farmers who rented all the land they worked outnumbered the part owners by more than six to one. Since the war, full tenancy has declined so rapidly and part owner-ship has become so attractive and necessary that in the 1964 census part owners will outnumber full tenants in the South for the first time, as they have in the North and West since 1954.

Some instances of full tenancy will always exist, but the practice is becoming a minor factor in Southern farming. The principal use of tenancy in the South was for cotton farming. With the near total elimination of hand and animal labor in this crop, it becomes logical for landlords to operate their places as complete units, using hired labor if necessary. Although the end result in tobacco is less clear at the moment, the tendency seems to be the same. The majority of Negro tenant farmers have already vacated, been displaced, or converted to hired work, and a majority of those tenants remaining will follow the same path.

The farmer who does not control the land he works does not control nis own destiny in the far-reaching changes now affecting agriculture. This puts the typical Negro farmer with his limited capital and lack of ownership experience at a disadvantage.

There is also the legacy of racial discrimination and distrust to combat.

With most land in the hands of white owners, Negroes have often found it difficult to be considered as potential buyers, unless the market was poor. For example, in the heart of the tobacco country in eastern North Carolina it was not uncommon in the 1950's for auctions of farmland to begin with a statement that bids would be received from white persons only.

In addition distrust by Negroes of white officials and of the white-controlled credit structures seems to be widespread. Conditions vary greatly from county to county, but all too many Negroes are apprehensive of attempting to purchase land or to encumber the land they may already have.

Since 1910 the amount of land owned by Negro farmers has gone steadily downward, with the exception of the period from 1940 to 1950. During that one decade, under the prosperous conditions of the war and immediate post-war period, there was a growth in both the number of Negro farmers who owned land and in the amount of land owned. Since that time, the gains of the 1940's have disappeared as far as agriculture is concerned. Some of the families who obtained land may continue to own it but no longer use it for farming.

Technological Changes Affecting Negro Farmers

Technological innovations are man-made, but the effects of technological change operate on most men in a very impersonal and neutral way. The effect of the rapid and continuing technological advance in agriculture is usually no different for Negro farmers as such than for any other farmers. But Negroes often are concentrated in those classes and types of farming that are most affected by technology.

The case of cotton, discussed earlier, is a prime example. The successful mechanization of this crop probably has had a more fundamental effect on the Negro farm population than any other event. Within the Southern states, where most Negro farmers live (excluding Texas and Oklahoma), the percentage of cotton mechanically harvested accelerated from 11 percent in 1957 to 55 percent in 1962. Experts of the Department of Agriculture expect that by the end of the 1960's only a very small percentage of Southern cotton will be hand harvested. Thus many more cotton tenants will be displaced, and certain adjustments will become logical for owners —such as larger and more consolidated fields—that lead toward fewer but larger farms.

The changes in tobacco farming have been much less than those affecting cotton, as yet. In the complicated process of harvesting, curing and marketing cigarette tobacco, a variety of time-consuming hand operations have been necessary. For example, in producing the flue-cured type of the South Atlantic States, the leaves are actually pulled from the stalk by hand. Furthermore, since the leaves ripen at different times the field has to be gone over ("primed") several times. Then the leaves have to be individually handled in preparing them for the curing barn and rearranged by hand in preparing them for auction. Tobacco requires 486 man hours of labor per acre, compared with seven for corn and forty-nine for all cotton (1960–62 averages). Naturally this tremendous labor requirement in tobacco farming stands as a challenge to agricultural engineers, and they are succeeding in ways to reduce it.

In the last few years machines have come into use which permit workers to ride through the fields while priming and preparing the leaves for the curing barn. In addition, new types of curing barns have been invented which reduce the handling of the crop. The major breakthrough is dependent upon the invention of a machine that will mechanically sever the ripe leaves from the plant and prepare them for curing—a so-called combine. Models of such machines are now in operation, and it appears only a matter of time before they are perfected for commercial use.

The mechanization of tobacco will not come overnight. The crop is geared much more to family sized farms and less to plantations than cotton was. But the initial effects have been evident since the mid-1950's, and the incentive for the larger operatives to procure reliable mechanical methods and free themselves from dependence on a labor pool is great. It seems inevitable that the direct and indirect pressures on Negro tobacco farmers to get larger or give up will become greater as this decade progresses.

In addition to the technological changes in their production, both cotton and tobacco are affected by recurring surplus supplies. Cotton is under pressure from competition of synthetic fibers. The price of synthetics such as rayon and nylon has been greatly reduced and there are many uses for which manufacturers can switch between cotton and synthetics, depending on prices. If the Government price support should be cut further, many of the higher-cost farmers concentrated in the Southeast could not grow cotton at a profit. There is almost no prospect of an increase in acreage allotments—most of which are now very small among Negroes—and always the threat of a loss of Government support if the public and the Congress become impatient with the subsidy burden.

In the case of tobacco, the finding by the Public Health Service that cigarette smoking is a health hazard has raised questions about the long-term future of the tobacco production. Per capita consumption has fallen, at least temporarily, and it seems likely that educational programs discouraging smoking will be directed at the public until such time as (and if) research can devise a benign cigarette. In addition, the quality of American cigarette tobacco has fallen in recent years from several reasons and the vital export market has been endangered. Owing to a build-up in supplies, the acreage farmers were permitted to raise of the principal cigarette tobaccos was cut by over 20 percent from 1963 to 1965.

Such are the effects of technological and related changes on the two crops that Negro farmers are most reliant on. Similar comments could be made about peanut farming.

The Effect of Rural Traditionalism in Racial Matters

As is evident from many sections of this chapter, the position and prospects of the Negro farmer cannot be divorced from the fact that he is almost entirely located in the South—and the inner part of the South at that. Within the South, the rural areas are for the most part more traditional and conservative in race relations than are the medium and large cities. The progress of the Negro in exercise of his civil rights, in desegregation or equalization of education, in the extension of social courtesies (the handshake, forms of address), in occupational opportunities, in interracial participation in civic life, and in public accommodations has been very limited in rural areas as compared with the cities.

Cowhig and Beale of the Department of Agriculture have shown that in most available measures of socio-economic status the already wide gaps between the white and nonwhite rural populations in the South have widened in recent years. This is true of income, proportion of young adults without a high school diploma, unemployment rate, proportion of workers in blue collar jobs, number of children born per women, proportion of young children living in households where the head is not their parent, proportion of people living in crowded housing and proportion living without hot and cold running water in the home. By contrast, in urban areas of the South there was some narrowing of the white-nonwhite gap in five of the measures mentioned.[4]

In rural communities it is easier for the white population to exercise informal and personal controls over the Negro population. The anonymity of large city populations is missing, as is the ease of organizing effective protest movements in the settled urban community. The low level of education and income in most rural areas is also a handicap. In addition, it is in rural counties that the Negro population most often constitutes a large segment of the population and thus poses a greater ultimate threat to the traditional structure of southern society. In such situations the white community feels less leeway in granting concessions and promoting change than is true tionin areas where Negroes are a smaller minority. The general racial conservatism of rural areas makes it difficult for Federal authorities—or even state authorities, if so inclined—to secure the impartial operation of Government-financed agricultural programs or economic development projects. By the nature of his occupation the farmer must carry on his business in the rural countryside, and in most instances live there as well. This is a basic handicap that the Southern Negro farmer seems destined to have to carry in comparison with his industrial or professionally-employed brother who can readily perform his occupation in the cities or in the North if he chooses.

The Status of Farming and Rural Life among Young People

Is it an exaggeration to suggest that the young Negro who goes into farming or farm work today is either a person with a great interest in agriculture and some resources to give promise of success, or else a person who is essentially indifferent in aspirations and social sensitivity? Undoubtedly the characterzation is oversimplified, but it would seem to have some truth. Observers in the South, both white and Negro, express the opinion that the propect of farming in the rural South has become emotionally unattractive to most rural Negro youth. It is urban and especially metropolitan life that has status. This attitude is not confined to Negroes. It is common among rural white youth as well. The image of agrarian life as the ideal and inherently best form of society, inherited from the Jeffersonian period, died a slow death, but research indicates that a large proportion of rural youth prefer to seek an urban life even without economic motivation. In the case of rural Negro youth in the South both the economic and social disadvantages of rural life are magnified, and the majority have been migrating away before they are twenty-five years old. This pattern has helped raise the average age of Negro farmers until the presently oncoming youth may, in turn, think of farm operation as an old man's job and a relic of an unpleasant past.

The Future Role of Negroes in American Agriculture

To be optimistic about the future of Negro farmers would be to disregard almost every facet of their past and present status and of the factors that impinge upon them. But then, the odds have always been against them even in the period when they reached their greatest number. The dissolution of their former concentration in farming was probably a precondition to the general advance of the race, so limiting were the semifeudal conditions of the rural South to social progress for the Negro.

The loss of one-half of all Negro farm operators in less than ten years (1950–59) impels the question of whether there is any future at all for them. Is the discussion in this chapter really an epilogue for a role that in fact has nearly vanished? To an extent—to a great extent—yes.

Of the 266,000 nonwhite farmers in the South in 1959, 44,000 (a sixth) were sixty-five years old and over and producing less than $2,500 of products for sale. They are essentially in retirement. Most of their farms have less than twenty acres of cropland and thus are not suitable as complete farms, although they might be useful as additions to other farms.

Another 130,000 farmers were classed as commercial but selling less than $5,000 of products a year. Few economists would give many of these much hope of becoming units capable of providing a decent income from farming alone, especially since two-thirds of them are tenant farms. About three thousand had one hundred or more days of off-farm work.

One-fourth of Southern nonwhite farmers (67,000) are small-scale operators who depend primarily on off-farm work (the "part-time" census class). Only half of them, however, have two hundred or more days of off-farm work per year and are thus employed on a relatively full-time basis.

Finally, there were somewhat less than 24,000 nonwhite southern farmers who produced and sold more than $5,000 of products. These men and their families would seem to be the core of the future potential of Negro farmers in commercial agriculture. But here again, less than one-third (7,000) own their land, and some of them who were tenants have undoubtedly already lost their lease or share arrangements since 1959.

In sum, there were in 1959 about 7,000 nonwhite owner operators with an adequate or marginally-adequate level of production, 3,000 owners with inadequate commercial production, but a fair amount of off-farm work, and 34,000 owners and renters who did not produce very much but had rather steady farm work. The sum of these groups (44,000) appears to be the total of the Negro farmers with a tangible expectation of obtaining a minimum adequate income from farming or a combination of farm and nonfarm work. They represent only 17 percent of the total number of Negro operators in 1959.

Perhaps others could successfully remain in farming or part-time farming if the land in the hands of small-scale owners could be combined through lease or purchase into larger units, or if Federal programs of assistance in land purchase could be made effective on a widespread basis for low-income landless farmers, or if additional nonfarm employment opportunities became available for rural Negroes.

Negro farm owners have about 4.7 million acres of land, but 2.0 million acres of it is in the hands of elderly and part-time noncommercial farmers, who are cultivating only half of their crop land. If more of this decidedly underused 2.0 million acres were channeled into the hands of aspiring tenants or commercial owners, as many as 10,000 additional commercial Negro farmers might have a reasonable chance for survival. But the trend has been for a decline in Negro-owned farm land, while the total of land in white-owned farms has been stable.

In addition to the groups mentioned, who in our judgment probably represent the maximum future potential number of Negro farm operators earning an acceptable income from all sources, there are other families who will remain in farming at the poverty level. Their numbers are diminishing rapidly, however.

A major effort by the Department of Agriculture to provide access to its programs impartially by all is basic to any successful future for Negro farmers as a class. Beyond impartial access it is necessary to schedule particular attention to the situation of Negro farmers to help offset the all too obvious effects of years of indifference to their problems.

Fortunately the passage of the Civil Rights Act of 1964 gives the Government the leverage as well as the obligation to act to remedy many of the prevailing conditions of Negro farmers' inadequate access to Federal programs. Shortly after the passage of the act, Secretary of Agriculture Orville Freeman called some 250 administrative officials of the Department of Agriculture to Washington to discuss those sections of the act affecting the department's work. In an uncompromisingly firm statement, Freeman said that ". . . there will be no delays in eliminating discrimination where it exists within the agencies of the Department; and . . . in the operation of any program carried out by the Department." "The time to put this legislation in effect is now," he said, "not tomorrow—or next week—or soon—but today."

Simultaneously, the U. S. Commission on Civil Rights was engaged in a long investigation of discrimination in the programs of the Department of Agriculture. Its report, issued in February 1965, was very critical of many conditions. The Commission concluded that ". . . the Department has generally failed to assume responsibility for assuring equal opportunity and equal treatment to all those entitled to benefit from its programs. Instead, the prevailing practice has been to follow local patterns of racial segregation and discrimination in providing assistance paid for by Federal funds."[5] The Commission recommended to the President an end to discriminatory practices, encouragement of full participation by Negroes in agricultural programs, and equal employment opportunities in programs.

The potential benefits for Negro farmers of the Civil Rights Act and the investigative report of the Commission on Civil Rights are great. But if the widespread and long entrenched disadvantages under which Negro farmers operate are not very soon corrected, Negro farmers may well disappear as a significant group in American agriculture before the end of the twentieth century. Here and there a number of fortunate and persistent operators would undoubtedly remain, but the presently high emigration rate of Negro farm people indicates that a continuation of present conditions is inimical to their general survival as farmers.

Paradoxically, the prospects for the future continuance of Negroes in hired farm work are high. Whereas in operation of a farm the race is being won by the strong who have the capital and organization to survive in modern agriculture, in hired farm work the race is being left to the weak.

TABLE X—Rural Negro Population in the United States, by Farm-Nonfarm
Residence, 1920–1963

Year	Population		
	Total rural	Rural nonfarm	Rural farm
	Thou.	Thou.	Thou.
1920	6,903.7	1,803.7	5,100.0
1930	6,697.2	2,016.7	4,680.5
1940	6,611.9	2,109.6	4,502.3
1950*	5,649.7	2,491.4	3,158.3
1960**			
Census	5,056.7	3,574.7	1.482.0
Revised	5,056.7	2,666.7	2,390.0
1963**	—	—	1,730.0

* The definition of rural was made more restrictive in 1950 than formerly, accounting for about 500,000 of the total rural decline from 1940–50.

** The definition of farm residence was made more restrictive in 1960, and the 1960 census obtained a distinct undercount of the Negro farm population. The revised figure shown is a more accurate estimate based on the Current Population Survey of the Bureau of the Census. The estimate for 1963 is also based on the Current Population Survey.

SOURCE: U.S. Censuses of Population, 1930, 1940, 1950, 1960, and *Farm Population,* Series Census-ERS (P–27), No. 34, Bureau of the Census and Economic Research Service, April 1964.

Because of the relatively unattractive conditions of much farm work, hired farm workers are being drawn from an increasingly atypical section of society. Except for a minority of well-paid supervisory or technical jobs, regular farm wage work has largely become a residual occupation hiring those who from poor education, lack of vocational training, or other limitations cannot succeed as farmers or do better in nonagricultural jobs. In the South and in migratory farm work the Negro worker best fits this description.

Although the chances for the continued existence of a large number of Negro farm operators in the United States are problematical, the persistence of several million Negroes in rural areas seems certain in the foreseeable future, in part because of their continuance in farm wage work. The rural nonfarm Negro population has increased in every decade since 1920 when first counted. In 1960 there were an estimated 2,655,000 rural nonfarm Negroes [6] up more than 6 percent from 1950 (Table X). Well over 90 percent are in the South. In addition to those who are in agriculture as hired workers, many work in agriculturally related industries such as food processing, woodcutting, and the making of lumber and other wood products. Other thousands engage in a variety of manufacturing, construction or service jobs.

The total Negro rural population—farm and nonfarm—declined from 1950 to 1960 by nearly 600,000 because of the heavy loss of farm people. But because the declining farm population is now smaller than the rural-nonfarm population, relatively heavy farm losses are no longer large enough to greatly offset rural nonfarm gains. It is quite possible that the Negro rural population will not drop below 4,500,000 and could begin an increase after about 1970–75.

Thus, whatever the fate of Negro farm operators, the total rural Negro population is expected to remain a numerous element. Its current rate of social and economic progress is far behind that of the urban Negro population or of the white rural population. Its problems are somewhat peculiar to their setting, as many rural problems are. They merit the continued attention not only of the Federal Government but also of the predominantly urban Negro leadership.

NOTES

[1] Paul B. Foreman and Mozell C. Hill, *The Negro in the United States: A Bibliography*, Bulletin of the Oklahoma A & M College, 44, No. 5 (February, 1947), 4.

[2] Morton Rubin, *Plantation County* (Chapel Hill: University of North Carolina Press, 1951), p. 64.

[3] For an example of the expression of such an attitude, see J. Sullivan Gibson, "Alabama Black Belt: Its Geographic Status." *Economic Geography*, January 1941. Gibson declares, "The negro (sic) farmer of this section, by nature and experience, is a cotton grower." "Lacking good judgment, a sense of thrift, and a feeling of responsibility, the average Black Belt negro is decidely incompetent as a stock farmer" (pp. 21 and 22).

[4] James D. Cowhig and Calvin L. Beale, "Relative Socio-economic Status of Southern Whites and Nonwhites, 1950 and 1960." *Southwestern Social Science Quarterly*, 45 (September 1964), p. 113–24.

[5] *Equal Opportunity in Farm Programs—An Appraisal of Services Rendered by Agencies of the United States Department of Agriculture*, United States Commission on Civil Rights, Washington, 1965, p. 100.

[6] Revision of 1960 census figures of 3,575,000, to accord with a more accurate estimate of farm population from the Current Population Survey.

BIBLIOGRAPHY

A Study of Negro Farmers in South Carolina. Atlanta: Southern Regional Council, 1962.

Beale, Calvin L., *Negro Farm Operators: Number, Location, and Recent Trends.* Washington: Agricultural Marketing Service, U.S. Department of Agriculture, 1958.

"Color, Race and Tenure of Farm Operator," *U.S. Census of Agriculture: 1959.* Washington: U.S. Bureau of the Census, 1962, Vol. II, Chap. X.

Cowhig, James D., and Beale, Calvin L., "Socioeconomic Differences Between White and Nonwhite Farm Populations in the South." *Social Forces*, 42 (March 1964), 354–62.

—— "Relative Socio-economic Status of Southern Whites and Nonwhites, 1950 and 1960." *The Southwestern Social Science Quarterly*, 45 (September 1964), 113–24.

Equal Opportunity in Farm Programs —An Appraisal of Services Rendered by Agencies of the United States Department of Agriculture, Washington: United States Commission on Civil Rights, 1965.

Jones, Lewis W., ed., *The Changing Status of the Negro in Southern Agriculture*, Rural Life Information Series, Bulletin No. 3 (Alabama: Tuskegee Institute, 1950).

Land Tenure in the Southern Region —Proceedings of Professional Agricultural Workers Tenth Annual Conference. Alabama: Tuskegee Institute, 1951.

Neal, Ernest E., and Jones, Lewis W., "The Place of the Negro Farmer in the Changing Economy of the Cotton South." *Rural Sociology*, 15 (March 1950), 30–41.

Rubin, Morton, *Plantation County.* Chapel Hill: University of North Carolina Press, 1951.

Schuler, Edgar A., *Social Status and Farm Tenure—Attitudes and Social Conditions of Corn Belt and Cotton Belt Farmers.* (Social Research Report, No. IV.) Washington: Bureau of Agricultural Economics, U.S. Department of Agriculture, 1938.

"The American Farmer." *Population Bulletin.* Washington: Population Reference Bureau, May 1963.

Woodson, Carter G., *The Rural Negro.* Washington: The Association for the Study of Negro Life, 1930.

AN OIL WORKER. (U.S. Dept. of Labor Photo)

Eli Ginzberg
and Dale L. Hiestand

chapter 4

Employment Patterns

of Negro Men and Women

Eli Ginzberg. Professor of Economics, Graduate School of Business, Columbia University, New York, New York. Director, Conservation of Human Resources Project, Columbia University. Author of *The Uneducated, The Negro Potential, The Nation's Children* and other books.

Dale L. Hiestand. Assistant Professor of Business Economics, Graduate School of Business, Columbia University, New York, New York. Research Associate, Conservation of Human Resources Project, Columbia University. Author of *Economic Growth and Employment Opportunities for Minorities.*

In a democratic society, based primarily on private enterprise, the work that an individual does largely determines his income, his status and his way of life. Hence, a major dimension of the role of Negro men and women in American society and more particularly the changes in their position can best be obtained by studying their experiences in the realm of work. Among the key factors are the proportion of adults who are in the labor force; the proportions of those in the labor force who are employed or, alternatively, unemployed; their occupational status; and the wages or salaries which they earn. A group may be better or worse off depending on the proportion that are employed; the types of occupational skills and opportunities which they possess; and the wages which they are able to earn.

Minorities in the Labor Force

Negroes are only one of several minority groups in the labor force. Women, both white and nonwhite, are often viewed as a minority group in the labor force, both because they account for less than one-third of all persons in paid employment, and because they are subject to discrimination in employment. But the term *minority* is usually restricted to persons identified on the basis of race, religion, color, national origin, or other ethnic or cultural distinction. Formerly, Catholics were a minority group in certain regions and localities, but they are now so widespread and economically well off that they can no longer be so classified.

Negroes comprise the largest single minority group in the United States. As Table I shows, in 1960 there were 6.8 million Negroes in the total American labor force, compared with 4.2 million foreign-born whites, 1.1 million whites of Spanish descent in the Southwest, 326,000 of Puerto Rican birth or parentage and lesser numbers of Japanese, American Indian, Chinese, Filipino and other nonwhites. Exactly comparable data are not available for Jews but that which is available suggests that their number in the labor force reached nearly 2.5 million in 1960. Of course, many of the above groups overlap one another.

The Negro Labor Force

The labor force includes all who work for pay or profit, and all who are seeking paid work. It includes the self-employed and those who work in family businesses or family farms. It includes the employees of profit-seeking firms, nonprofit enterprises such as hospitals, unions and civic associations, and Federal, state and local governments. It also includes members of the Armed Forces. It includes those who work full time or part time. Finally, it includes the unemployed.

The best way to introduce the reader to a consideration of the employment status of the Negro is to trace the growth which has occurred in the numbers of Negroes in the labor force; and to follow this with an evaluation of the occupational fields in which they are concentrated. Later stages of the analysis can then center around the income which Negroes are able to earn and the extent to which they are able to find employment, particularly on a year-round basis.

There are two closely related concepts of the labor force: one refers to the civilian labor force and the other refers to the total labor force which includes, in addition to civilians, the approximately 3 million persons who are currently in the Armed Forces. In 1960 the total labor force amounted to 69.9 million, of which 6.8 million or just under 10 percent were Negroes. However, if the male and female components of the total labor force are differentiated, one finds that Negro men accounted for only 8.7 percent of the men, while Negro women accounted for 12.0 percent of all women workers.

The growth of the labor force is conditioned by a great many different factors, including the number of adults in the population; the conventions governing the ages at which they enter upon or withdraw from employment; the job opportunities that prevail; social attitudes toward the employment of special groups such as young people, married women, and old persons, and still other factors.

Since the beginning of the century (Table II) the white labor force has been growing more rapidly than the Negro labor force. Different forces in different decades can help to explain this trend. Up to the outbreak of World War I, the white labor force grew very rapidly, among other reasons because of the very heavy immigration which characterized those years. For twenty years more, the white labor force continued to have significant incremental gains because the offspring of these earlier immigrants were reaching working age. During most of these decades the proportion of Negroes shifting from rural to urban areas was greater than for whites, and incident to such a shift was later entrance into the labor force and earlier retirement in urban areas than on the farm. Also, more and more white women tended, especially after 1940, to return to work in middle age. Although the Negro birth rate was rising more rapidly and the Negro death rate was falling more rapidly than the corresponding white rates, the above factors operating to accelerate the growth of the white labor force overbalanced the population factors that were increasing the size of the Negro labor force. Since 1950, however, the Negro labor force has been growing slightly more rapidly than white, primarily because during the 1930's and 1940's the reproduction rate was higher and increased more rapidly among Negroes than whites.

TABLE I—Various Minority Groups in the Labor Force, by Sex, 1960

	Total	Male	Female
Negro	6,806,968	4,116,194	2,690,774
Foreign-born white	4,159,006	2,869,060	1,289,946
Spanish-surname white *	1,114,688	819,271	295,417
Puerto Rican birth or parentage**	325,523	222,883	102,640
Japanese	202,405	125,239	77,166
American Indian	138,692	97,197	41,495
Chinese	104,368	75,805	28,563
Filipino	83,955	69,800	14,155

* In five Southwestern states.

** Includes less than 4 percent nonwhites; also includes some Spanish-surname whites in five Southwestern states, probably less than 5 percent.

SOURCE: U.S. Bureau of the Census, U.S. Census of Population, 1960: *Nonwhite Population by Race*, Tables 32–36; *Persons of Spanish Surname*, Table 6; *Puerto Ricans in the United States*, Table 5; *Employment Status and Work Experience*, Table 3.

TABLE II—Percentage Change in Labor Force, by Decades, by Sex and Race, 1890–1960

	1890 to 1900	1900 to 1910	1910 to 1920	1920 to 1930	1930 to 1940	1940 to 1950	1950 to 1960
Total labor force	25	29	14	15	7	14	16
White	24	30	15	16	8	14	15
Negro	30	19	6	9	−3	9	18
Male labor force	23	26	13	13	4	9	8
White	22	27	13	13	4	9	8
Negro	27	17	9	7	−4	7	10
Female labor force	33	40	16	24	17	29	35
White	32	46	20	27	21	31	35
Negro	36	22	1	13	−3	13	37

SOURCE: Based on data in U.S. Bureau of the Census, Census of Population: 1910, Vol 1V, *Occupation Statistics*, Table 15; *Negro Population, 1790–1915*, Table 3; *A Social-Economic Grouping of the Gainful Workers of the United States*, Tables 3 and 4; U.S. Census of Population: 1950, *U.S. Summary, Detailed Characteristics*, Table 195.

TABLE III—Negro and White Labor Forces, Urban and Rural, by Sex, 1960

	Percent Distribution	
	Negro	White
Urban total	78.4	72.2
Male	75.6	69.9
Female	82.8	77.2
Rural total	21.6	27.8
Male	24.4	30.1
Female	17.2	22.8
Total U.S.	100.0	100.0
Male	100.0	100.0
Female	100.0	100.0

SOURCE: U.S. Bureau of the Census, Census of Population: 1960, *United States Summary, Detailed Characteristics*, Table 194; *Nonwhite Population by Race*, Table 32.

The regional distribution of the Negro labor force has followed the population distribution set out in Chapter 2. As late as 1910 almost 90 percent of the Negro labor force continued to be concentrated in the South. World War I gave a substantial impetus to the northward migration of the Negro which had been underway since even before the Civil War. The 1920's saw a continuation of this trend, though at a reduced rate, and the same was true for the depressed 1930's. While there were no great numbers of jobs opening up for Negroes in the North between 1920 and 1940, the depressed status of Southern agriculture pushed many Negroes off the farm and many felt they were better off in the North, even if they had no more to look forward to than menial employment or a job on work relief. World War II ushered in an accelerated shift of the Negro labor force out of the South, both to the North and to the West. This continued after hostilities came to an end. By 1960 more than four out of every ten Negroes were employed outside of the South.

These gross movements mask some important additional shifts that took place. Many Negroes who left the South for the North and West did so as a result of a two-staged move. First they moved off a Southern farm into a Southern city; and only later, after they had become somewhat acclimated to urban ways, did they relocate outside of the South, again in urban centers. In fact, the Negro has tended both in the South and outside of the South to be disproportionately heavily represented in a selected number of large cities.

By 1960 the Negro population was more urbanized than the white population, more than three of every four Negroes being an urbanite (Table III).

TABLE IV—Occupations of Employed Negroes by Sex, 1960

	Number			Percent distribution		
	Total	Male	Female	Total	Male	Female
Total employed Negroes	6,099,089	3,643,949	2,455,140	100.0	100.0	100.0
Professional, technical, etc.	287,969	112,661	175,308	4.7	3.0	7.1
Managers, officers and proprietors, exc. farm	87,950	63,193	24,757	1.4	1.7	1.0
Clerical	360,598	178,920	181,678	5.9	4.9	7.4
Sales	82,768	46,685	36,083	1.4	1.3	1.5
Craftsmen, foremen, etc.	372,463	356,586	15,877	6.1	9.8	0.6
Operatives	1,197,667	887,434	310,233	19.6	24.4	12.6
Private household workers	915,494	27,288	888,206	15.0	0.7	36.2
Service, exc. pvt. hshld.	1,027,765	507,942	519,823	16.9	13.9	21.2
Laborers, exc. farm and mine	768,621	744,994	23,627	12.6	20.4	1.0
Farmers and farm managers	168,776	154,240	14,536	2.8	3.0	0.7
Farm laborers and foremen	326,193	256,698	69,495	5.3	7.0	2.8
Occupation not reported	502,825	307,308	195,517	8.2	8.4	8.0

SOURCE: U.S. Bureau of the Census, Census of Population: 1960, *United States Summary, Detailed Characteristics*, Table 205.

TABLE V—Occupations Employing Large Numbers of Negro Men, 1960

	Number	Percent of all employed Negro men
Janitors and porters	265,339	7.3
Truck drivers and deliverymen	248,276	6.8
Farm laborers, except unpaid, and farm foremen	237,108	6.5
Laborers (n.e.c.), construction	157,724	4.3
Lumbermen, raftsmen and wood choppers	111,603	3.0
Laborers (n.e.c.), wholesale and retail trade	56,881	1.6
Operatives (n.e.c.), food and kindred products mfg.	44,369	1.2
Automobile mechanics and repairmen	44,272	1.2
Laborers (n.e.c.), primary metal industries	44,113	1.2
Cooks, except pvt. household	42,998	1.2
Waiters, bartenders and counter workers	37,527	1.0

SOURCE: Same as for Table IV

TOBACCO WAREHOUSE WORKERS. (Standard Oil of N.J. Photo)

While a few Negroes joined the white rush to the suburbs during the 1950's, most of them remained locked in the central city, where they found it somewhat easier to secure, in the face of serious privation, at least the minimum housing which they required. Today the Negro labor force is more heavily concentrated than the white labor force in the larger cities of the South and the North.

The occupations that individuals pursue are determined by a variety of forces, including in particular the education and training which they have undergone, the job openings that exist in the communities where they grow up or to which they relocate and the extent to which their access to better jobs is facilitated or retarded by special forces, including such matters as segregation practices and discrimination. Conventionally, the occupational structure is viewed as a 10-stage hierarchy, from professional and related occupations at the top to laborers and farm workers at the bottom. Although some farmers do quite well, most have relatively low incomes, and they therefore may be classified at the bottom with farm laborers. It is also conventional to distinguish between white collar workers, including professional, managerial, clerical and sales workers, and blue collar workers, including craftsmen, operatives, laborers and service workers. Although there are a great many exceptions, the higher the proportion of a group in the white collar occupations at the top of the scale, the better their jobs, incomes, and status. The reverse is true for concentrations at the bottom of the hierarchy.

The Occupational Structure of the Negro Labor Force

The Negro labor force is substantially concentrated in the semiskilled, unskilled, service and farm occupations. This is true for both men and women. As Table IV indicates, over 70 percent of both Negro men and women are in these occupations. Among Negro men, one in four is an operative—typically a semiskilled worker in manufacturing or a truck driver—one in five a laborer, one in seven a service worker, one in ten a craftsman or foreman and another in ten a farm operator or worker. As Table V shows, one quarter of a million Negro men are employed as janitors and porters and another quarter million are truck drivers and deliverymen. Of the eleven largest occupations for Negro males, only one, automobile mechanics and repairmen, is above the semiskilled level.

Although Negroes comprise only 8.4 percent of total male employment, they comprise a far higher proportion in many occupations at the lower end of the scale, where skill, income and prestige are low. As Table VI shows, Negroes comprise one fourth or more of all male employees among janitors, longshoremen, laundry and dry cleaning operatives, and laborers in many industries. Other fields in which Negro men comprise a relatively high share of the male employees include various foundry occupations such as furnacemen and metal molders, plaster and cement finishers, elevator operators, taxicab drivers and chauffeurs, and operatives in sawmills, motor vehicle manufacturing and diverse other industries.

Among the higher ranking occupations, one third of all Negro men in the professional and technical occupations are teachers or clergymen (Table VII). Since many clergymen are not graduates of theological institutions and many lead very small congregations, their occupational status does not

TABLE VI—Occupations in Which a Large Percentage of the Male Employees Were Negro, 1960

Occupation	Negro men as a percent of all men
Private household workers	44.7
Janitors and porters	37.2
Laborers (n.e.c.), not specified mfg. industries	35.1
Longshoremen and stevedores	34.5
Laundry and dry cleaning operatives	33.3
Laborers (n.e.c.), misc. nonmanufacturing industries	31.2
Lumbermen, raftsmen and woodchoppers	30.8
Laborers (n.e.c.), communications, and utility and sanitary service	30.7
Laborers (n.e.c.), chemicals and allied products	30.2
Laborers, furniture, saw and planing mills, and misc. wood products	30.0
Laborers (n.e.c.) transportation equipment mfg.	27.9
Laborers (n.e.c.) railroads and railway express	27.8
Laborers (n.e.c.), primary metal mfg.	26.4
Laborers (n.e.c.), construction	25.9
Misc. specified laborers	23.7
Furnacemen, smeltermen and pourers	22.8
Laborers (n.e.c.) textile mill products and apparel mfg.	22.7
Farm laborers, exc. unpaid, and farm foremen	22.7
Molders, metal	22.3
Misc. service workers, exc. private household	22.1
Laborers (n.e.c.), food and kindred products mfg.	21.8
Plasterers and cement finishers	21.7
Cooks, except private household	21.5
Elevator operators	21.4
Laborers (n.e.c.), transportation, except railroad	21.0
Laborers (n.e.c.), stone, clay, and glass products	19.7
Operatives (n.e.c.), saw and planing mills and misc. wood products	18.8
Taxicab drivers and chauffeurs	18.3
Laborers (n.e.c.), fabricated metal industries	18.0
Laborers (n.e.c.), wholesale and retail trade	17.9
Sawyers	17.8
Operatives (n.e.c.), wholesale and retail trade	17.2
Packers and wrappers (n.e.c.)	15.4
Operatives (n.e.c.), primary metal mfg.	15.0
Operatives (n.e.c.), food and kindred products mfg.	14.7
Operatives (n.e.c.), misc. nonmfg. industries	14.7
Operatives (n.e.c.), motor vehicles and motor vehicles equipment mfg.	14.0
Laborers (n.e.c.), machinery mfg., including electrical	13.4
Truck drivers and deliverymen	12.7
Farm laborers, unpaid family workers	12.6
Stationary firemen	12.3
Waiters, bartenders, and counter workers	12.2
Shoemakers and repairmen, exc. factory	12.1
Operatives (n.e.c.), transport, commun., and other public utility	11.5
Masons, tile setters, and stone cutters	11.4
Sailors and deck hands	10.5
Mail carriers	10.4
Painters, exc. construction and maintenance	10.3
Operatives (n.e.c.), stone, clay and glass products mfg.	10.2
Bus drivers	10.1

SOURCE: Same as for Table IV

carry with it the usual prerequisites of such employment. Nearly four out of ten Negro male managers and proprietors are in wholesale and retail trade, primarily in eating and drinking places and food and dairy products stores. The latter stores also employ one in five Negro male sales workers. Clearly these are small establishments where the sales volume permits at best a relatively small net profit and correspondingly relatively small salaries. Over half of all Negro male clerical workers are postal clerks, shipping and receiving clerks, stock clerks, storekeepers, and mailmen.

Negro women are even more strongly concentrated in a few lower level jobs than are Negro men (Table IV). Seventy percent are in the two fields of service workers and operatives. Fully one third of all employed Negro women, or 848,000, were employed as private household workers in 1960 (Table VIII). Other leading occupations at the semiskilled and service

TABLE VII—Occupations Employing 10 Percent or more of the Negro Men within each Occupational Group, 1960

Occupation	Number	Percent distribution within group
Professional, technical and kindred	**112,661**	**100.0**
Teachers		
secondary	14,823	13.1
elementary	13,451	11.9
Clergymen	13,955	12.4
Managers, officials, & prop. exc. farm	**63,193**	**100.0**
Wholesale and retail trade		
Self-employed	17,791	28.2
Salaried	6,373	10.0
Clerical and kindred workers	**178,920**	**100.0**
Postal clerks	*	16.5
Shipping and receiving clerks		
Stock clerks and storekeepers	*	14.4
Mail carriers	20,050	11.2
Salesworkers	**46,685**	**100.0**
Retail trade—food and dairy products	*	20.2
Newsboys		
Insurance agents, brokers, underwriters	4,901	10.5
Hucksters and peddlers	*	10.3
Craftsmen, foremen and kindred	**356,586**	**100.0**
Carpenters	35,830	10.0
Automobile mechanics and repairmen	44,272	12.4
Operatives and kindred	**887,434**	**100.0**
Truck drivers and deliverymen	248,276	28.0
Service workers, exc. pvt. hshld.	**507,942**	**100.0**
Janitors and porters	265,339	52.2
Laborers, except farm & mine	**744,994**	**100.0**
Laborers (n.e.c.), construction	157,724	21.2
Lumbermen, raftsmen, and woodchoppers	35,870	4.8

* Actual count not available; percentage estimated from sample data.

SOURCE: U.S. Bureau of the Census, Census of Population: 1960, *United States Summary, Detailed Characteristics,* Table 205; *Occupational Characteristics,* Table 3.

EMPLOYMENT PATTERNS OF NEGRO MEN AND WOMEN 217

TABLE VIII—Occupations Employing Large Numbers of Negro Women, 1960

Occupation	Number	As percent of all employed Negro women
Private household workers, living out	848,334	34.6
Laundry and dry cleaning operatives	99,494	4.0
Cooks, except private household	80,980	3.3
Teachers: elementary school	75,695	3.1
Attendants, hospital and other institutions	66,997	2.7
Farm laborers, exc. unpaid and farm foremen	57,647	2.3
Waitresses, counter workers, etc.	54,123	2.2
Charwomen, janitors and porters	50,655	2.1
Operatives (n.e.c.), apparel and other fabricated textile products mfg.	34,550	1.4
Practical nurses and midwives	32,192	1.3
Nurses, professional	32,034	1.3
Hairdressers and cosmotologists	31,918	1.3
Saleswomen and sales clerks (n.e.c.), retail trade	28,691	1.2
Typists	27,142	1.1

SOURCE: Same as for Table IV

TABLE IX—Occupations in which a Large Percentage of the Female Employees Were Negro, 1960

Occupation	Negro women as a percent of all women
Private household workers	53.4
Farm laborers, exc. unpaid, and farm foremen	48.1
Laundry and dry cleaning operatives	35.9
Charwomen, janitors, and porters	25.0
Attendants, hospital and other institutions	23.2
Cooks, except private household	22.4
Operatives (n.e.c.), nonmanufacturing	17.9
Practical nurses and midwives	16.3
Operatives (n.e.c.), food and kindred products mfg.	16.0

SOURCE: Same as for Table IV

level include laundry and dry cleaning operatives, cooks, hospital attendants, waitresses, and charwomen. In contrast to the men, however, a substantially larger proportion of Negro women are in more desirable jobs, such as elementary school teacher, nurse, hairdresser or cosmetologist, sales clerk and typist.

Among all female workers, Negro women thus comprise half or more of the domestics and paid farm workers, one fourth or more of the laundry and dry cleaning operatives and charwomen, and one fifth of the cooks and institutional attendants (Table IX). Fully half of the Negro women in the professional and technical occupations are school teachers, and half of those who are managers and proprietors are in wholesale and retail trade (Table X). Negro women in managerial and sales positions are primarily in food and dairy products stores, as are Negro men. These white collar jobs do not necessarily carry high earnings or high prestige. Substantial numbers of Negro women clerical workers, whether typists, secretaries or in miscellaneous other fields, are governmental employees.

If the occupational distribution of the Negro male population is studied on a regional basis one does not find any striking variations from one region to another (Tables XI and XII). The major difference is that in the South about 17 percent of the men are still in farming compared to less than three percent in the Northeast, North Central and Western regions. Also, 24 percent of all Negro male workers in the South are laborers, compared with 15 to 18 percent in the three other regions. The South does not differ strikingly from the other regions in terms of the proportion of Negro men employed in the operative, professional, proprietary or sales categories. The South does employ relatively fewer Negroes than all the other regions in service, skilled and clerical occupations. However, only in the clerical field

TABLE X—Occupations Employing 10 percent or More of the Negro Women within each Occupational Group, 1960

Occupation	Number	Percent distribution within group
Professional, technical and kindred	**175,308**	**100.0**
Teachers		
elementary school	75,695	43.1
secondary school	18,194	10.4
Mgrs., officials and prop., exc. farm	**24,757**	**100.0**
Wholesale and retail trade		
self-employed	10,023	40.5
salaried	2,831	11.4
Clerical and kindred	**181,678**	**100.0**
Typists	27,142	15.0
Clerical and kindred workers (n.e.c.),		
public administration	*	12.9
Secretaries	20,650	11.4
Sales workers	**36,083**	**100.0**
Retail trade	28,691	79.5
Food and dairy prod. stores	*	22.7
General mdse.	*	19.4
Apparel and accessories	*	11.1
Operatives	**310,233**	**100.0**
Laundry and dry cleaning	99,494	32.0
Apparel and other fabricated textile products	34,550	11.1
Service, exc. pvt. household	**519,823**	**100.0**
Cooks, except pvt. hshld.	80,980	15.6
Chambermaids and maids, exc. pvt. hshld.	*	19.1
Attendants, hospital and other institutions	66,997	12.9
Waitresses, bartenders and counter workers	54,123	10.4

* Actual count not available; percentage estimated from sample data.

SOURCE: Same as for Table VII

is the discrepancy relatively marked. There are fewer Negro men employed in the South in this field than in other regions.

The differences among the regions are more marked in the case of the employment patterns for Negro women. Although nearly 5 percent of employed Negro women in the South are in farming, compared to almost none in the other regions, this is but one of the sharp contrasts that exist between the South and the rest of the country. Marked discrepancies occur in the area of clerical work, in which only 4 percent of the Negro women in the South, but 13 percent in the other regions, are employed; in the operatives category, in which less than 9 percent are employed in the South, but from 13 to 22 percent in the other regions; and in private household service, which accounts for roughly 25 percent of the Negro women in the Northeast, North Central and West, but as much as 45 percent in the South.

On the other hand, the South is in some regards much like the other regions. For instance, relatively few Negro women in the South, as elsewhere, are sales workers, business managers and proprietors, craftsmen and foremen, and unskilled laborers. Both in the South and elsewhere a substantial proportion are employed in nonhousehold service work (18 to 26 percent) and in the professions (6 to 8 percent).

TABLE XI—Occupations of Employed Negroes, by Sex, for Regions, 1960

	Northeast	North Central	South	West
Total males	**638,866**	**678,393**	**2,118,185**	**208,505**
Professional, technical, etc.	23,256	20,595	59,429	9.381
Managers, offs. & prop. except farm	17,035	12,144	29,155	4,859
Clerical	56,946	45,913	61,062	14,999
Sales	12,456	10,568	20,176	3,485
Craftsmen, foremen, etc.	73,272	74,954	181,516	26,844
Operatives	174,359	196,646	472,752	43,677
Private household workers	5,347	3,515	17,184	1,242
Service, exc. pvt. hshld.	99,847	101,757	269,288	37,050
Laborers, exc. farm & mine	97,206	119,689	490,102	37,997
Farmers and farm mgrs.	698	1,580	151,014	948
Farm laborers & foremen	4,982	4,596	242,309	4,811
Occupation not reported	73,462	86,436	124,198	23,212
Total females	**486,506**	**414,098**	**1,414,932**	**139,604**
Professional, technical, etc.	31,192	28,147	105,458	10,511
Managers, offs. & prop. except farm	4,377	4,623	13,967	1,790
Clerical	61,222	51,797	50,110	18,549
Sales	10,526	8,900	14,344	2,313
Craftsmen, foremen, etc.	4,684	3,795	6,082	1,316
Operatives	108,146	62,460	120,943	18,684
Private household workers	120,524	91,370	637,273	39,039
Service, exc. pvt. hshld.	87,323	106,078	295,094	31,328
Laborers, exc. farm & mine	3,670	5,658	12,865	1,434
Farmers and farm mgrs.	65	118	14,312	41
Farm laborers & foremen	738	653	67,536	568
Occupation not reported	54,039	50,499	76,948	14,031

SOURCE: U.S. Bureau of the Census, Census of Population: 1960, *United States Summary, Detailed Characteristics*, Table 257.

TABLE XII—Percentage Distribution of Employed Negroes by Sex and Occupation, for Regions, 1960

	Northeast	North Central	South	West
Total males	100.0	100.0	100.0	100.0
Professional, technical, etc.	3.6	3.0	2.8	4.5
Managers, offs. & prop. exc. farm	2.7	1.8	1.4	2.3
Clerical	8.9	6.8	2.9	7.2
Sales	1.9	1.6	1.0	1.7
Craftsmen, foremen, etc.	11.5	11.0	8.6	12.9
Operatives	27.3	29.0	22.3	20.9
Private household workers	0.8	0.5	0.8	0.6
Service, exc. pvt. hshld.	15.6	15.0	12.7	17.8
Laborers, exc. farm & mine	15.2	17.6	23.1	18.2
Farmers and farm mgrs.	0.1	0.2	7.1	0.5
Farm laborers & foremen	0.8	0.7	11.4	2.3
Occupation not reported	11.5	12.7	5.9	11.1
Total females	100.0	100.0	100.0	100.0
Professional, technical, etc.	6.4	6.8	7.5	7.5
Managers, offs. & props. exc. farm	0.9	1.1	1.0	1.3
Clerical	12.6	12.5	3.5	13.3
Sales	2.2	2.1	1.0	1.7
Craftsmen, foremen, etc.	1.0	0.9	0.4	0.9
Operatives	22.2	15.0	8.5	13.4
Private household workers	24.8	22.0	45.0	28.0
Service, exc. pvt. hshld.	17.9	25.6	21.0	22.4
Laborers, exc. farm & mine	0.8	1.4	0.9	1.0
Farmers and farm mgrs.	0.0	0.0	1.0	0.0
Farm laborers & foremen	0.2	0.2	4.8	0.4
Occupation not reported	11.1	12.2	5.4	10.0

SOURCE: Same as for Table XI

There is a widespread but erroneous notion that there are deeply ingrained patterns of Negro employment which prevail for long periods of time in different regions of the country. Even in the South, however, study after study has revealed that while a general pattern could be discerned, significant exceptions existed in almost every community. Moreover, the general patterns can best be described in terms of the gross proportions of Negroes in the major occupational fields and industries, for considerable variability within the general patterns can be discerned. For instance, while it is true that the proportion of Negro women among operatives in the South is relatively small, there are localities where their proportion is very large. Moreover, while certain industries may have very few such operatives, other industries may have a substantial number.

Occupational Trends

There is a tendency for occupational trends to shift relatively slowly. This reflects the fact that the technological and economic factors in the several sectors of the economy, the geographical distribution of various population groups and the educational, political and social factors that affect their

TABLE XIII—Occupational Distribution of Negro Workers, by Region, 1940, 1950, and 1960

	South			Other Regions		
	1940	1950	1960	1940	1950	1960
Total Negro male employment *	100.0	100.0	100.0	100.0	100.0	100.0
Professional, technical and kindred	1.6	2.0	3.0	3.1	2.6	4.0
Managers, officials and proprietors	0.9	1.4	1.5	2.8	3.0	2.5
Clerical and sales	1.2	2.4	4.1	5.6	7.8	11.0
Craftsmen and foremen	3.6	6.4	9.1	7.7	10.8	13.0
Operatives	10.9	18.6	23.7	19.6	27.4	30.8
Service	11.2	11.2	14.4	32.6	21.4	18.5
Nonfarm laborers	20.6	23.6	24.6	24.5	24.9	18.9
Total nonfarm	50.0	65.6	80.3	95.9	97.9	98.8
Farmers and farm workers	50.0	34.4	19.7	4.1	2.1	1.2
Total Negro female employment *	100.0	100.0	100.0	100.0	100.0	100.0
Professional, technical and kindred	4.4	6.3	7.9	3.7	4.6	7.6
Managers, officials and proprietors	0.6	1.3	1.0	1.1	1.4	1.2
Clerical and sales	0.9	3.5	4.8	3.0	9.0	16.7
Craftsmen and foremen	0.1	0.4	0.4	0.3	1.1	1.0
Operatives	5.0	9.5	9.0	10.6	24.7	20.5
Service workers, private household	58.8	45.4	47.6	64.4	35.8	27.2
Other service workers	8.9	18.2	22.0	15.9	20.9	24.4
Nonfarm laborers	0.9	1.2	1.0	0.8	2.1	1.2
Total nonfarm	79.6	85.8	93.9	99.8	99.6	99.8
Farmers and farm workers	20.4	14.2	6.1	0.2	0.4	0.2

* Those for whom no occupation was reported are distributed proportionately among the occupational groups.

SOURCE: Eli Ginzberg, *The Negro Potential,* New York, Columbia University Press, 1956, pp. 23 and 28.

access to various occupations are all likely to change relatively slowly. In reviewing the occupational trends of the Negro population since the outbreak of World War II, one finds both relative stability and substantial changes. For instance, in 1940 as in 1960 the major difference between the South and the North lay in the heavier concentration of Negro males in farming in the South. At that time, as Table 13 shows, 50 percent of all Negro men in the South were in farming, 11 percent were in service occupations and another 11 percent were operatives, whereas in the rest of the country only 4 percent were in farming, but 20 percent were operatives, and 33 percent were in service occupations. However, in the years intervening, the Southern Negro male labor force has been shifting out of farming primarily in the direction of semiskilled and skilled work. In the North, the more important trends have been the decline in the relative importance of service and unskilled labor and the increased importance of semiskilled, skilled and clerical work. On the other hand the relative importance of the professions and management has changed very little, although such changes as have occurred have been more pronounced in the South than in the rest of the country.

Over the last two decades, there have not been striking changes in the occupational distribution of Negro women in the South. During the 1940's, there was a substantial reduction in the proportions employed as private household workers and to a lesser extent on farms. The major growth areas were among nonhousehold service occupations and semiskilled operatives. In the 1950's, a major decline occurred in farm occupations, with minor growth in service employment. Over both decades, there were also significant although not large increases in the proportion of Negro women in the South employed in professional, clerical and sales occupations.

The shifts in the occupational distribution of Negro women in the rest of the country were somewhat more dramatic. The proportion employed as domestics declined from 64 to 36 percent between 1940 and 1950, and declined further, down to 27 percent, by 1960. The major increase was a growth from 3 to 17 percent in clerical and sales work. The proportion employed as operatives first increased dramatically from 11 to 25 percent, but then declined to 17 percent. There were more sustained increases in the proportion employed as service workers other than in households and in professional and related fields.

The continuing shift of the Negro population from the Southern farm to the Southern city and to the urban centers in the North and West, as well as the continuing improvement of their occupational position within each region, has profoundly altered their overall occupational distribution. Each improvement in the position of the Negro lays the basis for further gains. As the incomes of Negroes have grown, opportunities in Negro owned businesses have increased. Improvements in the political and economic position of the Negro in both the South and the North have facilitated his increased employment in government. The result has been a fairly steady and long-run upgrading in the total Negro labor force.

As Table XIV shows, in 1910 half of the Negro labor force was in

TABLE XIV—Percent Distribution of White and Negro Employed by Occupational Fields, 1910–1960

	1910		1920		1930		1940		1950		1960	
	White	Negro	White	Negro	White	Negro	White	Negro	White	Negro	White	Negro
All sectors	100.0	100.0	100.0	100.0	100.0	100.0	100.0*	100.0*	100.0*	100.0*	100.0*	100.0*
Nonfarm, total	72.0	49.6	76.0	53.4	80.6	63.9	82.3	66.6	81.6	79.5	89.6	83.6
White collar sector, total	23.8	3.0	27.8	3.6	33.0	4.6	35.7	6.0	39.9	10.2	44.1	13.4
Professional & tech.	4.8	1.4	5.3	1.5	6.5	2.1	8.0	2.7	8.6	3.4	11.9	4.7
Props., mgrs. & offcls.	7.4	0.8	7.4	0.8	8.3	1.0	9.0	1.3	9.8	2.0	9.1	1.4
Clerical & sales	11.6	0.8	15.1	1.3	18.2	1.5	18.7	2.0	21.5	4.8	23.1	7.3
Manual & service sector	48.2	46.6	48.2	49.8	47.6	59.3	46.6	60.6	47.7	69.3	45.5	70.3
Skilled	13.0	2.5	14.5	3.0	14.2	3.2	12.2	3.0	14.4	5.5	14.3	6.1
Semiskilled & operative	16.1	5.4	16.8	7.3	17.2	9.4	19.0	10.3	20.3	18.3	18.3	19.6
Laborers	14.3	17.4	13.4	20.8	11.7	21.6	6.1	14.3	5.0	15.7	4.0	12.6
Service	4.8	21.3	3.5	18.7	4.5	25.1	9.3	33.0	8.0	29.8	8.9	31.9
Farm, total	28.0	50.4	24.1	46.6	19.4	36.1	16.7	32.8	11.1	19.0	5.9	8.1

* Sum of items does not equal 100.0 because of those for whom no occupation was reported.

SOURCE: Dale L. Hiestand, *Economic Growth and Employment Opportunities for Minorities*, New York, Columbia University Press, 1964, p. 42 and U. S. Bureau of the Census, *Census of Population: 1960, U. S. Summary, Detailed Characteristics*, Table 205.

DRAFTSMEN. (U.S. Dept. of Labor Photo)

ACCOUNTING SUPERVISOR. (Ohio Bell Telephone Photo)

farming, as compared to only 28 percent of the white labor force. This discrepancy no longer prevails, for only 7 percent of the white labor force and 11 percent of the Negro labor force were in farming in 1960. As the white labor force transferred out of farming, its major growth area was in white collar work. The proportion of the white labor force in manual and service work has remained remarkably stable since 1910 at almost 50 percent. In contrast, as the Negro labor force shifted out of farming, it went until 1940 almost wholly into manual and service work. Since then, the shift has been evenly divided, with white collar work being as important as manual and service. Over the decades, the proportion of the Negro labor force in manual and service work has increased from 47 to 73 percent, while the proportion in white collar work has increased from 3 to 15 percent.

Each decade is more or less unique in terms of the major occupational opportunities which open up to Negroes. Between 1910 and 1920, for instance, Negroes found substantial opportunities in unskilled labor but also made a sizeable breakthrough into semiskilled work. The 1920's were noted chiefly for substantial withdrawals from Southern agriculture to service work, but also saw a significant expansion in semiskilled employment. The depression of the 1930's hit Negroes severely as job opportunities declined severely even in such traditional fields as service and unskilled labor. As a result not only did total Negro employment decline between 1930 and 1940, but the total number of Negroes in the labor force also declined. During the 1940's their major improvements occurred at the operative level. These fields accounted for 10 percent of all Negro employment in 1940 but over 18 percent in 1950. The 1940's also marked the beginning of significant employment at the clerical and skilled level. The 1950's saw continued improvement at the semiskilled and higher levels, particularly at the clerical level. There has been a slow but steady growth in the relative importance of the professional and related occupations for Negroes, but no significant increase has occurred as yet at the managerial level.

Trends Toward Occupational Equality

Throughout all earlier generations, there were striking differences in the occupational patterns of Negro and white workers, not only on the basis of national comparisons, but also even when comparisons were made in the same region. Originally these differences reflected such overriding institutions as slavery and later racial segregation, particularly in the farming communities of the South, where most Negroes lived and worked. In recent decades, Negroes have relocated to areas where the labor market has been less sharply differentiated on a racial basis. Moreover, there is much greater concern and efforts are now being made to open employment opportunities to the Negro from which he had previously been barred. These developments bring into focus the question of the trends towards occupational equality between whites and Negroes.

While Negroes have moved increasingly into high-level occupations, whites have also been shifting from farming and the lesser skilled fields into these higher level occupations. The question whether Negroes have achieved a greater measure of occupational equality must consider not only their gains, but also the gains that the whites have been able to make. The data in Table XV provide one way of looking at this. This table traces out the

TABLE XV—Ratio of White to Negro Workers* by Occupational Field and Sex, 1910–1960

	Male						Female					
	1910	1920	1930	1940	1950	1960	1910	1920	1930	1940	1950	1960
All sectors	1.0	1.0	1.0	1.0	1.0	1.0	1.0	1.0	1.0	1.0	1.0	1.0
Nonfarm, total	1.5	1.4	1.3	1.3	1.1	1.1	1.3	1.6	1.3	1.2	1.1	1.0
White collar sector, total	6.8	6.6	6.3	3.4	3.8	2.9	12.7	12.7	10.5	7.8	4.5	3.5
Professional & technical	2.9	2.9	2.8	3.2	3.1	3.7	6.6	5.9	4.8	3.4	2.3	2.4
Props., mgrs., & officials	8.1	8.7	7.8	6.4	5.1	6.8	4.9	4.6	4.7	5.7	3.4	2.9
Clerical & sales workers	10.1	8.1	8.3	6.4	3.4	2.0	43.2	34.2	30.5	21.3	6.9	4.7
Manual & service sector, total	1.1	1.0	0.9	0.9	0.8	0.7	1.0	0.8	0.6	0.6	0.5	0.5
Skilled workers & foremen	4.3	4.0	3.7	3.6	2.4	2.1	30.5	13.9	12.1	7.1	2.5	1.6
Operatives & semiskilled	2.5	2.0	1.7	1.5	1.0	0.8	5.2	3.5	2.6	2.1	1.3	1.0
Laborers	0.7	0.5	0.5	0.4	0.3	0.3	1.5	0.9	0.8	1.1	0.5	1.4
Service workers	0.2	0.2	0.2	0.4	0.4	0.4	0.4	0.3	0.3	0.3	0.3	0.3
Farm, total	0.6	0.6	0.6	0.5	0.6	0.6	0.2	0.2	0.2	0.1	0.3	0.4

* Relative to their number in total work force.

SOURCE: Same as for Table XIV, Hiestand, p. 48.

changes in the relative number of white and Negro workers in the various fields, account having been taken of relative size of each group.

This table shows that throughout the past half-century, white men have been and continue to be present in white collar occupations in relatively greater numbers than Negro men. In 1910, white men were seven times more numerous in white collar work than Negro men, and they were still relatively three times more numerous in 1960. The position of white men in clerical and sales work has declined from ten times to two times the proportion of Negro men. On the other hand, there has been little change over the long run in the relative position of white men in the professions, for they have had a threefold lead over Negroes throughout the half-century, a lead that increased slightly during the last decade. The relative position of white men in the managerial fields decreased from eightfold to fivefold between 1910 and 1950 but increased to sevenfold by 1960.

In the manual and service sector, quite diverse patterns can be found. Among operatives, Negro men are now overrepresented, where they were formerly underrepresented. The relatively greater number of white men among skilled workers and foremen has declined, from fourfold to twofold. Among laborers and service workers, Negro men continued to be overrepresented, although the extent thereof has increased among laborers and decreased among service workers. The relative underrepresentation of white men in farming continued at approximately the same level throughout the half-century.

In comparing Negro and white women, the trend toward equality in the white collar sector has been even stronger than among men, particularly in the professional and in the clerical and sales categories. Among women in manual and service categories, a position of relative equality prevailed in 1910. Negro women are now relatively more prominent in this sector, although the degree to which this is true has changed little since 1930. Among operatives, white women were once relatively five times as numerous, but now a position of "equality" prevails. The underrepresentation of white women in the service occupations, as well as in farming, has changed little over the past half-century.

Despite, or perhaps because of these differing trends in the several occupational groups the search for a clear answer to the question of whether the Negro has been improving his position relative to the white continues. The data in Table XVI provide one answer to this question. This provides an index of relative occupational position, which takes into consideration the respective distribution of whites and Negroes at various occupational levels, but does not reflect changes in earnings in these several fields. The index reflects the shifts in the distribution noted in Table XIV.

TABLE XVI—Index of Occupational Position of Negroes
Relative to Whites, by Sex, 1910–1960

	Men	Women
1910	78.0	78.0
1920	78.1	71.3
1930	78.2	74.8
1940	77.5	76.8
1950	81.4	81.6
1960	82.1	84.3

SOURCE: Dale L. Hiestand, *Economic Growth and Employment Opportunities for Minorities*, New York, Columbia University Press, 1964, p. 53.

As Table XVI shows, the occupational position of Negroes relative to whites has improved very slightly over the long run. The index for men hardly changed between 1910 and 1930. Between 1930 and 1940, the position of Negro men relative to whites actually deteriorated. The major improvement in the position of Negro men relative to whites has occurred since 1940 and nearly all of it during the 1940–50 decade.

A different pattern is found among women. The occupational position of Negro women relative to whites deteriorated greatly between 1910 and 1920, but has improved significantly in each decade since then. As a result, a smaller gap between the races now prevails among women than among men.

Regional Differences in Relative Occupational Status

While these national comparisons are illuminating and useful for certain purposes, there is the question of whether important regional and state differences lurk back of the national figures. Are there areas in the United States where the Negro has moved toward occupational equality with the white population, or did the trend toward equality found in the national data fail to appear in some regions and states? The data in Table XVII, computed in a slightly different way from those in Table XVI, provide an answer.

These data confirm the finding that Negro men made significant progress in closing the occupational gap during the 1940's, but their rate of progress relative to white men slowed down considerably during the 1950's. More

TABLE XVII—Index of Occupational Position of Negro Relative to White Males, by States,* 1940–1960

	1940	1950	1960
United States, total	**70**	**77**	**81**
Northeast			
Massachusetts	81	84	88
Connecticut	82	84	83
New York	85	86	87
New Jersey	78	80	83
Pennsylvania	85	85	86
North Central			
Ohio	87	86	86
Indiana	92	90	89
Illinois	89	88	88
Michigan	91	90	88
Missouri	87	88	86
South			
Maryland	71	75	78
District of Columbia	75	77	79
Virginia	73	76	76
North Carolina	71	72	73
South Carolina	62	65	69
Georgia	71	73	73
Florida	68	67	69
Kentucky	93	89	83
Tennessee	84	83	79
Alabama	75	77	74
Mississippi	63	66	64
Arkansas	73	74	77
Louisiana	66	70	74
Oklahoma	77	78	82
Texas	73	77	79

* Actually index of nonwhite to white; includes all states with 100,000 or more Negroes in 1960 except California where such a ratio may not be representative of Negroes.

SOURCE: U.S. Senate, Subcommittee on Employment and Manpower, Hearings on *Equal Employment Opportunity*, 1963, p. 323.

importantly, the data in Table XVII show that in not a single state was the improvement in relative occupational position as great as in the nation as a whole. The improvement was particularly marked in Louisiana, South Carolina, Massachusetts and Maryland. In some cases, this reflects a relatively rapid growth in employment opportunities in higher level occupations; in others it reflects a rapid reduction of employment in farming and other low paying occupations as a result of outmigration.

The relative occupational position of Negro men improved in most states. In a number of states—notably in all of the North Central states—their relative occupational position declined slightly between 1940 and 1960. During this period, these states experienced substantial inflows of Negro manpower.

This points up the fact that the rapid improvement of the Negro position reflects two trends: their relative improvement within specific states, and their migration from states in the South where they have done relatively poorly to states in the North where they do relatively better, even though they remain at a disadvantage.

The analysis up to this point has been concerned almost exclusively with the position of the Negro in the civilian labor force. However, as was pointed out at the beginning of this chapter, nearly three million white and Negro

TABLE XVIII—Total and Negro Personnel by Grade, and Negro Personnel as a Percent of Total Personnel in Each Grade, for Each Service (1962)

Pay grade	Army			Air Force*		
	Total personnel	Negro personnel	Percent Negro	Total personnel	Negro pesonnel	Percent Negro
Officers						
General	15			6		
Lieutenant general	35			27		
Major general	197			142	1	0.7
Brigadier general	248			172		
Colonel	5,127	6	0.1	4,066	6	0.1
Lieutenant colonel	12,309	117	1.0	12,337	67	0.5
Major	17,100	424	2.5	20,395	124	0.6
Captain	29,397	1,532	5.2	35,180	615	1.7
1st lieutenant	14,978	650	4.3	20,292	317	1.6
2nd lieutenant	18,559	421	2.3	11,664	170	1.5
Total	**97,965**	**3,150**	**3.2**	**104,281**	**1,300**	**1.2**
Warrant officers						
Chief (W-4)	1,140	28	2.5	383		
Chief (W-3)	2,674	102	3.8	969	15	1.6
Chief (W-2)	4,383	158	3.6	1,058	13	1.2
Warrant officer	1,523	33	2.2	1		
Total	**9,720**	**321**	**3.3**	**2,411**	**28**	**1.2**
Enlisted personnel						
Sergeant major	2,549	76	3.0	3,813	32	0.8
Master or 1st sergeant	10,239	586	5.7	8,358	140	1.7
Platoon sergeant or sergeant 1st class	41,107	3,143	7.6	24,629	616	2.5
Staff sergeant	82,951	10,496	12.7	50,374	2,115	4.2
Sergeant	134,457	21,892	16.3	110,152	10,287	9.3
Corporal	173,188	21,133	12.2	114,768	14,321	12.5
Private first class	286,597	26,985	11.9	124,158	11,505	9.2
Private	102,332	10,836	10.6	67,921	6,951	10.2
Recruit	75,778	8,456	11.2	3,476	597	17.1
Total	**849,198**	**103,603**	**12.2**	**507,549**	**46,564**	**9.2**
Grand total	**956,883**	**107,074**	**11.2**	**614,241**	**47,892**	**7.8**

* Represents 75 percent of total strength

SOURCE: U.S. Commission on Civil Rights, *1963 Report*, Washington, 1963, p. 219.

men and women are in the Armed Forces. For many, such service is the equivalent of a career in the civilian sector of the economy.

But the Armed Forces have a significance that transcends the fact that they offer employment for considerable numbers of white and Negro workers. Even those who remain for only one or two tours of duty and then return to civilian life will have a better or worse opportunity to find a desirable job, depending on the training, skills and experiences that they had while on active duty.

The experience of Negroes in the Armed Forces has therefore a twofold significance: as an area of employment while they are in service, and as a factor in facilitating or retarding the type of employment which they can secure when they return to civilian life.

In many respects, the Armed Forces have made greater progress than any other sector in providing more equal employment opportunities for Negroes. This advance has been most conspicuous with respect to enlisted men and noncommissioned officers, although opportunities for Negroes at officer levels have also expanded rapidly. The major improvement in the position of Negroes in the Armed Forces has occurred in the Army and Air Force, with the Navy particularly, and the Marines to a less extent, lagging. As Table XVIII shows, in 1962 Negroes accounted for more than 11 percent of all Army personnel, 8 percent in the Air Force, 7 percent in the Marines, and less than 5 percent in the Navy. The most striking differences occur at the officer level, with Negroes comprising 3 percent of all Army officers, one percent in the Air Force and only 0.3 and 0.2 percent respectively in the Navy and Marines.

Significant numbers of Negroes had achieved relatively high positions. One was a major general in the Air Force, six were colonels in the Army and an additional six were at this level in the Air Force, while those at lieutenant colonel or equivalent level numbered 117 in the Army, 67 in the Air Force and 3 in the Navy.

Over the past several decades, the Army has consistently had a higher proportion of Negro personnel than the other services, while the Air Force, since it became independent in 1948, has ranked second. The Navy has changed little over the years, while the Marines, who formerly trailed, now utilize Negroes relatively more than the Navy (Table XIX).

TABLE XIX—Negroes as a Percent of Officers and Enlisted Personnel for Each Service, for Selected Dates (1945, 1949, 1954, and 1962)

	1945	1949	1954	1962
Officers				
Army ⎱	0.7	1.7	2.9	3.2
Air Force ⎰		0.6	1.1	1.2
Navy	(1)	(1)	0.1	0.3
Marines	N.A.	(1)	0.1	0.2
Enlisted personnel				
Army ⎱	10.3	9.6	12.3	12.2
Air Force ⎰		5.1	8.6	9.2
Navy	4.8	4.5	3.6	5.2
Marines	N.A.	2.1	6.5	7.6

.1 Less than 0.5 percent.
N.A.—Not available.

SOURCE: U.S. Commission on Civil Rights, *1963 Report*, Washington, 1963, p. 221.

TABLE XX—Part 1—Negroes as a Percent of Total in Selected Fields,
for Civilian Employment Compared to Armed Forces

	Male[1] civilian employment, 1960	Armed Forces, 1962				
		Total	Army	Air Force	Navy	Marines
	Professional and managerial versus military officers					
1 Legal	1.0	0.7	1.0	0.8	..	N.A.
2 Chemical and scientific	2.0	2.8	5.1	1.7	..	..
3 Electrical engineers, signal, electronics, etc.	0.7	2.2	3.1	1.8	0.1	0.2
4 Civil, aeronautical and other engineers	0.6	1.4	2.6	1.0	0.0	..
5 Finance, accountants, auditors, etc.	0.9	1.5	1.8	1.4	N.A.	0.5
6 Supply, transportation and misc. managers	0.9	2.2	3.8	1.6	0.1	0.4
7 Physicians, medical corps	2.0	1.2	1.7	1.2	0.6	N.A.
8 Dentists	2.5	1.6	1.9	2.4	0.4	N.A.
9 Nurses	[1]5.4	3.4	3.8	4.5	1.3	N.A.
10 Clergymen, chaplains	7.1	1.9	3 2	1.6	0.4	N.A.
11 Air pilots and navigators	0.4	0.7	N.A.	0.4	0.2	0.2
12 Policemen, etc.; officers in military police, etc.	[2]3.4	3.2	3.7	1.8	N.A.	..

TABLE XX—Part 2—Negroes as a Percent of Total in Selected Fields,
for Civilian Employment Compared to Armed Forces

	Male[1] civilian employment, 1960	Armed Forces, 1962				
		Total	Army	Air Force	Navy	Marines
	Technicians, craftsmen, clerical, and service versus enlisted men					
1 Electronic technicians including television repair	2.9	4.7	8.8	4.8	2.0	1.9
2 Other technical	[1]3.1	8.5	12.1	6.5	4.7	3.4
a. Medical and dental	[1]7.1	11.0	16.0	8.6	5.2	N.A.
b. Draftsmen and related	1.1	5.4	4.4	7.1	2.9	6.6
3 Clerical and related	[1]3.9	10.6	10.0	14.2	4.6	6.3
4 Mechanics and repairmen	4.4	5.8	9.6	5.3	3.7	4.8
a. Aircraft and engine	2.9	4.6	4.6	4.9	3.8	3.9
b. Electricians, linemen, etc.	1.4	9.9	12.4	7.2	1.5	7.9
c. Automotive	6.5	8.4	11.5	10.7	4.8	6.3
5 Miscellaneous craftsmen	5.7	8.4	11.5	10.7	4.8	6.3
a. Construction and related	6.2	10.1	12.1	13.5	3.9	7.0
b. Printing	2.2	9.6	6.0	11.1	3.3	5.3
6 Service occupations	[1]18.9	16.6	15.6	15.4	22.9	15.6
a. Food service	[1]11.5	19.9	17.7	18.4	23.9	20.3

[1] Most figures for civilian occupations include males only; noted figures include females on the assumption that a significant number of the Armed Forces personnel in the field are female.

[2] The civilian figure includes all policemen, sheriffs, and marshals and would undoubtedly be much smaller if it included only those in grades of lieutenant or above, or equivalent, as do the military figures.

N.A.—Not available or not applicable.
Blanks indicate no Negroes in these occupational fields.

SOURCE: U.S. Commission on Civil Rights, *1963 Report*, Washington, 1963, p. 223

Both Negro enlisted men and officers enjoy relatively better occupational opportunities than do Negroes in civilian employment. As Table XX shows, Negroes comprise a higher percentage of the enlisted men than they do of the civilians in every clerical, technical and skilled field for which a comparison is possible. These include such occupations as electronic, medical and dental, drafting and other kinds of technicians; aircraft and automotive mechanics; electricians and communications linemen, construction and related craftsmen and printing craftsmen. Negroes comprise 9 percent of those who might be considered as craftsmen and foremen, compared to only 5 percent in civilian life.

A slightly different pattern emerges among officers, Negroes comprise a smaller proportion of military than civilian personnel in such fields as law, medicine, dentistry, nursing and the clergy—traditionally the major fields of professional employment because those so employed serve the Negro community. However, in a number of fields Negroes represent a larger proportion in the Armed Forces than in civilian life. This is true in engineering, the applied sciences, finance and accounting, aviation and navigation and a wide variety of management fields.

There are marked differences among the services in the occupational levels of their Negro personnel. The better opportunities in military life primarily reflect Army and Air Force practice. In nearly all of the clerical, technical and skilled fields, the Army's proportion of Negroes is at least two and sometimes four times higher than in comparable civilian jobs. The Army also has a higher proportion of Negroes in most professional, scientific and managerial fields than does the civilian economy. The Air Force presents substantially better patterns than the civilian labor market in most occupational categories.

The Navy is the only service that does not utilize Negroes as heavily as the civilian economy in almost every occupational category, from the professional, scientific and managerial to medical and dental technicians, general mechanics and repairmen, administrative and clerical personnel and construction and utility craftsmen. Negroes in the Navy are heavily con-

TABLE XXI—Median Income of Experienced Civilian Labor Force, by Occupation, Sex and Color, 1960

	Men		Women	
Occupational group	Total	Nonwhite	Total	Nonwhite
Total	4,621	$2,703	$2,257	$1,219
Professional, technical, etc.	6,619	4,563	3,625	3,571
Farmers and farm managers	2,169	778	836	589
Mgrs., offs. and prop., exc. farm	6,664	3,869	3,355	1,927
Clerical	4,785	4,072	3,017	2,993
Sales	4,987	2,809	1,498	1,562
Craftsmen	5,240	3,480	2,927	2,314
Operatives	4,299	3,040	2,319	1,829
Private hshld. worker	1,078	1,216	684	704
Service workers exc. pvt. hshld.	3,310	2,529	1,385	1,365
Farm laborers and foremen	1,066	816	602	553
Laborers exc. farm and mine	2,948	2,394	1,872	1,444

SOURCE: U.S. Bureau of the Census, Census of Population: 1960, *United States Summary, Detailed Characteristics*, Table 208.

TABLE XXII—Median Income of White and Nonwhite Wage and Salary Workers, by Sex, 1939 and 1947–1962

	Male			Female		
	White, in dollars	Nonwhite		White, in dollars	Nonwhite	
		In dollars	As percent of white		In dollars	As percent of white
1939	$1,112	$ 460	41.4	$ 676	$ 246	36.4
1947	2,357	1,279	54.3	1,269	432	34.0
1948	2,711	1,615	59.6	1,615	701	43.4
1949	2,735	1,367	50.0	1,615	654	40.5
1950	2,982	1,828	61.3	1,698	626	36.9
1951	3,345	2,060	61.6	1,855	781	42.1
1952	3,507	2,038	58.1	1,976	814	41.2
1953	3,760	2,233	59.4	2,049	994	48.5
1954	3,754	2,131	56.8	2.046	914	44.7
1955	3,986	2,342	58.8	2,065	894	43.3
1956	4,260	2,396	56.2	2,179	970	44.5
1957	4,396	2,436	55.4	2,240	1,019	45.5
1958	4,569	2,652	58.0	2,364	1,055	44.6
1959	4,902	2,844	58.0	2,422	1,289	53.2
1960	5,137	3,075	59.8	2,537	1,276	50.2
1961	5,287	3,015	57.0	2,538	1,302	51.3
1962	5,642[a]	3,023[a]	53.6[a]	b	b	b

[a] Preliminary.   [b] Not available.

SOURCE: *Manpower Report of the President*, March, 1964, Table H-10; U.S. Bureau of the Census, *Current Population Reports*, Series P-60, annual issues.

centrated in the service occupations, although it is said the Navy is trying to change this traditional pattern. As yet, however, little success has been achieved, among other reasons because the Navy has accepted a smaller proportion of Negroes than the other services.

Incomes of Negro Workers

The preceding analysis of occupational status has been important not only in its own right but also because the type of work that an individual performs largely determines what he is able to earn, which in turn determines how he can live and maintain his family. However, an occupational analysis by itself can at best shed only indirect light on the question of income. More direct information on incomes is presented in Tables XXI and XXII.

The improvement of the occupational position of the Negro in the American economy has been matched only partially by an improvement in their income position. The occupational indexes previously developed treated all workers within a given occupational group as equal. But Table 21 emphasizes that Negroes tend to be concentrated in the lower-paying positions within each occupational field. In almost every field Negroes tended to earn less than whites. This was particularly true among men. Nonwhite women earned more than white women in sales and private household work, and almost as much in professional, clerical and service employment. Among men this occurred only in the relatively small field of private household work.

Relative incomes provide a better index of the changing economic position of Negroes in relation to white workers than do relative occupational

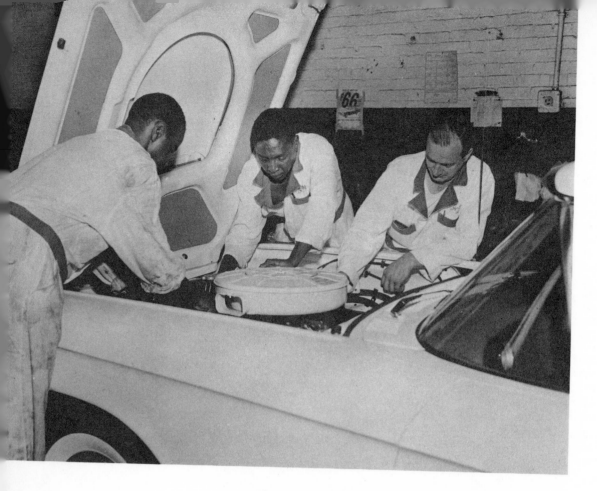

AUTOMOBILE PLANT WORKERS. (U.S. Dept. of Labor Photo)

CARPENTERS. (U.S. Dept. of Labor Photo)

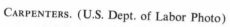

positions. As Table XXII indicates, the average income of Negro male workers was only 41 percent of that of white male workers in 1939. Between 1939 and 1947, there was a substantial improvement in the relative income position of Negro men to 54 percent. Since then, however, the ratio of Negro to white male income has fluctuated between 54 and 62 percent. The low points have been somewhat associated with years of high unemployment, although there has been no clear-cut pattern. Neither has there been any consistent trend in these ratios over time.

For Negro women, the pattern has been somewhat different. The pre-war ratio of the average incomes of Negro to white women workers amounted to 36 percent. From 1939 to the immediate post-war period, there was little change. Since then, the ratio has increased to over 50 percent.

TABLE XXIII—Percent of employed persons with two or more jobs, May, 1962

	Both sexes	Male	Female
Total	4.9	6.4	2.0
White	4.9	6.5	1.8
Nonwhite	4.6	5.6	3.1

SOURCE: U.S. Department of Labor, "Multiple Job Holders in May 1962." *Special Labor Force Report*, No. 29, Table A.

These shifts in relative income positions reflect a great many different forces that have been interacting upon one another. They reflect shifts in occupational patterns previously noted, but they also reflect shifts in prevailing incomes in various occupations, in unemployment rates, in multiple job-holding rates and in the importance of part-time versus full-time work. As the nation moved from the depressed economic conditions of the 1930's to higher price and wage levels after World War II, wage rates in low paying jobs increased more rapidly than those in high paying jobs. Since Negroes were concentrated more heavily in the lower paying jobs, their incomes tended to increase more rapidly than those of whites. Indeed, there is evidence that there was a long-run tendency extending over the period from before World War I to after World War II for relative income differentials to decline; that is, for incomes to increase more rapidly in the occupations and regions (i.e., the South) where they were relatively low. However, this decline in relative income differentials has not continued in the last decade. In this connection one should recall the shift of the Negro out of the South to regions where he has found greater opportunities to work at a higher occupational level. This internal migration probably accounted for much more of his total gains than a move towards equality within particular regions.

Employment, Unemployment and Labor Force Participation Rates

One aspect of the lower income position of Negroes than whites is that they are employed to a lesser extent than whites. This can be shown in a variety of ways. Among employed men, Negroes are less likely than whites to hold two or more jobs (Table XXIII). On the other hand, Negro women are more likely than white women to hold two or more jobs, which helps

TABLE XXIV—Unemployment Rates, by Color and Sex: Annual Averages, 1948–62

	White			Nonwhite		
	Both Sexes	**Male**	**Female**	**Both Sexes**	**Male**	**Female**
1948	3.2	3.1	3.4	5.2	5.1	5.2
1949	5.2	5.2	5.2	8.2	8.8	7.2
1950	4.6	4.5	4.9	8.5	8.9	7.8
1951	2.8	2.4	3.7	4.8	4.4	5.4
1952	2.4	2.2	2.9	4.6	4.5	4.8
1953	2.3	2.2	2.6	4.1	4.4	3.7
1954	4.5	4.4	4.9	8.9	9.2	8.2
1955	4.6	4.8	4.3	10.1	11.3	8.1
1956	3.3	3.1	3.8	7.5	7.3	8.0
1957	3.9	3.7	4.3	8.0	8.4	7.4
1958	6.1	6.1	6.2	12.6	13.7	10.8
1959	4.9	4.6	5.3	10.7	11.5	9.5
1960	5.0	4.8	5.3	10.2	10.7	9.5
1961	6.0	5.7	6.5	12.5	12.9	11.9
1962	4.9	4.6	5.5	11.0	11.0	11.1

SOURCE: *Manpower Report of the President*, March 1964, Table A-10.

to explain the large number of occupational fields in which Negro women earned approximately as much per year as white women.

The lesser degree of employment among Negroes is attested in another way in Table XXIV. In recent years, unemployment rates for Negroes have tended to run slightly more than twice as high as whites. This is, in fact, a slightly higher differential than prevailed prior to about 1955. In earlier years, the Negro rate tended to be slightly less than twice as great as the white rate. Since 1957, the unemployment rate for the entire labor force has tended to be higher than formerly. Thus, as unemployment rates have increased, those among Negroes have increased even more rapidly than those among whites.

Higher unemployment rates among Negroes are in part a reflection of the fact that they tend to be concentrated in the low paying, low skilled jobs in which employment is more unstable. This is not the only factor, however, for, as Table XXV shows, Negroes tend to suffer higher unemployment rates than whites at each occupational level.

The unemployment statistics do not provide an adequate picture of the extent of joblessness among Negroes. In terms of their relationship to paid employment, the population may be divided into three groups. First are the employed. Second are the unemployed who are defined as those without a job who are looking for work. The employed and the unemployed comprise the labor force. There is a third group—those who neither work nor look for work. They are not counted as part of the labor force. Many who do not look for work may do so as a matter of choice, because they have no need or desire for a job.

Some who do not look for work may fail to do so because they know or believe that no job opportunities are available to them. Such persons are clearly unemployed, but there is reason to believe that many, and perhaps an increasing number, are not counted as being in the labor force. This is suggested by Table XXVI, which presents labor force participation rates for men and women at different age levels in 1940, 1950 and 1960. These describe the percentage of persons in the respective groups who are employed or looking for work. The reciprocal of these figures would be the percentages of those in the respective groups who neither worked nor looked for work.

Several quite striking points arise in comparing labor force participation rates of Negro and white men and women over the last several decades. In the first place, the labor force participation rates have tended to be higher among white than Negro men throughout the age range from twenty-five to sixty years. These differences, moreover, have tended to widen with time. The rates for Negro men have declined slightly since 1940, while those for whites have tended to increase slightly. This pattern was even sharper among teenage Negro boys, who once were more likely than white boys to be in the labor force, but now are less likely. The tendency toward a higher proportion of white boys to be in the labor force has occurred despite the fact that more of them attend school.

Among older men, the reduction in labor force participation rates has also been sharper among Negroes than whites. As a result, while formerly relatively more Negro than white men worked throughout the range from sixty to seventy-four years of age, now labor force participation rates are higher for whites than for Negroes. The fact that there has been a tendency for relatively fewer Negroes to be in the labor force at the same time that their unemployment rates have increased substantially faster than whites, suggests that many are not in the labor force because there is no work for them. To the extent this is true, they represent unemployed manpower and the unemployment rates referred to earlier really understate the true figure.

TABLE XXV—Unemployment Rates by Occupational Group, Sex, and Color, 1960

Occupational group	Male		Female	
	White	Nonwhite	White	Nonwhite
Total	4.5	8.4	4.7	7.9
Professional and technical	1.4	2.3	1.4	2.2
Managers, officials, and proprietors, exc. farm	1.4	2.9	1.8	2.5
Clerical	3.2	5.6	3.1	5.8
Sales	2.5	5.6	4.8	8.0
Craftsmen and foremen	5.2	8.3	5.6	9.2
Operatives	6.2	8.2	9.6	12.3
Private household workers	5.8	6.4	4.6	6.0
Service, exc. pvt. hshld.	4.9	7.1	5.3	7.9
Laborers, exc. farm and mine	11.8	12.5	10.9	16.6
Farmers and farm mgrs.	0.7	1.7	0.8	5.2
Farm laborers and foremen	6.6	7.4	6.1	17.4

SOURCE: Same as for Table IV

Somewhat comparable tendencies can be found among women workers. The proportion of Negro women who work has always tended to be higher than among white women. There has been an increase in the proportion of Negro women above the age of thirty-five who are employed. This has been particularly so since 1950. The proportion of white women in the middle and higher age brackets who are in the labor force increased even more rapidly during the 1940's and the 1950's. As a result, the current differences between the labor force participation rates of white and Negro women in these higher age ranges, while sizeable, are not really distinctive.

Among women of childbearing age, from twenty to thirty-five among white women and eighteen to thirty-five among Negro women, there has been very little change in their labor force participation rates in recent years. In the still younger age group, among teenagers, one finds that relatively more white girls and fewer Negro girls have entered the labor force than in the past. As a result, teenage white girls are now more likely to be employed than are teenage Negro girls.

TABLE XXVI—Percent in the labor force by age group, sex, and color, 1940–1960

Age in years	Nonwhite			White		
	1940	1950	1960	1940	1950	1960
			Men			
14 and 15 years	19.3	20.2	12.5	6.7	14.9	16.5
16 and 17 years	46.1	43.0	28.8	27.4	34.9	37.8
18 and 19 years	73.1	68.7	58.8	65.0	66.5	67.2
20 to 24 years	88.5	80.3	82.0	88.0	82.1	86.7
25 to 29 years	92.1	84.5	87.6	95.1	91.0	94.7
30 to 34 years	92.7	88.2	89.1	95.7	94.5	96.6
35 to 39 years	92.9	90.4	89.7	95.4	95.1	96.5
40 to 44 years	91.7	90.7	89.6	94.3	94.7	95.0
50 to 54 years	88.9	86.9	85.9	91.1	91.0	92.8
55 to 59 years	87.7	82.9	80.6	87.9	87.0	88.5
60 to 64 years	80.5	76.0	68.7	78.9	79.7	78.4
65 to 69 years	64.3	56.1	40.8	59.0	60.0	44.1
70 to 74 years	43.7	40.2	27.4	38.0	38.6	28.8
75 years and over	23.5	21.9	15.7	17.8	18.4	15.5
Age in years			Women			
14 and 15 years	7.8	7.2	5.4	1.6	4.8	7.1
16 and 17 years	20.3	16.5	14.0	12.4	17.9	21.8
18 and 19 years	36.7	30.9	34.8	40.6	45.6	47.9
20 to 24 years	44.9	39.6	45.4	45.7	43.6	44.8
25 to 29 years	46.1	42.9	46.9	34.2	31.3	33.5
30 to 34 years	46.2	46.3	50.2	29.1	29.1	33.5
35 to 39 years	45.7	48.6	54.7	26.1	32.1	38.5
40 to 44 years	44.3	48.1	57.0	24.0	34.9	43.9
45 to 49 years	41.8	45.3	56.5	21.9	33.6	46.4
50 to 54 years	37.6	40.9	52.6	19.8	29.8	45.1
55 to 59 years	33.6	34.9	44.8	17.4	25.2	39.1
60 to 64 years	27.8	27.6	34.2	13.9	20.0	29.0
65 to 69 years	18.5	16.4	19.6	8.8	12.5	16.3
70 to 74 years	9.5	8.4	11.5	4.8	6.5	9.4
75 years and over	4.9	3.8	5.5	2.1	2.5	4.1

SOURCE: U.S. Bureau of the Census, Census of Population: 1960, United States Summary, Detailed Characteristics, Table 195.

TABLE XXVII—Labor Force Participation Rates by Age, Sex, Marital Status and Color, 1960

Age group (in years)	Single		Married spouse present		Other marital status	
	Total	Nonwhite	Total	Nonwhite	Total	Nonwhite
Males						
14 to 17	26.2	20.2	81.1	69.8	35.6	37.0
18 to 19	63.9	56.2	95.4	92.4	77.8	69.6
20 to 24	78.3	74.7	96.3	95.1	83.6	76.6
25 to 29	83.8	75.6	97.8	96.4	82.1	75.5
30 to 34	84.0	74.0	98.6	96.3	82.1	74.7
35 to 44	80.3	72.1	98.2	95.8	81.7	76.4
45 to 64	75.8	69.6	96.2	92.8	79.8	76.9
55 to 64	65.2	61.7	87.3	82.0	68.2	64.2
65 to 74	28.9	28.3	41.1	40.3	27.5	28.8
75 and over	14.2	15.2	19.0	19.1	11.1	12.7
Females						
14 to 17	13.9	8.8	16.4	18.1	22.0	22.6
18 to 19	53.6	37.4	29.2	25.7	43.6	34.8
20 to 24	73.2	59.4	31.1	34.0	53.9	48.7
25 to 29	79.1	66.8	26.8	38.2	58.2	56.3
30 to 34	79.4	68.1	29.0	43.0	62.2	62.4
35 to 44	78.2	68.1	36.5	48.7	68.2	67.7
45 to 54	76.1	66.0	39.3	47.2	67.3	65.3
55 to 64	64.8	49.5	25.2	33.6	47.6	46.2
65 to 74	30.5	27.9	7.7	12.7	15.8	17.3
75 and over	10.2	14.5	3.0	6.5	3.9	5.0

SOURCE: U.S. Bureau of the Census, Census of Population: 1960, *Employment Status and Work Experience*, Table 6.

A substantial part, but by no means all, of the differences in labor force participation rates is related to differences in the marital status of the Negro and white population. Among men of both races, labor force participation rates are higher among those who are married and whose spouse is present than among those who are single or who are divorced, widowed, or separated. Among women, those who are single are more likely to be in the labor force than those who are divorced, widowed or separated, while those who are married are the least likely to work.

Negroes are more likely than whites to be divorced, widowed or separated. This is associated with higher labor force participation rates in general among Negro than white women, but lower labor force participation rates in general among Negro men than white men.

Differences in marital status do not, however, account for all of the differences in labor force rates. As Table XXVII shows, in all three types of marital status, Negro men are almost consistently less likely than white men in the same age range to be in the labor force. The same is true in comparing Negro and white women who were single or divorced, widowed or separated. The exception is women with spouse present, among whom Negroes are more likely than whites to work.

The cause and effect between work and marital status is difficult to unravel. On the one hand, men who are single or not with their spouse

TABLE XXVIII—Two Indexes of Work Experience in 1962 for Whites and Nonwhites, by Age and Sex.

Age group	Percent of population with no work experience in year		Percent of workers with full-time full year jobs	
	Male	Female	Male	Female
14–19 years				
White	41.9	56.0	6.6	8.3
Nonwhite	55.1	65.0	11.0	4.8
20–24 years				
White	7.4	36.0	45.1	34.6
Nonwhite	10.0	41.7	46.8	30.7
25–64 years				
White	3.7	49.5	77.7	44.0
Nonwhite	7.2	35.5	61.7	37.3
65 years and over				
White	61.4	86.1	38.6	26.7
Nonwhite	63.9	81.3	27.9	12.9

SOURCE: U.S. Department of Labor, "Work Experience of the Population in 1962," *Special Labor Force Report*, No. 38, Table A-9.

may have less pressure on them to seek or find work. On the other hand, those who are unable to find work, for whatever reason, may be less likely to marry or, if they marry, to maintain a stable family relationship. Thus, the high proportion of Negro men who are unemployed or out of the labor force may cause or it may reflect the fact that many of them have a broken marital status. The fact that many more Negro than white women work is undoubtedly due to their broken marital status, although even here some may be able to leave unhappy situations because they have jobs. Higher labor force participation rates among Negro than white women even when their spouse is present undoubtedly reflect their greater need for income because their husband is more likely to be unemployed or in a low paying job.

The previous data on unemployment and labor force participation refer to data collected at a particular point in time. There are also data available that show that a higher proportion of Negroes than white men tend to be unemployed or out of the labor force during longer periods of time. As Table XXVIII shows, at every age level, Negro men were less likely than whites to have held a job during 1962. Among men in the prime working ages of twenty-five to sixty-four years, over 7 percent of the Negroes but less than 4 percent of the whites did not hold any job during 1962. Among those who did hold a job during the year, 78 percent of the white men worked full time the year round, while only 62 percent of the Negroes were able to do so.

Among girls and young women under twenty-four years of age, relatively more Negroes did not hold a job during the year. Among older women, however, Negro women were more likely than whites to have worked. Indeed, two out of every three Negro women in the age range twenty-five to sixty-four worked at some time during the year, compared to only half the white women. Regardless of their age, Negro women workers were less likely, however, than whites to have held a full time job the year round.

Another evidence of the instability in the employment of Negroes is that they tend to have, on the average, a shorter period of tenure on their jobs. There are in fact few differences between Negro and white women on this score. As Table XXIX shows, however, the average white male worker in 1963 had been on his current job for nearly six years, while the average Negro male worker had been on his job little more than four years, or a difference of nearly two years. As workers grow older, there is obviously a greater opportunity for this difference to be larger, and it reached nearly four years among white and Negro men aged fifty-five to sixty-four. In addition to unemployment, the fact that relatively more Negroes than whites migrated in the last few decades tends to shorten the average job tenure of the Negro worker.

The Causes of Negro Disadvantage

The simplest and most obvious reason for the inferior economic and occupational position of Negroes is, of course, discrimination. But discrimination takes many forms, both direct and indirect. In addition, the Negro is handicapped by additional factors that cannot be labeled as discriminatory.

In the first place, the job opportunities available to Negroes have been profoundly affected by their geographic distribution. Negroes at the end of the Civil War were heavily concentrated in the rural South. The fact that the South was agricultural, that it industrialized slowly and that education and other public services have lagged in that region has affected Southern whites and Negroes alike. Much of the gap between the economic position of the Negro and white populations stems from this historical circumstance.

TABLE XXIX—White and Nonwhite Workers: Median Years on Current Job, by Age and Sex, January 1963

Age	Both sexes			Male			Female		
	Total	White	Non-white	Total	White	Non-white	Total	White	Non-white
Total, 14 years and over	4.6	4.7	3.6	5.7	5.9	4.1	3.0	3.0	2.9
14 to 24 years	0.8	0.8	0.6	0.8	0.9	0.7	0.8	0.8	0.5
25 to 34 years	3.0	3.1	2.4	3.5	3.6	2.6	2.0	2.0	2.1
35 to 44 years	6.0	6.1	5.0	7.6	7.7	6.5	3.6	3.6	3.7
45 to 54 years	9.0	9.3	7.3	11.4	11.6	9.6	6.1	6.1	5.7
55 to 64 years	11.8	12.1	8.8	14.7	15.1	11.2	7.8	7.9	6.4
65 years and over	13.8	13.6	17.3	16.6	16.3	19.7	8.8	8.4	(1)

[1] Median not shown where base is less than 100,000.

SOURCE: U.S. Department of Labor, "Job Tenure of American Workers, January 1963," *Special Labor Force Report*, No. 36, Table 2.

EMPLOYMENT PATTERNS OF NEGRO MEN AND WOMEN   241

The impact of geography on the occupational structure of Negroes in recent years has been much moderated. True, Negroes are still relatively heavily concentrated in the South. And in the North they are found predominantly in the central city rather than in the suburb. The fact that they did not follow the whites to the suburbs has had a twofold impact

TABLE XXX—Occupational Distribution of White and Nonwhite College, High School and Elementary School Graduates,[a] by Sex, 1960

Years of School Completed	Male		Female	
	Nonwhite	White	Nonwhite	White
College—4 years				
Total	100.0	100.0	100.0	100.0
Professional and technical	47.4	42.5	73.6	68.9
Mgrs., officials, and props. exc. farm	7.9	24.4	1.7	4.5
Clerical	12.7	6.7	11.2	16.1
Sales	3.6	12.5	0.9	2.9
Craftsmen and foremen	5.2	5.5	0.2	0.5
Operatives	5.1	1.7	2.1	0.8
Service workers	6.7	1.0	4.9	1.9
Laborers, exc. farm and mine	2.7	0.4	0.1	0.0
Farmers	0.9	1.8	0.0	0.3
Farm laborers and foremen	0.4	0.2	0.1	0.1
Occupation not reported	7.3	3.2	5.1	3.8
High School—4 years				
Total	100.0	100.0	100.0	100.0
Professional and technical	3.2	7.1	5.8	7.5
Mgrs., officials and props., exc. farm	3.8	15.1	1.7	5.3
Clerical	11.6	9.8	19.7	47.9
Sales	2.5	8.8	3.0	9.9
Craftsmen and foremen	14.1	24.8	1.1	1.3
Operatives	23.9	16.8	16.0	10.8
Service workers	15.7	4.7	42.7	11.5
Laborers, exc. farm and mine	12.1	3.0	0.8	0.3
Farmers	1.7	5.2	0.2	0.4
Farm laborers and foremen	1.4	0.7	0.7	0.7
Occupation not reported	9.8	4.0	8.1	4.4
Elementary—8 years				
Total	100.0	100.0	100.0	100.0
Professional and technical	0.9	1.4	0.8	1.8
Mgrs., officials, and props., exc. farm	2.2	7.9	1.1	3.7
Clerical	3.1	4.3	1.7	12.5
Sales	1.0	4.0	1.5	10.0
Craftsmen and foremen	12.7	26.2	0.6	2.0
Operatives	27.6	25.8	15.8	31.6
Service workers	16.1	6.6	65.6	28.6
Laborers exc. farm and mine	20.5	7.3	0.9	0.8
Farmers	3.2	10.5	0.6	1.1
Farm laborers and foremen	3.7	2.0	2.4	1.7
Occupation not reported	9.0	3.8	8.9	6.2

[a] Employed persons aged 25 years or more.

SOURCE: U.S. Bureau of the Census, Census of Population: 1960, *Educational Attainment*, Table 8.

on their position in the labor market. It has kept them closer to certain jobs, but it has put a gulf between them and the many service jobs that have developed in the white suburbs.

The fact that Negroes have received less education than whites, and that it has been of inferior quality (see Chapter 7) has obvious occupational implications. In both the North and the South, Negroes receive poorer education than whites. In addition, even among Negroes living in the North, many were originally educated in the South, which means that they carry with them a serious educational deficiency.

In addition, Negroes generally secure less desirable employment than whites with comparable education and background, even after some allowance is made for the poorer quality of Negro education. Table XXX shows that among male college graduates, 20 percent of the nonwhites were skilled, semiskilled, service or unskilled workers, compared to 9 percent of the whites. At the other extreme, 24 percent of the whites but only 8 percent of the nonwhites were managers, officials and proprietors. A slightly higher proportion of nonwhites than whites were in professional and technical occupations, but closer examination reveals that the whites are more likely to be in such higher paying professions as medicine, law, engineering and the sciences, while the nonwhites are concentrated in teaching and the clergy. Most of the remaining Negro men who are college graduates are in low paying clerical jobs, while the remaining white men who finished college are in sales work where they may earn quite large salaries.

Among male high school graduates, nearly 40 percent of the whites were in white collar jobs, including nearly 15 percent who were salaried or self-employed managers, compared to only 21 percent among the nonwhites, almost none of whom were managers. In addition, 25 percent of the white men but only 14 percent of the Negro men were employed as craftsmen and foremen. Negro high school graduates were far more likely than whites to become operatives, service workers or laborers. Over 60 percent of the nonwhites, but only 25 percent of the whites entered these positions.

The discrepancy remains even among those who complete only grade school. Nonwhite men were far more likely to become service or unskilled workers, while the whites had far greater than proportionate concentrations among craftsmen, foremen and managers.

Among women college graduates, there was little difference between the occupational distributions of whites and nonwhites. Among high school graduates, white women tended strongly to become clerical workers, while Negro women tended to enter service jobs. Among those who finished only elementary school, nearly two-thirds of the Negro women but little more than one-fourth of the white women entered service occupations. Over 30 percent of the white women but only half that many Negro women entered semiskilled jobs. In addition, 28 percent of the white women but only 5 percent of the Negro women were employed as clerical, sales and other white collar workers.

From these figures it is reasonable to conclude that discrimination in employment represents the major reason for the less favorable employment patterns of Negroes. The varieties of employment discrimination are too many and complicated to be set forth here. They exist at every turn.

They may be overt or covert; they may be unconscious or simply a matter of indifference. They may reflect the fact that Negroes have great difficulty in learning about job opportunities. They may also reflect the fact that standards of selection or practices used in hiring, placement, promotion and admission to training opportunities may work to the disadvantage of Negroes. The policies of trade unions, employment agencies and the other private or public organizations may have adverse effects on Negro employment, which may also be true for the behavior of workers, customers or others who affect the course of business.

These economic realities, by affecting the attitudes and actions of Negroes, set up a reinforcement mechanism that helps to compound the situation. There is, in fact, no way to disentangle the role of any individual factors, for they are linked together in a vicious circle. Lack of opportunities discourages favorable work attitudes, while poor work attitudes help to provide a rationalization or justification for discrimination. The vocational value of additional education is not as clear for a Negro, particularly in the case of men, as it is for whites. Apparently for this reason, Negroes do not aspire to as much education as do whites, and this is particularly true of Negro men. Their relative lack of education thus helps to explain their lower occupational levels. Many Negro families are broken as a result of low income and high geographical mobility, and for other reasons. In many broken families youngsters may not receive the emotional and economic support necessary for the development of work attitudes and skills essential for proper performance on the job.

Programs and Policies for Greater Opportunity

Just as this analysis cannot deal with all the causes and ramifications of the limited opportunities of Negroes, so it cannot deal with all of the ways in which disadvantage and discrimination may be successfully attacked.[1] The following will suggest some of the programs and policies which may have a direct effect on expanding the employment opportunities of Negroes. In the first place, broadened employment opportunities for Negroes depend on the establishment and maintenance of full or nearly full employment. Given the rapid growth in the labor force and the continued displacement of labor through changes in technology, a high level of employment requires rapid economic growth. The policies best able to promote full employment and economic growth fall beyond the confines of this analysis, but there can be no doubt whatever that if it were achieved it would greatly reduce the heavy burden of unemployment on Negroes.

Rapid economic growth which would involve the emergence and expansion of newer occupations would help to open up job opportunities for Negroes. In the past, the pattern has been for employment to expand more rapidly for Negroes than whites in rapidly growing fields. Such opportunities, while not numerically great, have been significant in developing beachheads for future expansion. At the same time, the past pattern has been for large numbers of whites to move up to higher level occupations, leaving opportunities for more Negroes to enter occupations in the intermediate range of the job hierarchy. This is necessary if Negroes, who are displaced more rapidly than whites from any declining fields, are to find reemployment.[2]

AIRLINE HOSTESSES. (Plans for Progress Photo)

TABLE XXXI—Employment in the Federal Government, by Pay Category,
Grade and Salary groups, and Race, June 1961 and June 1962[a]

Pay Category	June 1961			June 1962		
	Total	Negro		Total	Negro	
	Employees	Number	%	Employees	Number	%
Total	2,197,360	282,616	12.9	2,259,993	293,353	13.0
Total Class. Act or Similar	1,012,447	89,784	8.9	1,065,420	96,711	9.1
GS-1 thru 4	355,446	64,242	18.1	363,970	66,101	18.2
GS-5 thru 11	503,058	24,505	4.9	532,888	29,204	5.5
GS-12 thru 18	153,943	1,037	0.7	168,562	1,406	0.8
Total Wage Board	568,835	106,853	18.8	569,116	105,784	18.6
Up to $4,499	N.A.	N.A.	N.A.	104,210	44,680	42.9
$4,500 to $7,999	N.A.	N.A.	N.A.	441,198	60,953	13.8
$8,000 and over	N.A.	N.A.	N.A.	23,708	151	0.6
Total Postal Field Service	566,151	83,187	14.7	576,047	86,842	15.1
PFS-1 thru 4[b]	487,407	78,981	16.2	497,396	81,887	16.5
PFS-5 thru 11	74,980	4,195	5.6	75,016	4,939	6.6
PFS-12 thru 18	3,764	11	0.3	3,635	16	0.4
Total Other Pay Categories	49,927	2,792	5.6	49,410	4,016	8.1
Up to $4,499	N.A.	N.A.	N.A.	12,635	2,691	21.3
$4,500 to $7,999	N.A.	N.A.	N.A.	20,825	1,104	5.3
$8,000 and over	N.A.	N.A.	N.A.	15,950	221	1.4

[a] 1961 data covers all employment worldwide. 1962 data excludes employment in Alaska, Hawaii, and Puerto Rico. Overseas data is as of July 31, 1962 and covers U.S. citizens only in Department of State (including Agency for International Development and Peace Corps), Department of Defense, U.S. information Agency, Panama Canal Co. and Canal Zone Government.
[b] Includes 4th Class Postmasters and Rural Carriers.
N.A.—Not available.

SOURCE: President's Committee on Equal Employment Opportunity, unpublished data.

But economic growth alone is not enough to assure equal employment opportunities for Negroes. What is also required are changes in the whole range of policies that affect the employment process.

Much has been happening on this front. More and more employers have been moving in the direction of providing greater opportunities for Negroes. Sometimes this is a policy which management initiates on its own. For several decades, a number of nationally known companies, such as the International Harvester Company, Pitney-Bowes, Inc., and the Radio Corporation of America have actively worked toward this end, sometimes in hostile environments. This has also been true of a number of trade unions.

Increasingly, governments have become directly involved in programs to improve employment opportunities for minorities. This has proceeded on two fronts. In the first place, governments as large employers can themselves unilaterally improve Negro employment opportunities. Governments can also influence employment opportunities in private employment, either through persuasion or compulsion. Compulsion, moreover, has many facets, for in addition to forcing the recalcitrant to change, it may also provide the stimulus to help those who want to change.

The Federal Government's efforts to improve opportunities within its own operations have proceeded along two lines. The strong push toward more equal opportunity in the Armed Forces and its substantial success has been previously noted and dealt with at length in Chapter 15. In addition, the Federal Government, through the Civil Service Commission, the President's Committee on Equal Employment Opportunity and the operating agencies, has sought to improve opportunities in its employment of civilians. There are no precisely comparable data over any long period which would reveal exactly how much progress has been made. Such evidence as is available indicates that the opportunities for Negroes have improved substantially over the last three decades, after declining materially during the preceding twenty-five years or so. The most recent distribution of Negro employment in the Federal Government is presented in Table XXXI.

Many state and local governments have also made strides in opening up opportunities in their own work force. Again little in the way of data is available. Overall, however, governments can be seen to be major areas of expansion for Negro employment between 1950 and 1960 (Table XXXII). The employment of Negroes in Federal, state and local governments increased by over 400,000 between 1950 and 1960, an amount equal to 40 percent of the net increase in total employment of Negroes. In so doing, Negroes increased from 8.7 percent to 11.2 percent of all governmental workers. They also markedly increased their relative importance among all governmental employees in every occupational group.

The impact of government on private employment policy has been through requiring contractors selling goods and services to government to follow nondiscriminatory policies and through regulatory activities directed toward other employers to do likewise.

The most far-reaching effort is the Federal executive order that nearly all contracts entered into by the Federal Government must contain a provision that the contractor and his subcontractors follow fair employment practises. The enforcement of this clause has been left primarily to the

TABLE XXXII—Nonwhite Governmental Employees by Occupational Groups, 1950 and 1960

Occupational group	1950		1960	
	Number	As percent of total in group	Number	As percent of total in group
Total	**479,190**	**8.7**	**879,704**	**11.2**
Professional and technical	105,780	6.2	210,987	8.0
Managers and officials	5,280	1.6	12,282	2.8
Clerical	94,200	6.9	191,948	10.3
Craftsmen and foremen	23,070	4.7	49,754	7.3
Operatives	49,950	13.6	80,463	17.9
Service workers exc. pvt. household	118,740	14.2	224,287	17.3
Laborers exc. farm and mine	75,660	22.4	88,583	25.5
Other and not reported	6,540	a	21,400	a

a Not relevant.

SOURCE: U.S Bureau of the Census, Census of Population: 1960, *Occupational Characteristics*, Table 21, Census of Population: 1950, Table 13.

contract agency. Enforcement has not been very successful. A succession of five Presidential committees have also had a measure of responsibility for enforcement. In the only comprehensive review of this program, Norgren and Hill conclude "that the earlier committees did not effect any significant abatement of employment discrimination. The currently functioning committee [the President's Committee on Equal Employment Opportunity], however, has a somewhat better record of accomplishment."[3]

There are, in addition, fully enforceable fair employment practices laws in twenty-one states and many municipalities. In ten of these states, laws have been in effect for more than a decade. Norgren and Hill conclude, however, that very few of the administering commissions are supplied with adequate funds to deal effectively with the problem. In New York and several other states, the commissions' efforts in dealing with selective employers were viewed as successful. The effort to deal with employment agencies and labor unions was deemed considerably less successful.[4]

Conclusion

It is not easy to summarize what has emerged from the critical review of the multiple dimensions of the work status of the Negro in the United States as of the 1960's. There is much that provides ground for optimism, if only guarded optimism. Negroes have succeeded during the past half-century in flowing from the major declining industry to which they were overwhelmingly attached—agriculture—and latching on to jobs in the expanding industrial sectors. What is more, they have relocated in large numbers from the South, where their opportunities were more constricted, to the North and West, where they were broader. Finally, they have benefited from certain wage trends which have helped to narrow the differentials that previously existed between the higher paying jobs where they were underrepresented, and the lower paying jobs, where they were overrepresented. All these were favorable developments and have helped the Negro to improve his occupational status and his earnings, and further to narrow the gap between himself and his white fellow citizens.

But there are other signs that are less favorable. The Negro was so far behind at the start of this century that despite his progress he remains today still very far behind. In fact the relatively slow pace at which the occupational gap is being closed reflects increasingly the educational gap between Negroes and whites, for increasingly education has come to determine what one can accomplish in the job market. Moreover, being the most vulnerable group in the labor market Negroes have been particularly hard hit by the general easing in the employment situation during the past decade. And the future is even more ominous because of the much larger numbers of better educated whites who will be competing for the available jobs. Hence the continuance of a slack labor market is a major danger to the Negroes' occupational future.

Aside from these favorable and unfavorable forces playing on the Negro community as a whole, it is important not to lose sight of the individual Negro and his preparation for and access to employment. The United States is moving with varying degrees of speed to remove overt and covert discrimination in education and employment and in housing, which is directly related to both. The faster the progress which it makes on these crucial fronts to eliminate discrimination, the faster the opportunity for the individual Negro to prepare himself adequately for work and to secure the full benefits of work preparation. This is the challenge that faces the nation as a whole, as well as every individual Negro.

NOTES

[1] For one view on approaches to improving the situation, see Ginzberg, *et al.*, *The Negro Potential.* (New York: Columbia University Press, 1956).

[2] This pattern is set out more fully in Hiestand, *Economic Growth and Employment Opportunities for Minorities.* (New York: Columbia University Press, 1964).

[3] Norgren and Hill, *Toward Fair Employment,* Columbia Univ. Press, p. 10.

[4] *Ibid,* Ch. 5, passim.

BIBLIOGRAPHY

Becker, Gary S., *The Economics of Discrimination.* Chicago: University of Chicago Press, 1957.

Dewey, Donald, "Negro Employment in Southern Industry." *Journal of Political Economy,* LX (August, 1952), pp. 279–293.

Edwards, G. Franklin, *The Negro Professional Class.* Glencoe, Illinois: The Free Press of Glencoe, 1959.

Feldman, Herman, *Racial Factors in American Industry.* New York: Harper & Brothers, 1931.

Frazier, E. Franklin. *The Negro in the United States,* rev. ed. New York: Macmillan, 1957.

Ginzberg, Eli, *et al.*, *The Negro Potential.* New York: Columbia University Press. 1956.

Henderson, Vivian, "The Economic Imbalance. An Inquiry into the Economic Status of Negroes in the United States, 1935–1960, with Implications for Negro Education." *Quarterly Review of Higher Education Among Negroes,* XXVIII (April, 1960), pp. 84–98.

———. *The Economic Status of Negroes: In the Nation and in the South.* Atlanta: Southern Regional Council, c. 1963.

Hiestand, Dale L., *Economic Growth and Employment Opportunities for Minorities.* New York: Columbia University Press, 1964.

Hope, John, II, "The Employment of Negroes in the United States by Major Occupation and Industry." *The Journal of Negro Education,* XXII Summer Issue, 1953, pp. 307–21.

Myrdal, Gunnar, *An American Dilemma.* New York: Harper & Co., 1944.

National Manpower Council, *Womanpower.* New York: Columbia University Press, 1957.

National Planning Association, Committee of the South, *Selected Studies of Negro Employment in the South* (Report No. 6). Washington, National Planning Association, 1955.

Norgren, Paul H., and Samuel E. Hill, *Toward Fair Employment.* New York: Columbia University Press, 1964.

U.S. Bureau of the Census, *Sixteenth Census of the United States, 1940, Population,* "Comparative Occupation Statistics for the United States, 1870 to 1940" (by Alba M. Edwards). Washington: Government Printing Office, 1943.

———. *Negroes in the United States, 1920–32.* Washington: Government Printing Office, 1935.

U.S. Commission on Civil Rights, *Civil Rights '63,* 1963 Report of the Commission, "The Negro in the Armed Forces." Washington: Government Printing Office, 1963, pp. 169–83, 214–24.

U.S. Department of Labor, *The Economic Situation of the Negro in the United States* (Bulletin S3). Washington: Government Printing Office, October, 1960.

———, *Negroes in the United States: Their Employment and Economic Status* (Bulletin No. 1119). Washington: Government Printing Office, 1952.

U.S. Senate, Committee on Labor and Public Welfare, Subcommittee on Employment and Manpower, *Hearings: Equal Employment Opportunity.* 88th Congress, First Session, 1963, Washington: Government Printing Office, 1963.

Vance, Rupert B., and Nicholas J. Demerath, eds., *The Urban South.* Chapel Hill: University of North Carolina Press, 1954.

Wagley, Charles, and Marvin Harris, *Minorities in the New World.* New York; Columbia University Press, 1958.

Weaver, Robert C., *Negro Labor, A National Problem.* New York: Harcourt, Brace, 1946.

chapter 5

Andrew F. Brimmer

The Negro

in the National Economy

Andrew F. Brimmer.   Assistant Secretary for Economic Affairs, United States Department of Commerce, Washington, D. C. Formerly Assistant Professor of Finance, Wharton School of Finance, University of Pennsylvania. Author of *Life Insurance Companies in the Capital Market.*

INTRODUCTION

The Negro lives and works in the backwaters and eddies of the national economy in the United States. This has been true since he arrived on these shores long before the colonies became a nation. In recent years, Negroes have made a number of vigorous advances in their efforts to enter the mainstream of economic activity. However, they remain at best a marginal factor in virtually every field, except those protected by the legacy of racial segregation and discrimination. Yet, the winds of change are blowing across the land, shaking old arrangements and creating new opportunities for men with imagination and enterprise. The objectives in this chapter are to identify and explain the forces which are re-making the economic world of the American Negro.

An appraisal of the Negro's role in the national economy can be approached in a number of ways. One alternative is to chronicle the progress the Negro has made within the long-term development of the economy as a whole. This approach would be primarily historical and descriptive. Since the record of the Negro's progress is impressive, the result might be both a colorful document and a monument to perserverance against great obstacles.

Another alternative is to highlight the strategic factors influencing the conditions under which Negroes participate in the economy and share the benefits of national production. This approach, which is basically analytic and statistical, emphasizes the Negro's adaptation to the malfunctioning of the market place. In general, both resource allocation and income shares are determined by the price system in an economy such as that found in the United States. But the existence of racial discrimination and the mosaic of social disorganization associated with segregation have severely restricted the Negro's opportunities to acquire skills and property and to offer them in exchange for income. Partly because of the resulting limited ability to earn—but also because of additional barriers—the Negro in turn has a restricted access to the market for consumer goods and services.

The effect of these constraints has been essentially the same as that produced by a protective tariff in international trade: two markets have emerged. One is open to the white public virtually without limitations, and whites are free to purchase both goods and services with complete freedom of choice. However, for Negroes entry into this market is extremely circumscribed. While they enjoy considerable freedom of choice in the purchase of goods (except housing), a wide range of services (especially personal services) offered to the general market is unavailable to them. Consequently, a second market has arisen. This is basically a Negro market, and the provision of personal services lies at its core. Thus, the Negro market is entirely derivative; it has evolved behind the walls of segregation to meet a demand left unfilled by business firms operating in the general market.

As background for the rest of the Chapter, it would be helpful to begin with a brief introduction to the general market economy in the United States, with special reference to the way it affects the Negro. Chart I, presenting a schematic view of the circular flow of economic activity, makes it clear that the Negro's role is both critical and marginal: he is a critical factor in the labor market and in the market for goods and services. On the other hand, the Negro makes little impact on the national economy in his role as an entrepreneur.

In general, the economy can be visualized as consisting of the four sec-

252   THE NEGRO IN THE NATIONAL ECONOMY

Chart I

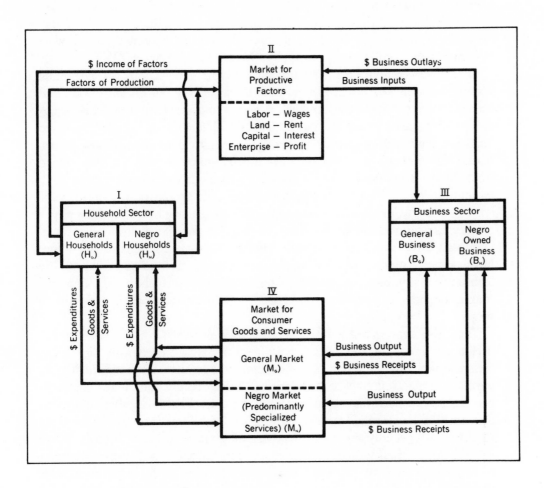

tors described in Chart I: (I) the household sector; (II) the market for productive resources; (III) the business sector and (IV) the market for consumer goods and services.[1] The schema rests on two principal assumptions: (1) that the dominant motivating forces in the economy are the attempts of households to maximize consumer satisfaction and the attempts of business firms to maximize profits; (2) the primary way to obtain income is to work for it. These assumptions lead to the first link traced in Chart I between the household sector (I) and the market for productive factors (II). (In tracing the flows, it should be noted that the movement of money is marked by $). To obtain income, households offer their resources in the market to those willing to employ them. For convenience, we can group these productive factors into four classes according to the types of income they receive. The most important factor of production is *labor,* and its income consists of *wages* (including salaries). Owners of *land* (including buildings and other improvements) receive *rent.* Owners of *capital* (defined broadly as loanable funds) receive *interest.* Finally, persons who take the risk of operating an *enterprise* (including common stockholders) receive *profits* (or bear *losses*). In our economy, the private business sector employs the vast proportion of the labor force; it rents or owns most of the land and structures, and it borrows most of the loanable funds. Thus, as labor and other resources flow from the market for factors into the business sector (III), they account for the bulk of business outlays. These business inputs are required to produce the output of goods and services demanded by, and sold to, consumers in the retail market (IV).

At this stage, however, a significant branching occurs in the economic stream as far as Negroes are concerned. Because Negroes do not have equal access to all sectors of the market for goods and services, a partially separate and parallel structure has emerged. This consists of Negro-owned business firms selling primarily through a Negro market to Negro households. The manner in which the structure is linked together can be traced from Negro households (H_N in sector I) through the Negro market (M_N in sector IV) to Negro-owned business (B_N in sector III). This parallel structure is the predominantly segregated Negro market. It is basically a market for services. It is the place of practice for the Negro professional (lawyers, physicians, dentists, undertakers). It is the counter for the Negro businessmen (owners of retail outlets, real estate dealers and brokers, life insurance companies, cosmetics manufacturers). And above all, it is the source of personal services purchased by Negroes (barber and beauty shops).

Thus, this segregated market, serving as a protective tariff, is the foundation for much of the Negro middle class. However, while the Negro businessman generally has few customers other than Negroes, he by no means has the Negro market to himself. Traditionally the Negro customer has made most of his expenditures for goods (both durable and nondurable) in those retail outlets serving the public at large. And in many localities (especially in the great urban centers of the North) white people have usually owned the more substantial retail stores catering to Negroes. In recent years, a considerable number of firms producing for the general market have begun to pursue the Negro consumer with extra vigor.[2] The result is that the consumption behavior of Negro households is increasingly merging with that of the rest of the population. But in the meantime, the historic dichotomy created by the limited access of Negroes to personal services persists and imparts a peculiar flavor to the participation of the Negro in the Nation's economy.

In Chapter 4, dealing with the Employment Patterns of Negro men and women, the changing occupational structure among Negroes has already been discussed. However, that chapter, designed with a different orientation, contains little discussion of the size, composition, trends and determinants of the income of the Negro community. Consequently, a look at the income picture is the point of departure in this chapter. The next task is the explanation of the changing pattern of expenditures by Negro consumers. A principal objective of the analysis is to weigh the implications of these emerging trends of consumer behavior for the future of the Negro market.

The remainder of the chapter is given to an examination of the changing environment in which Negro-owned businesses must operate and the prospects for careers as corporate officials. In the final section, the results are summarized and the principal conclusions are restated briefly.

Income of the Negro Community

In a price-directed, free-market economy, the size and distribution of income are prime indicators of economic progress and the well-being of citizens. Measured by either of these indicators, American Negroes, since World War II, have made mixed progress: as a group their incomes have grown both in absolute terms and as a share of the nation's aggregate income. However, because of the rapid strides made by white families, taken as a group, little actual improvement in the Negro's relative position was registered.

This experience is clearly evident from Table I, which shows the estimated aggregate income of families and individuals, by color, for the United States from 1947 through 1963. The personal income of nonwhites (about 92 percent of whom are Negroes) amounted to $23.6 billion in 1963, or 6.4 percent of total personal income. This was a record by both measurements. However, the most striking feature of Table I is the stag-

Chart II

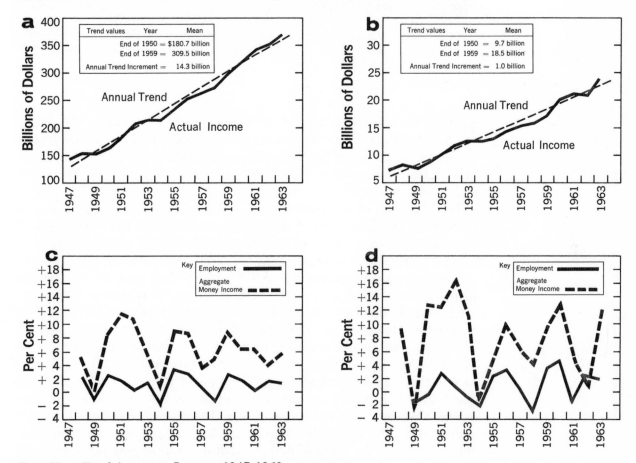

Chart IIa   Total Aggregate Income, 1947-1963
Chart IIb   Nonwhite Aggregate Income, 1947- 1963
Chart IIc   Annual Percentage Changes in Total Employment and Total Personal Income, 1948-1963
Chart IId   Annual Percentage Changes in Nonwhite Employment and Nonwhite Personal Income, 1948-1963

SOURCE: U.S. Department of Labor, *Manpower Report of the President,* March,

TABLE I—Estimated Aggregate Income of Families and Unrelated Individuals, by Color, for the United States, 1947–1963

Year	Aggregate Money Income (Billions)			Percent		
	Total	White	Nonwhite	Total	White	Nonwhite
1947	$147.0	$139.8	$7.2	100.0	95.1	4.9
1948	154.4	146.5	7.9	100.0	94.9	5.1
1949	153.9	146.2	7.7	100.0	95.0	5.0
1950	167.3	158.6	8.7	100.0	94.8	5.2
1951	186.2	176.4	9.8	100.0	94.7	5.3
1952	205.5	194.1	11.4	100.0	94.5	5.5
1953	215.4	202.7	12.7	100.0	94.1	5.9
1954	216.1	203.6	12.5	100.0	94.2	5.8
1955	235.1	222.0	13.1	100.0	94.4	5.6
1956	254.4	240.0	14.4	100.0	94.3	5.7
1957	263.3	248.0	15.3	100.0	94.2	5.8
1958	276.2	260.3	15.9	100.0	94.2	5.8
1959	301.2	283.8	17.4	100.0	94.2	5.8
1960	319.5	299.8	19.7	100.0	93.8	6.2
1961	339.1	318.3	20.8	100.0	93.9	6.1
1962	351.5	330.4	21.1	100.0	94.0	6.0
1963	371.1	347.5	23.6	100.0	93.6	6.4

SOURCE: U.S. Department of Commerce, Bureau of the Census, *Current Population Reports*, series P–60, annual issues. (Washington, D.C., Government Printing Office)

nation in the relative position of nonwhites between 1953 and 1960, during which years their share of personal income was frozen at approximately 5.8 percent of the total. This retardation is partly explained by the sluggishness of the economy as a whole from the end of the Korean War to the end of the decade.

This slow rate of economic growth had a particularly adverse effect on nonwhites. The dimensions of this impact are compared in Chart II; panels (a) and (b) trace the level and trend of total and nonwhite personal income from 1947 through 1963. As the trend lines indicate, total personal income increased by an average of $14.3 billion each year, and the income of nonwhites rose by an average of $1.0 billion. This represented an annual average rate of growth of 6.0 percent for the total and 7.7 percent for nonwhites. However, for the years of relative stagnation (1954–59 inclusively), the annual average growth rate of total income eased off to about 5.9 percent. In sharp contrast, during this same period, the growth rate in the income of nonwhites dropped to 5.4 percent. The result was a much greater gap between potential and actual level of income for nonwhites than for the nation as a whole. The size of this gap is roughly indicated by the spread between actual income and the trend lines. By this benchmark, the accumulated shortfall in total personal income during these six years amounted to about $86 billion, or about 5.8 percent less than the higher growth rate would have produced. For nonwhites, the accumulated shortfall in income was around $6.9 billion, representing a difference of 7.8 percent. Put differently, the sluggish behavior of the economy in the last half of the 1950's cost nonwhites the equivalent of 3.5 months' income at the 1963 rate, compared with just over 2.8 months' income for the entire economy.

The much greater impact of postwar business cycles on the employment and incomes of nonwhites also is graphically marked in Chart II. Panel (c) shows the annual percentage changes in total employment and total personal income over the years 1948–63; panel (d) shows the same information for nonwhites (except that estimates of changes in nonwhite employment are not available for 1949).[3] The effects of the four postwar recessions are clearly visible. The lowest levels in employment were reached in 1949, 1954, 1958 and 1961, respectively. During the first three recessions, the level of total employment declined by one-two percent; but no actual decrease in the level of total employment occurred in 1961. In contrast, the level of nonwhite employment dropped by approximately 2 percent in each of the recessions, and the decline was close to 3 percent in 1958. On the other hand, the return of better conditions also benefited nonwhites relatively more than the country as a whole. For instance, while total employment advanced by an average of 2.4 percent in the first year following each recession (excluding the 1949 setback), the corresponding increase in nonwhite employment was 2.7 percent. Moreover, for non-whites, the largest percentage gains in employment were registered in the second year of recovery, rather than in the first year as was the case for total employment. This tendency for nonwhite employment to lag may well be further evidence of the apparent habit for nonwhites to be "the last hired."

The more volatile behavior of nonwhite income is also traceable. The first thing to note, however, is that total personal income and the incomes of nonwhites are considerably more stable than the level of employment. This undoubtedly reflects the short duration of postwar recessions, as well as the influence of unemployment compensation, welfare payments and other sources which prevent incomes from falling in tandem with employment during recessions. In fact, total personal income declined absolutely only during 1949, and it actually rose by 5–7 percent in 1958 and 1961. Moreover, in the first year following each recession, total personal income climbed by an average of 7.6 percent. Nonwhite incomes displayed significantly more instability. A decline of about 2 percent was registered in both 1949 and 1954. While nonwhite incomes also showed advances in 1958 and 1961, the gains were substantially less than for the total. Increases during the first year of recovery after each recession were also less—averaging about 7 percent.

In summary, we can conclude that both business cycles and the relatively slow growth of the economy in the decade of the 1950's affected nonwhites considerably more adversely than all citizens combined. Since the evidence in Chapter 4 (Patterns of Employment of Negro Men and Women) suggests that little fundamental improvement is occurring in the relative position of the Negro in industry, we can expect nonwhites to continue to bear a disproportionate share of the burden of economic instability in the future.

We must now look behind these aggregate figures to the behavior of family and individual incomes, for it is at this more personal level that the welfare of the Negro community must be judged. Table II presents the median income [4] of families and individuals, by color, for the years 1947 through 1963. The general advance of family income is striking. Between 1947 and 1963, median family income, for both total and nonwhite families, just about doubled. For all families, the median rose from $3,031

TABLE II—Median Income of Families and Unrelated Individuals, by Color, for the United States, 1947–1963

	Families				Unrelated Individuals			
Year	Total	White	Nonwhite	Ratio of Nonwhite to white	Total	White	Nonwhite	Ratio of Nonwhite to white
1947	$3,031	$3,157	$1,614	0.51	$ 980	$1,035	$ 746	0.72
1948	3,187	3,310	1,768	.53	996	1,053	789	.75
1949	3,107	3,232	1,650	.51	1,050	1,134	819	.72
1950	3,319	3,445	1,869	.54	1,045	1,115	817	.73
1951	3,709	3,859	2,032	.53	1,195	1,258	929	.74
1952	3,890	4,114	2,338	.57	1,409	1,519	1,051	.69
1953	4,233	4,392	2,461	.56	1,394	1,473	1,161	.79
1954	4,173	4,339	2,410	.56	1,224	1,317	875	.66
1955	4,421	4,605	2,549	.55	1,316	1,402	935	.67
1956	4,783	4,993	2,628	.53	1,426	1,466	1,087	.74
1957	4,971	5,166	2,764	.54	1,496	1,592	1,013	.64
1958	5,087	5,300	2,711	.51	1,486	1,592	1,080	.68
1959	5,417	5,643	2,917	.52	1,556	1,663	1,075	.65
1960	5,620	5,835	3,233	.55	1,720	1,860	1,064	.57
1961	5,737	5,981	3,191	.53	1,755	1,885	1,160	.62
1962	5,956	6,237	3,330	.53	1,753	1,876	1,251	.67
1963	6,249	6,548	3,465	.53	1,800	1,887	1,294	.69

SOURCE: U.S. Department of Commerce, Bureau of the Census, "Current Population Reports", series P–60, annual issues. (Washington, D.C., U.S. Government Printing Office)

in 1947 to $6,249 in 1963. The advance for nonwhites was from $1,614 in 1947 to $3,465 in 1963. Equally striking, however, is the evidence that nonwhite families made virtually no net improvement in their income position relative to white families. In fact, the slight closing of the income gap which occurred between 1947 and 1952 was actually reversed over the next decade. Thus, by 1963, the median income of nonwhite families was 53 percent of that for white families—compared with 51 percent in 1947. The ratio had climbed to 57 percent in 1952, but it had also shrunk to a low of 51 percent in 1958. This deterioration further reflects the erosion of the Negro's position during the years of slack economic growth beginning in the mid-1950's. The more burdensome consequences of this slow-down on nonwhite families is also reflected in Table II. For instance, during the post-war period as a whole, the annual average rate of growth in median income was about the same for white and nonwhite families—4.7 percent and 4.8 percent, respectively. But during the years when nonwhites registered their largest relative gains (1947–52), the annual growth rate in their incomes was 7.7 percent, compared with 5.4 percent for white families. In contrast, during 1953–63, the order was reversed: the growth rate was 4.4 percent for whites and 3.6 percent for nonwhites. Again, the explanation for this weakness in the Negro's income position is to be found in the host of factors (including automation in industry and the continued ravages of racial discrimination) discussed in Chapter 4.

For the average American, education is undoubtedly the most promising escalator for advancement from low to high income status. For Negroes, education has been virtually the only escalator. However, the financial advantage for Negroes of an additional year of educational attainment is just over half that of whites. The general relationship between education and expected lifetime earnings of men, by color, is shown in Table III. Perhaps the most striking feature of these statistics is the fact that a nonwhite man must have between one and three years of college before he can expect to earn as much as a white man with less than eight years of schooling, over the course of their respective working lives. Moreover, even after completing college and spending at least one year in graduate school, a nonwhite man can expect to do about as well as a white person who only completed high school.

A number of considerations may account for the observed differentials. In the first place, whites and nonwhites reporting the same years of schooling undoubtedly have received educations differing vastly in quality. The historical pattern of legal and *de facto* school segregation, plus the cultural deprivation associated with it, have generally meant inherently unequal educational opportunities for nonwhites. The result has been a serious deficiency in the level of qualifications which nonwhites have been able to achieve in a wide range of occupations. Nevertheless, the corrosive effects of racial discrimination on earnings differentials for white and nonwhite men are also evident—even after one allows for differences in the quality of education. This is clearly illustrated by data relating to carpenters, truck drivers and semiskilled factory workers with less than eight years of schooling. Among these workers, the influence of differential quality in education is probably minimized. The expected lifetime earnings of nonwhite carpenters amount to 60 percent of that of white carpenters, or $91,000 versus $152,000. For truck drivers, the ratio was the same— $97,000 to $162,000. For factory workers, white and nonwhite lifetime

TABLE III—Education and Differential Lifetime Earnings of Men, by Color *

(Thousands of Dollars)

Level of Education	White	Nonwhite	Nonwhite as Percent of white
Elementary School:			
Less than 8 years	$157	$ 95	61
8 years	191	123	64
High School:			
1 to 3 years	221	132	60
4 years	253	151	60
College:			
1 to 3 years	301	162	54
4 years	395	185	47
5 years or more	466	246	53

* For men aged 18 to 64. Derived from 1960 Census data. See U.S. Senate, 88th Congress, 1st Session, *Hearings Before the Committee on Labor and Public Welfare on Bills Relating to Equal Employment Opportunities*, July and August, 1963.

earnings were $167,000 and $120,000, respectively, or a ratio of 72 percent. Within this structure, there was considerable variation, but the ratios of nonwhite to white earnings were generally lowest in the South and highest in the North and West. Moreover, U.S. Census Bureau figures relating to about twenty-seven other occupations reveal essentially the same pattern of variation. Thus, it seems that, even given about the same educational attainments, the money value of a nonwhite man is about two-fifths less than that of a white man when weighed in the general market for skills.

Poverty and Prosperity Among American Negroes

For a large number of Negro families, poverty is the normal state of existence. However, contrary to popular belief, the entire Negro community is certainly not poverty stricken—no matter what standard of measurement is applied. In fact, a substantial proportion of such families enjoys a standard of living thoroughly comparable to that enjoyed by the white middle class, and a fairly sizable number can afford the luxuries which cushion the lives of some of the nation's most well-off households.

TABLE IV—Selected Characteristics of Families with Incomes Under
$3,000 in 1959 for the United States, 1960 (Numbers in Thousands)

Selected Characteristics	All Families		White Families		Nonwhite Families	
	Number	Percent	Number	Percent	Number	Percent
All families	9,650	100.0	7,616	100.0	2,034	100.0
Male head	**7,573**	**78.5**	**6,190**	**81.3**	**1,383**	**68.0**
Head under 65 years	5,073	52.6	3,948	51.8	1,125	55.3
Husband-wife families	4,846	50.2	3,784	49.7	1,062	52.2
No earners	541	5.6	461	6.1	80	3.9
1 earner or more; head not earner	287	3.0	224	2.9	62	3.1
Head worked 50 to 52 weeks	1,945	20.2	1,544	20.3	401	19.7
Farmers and farm managers	570	5.9	525	6.9	46	2.2
Craftsmen, operatives, and kindred workers	479	5.0	357	4.7	122	6.0
Service workers, including private household	129	1.3	69	0.9	60	2.9
Laborers, except mine	290	3.0	170	2.2	121	5.9
All other occupation groups	476	4.9	423	5.6	53	2.6
Head worked less than 50 weeks	2,073	21.5	1,555	20.4	519	25.5
Farmers and farm managers	184	1.9	138	1.8	46	2.2
Craftsmen, operatives and kindred workers	867	9.0	705	9.3	162	8.0
Service workers, including private household	128	1.3	82	1.1	46	2.3
Laborers, except mine	549	5.7	329	4.3	220	10.8
All other occupation groups	345	3.6	300	3.9	45	2.2
Other male head families	226	2.3	164	2.2	62	3.1
No earners	44	0.5	34	0.4	10	0.5
1 earner or more	182	1.9	130	1.7	52	2.6
Head 65 years and over	2,500	25.9	2,242	29.4	258	12.7
No earners	1,545	16.0	1,434	18.8	111	5.5
1 earner or more	955	9.9	808	10.6	147	7.2
Female Head	**2,077**	**21.5**	**1,426**	**18.7**	**651**	**32.0**
Head under 65 years	1,625	16.8	1,066	14.0	559	27.5
No earners	584	6.1	409	5.4	175	8.6
1 earner or more	1,041	10.8	658	8.6	383	18.8
Head 65 years and over	452	4.7	360	4.7	92	4.5
No earners	229	2.4	195	2.6	34	1.7
1 earner or more	223	2.3	165	2.2	58	2.8

SOURCE: U.S. Department of Commerce, Bureau of the Census. *U.S. Census of Population*, 1960, PC(2)–4C, "Sources and Structure of Family Income", Tables 1, 2A, and 2B. (Washington, D.C., U.S. Government Printing Office).

TABLE V—Color and Farm—Nonfarm Residence: Families and Unrelated Individuals by Total Money Income in 1963, for the United States: 1964

Total Money Income	Families					Unrelated Individuals				
	United States			Nonfarm	Farm	United States			Nonfarm	Farm
	Total	White	Nonwhite			Total	White	Nonwhite		
Total										
Number—thousands	47,436	42,663	4,773	44,343	3,093	11,182	9,725	1,457	10,817	365
Percent	100.0	100.0	100.0	100.0	100.0	100.0	100.0	100.0	100.0	100.0
Under $1,000	3.8	3.2	9.2	3.3	11.1	28.2	26.2	41.1	27.7	44.4
$1,000 to $1,499	3.2	2.6	8.3	2.9	8.1	15.9	16.0	15.2	15.7	22.6
$1,500 to $1,999	3.6	3.2	8.0	3.3	8.9	9.8	10.0	8.9	9.8	9.3
$2,000 to $2,499	4.2	3.6	9.6	4.0	8.5	7.2	7.2	7.3	7.3	5.2
$2,500 to $2,999	3.7	3.3	8.0	3.5	6.8	4.7	4.5	6.1	4.8	3.3
$3,000 to $3,499	4.6	4.3	7.4	4.4	7.7	4.0	3.9	4.2	4.0	4.4
$3,500 to $3,999	4.1	3.9	6.1	4.1	5.4	4.2	4.3	3.6	4.2	3.7
$4,000 to $4,999	9.0	8.8	10.9	8.9	10.3	7.8	8.0	6.1	7.9	3.7
$5,000 to $5,999	11.1	11.3	8.7	11.2	8.9	6.2	6.6	3.7	6.4	1.1
$6,000 to $6,999	10.2	10.5	7.3	10.5	5.5	4.0	4.3	1.6	4.1	0.7
$7,000 to $7,999	9.1	9.6	4.7	9.4	4.7	2.8	3.0	1.6	2.9	—
$8,000 to $9,999	13.4	14.2	6.1	13.9	6.2	2.6	2.9	0.6	2.7	0.7
$10,000 to $14,999	14.5	15.6	4.1	15.0	5.9	1.8	2.1	—	1.9	0.7
$15,000 and over	5.4	5.9	1.6	5.7	2.1	0.7	0.8	0.2	0.7	—
Median income	$6,249	$6,548	$3,465	$6,427	$3,435	$1,800	$1,887	$1,294	$1,839	$1,123
Head Year-Round Full-Time Worker										
Percent of total	64.7	66.1	51.6	64.5	66.4	33.1	33.8	28.2	33.3	28.2
Median income	$7,458	$7,664	$4,847	$7,644	$4,107	$4,343	$4,486	$2,840	$4,411	(B)

— Entry rounds to zero.
(B) Median not shown where base is less than 200,000

SOURCE: U.S. Department of Commerce, Bureau of the Census, "Consumer Income", *Current Population Reports,* Series P–60, No. 42, (Washington, D.C., Government Printing Office June 1964.)

But taken as a group, Negroes are about two and one-half times more likely than white families to be found among the poor (see Table IV). Of course, it is virtually impossible to define precisely the boundaries of poverty, and it is almost as difficult to obtain general agreement on any definition adopted. For the purpose of this brief analysis, it is useful to follow the rough benchmark set by the Council of Economic Advisers.[5] Thus, a family of four with $3,000 or less per year can be considered "poor." Unattached individuals with incomes of $1,500 or less also can be considered "poor." These are obviously arbitrary cut-off figures, and they could be refined in a variety of ways to permit income variations according to size of family, location, age and other factors influencing household needs and living costs. But the $3,000 income figure for families does provide a crude yardstick for measuring the incidence of poverty among different groups in the population. Translated another way, an annual income of $3,000 means a weekly pay of about $60, compared with an average factory pay of around $100 per week in 1963. It means only $15 per week per person for a family of four. In the case of unattached individuals, an annual income of $1,500 implies a weekly income of less than $30. Clearly, these criteria are by no means generous, and if anything they probably understate the real incidence of poverty in the United States.

By the $3,000-income criterion, there were about 8.8 million poor families in 1963 (see Table V). This represented about 19 percent of the 47.4 million families in the country in that year. There were also about 3.9 million poor individuals in 1963, when the $1,500 income limit is used. The proportion of nonwhite families and individuals in the poverty group was considerably higher. For example, in 1963, there were 4.8 million nonwhite families; yet 2.1 million (or 43 percent) were poor. In fact, nonwhite families constituted just over 10 percent of all families in the country, but they represented about 23 percent of all the poor families. In 1963, there were 1,457 thousand nonwhite individuals, and they accounted for an even larger share (56 percent) of all poor and unattached individuals.

Poverty among Negroes is about three times more prevalent in the South than in the rest of the country. For example, of the 2,060 thousand Negro families with incomes under $3,000 in 1959, almost three-fourths lived in the South; less than one-fourth lived in the North; and only 4 percent lived in the West.[6] Within the South, well over half of the poor Negro families resided in urban areas; about one-third were rural families not on farms, and 15 percent lived on farms. The situation was sharply reversed in the North and West. Virtually all (95 percent) of the poor Negro families in these regions lived in cities. Among cities, however, the incidence of poverty among Negroes also varied widely. As Table VI shows, in generally poor areas of the country, the economic gap between nonwhites and the population at large is likely to be particularly wide. Thus, in New Orleans, where just over one-fourth of all families had incomes of $3,000 or less in 1959, about half of the nonwhite families were in that category. Moreover, nonwhites represented one-third of all families in New Orleans, but they accounted for three-fifths of all poor families in the city. Of the cities shown, the smallest gap between nonwhite and whites existed in Los Angeles, with Washington, D.C., second.

It is not possible here to offer a full explanation of the much greater incidence of poverty among Negroes. However, it seems evident that Negroes—far more than any other ethnic group (with the possible exception of American Indians)—suffer from the vicious circle of hereditary poverty. Because of the legacy of slavery, racial discrimination and the historical alienation of Negroes from the economic mainstream, the typical Negro family has long suffered from low and unstable incomes and the inadequate living standards made possible by such meager earnings. These circumstances have also meant that generation after generation of Negro children have been reared in an environment which heretofore has placed a low premium on education and the acquisition of technical skills which in turn form the basis of higher earning capacity. Numerous other elements help define and explain this mosaic of social disorganization and economic dependence which characterize poverty among Negroes, but the aim here is to present only a panoramic view within a general discussion of the income of the Negro community.

Although the Negro community can claim only a handful of millionaires, it can boast of a fairly large number of prosperous families and individuals. For example, as shown in Table V, in 1963, 274,000 nonwhite families had incomes of $10,000 or over, and more than one quarter of these earned in excess of $15,000. Between 1959 and 1963, the number of nonwhite families

in the $10,000-and-over group rose by about 93,000, or about 50 percent. In contrast, the corresponding rise for all families was about 2,700,000, or 40 percent. In 1963, these relatively high income nonwhite families represented just under 3 percent of all families with incomes over $10,000, compared with about 2.5 percent in 1959. Yet these figures clearly demonstrate that a sizable number of Negroes dwell well beyond the margin of subsistence. With incomes of this level, such families not only can afford comfortable housing (when they can manage to purchase it in an essentially segregated market), but they can also provide a college education for their children. They can entertain graciously and participate in a variety of cultural activities. They can travel widely at home and abroad. In fact, a number of travel agencies have grown up (and prospered) through serving predominantly Negro middle class customers. As a matter of fact,

TABLE VI—Relative Poverty Among White and Nonwhite Families in Selected Cities

A. All Families and Families with Income of $3,000 or less, 1959

	Total			Nonwhite		
		Poor Families			Poor Families	
City	Total Families	Number	Percent of Total	Total Nonwhite	Number	Percent of Total
Chicago	909,204	123,214	13.6	184,682	52,341	28.3
Los Angeles	636,522	91,513	14.4	98,653	23,778	24.1
Baltimore	229,069	42,493	18.6	68,229	21,719	31.8
Washington	173,695	30,077	17.3	91,058	21,614	23.7
New Orleans	152,518	42,381	27.8	50,678	25,471	50.3

B. Relative Position of Total and Nonwhite Families, 1959

	All Nonwhite Families As Percent of Total Families	Poor Nonwhite Families As Percent of Total Poor Families
Chicago	20.3	42.5
Los Angeles	15.5	26.0
Baltimore	29.8	51.1
Washington	52.4	71.9
New Orleans	33.2	60.1

SOURCE: U.S. Census of Population, 1960.

a substantial portion of the advertising in *Ebony* Magazine reflects the tastes and aspirations of a rising Negro middle class—and their increasing ability to purchase the goods and services which support a middle class existence.

But this relatively broad carpet of prosperity among middle class non-whites rests heavily on the labor of multiple earners. For instance, of the 181,000 nonwhite families earning $10,000 or over in 1959, 161,000—or almost 90 percent—had two or more earners.[7] Among all families in that income bracket, multiple-earner families accounted for just under two-thirds of the total. Thus, it seems evident that a nonwhite family head has a slim chance to attain a middle class plane of living if he is the only breadwinner. In fact, an extra worker in a nonwhite household makes a contribution to the family budget which is worth approximately one and one half times as much as that contributed by an extra earner in house-holds in general. In 1959, the median income of nonwhite families with only one earner was $2,903; in nonwhite families with two or more earners, the figure was $4,370 or 50 percent greater. For all families in the country, the respective median incomes were $5,326 and $7,009—suggesting only a one-third gain attributable to the presence of one or more additional earners.

Income Distribution

A particularly distressing trend is evident in the distribution of income within the Negro community: the middle and upper income groups are getting richer, while the lowest income group is getting poorer. The basis for this conclusion can be readily seen in Table VII and Chart III. Table

VII shows the percentage distribution of families and aggregate money income, by color, in 1947 and 1960. It will be observed that in both the white and nonwhite communities, the middle income groups made sizable gains in their share of total income. While such gains were made at the expense of both extremes of the income spectrum, the shrinkage in the relative share of the lowest fifth of nonwhite families is especially noticeable.

Chart III provides a visual perspective on the changing pattern of income distribution among white and nonwhite families since World War II. Panels (a) and (b) of the chart give a graphic picture (known technically as a "Lorenz Curve") of the distribution of total money income among the white and nonwhite families in 1947 and 1960. These are the same figures shown in Columns (4) and (8) of Table VII. For example, reading along the bottom of panel (a), one can see that in 1947 the lowest fifth (or 20 percent) of white families received about 5.5 percent of the income (shown along the vertical axis of the chart). The corresponding

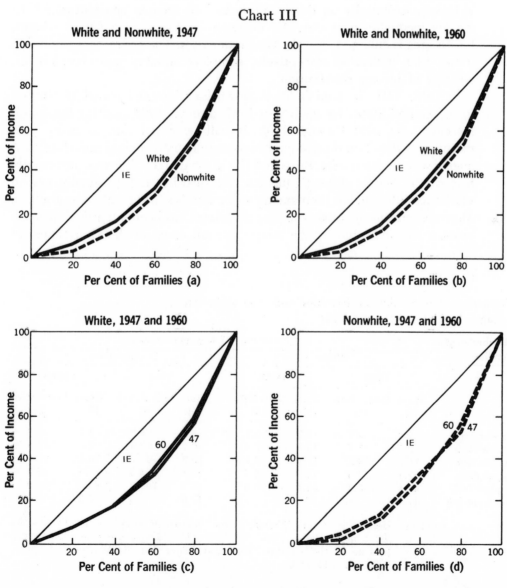

Chart III

figures were about 4.8 percent for the lowest 20 percent of nonwhite families. The second fifth of white families in 1947 received 12.2 percent of aggregate income, making a total of 17.7 percent for the lowest 40 percent of the white families combined. For the lowest two-fifths of nonwhite families, the proportion was 13.5 percent in 1947. Thus, by plotting successive fifths of the families along the horizontal axis and indicating the relative share of total income received along the vertical axis, one completes the Lorenz Curve.

This curve is a handy tool with which to examine the extent of income equality within any specified group. For instance, if incomes were equally distributed, the Lorenz Curve would be the diagonal line rising from the lower left of each panel. It would mean that 20 percent of the families received 20 percent of the income; 60 percent of the families received 60 percent of the income—and so on. Consequently, the deviation of the actual pattern of income distribution from this diagonal line is a measure of the degree of income inequality within a particular community. In fact, this degree of inequality can be stated with considerable precision. It is the ratio of the area between the diagonal line and the actual Lorenz Curve [marked by IE in panel (a)] to the area of the triangle X, Y, Z. This ratio is known technically as the "Gini Index" of income concentration.[8] As income inequality increases, the deviation of the Lorenz Curve widens, the IE area is enlarged, and the Gini Index rises. The Index varies between 0 and 1.00, indicating respectively, complete equality and complete inequality of income distribution.

In Table VIII, the Gini Index is shown for white and nonwhite families in the United States for each year 1947 through 1960, and for the South for each year 1953 through 1960. It will be noted that in every year income was distributed considerably more unequally among nonwhite than among white families [see also panel (b) of Chart III]. This was particularly true of the South, although income was distributed less equally among southern white families than among white families in the nation as a whole. Moreover, income inequality among nonwhites has been intensified over the years, a fact indicated by the steady upward creep of the Gini Index. In

TABLE VII—Percentage Distribution of Families and Aggregate Money Income, by Color, 1947 and 1960

Distribution of Families	Percentage of Aggregate Income							
	White				Nonwhite			
	1947		1960		1947		1960	
	Share (1)	Cumulative (2)	Share (3)	Cumulative (4)	Share (5)	Cumulative (6)	Share (7)	Cumulative (8)
Lowest Fifth	5.5	5.5	5.3	5.3	4.8	4.8	3.9	3.9
Second Fifth	12.2	17.7	12.4	17.4	10.2	15.0	9.6	13.5
Middle Fifth	16.9	34.6	17.5	35.2	15.7	30.7	16.4	29.9
Fourth Fifth	22.8	57.4	23.3	58.5	23.6	54.3	25.4	55.3
Highest Fifth	42.6	100.0	41.4	100.0	45.7	100.0	44.7	100.0
Top 5 percent	17.4	—	16.7	—	17.0	—	16.2	—

SOURCE: Herman P. Miller, *Trends in the Income of Families and Persons in the United States: 1947 to 1960.* (U.S. Department of Commerce, Bureau of the Census, Technical Paper No. 8, Washington, D.C. 1963, pp. 168–189.

TABLE VIII—GINI Index of Income Concentration, by Color, for the United States and the South, 1947-1960

Year	White Families		Nonwhite Families	
	U.S.	South	U.S.	South
1947	.363		.406	
1948	.361		.406	
1949	.367		.415	
1950	.372		.402	
1951	.352		.405	
1952	.359		.365	
1953	.353	.380	.393	.400
1954	.359	.415	.402	.418
1955	.358	.394	.388	.400
1956	.347	.367	.396	.401
1957	.345	.364	.405	.433
1958	.340	.364	.412	.425
1959	.349	.377	.414	.422
1960	.357	.394	.414	.437

SOURCE: Herman P. Miller, *Trends in the Income of Families and Persons in the United States: 1947 to 1960.* (United States Department of Commerce, Bureau of the Census, Technical Paper No. 8, Washington, D.C. 1963), pp. 168–189.

contrast, the trend was toward greater equality among white families as witnessed by the slight downward drift of the Gini Index. These trends are also shown graphically in panels (c) and (d) of Chart III. The Lorenz Curves in panel (c) for white families indicate a moderate shift to greater equality, because the 1960 curve lies on the 1947 curve, or slightly to its left toward the upper end of the distribution. The picture for nonwhite families, shown in panel (d) is quite different: over most of the distribution, the 1960 Lorenz Curve lies to the right of the 1947 curve, signifying increased inequality in income distribution. Only in the upper income range, where the 1960 curve is closer to the diagonal line, was there evidence of a tendency toward greater income equality.

This drift toward further income inequality among nonwhite families is exhibited even more clearly in Table IX, showing the percentage distribution of families and mean family income, by color, for 1947 and 1960. First, it will be observed that nonwhite families as a whole made moderate gains relative to white families, reflected in the rise in the income ratio from 54.2 percent in 1947 to 58.8 percent in 1960. Even larger percentage advances were registered by those in the middle-through-highest fifth of families. The top 5 percent of nonwhite families also did moderately well in relation to their white counterparts. However, the story was far different for those nonwhite families at the bottom of the income ladder. For them, the income ratio actually dropped, falling from 47.4 percent of white family incomes in 1947 to 43.2 percent in 1960. Although the mean income of the lowest group of nonwhite families more than doubled between 1947 and 1960, it still amounted to only $764 in the latter year. In fact, the relative gap between the lowest and highest nonwhite income groups widened appreciably, while the relative income spread between the lowest and highest white families remained virtually unchanged.

While it is comparatively easy to describe the deterioration in the

TABLE IX—Percentage Distribution of Families and Mean Family Income,
by Color, 1947 and 1960

Distribution of Families	1947			1960		
	White	Nonwhite	Nonwhite as Percent of White	White	Nonwhite	Nonwhite as Percent of White
All Families	$3,718	$2,016	54.2	$6,674	$3,921	58.8
Lowest Fifth	1,022	484	47.4	1,769	764	43.2
Second Fifth	2,268	1,029	45.4	4,138	1,882	45.5
Middle Fifth	3,142	1,583	50.4	5,840	3,216	55.1
Fourth Fifth	4,238	2,380	56.2	7,775	4,980	64.1
Highest Fifth	7,919	4,619	58.3	13,815	8,766	63.5
Top 5 Percent	12,938	6,858	53.0	22,293	12,677	56.9
Total Number of Families (thousands)	34,158	3,121	—	41,104	4,331	—
Aggregate Income (millions)	$126,999	$6,292	—	$274,328	$16,982	—

SOURCE: Herman P. Miller, *Trends in the Income of Families and Persons in the United States: 1947 to 1960.* (United States Department of Commerce, Bureau of the Census, Technical Paper No. 8, Washington, D.C. 1963), pp. 168–189.

relative position of the nonwhite families at the bottom of the income distribution it is far more difficult to explain it. Initially, however, it seems to reflect the same complex of factors described in Chapter 4. The handicaps of limited education, the changing demand for skills, and the effects of racial discrimination—all seem to interact to trap a vast number of nonwhite families in the dismal poverty so characteristic of the backwaters of the nation's economic life. And there they seem to remain, while others move ahead, including an increasing number of better-equipped nonwhites. Clearly, some large-scale, national economic and community development effort is required to break the cycle of poverty in the United States— especially among nonwhites.

The Economic Cost of Racial Discrimination

It is appropriate to conclude this discussion of the income of the Negro community by an assessment of the overall economic cost of racial discrimination. In 1962, the Council of Economic Advisers [9] estimated this cost at about $17.3 billion, or roughly 3.2 percent of a gross national product (GNP) which totaled $554.9 billion in that year. Using a different estimating procedure, the U.S. Bureau of the Census has prepared a similar estimate for each year 1949 through 1963. The results are shown in Table X. Before examining these figures, it should be pointed out that these estimates are tentative, because it is not possible to measure with any degree of certainty the full effects of non-discriminatory employment practices on the relative distribution of jobs, occupations, and earnings among whites and nonwhites. Moreover, the estimates approximate only the economic cost of racial discrimination, which is but a minor part of the damage done to the entire community—Negro and white—by the ravages of racial discrimination.

The estimates attempt to account for the economic losses arising from two sources: (1) inefficiencies in the use of the labor force resulting from failure to utilize fully the *existing* experience and skills of our population; (2) failure to develop *potential* experience and skills fully. The losses are described in terms of the gains that might accrue to GNP if discrimination were eliminated—or had been eliminated in the past. However, because the legacy of past discrimination affects today's occupational, geographic and capital structure, and the skills, training and education of the nonwhite labor force, the gains would accrue only over time as the economy adjusts and the labor force is upgraded.

As Table X shows, the economy has been losing between 1.9 percent and 2.4 percent in GNP simply because racial discrimination prevents the full use of the *present* educational attainment of nonwhites. In 1963, this loss amounted to 1.9 percent of GNP or $11.1 billion. However, this source of loss in GNP has declined compared with the six years 1949–54, when it amounted to 2.4 percent of the value of total output of goods and services. Behind this loss in GNP is a number of interrelated factors. In the first place, discrimination limits nonwhites primarily to job categories in which they cannot fully use their qualifications. If discrimination were lessened, nonwhites could migrate more readily from low to high productivity positions. The result would be an increase in the total output of goods and services. Moreover, a more rational utilization of the labor force probably would also require greater additions to the capital stock; plant and equipment expenditures would rise—further boosting the gain in output. Thus, capital as well as labor income would be enhanced, and the larger earnings of capital would also expand GNP. Self-employed entre-

TABLE X—Estimated Gains in Gross National Product from the Elimination of Racial Discrimination (Amounts in Billions of Dollars)

Year	Actual GNP	Gains in GNP from Full Use of Present Educational Attainment of Nonwhites		Gains in GNP from Raising the Educational Level of Nonwhites		Gains in GNP from Raising and Fully Using the Educational Level of Nonwhites	
		Amount	Percent	Amount	Percent	Amount	Percent
1949	$258.1	6.2	2.4	3.2	1.2	9.4	3.6
1950	284.6	6.8	2.4	3.1	1.1	10.1	3.5
1951	329.0	7.9	2.4	3.5	1.1	11.4	3.5
1952	347.0	8.4	2.4	3.5	1.0	11.9	3.4
1953	365.4	8.9	2.4	2.9	0.8	11.8	3.2
1954	363.1	8.8	2.4	3.4	1.0	12.2	3.4
1955	397.5	7.5	1.9	5.8	1.4	13.3	3.3
1956	419.2	7.9	1.9	6.3	1.5	14.2	3.4
1957	442.8	8.3	1.9	6.7	1.5	15.0	3.4
1958	444.5	8.4	1.9	6.3	1.4	14.7	3.3
1959	482.7	9.2	1.9	7.9	1.6	17.1	3.5
1960	502.6	9.5	1.9	6.2	1.4	16.7	3.3
1961	518.2	9.9	1.9	7.7	1.5	17.6	3.4
1962	554.9	10.6	1.9	9.1	1.7	19.7	3.6
1963	583.9	11.1	1.9	9.0	1.6	20.1	3.5

SOURCE: U.S. Department of Labor, *Manpower Report of the President,* March, 1964, Table A–3, p. 197.

preneurs (especially nonwhites) would have more open access to markets, and thus become more efficient, in the absence of racial discrimination; and their incomes would reflect their higher productivity. This is another source of the improvement in GNP resulting from a decline in racial discriminaton.

We can express in other ways the magnitude of the loss in GNP attributable to the failure to use efficiently the present educational achievements of the nonwhite labor force. For example, nonwhites account for about 10 percent of the country's total civilian population aged fourteen and over and for approximately 11 percent of the labor force. Consequently, the country is wasting about one-fifth of the potential productivity and contribution of nonwhites to the national economy. Put still another way, the $11.1 billion lost to the nation in 1963 because of racial discrimination—ironically—is almost identical to the amount which the Council of Economic Advisers estimated would be required for the conquest of poverty in the United States.[10] Using an annual income of $3,000 or less as a poverty benchmark, it would require about $11 billion to lift all poor families to a minimum standard of well-being.

If Negroes and other nonwhites could also achieve the same educational levels obtained by the white population—and if discrimination did not hamper their full participation in the economy—GNP might be expanded by about 3.5 percent. In 1963, this was equivalent to $20.1 billion. This figure includes the previous gain of $11.1 billion which might accrue from the eradication of discrimination. Thus, equal education for nonwhites in a nondiscriminatory economy could be valued roughly at $9 billion in terms of 1963 GNP. Moreover, the proportion of the total loss in GNP accounted for by the differences in the level of education of whites and nonwhites has risen sharply. It was around one-third in the years 1949–52, and it dropped to about one-fourth in 1953–54. However, since 1956, it has remained well above two-fifths.

Finally, one could aggregate the loss in GNP accruing from racial discrimination over the years. During the period 1946–1963, the failure to use fully present skills of nonwhites cost the nation approximately $129.4 billion; the persistence of educational differences (which itself reflects the legacy of discrimination) added a further loss of $85.8 billion. These two sources combined were responsible for aggregate losses in GNP of $215.2 billion, or 3.4 percent of the total output of goods and services during these years. Everyone can visualize easily the improvements in the general welfare which could have resulted from such a windfall gain in the nation's output of goods and services.

CONSUMER EXPENDITURES AND THE NEGRO MARKET

Historical Divergence in Negro-White Consumption Patterns

In the past, the pattern of expenditures among Negroes has diverged sharply from that of the general population. This divergence has resulted from a number of circumstances, but low incomes and the restrictions of racial discrimination have been principally responsible. Because of low incomes, the typical Negro family has had to spend a somewhat larger proportion of its paycheck for basic necessities, such as food, clothing and housing, than have white families. Because of limited access to public accommodations, Negroes have tended to entertain more at home than white families in the same income group. Moreover, Negroes seem to be particularly brand conscious; and (when they can afford them) they appear to lean toward higher priced items in any specific line. Finally, expenditures in personal care (including the costs of cosmetics and patronage at beauty and barber shops) normally run much higher for Negroes than for whites in the same income category.

In some cases it is possible to obtain a reasonably good quantitative estimate of the effects of racial discrimination on Negro consumption expenditures. The effects are particularly noticeable in the pattern of spending for the services of the amusement, restaurant, hotel and motel industries. Here the availability or nonavailability of desegregated facilities seems to outweigh any special kinds of taste or conspicuous consumption in shaping the behavior of Negro consumers. The differential effects of the segregated market are clearly discernible in Table XI, showing average Negro and white family expenditures for "admissions," which is a good proxy for patronage of theaters and recreational facilities; "food eaten away from home," which covers restaurants, diners and other eating places; and "automobile operations," that is, the cost of driving and maintaining a car—a key to travel, including the use of hotels and motels. From these data it is clear that Negroes in large Northern cities spend considerably more than Southern Negroes of the same income bracket for each of the services listed in Table XI; on the other hand Northern city white families

TABLE XI—Average Family Expenditures for Admissions, Food Eaten Away from Home, and Automobile Operations, for 3 Income Classes, Large Northern and Southern Cities, by Race, 1950.

Income Class and Region	Admissions			Food Eaten Away From Home			Automobile Operation		
	Negro	White	Negroes Percent of Whites	Negro	White	Negroes Percent of Whites	Negro	White	Negroes Percent of Whites
$2,000 to $3,000:									
Large Northern Cities	$31	$29	107	$148	$184	80	$52	$86	60
Large Southern Cities	$23	$36	64	$113	$194	58	$52	$95	55
Northern Expenditures as Percent of Southern	135	81	—	131	95	—	100	91	—
$3,000 to $4,000:									
Large Northern Cities	$45	$37	122	$138	$170	81	$67	$158	42
Large Southern Cities	$37	$39	95	$117	$180	65	$86	$170	51
Northern Expenditures as Percent of Southern	122	95	—	118	94	—	78	93	—
$4,000 to $5,000:									
Large Northern Cities	$57	$48	119	$182	$234	78	$148	$220	67
Large Southern Cities	$39	$45	87	$166	$257	65	$136	$225	60
Northern Expenditures as Percent of Southern	146	107	—	110	91	—	109	98	—

SOURCE: "Study of Consumer Expenditure Income and Saving," tabulated by Bureau of Labor Statistics, U.S. Department of Labor, for Wharton School of Finance and Commerce, University of Pennsylvania, Philadelphia, Pa., 1956–57.

TABLE XII—Summary of Family Expenditures, Income, and Savings, by Race, All Urban Families and Single Consumers, United States, 1950 and 1960–61

	1950		1960–61	
	Total	**Negro**	**Total**	**Negro**
Family Characteristics:				
Number of families ('000)	31,539	2,965	40,132	4,398
Percent of families	100.0	9.4	100.0	11.0
Average				
Family size	3.0	3.1	3.1	3.2
Money income before taxes	$4,237	$2,709	$6,691	$4,133
Net change in assets and liabilities	−74	−116	$ 177	$ 23
Number of full-time earners	0.9	0.8	0.8	0.7
Age of head	47	45	47	46
Education of head	10	9	11	8
Number of children under 18 years			1.2	1.4
Percent				
Homeowners, all year	48	32	53	31
Auto owners, end of year			73	43
Reporting savings increase			52	43
" " decrease			41	43
" " no change			7	14
With children under 18 years			50	50
With persons 65 years and over			23	19
Average income, expenditures and savings:				
Total receipts	$5,237	$3,125	$7,747	$4,512
Money income after taxes	3,910	2,605	5,906	3,840
Other money receipts	49	15	82	33
Decrease in assets	753	153	897	128
Increase in liabilities	525	352	862	511
Account balancing difference	−117	−64	−207	−210
Total disbursements	$5,354	$3,189	$7,954	$4,722
Increase in assets	955	291	1,423	346
Decrease in liabilities	249	98	514	316
Personal insurance	177	106	324	203
Gifts and contributions	165	81	303	150
Expenditures for current consumption	$3,808	$2,614	$5,390	$3,707

SOURCE: Data for 1950 are from *Study of Consumer Expenditures, Incomes and Savings,* Statistical Tables, Urban—1950 (University of Pennsylvania, 1956–57.) Data for 1960–61 are from *Consumer Expenditures and Income, Urban United States, 1960–61* (U.S. Department of Labor, Bureau of Labor Statistics), Supplement 1 to BLS Report No. 237–38, Washington, D.C. April, 1964.)

spend less than Southern city families. Within the same income class, Negroes in the North spend more than whites in the North for "admissions." But Southern Negroes spend less than either Southern whites or Northern Negroes. In both the North and South, Negroes spend less on "food eaten away from home" than white people in the same income categories. However, the differential is much greater in the South. The table also indicates that both Northern and Southern Negroes spend much less than whites of the same income class on "automobile operations"—40 to 60 percent less.

These summary statistics certainly suggest that Negroes are less likely than whites to be patrons of cultural events, customers of restaurants or tourists along the open road. Since Negroes spend close to the same amount, on the average, for the purchase of automobiles as did whites of the same income level (and proportionately more for food) it seems evident that their limited access to adequate facilities historically has distorted their overall pattern of consumption.

Recent Trends in Negro Consumption Behavior

In recent years, however, Negro consumers have displayed a marked tendency to behave like other consumers with similar incomes and education. In Tables XII and XIII, one can observe the broad trends in Negro-white expenditure patterns in the last decade and a half. For example, between 1950 and 1960–61, the average urban Negro family increased its spending for current consumption by 42 percent. In the process, the distinguishing characteristics of the Negro market were blurred substantially. While the overall pattern of expenditures by Negro families continues to be typical of that generally found among low income groups, there is also evidence of rapidly emerging middle class spending habits.

In 1960–61, the average urban Negro family spent about $3,707 for annual living expenses (see Table XII). This amount was just over two-thirds that spent by the average family in the Nation as a whole—a ratio which was virtually unchanged from 1950. Also in 1960–61, the average Negro family paid $293 in income and other personal taxes; channeled about $203 into life insurance and retirement funds and made gifts and contributions of approximately $150. Finally, such families typically increased both their assets and liabilities. But on balance, they registered net savings of $23 compared with an increase of $116 in net indebtedness in 1950.

The income of average urban Negro families, both before and after taxes, registered a sizable gain. Before taxes, their income in 1960–61 was $4,133, a rise of about 53 percent. However, increases in taxes held their after-tax income to $3,840, representing an advance of 47 percent. For all urban families in 1960–61, average before tax income was $6,691, and after taxes the figure was $5,906. However, after adjusting for the increase in consumer prices during the 1950's, the gain in aftertax income for urban families as a whole was 22 percent and in expenditures 14 percent.

Negro families, along with other families in the Nation, increased their total outlay for consumption between 1950 and 1960–61. But there were notable shifts in the proportion of their expenditures devoted to different purposes. (See Table XIII.) The share spent for food dropped from 32 percent to 25 percent—with the biggest decline occurring in spending on food consumed at home. By 1960–61, there was little difference on the average between the share of expenditures devoted to home consumption of food by Negro families and those in the society at large. Another sizable shift occurred in the pattern of spending on housing. Total housing outlays absorbed about 31 percent of the current consumption expenditures for Negro families in 1960–61, compared with 28 percent in 1950. The sharp advance in the proportion spent by the home-owning group was parallel to that of all families. But among Negro families, spending on rented dwellings also expanded relatively, while the trend was slightly downward for all renters combined. Part of this changing pattern of housing expenditures undoubtedly reflects inflation in rents and construction costs during the last decade, but even after adjusting for price increases the overall tendency to spend relatively more on housing would probably remain.

There is other evidence of up-grading in the consumption behavior of Negro families. Their purchase and operation of automobiles rose from 7.0 percent to 9.5 percent of their total expenditures for current consumption. Although this proportion is still substantially below that for white families (13.3 percent), the relative gain for Negro families was considerably larger than for white families in urban areas. Spending by Negro families on personal care remains comparatively higher than for families in general, but for the former such outlays are growing less rapidly than for the latter. In contrast, the spread between the percentage of expenditures for medical care made by Negro and white families narrowed somewhat, because Negro families increased the proportion devoted to medical care at a greater rate.

Alcoholic beverages and tobacco have traditionally accounted for a larger

TABLE XIII—Distribution of Expenditures for Current Consumption, Negro and White Families, Urban United States, 1950 and 1960–61

| | Negro Families | | | | White Families | | | |
| | Amount | | Percentage Distribution | | Amount | | Percentage Distribution | |
	1950	1960–61	1950	1960–61	1950	1960–61	1950	1960–61
Expenditures for Current Consumption:								
Total	$2,614	$3,707	100.0	100.0	$3,938	$5,610	100.0	100.0
Food, total	834	929	31.9	25.1	1,162	1,357	29.5	24.2
Food prepared at home	720	760	27.5	20.5	936	1,070	23.7	19.1
Food away from home	114	169	4.4	4.6	227	287	5.8	5.1
Clothing, materials, services	356	464	13.6	12.5	446	571	11.3	10.2
Housing: total	723	1,163	27.7	31.4	1,069	1,647	27.1	29.3
Shelter	296	554	11.3	14.9	453	775	11.5	13.8
Rented dwelling	213	389	8.1	10.5	230	316	5.8	5.6
Owned dwelling	77	159	2.9	4.3	198	416	5.0	7.4
Other shelter	6	6	0.2	0.2	26	43	0.7	0.8
Fuel, light, refrigeration, water	132	178	5.0	4.8	161	253	4.1	4.5
Household operations	107	228	4.1	6.1	186	332	4.7	5.9
Household furnishings and equipment	188	203	7.2	5.5	269	287	6.8	5.1
Transportation	253	435	9.7	11.7	538	839	13.7	15.0
Automobile purchase and operation	184	352	7.0	9.5	470	745	11.9	13.3
Other travel and transportation	69	83	2.6	2.2	67	94	1.7	1.7
Medical and personal care	175	319	6.7	8.6	294	537	7.5	9.5
Medical care	96	178	3.7	4.8	208	378	5.3	6.7
Personal care	79	141	3.0	3.8	86	157	2.2	2.8
Alcoholic beverages and tobacco	117	155	4.4	4.2	135	189	3.5	3.3
Alcoholic beverages	61	75	2.3	2.0	66	92	1.7	1.6
Tobacco	56	80	2.1	2.2	69	97	1.8	1.7
Recreation	95	130	3.6	3.5	176	228	4.5	4.1
Reading and Education	29	55	1.1	1.4	61	117	1.5	2.1
Reading	21	31	0.8	0.8	36	52	0.9	0.9
Education	8	24	0.3	0.6	25	65	0.6	1.2
Other Expenditures	30	57	1.1	1.5	58	127	1.5	2.3

SOURCE: Data for 1950 are from *Study of Consumer Expenditures, Incomes and Savings,* Statistical Tables, Urban—1950 (University of Pennsylvania, 1956–57.) Data for 1960–61 are from *Consumer Expenditures and Income, Urban United States,* 1960–61 (U.S. Department of Labor, Bureau of Labor Statistics, Supplement 1 to BLS Report No. 237–38 Washington, D.C. April, 1964.

TABLE XIV—Percentage Change in Selected Consumption Expenditures in
Response to Percentage Change in After-Tax Income for
Negro and White Families, 1950 and 1960–61

Expenditure Item	Negro Families	White Families
1. Education	4.22	3.06
2. Household Operation	2.39	1.50
3. Housing: Owned Dwelling	2.25	2.11
4. Automobile	1.93	1.12
5. Medical care	1.80	1.56
6. Housing: Rented Dwelling	1.74	0.72
7. Personal care	1.66	1.58
8. Food away from home	1.02	0.51
9. Reading	1.00	0.85
10. Tobacco	0.91	0.78
11. Recreation	0.78	0.56
12. Fuel, light, etc.	0.73	1.09
13. Clothing	0.64	0.54
14. Alcoholic beverages	0.49	0.75
15. Transportation (exc. auto)	0.43	0.77
16. House furnishings	0.17	0.13
17. Food (at home)	0.12	0.27
18. Total Consumption	0.80	0.81

SOURCE: Computed from TABLES XII and XIII.

share of expenditures by Negro families than of expenditures by white families. Between 1950 and 1960–61, this pattern of spending was modified. Negro families' relative outlays on alcoholic beverages eased off, but those for tobacco edged up slightly. For white families, both categories registered modest losses on a relative basis.

Expenditures by both white and Negro families for recreation lost a bit of ground relatively, but the loss for white families was moderately large. Recreation includes purchases of TV sets, as well as the cost of admission to theaters, sports events, concerts, etc. The share of spending represented by admissions to motion pictures undoubtedly declined over the decade, while the share of TV sets rose sharply. Spending for reading matter accounted for about the same percentage of expenditures for current consumption in both Negro and white families, and its relative position in both sets of family budgets remained unchanged between 1950 and 1960–61. However, both Negro and white families just about doubled the percentage of expenditures devoted to education.

In general, this shifting pattern of outlays by Negro families represents a gradual conversion toward the consuming behavior of white families. The implications of these changing preferences may be quite serious from the point of view of the future composition of the Negro market. Table XIV highlights the main tendencies which will basically shape the Negro market in the years ahead. This table shows the percentage increase between 1950 and 1960–61 in consumer expenditures for selective categories of goods and services in response to the percentage increase in family incomes after taxes. (In economists' language, this is a rough measure of the income elasticity of consumption. A ratio greater than 1.00 indicates a stronger than average preference for a particular item.) The expenditure categories have been ranked according to the strength of the response of consumption for Negro families to the rise in their income. The corresponding measure for white families is also shown. It will be noted that for both Negro and white families, the percentage increase in total consumption was about four-fifths that of the percentage increase in income. Spending for education by Negro families had the strongest response—a gain of 4.22 percent for each 1.00 percent increase in income. Spending for food consumed at home by Negro families had the lowest response at 0.12 percent.

In general, the figures in Table XIV suggest that, in the future, Negro families will register the strongest demand in those areas associated with overall upgrading in their standard of living. There should be a strong market for housing and household operation, automobiles and medical and personal care. Those areas which have traditionally received a good share of the Negro's patronage—tobacco, clothing, alcoholic beverages and food —will probably be characterized by relatively slow growth.

Potential Expansion of the Negro Market

Another perspective on the Negro market can be provided by linking the potential gains in income from eliminating racial discrimination shown in Table X with the pattern of consumer expenditures shown in Table XII.

On the basis of calculations discussed above, it was estimated that the nation lost about $11 billion in gross national product in 1963 because racial discrimination prevented the efficient use of the present educational attainment of nonwhites. If we included the gains which would result from raising the educational levels of nonwhites to that of the rest of the population, GNP could have been further increased by $9 billion. Thus, an additional $20 billion could have been added to a GNP of $584 billion in 1963, raising the total by almost 3.5 percent. These global gains in the output of the nation's goods and services can be translated into rather striking implications for the Negro market. For example, if racial discrimination were removed, by how much would the income of the nonwhite population increase? What would be the effect of the increase in income on the level of consumer spending? What would this increased spending mean in terms of the market for food, clothing, housing and automobiles? What would be the effect on the level of savings? The answers are roughly as follows:

Personal income of nonwhites after taxes, which amounted to about $21.9 billion in 1963, would increase by $14.7 billion to a new level of approximately $36.6 billion. This is a gain of two-thirds.

The level of consumer expenditures by nonwhites would increase by roughly $11.8 billion, rising from $21.1 billion to $32.9 billion. This is an advance of 56 percent.

Outlays on food would rise by $3.0 billion, from $5.3 billion to $8.3 billion. This is an increase of 57 percent.

Clothing expenditures would rise by $1.5 billion, raising the level from $2.6 billion to $4.1 billion. This also represents an increase of about 57 percent.

Money spent on household operations, which amounted to $6.6 billion in 1963, would increase by $3.7 billion to a new level of $10.3 billion. This represents a gain of 56 percent.

In 1963, nonwhites spent about $2 billion in the operation of automobiles.

Another $1.1 billion would be added, raising the total to $3.1 billion. This represents a gain of 55 percent.

The level of current savings by nonwhites was roughly $800 million in 1963. This would make a spectacular jump of $2.9 billion to a new level of $3.7 billion. Thus, savings would advance by a remarkable 364 percent.

We could go on describing the beneficial economic effects of the elimination of racial discrimination. However, enough has been said to demonstrate that the economy as a whole—and not Negroes alone—would reap immense advantages if the legacy of racial discrimination could be erased from the face of the land.

Economic Consequences of the Changing Negro Market

The shifting pattern of consumer expenditures described above has had a significant impact on the fortunes of those professionally involved in developing the Negro market. Expressed succinctly, it appears that nonwhites depending directly on the Negro market made only spotty progress during the last decade. In contrast, those who have found new opportunities in the marketing channels for the economy as a whole made substantial

TABLE XV—Number of Sales Workers, All Professional and Employed Workers, Experienced Civilian Labor Force by Color, 1950–1960 — Rate of Growth, 1950–1960

	1950 Total	1950 Nonwhite	1960 Total	1960 Nonwhite	% Dist 1950 Total	% Dist 1950 Non-white	% Dist 1960 Total	% Dist 1960 Non-white	% Change Total	% Change Non-white	Ann. Avg Rate Growth Total	Ann. Avg Rate Growth Non-white
Sales Workers	4,014,210	77,400	4,807,637	116,907	100.0	100.0	100.0	100.0	+ 19.8	+ 51.0	+ 1.8	+4.2
Advertising Agents & Salesmen	35,370	480	33,785	208	0.9	0.6	0.7	0.2	− 4.5	− 56.7	− 0.5	−8.0
Auctioneers	5,430	120	4,267	—	0.1	0.2	0.1	—	− 21.4	—	− 2.4	—
Demonstrators	14,130	480	25,909	262	0.4	0.6	0.5	0.2	+ 83.3	− 45.4	+ 6.2	−5.9
Hucksters and Peddlers	23,370	3,580	54,290	3,116	0.6	4.6	1.1	2.7	+132.3	− 13.0	+ 8.8	−1.3
Insurance Agents, Brokers and Underwriters	305,130	7,860	370,982	8,933	7.6	10.2	7.7	7.6	+ 21.6	+ 13.7	+ 2.0	+1.3
Newsboys	180,270	4,020	200,032	9,568	2.7	5.2	4.2	8.2	+ 11.0	+138.0	+ 1.1	+9.1
Real Estate Agents & Brokers	141,030	3,480	200,070	4,365	3.5	4.5	4.2	3.7	+ 41.9	+ 25.4	+ 3.6	+2.3
Stock and Bond Salesmen	11,100	240	30,796	388	0.3	0.3	0.6	0.3	+177.4	+ 61.7	+10.7	+4.9
Salesmen and Clerks (nec)	3,370,380	58,140	3,887,506	90,067	84.0	75.1	80.9	77.0	+ 15.3	+ 54.9	+ 1.4	+4.5
Manufacturing	321,090	1,860	474,865	4,134	8.0	2.4	9.9	3.5	+ 47.9	+122.3	+ 4.0	+8.3
Wholesale Trade	406,050	2,370	506,377	5,574	10.1	3.1	10.5	4.8	+ 24.7	+135.2	+ 1.5	+8.9
Food & Related Prods.			86,861	937			1.8	0.8				
Other Wholesale Trade			419,516	4,637			8.7	4.0				
Retail Trade	2,510,730	51,060	2,719,796	76,540	62.5	66.0	56.6	65.5	+ 8.3	+ 49.9	+ 0.8	+4.1
Food & Dairy Product Stores			519,859	26,667			10.8	22.8				
Genl. Mdse Retailing			595,195	12,789			12.4	10.9				
Ltd. Price Variety Stores			185,210	4,292			3.9	3.7				
Apparel & Accessories			340,830	7,647			7.1	6.5				
Motor Vehicles & Access. Retailing			228,250	3,213			4.7	2.7				
Other Retail Trade			850,452	21,932			17.7	18.8				
Other Industries (incl. not reporting)	132,510	2,850	186,468	3,819	3.3	3.7	3.9	3.3	+ 40.7	+ 34.0	+ 3.5	+3.0
Total Employed Persons	58,550,700	6,083,340	68,006,553	7,216,836					+ 16.1	+ 18.6	+ 1.5	+1.7
All Professional Workers	4,937,790	191,970	7,324,906	360,070					+ 48.3	+ 87.6	+ 4.0	+6.5

SOURCE: *U.S. Census of Population, 1950*, Special Reports, "Occupational Characteristics," 1956, p. IB–29–36. *U.S. Census of Population, 1960*, "Occupational Characteristics," pp. 21–30.

TABLE XVI—Median Income of Sales Workers, All Professional Workers,
and All Employed Persons, by Color, 1949 and 1959 (Amounts in Dollars)

	1949 Total		1949 Nonwhite		1959 Total		1959 Nonwhite		Percentage Change, 1949–1959 Total		Percentage Change, 1949–1959 Nonwhite	
	Male	Female	Male	Female	Male	Female	Male	Female	Male	Female	Male	Female
Sales Workers	3,026	1,243	1,659	1,923	5,119	1,619	2,845	1,582	69.2	30.2	71.5	70.8
Advertising Agents and Salesmen	3,750	2,060	—	—	6,417	3,572	—	—	71.1	73.4	—	—
Auctioneers	3,266	—	—	—	5,398	—	—	—	65.3	—	—	—
Demonstrators	—	845	—	—	4,333	853	—	—	—	0.9	—	—
Hucksters and Peddlers	1,404	—	—	—	2,826	758	1,815	769	101.3	—	—	—
Insurance Agents, Brokers and Underwriters	3,711	2,168	2,300	—	6,331	3,367	3,947	2,021	70.6	55.3	71.6	—
Newsboys	320	478	—	—	567	709	556	—	77.2	48.3	—	—
Real Estate Agents and Brokers	3,712	2,000	—	—	6,508	3,188	5,037	2,555	75.3	59.4	—	—
Stock and Bond Salesmen	4,386	—	—	—	7,730	4,096	—	—	76.2	—	—	—
Salesmen and Clerks (nec)	2,974	1,227	1,692	920	5,101	1,597	3,052	1,577	71.5	30.2	80.4	71.4
Manufacturing	3,868	1,485	—	—	6,835	1,768	4,008	1,953	76.7	19.1	—	—
Wholesale Trade	3,635	1,722	—	—	6,146	2,451	4,431	—	69.1	42.3	—	—
Food & related prods.					5,545	1,773	—	—	—	—	—	—
Other Wholesale Trade					6,329	2,553	4,370	—	—	—	—	—
Retail Trade	2,543	1,221	1,629	921	4,027	1,585	2,874	1,575	58.4	29.8	76.4	71.0
Food & Dairy Products Stores					2,955	1,459	2,599	1,294				
General Merchandise Retailing					3,977	1,710	2,862	1,895				
Limited Price Variety Stores					2,114	1,106	—	1,263				
Apparel and Accessories					3,829	1,740	2,969	1,924				
Motor Vehicles and Accessories Retailing					4,947	2,193	3,730	—				
Other Retail Trade					4,256	1,661	2,950	1,453				
Other Industries (including not reporting)	3,152	1,157	—	—	5,590	1,503	2,897	1,083	77.3	29.9		
Total Employment	2,668	1,575	1,483	786	4,720	2,333	2,750	1,320	76.9	48.1	85.4	67.9
Professional	3,949	2,265	2,269	1,923	6,778	3,711	4,640	3,587	71.6	63.0	104.5	86.5

SOURCE: *U.S. Census of Population: 1950*, Special Reports, "Occupational Characteristics" 1956, IB–183–198 and IB–215–230. *U.S. Census of Population: 1960*, "Occupational Characteristics," pp. 296–335.

progress. This impression is sustained by the evidence relating to the structure of employment and income in marketing.

Table XV shows the number and distribution of sales workers by major fields of activity in 1950 and 1960. It will be observed that a substantial number of opportunities were opened in marketing during the 1950's. However, such jobs for nonwhite workers grew at a much faster rate than for all employees as a group. The bulk of the new sales opportunities as far as nonwhites are concerned was concentrated in the semiskilled category consisting of counter salesmen and clerks. These were employed primarily by department stores and other retail outlets serving the general market. In contrast, among nonwhite professional salesmen who work almost exclusively in the Negro market, the growth rate lagged considerably behind that for professional sales workers in the rest of the economy.

For example, the number of nonwhite sales workers grew by 50 percent, while the number of total sales workers expanded by one-fifth. In the professional category, the total number of stock and bond salesmen rose by 177 percent, but the number of nonwhites in this occupation increased by 62 percent. The corresponding figures for insurance agents, brokers and underwriters were: total up 22 percent, nonwhite up 14 percent; real estate agents and brokers: total up 42 percent, nonwhite up 25 percent. While the number of advertising agents and salesmen declined for both groups, the percentage decrease was greater for nonwhites than for whites: down 57 and 5 percent, respectively.

The growth profile for the clerical group was exactly opposite to that for the professional category. The total number of salesmen and clerks grew by 15 percent, compared with 55 percent for nonwhites. Clerks employed in manufacturing industry expanded by 48 percent, as against 122 percent for nonwhites. In wholesale trade, the corresponding figures were 25 percent for the total and 135 percent for nonwhite. Total clerical employment in retail stores grew by 8 percent, while the number of nonwhites employed in such stores rose by one-half.

This slower improvement in the position of nonwhite professionals in the marketing field is also documented in the income figures. Table XVI shows the median income of sales workers, of professional workers and of employed persons by color in 1949 and 1959. The first thing to note is that over the decade a substantial improvement occurred in all types of incomes. However, the largest increase was registered by nonwhite male professional workers taken as a group; for them, the increase was 105 percent compared with 72 percent for all male professional jobholders. But in the marketing group, the percentage gains for nonwhite men holding professional positions was about the same as the total. This is typified by the 72 percent increase for those in the insurance area. In contrast, the increase in median income of nonwhite male clerical workers exceeded that for the total—80 percent versus 72 percent. Among female clerical workers (virtually none of whom were in the professional class in 1949), the percentage increase was 71 percent compared with only 30 percent for all female sales workers.

Moreover, the greatest relative gains were made by nonwhite female workers. In 1949, their median income was about 75 percent of that of all female sales workers. By 1959, the ratio had climbed to 98 percent. On the other hand, nonwhite female insurance agents in 1959 had a median income only 60 percent of that of all females employed as insurance agents. The relative income position of nonwhite males in the marketing field registered only a modest improvement over the decade. For all sales workers, the median income rose from 55 percent to 56 percent of the median income for all males. Among male clerical workers, the ratio rose from 57 percent to 60 percent. On the other hand, for nonwhite male insurance agents, the figure was virtually unchanged—62 percent in 1949 and 63 percent in 1959.

Taken together, the above statistics on employment and income trends in the marketing field appear to lead to an inescapable conclusion: nonwhite professional salesmen, concentrating on the development of the Negro market, have made new gains, but they have been relatively modest.

Within this framework, it may be interesting to examine the employment and income position of public relations men and publicity writers. The experience of this group is probably typical of the professional workers engaged in marketing. Table XVII shows the number of public relations men and publicity writers by color and industry of employment in 1960. It will be noted that the nonwhite workers in this category were concentrated in only a few industries. Manufacturing accounted for 28 percent

TABLE XVII—Number of Public Relations Men and Publicity Writers, by Color and Industry of Employment, 1960

Industry	Nonwhite		Total Employment	
	Number	Percent of total	Number	Percent of total
All Industry	**142**	**100.0**	**21,434**	**100.0**
Agriculture, forestry and fisheries	none	—	20	0.1
Mining	none	—	183	0.9
Construction	none	—	241	1.1
Manufacturing: total	40	28.2	5,097	23.8
Food and kindred products	20	14.1	785	3.7
Misc. durable goods	20	14.1	402	1.9
All other manufacturing	none	—	3,910	18.2
Railroads and RR express	none	—	299	1.4
Other transportation	none	—	703	3.3
Communications	21	14.7	1,304	6.1
Utilities	none	—	688	3.2
Wholesale trade	20	14.1	851	4.0
Retail trade	none	—	567	2.6
Finance, insurance and real estate	none	—	2,477	11.6
Business services	21	14.7	2,078	9.7
Personal services	20	14.1	141	0.7
Other services	none	—	204	1.0
Education services, government	20	14.1	551	2.6
All other industries	none	—	5,980	27.9

Source: *U. S. Census of Population: 1960*, "Occupational Characteristics," Table 37, pp. 519–530. Bureau of the Census, U. S. Department of Commerce.

—divided equally between food and miscellaneous durable goods. Communications (especially radio and TV), wholesale trade, business services, personal services and educational services—each accounted for about 14 percent. Aside from communications and educational services, neither of these industries is currently experiencing a particularly rapid rate of growth. In contrast, public relations men and publicity writers in the economy as a whole were widely distributed among industries. There was a good scattering in the rapidly growing areas of finance, communications, real estate and the newer types of manufacturing industries.

The distribution of public relations men and advertising agents and salesmen by income class in 1959 is shown in Table XVIII. The first point to observe is that public relations men seem to do much better than advertising agents and salesmen. This is true for nonwhites, as well as for the total. The median income of all PR men in 1959 was about $8,000. For nonwhites, the figure was between $6,000 and $7,000. The corresponding figures for advertising agents were $6,400 for the total and between $3,000 and $4,000 for nonwhites. Moreover, the gap between the median income of nonwhites and all PR men taken as a group seems to be much smaller than that for advertising agents. In 1959, the median income for nonwhite PR men was equal to about 80 percent of the median income for all PR men combined. Among advertising agents, the corresponding figure was approximately 54 percent.

Against this background, it may be interesting to look more closely at those professionals engaged principally in the Negro market. A substantial number of these hold membership in the National Association of Market Developers. Thus, a profile of NAMD members provides considerable insight into their perception of the Negro market. In Table XIX, a rough estimate is made of the distribution of NAMD membership by industry and type of employment, ownership of firm and the market focus of members. (However, no lists were available for NAMD chapters in Atlanta, Baltimore and New York.)

Several features of the table are striking. Of the 400-odd members represented, over four-fifths were salaried employees and the remainder were self-employed. More than one-third of the total (and over two-fifths of the salaried members) were concentrated in the distribution of food and kindred products. Here, the heaviest concentration was in alcoholic beverages, and soft drinks also accounted for a sizable proportion. There was only modest representation in the rapidly growing field of automobiles, other forms of travel and petroleum products.

Approximately 10 percent were associated with communications media, with newspapers having the largest representation. About 4 percent of the total list was employed in public relations firms. The self-employed members were almost exclusively concentrated in public relations and newspaper work.

It comes as no surprise to observe that the vast majority of the NAMD membership is employed by large corporations serving the economy as a whole. Where a member was employed in a Negro-owned firm, there is a good chance that the business was a bank, newspaper, magazine or public relations firm. Yet according to our estimate, about 80 percent of the

TABLE XVIII—Median Income of Public Relations Men and Advertising Agents, by Color, 1960

Income Class	Public Relations Men and Publicity Writers		Advertising Agents and Salesmen	
	Total	Nonwhite	Total	Nonwhite
Total Persons with Income	23,855	203	28,487	166
$1–999	285	20	775	41
1,000–1,999	710	—	1,304	22
2,000–2,999	627	—	1,237	—
3,000–3,999	733	63	2,136	20
4,000–4,999	1,456	—	3,268	21
5,000–5,999	2,395	—	4,061	20
6,000–6,999	2,699	20	3,509	—
7,000–7,999	2,793	60	2,737	21
8,000–9,999	3,679	—	3,504	—
10,000–14,999	5,352	40	3,548	21
15,000 and Over	3,126	—	2,408	—
Median	$8,125	$6,000–6,999	$6,417	$3,000–3,999

SOURCE: *U.S. Census of Population: 1960,* "Occupational Characteristics," U.S. Department of Commerce, Bureau of the Census, pp. 296–335.

NAMD membership was active almost exclusively in the development of the Negro market, as opposed to the general market. Virtually all of those employed in the food industry were concentrating on the Negro market. In fact, only those active in marketing automobiles, petroleum products, and banking and financial services, appear to be primarily active in the market catering to consumers as a whole. About one-third of the members active in the newspaper field were associated with newspapers with a readership substantially wider than the Negro community.

Of course, one must be extremely cautious in attempting to draw any overall conclusions about the activities of all Negro professional marketeers on the basis of data presented in Table XIX. As mentioned earlier, the NAMD membership list is incomplete, and the classifications were made on the basis of the business affiliations identified in the membership roster. Moreover, NAMD itself does not represent all Negro professionals engaged in the Negro market.

But on this broad canvas, a rough profile begins to emerge. Tentatively, we can conclude that Negro professionals seem to be concentrating primarily in those sectors of the market for consumer goods and services which are not spearheading the growth of the economy as a whole. We might also conclude that the most promising marketing careers in the future will be found in rapidly growing fields such as housing, automobiles, travel and other services indicative of an evolving middle class mode of living.

TABLE XIX—Estimated Distribution of NAMD Membership, by Industry and Type of Employment, Ownership of Firm and Market Focus of Member

Industry and Type of Employment	Total List		Market Focus of Member		Ownership of Firm	
	Number	Percent of Total	Negro Market	General Market	Negro	Other
Salaried	343	84.3	278	65	67	276
Food and kindred products	148	36.4	147	1		148
Beer and whiskey	120	29.5	119	1		120
Soft drinks	28	6.9	28			28
Tobacco	12	2.9	12			12
Automobiles	10	2.5		10		10
Petroleum Products	9	2.2		9		9
Travel	3	0.7	2	1	1	2
Banks and Savings and Loan Assns.	11	2.7	3	8	10	1
Government and Nonprofit	11	2.7		1		11
Other industry	76	18.7	61	15	16	60
Media	46	11.3	38	8	26	20
Newspapers	22	5.4	15	7	17	5
Magazines	8	2.0	8		8	
Radio-TV	16	3.9	15	1	1	15
Agency	17	4.2	15	2	14	3
Advertising	2	0.5		2		2
Public Relations	15	3.7	15		14	1
Self-Employed	64	15.7	52	12		
Public Relations	27	6.6	27			
Newspapers	30	7.4	18	12		
Other	7	1.7	7			
Totals	407	100.0	330	77		

SOURCE: National Association of Market Developers Membership Roster, 1964. Lists of members were unavailable for Chapters in Atlanta, Baltimore, and New York.

Negroes as Entrepreneurs

Trends in General Business

As mentioned above, segregation has served the Negro businessman in the same way a tariff protects an infant industry. With the removal or reduction of a tariff wall, major adjustments must be made by those who have benefited from its existence. The Negro businessman is faced with such an adjustment. As the process of desegregation permeates the marketplace, Negro-owned businesses (the vast majority of which concentrate on providing personal services in a segregated market) are faced with increased competition from firms catering to buyers with a decreasing reference to race.

The consequences of this process are already evident. Because we have only fragmentary statistics on Negro-owned business, it is difficult to chart these trends with precision. However, since the vast majority of Negro businesses are single proprietorships—rather than partnerships or corporations—Bureau of the Census statistics on self-employed managers, proprietors and officials give a fair indication of the scope of Negro business. These statistics are summarized in Table XX.

Even a cursory analysis of the evidence clearly demonstrates the heavy dependence of Negro businessmen on the segregated Negro market. Where Negro customers have relatively free access to goods and services sold in the general marketplace, Negro businessmen have made little headway against the strong competition of white firms. In 1960, Negroes constituted about 2.5 percent of all self-employed businessmen, but this ratio varied greatly among different industries. Their largest share of a major industry was personal services (3.4 percent); at the bottom of the spectrum was banking and finance, where Negroes represented less than two-tenths of one percent of the total. But behind the array of ratios is an interesting and significant story. If we divide the retail trade sector according to the principal types of stores, we see immediately the importance of segregation in providing opportunities for Negro entrepreneurs. For example, in 1960, Negroes operated 2.6 percent of all retail outlets—but 5.6 percent of the eating and drinking establishments. They also had 4.1 percent of the food stores; this is a reflection of the fact that such stores (especially smaller ones) are typically located in or near segregated residential areas.

In sharp contrast, Negroes owned much less than one percent of the retail establishments selling apparel, furniture, hardware or motor vehicles. In these categories, the meager ownership role played by Negroes can be attributed partly to the fact that few of them can obtain the relatively large amount of capital required for successful operation. Another factor appears to be the sizable volume of sales necessary to sustain such a business. However, the most basic explanation seems to be the freedom Negro customers have to shop for these items in stores catering to the general market. The slightly stronger position of Negroes as operators of gasoline stations is due primarily to the vigorous and competitive efforts of the leading petroleum companies to establish franchise outlets in or near the geographical areas occupied by Negroes in the key population centers. Outside of retail trade, the provision of personal services to Negro customers has been a mainstay of Negro businessmen. The most outstanding examples are owners of barbershops and beauty salons. In fact, this area alone has generated a complex of interrelated activities by Negro businessmen shown under other headings in Table XX. For instance, the majority of the 1,300 Negroes who owned manufacturing firms in 1960 were probably producing cosmetics and barber and beauty shop supplies especially for the Negro trade. Undoubtedly, a fairly large proportion of the 2,600 Negro businessmen engaged in wholesale trade were distributing these items to local shops. Still other businessmen (e.g., insurance and real estate brokers, and those providing a variety of business services) were probably only slightly less dependent on the segregated Negro market. On the other hand, Negroes owning automotive repair facilities, running transportation (such as taxis and local haulage), and doing construction jobs normally would find their customers in the community at large—although Negro customers may provide their ultimate base of support.

But this configuration of Negro-owned businesses is changing drastically as Negro consumers are increasingly attracted to the general market. Between 1950 and 1960, the total number of Negro businessmen shrank by more than one-fifth. While there was a similar decrease in the total number of self-employed businessmen during the decade, the proportion was smaller. Moreover, much of the decline in the overall number was accounted for by the change to the corporate form of organization. This was much less true for Negroes.

Furthermore, with few exceptions, the incidence of decline was greater for Negroes, compared with the total, in those fields where segregation and discrimination imposed the least constraints on Negro customers. For instance, the annual average percentage changes between 1950 and 1960 in several key areas for Negroes and the total self-employed, respectively, were: communications, utilities and sanitary services, -11.2 vs. $+1.2$; transportation, -6.5 vs. -2.9; furniture and housefurnishings, -6.1 vs. -2.9; apparel and accessories, -5.9 vs. -3.6; hardware and building materials, -3.9 vs. -1.6. It is difficult to account for the causes underlying these specific decreases, but several considerations can be cited. The sharp drop in the number of Negroes in the private sanitary services (and the growth in the total number of businessmen engaged in this activity) probably reflects the increased competition from large firms which move trash for restaurants, department stores and similar establishments on a contract basis. A similar explanation probably applies in the case of transportation. In the past, numerous small Negro businesses were formed around one or two trucks, with the owner and a few helpers providing local moving and job-by-job transportation services. However, with the growing unionization of the trucking industry, even extending into purely local transportation, the rising wage levels have made such opportunities increasingly attractive to white men. The trend toward the use of more sophisticated equipment (such as refrigerator trucks and other speciality vehicles) has also necessitated the accumulation of considerably more capital than most Negro truckers could raise. In addition, the number of Negro taxi owners in the major cities (with the possible exception of Washington, D.C.) has shrunk as gigantic corporations have acquired franchises to operate fleets of several thousand vehicles. The decline in the retail outlets undoubtedly reflects the diffusion of mass marketing throughout the economy; this has made it exceedingly difficult for the small Negro retailer (along with similarly situated white merchants) to compete with the super market, large department stores and discount houses.

Several other types of traditional Negro businesses, although not shown

Industry	1950			1960			Annual Average Percentage Rate of Growth 1950–1960		Median Income 1949		Median Income 1959	
	Total[1]	Negro	Negro as % of Total	Total	Negro	Negro as % of Total	Total	Negro	White Males	Non-white Males	White Males	Non-white Males
Construction	191,820	3,390	1.7	222,601	3,978	1.8	1.7	1.6	$3,873	$1,922	$6,756	$3,239
Manufacturing	231,210	1,050	0.4	168,395	1,376	0.8	−3.1	2.7	4,700	2,250*	7,998	3,503
Transportation	50,940	2,430	4.7	38,223	1,241	3.2*	−2.9	−6.5	3,535	2,250*	6,638	2,792
Communications, utilities & sanitary serv.	4,260	270	6.3	4,812	82	1.7	1.2	−11.2	3,310	2,500	7,138	3,500*
Wholesale trade	174,240	2,640	1.5	133,607	2,610	1.9	−2.6	−0.1	4,336	1,250*	7,813	2,693
Retail trade	1,349,190	38,730	2.8	994,425	26,303	2.6	−3.0	−3.8	3,277	1,838	5,332	3,511
Food & dairy prods.	376,350	14,520	3.9	214,758	8,740	4.1	−5.5	−4.9	2,875	1,819	4,464	3,487
Eating & drinking places	270,720	15,030	5.5	203,830	11,344	5.6	−2.9	−2.9	3,114	1,870	4,990	3,170
Genl. mdse. & ltd. price variety	63,690	750	1.2	46,406	640	1.3	−3.1	−1.6	3,211	2,000	5,416	2,500*
Apparel & accessories	82,140	600	0.7	56,722	321	0.6	−3.6	−5.9	4,725	1,250*	7,292	4,500*
Furniture & homefurn.	66,210	360	0.5	49,946	182	0.4	−2.9	−6.1	3,931	2,250*	6,923	5,500*
Motor vehicles & access.	58,590	180	0.3	55,476	163	0.3	−0.5	−0.9	6,367	2,000	7,460	3,500*
Gasoline service stations	143,010	1,290	0.9	152,294	2,153	1.4	0.6	5.3	2,906	2,250*	4,657	4,030
Hardware, bldg. materials	79,020	120	0.2	67,002	80	0.1	−1.6	−3.9	4,427	1,750*	6,552	2,500*
Other retail trade	209,460	5,880	2.8	147,991	2,680	1.8	−3.3	−7.5	3,330	1,717	5,794	3,737
Banking and finance	20,910	90	0.4	22,076	41	0.2	0.6	−7.5	8,277	n.r.	14,527	12,500*
Insurance & real estate	44,910	600	1.3	49,232	794	1.6	1.0	2.8	5,727	2,250*	10,393	5,500*
Business services	33,390	570	1.7	37,020	890	2.4	1.1	4.6	4,250	2,250*	7,626	4,500*
Automotive repair & garages	59,610	870	1.5	38,528	1,083	2.8	−4.2	2.2	3,183	2,000	5,237	3,564
Misc. repair services	29,070	450	1.5	19,317	414	2.1	−4.1	−0.8	2,713	1,750*	4,851	3,500*
Personal services	135,720	5,970	4.4	127,356	4,349	3.4	−0.7	−3.1	3,114	2,174	5,060	3,296
Other industries	97,080	2,760	2.8	95,311	3,239	3.4	−0.2	1.6	3,433	1,250*	5,777	2,508
Total	2,422,350	59,820	2.5	1,954,903	46,400	2.4	−2.1	−2.4	3,502	1,860	5,932	3,368

TABLE XX—Self-Employed Businessmen, by Race and Industry, 1950 and 1960

[1] White and Negro only.
* Estimated at mid-point of income class interval.
n.r. not reported

SOURCE: *U.S. Census of Population, 1950*, Special Reports, "Occupational Characteristics," 1956, IB Table 13. *U.S. Census of Population, 1960*, "Occupational Characteristics," 1963, Table 3.

explicitly in Table XX, also experienced absolute decline or a severe slackening in the rate of growth. For example, the number of funeral directors dropped by 6 percent between 1950 and 1960, and the number of barbers decreased by over 16 percent. While the number of Negro-owned hotels and motels has continued to expand, they have lost a sizable proportion of their most desirable clientele—a loss only partly made up by the growth of luxury and semiluxury resort and vacation sites.

On the other hand, Negro businessmen made significant strides in several new or revitalized fields. The number of self-employed in construction climbed by more than 17 percent, about the same rate achieved by this category as a whole. Substantial gains were also registered in the ownership of gasoline service stations, automotive repair shops and garages. In manufacturing, modest expansion occurred. This gain was made despite the capture by large corporations of a fairly sizable share of the cosmetics market among Negro customers, which traditionally accounted for virtually all of the output of Negro manufacturing firms. Many of the more recent ventures in manufacturing include plastics, apparel, food processing and other relatively new areas.

In analyzing these general trends in Negro-owned businesses during the last decade or so, the intention is not to paint a bleak picture of total stagnation and decline. On the contrary, a great number of individual Negro businesses have been launched and have achieved considerable success. Moreover, many established firms have made substantial progress. Indeed, without much difficulty, one can find exceptionally prosperous businessmen whose enterprises stand out against the general trend in any of the areas described here. Nevertheless, when the basic trends are viewed against the panorama of the overall business landscape, one cannot escape concluding that Negro businessmen taken as a group have lost considerable ground and are facing an uncertain future.

Trends in the earnings of Negro businessmen also support this general conclusion. Again the historical paradox of segregation as a protective shield is evident: nonwhite businessmen concentrating in the segregated market tend to earn relatively more, compared with all self-employed entrepreneurs, than their colleagues competing in the open market. For example, in 1949, the median income of nonwhite professional workers taken as a group was $2,269, about 58 percent of the median income of all professionals ($3,949). Among salaried managerial personnel, total and nonwhite median incomes were $4,403 and $2,134, respectively, yielding a ratio of 49 percent. Among self-employed businessmen, the income figures were: total, $3,502 and nonwhite, $1,860, for a ratio of 53 percent. But nonwhites providing personal services to a segregated market (barbers, beauticians, etc.) had a median income of $2,174 in 1949, equal to 70 percent of that earned by all those offering personal services. For operators of retail food stores in predominantly Negro neighborhoods, the ratio was 63 percent, and for nonwhite restaurant owners it was 60 percent. By 1959, virtually all of these proportions had risen. However, the extra advantage derived by Negro businessmen from the segregated market was still visible. The ratio of nonwhite to total median income of self-employed owners was 56 percent; it was 78 percent for food outlets and about 65 percent for personal services and eating and drinking places. In contrast, in the more open manufacturing and transportation sectors, the proportions were much smaller—44 percent and 42 percent, respectively.

In interpreting the above figures, however, the reader should not conclude that self-employment is an easy way for Negroes to become rich. In fact, one can infer that the financial return to Negro risk-takers in general is probably substantially less than for the total population when appraised in terms of alternative opportunities. Yet, the gap appears to be smaller for nonwhite businessmen than for professionals. For instance, in 1959 self-employed nonwhites had a median income of 73 percent of that for all nonwhite professional workers. Comparable figure for all self-employed was 87 percent. Expressed differently, the typical nonwhite businessman in 1959 earned about $65 per week, while the average nonwhite professional worker earned approximately $90 per week. Among the total population the corresponding figures were $114 and $130, respectively. Once these figures are adjusted to reflect what Negro businessmen typically bring to their enterprises, the discrepancy seems to disappear. Of course, nothing is known about the amount of capital invested by either group of businessmen or professionals. Consequently, it is impossible to estimate the profitability of either type of activity; to do this figures on rate of return would be needed. However, the information available on educational attainment suggests that Negro businessmen do seem to enjoy a higher income per year of schooling than do Negro professionals. Self-employed nonwhite businessmen (with an average of 9.0 years of school completed) have just over half as much education as nonwhite professionals (with 16.3 years of schooling). In contrast, the comparable educational attainment for all self-employed businessmen was nearly three-quarters of that for all professionals—12.1 years and 16.3 years. Nevertheless, the median income of the nonwhite business group in 1959 was in the neighborhood of three-quarters of that for nonwhite professionals. Thus, there is a strong suggestion that part of the income of Negro businessmen is a reflection—not exclusively of their investment in capital and education—but also is a reflection of the partial protection afforded by a segregated market.

Banking and Finance

Even a cursory look makes it evident that Negroes cast a pale shadow on the financial landscape. At the end of 1963, Negroes owned or controlled thirteen banks and about fifty life insurance companies. They also had thirty-four Federally-insured savings and loan associations, of which twenty had charters granted by the Federal Government. The combined assets of these three groups of financial institutions amounted to $764 million, or only 0.12 percent of the total assets held by similar financial enterprises in the country as a whole. While a number of the individual businesses have been strikingly successful, their collective impact has been insignificant.

This indifferent progress cannot be attributed to the reluctance of Negroes to venture onto the financial terrain. Indeed, even before the Civil War, Negroes made numerous attempts to launch banks. The Freedmen's Savings

TABLE XXI—Assets and Rate of Growth of Negro-owned Banks, 1957– 1963

Name of Bank	Total Assets		Annual Average Rate of Growth 1957–1960
	1957	1963	(Percent)
Carver State Bank, Savannah, Ga.	$ 928,809	$ 1,643,904	10.0
Citizens and Southern, Phila., Pa.	3,541,965	5,823,293	8.4
Citizens Savings Bank and Trust Co., Nashville, Tenn.	2,494,140	3,313,879	4.9
Citizens Trust Co., Atlanta, Ga.	8,128,457	12,443,533	7.4
Consolidated Bank and Trust Co., Richmond, Va.	4,915,286	6,319,428	4.2
Crown Savings Bank, Newport News, Va.	3,188,498	6,221,454	11.8
Douglas State Bank, Kansas City, Kansas	2,501,053	4,754,632	11.3
First State Bank, Danville, Va.	2,064,146	3,016,630	6.6
Industrial Bank of Washington, D. C.	7,780,327	12,573,741	8.4
Mechanics and Farmers Bank, Durham, N. C.	7,144,257	13,112,958	10.7
Tri-State Bank, Memphis, Tenn.	3,056,718	4,717,471	7.5
Victory Savings Bank, Columbia, S. C.	916,203	1,421,368	7.6
Farmers' State Bank, Boley, Oklahoma	129,748	—	—
Riverside National Bank, Houston, Texas	—	1,502,077	—
All Negro-Owned Banks	46,789,607	76,864,368	8.6
All Banks in the United States (amounts in millions)	257,864	363,678	5.9

SOURCE: "All Banks," U.S. Bureau of the Census, *Statistical Abstract*, 1960, p. 436; 1964, p. 449. Emmer M. Lancaster, *Negro-owned Banks, Annual Report of Banking Institutions Owned and Operated by Negroes*, (Washington, D.C., 1957 and 1963 National Bankers Association.)

Bank and Trust Company, sponsored by the Freedmen's Bureau, was the most ambitious effort. In its heyday, it had a network of branches in thirty-six cities, and its deposits reached a peak of $57 million. While the bulk of its deposits was backed by United States Government bonds, its reserve funds apparently were not managed well. In any case, the failure of the bank in the depression of 1874 greatly damaged the confidence of Negro depositors in Negro-owned institutions.[11] Yet, during each subsequent period of sustained prosperity, a new crop of Negro banks appeared. But again and again, the end of prosperity brought another epidemic of bank failures and widespread losses to depositors. While this pattern was also typical of the behavior of the banking system as a whole, the legacy in the poverty-stricken Negro community was particularly discouraging.

Among Negro-owned insurance companies, the record is somewhat better. The primary explanation, of course, is the protection provided by the discriminatory practices of the principal insurance companies serving the community at large.

In this section, recent trends in the Negro's participation in banking and finance are appraised. Because of the greater availability of data, the primary emphasis is on banking and insurance.

Negro-Owned Banks

As shown in Table XXI, the combined resources of the thirteen Negro banks amounted to about $77 million at the end of 1963, compared with $364 billion of total assets held by the 14,079 banks in the country as a

TABLE XXII—Distribution of Bank Assets and Liabilities, 1956 and 1963

| Category | All Banks (Mill. of Dollars) | | Negro-owned Banks (Thous. of Dollars) | | Percentage Distribution | | | |
| | | | | | All Banks | | Negro-owned Banks | |
	1956	1963	1956	1963	1956	1963	1956	1963
Assets								
Cash	49,836	51,677	7,355	11,087	19.8	14.2	16.4	14.4
U.S. Government securities	66,795	69,223	12,526	14,905	26.5	19.0	27.8	19.4
State and local government sec.	13,637	30,289	3,865	7,172	5.4	8.3	8.6	9.3
Corporate securities	6,920	10,291	1,264	3,116	2.8	2.7	2.8	4.1
Loans and discounts	110,632	193,442	19,314	38,531	43.9	53.2	42.9	50.1
Bank premises	2,111	4,300	504	1,492	0.8	1.2	1.1	1.9
Other real estate	195	491	30	126	0.1	—	0.1	0.2
Other assets	1,839	3,965	143	436	0.7	1.4	0.3	0.6
Total assets	**251,965**	**363,678**	**45,001**	**76,865**	**100.0**	**100.0**	**100.0**	**100.0**
Liabilities								
Deposits	228,579	320,746	40,613	69,035	90.7	88.2	90.3	89.8
Capital stock	5,007	7,616	1,750	2,551	2.0	2.1	3.9	3.3
Undivided profits and reserves	4,367	7,192	844	1,215	1.7	2.0	1.9	1.6
Surplus	9,976	15,155	1,441	2,949	4.0	4.1	3.2	3.8
Other liabilities	4,036	12,969	353	1,115	1.6	3.6	0.7	1.5
Total liabilities	**251,965**	**363,678**	**45,001**	**76,865**	**100.0**	**100.0**	**100.0**	**100.0**

SOURCE: "All Banks," U.S. Bureau of the Census, *Statistical Abstract*, 1960, p. 436; 1964, p. 449. Emmer M. Lancaster, op. cit. as shown in Table XXI ante.

whole. Thus, Negro banks represented only 0.021 percent of the nation's banking business. But even this small figure reflected an improvement, because in 1957, their share was 0.018 percent. In the intervening years, the Negro banks as a group experienced an annual average rate of growth of 8.6 percent, compared with 5.9 percent for all banks in the nation. While the Negro banks' faster expansion partly reflected their small size (thus permitting even a modest absolute gain to be registered as a large percentage), much of their progress was genuine. Moreover, in 1964 six Negro banks received charters or actually opened for business, and three others were seeking charters. All except two of these new institutions were national banks, reflecting a substantial liberalization of policy by Federal banking officials. Nevertheless, Negro banks remain modest institutions.

The distribution of their assets and liabilities, as Table XXII shows, is essentially the same as that for all banks. Yet, a few significant variations are evident. In relation to total assets, Negro banks tend to hold a slightly smaller proportion of loans and a slightly larger proportion of securities and real estate. The lighter emphasis on loans may well reflect the higher risk inherent in a small bank lending to small borrowers. The average Negro bank, with $5.6 million, was only one-fifth as large as the average bank in the country as a whole, which had about $25.8 million in assets at the end of 1963. While we do not know the size of typical borrowers at Negro banks, they are obviously small. Moreover, as mentioned above, Negro businesses are highly concentrated in a narrow range of retail activities focused on the segregated Negro market. Thus, the Negro banker has little opportunity to reduce his risk through loan diversification. Consequently, he would naturally turn to securities for added diversification—although the net rate of return may be less than on loans. The higher percentage of real estate owned by Negro banks may reflect a similar effort to diversify their holdings. But it may also reflect a higher incident of mortgage foreclosures among Negro homebuyers.

The liabilities of Negro banks also exhibit a few distinguishing features compared with all banks combined. While the ratio of deposits to total liabilities is about the same for both groups, Negro banks seem to be somewhat more heavily capitalized. On the other hand, Negro banks in the past appear to have retained a smaller proportion of their profits to build up reserves and surplus.

The combined balance sheet summarized in Table XXII provides a fair description of the overall features of Negro banks, but it is basically a static picture. It would be particularly helpful to have an insight into their dynamic role of mobilizing savings and channeling them into various sectors of the economy. This role can be highlighted by the application of the "Sources and Uses of Funds" accounting system. Conceptionally, this method of accounting is derived by calculating changes between two or more dates in the combined balance sheets of the institutions. Table XXIII shows the sources and uses of funds of Negro-owned banks and all banks in the country over the period 1956–63. Basically, two questions are posed: First, how did the banks expand their resources during the years indicated, or what were the *sources* of the increase in their loanable funds? Second, what was the composition of the increase in the banks, assets, or what *use* did they make of their greater resources? To answer the first question, one must look at changes in the banks' liabilities; to answer the second, one must examine changes in their assets. As in the case of the traditional balance sheet in

TABLE XXIII—Sources and Uses of Bank Funds, 1956–1963

Category	All Banks		Negro-owned Banks	
	Amount (Millions of Dollars)	Percent of total	Amount (Thousands of Dollars)	Percent of total
Sources of Funds				
New Capital	2,609	2.3	801	2.5
Deposits	92,167	82.5	28,422	89.2
Undistributed Profits	2,825	2.5	371	1.2
Surplus	5,179	4.6	1,508	4.7
Other sources	8,933	8.1	761	2.4
Total sources	**111,713**	**100.0**	**31,863**	**100.0**
Use of Funds				
Cash	1,841	1.6	3,732	11.7
U. S. Government Securities	2,428	2.2	2,380	7.5
State and local Govt. Sec.	16,652	14.9	3,307	10.4
Corporate securities	3,371	3.0	1,852	5.8
Loans	82,810	74.1	19,217	60.3
Real estate	2,485	2.2	1,085	3.4
Bank Premises	2,189	2.0	988	3.1
Other real estate	296	0.2	97	0.3
Other uses	2,126	1.9	291	0.9
Total uses	**111,713**	**100.0**	**31,863**	**100.0**

SOURCE: Calculated from Table XXI

which liabilities must equal assets, sources of funds must equal uses of funds.

Table XXIII again puts into sharp focus the similarities and differences between Negro-owned banks as a group and those in the nation at large. The sources of funds for the two sets of institutions are virtually the same. During the period 1956–63, both types of banks relied on sales of new equity securities for roughly the same proportion (about 2.5 percent) of their total sources. However, since capital stock accounted for a larger proportion of Negro banks' assets in 1956, this implies that they sold new stock issues at a slower rate (in relation to their earlier position) than did banks as a group. Increased deposits were, of course, the principal source of funds for banks in general, but they were of more importance for Negro institutions. Because deposits are the primary means used by banks to mobilize financial resources which they lend to borrowers, it would be helpful to examine this source in greater detail. This is done in Table XXIV listing the type and ownership of bank deposits in 1963. As one would expect, demand deposits represent a smaller proportion of total deposits in Negro banks than in all banks combined. This is a reflection of the lesser use of checks by Negroes in day-to-day transactions and in paying bills, a mode of behavior typical of low-income status. On the other hand, time deposits constitute a larger share of Negro-owned banks' total deposits. For Negro banks, these are primarily savings deposits of individuals, mirroring the normal way in which most resources of small savers are held. Individuals' savings accounts also make up the bulk of total time deposits. However, a fairly large component is owned by partnerships and corporations as a temporary means of holding funds accumulated as working capital or to pay income taxes.

Negro-owned banks and banks in general are about equally dependent on government deposits as a source of funds. Deposits of state and local governments are more important than those of the Federal Government. The U. S. Treasury Department tries to keep its cash holdings to a minimum and also holds its immediate working balances in Federal Reserve Banks. This ability to attract government deposits is a mark of considerable financial maturity, because such deposits are nearly always restricted to those institutions which have demonstrated a high level of stability. At the end of 1963, all except one of the thirteen Negro-owned banks held Federal Government deposits, and only three of them held none for state and local governments.

Finally, Negro-owned banks held a relatively smaller amount of interbank deposits, compared with banks as a whole. Such deposits are usually the basis of a rather sophisticated correspondence system in which big-city banks perform services for institutions in outlying areas. Among such services are purchases and sales of securities, foreign exchange and other international transactions, and marketing research. So far, because of the restricted nature of their customers' requirements, Negro banks have shown little need for interbank deposits. Where such deposits are held, they are typically owned by savings and loan associations which use them to cover unusual cash withdrawals.

If we look back to Table XXIII, it is again evident that Negro banks, during the period under review, retained a smaller proportion of their profits to strengthen the institution. This tendency may be attributable to the greater necessity to pay dividends in order to attract capital. The increment in surplus was relatively the same for both sets of banks.

When we examine the uses of bank funds between 1956 and 1963, the differences between Negro-owned and other banks are far more marked. The Negro institutions put a much larger percentage of their increased resources in liquid assets. Cash and U. S. Government securities combined represented almost one-fifth of their total uses of funds, compared with only 4 percent for all banks. While the banking industry in general channeled

TABLE XXIV—Type and Ownership of Bank Deposits, 1963

Type and Ownership of Deposits	All Banks Amount (Billions of Dollars)	Percent of total	Negro Banks Amount (millions of Dollars)	Percent of total
Demand deposits of individuals, partner-ships and corporations	125.4	39.1	25.7	37.3
Time deposits of individuals, partnerships and corporations	147.6	46.1	35.1	51.0
U.S. Government deposits	7.0	2.2	1.5	2.2
State and local government deposits	20.3	6.3	4.4	6.3
Interbank deposits	15.8	4.9	1.7	2.4
Other deposits	4.5	1.4	0.6	0.8
Total deposits	**320.7**	**100.0**	**69.0**	**100.0**

SOURCE: Same as Table XXI.

three-fourths of its new funds into loans, the proportion for Negro banks was about three-fifths. Again, this distribution of loanable funds is consistent with the differential risks of lending faced by Negro banks which was described above.

Negroes, of course, are attracted to the banking business by the same objectives which attract other investors: to make a profit. But here, as with many other pursuits in the field of business, the Negro appears to be less successful than his white counterpart in achieving his goal. Negro banks, taken as a group, seem to have higher operating expenses, lower rates of return on their resources—and thus lower rates of profit. However, what may come as a surprise to many readers, actual losses suffered by Negro banks on bad loans appear to be smaller, in relation to the volume of loans outstanding, than for banks in the economy as a whole.

Operating Ratios for Negro Banks

These general conclusions are amply supported by the evidence in Table XXV showing operating ratios for Negro-owned and member banks of the Federal Reserve system.[12] Because these ratios in many instances vary by size of bank, the Negro institutions are also compared with the smaller units in the Federal Reserve System. Operating ratios provide a convenient tool with which to appraise the performance of banks classified by type and size. Given the ratios for any particular class of bank, an individual banker (or his stockholders) has a standard to measure his own achievement. Some of the ratios are calculated by expressing various items from a bank's profit and loss statement as percentages of key components of the bank's balance sheet. For example, income may be divided by the total capital account to indicate the rate of return on stockholders' investment. Other ratios may be calculated to show the sources and disposition of the bank's income.

The summary operating ratios shown at the top of Table XXV clearly suggest that a dollar invested in Negro banks earns only about three-quarters as much as it would in a typical bank serving the community at large. For Negro banks, net current earnings before income taxes in 1963 were 9.9 percent of invested capital, compared with 13.6 percent for all Federal Reserve member banks. Even when compared with the smaller institutions in the Federal Reserve System, the Negro banks' performance was not greatly improved. After paying income taxes, Negro banks earned about 6.2 percent on their employed capital, against 8.2 percent for all Federal Reserve member banks and 7.4 percent for banks of comparable size. However, Negro owners received proportionately less in cash dividends than did other investors in bank stocks. When total assets are used as a benchmark, the less vigorous performance of Negro banks is also evident.

This squeeze on the profits of Negro banks can be explained by the second group of operating ratios in Table XXV describing the sources and disposition of income. First, it will be noted that Negro banks receive a smaller share of their revenue from loans and securities than do other banks. On the other hand, they depend more heavily on receipts from service charges; this means that customers of these institutions pay relatively more for what is likely to be a less complete range of services. Moreover, revenue from other sources (such as the rental of real estate) is particularly important for the Negro banks. But the most significant figure bearing on the profits squeeze is the expense ratio. In Negro-owned banks, total expenses absorbed about eighty-four cents of each dollar of revenue; in other institutions the comparable figure was only seventy-five cents. In every expense category, Negro banks had higher operating costs than other banks. The extra pressure of salaries and wages on their operating revenue was especially noticeable. Of course, this does not mean that officers and employees of Negro banks are

TABLE XXV—Operating Ratios of Negro-Owned and Federal Reserve Member Banks,* 1963 (Percentages)

	Federal Reserve Member Banks		Negro-owned Banks
Item	All Member Banks	Banks with Total Deposits of $1 mill. to $25 million	
Number of Banks	1	2	3
1 Summary ratios:			
Percentage of total capital accounts:			
Net current earnings before income taxes	13.6	12.1	9.91
Net income before related taxes	11.9	10.5	7.96
Net income	8.2	7.4	6.22
Cash dividends declared	3.1	2.8	1.97
Percentage of total assets:			
Total operating revenue	4.69	4.72	5.31
Net current earnings before income taxes	1.18	1.15	.86
Net income	.71	.71	.54
2 Sources and disposition of income:			
Percentage of total operating revenue:			
Interest and dividends on:			
U.S. Government securities	22.0	22.8	13.1
Other securities	6.8	5.9	6.3
Revenue on loans	61.7	62.2	58.7
Service charges on deposit accounts	5.9	5.7	6.7
All other revenue	3.6	3.4	15.2
Total revenue	**100.0**	**100.0**	**100.0**
Salaries and wages	29.0	29.1	33.0
Interest on time deposits	25.4	22.5	25.9
Other current expenses	20.1	16.7	24.8
Total expenses	**74.5**	**75.3**	**83.7**
Net current earnings before income taxes	**25.5**	**24.7**	**16.3**
Net losses (or recoveries and profits +)	1.4	1.6	1.2
Net increase in valuation reserves	1.6	1.2	1.9
Taxes on net income	7.0	6.4	2.8
Net income after taxes	15.5	15.4	10.2
3 Rates of return on securities and loans:			
Return on securities:			
Interest on U.S. Government securities	3.48	3.50	3.53
Interest and dividends on other securities	3.23	3.45	1.39
(Net losses or recoveries and profits +)	+ .07	0.05	.01
Return on loans:			
Revenue on loans	6.71	6.92	6.55
Net losses	.17	.18	.11

* For Federal Reserve Member banks, averages of individual ratios expressed as percentages. For Negro-owned banks, ratios are for all banks combined.

SOURCE: For Negro-owned banks, same as Table XXI; for Federal Reserve Member banks, Federal Reserve Bulletin, April, 1964.

HEADQUARTERS OF NORTH CAROLINA MUTUAL LIFE INSURANCE COMPANY, largest Negro owned business in the United States. *". . . the life insurance field remains the outstanding example of Negro enterprise."* (Welton Becket and Associates Photo)

exceptionally well-paid. (In fact, the median income of salaried Negro bank officials in 1959 was less than 90 percent of that for all such officials.) Rather, it indicates that their small size and generally poor marketing area severely limit the cash inflow of Negro-owned banks. On this meager revenue stream, it is difficult to sustain even the modest salaries they pay their employees. The higher ratio of interest on time deposits to total revenue is due primarily to the fact that most Negro banks are located in the South where interest rates generally exceed those in the rest of the nation (with the exception of the far West). Finally, other current operating expenses of Negro banks (such as local taxes, stationery, building maintenance, etc.) appear to be much higher proportionally, even after allowing for the relatively small size of their enterprises. No explanation for this divergence is readily apparent. But, in any case, the impact of these differential operating expenses in 1963 left Negro banks with about sixteen cents of net earnings per dollar of revenue, compared with twenty-five cents for banks in general. After adjustment for taxes, additions to security reserves and losses on loans and investments, these figures were reduced to about ten cents and fifteen cents, respectively.

Finally, the third set of operating ratios reveal that, despite the fact that Negro banks primarily with customers whose economic position is particularly weak, their losses are proportionally smaller than banks in general. In 1963, losses on securities were 0.01 percent for Negro banks; they were 0.07 percent for all Federal Reserve members and 0.05 percent for the smaller members of the system. While losses due to bad loans were somewhat larger than on securities for both Negro-owned and other banks, the Negro banks still had a smaller loss ratio. This differential loss experience seems to pose a paradox: in view of their small size and the more economically unstable environment in which they operate, one might conclude that the loans made by Negro banks are inherently more risky. Yet, their loss experience seems to suggest the opposite. Actually, this apparent paradox may not exist at all. Exactly because of the inherently greater risk of lending to small business borrowers with an uncertain future, Negro banks seem to take extra precautions in extending loans. They generally accept a smaller percentage of applications and require proportionately more (and more easily marketable) collaterial as security for loans. By thus restricting their loans to the best of the prospective borrowers, they may maintain a loan portfolio whose average quality actually exceeds that achieved by banks in the economy as a whole.

The Significance of Negroes in Banking

Against the above analysis of the role of Negroes in banking, one might still ask just how crucial is the entire effort. The reply, of course, must be that these institutions represent a vital link in the process of economic development in the Negro community. One can trace very briefly the basic features of this link. As is widely known, Negro businessmen have typically found it especially difficult to obtain sufficient credit to finance their operations. While other obstacles (such as insufficient management know-how, small markets and the inability to attract and hold enough capable employees) have also existed, the lack of credit certainly has posed one of the most difficult limitations. Furthermore, although these difficulties are typically faced by all small businessmen, white as well as Negro, they seem to be particularly distressing for Negroes.

Thus, the most vital function a strong bank can perform is to help finance the growth and expansion of those Negro businessmen who possess an idea and who can combine it with the knowledge and imagination to develop a market. Needless to say, the author by no means is advocating a segregated banking system to support a segregated Negro business sector. On the contrary, Negroes along with other businessmen will continue to look for financial accommodation at banks serving the general community. What is being stressed is that competition from strong Negro-owned banks can make just that margin of difference which will encourage leading institutions serving the general market to be somewhat more sympathetic and sensitive to the financial needs of potential Negro customers. In numerous cities (especially in Atlanta, Georgia, and Durham, North Carolina) there appears to be evidence that white bankers have become more liberal in both the size and terms of loans to Negro customers with the growth and expansion of Negro-owned institutions.

This beneficial influence stemming from the presence of Negro banks has not always been recognized. In fact, a definitive book on the Negro in America, which appeared in the early 1940's, not only failed to foresee this possibility—it actually concluded that the best course for Negroes in the field of banking was to seek fuller employment opportunities and the greater availability of credit at white-owned institutions.[13] Needless to say, the author does not share this pessimistic view. Instead it is vitally important for Negroes to be owners and risk-takers in banking as well as for them to seek a greater number of positions of dignity as employees of white-owned institutions.

As far as expanding banking employment is concerned, it is clear that the bulk of such opportunities must be sought primarily in white-controlled institutions. For example, between 1950 and 1960, the number of self-employed Negro bankers shrank from ninety to forty-one. The number in insurance and real estate climbed from 600 to 794. Over the same decade, the number of salaried Negro officials in all three fields rose from 183 to 293. However, only a handful of these Negro officials have found senior staff positions in white-owned banks. While the number is growing daily, this is still clearly an area where considerable strides can and should be made.

Negro-Owned Life Insurance Companies

The field of life insurance provides a classic illustration of the origins and rationale of Negro business: the exclusive and discriminating practices of the companies serving the national market created a protected environment in which the Negro institutions could develop. Beginning in the 1880's, most of the leading insurance firms began to employ a separate mortality table to estimate risks of insuring Negro lives; this separate table resulted in substantially higher premiums for Negroes for the same amount of coverage.[14] Still other companies refused to insure Negroes under any circumstances. Since many Negroes, along with other citizens, foresaw the desirability of insurance coverage, the conditions were set for the growth of Negro life insurance companies. While the record is replete with numerous failures (which is also true of white-owned and controlled companies), the life insurance field remains the outstanding example of Negro enterprise.

At the end of 1963, Negroes owned some fifty-odd legal reserve life insurance companies. They also maintained more than thirty burial and mutual aid societies. All of the latter are small, localized ventures, with a total of only $1 million of assets in 1962. Moreover, accurate statistics are available for only the twenty or so largest companies which hold virtually all of the assets owned by Negro institutions. Consequently, the following analysis is based on these companies. A detailed description of these companies is given in Tables XXVII, XXVIII and XXXI. But for the purpose of examining their structure and performance, a general summary is sufficient. This summary is provided in Table XXVI.

TABLE XXVI—Selected Characteristics of all Life Insurance Companies and Negro-Owned Life Insurance Companies, 1962

Selected Characteristics	All Companies		Negro Companies	
	Amount (Millions of Dollars)	Percent of Total	Amount (Millions of Dollars)	Percent of Total
Assets				
Cash	1,457	1.1	8,595	2.8
Bonds	63,722	47.8	165,349	53.2
Stocks	6,302	4.7	15,887	5.1
Mortgages	46,902	35.2	86,718	27.9
Policy Loans	6,234	4.7	11,743	3.8
Other Assets	8,674	6.5	22,553	7.2
Total Assets	133,291	100.0	310,845	100.0
Obligations				
Policy Reserves	108,384	81.3	237,287	76.3
Capital	978	0.7	9,503	3.1
Special Surplus Funds	2,352	1.8	6,765	2.2
Unassigned Surplus	7,926	6.0	27,806	8.9
Other Obligations	13,651	10.2	29,484	9.5
Total Obligations	133,291	100.0	310,845	100.0
Life Insurance in Force Dec. 31, 1962				
Ordinary	389,150	57.5	614,891	37.4
Industrial	39,638	5.9	1,029,055	62.6
Other	247,189	36.6	6	
Group	209,178	31.0		
Credit	38,011	5.6		
Total	675,977	100.0	1,643,952	100.0
Life Insurance Purchases 1962	79,577		592,359	
Death Benefits Paid 1962	3,878		8,520	
Ratio of Death Benefits to Purchases (Percent)		4.9		1.4
Income Received				
Premium Income	19,373	74.5	74,221	83.5
Investment and Other Income	6,627	25.5	14,619	16.5
Total	26,000	100.0	88,840	100.0

SOURCE: All Companies, *Life Insurance Fact Book, 1964*. Negro-Owned Companies, based on a preliminary data compiled by Emmer M. Lancaster, supplemented with statistics from *Best's Life Insurance Reports*.

As the Table shows, the twenty leading Negro companies had total assets of $311 million in 1962. This represented about 0.23 percent of the $133 billion of total assets owned by all life insurance companies. Thus, compared with Negro-owned banks (which held only 0.021 percent of total banking assets at the end of 1963), the relative position of the Negro insurance companies in the financial community is considerably stronger. However, the table also suggests some basic differences in the life insurance business operated by Negroes and the industry as a whole.

Life Insurance in Force in Negro Companies

Perhaps the most striking difference between Negro and other companies is the type of life insurance coverage. Industrial life insurance represented more than three-fifths of the total life insurance in force with Negro companies. Among all companies in the nation, industrial policies accounted for only 6 percent of total life insurance in force. Industrial life insurance is issued in small amounts, usually not over $500, with premiums payable on a weekly or monthly basis. The premiums, which may be as low as twenty-five cents per week, are generally collected at the policyholders' home by an agent of the company. In 1962, industrial life insurance outstanding with Negro companies amounted to $1,029 million. This represented 2.5 percent of the industry total, by far the largest share which Negroes controlled of any part of the insurance business.

Ordinary insurance constituted 37 percent of the face value of all policies outstanding with the Negro companies, compared with 58 percent for the industry. Ordinary insurance (which is also called whole or straight life insurance) forms the backbone of the life insurance business. It is usually issued in amounts of $1,000 or more. Premiums are payable on an annual, semiannual, quarterly or monthly basis. The premiums, in turn, are calculated on the "level premium" basis. This means the cost of the coverage is distributed evenly over the period during which premiums are paid. Because the premium remains the same from year to year, it is more than the actual cost of protection in the earlier years of the policy and less than the actual cost in the later years. The excess paid in the early years builds up the reserve. This reserve, of course, is a fund of policyholders' savings. This latter feature makes ordinary life insurance the key to the role of life insurance companies as leading sources of funds to finance residential construction and the acquisition of plant and equipment by the business sector. Yet, because ordinary insurance with its large savings component occupies such a minor position in the affairs of Negro life insurance companies, the latter also can play only a minor role in the financing of long-term capital formation in the Negro community.

Negro life insurance companies have made virtually no headway in the relatively new fields such as group and credit life insurance. Group coverage is issued, usually without medical examination, on a group of persons under a single master policy. It is normally issued to an employer for the benefit of employees, and individual members of the group hold certificates stating their coverage. Group insurance has been one of the fastest-growing segments of the industry; by the end of 1963, there were $228.5 billion of group life insurance outstanding, accounting for 31 percent of all life insurance in force in the United States. Negro companies provided none of this group protection. The explanation is simple: group contracts are typically issued to relatively large employers (although some are also written for trade unions and professional associations), and their size is generally well beyond the financial and managerial capacity of all except the two or three largest Negro companies. For example, at the end of 1963, the $228.5 billion of group life insurance outstanding had been written under 203,000 master contracts. These master contracts represented 50.9 million individual certificates, or an average of $4,490 per certificate. Thus, these figures imply that the average group consisted of about 250 individuals, with a group coverage of over $1 million. Since Negro companies write policies almost exclusively on Negro lives—and since there are only a handful of Negro firms employing even close to 250 workers—the group insurance market is extremely limited for these institutions. While Negro churches, fraternities and similar organizations do offer some potential for group insurance, little progress has been made in developing it.

Credit life insurance, designed to repay debt in case borrower should die, is the fastest-growing of all forms of life insurance, with the amount outstanding doubling every three years. But Negro companies have not even entered the field. By the end of 1963, about $43.6 billion of credit insurance were outstanding. This type of coverage has greatly reduced the risk of borrowing. By guaranteeing repayment of installment-plan debt or a personal loan in case the borrower should die, credit life insurance protects the borrower and his family as well as the bank, finance company, credit union or retailer that lent the money. However, because credit insurance is issued by life insurance companies through lending agencies, it is understandable that Negro insurance companies have not been able to penetrate this part of the life insurance market.

The reader should keep in mind, however, that the above discussion is focused on life insurance outstanding with Negro companies—and not on the ownership of life insurance by Negroes. While we have no firm estimates of the amount of protection purchased by Negroes, we do know that the great bulk of such coverage is provided by the leading insurance companies serving the general community. In fact, any one of the largest companies (such as Metropolitan or Prudential) probably has on its books far more coverage on Negro lives than the amount outstanding with all Negro-owned companies combined. In addition, we know that the proportion of Negro families covered by life insurance of any kind is still considerably below that for all families in the nation—although the gap has been closing in recent years. In 1963, about 67 percent of all heads of families owned individual life insurance, and the proportion rose to 85 percent with the inclusion of those holding group, veterans, fraternal and other types of insurance. For those with individual policies, the mean amount owned was $7,604; and the figure for all types of insurance was $10,600. Taking all families in the country, the average protection in 1963 was approximately $12,200, or roughly equivalent to 22 months of the average family's disposable personal income.

We do not have similar statistics for Negroes alone. However, among families with incomes below $3,000 (and about two-fifths of all Negro families had incomes below this figure in 1963), only 71 percent had insurance coverage of any kind, compared with 89 percent for the nation's families taken together. The proportions among Negroes were undoubtedly much smaller. We can get a slightly better feeling for the probable size of individual policies held by Negro families. In Table XII, it was shown that Negro

TABLE XXVII—Selected aspects of Negro Life Insurance Companies' operation, 1962

| | Type of Company | Life Insurance in Force, December 31, 1962 | | | | Life Insurance Purchases 1962 | Death Benefits Paid, 1962 |
		Total	Ordinary	Industrial	Other		
North Carolina Mutual Life Insurance Co., Durham, N.C.	Mutual	337,013,000	158,993,000	178,020,000	None	133,310,000	1,212,765
Atlanta Life Insurance Co., Atlanta, Ga.	Stock	182,126,000	59,795,000	122,331,000	None	46,768,000	1,189,630
Supreme Life Insurance Co. of America, Chicago, Ill.	Stock	195,175,000	68,045,000	127,130,000	None	57,730,000	1,134,019
Universal Life Insurance Co., Memphis, Tenn.	Stock	140,226,000	27,573,000	112,653,000	None	77,903,000	830,798
Golden State Mutual Life Insurance Co., Los Angeles, Calif.	Mutual	161,060,178	110,982,000	50,078,000	178	43,613,000	553,015
Chicago Metropolitan Mutual Assurance Co., Chicago, Ill.	Mutual	126,073,000	20,425,000	105,643,000	5,000	42,550,000	683,339
Mammoth Life and Accident Insurance Co., Louisville, Ky.	Stock	116,082,000	34,129,000	81,953,000	None	62,606,000	678,829
Pilgrim Health Life Insurance Co., Augusta, Ga.	Stock	55,961,000	17,740,000	38,221,000	None	17,788,000	383,094
Afro-American Life Insurance Co., Jacksonville, Fla.	Stock	52,753,000	11,840,000	40,913,000	None	25,899,000	417,878
Great Lakes Mutual Life Insurance Co., Detroit, Mich.	Mutual	71,960,000	24,818,000	47,142,000	None	19,788,000	247,953
Victory Mutual Life Insurance Co., Chicago, Ill.	Mutual	34,559,000	34,559,000	None	None	N.A.	185,493
United Mutual Life Insurance Co., New York, N.Y.	Mutual	31,014,000	18,701,000	12,313,000	None	4,503,000	222,617
Booker T. Washington Life Insurance Co., Birmingham, Ala.	Stock	61,720,932	8,684,000	53,036,000	932	23,105,000	261,833
Mutual Benefit Society of Maryland, Baltimore, Md.	Mutual	13,348,000	1,366,000	11,982,000	None	3,843,000	126,390
Southern Aid Insurance Co., Richmond, Va.	Stock	15,726,000	4,622,000	11,104,000	None	4,764,000	121,139
Virginia Mutual Benefit Life Insurance Co., Richmond, Va.	Mutual	16,054,000	3,483,000	12,571,000	None	8,854,000	76,062
Union Protective Life Insurance Co., Memphis, Tenn.	Stock	15,588,000	1,025,000	14,563,000	None	10,976,000	112,651
Guaranty Life Insurance Co., Savannah, Ga.	Stock	7,492,234	1,033,000	6,459,000	234	3,352,000	49,148
Southern Life Insurance Co., Baltimore, Md.	Stock	2,943,000	None	2,943,000	None	1,154,000	27,273
Crusaders Life Insurance Co., Kansas City. Kans.	Stock	7,078,000	7,078,000	None	None	3,863,000	6,263
Total		**1,643,952,344**	**614,891,000**	**1,029,055,000**	**6,344**	**592,359,000**	**8,520,189**

SOURCE: All Companies, *Life Insurance Fact Book*, 1964.

TABLE XXVIII—Assets of Negro Life Insurance Companies

| Income Received | | Total Assets | Cash | Bonds | Stocks | Mortgages | Policy Loans | Other Assets |
Total	Premium							
21,981,281	16,028,184	76,762,500	2,054,398	41,317,359	5,531,834	20,843,094	2,905,174	4,110,641
12,307,242	10,458,800	58,778,286	1,451,066	43,341,421	5,755,433	6,565,879	1,851,957	1,812,530
8,663,976	7,396,907	31,718,921	854,954	13,200,367	311,182	13,057,926	1,659,040	2,635,452
7,605,042	6,740,561	23,803,449	468,873	9,797,113	764,631	10,248,262	808,758	1,715,812
8,198,131	7,378,388	20,449,143	534,272	6,739,719	826,580	8,665,302	1,564,856	2,118,414
5,179,383	4,493,343	16,497,977	283,831	8,379,252	100,000	6,702,076	157,950	874,868
5,980,436	5,470,851	16,114,327	301,120	9,270,214	239,877	4,520,020	156,785	1,626,311
3,122,542	2,703,432	12,094,479	378,674	8,013,326	1,174,986	1,626,266	456,874	444,353
3,366,983	2,971,440	11,177,673	201,249	6,142,300	812,712	2,384,178	272,577	1,364,657
2,440,763	2,123,175	9,379,146	465,632	6,124,156	150,476	760,538	341,110	1,537,234
1,217,381	982,968	7,520,049	180,389	2,703,972	74,836	2,770,981	1,119,447	670,424
1,148,795	923,675	6,112,608	258,112	3,714,676	10,500	1,613,712	248,481	267,127
2,180,951	2,040,808	4,446,784	231,369	540,370	662,788	1,287,322	41,379	1,683,556
839,371	704,781	4,173,811	174,971	702,130	1,110,520	1,504,775	18,120	662,185
1,062,985	904,856	4,040,120	142,131	1,841,696	148,610	1,647,535	45,882	214,266
1,684,966	1,210,630	3,095,037	378,917	1,648,775	None	761,351	52,043	253,951
1,055,591	988,820	2,061,070	97,879	523,013	115,844	1,154,202	466	169,666
486,480	423,721	1,668,710	69,991	1,068,456	75,964	363,179	27,390	63,730
156,383	137,000	587,644	17,980	177,651	None	111,878	4,407	275,728
161,315	139,147	362,969	49,309	102,221	20,000	129,748	9,990	51,701
88,839,997	74,221,487	310,844,703	8,595,117	165,349,297	15,886,773	86,718,224	11,742,686	22,552,606

SOURCE: All Companies, *Life Insurance Fact Book, 1964.* Negro-Owned Companies, based on a preliminary data compiled by Emmer M. Lancaster, supplemented with statistics from *Best's Life Insurance Reports.*

families spent about $203 for personal insurance in 1960–61, compared with $324 spent by all families combined. These amounts represented 5.3 percent and 5.5 percent, respectively, of the after-tax personal incomes of Negro and all families. If a dollar of premiums purchased the same amount of protection for both groups, the average value of individual policies held by Negroes would have been about $5,150 in 1963, against $8,178 for all families. However, because a large proportion of coverage owned by Negroes consists of industrial insurance (where costs are much higher per dollar of coverage compared with ordinary insurance), the actual size of the average Negro-owned policy is probably much smaller than $5,000.

Operation of Negro Life Insurance Companies

The operations of Negro-owned companies are sketched in Table XXVI. In 1962, the 20 largest Negro institutions sold $592.3 million of new life insurance coverage. In the same year, industry sales amounted to $79.6 billion. Expressed another way, the average Negro company sold about $30 million of new life insurance coverage in 1962, compared with $54.1 million sold by the average company in the industry. So Negro companies accounted for 0.75 percent of total industry sales, a proportion more than three times their share of industry assets. Thus, while Negro companies remain small, collectively they are expanding their operations somewhat more rapidly than the industry as a whole. However, this is due partly to their small size, because the smaller units in the industry in general have made larger percentage gains in recent years than have the bigger institutions. But part of the growth undoubtedly reflects the expanding demand for insurance by Negro families as their incomes rise.

Negro companies paid about $8.5 million in death benefits in 1962. This represented about $425,000 per company. For the industry as a whole, death benefits amounted to $3.9 billion, or $2,620,000 per company. These figures indicate that for Negro companies, death benefits constituted 1.4 percent of new sales; for all companies combined the corresponding figure was 4.9 percent. The small ratio for Negro companies apparently reflects the mechanics in which industrial insurance plays a dominant role. When such policies are sold, their full face value is added to life insurance in force. The lapse rate for such policies is exceptionally high, and the proceeds paid on those which actually mature are relatively small. Death benefits are the primary form of payment made by Negro-owned companies to beneficiaries. This is far less true for the industry generally. For instance, in 1963 total life insurance benefit payments in the United States amounted to $10,028 million. Death benefits were only $4,209 million, or 42 percent. The remaining $5,819 million, or 58 percent, went to living policyholders. About $809 million were paid in matured endowments, $155 million in disability payments and $902 million in annuity payments. Dividends paid to policyholders amounted to $2,165 million, and policies surrendered for cash had a value of $1,789 million.

Negro life insurance companies had an income of about $89 million in 1962. Premium income provided $74 million, or 83.5 percent of the total. Investments and other sources provided $14.6 million, making up the remaining 16.5 percent. For the entire industry, total income amounted to $26.0 billion, of which $19.4 billion, or 74.5 percent, arose from premiums; investment and other income came to $6.6 billion, or 25.5 percent of the total. These income figures reveal a number of distinctions between Negro companies and the rest of the industry. The lesser importance of investments as a source of income is a further reflection of their modest status as financial intermediaries. The factors underlying this situation are explored more fully below. Another feature accounting for the difference in premiums as a source of income for Negro companies is their lack of participation in the market for group insurance. Group policies, which have been expanding rapidly, usually carry relatively low reserves, low premiums and no cash surrender values. Another factor has been the rise in family plan and family income policies, which with their term insurance features, also have relatively low premiums and no cash values on their term elements. All of these factors have combined to dampen the growth of premium income for industry as a whole. But since Negro companies for the most part have not joined in these innovations, premiums remain for them a far more important source of income.

The obligations of Negro-owned companies also exhibit a few differentiating features. (See Table XXIX) Their policy reserves amounted to

TABLE XXIX—Obligations of Negro Life Insurance Companies

	Total Obligations	Policy Reserves	Capital	Special Surplus Funds	Unassigned Surplus	Other Obligations
North Carolina Mutual life Insurance Co., Durham, N. C.	76,762,500	60,146,961	None	4,136,342	5,550,000	6,929,197
Atlanta Life Insurance Co., Atlanta, Ga.	58,778,286	36,103,703	4,000,000	1,000,000	10,080,452	7,594,131
Supreme Life Insurance Co. of America, Chicago, Ill.	31,718,921	26,996,676	1,665,000	200,000	1,001,486	1,855,759
Universal Life Insurance Co., Memphis, Tenn.	23,803,449	19,905,604	1,565,650	None	1,481,819	850,376
Golden State Mutual Life Insurance Co., Los Angeles, Calif.	20,449,143	16,359,533	None	98,949	1,350,000	2,640,661
Chicago Metropolitan Mutual Assurance Co., Chicago, Ill.	16,497,977	12,685,055	None	None	2,053,865	1,759,057
Mammoth Life and Accident Insurance Co., Louisville, Ky.	16,114,327	11,467,259	600,000	488,943	844,222	2,713,903
Pilgrim Health Life Insurance Co., Augusta, Ga.	12,094,479	9,789,942	200,000	300,000	1,244,980	559,557
Afro-American Life Insurance Co., Jacksonville, Fla.	11,177,673	9,462,161	500,000	None	438,217	777,295
Great Lakes Mutual Life Insurance Co., Detroit, Mich.	9,379,146	7,835,296	None	200,000	458,271	885,579
Victory Mutual Life Insurance Co., Chicago, Ill.	7,520,049	6,818,664	None	1,233	325,600	374,552
United Mutual Life Insurance Co., New York, N. Y.	6,112,608	5,514,679	None	None	240,277	357,652
Booker T. Washington Life Insurance Co., Birmingham, Ala.	4,446,784	3,513,621	100,000	None	607,685	225,478
Mutual Benefit Society of Maryland, Baltimore, Md.	4,173,811	2,609,619	None	None	568,793	995,399
Southern Aid Insurance Co., Richmond, Va.	4,040,120	2,697,186	300,000	150,000	636,476	256,458
Virginia Mutual Benefit Life Insurance Co., Richmond, Va.	3,095,037	2,335,498	None	None	351,421	408,118
Union Protective Life Insurance Co., Memphis, Tenn.	2,061,070	1,294,024	200,000	100,000	308,706	158,340
Guaranty Life Insurance Co., Savannah, Ga.	1,668,710	1,105,568	200,000	89,404	200,000	73,738
Southern Life Insurance Co., Baltimore, Md.	587,644	479,959	10,000	None	38,078	59,607
Crusaders Life Insurance Co., Kansas City, Kans.	362,969	166,274	162,271	None	25,068	9,356
TOTAL	310,844,703	237,287,282	9,502,921	6,764,871	27,805,416	29,484,213

TABLE XXX—A comparative analysis of investment portfolios of selected life insurance companies

Selected Assets as Percentage of Total Admitted Assets

Rank	Name and State	Total Assets Dec. 1961 (Thousands of $)	Cash	Bonds Total	Bonds U.S. Govt.	Stocks Total	Stocks Pref'd	Stocks Common	Mortgages	Annual Growth Rate Period	Annual Growth Rate %
1	North Carolina Mutual, North Carolina	$ 71,134	1.6	58.1	3.0	6.4	0.2	6.2	24.3	1951–61	7.8
2	Atlanta Life, Georgia	56,837	1.9	73.9	20.7	6.2	1.2	5.0	11.6	1951–61	7.9
3	Supreme Life, Illinois	30,688	1.2	32.5	1.7	0.5	0.4	0.1	36.2	1951–61	9.9
	Old Republic, Illinois	30,433	35.2	46.3	21.5	4.3	None	4.3	0.5	"	17.9
4	Universal Life, Tennessee	22,496	1.8	42.5	7.3	1.3	0.9	0.4	42.6	1951–61	9.3
5	Golden State Mutual, California	18,873	3.4	28.9	1.4	3.0	0.4	2.6	45.4	1951–61	12.5
	Pierce Insurance Co., California	18,078	4.3	43.8	39.2	3.1	1.1	2.0	38.6	"	17.6
6	Chicago Metro, Illinois	15,461	1.2	52.0	5.9	None	None	None	41.1	1951–61	10.9
	Globe Life, Illinois	15,047	1.6	49.2	11.7	2.9	1.7	1.2	38.9	"	8.6
7	Mammoth Life, Kentucky	15,234	1.9	57.0	12.4	0.6	0.3	0.3	29.7	1951–61	15.7
8	Pilgrim Health, Georgia	11,790	3.5	66.9	4.3	9.2	N.A.	N.A.	12.7	1951–61	6.8
	General Fidelity, Georgia	10,316	81.7	8.8	3.0	0.1	None	0.1	None	1955–61	25.0
9	Afro-American, Florida	10,915	1.8	55.7	11.0	5.4	1.9	3.5	20.4	1951–61	6.2
	American Bankers, Florida	12,702	9.2	26.6	6.7	8.1	8.0	0.1	29.4	1952–61	40.0
10	American Woodman, Colorado	9,350	1.3	77.1	33.9	None	None	None	13.9	1951–61	3.3
	National Farmers Union, Colorado	9,920	4.0	31.6	2.1	0.1	None	0.1	27.2	"	17.0
11	Great Lakes Mutual, Michigan	8,892	4.3	67.4	10.9	1.3	1.3	None	10.8	1951–61	13.0
12	Victory Mutual, Illinois	7,408	2.8	33.8	3.3	0.9	0.8	0.1	38.0	1951–61	7.0
	Horace Mann, Illinois	7,465	7.0	46.9	14.2	6.4	3.0	3.3	23.3	"	44.0
13	United Mutual, New York	5,802	3.1	63.0	2.6	None	None	None	25.1	1951–61	9.0
14	Southern Aid, Virginia	4,005	4.1	43.7	8.0	3.6	3.6	None	42.1	1951–61	3.5
15	Booker T. Washington, Alabama	3,969	5.8	13.3	2.2	15.9	0.2	15.7	30.5	1952–61	12.9
	Loyal American, Alabama	3,486	3.8	23.6	5.0	15.4	0.8	14.7	22.1	1956–61	27.0
16	Unity Mutual, Illinois	3,000	11.1	42.1	3.0	None	None	None	39.0	1951–61	16.1
17	Virginia Mutual, Virginia	2,984	9.2	54.5	6.9	0.7	N.A.	N.A.	26.3	1954–61	7.9
	North American Assurance, Virginia	2,861	6.7	69.3	6.9	12.4	1.7	10.7	5.6	1951–61	10.4
18	Union Protective, Tennessee	1,935	10.0	25.5	13.2	None	None	None	51.7	1952–61	9.0
	American Old Line, Tennessee	1,982	48.5	35.4	35.4	None	None	None	15.1	1960–61	27.1
19	Guaranty Life, Georgia	1,631	1.1	65.3	12.0	4.4	4.0	0.4	21.4	1951–61	4.0
	Farmers National, Georgia	1,729	15.6	51.3	43.3	1.0	0.5	0.5	8.6	1959–61	55.0
20	Southern Life, Maryland	584	3.4	27.6	25.2	3.3	None	3.3	36.1	1960–61	2.1
	Industry Totals[1] (Amounts in Millions of Dollars)	126,816	1.1	48.0	4.9	4.9	1.6	3.3	34.9	1951–61	6.4

[1] *Life Insurance Fact Book, 1963*
N.A. Not Available
SOURCE: *Best's Life Insurance Reports*, 1962.

$237 million at the end of 1962, representing 76.3 percent of their total obligations. For the industry as a whole, policy reserves totaled $108.4 billion and accounted for 81.3 percent of total obligations. These reserves have been set aside to meet the life insurance companies' future obligations to policyholders and their beneficiaries. State laws require each company to maintain its policy reserves at a level sufficient to ensure payment of all policy obligations as they become due. The amount of reserves required for this purpose is calculated actuarially, taking into account the additional funds forthcoming from future premium payments and investment earnings. In 1962, the $1,644 million of life insurance in force with Negro companies were backed by policy reserves amounting to 14 percent. For all companies combined, the ratio of policy reserves to life insurance in force was 16 percent. Again the smaller ratio for Negro companies can be attributed partly to their concentration on industrial policies.

Capital stock constitutes a much larger share of the obligations of the combined Negro companies than is true for the industry as a whole. The ratios were 3.1 percent and 0.7 percent, respectively, in 1962. This clearly reflects the fact that the 12 Negro institutions which are stock companies are a far more important segment of the Negro insurance sector than is true of stock companies in the industry generally. For example, in mid-1963, there were 1,347 companies owned by stockholders, and 156 were mutual companies owned by their policyholders. However, the 156 units (only one-tenth of the total) were generally older and larger. They accounted for about 60 percent of the life insurance in force, and for about 70 percent of the assets of all life insurance companies in the United States. Among the twenty Negro companies in 1962, the twelve owned by stockholders accounted for about 51 percent of insurance in force with the group as a whole, and for around 54 percent of the assets.

Investment Behavior of Negro Life Insurance Companies

Negro life insurance companies tend to be much more conservative in their investment policies than the industry as a whole. They tend to hold relatively more cash and government bonds and a relatively smaller proportion of common stocks. The net result is that the Negro companies, as mentioned above, play a somewhat less important role (even after allowing for their small size) as sources of funds to finance long-term capital formation by private borrowers.

At the end of 1962, Negro life insurance companies held 2.8 percent of their total assets in cash, or two and one-half times the proportion for all companies. As was true of Negro banks, their cash and bond holdings made them much more liquid than other institutions. Again, as with banks, their higher liquidity ratios reflect a limited range of investment opportunities in the private business sector—especially if the company attempts to strengthen its life insurance market by lending in the Negro community. But the extra risk inherent in lending to Negro borrowers (an extra risk associated with the instability of family incomes and the uncertain conditions under which Negro entrepreneurs operate) is a major factor restraining the acquisition of mortgages by Negro life insurance companies.

The investments of Negro life insurance companies in 1962, grouped by broad category, are shown in Table XXVIII. These assets, as in other companies, are held primarily to meet future obligations to policyholders. But the distribution of life insurance assets also provides a fairly clear insight into the role of life insurance companies as financial intermediaries. By tracing changes in this distribution over time, it is possible to gauge their impact on the market for long-term funds.[15]

To go behind the broad contours of portfolio management in Negro-owned life insurance companies, statistics were collected for 1961, the latest year for which detailed figures were available from reliable industry sources. These statistics are shown in Table XXX. The Negro companies shown in the table are essentially the same ones included in earlier tables. However, because of differences in state investment laws, where possible each Negro company has been compared with another company of similar size in the same state.

Several broad features stand out in Table XXX. As mentioned above, the Negro-owned companies appear to be somewhat more conservative in their ownership of common stock than other companies of similar size. This is less true of other assets. Having adjusted for size of company, it appears that their cash holdings, while still high relative to the industry, are slightly lower than for other companies with comparable total assets. While Negro companies' bond holdings tend to be relatively smaller than for other companies in the same size group, the composition of their holdings varies significantly. United States Government bonds make up a somewhat smaller proportion of the portfolios of Negro companies. Instead, considerable emphasis is placed on other types of debt obligations, especially bonds sold by state and local governments. The tax-exemption of the income from these securities makes them particularly attractive to some institutions. In addition, compared with other small companies, the Negro institutions also seem to have above average commitments in mortgages—just the opposite of the situation when they were contrasted with the industry as a whole.

The conservatism of Negro-owned companies with respect to equity securities is clearly evident in their holdings of common stocks. As a rule, the ratio of common stocks to total assets in Negro-owned companies is well below the average for both the industry and other institutions of comparable size. This pattern may be related to the fact that the management of a portfolio of common stocks requires the command of an expertise which most small companies (Negro-owned companies among them) find it difficult to employ. Furthermore, the required diversification of a common stock portfolio is hard to achieve in the typical small company.

However, many small companies rely on the expert guidance of outside investment advisers to assist them in portfolio planning. A number of Negro-owned companies are among them. If more companies were to employ such advisers, common stocks could be acquired by a greater number of institutions. In limited amounts, and provided seasoned and amply diversified stocks (although not necessarily blue chip stocks) are selected, common stocks are an advantageous investment outlet for these institutions. Because of the long-term nature of their liabilities and steady cash inflow, they are seldom—if ever—forced to liquidate assets to meet claims. Thus, they are free to hold common stocks primarily as a source of income. Over a period of time, and after allowing for occasional small capital losses, common stocks can make a major contribution to building up the net earnings of life insurance companies.

It will also be noted from Table XXX that, as a rule, the rate of growth of Negro-owned companies in the decade of the 1950's was somewhat below that for other companies of comparable size. Of course, this was not universally true, because the rate of growth in several Negro-owned companies was well ahead of that for the industry as a whole.

THE FUTURE OF NEGROES IN BUSINESS

If the fields in which Negro businessmen have traditionally concentrated are less promising than in the past, what alternative opportunities are likely to appear in the future? For Negroes, as for other citizens in the business world, such opportunities are likely to be found primarily as managers and officials employed by our medium and large corporations and public enterprises. That Negroes have made little progress in this field is common knowledge. For example, in 1960, about 8 percent of the total civilian labor force of 68 million was engaged as non-farm managers, officials and proprietors. Less than 1.5 percent of the 6.6 million Negroes in the labor force were so engaged. If the percentages had been approximately equal, there

NEW YORK FRANCHISEE: The first franchise acquired by a Negro under the Department of Commerce's Franchise Service for Minorities was made possible by loans from the Freedom National Bank of New York City ($2,500), the Small Business Administration ($7,500) and the investment of personal funds ($8,000) by the franchise, William Bailey. Shown at ceremonies awarding the SBA grant are (left to right) William Hudgins, President of Freedom National Bank; A. L. Tunick, President of Chicken Delight, Inc.; Under Secretary of Commerce Franklin D. Roosevelt, Jr.; Mr. Bailey; SBA Administrator Eugene Foley and Assistant Secretary of Commerce Andrew F. Brimmer.

(Task Force for Equal Opportunity in Business Photo)

CHICAGO CLEANING CONTRACTOR: The president of the Village Maid Service had worked as a domestic prior to the establishment of her own business.

(Small Business Administration Photo)

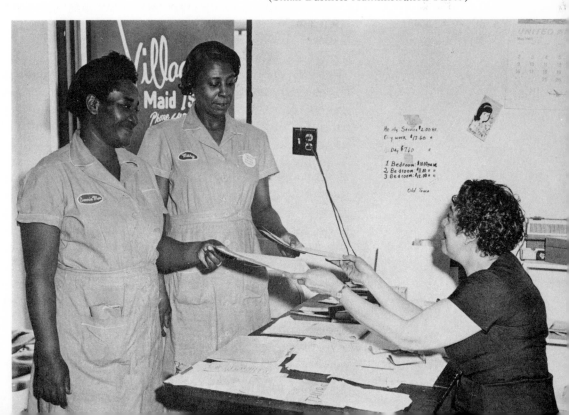

would have been about 525 thousand—rather than the actual 191 thousand —Negroes in the managerial class. Furthermore, over half of the Negro managerial group was self-employed, compared with just over one-third of all managers in the country.

Thus, from these data a clear inference can be drawn: with a change in aspirations among potential Negro businessmen, better preparation on their part and a genuine commitment to equal opportunity by leaders in the corporate business community, the future could be promising for a number of Negro businessmen.

Some progress is already being made in this direction, although few corporate executives would claim that the pace has been rapid. A rough indication of the current trends is given by the experience of those companies which participate in "Plans for Progress." This is a voluntary program to expand access to jobs, operated in conjunction with the President's Committee on Equal Opportunity. In a report covering the period when the companies joined Plans for Progress through mid-July, 1964, 103 of these firms reported that their total employment increased by 300,796 or 7.6 percent. Just over two-fifths of this gain represented an expansion in white collar employment. During the same period, these companies added 40,938 employees from minority groups. This represented about 13.6 percent of the expansion in total employment. On the other hand, nonwhites filled about 11.0 percent of the increase in white collar jobs.

When these companies joined Plans for Progress, nonwhites constituted about 5 percent of their total labor force, and they represented approximately 1.2 percent of those in the managerial group. In the subsequent expansion in employment, nonwhites obtained about 3,000 (or 2 percent) of the new jobs in the management category. While this gain is obviously very small, it does represent about 1,000 more managerial and technical positions for nonwhites than might have been expected on the basis of the companies' traditional employment practice.

Simultaneously, many corporations are making a special effort to recruit and train Negroes and other minority group citizens for corporate positions. Some of this effort undoubtedly can be written off as "image-making" by some firms, who would like to point to their recruiting efforts which have —unfortunately—failed to produce "qualified" candidates. On the whole, however, the vast majority of corporate recruiters seem to be making a genuine effort to identify and to enroll promising minority group candidates. On the other hand, given the criteria which the typical corporation uses in selecting its managerial personnel, most corporate recruiters are undoubtedly finding it difficult to locate qualified personnel. The sources of these difficulties are widely known. They spring from the vicious circle created by a history of discriminatory employment practices; poor undergraduate training provided by the archaic curricula of basically segregated institutions attended by many Negro college students; a resulting peculiar pattern of occupational preferences stressing medicine, law, teaching and the ministry; a reluctance to venture into the expanding fields of business administration and related social sciences, engineering and other technical areas—which result in only marginal preparation for management careers in business.

Pattern of Corporate Demand for Nonwhite Professional Personnel

In the meantime, it may be helpful to provide a profile of the types of skills for which corporations are searching among Negroes and other minority group members. A rough outline can be sketched by an analysis of the recruiting visits which corporations are currently making on predominantly Negro college campuses. For this purpose, the experience of Howard University may be taken as a prototype. (Of course, the Howard University experience is undoubtedly biased because its curricula are most varied and its program in engineering and the physical sciences probably far surpasses that of all other predominantly Negro schools; its program in business administration also ranks high among the three or four genuine programs to be found on Negro college campuses. But, if we keep in mind these limitations of the Howard data, we can gain an insight into the types of professions demanded by corporations.)

Table XXXI summarizes the Howard University experience for the academic year 1963–64. During that period, Howard's placement office received visitors from about 160 corporations and about 20 government departments and independent agencies. These companies represented a variety of industries, but the heaviest concentration was in chemicals, transportation equipment, and communications and utilities. Among government agencies, the Defense Department was the most frequent visitor.

Together, these potential employers made more than seven hundred requests about some forty-odd occupational categories. The engineering field accounted for about two-fifths of the total, with electrical and mechanical engineering being most frequently specified. Somewhat over one-fifth of the inquiries sought graduates in the physical sciences, with chemists and physicists taking the lead. Thus, more than three-fifths of all of the requests were concentrated in the engineering and technical fields. If the closely related field of mathematics is added, about 70 percent of the total inquiries were for candidates with highly technical undergraduate training.

In contrast, requests for personnel in the field of business administration represented only 15 percent of the total. General business administration and accounting each attracted 5 percent, and marketing about 4 percent. If we add inquiries for graduates in the social sciences—which frequently serve as a pool of skills that can be reshaped for business administration purposes—the share accounted for by the business area would rise to only one-sixth of the total.

A number of inferences can be drawn from these data, but one implication seems clear: if we can generalize the Howard experience, corporations (and to some extent government agencies) have directed their recruitment efforts on Negro campuses more to the technical and scientific fields and less to those which lead directly into key managerial functions in corporate enterprise. While engineers, chemists and other technicians (with years of experience) do frequently move into positions of general management responsibility, the more likely routes through the corporate hierarchy typically begin in the nontechnical fields, such as financial administration, accounting and marketing.

TABLE XXXI—Structure of Corporate Demand for Nonwhite Professional Personnel

INDUSTRY DISTRIBUTION OF REQUESTS

Professions	TOTAL INQUIRIES		Manufac-turing	Research and Development
	Number	Percent of Total		
Engineering:	**284**	**40.4**	**165**	**17**
Engineer, General	99	14.1	58	5
Electrical Engineer	77	11.0	41	7
Mechanical Engineer	82	11.7	48	5
Civil Engineer	16	2.3	8	—
Chemical Engineer	6	0.9	6	—
Industrial Engineer	4	0.6	4	—
Physical Sciences:	**157**	**22.3**	**94**	**9**
Scientist, General		3.0	18	2
Chemist	50	7.1	33	2
Physicist	57	8.1	34	5
Biologist	22	3.1	5	—
Pharmacist	6	0.9	4	—
Geologist	1	0.1	—	—
Mathematician	**51**	**7.3**	**20**	**3**
Business Professions:	**106**	**15.1**	**49**	**—**
Business Administration, General	36	5.1	16	—
Accountants	38	5.4	21	—
Management trainees	6	0.9	—	—
Marketing, General	14	2.0	7	—
Buyers	1	0.1	—	—
Sales and Advertising	11	1.6	5	—
Social Sciences:	**19**	**2.7**	**3**	**—**
Social Scientist, General	2	0.3	—	—
Economist	8	1.1	1	—
Statistician	7	1.0	2	—
Sociologist	1	0.1	—	—
Psychologist	1	0.1	—	—
Other Professions:	**60**	**8.5**	**19**	**1**
Liberal Arts, General	33	4.7	12	1
Lawyer	4	0.6	3	—
Home Economist	5	0.7	2	—
Religious Worker	2	0.3	—	—
Architect	2	0.3	—	—
Education—University Professor	3	0.4	—	—
Primary and Secondary Teachers	6	0.9	—	—
Social Worker	2	0.3	—	—
Medical Personnel (premed.)	3	0.4	2	—
Humanities:	**6**	**0.9**	**—**	**—**
Art	4	0.6	—	—
Music	1	0.1	—	—
Drama	1	0.1	—	—
Miscellaneous:	**20**	**2.8**	**2**	**—**
Men (unspecified)	11	1.6	1	—
Women (unspecified)	6	0.9	—	—
Recreation Workers	3	0.4	1	—
GRAND TOTAL	**703**	**100.0**	**352**	**30**
Percent of Grand Total	100.0	—	50.1	4.3
Memo: Number of Companies and Government Agencies	179	—	90	11

Communications	Wholesale and Retail Trade	Financial	Business Services	Education and Social Services	Government
5	2	—	—	—	66
2	2	—	—	—	24
3	—	—	—	—	18
—	—	—	—	—	17
—	—	—	—	—	7
—	—	—	—	—	—
—	—	—	—	—	—
34	1	—	—	—	52
10	1	—	—	—	—
11	—	—	—	—	14
12	—	—	—	—	18
1	—	—	—	—	17
—	—	—	—	—	2
—	—	—	—	—	1
—	—	—	—	—	27
1	20	9	—	—	17
—	3	5	1	—	9
—	5	—	1	—	8
—	4	2	—	—	—
—	4	2	—	—	—
—	1	—	—	—	—
1	3	—	1	—	—
1	2	—	—	—	13
—	—	—	—	—	2
1	1	—	—	—	5
—	1	—	—	—	4
—	—	—	—	—	1
—	—	—	—	—	1
4	4	6	—	20	6
1	4	6	—	6	3
1	—	—	—	—	—
2	—	—	—	—	1
—	—	—	—	2	—
—	—	—	—	—	2
—	—	—	—	3	—
—	—	—	—	6	—
—	—	—	—	2	—
—	—	—	—	1	—
—	—	—	1	2	3
—	—	—	1	2	1
—	—	—	—	—	1
—	—	—	—	—	1
1	—	1	—	8	8
—	—	—	—	4	6
1	—	1	—	4	—
—	—	—	—	—	2
47	29	16	7	30	192
6.7	4.1	2.3	1.0	4.3	27.3
19	11	8	5	15	20

Of course, the chance to go into business for themselves is an option which will remain open to Negroes along with other citizens. However, before this option is taken up in the future, potential Negro business should give careful consideration to several factors that are rapidly reshaping the environment in which they will have to operate. While the majority of Negro businessmen are correct in assuming that (within the foreseeable future) they will have to rely primarily on Negro customers for their patronage, they apparently do not realize that in the future they will have to compete in a wholly different type of market. As mentioned above, the desegregation of places of public accommodation, such as restaurants, theaters, hotels and similar establishments, will have a serious impact on many of the sheltered businesses which most Negro businesmen have operated behind the barriers induced by segregation. With greater access to facilities provided for the public in general, Negro customers will increasingly demand that Negro businesses compete in terms of quality of services provided at competitive prices.

Further, there is a prime need to shift from the single proprietorship form of organization, which is so dominant among Negro businessmen, to the corporate form which is the key to financing business expansion. The superiority of the corporation over unincorporated enterprises as a medium for expanding business has been clearly demonstrated, and growth as opposed to stagnation has always been a measure of business health. Recent data on the distribution of firms by type of organization and the relative share of receipts and profits show that relatively few companies account for the major share of the nation's business, and these are the large and ever-growing corporations. For example, in 1960, corporations constituted about 10 percent of the total number of businesses in existence. However, the total receipts of corporations were $803 billion, representing over three-quarters of the total. Their net profits, after allowing for losses, amounted to $44 billion, or three-fifths of the total net profits of business enterprises.

But whatever form of organization a businessman chooses for his operation, several conditions must be met if success is to be realized. In the first instance, a businessman must perceive a market for a product or service. Next, steps must be taken to translate this idea into a practical production process. Thirdly, technical and managerial know-how must be sufficient to establish and conduct an enterprise. Financial resources, especially equity capital, must be available or acquired. A skilled labor force must exist or must be trained. Finally, the businessman must possess enough marketing know-how to find and maintain customers in the face of competition from other products and services. As we all know, the typical Negro-owned firm is deficient in all or most of these vital requirements.

While there is no shortage of potential Negro businessmen, there is a severe shortage of technical know-how outside the traditional areas of trade and personal services. This lack of mastery over technical requirements may well be an obstacle as great as the lack of equity capital. To help fill this gap, a number of economic development and business service centers (including centers at Atlanta University and Howard University) were established in 1964. The objectives of these projects include:

—The provision of technical and management assistance to establish or expand businesses, particularly those that are Negro-owned or managed and have a preponderance of Negro employees.

—The provision of technical training and services to groups and communities, particularly Negro, in the field of economic development which will enable them to take a more active role in the creation of new enterprises and new job opportunities.

Such centers could become the locus of the kind of economic and technical research and guidance so necessary for economic development and successful business enterprise. Finally, they would provide for both students and faculty exposure to the variety and complexity of managerial problems with which virtually every future businessman must deal.

The above observations focus on only a few of the growing opportunities for Negro businessmen to participate in the future growth of the country. Above all, there will undoubtedly be a variety of ventures engaged in the production and distribution of goods and services for the community as a whole. Moreover, there will undoubtedly be growing opportunities for Negroes to participate in the management activities of large corporations which are also oriented to the general market. It should be emphasized again that desegregation of the marketplace which is already well under way will require desegregation in the ownership and management of business enterprises as well. While the future of a segregated Negro-owned business, existing in a segregated market, appears not to be bright, the future of Negroes in the business life of the country in general does appear to be more promising than ever before.

SUMMARY AND CONCLUSIONS

The principal conclusions reached in this chapter have been stated at the end of each section. However, the highlights can be summarized here. The basic theme is this:

General Position of the Negro in the Economy

Segregation has created a dual market for personal services in the United States. This in turn has created a Negro subsector of the national economy. This is the foundation of Negro business and of the Negro middle class.

Income of the Negro Community

Trends in personal income, the best overall indicator of economic well-being, suggest that Negroes as a group have shared in the long period of post-war prosperity along with the rest of the economy. However, both business cycles and the relative slowdown of the economy in the decade of the 1950's affected nonwhites considerably more adversely than the country at large. The net result was that Negroes made little progress in closing the income gap between themselves and the rest of the population. In 1947 the median income of nonwhite families was 51 percent of that of white families; in 1963 the ratio was still only 53 percent.

Within the Negro community, unlike the country at large, the distribution of income has become more unequal in the post-war period. Middle class Negroes have greatly improved their relative position during the last one and a half decades. But those at the bottom of the income ladder experienced some deterioration. In 1947, the lowest fifth of the nonwhite population received 4.8 percent of the aggregate family income; by 1960 their share had dropped to 3.9 percent. Among white families, the lowest fifth received 5.5 percent and 5.3 percent in 1947 and 1960, respectively. Thus, the relative deterioration was much sharper for nonwhite families.

This deterioration in the position of the lowest nonwhite income group both reflects and contributes to the lingering poverty among Negroes in America. By almost any standard, poverty is the normal state of existence of most Negroes. Using the rough benchmark of $3,000 as a rough poverty line, Negroes are about two and one-half times more likely than white families to be found among the poor. While about one-fifth of the nation's 47.4 million families are poor, 43 percent (or 2.1 million) of the 4.8 million nonwhite families are poor.

At the opposite end of the income scale, the Negro community can claim only a handful of millionaires. But it can boast of a fairly large and growing number of prosperous families and individuals. For example, in 1963 approximately 274,000 nonwhite families had incomes of $10,000 or more. Between 1959 and 1963 the number of nonwhite families in the $10,000-and-over group rose by about 50 percent compared with 40 percent for all families. However, a much larger proportion of the nonwhite families than of white families in the higher income brackets depend on the earnings of two or more workers.

While racial discrimination clearly imposes a severe burden on the nation's economy, its economic costs have been difficult to assess. However, using the differential in education and occupation distribution between the whites and nonwhite, a rough estimate was made of this cost in terms of lost gross national product (GNP). The general findings are: if the present educational achievement of nonwhites were fully utilized, GNP would rise by 1.9 percent. If educational levels were equalized, GNP would rise further by 1.6 percent. Translated into the value of output, these percentage gains imply an increase of $11 billion and $9 billion, respectively, or a total increase of $20 billion, based on a GNP of $585 billion in 1963.

Consumer Expenditures and the Negro Market

An examination of trends in consumer expenditures shows a rapid conversion of Negro and white consumption patterns. With rising incomes, Negro families are spending proportionately more on goods and services typically purchased by middle-class consumers and proportionately less on the basic necessities to which low-income groups are restricted. Similarly, the erosion of segregation and discrimination is providing Negroes with greater access to places of public accommodation, and their expenditure pattern reflects this change.

But these shifting consumption patterns are also effecting drastic changes in the Negro market. Salesmen and other middle men who have earned their livelihood through developing the traditional Negro market are progressing more slowly than those who have detected the emerging trends and have moved into new channels of distribution.

They said it couldn't be done.
It couldn't.

We tried. Lord knows we tried. But no amount of pivoting or faking could squeeze the Philadelphia 76ers' Wilt Chamberlain into the front seat of a Volkswagen.

So if you're 7'1" tall like Wilt, our car is not for you.

But maybe you're a mere 6'7".

In that case, you'd be small enough to appreciate what a big thing we've made of the Volkswagen.

There's more headroom than you'd expect. (Over 37½" from seat to roof.)

And there's more legroom in front than you'd get in a limousine. Because the engine's tucked over the rear wheels where it's out of the way (and where it can give the most traction).

You can put 2 medium-sized suitcases up front (where the engine isn't), and 3 fair-sized kids in the back seat. And you can sleep an enormous infant in back of the back seat.

Actually, there's only one part of a VW that you can't put much into.

The gas tank.

But you can get about 29 miles per gallon out of it.

Under the same set of dynamic forces, the Negro business sector is also changing rapidly. Since racial segregation has served Negro businessmen as a protective tariff, the decline of segregation is affecting them in the same way a reduction in a tariff affects domestic industry. In general, Negro businessmen have concentrated on providing a variety of personal services which were unavailable to Negroes from establishments catering to the public at large. In those areas in which Negro consumers have relatively free access to retail establishments (such as department stores, hardware, furnishings and similar outlets), Negro businessmen have not found fertile soil. On the other hand, in those areas where segregation has provided a shield (such as restaurants, barber shops, hotels, undertaker establishments, etc.), Negro businessmen in the past have made their greatest gains. They have made little headway in construction, transportation, public utilities, and similar fields. In manufacturing, which typically requires large investments of capital and a wide market, few Negro-owned enterprises exist. The few exceptions are principally cosmetic firms which produce for the segregated market provided by Negro barber and beauty shops. However, even these firms are beginning to feel the impact of competition from large nation-wide manufacturing enterprises who recognize the expanding market based on rising Negro incomes. In recent years, however, the number of Negro businessmen has been expanding in relatively new fields, such as automobile repair and service stations and automotive distribution. Gains have also been registered in a variety of business services.

The field of banking and finance has not been a growth area for Negroes. While they own or control about twenty banks, fifty-odd insurance companies, and thirty-odd federally insured savings and loan associations, these institutions combined hold only about 0.12 percent of the total assets held by these financial intermediaries in the nation at large. However, the Negro banks do serve two useful purposes: their presence and the potential competition this implies induce the large white-controlled banks to be more liberal in considering the credit needs of the Negro borrower. They also provide a marginal amount of funds to meet the requirements of Negro businessmen and home buyers. In general, the Negro banks appear to hold a higher percent of liquid assets than do other banks of the same size. While their operations seem to be basically similar to those conducted by other institutions, there are differences derived from lending to borrowers exposed to inherently greater risks. But by modifying their lending practices, Negro banks have been able to achieve loss ratios which are actually below those of other banks of comparable size. Nevertheless, Negro banks tend to have lower rates of profit than banks in general.

Life insurance companies represent the classic example of Negro businesses which have grown up behind the walls of segregation. Beginning in the 1880's, most leading life insurance companies either refused to sell coverage to Negroes or did so on the basis of separate mortality tables which meant higher costs. These discriminatory practices provided Negroes with the opportunity and incentive to meet the insurance demands of Negro citizens. The growth of Negro life insurance companies has been based primarily on sales of industrial insurance which accounts for about two-thirds of their business. In contrast, ordinary insurance is the backbone of the nation's life insurance industry, representing about three-fifths of the total amount of life insurance in force. Because of the high incidence of poverty among Negroes, industrial insurance (sold in small amounts by door-to-door salesmen who collect premiums on even a weekly basis) was virtually the only type of insurance which the typical Negro family could afford. With the rise in income, Negro families are becoming attractive prospects for the large national insurance companies. In fact, they are increasingly employing Negro salesmen to facilitate penetration of the Negro market.

As financial institutions, Negro life insurance companies tend to be quite conservative, and they hold relatively more liquid assets than other companies. Partly because of the inherently greater risks of lending to low-income Negro borrowers seeking to purchase homes or to small Negro businessmen, Negro life insurance companies hold a lower percentage of mortgages than do companies in the industry at large. Instead, they concentrate more heavily on bonds—especially on state and local government issues, the income from which is exempt from Federal income taxes. But with some liberalization in portfolio management (particularly the acquisition of more common stocks), life insurance companies could greatly improve their investment position. While Negro insurance companies will undoubtedly continue to exist, their future prospects will be dampened by the continued competition from the large companies. This clearly suggests that the Negro institutions may have to turn increasingly to the larger market beyond the Negro community.

The Future of Negroes in Business

Since the fields in which Negro businessmen have traditionally served are less promising than in the past, they must look for other opportunities. For Negroes as for other citizens in the business world, such opportunities are likely to be found primarily as managers and officials employed by our medium and large corporations and public enterprises. While Negroes have made some progress in the executive suite, the gains are exceptionally modest compared with their progress in other areas of the economy. In an effort to remedy this situation, a number of corporations are attempting to recruit promising Negro college graduates. However, it appears that so far the main focus has been on technical fields (such as engineering, chemistry, physics, mathematics and other hard sciences) in which the number of Negro graduates remains relatively small. In contrast, the typical white entrant into corporations at the management level is employed as a management trainee. Moreover, he is recruited from a variety of fields which are predominantly nontechnical. These include business administration, economics and the other social sciences. It is precisely in these latter fields that the majority of Negro college graduates are found. Thus it appears evident that the future opportunities for Negroes in the corporation will depend heavily on the willingness of corporations to modify their recruitment practices. Simultaneously, however, these opportunities will also depend on substantial upgrading in the quality of training received by Negro college graduates—a predominant number of which still attend largely segregated Negro institutions.

Of course, the chances to go into business for themselves is an option which will remain open to Negroes along with other citizens. But in electing this option, Negroes will have to give careful consideration to the changing environment in which they must operate in the future if they wish to succeed. No longer will segregation provide relative security for ventures into traditional types of business. With the desegregation of places of public accommodation, Negro businessmen in these traditional fields will have to weather the competition of firms serving the community as a whole. Secondly, there is a prime need for Negro businessmen to adopt the corporate form of organization. Traditionally, the typical Negro enterprise has been a single proprietorship or a partnership owned by members of the same family. This arrangement has imposed several limitations on the development of managerial talents and the mobilization of financial resources to underwrite expansion. The corporation is an excellent instrument to overcome these handicaps.

While there is no shortage of potential Negro businessmen, there is a severe shortage of technical know-how outside the traditional areas of retail trade and personal services. This lack of mastery over technical requirements may well be an obstacle as great as the lack of equity capital —which has long been recognized as a basic problem facing Negro businessmen along with all other small entrepreneurs. In 1964 a number of economic development and business service centers (including centers at Atlanta University and Howard University) were established to help fill this gap. With the acquisition of greater technical know-how, and with the increased availability of credit which is coming about, there will be growing opportunity for Negro businessmen to participate in the future growth of the country. But it should be emphasized again that desegregation of the marketplace which is already well under way will require desegregation in the ownership and management of business enterprises as well.

NOTES

[1] The actual structure of the economy is clearly more complicated. The present description neglects a number of strategic roles, of which that of government, trade unions and nonprofit institutions are perhaps the most important. Moreover, the business sector could be broken down to show the market for capital goods and the financial system. But for the present summary analysis, greater detail appears not to be necessary.

[2] In fact, an entire fraternity of marketing specialists, the National Association of Market Developers, has grown up, and its members are employed in helping many leading corporations to penetrate the Negro market.

[3] See Technical Note 1

[4] "Median income" is that figure which divides the number of income recipients into two equal groups.

[5] Council of Economic Advisers, *Economic Report of the President,* January 1964, p. 58.

[6] See Deborah P. Wolfe and Andrew F. Brimmer, Editors, *Poverty in the United States,* Committee on Education and Labor, House of Representatives, 88th Congress, 2nd Session, April 1964, Tables C, D, and E, p. 29.

[7] U.S. Department of Commerce, Bureau of the Census, *U.S. Census of Population,* 1960, PC (2)–4C "Sources and Structure of Family Income", (Washington, D.C., Government Printing Office 1964), Table 1.

[8] The technique of computing the Index is explained in Herman Miller's *Trends in the Income of Families and Persons in the United States: 1947 to 1960,* United States Department of Commerce, Bureau of the Census, Washington, D.C. 1963), p. 26.

[9] See Press Release, September 25, 1962.

[10] *Economic Report of the President,* January, 1964, p. 77.

[11] Gunnar Myrdal, *An American Dilemma,* (New York: Harper & Bros., 1944), Vol. I, p. 314.

[12] These data are available in sufficient detail only for those banks which are members of the Federal Reserve System. The ratios were used only as rough benchmarks. Two Negro banks were members of the Federal Reserve System at the end of 1963.

[13] G. Myrdal, *An American Dilemma* (New York: Harper & Brothers, 1944), Vol. I, p. 318.

[14] Myrdal, *op. cit.,* Vol. I, p. 316.

[15] See Andrew F. Brimmer, *Life Insurance Companies in the Capital Market.* East Lansing: Michigan State University, Bureau of Business and Economic Research, 1962.

TECHNICAL NOTE 1.

Calculation of Nonwhite Labor Force Data, 1948–1953

The U.S. Bureau of Labor Statistics has not published nonwhite labor force figures for years prior to 1954. The estimates shown in this chapter were calculated in the following manner:

Multiply the total number [1] of nonwhite males and females over fourteen years of age, excluding military, by the labor force participation rates [2] for the individual years. The products, added together, will give an approximation of the total nonwhite, civilian noninstitutionalized labor force. The unemployment figures are derived by multiplying the estimated total labor force figure by the published unemployment rates.[3] Subtract this estimated number employed. The results are shown below:

Estimated Nonwhite Labor Force Data, 1948–53 (Thousands)

Year	Estimated Labor Force	Estimated Employment	Estimated Unemployment
1948	6,891	6,533	358
1949	7,011	6,436	575
1950	7,006	6,411	595
1951	6,936	6,603	333
1952	6,997	6,675	322
1953	6,921	6,637	284

TECHNICAL NOTE 2.

Estimation of the Economic Cost of Racial Discrimination

1. *Estimation of the gain in gross national product (GNP) resulting from using more fully the* present *educational achievement of nonwhites.*

In making this estimate, the U.S. Bureau of the Census used income data from the 1950 and 1960 Census of Population. For each age-sex group, the mean income of nonwhites was changed to equal the mean income of whites reporting the same number of years of school completed. These calculations provided the percentage increase in total money income shown in Column (1) of Table A. In the second step, the wage or salary component (including supplements) of GNP was raised by the percentage increase in total money income; the results are shown in columns (2) and (3). In the third step, the entrepreneurial component of GNP was raised by one half the percentage increase in wage or salary income. Columns (4) and (5) show the results. In the final step, columns (2) and (4) were combined to produce columns (6) and (7), showing, respectively, the total amount and percentage increase in GNP.

The 1950 Census relationships were applied to the GNP figures for the years 1949 through 1954; the 1960 Census relationships were applied to the GNP figures for the years 1955 through 1963.

[1] U.S. Department of Commerce, Bureau of the Census, *Current Population Reports,* Series P–25, No. 98, Table 2; *Current Population Reports,* Series P–25, No. 265, Table A–3 and Table 3; *Current Population Reports,* P–25, No. 276, Table 3.

[2] U.S. Department of Labor, *Manpower Report of the President,* March, 1964, Table A–3, p. 197.

[3] U.S. Department of Labor, *Manpower Report of the President,* March, 1964, Table A–10, p. 201.

TABLE A—Estimates of Gain in GNP Based on the Assumption that the Present Educational Achievement of Nonwhites is Fully Used: 1949 to 1963 (Absolute numbers in billions of dollars)

Year	Percent Increase in Total Money Income	Applied to Compensation of Employees (wages)		Applied to entrepreneurial Income (other than wages)		Total Increase in the Gross National Product	
		Added Amount	Percent Increase	Added Amount	Percent Increase	Added Amount	Percent Increase
1963	2.4	$8.2	2.4	$2.9	1.2	$11.1	1.9
1962	2.4	7.8	2.4	2.8	1.2	10.6	1.9
1961	2.4	7.3	2.4	2.6	1.2	9.9	1.9
1960	2.4	7.0	2.4	2.5	1.2	9.5	1.9
1959	2.4	6.7	2.4	2.5	1.2	9.2	1.9
1958	2.4	6.2	2.4	2.2	1.2	8.4	1.9
1957	2.4	6.1	2.4	2.2	1.2	8.3	1.9
1956	2.4	5.8	2.4	2.1	1.2	7.9	1.9
1955	2.4	5.4	2.4	2.1	1.2	7.5	1.9
1954	3.1	6.4	3.1	2.4	1.6	8.8	2.4
1953	3.1	6.5	3.1	2.4	1.6	8.9	2.4
1952	3.1	6.0	3.1	2.4	1.6	8.4	2.4
1951	3.1	5.6	3.1	2.3	1.6	7.9	2.4
1950	3.1	4.8	3.1	2.0	1.6	6.8	2.4
1949	3.1	4.4	3.1	1.8	1.6	6.2	2.4

2. *Estimation of the gain in gross national product from using the potential contributions of nonwhites by raising their educational level to that of whites.*

The calculation is based on the Census Bureau's "Current Population Survey" data for each year. First, the mean income of nonwhite families was changed to equal the mean income of white families, and the mean income of nonwhite unrelated individuals was changed to equal that of white unrelated individuals. Next, the increase in GNP was obtained in the same manner as described above. The results are shown in Table B.

TABLE B—Estimates of Gain in GNP Based on the Assumption that the Achievement of Nonwhites is the Same as That of Whites: 1949 to 1963 (Absolute numbers in billions of dollars)

Year	Percent Increase in Total Money Income	Applied to Compensation of Employees (wages)		Applied to entrepreneurial Income (other than wages)		Total Increase in the Gross National Product	
		Added Amount	Percent Increase	Added Amount	Percent Increase	Added Amount	Percent Increase
1963	4.4	$15.0	4.4	$5.4	2.2	$20.4	3.5
1962	4.5	14.5	4.5	5.2	2.3	19.7	3.6
1961	4.3	13.0	4.3	4.6	2.2	17.6	3.4
1960	4.2	12.3	4.2	4.4	2.1	16.7	3.3
1959	4.5	12.5	4.5	4.6	2.3	17.1	3.5
1958	4.2	10.8	4.2	3.9	2.1	14.7	3.3
1957	4.3	11.0	4.3	4.0	2.2	15.0	3.4
1956	4.3	10.4	4.3	3.8	2.2	14.2	3.4
1955	4.3	9.6	4.3	3.7	2.2	13.3	3.3
1954	4.3	8.9	4.3	3.3	2.2	12.2	3.4
1953	4.1	8.6	4.1	3.2	2.1	11.8	3.2
1952	4.4	8.6	4.4	3.3	2.2	11.9	3.4
1951	4.5	8.1	4.5	3.3	2.3	11.4	3.5
1950	4.6	7.1	4.6	3.0	2.3	10.1	3.5
1949	4.7	6.6	4.7	2.8	2.4	9.4	3.6

chapter **6**   *Joseph H. Douglass*

The Urban Negro Family

Joseph H. Douglass.   Chief, Program Analysis and Scientific Communications Staff, Office of the Director, National Institutes of Health, Public Health Service, United States Department of Health, Education and Welfare. Formerly Fulbright Lecturer, Cairo, Egypt. Author of *The Negro Family's Search for Economic Security* (monograph of U. S. Department of Health, Education and Welfare); "Aspects of Marriage and Family Relations Among the Fellaheen," *Journal of Marriage and Family Relations* (April 1954).

Introduction *

Today, as a result of large-scale urbanization, the Negro family [1] in the United States is in the process of transition. In their earliest experiences in the United States, Negroes were concentrated in rural areas, placed in the lowest rungs of the socio-economic ladder, rendering service as slaves or indentured servants. Over the years, however, the Negro family has come increasingly to approximate general American family patterns, becoming more urban and less identified with agricultural pursuits or with non-urban jobs in sawmills, turpentine plants and the like.

Growth and mobility have been characteristic of the population of the United States in general and of the Negro group in particular. For the past two decades the Negro population has been increasing at a significantly faster rate than has the white. The 1960 census showed nearly 20.5 million nonwhites in the United States. As of 1962 Negroes constituted approximately 12 percent of the total population. [2] Six states now have a Negro population in excess of one million. Outside the Deep South, the Negro population has increased fivefold since 1910, nearly tripling since 1940. Part of this expansion has come from natural increase and part from the movement of Negroes from the South to other regions.

Fifty years ago approximately three-fourths of the Negro population lived in areas classified as rural; now the order is reversed. [3] Now three out of four Negro families live in the city.

Negroes have not only left the South; they have left the farms also. The heaviest movements between 1950 and 1960 were out of the states of Mississippi, Alabama and South Carolina and into the urban centers in California, New York, and Illinois. [4] Within the South itself Negroes have been moving to the cities; apparently the city, no matter where it is, is believed to hold greater opportunities.

In the decade 1950–60 there were dramatic shifts in the color composition of the population in metropolitan areas. In each of the fifty largest cities in conterminous United States there were higher proportions of Negroes in 1960 than ten years earlier.

Although all of the country's largest cities had a higher proportion of nonwhites in 1960 than in 1950, the reasons for this distribution varied. In each of the largest Northeastern cities, and in all but two of the largest sixteen cities in the North Central region, the changing balance between color groups was due to losses in the number of whites. The outward flow of whites and the influx of nonwhites to these cities represented a sharpening of a trend which had been in process for a considerable period. In thirteen of the fifty largest cities, however, both whites and nonwhites increased in absolute numbers; in these cities the rise in the proportion of nonwhites reflected both a more rapid natural increase as compared to whites as well as in-migration of nonwhites. †

The experience of the South is in sharp contrast to that of the other regions, as over six out of every ten Southern metropolitan areas showed lower proportions of nonwhites in 1960 than in the previous ten years. These Southern communities have become progressively more "white" during the last decade.

---

* The author wishes to acknowledge with grateful appreciation the assistance of his friend and colleague, Dr. Israel Light, in the preparation of this paper.

† For an extended discussion of this point see Karl and Alma Taeuber, "The Negro Population in the United States," earlier in this volume.

Negro families in urban areas have gravitated into the "core" or "central city." In 1960 some 10.3 million, or slightly more than half the nonwhite population, lived in central city—a gain of 63 percent over 1950. In the nation's 212 Standard Metropolitan Statistical Areas 78 percent of nonwhites lived in the central cities, with only 22 percent in the suburbs; 52 percent of whites lived outside of the central cities. Only in the South do more whites live in central cities than in the suburbs.

The increased urbanization of Negro families has not extended to the suburbs. Only one in five Negroes in the Standard Metropolitan Areas in the United States live in the suburbs. In contrast one half of the whites live in the suburbs.

White families as they have become affluent have looked to the suburbs as an area where they can achieve what to them represents the highest living standards America offers. Some Negro families with the same aspirations as the white suburban families have found a place in the suburbs. Their proportion to the total Negro population, however, is smaller than is the case for white families; even though they often have the means to buy better homes outside the heart of the city, they are unable to do so largely for reasons of racial prejudice. Thus more and more Negro families —poor and better off—have been squeezed together in central city ghettoes irrespective of the wide social distance between them.[5] More and more in the use of such public facilities as parks, hospitals, schools, etc., their geographical separation has led to *de facto* segregation of increasing intensity. One glaring example of this is Washington, D.C., where effective racial exclusion of Negroes from the suburbs has resulted in a city school system with a school population 83 percent Negro.

Family Characteristics

In the city the Negro family is retaining many of the primary group characteristics of rural families. Nonwhite households contained a larger proportion of children in 1960 than white households. The Negro households had more than three times as many grandchildren living with grandparents as white households in 1950; by 1960 this proportion had become five times as large. Although the percentage of lodgers in nonwhite households was sharply reduced in the 1950's, it was still twice as large in 1960 as that in white households.

Nonwhite women who married averaged more children per woman than white women of the same status, but the amount of the difference was affected by the large number of children born, the proportion of nonwhite women with five or more children being much larger than that of white women.

During the 1950's the marriage rate for nonwhites also showed a reverse pattern to that of the white population, with an increase in the percentage single, and a decrease in the percentage married, for the decade.

Nonwhite women become widows at an earlier age than white women. About 20 percent of all nonwhite females between fourteen and thirty-five years of age, as compared with 6.9 percent of white females of the same age group, were widows in 1960.[6]

The nonwhite population has substantially higher percentages of divorced persons; in the proportion of those separated the percentage of nonwhite separated males is more than five times, and of females more than six times, that of the corresponding white population. These figures, however, do not give a complete picture of the greater tendency of nonwhite marriages to break up, because death contributes in considerable measure to the difference between whites and nonwhites in the number of broken family units.

Thus, while nonwhite families were slightly less than 10 percent of all families in 1960, they were only 8 percent of families with both husband and wife present in the home. They represented 21.0 percent of all families with a female head.[7] While one in eleven white families was headed by a female, one in five nonwhite families had a female head.

Educational Attainment

Gains have been made during the past two decades in reducing the educational gap between Negroes and whites. By 1962 the average white person twenty-five to twenty-nine years of age had completed 12.5 years of schooling compared with 11.2 years by the average nonwhite person. For nonwhite men this represented a gain of some four and one-half years of school since 1940; for whites the average gain was two years.[8] The narrowing of the educational gap can be attributed largely to the increased number of Negro youth who have enrolled in school.[9]

At the elementary school level, the differential has been markedly reduced as practically all children of elementary school age were in school in 1961.[10] At the high school level, however, the percentage of nonwhites attending school was appreciably below that of white students.[11]

Proportionately fewer Negroes than whites go to college, although by 1960, approximately 40 percent of the nonwhite population had acquired some high school or college education, compared to 62 percent of the white population.[12] The number of Negro college graduates is rising at a faster rate than the overall increase in the total nonwhite population.

Educating any child in a central city environment always presents difficult school problems. These problems are usually more acute for the Negro child. Holsey observes that "One has only to listen to children's tragic expressions on how they feel about belonging to a discriminated against minority group to know the bitterness it engenders." Repeated blows to self-esteem unquestionably interfere with the ability to learn.[13]

As a consequence of barriers to learning, school dropouts have become a serious problem for Negro families.[14] As an example, Negroes constituted 20 percent of the 350,000 youth, sixteen to twenty-four years old, who left school between January and mid-October of 1961. Many of these failed to get jobs; and 80 percent of Negroes who did find employment were working in unskilled laboring or service jobs, compared with 45 percent of the employed white dropouts.[15]

As Holsey points out, the parents of such children frequently are emotionally and materially deprived. In speaking of Negro parents she states:

> Many of them . . . have sunk into despair because they are cut off from the mainstream of opportunity in our society. Many had their origins in a very different kind of life than the life they are faced with in the crowded core of a great metropolis . . . a few apparently do not care what happens to their children or get their satisfactions from victimizing them.[16]

In the beginning of the Negro shift to the city the principal job opportunities open to them as well as the kinds of jobs they were prepared to hold down were unskilled and low paid. This pattern was similar to that experienced by European migrants to the United States at the turn of the century. But unlike the white European, the Negro families did not, for a complex of reasons, escape in large numbers from their occupational ghetto.

It was not until the World War II period and after that there developed wider occupational distribution in the employment patterns for Negroes. Despite the gradual movement of nonwhite workers into higher skilled and better paying jobs, great differentials still persist between them and white workers. Although professional and clerical occupations have provided a major source of both white and nonwhite employment growth since the mid-1950's, Negroes continue to be overrepresented in such occupations as domestic servants, laborers, and semiskilled operatives. Nonwhites are still seven times as likely as white workers to be employed as private household workers (including maids, babysitters, housekeepers, chauffeurs, laundresses). Less than 5 percent of nonwhites were employed as managers, officials, proprietors and sales workers in 1962, whereas the proportion of white workers in these occupations in 1962 was almost 20 percent.[17]

The educational lag of Negroes is clearly reflected in the types of occupations most common to the two races in 1960. The U.S. Department of Labor continues to report that educational and training specifications for jobs in today's labor market underscore the poor education, inadequate training and low skills of many Negro workers. The gap is steadily widening between Negro worker qualifications and hiring requirements, particularly in those occupations with a growing demand for workers.

Goodwin, for example, writes:

> Many Negro families are trapped in what can only be called a vicious circle: Job discrimination and lack of educational opportunity or educational quality limit their employment opportunities and result in low and unstable incomes. Low incomes, combined with discrimination, reduce attainable levels of health and skills, and thus limit occupational choice and income in the future. And limited job opportunities result in limited availability of education and apprenticeship training, thus completing the circle.[18]

In the urban population where approximately 23 percent of the white workers are in professional, technical, or management positions, roughly only 8 percent of the nonwhites are similarly employed. Among the skilled craftsmen the ratio of whites employed—14 percent—is double that for nonwhites, 7 percent.

In addition, nonwhite workers of both sexes are less frequently employed at full-time jobs than white workers, are about twice as likely as whites to have reduced workweeks, and about five times as likely as the white worker to face under-employment.[19] Related to this is the fact that Negroes also tend to have a somewhat larger number of wage earners per family unit and higher rates of labor force participation than whites. Reflecting the heavy concentration of Negro women in household service occupations, about 30 percent of the nonwhite married women in the labor force in March, 1960, were part-time workers, compared with only about 20 percent of white married women.

Nonwhite workers are subject also to more frequent periods of unemployment. About three of every ten nonwhite men who had been unemployed sometime during the year were subject to three periods or more of unemployment in 1961, compared with two of every ten white men who had some employment. Moreover, nonwhite workers spend a considerably longer period of time on layoff or looking for work between jobs.

Nonwhite married women are more likely to be in the work force than white married women, regardless of the presence and age of children or income of husband. Approximately two-fifths of all white women twenty-five to sixty-four were in the labor force in 1962, compared with nearly three-fifths of nonwhite women of the same ages.[20]

Nonwhite boys and girls fourteen to nineteen years of age evidence one of the highest jobless rates of any age-color group. In 1962 the unemployment rate of nonwhite teenagers remained near 25 percent, compared with about 12 percent for white youth. Since 1955, the jobless rate of nonwhite teenagers has increased faster than that of white youngsters—up to about 60 percent among nonwhites compared with a 30 percent rise for white youth.

Income

The nature of the labor force participation of Negro family members has a direct bearing on income. The great disparity in income distribution between Negroes and whites is indicated in the following table.[21]

TABLE I—Relative Income Groups: Nonwhite—White

Income	Percent families	
	Nonwhite	White
Less than $4,000	60	26
$6,000–$14,999	19	47
More than $15,000	1	5

SOURCE: U.S. Department of Commerce, Bureau of the Census, *Current Population Reports Consumer Income*, Series P–60, No. 41, October 21, 1963. See especially Tables 1 and 16.

Housing

Negro families are concentrated in the low rent areas of the larger cities and housing is one of the most critical aspects of the socio-economic status of Negro families. More than any other variable it symbolizes for many Negroes their "have-not" status.

Out of the 3.7 million nonwhite families who moved between 1950 and 1960, only 23 percent moved into units built during that decade. By contrast, out of 19 million white families, 58 percent moved into a house or apartment built between 1950 and 1960.[22]

Thus "Negro districts" commonly are in the slum areas adjacent to the central business and older sections of the city abandoned by the white population. This concentration of Negro families in central cities reflects not only economic necessity but also the lack of open occupancy in new suburban housing.

Within urban areas nonwhite households have an average of 3.63 persons versus 3.13 for white households. The HHFA data indicate that (with some variations) between 1950 and 1960 a better matching of nonwhite families with housing units gave more of them increased space by 1960. Yet, the number of overcrowded units among nonwhite families increased by more than a quarter over the decade from nearly one million in 1950 to 1.3 million in 1960, while the number of overcrowded white families decreased by almost a quarter or about 0.2 million.

The contrast between white and nonwhite families is sharper in reference to seriously overcrowded units; among nonwhites these decreased from 18 to 13 percent, but among whites they fell from 4.3 to 2.4 percent.

While the rents paid by nonwhite tenants and the value of homes owned by nonwhites more than doubled between 1950 and 1960, they were still far below comparable figures for housing occupied by white families. The lower level of rents and values reflects the poorer quality of much of the housing available to Negro families. Because of limitations in the availability of housing, the rents and values of units occupied by Negroes often run well above the costs at which houses of comparable quality can be obtained by white families. Although Negroes have improved their home ownership position, increasing from 35 percent in 1950 to 38 percent in 1960, the improvement was not as great as that of white householders where the proportion of owners increased from 57 to 64 percent.

Mortality[23]

Since the turn of the century the mortality rate among nonwhites has been reduced more than half; but compared with mortality rates of the total population, those of the nonwhites continue to be excessive at nearly all age levels. In 1960 mortality rates of the nonwhites were 1.5 or more times as high as those of the total population during early childhood and the period twenty to sixty-four years of age. The Negro infant mortality rate in 1960 exceeded that in the total population by 66 percent (compared with an excess of 52 percent in 1950.)[24]

Today both Negroes and whites may expect to live longer than in previous years. Since 1900, life expectancy has increased by more than twenty years for the total population and by about thirty years for nonwhites.[25] In 1960 the average expectation of life at birth in the United States was 63.6 years for the nonwhite group and 69.7 years for the total population, a difference of 6.1 years, in contrast to a differential of 7.4 years in 1950. The recent increase in the proportion to the total population is due to the drop in the Negro death rate as well as the increasing birth rate. Hayes[26] indicates that much of this is due to improved health measures, particularly those that led to the near eradication of tuberculosis and typhoid, and to large reductions in the deaths of mothers and children. A major cause of the continuing disparity in health between nonwhites and the rest of the population is the relatively low economic status of the nonwhite group.

Probably one-quarter of the Negro families continue to be subjected to marginal employment opportunities, accompanied by sporadic work experience and unemployment. With roughly half of the income of white families, the Negro family is placed in a severely disadvantaged competitive position for the attainment of the necessities of life.

Poverty and Dependency

A disproportionately large number of Negro families thus live at the poverty level. While Negroes constitute approximately 12 percent of the population, they comprise 22 percent of the poor families. A recent report describes the life of the urban poor:

> There are poor people in Washington who get water by carrying a bucketful from a gas station, who obtain light by running extension cords across an alley to a neighbor's home, who live like rats in enclosures under porches. . . . In the heart of the city, some of the poor try to make a living by "picking"— picking up discarded papers and bottles to be sold to the junkman, picking over gutter debris to see if last night's drunk lost any coins, picking at the slots of vending machines for a stray dime.[27]

As compared with whites, some of the evidences of the poverty status of Negro families are their generally higher dependence upon public maintenance programs and disproportionate numbers of children born out of wedlock. Walker observes that "faulty parent-child relationships, instability of parents and a harmful social environment, crowded living conditions, inadequacy of food and clothing, lack of supervised recreational facilities, racial hostility, and segregation are all factors provocative of illegitimacy."[28] Available data appear to support these observations.[29] For example, in 1961 22 percent of all nonwhite babies were born out of wedlock as compared with 2.5 percent of all white babies, and 62 percent of all illegitimate births were nonwhite.

For both mothers and children the problems of illegitimacy and poverty are compounded by the fact that two out of five mothers of babies born out of wedlock are under twenty years of age, and about 2 percent are under fifteen years.

Aid to Families with Dependent Children [30]

In 1961 the Bureau of Family Services, in cooperation with state public welfare agencies, studied the characteristics and financial circumstances of the 910,000 families then receiving Aid for Dependent Children. It found that most of the dependent families have limited educational opportunity, lack skills needed for available work and live in crowded housing. Often they have been cut off by poverty and discrimination from constructive influences and community life.

Among all white children, 23 of each 1,000, and among all nonwhite children, 136 of each 1,000, needed AFDC at the time of the study.

The AFDC payments made up the largest part of the income of most dependent families, and more than half of the families (55 percent) had no income from any other source. These families had an average income of roughly 408 dollars a year per person, which was less than one-fourth of the national per person income at the time.

In one-third of the families there were four or more children. Three-

Nonwhite households contain a large proportion of children.
(Haryou-Act Still Photography Workshop, Photo by Gene Ward)

fourths of the AFDC homes were fatherless. Fathers were away from the home in two-thirds of the cases. The fathers were dead in 7.7 percent of the cases. Nearly one-fifth of the families were in need because fathers were disabled. In another one-fifth, parents were not married. Separation, divorce and desertion, therefore, figure in approximately two-fifths of the families.

Few AFDC fathers had held, or were able to hold, jobs with high status or income. Only 3 percent had white collar employment experience, compared with almost 35 percent in this category among all employed males. Only 7 percent had worked in industry in such jobs as craftsmen or foremen, compared with 20 percent of all working men. About 34 percent were unskilled laborers, compared with 7 percent of all employed males. Some 3 percent of AFDC fathers had never held any full-time job. Thus, disability and low level of education go hand in hand with unemployment and dependency. Two large groups of AFDC fathers are to be found living in the home with the children—the incapacitated and the unemployed.

In the central cities, 63 of every 1,000 children under eighteen received AFDC. Almost 70 percent of all the assisted families lived in rented quarters, and 51 percent were crowded; the crowding was serious for almost half of these.

Old Age Assistance

A study of old-age benefit recipients in 1958 showed that 45 out of every 100 nonwhite aged persons in the United States received old-age assistance as compared to 17 out of every 100 white aged persons. The lower rate of insurance beneficiaries among the nonwhites is an important reason for the higher old-age assistance recipient rates. Nonwhites are more likely than whites to reach age 65 without sufficient income or savings, and must rely to a greater degree on public assistance payments.[31]

How the Poor Negro Family Sees Itself [32]

Low income, poor housing, lack of education, broken homes, and discrimination and segregation all affect the Negro adversely. The central problem—to which all others are related—is that of racial discrimination, which, psychologically, produces a self-image of low self-esteem as a result of the behavior and attitudes of whites toward him from childhood and its consequences for certain aspects of the Negro's ability to live at ease with his white fellowman. Among many Negro families this low self-esteem apparently often displays itself in numerous apathetic reactions and the search for the material pleasures of the day without regard for the future.

The Negro family suffers also, especially the lower-class family, from early death, abandonment or divorce, as well as discrimination. Children are the prime target of such social disorganization, and their intrafamily relationships are warped. Sibling rivalry mounts with increasing material scarcity. Youngsters are "farmed out" to relatives for custody because of a broken home. The parent or "relative" is a member of a despised and discriminated-against group, and the child cannot identify with his parents because such identification carries with it a guarantee of external and reflected hatred.[33] The broken home often makes the mother the object and the children the victims of dependency. Therefore, the male child either has no father image or model to look to or otherwise sees this model condemned.

Lacking status in the social community, the Negro parent is inclined to overwhelming dominance within the family. If the mother should be alone to head the family, her need to make a living leaves her little time to indulge the children. In the eyes of the children she thus frequently becomes someone ambivalently to fear and to rely upon.

If the broken home is the setting, there are apt to be few useful and positive parental models with consequent injury to family life. As a result, the tough competitive and segregated world provides the main source of satisfactions and values. The mores of the street often make school attendance quite irrelevant and crime the desired path to success.

As child or adult, the Negro often cannot identify. If parents are the model, they are either not at home or are discredited and vilified by the white world. If whites are the ideal, acceptance often results in self-hatred, frustration and unrealistic goals.

The so-called white ideal is particularly oppressive to the middle and upper class Negro family where ambition is heightened, marriage is more stable, material comforts have been acquired and time and energy are available to be conventional and respectable. But white idealization must be linked with segregation and discrimination.

These Negro individuals and families are caught in the middle of the ladder of life. They will not move down to lower-class Negro standards, but they are blocked from moving up to the white ideal.

Historically, two sets of factors have affected the Negro urban family. One relates to the circumstances of migration; the other, to the continuing handicaps of the Negro group.

In emigrating, Negro families have had to give up old patterns of behavior and leave old associates behind. In their new environment they had to learn new ways of doing things. Problems had to be faced in breaking through limited and marginal employment, in upgrading low educational levels and in overcoming various forms of personal and social maladjustment.

Old and unproductive family members often became a burden in the cramped tenement houses of the city, in contrast with a more viable status in the more kinship-oriented environment of rural areas.

Vice, crime and asocial behavior are much more in evidence in the big cities than in the rural places. Births out of wedlock, for example, are more likely to become apparent in urban areas.

Thus, Negro families have had experiences typical of a folk or peasant people adjusting to an urban way of life. Historically, the cities have provided the loci for integrating immigrants into the American culture. The experience has proved to be one in which each immigrant group has improved its socioeconomic status. A similar rise in social and economic status, however, has not yet been achieved in the case of a majority of Negro families. This is also true of other minorities in the United States, notably the Puerto Ricans.[34]

The slowness of the rate of progress of Negroes in urban society is due in large degree to the special handicap of race imposed upon them by the majority group.

"Fifty years ago approximately three-fourths of the Negro population lived in areas classified as rural; now the order is reversed. Now three out of four Negro families live in the city."

(Haryou-Act Still Photography Workshop, Photo by Laura Brown)

Despite an unfavorable social environment great "social distance" exists among Negro urban families. The overall urban experience of Negro families is not uniform. Among urban Negroes there are, at one extreme, families which are third-generation urban residents. At the other extreme, many have come to urban centers only within the last decade. The success achieved by Negro families in the cities thus is related to (a) length of urban residence, (b) the particular urban areas to which they migrated, (c) their educational levels, skills or other "equipment" for competition, and (d) their particular experience with racial discrimination.

For some Negro families the migration and adaptation to urban living have been successful. They have achieved relatively high income status, high levels of education, family integrity and solidarity, and economic security. For these families the cities have provided opportunities for them to achieve middle- and upper-class status. Some Negro families have been urbanized for a period of fifty years preceding the World War I exodus of rural migrants to urban areas. In Washington, D.C., New York, Chicago, Philadelphia and Detroit, for example, many of these older Negro residents have well-established neighborhoods, stable families and moderate to high income levels. In this group are physicians, bankers, lawyers and teachers. Many appear to have no rural antecedents.

Sutherland observed that a sizeable proportion of Negro families have "shared in the American dream." As he stated several years ago:

> Some Negro youth have been so completely surrounded by middle-class patterns that their expectation of achieving advanced degrees, high professional standing, and an income which will enable them to live as well as, or better than their parents is taken for granted.[35]

The majority of Negro families, however, have not yet made a successful transition to urban life. A disproportionately large number of these families are of low socio-economic status and live in the cities at the poverty level.[36] Therefore, as families and as individuals, they continue to show high rates of personal and social disorganization.

It is the accumulation and circular effects of disadvantages that accentuate the problems faced by the Negro family in the city. As one observer has stated:

> Some of the problems of the transplanted migrants are inevitable, for movement across centuries of experience can not occur painlessly within a few years. Some are associated directly with conditions of living in the initial areas of settlement. And some are associated with the barriers to mobility that lead to increasing density and more intense personal and social problems in areas of concentrated Negro settlement.[37]

Summary and Conclusion

In its development of a middle-class orientation, the Negro family is beginning to approximate the major trend affecting all American families in its movement toward urban centers. The urban location is producing an increasing dependence upon money income and is changing the older familial model of three generation groups (that is grandparents, parents and children living in one household), to two- and one-generation groups. As a consequence, numerous intrafamilial expectations are changing.

Brimmer has observed that while the overall pattern of expenditures by Negro families continues to be typical of that generally found among low-income groups, there is also evidence of rapidly emerging middle-class spending habits. In 1960–61, the average urban Negro family spent about $3,707 for annual living expenses. This amount was just over two-thirds that spent by the average family in the Nation as a whole—a ratio which was virtually unchanged from 1950.[38]

In many respects the Negro family has moved from one disadvantaged circumstance into another in its striving for urban status. The "core" and "gray" areas of the larger metropolitan areas most often are the locus of obsolescence and social and economic deterioration. The pattern of location of new "urbanites" has produced racial ghettoes. Concomitant with a general movement of the white population from these central portions of the city to suburban areas, the result most often has been a feeling on the part of the Negro population of at least psychological discrimination even when community efforts have been made to desegregate schools, or to undertake urban renewal programs, or to effect improved placement of groups. For example, even after efforts at desegregation, school populations have become resegregated. Churches, recreational areas and even business establishments have become largely identified with use by a particular group.

The recent shifting of Negro families to urban areas is related to the groups' growing protest movements. Negroes have become increasingly dissatisfied with their socio-economic status, and they point to housing restrictions, segregated education, discriminatory policies in trade unions and apprenticeship opportunities and other circumstances, as prohibitive of their achieving equal status. While the urban life of metropolitan areas appeared to have promised the Negroes greater freedom, the facts of everyday living are such that discrimination on the basis of race continues. Increased tension between Negroes and whites is the result.

Like the white family, the Negro family is beset with dynamic influences for which it is difficult to make adequate psychosocial preparation. Major social forces, such as the impact of automation on the labor force, the increasing reliance of society upon technically or professionally trained personnel and the continuing high levels of unemployment (even within a full economy) make it very difficult for families to prepare their members for the future.[39]

Today, however, the environment in which the urban Negro family lives contains numerous elements which result in "cultural deprivation" and social impoverishment; possibly half of the Negro youth live in such a situation.

Economic deprivation is conducive to cultural deprivation. The training ground for good citizenship, such as college education, adequate health protection, adequate recreation, reading, travel and involvement in community affairs, is not readily available to those at the bottom of the economic ladder.

It is difficult to assess the hopes and expectations of Negro youth, but it is reasonable to assume that the lack of opportunity open to them in American society results in considerable frustration. Their level of opportunity is far below their potential for personal and social achievement.

As families and as individuals Negroes have become dissatisfied with their

SUCCESS MODELS: "Striver's Row," luxury housing of another era in Harlem and today's fashionable Lenox Terrace. (Photos by Roland Mitchell)

TABLE II—"Balance Sheet" on Selected Aspects of Whites and Nonwhites

Item	White	Nonwhite
Population		
Size—growth—gains		
1960 total national	88.5%	11.5%
1940—50 gains	14.1%	17.1%
1950—60 gains	17.5%	26.7%
Outside the South		tripled since 1940
Migration		
From South	steady	marked
Rural to urban	steady	marked
To suburbia	major	minor
Concentration		
North Central cities	less	gain
Central or core city	out of	into
Family characteristics		
Units (household)		
Number households, 1960	47.9 million	5.2 million
Increase, 1960 over 1950	16.4%	21%
Living in urban areas, 1960	72%	77%
Marital Status		
Divorced males	2.1%	2.4%
Divorced females	2.7%	3.6%
Proportion separated males		over 5 × the whites
Proportion separated females		over 6 × the whites
Widows, ages 14—35	6.9%	20%
Total—separation, death, divorce		
Males	6.8%	15.7%
Females	16.7%	31.2%
Family Composition		
Size of household	3.23 persons	3.85 persons
Headed by male	9 of 10	3 of 4
Headed by female	1 of 11	1 of 5
Fertility		
Rate, 1961, age 15—44	112.3	153.8
Women not given birth	16.0%	21.3%
Proportion with 5—6 children		much larger than white
Proportion with 7 plus children		3 × the white
Babies born out of wedlock, 1961	2.5%	22.0%
Life expectancy, 1960	69.7 years	63.6 years
Mortality, 1960, early childhood and 20—64		1.5 × the white
Housing		
Home ownership		
Moved into new suburban housing 1950—60	58% of 19 million	23% of 3.7 million
Increase in 1950's	57%—64%	35%—38%

traditional status in the United States and they are participating in large-scale protest led in the main by the group's younger elements.

As examples:

The "sit-in" movement had its genesis in the Negro population of college age.

Item	White	Nonwhite
Standardized units occupied in 1950's	68%–87%	25%–50%
Overcrowded units in 1950's	decreased 0.2 million	increased 0.3 million
Education		
Years of school completed, 1962, 25–29 age group	12.5 years	11.2 years
Gain since 1940 in school years completed	2 years	4.5 years
Elementary School enrollment, 1961	99.5%	98.2%
High School enrollment, 1956–61, increase for ages 14–17	89% to 92%	81% to 87%
Some College, total population	62%	40%
Labor Force participation		
White collar		
Increase, 1955–62	47%	17%
Managers, officials and proprietors, 1962	20%	5%
Service industries, 1960	8%	23%
Skilled		
Clerical, professional, technical and managerial	6%	20%
Professional and technical, 1962	12.5%	5%
Manufacturing, 1962	28%	18%
Professional, technical, managerial, 1960, urban	23%	8%
Unskilled and semiskilled		
Male, nonfarm	33%	75%
Females, proportion of		
Age 25–64, 1962	40%	58.5%
Part-time, married, 1960	20%	30%
All domestic and service, 1960	20%	60%
Income		
Median		
National, 1962	$6,200	$3,300
Males	$4,700	$2,300
Under $4,000, family	26%	60%
$6,000–$14,900, family	47%	19%
$15,000– , family	5%	Less than 1%
Unemployment		
Age 25–44, 1962	3%	9%
Dropouts in unskilled and services	45%	80%
Teenagers, 1962	12%	25%
Teenagers, since 1955	up 30%	up 60%
Old Age assistance, recipients		
per 100 in all ages	17	45

The hopes, plans and demands of the Negro population are being sharpened and lifted with the expectations that the rewards of American society will be forthcoming on a basis of racial equality.

The Negro family can now point to success models within the group in many walks of life.

The parental generation expects for its children opportunities much greater than any they might realize.

Thus, one consequence of urbanization appears to be an increasing sophistication and articulation on the part of Negro families; they are using techniques such as political participation, involvement in community organization and community processes and "movements" of various types to express their discontent and to effect widespread social change. The *Washington Post* reports:

> The Negro demands an end to housing shortages, limited job opportunities, the problems of slums. He sees symbols of discrimination everywhere—the all-white suburbs, his hand-me-down churches that whites have fled, the overcrowded and overaged schools that are now resegregated. . . . The Negro concedes the door to full equality is ajar. He demands that it open wide.[40]

The many trends affecting the American family generally, such as rising levels of health, increasing levels of educational attainment, improved occupational distribution, improved housing conditions and increased security through participation in public programs, are all having their beneficial effects on the Negro family. In part as a result of their determination to eliminate racial discrimination and achieve equality on all fronts, it is to be expected that in the future fewer and fewer distinctions may be drawn between the great mass of Negro families and those of the general population.

NOTES

[1] The family, as such, hardly existed for Negroes during at least two-thirds of their history in this country; and matriarchal aspects of family organization, which are so prominent in Negro families, were largely an outgrowth of the institution of slavery. The slave had no property rights, no rights as a human being before the law, no legal recognition of marriage, no recognition of lineage. The only group tradition was that of bondage. Roots of the Negro family have been grounded in a strong maternal affiliation because it was the mother who provided such nurturing of the young as was possible in a slave society. Vestigial evidence of this matriarchal form continues to the present day.

[2] U.S. Department of Health, Education, and Welfare, *Trends,* (Washington, D.C.: Government Printing Office, 1963 edition) p. 27.

[3] Tobia Bressler, "Some Population Trends Involving and Affecting the Negro—Implications." Address, Association of Social Science Teachers, Nashville, Tennessee, March 22, 1962.

[4] U.S. Housing and Home Finance Agency, *Our Nonwhite Population and its Housing: The Changes Between 1950 and 1960,* (Washington, D.C.: Government Printing Office, July, 1963).

[5] U.S. Housing and Home Finance Agency, op. cit., p. 3. This report goes on to state, "As the examination into the housing condition of the nonwhites will demonstrate, the failure of many nonwhite families to move into suburban communities was not necessarily due to a preference for the central city environment. Rather it reflected a lack of housing available to them in most suburban areas."

[6] G. Franklin Edwards, "Marriage and Family Life Among Negroes." *The Journal of Negro Education Yearbook,* XXXII (Fall, 1963). Washington, D.C.: The Howard University Press.) p. 451.

⁷ Edwards, *ibid.*

⁸ Robert G. Goodwin, *America Is For Everybody* (U.S. Department of Labor, Bureau of Employment Security, Washington, D.C.: Government Printing Office, 1963).

⁹ Cognizance should be taken of the observation that despite the increasing rate of educational attainment by Negroes, there continues to be significant variance in the quality of education obtained in various sections of the United States.

¹⁰ Marion Hayes, "A Century of Change—Negroes in U.S. Economy 1860–1960." *Monthly Labor Review*, U.S. Department of Labor (December, 1962).

¹¹ U.S. Department of Commerce, Bureau of Census, *Current Population Reports, Population Characteristics*, Series P–20, No. 115 (Washington, D.C.: Government Printing Office, February 7, 1962).

¹² Goodwin, *op. cit.*

¹³ Eleanor Holsey, "Culturally Deprived Children in Day-Care Programs." *Children*, 10, No. 5 (September–October, 1963). Dr. Carl F. Hansen, Superintendent of Schools, Washington, D.C., writes in the *Washington Post*, October 27, 1963: "In the cultural Siberia in which many Negro children live, they acquire too little that is educationally helpful before they come to school, and as a result teachers must supply many of the experiences and learnings which children should get as a matter of course in home and family life. The wonder is, then, that so many of the Negro children who have had so little in their homes have gained so much in school. . . ."

¹⁴ Added difficulties which school dropouts will face are discussed in recent studies by the Department of Labor's Bureau of Labor Statistics. See "Employment of High School Graduates and Dropouts in 1961." *Monthly Labor Review* (May, 1962), and "Out of School Youth" February 1963, Parts I and II reprinted from the *Monthly Labor Review* November and December, 1964 (Reprints 2448 and 2452).

¹⁵ Goodwin, *op. cit.*

¹⁶ Holsey, *op. cit.*

¹⁷ Matthew A. Kessler, "Economic Status of Nonwhite Workers 1955–62." *Monthly Labor Review*, Preprint No. 2419, U.S. Department of Labor, July, 1963.

¹⁸ Goodwin, *op. cit.*

¹⁹ Robert L. Stein and Jane L. Meredith, "Growth and Characteristics of the Part-Time Work Force, No. 10." *Monthly Labor Review*, Reprint No. 2356, U.S. Department of Labor (November, 1960). Margaret L. Plunkett observes that "The proportion of Negro men with some college education who work in comparatively low-paying service and laborer jobs is almost five times greater than for whites. Among the least educated (no high school) 34 percent of nonwhite men work as nonfarm laborers compared with only 10 percent of whites with a similar educational level.

"The same general situation applied to Negro women who work. Ten percent of Negro women who have gone to college work as domestics compared with about one percent of other college women. About 44 percent of white women who have attended high school become office workers of various kinds compared with only 12 percent of nonwhite women. Almost two-thirds of the Negro high school group work as domestics or in other types of service jobs as against only 17 percent in the comparably educated white group." See U.S. Senate, 86th Congress, 2nd session, Special Committee on Unemployment Problems, *Studies in Unemployment* (Washington, D.C.: Government Printing Office, 1960), p. 89.

²⁰ Kessler, *op. cit.* John Hope states that "Although a greater share of nonwhite girls are participants at ages 14, 15, and 16 than are white girls, at ages 17 to 23 a larger proportion of white girls is in the labor force. This may be explained by the fact that white girls have more job opportunities at these ages, and because nonwhite girls marry earlier than white girls. At age 20 the rate for white women decreased while that of nonwhite women continued to rise, reaching a maximum of 48 to 49 percent at ages 35 to 44 years." See U.S. Senate, 86th Congress, 2nd session, Special Committee on Unemployment Problems, *Studies in Unemployment* (Washington, D.C.: Government Printing Office, 1960), p. 175.

²¹ The relatively low nonwhite median income in 1962 reflects in part the fact that about one-half of nonwhite families still live in the South where average family income is relatively low for both the white and nonwhite populations. For regions outside the South, this ratio was about two-thirds in 1962, whereas for the South it was less than one-half.

²² Unless otherwise noted, the data on housing are from U.S. Housing and Home Finance Agency (HHFA) materials, *op. cit.*

²³ The data on mortality are derived mainly from Marcus S. Goldstein, "Longevity and Health Status of the Negro American." *Journal of Negro Education* (Washington, D.C. Howard University Press, Fall, 1963), pp. 337–48.

²⁴ For 1960 U.S. Department of Health, Education, and Welfare *Trends*, 1963, p. 27,

indicate that the infant mortality rate was 40.7 for nonwhites, and 22.4 for whites.

[25] U.S. Department of Health, Education, and Welfare, *Trends, op. cit.*

[26] Hayes, *op. cit.*

[27] Eve Edstrom, "They're All Scufflin'—Like Me," *Washington Post,* January 12, 1964.

[28] I. Walker, and Eugenia Sullivan, *New Directions in Health, Education, and Welfare,* 1st edition, U.S. Department of Health, Education, and Welfare, 1963, p. 46.

[29] Helen E. Martz, "Illegitimacy and Dependency," *Indicators,* U.S. Department of Health, Education, and Welfare, Reprint, September, 1963. Mrs. Martz indicates that, taken alone, these facts can be misleading. For example, since 1956, the annual rate of increase of white illegitimate babies has been greater than for nonwhite illegitimate babies. In 1961, an estimated 8,600 more white babies than in 1960 were born out of wedlock as compared to 7,300 more nonwhite babies. The 1960–61 nonwhite increase was 5 percent whereas the white increase was twice as great—over 10 percent. Also, there is a disproportionate number of nonwhites in the lower social and economic groups, where most reported illegitimacies occur. Another misleading factor may be that middle-class white women can get abortions done more readily under secret and safe circumstances.

[30] U.S. Department of Health, Education, and Welfare, Welfare Administration, Bureau of Family Services, *Dependent Children and their Families.* (Washington, D.C.: Government Printing Office, 1963.)

[31] U.S. Department of Health, Education, and Welfare, Social Security Administration, *Social Security Program Statistics Relating to Nonwhite Families and Children,* Note No. 29 (September 8, 1958).

[32] For an excellent discussion of the psychodynamics of the Negro personality see Abram Kardiner, and Lionel Ovesey, *The Mark of Oppression: A Psychosocial Study of the American Negro* (New York: W. W. Norton & Company, Inc.), 1951.

[33] Claire Hancock states that, "The more frequent and less pathological forms of exploitation also adversely affect children. Children may be overworked, or expected to take unreasonable responsibility for household tasks and care of younger children. Children who are kept out of school or denied time for normal school recreational activities are deprived of important opportunities for intellectual and social development. It is important to recognize the difficult task faced by parents who must live in slum areas where children are exposed to many dangers. Overcrowded households force children into the streets and sometimes into places where they may become victims of juvenile delinquency or adult degradation. . . . In some isolated rural areas, there are groups who are so withdrawn from contact with the larger community that inbreeding and deteriorated family and social life may result." (*Children and Neglect,* U.S. Department of Health, Education, and Welfare, Washington, D.C.: Government Printing Office, 1963).

[34] For an extended discussion of racial comparisons between whites and nonwhites, of income, economic status, working wives, etc., see Herman P. Miller, *Rich Man, Poor Man* (New York: Thomas Y. Crowell Company, 1964).

[35] Robert L. Sutherland, *Color, Class and Personality,* American Council on Education, Washington, D.C.

[36] For an excellent analysis of the class structures within the Negro group, see John R. Rohrer and M. S. Edmonson, eds., articles by Harold Lief; Daniel Thompson; and William Thompson, *The Eighth Generation,* (New York: Harper and Brothers, 1960). There it is observed (p. 54) that "the social structure of the lower class is less organized, less stable, and less coordinated than that of the middle class. Its family life is predicated on unstable (frequently 'common law') marriage and frequent desertion. The mother is often the chief breadwinner, augmenting her own earnings with what she can wheedle or extort from her current husband, and the discipline exercised over the children is apt to be harsh and inconsistent, with both parents frequently out of the home."

[37] Irene B. Taeuber, "Migration, Mobility, and the Assimilation of the Negro." *Population Bulletin,* XIV, No. 7, U.S. Department of Commerce, (November, 1958), pp. 127–151.

[38] Andrew F. Brimmer, remarks before the 11th Annual Conference of the National Association of Market Developers. (Press release of May 15, 1964, U.S. Department of Commerce, Washington, D.C.)

[39] See Margaret Mead, "The Changing American Family," *Children,* 10, No. 5 (September–October, 1963).

[40] Robert E. Baker, "Covert Segregation Galls D.C. Negroes," *Summer of Discontent,* VII, *Washington Post,* August 16, 1963.

BIBLIOGRAPHY

Baker, Robert E., "Housing Restrictions Top Grievance List of Washington Negroes," *Summer of Discontent*, II, *Washington Post* (August 12, 1963).

———, "Covert Segregation Galls D.C. Negroes," *Summer of Discontent*, VII, *Washington Post*, August 16, 1963.

Bressler, Tobia, "Some Population Trends Involving and Affecting the Negro—Implications." Address, Association of Social Science Teachers,

Nashville, Tennessee, March 22, 1962.

Coe, Paul F., "Nonwhite Population Increases in Metropolitan Areas." *Journal of the American Statistical Association,* 50, No. 270 (June, 1955).

Conant, James B., "Social Dynamite in Our Large Cities." *Children,* 8, No. 5 (September–October, 1961).

Deutsch, Martin P., "The Disadvantaged Child and the Learning Process," in Passow, A. Harry (ed.), *Education in Depressed Areas.* New York: Teachers College, Columbia University Press, 1963.

Douglass, Joseph H., *The Negro Family's Search for Economic Security,* U.S. Department of Health, Education, and Welfare, Washington, D.C., July, 1956.

Edstrom, Eve, "They're All Scufflin' Like Me," *Washington Post,* January 12, 1964.

Edwards, G. Franklin, "Marriage and Family Life Among Negroes." *The Journal of Negro Education, Yearbook* No. XXXII, Washington, D.C.: The Howard University Press, 1963. p. 451.

Frazier, E. Franklin, *The Negro Family in the United States.* Chicago: University of Chicago Press, 1939.

Gist, Noel P. and Bennett, William S., Jr., "Aspirations of Negro and White Students." *Social Forces,* 41, No. 1 (October, 1963).

Goldberg, Miriam L., "Factors Affecting Educational Attainment in Depressed Urban Areas," in Passow, A. Harry (ed.), *Education in Depressed Areas.* New York: Teachers College, Columbia University Press, 1963.

Goldstein, Marcus S., "Longevity and Health Status of the Negro American." *Journal of Negro Education,* Fall, 1963.

Goodwin, Robert G., *America Is For Everybody.* U.S. Department of Labor, Washington, D.C.: Government Printing Office, 1963.

Hancock, Claire, *Children and Neglect—Hazardous Home Conditions,* U.S. Department of Health, Educa-

tion, and Welfare, Washington, D.C., 1963.

Handlin, Oscar, *The Newcomers—Negroes and Puerto Ricans in a Changing Metropolis.* Cambridge: Harvard University Press, 1959.

Hayes, Marion, "A Century of Change—Negroes in the U.S. Economy 1860–1960." *Monthly Labor Review,* U.S. Department of Labor, December, 1962.

Holsey, Eleanor, "Culturally Deprived Children in Day-Care Programs." *Children,* 10, No. 5 (September–October, 1963).

Kardiner, Abram and Ovesey, Lionel, *The Mark of Oppression: A Psychosocial Study of the American Negro.* New York: W. W. Norton and Company, Inc., 1951.

Kessler, Matthew A., "Economic Status of Nonwhite Workers 1955–62." *Monthly Labor Review,* Preprint No. 2419, U.S. Department of Labor, July, 1963.

Lewis, Hylan, "The Changing Negro Family," *The Nation's Children,* Vol. 1. New York: Columbia University Press, 1960.

Lewis, Hylan and Hill, Mozell, "Desegregation, Integration, and the Negro Community." *The Annals of the American Academy of Political and Social Science,* 304, March, 1956.

John H. Rohrer and M. S. Edmonson, eds.; co-authors Lief, Harold; Thompson, Daniel; and Thompson, William, *The Eighth Generation.* New York: Harper and Brothers, 1960.

Mead, Margaret, "The Changing American Family." *Children,* 10, No. 5 (September–October, 1963).

Miller, Herman P., *Rich Man, Poor Man.* New York: Thomas Y. Crowell Company, 1964.

National Association of Intergroup Relations Officials, *Public School Segregation and Integration in the North.* Washington, D.C. (November, 1963).

Pollack, Otto, "Some Challenges to the American Family." *Children,* 11, No. 1 (January–February, 1964).

Schiffman, Jacob, "Marital and Family Characteristics of Workers, March, 1960." *Monthly Labor Review*, Reprint No. 2364, U.S. Department of Labor (April, 1961).

Schnore, Leo F. and Sharp, Harry, "Racial Changes in Metropolitan Areas, 1950–1960." *Social Forces*, 41, No. 3 (March, 1963).

Silberman, C. E., "The City and the Negro," *Fortune*, LXV, No. 3, 65:88–91 (March, 1962).

Stein, Robert L. and Meredith, Jane L., "Growth and Characteristics of the Part-Time Work Force, No. 10." *Monthly Labor Review*, Reprint No. 2356, U.S. Department of Labor (November, 1960).

Sutherland, Robert L., *Color, Class and Personality*, American Council on Education, Washington, D.C., 1942.

Taeuber, Irene B., "Migration, Mobility, and the Assimilation of the Negro." *Population Bulletin*, XIV, No. 7, U.S. Department of Commerce, November, 1958.

U.S. Department of Commerce, Bureau of Census, *Current Population Reports, Population Characteristics*, Series P–20, No. 115 (February 7, 1962).

U.S. Department of Commerce, Bureau of Census, *Current Population Reports, Population Characteristics*, Series P–20, No. 118 (August 9, 1962).

U.S. Department of Commerce, Bureau of Census, *Current Population Reports, Consumer Income*, Series P–60, No. 41 (October 21, 1963).

U.S. Department of Commerce, "Negro Population for Selected Standard Metropolitan Statistical Areas: 1960," *Appendix* (release of February 26, 1961).

U.S. Department of Commerce, "Negro Population of the 25 Largest Cities in United States: 1960" (release of March 14, 1961).

U.S. Department of Commerce, *Summary Population Characteristics*, Final Report PC (1)–1D, Washington, D.C.: Government Printing Office, 1963.

U.S. Department of Health, Education, and Welfare, Welfare Administration, Bureau of Family Services, *Dependent Children and Their Families*. Washington, D.C.: Government Printing Office, 1963.

U.S. Department of Health, Education, and Welfare, *Indicators*. February, 1964.

U.S. Department of Health, Education, and Welfare, Office of the Secretary, *New Directions in Health, Education, and Welfare*, 1963.

U.S. Department of Health, Education, and Welfare, Social Security Administration, *Social Security Program Statistics Relating to Nonwhite Families and Children*, Note No. 29, September 8, 1958.

U.S. Department of Health, Education, and Welfare, *Trends*, 1963 edition.

U.S. Department of Labor, Bureau of Labor Statistics, *Economic Status of Nonwhite Workers, 1955–62*, Special Labor Force Report No. 33, Preprint No. 2419.

U.S. Department of Labor, "Employment of High School Graduates and Dropouts in 1961." *Monthly Labor Review* (May, 1962).

U.S. Housing and Home Finance Agency, *Our Nonwhite Population and its Housing: The Changes Between 1950 and 1960*, July, 1963.

U.S. Senate, 86th Congress, 2nd Session, Special Committee on Unemployment Problems, *Studies in Unployment*, Washington, D.C.: Government Printing Office, 1960.

Wagner, Robert F., Remarks at the Annual Civil Rights Conference of the New York City Central Labor Council, March 9, 1963. From *Congressional Record Appendix*, March 14, 1963.

Walker, I. and Sullivan, Eugenia, *New Directions*, 1st edition, U.S. Department of Health, Education, and Welfare, 1963.

Washington Post, Editorial (January 27, 1964).

White, Theodore H., "Racial Collision in the Big Cities," *Life*, 55:100–2 (November 22, 1963).

chapter **7**

Virgil A. Clift

Educating the American Negro

Virgil A. Clift.   Professor of Education, New York University, New York, New York. Formerly Member of U. S. State Department Mission to Pakistan. Editor of the Sixteenth Yearbook of the John Dewey Society, *Negro Education in America.*

The story of the education of the American Negro has raised fundamental questions throughout our history as to the extent and quality of his cultural integration. The ordeal of slavery, followed by a century of segregation and discrimination, forced the Negro to live in a cultural no man's land. He was stripped of his African culture, language and religion; and, at the same time, by exclusion and denial was not permitted to enter the mainstream of American life. Yet, in spite of differential treatment, inequality before the law and often intense, harsh and brutal treatment, he developed a devotion, loyalty and attachment to America. Therefore, one must understand the historical paradox of the Negro's life in America in order to gain insight into his past and present education. Historically, the development of schools and programs of education for Negroes has represented largely the influences of social forces outside the Negro community and over which he had little or no control.

EDUCATION DURING THE COLONIAL PERIOD

Since the introduction of the first Negro slaves (c. 1619) into the Jamestown colony, the question of Negro education has been a subject of controversy in America. During the colonial period, the institution of slavery was recognized as being incompatible with education. If made available to slaves, education would be a factor in destroying slavery. There are reports of instances, however, where organizations sought to provide some education for slaves. After 1740, the Society for the Propagation of the Gospel in Foreign Parts sought to raise the level of living among both whites and Negroes in the South. The missionaries of this organization urged the masters to provide opportunity for their slaves to be converted. They suggested that slaves be given time to study the Scriptures and to learn to read and write. Occasionally, they taught the slaves themselves and, in one notable instance, they fostered the establishment of a school for Negroes in Charleston, South Carolina, in which the teachers themselves were slaves owned by the society.[1]

"The Christianization of the Negro proceeded as the first great step in his larger American education."[2] There is considerable evidence that the Puritans favored conversion. In a tract published in London in 1673, Richard Baxter favored Christian instruction of slaves. In 1674, John Eliot, who had done much to improve life among the Indians, turned his attention to instructing Negroes. Cotton Mather, busy with writing and teaching, took time to instruct Negroes and, in 1717, began his evening school for Indians and Negroes. Samuel Sewall, a judge in Massachusetts, not only favored instruction but also was quite outspoken against slavery, believing it to be a curse against God and humanity. In 1728, Nathaniel Pigott announced that he was opening a school for the "instruction of Negroes in reading, catechizing, and writing," but there is no record of its success or failure.

The most conscientious effort to improve conditions among slaves was made by the Quakers. They not only took steps to abolish slavery, but some leaders such as George Fox urged owners of slaves to give religious instruction to them. In 1700, William Penn was instrumental in getting a Monthly Meeting established for Negroes. During this time many colonists were teaching their slaves and free Negroes; indeed, Paul Cuffee, a prosperous Negro, set up a school in Massachusetts in the eighteenth century. John Woolman's influence was especially noteworthy among Quakers.

Important also was the influence of Anthony Benezet, who began an evening school in his home in Philadelphia in 1750 and continued instruction there for twenty years. Regarded among his contemporaries as a highly enlightened man of letters, his views had much significance when he spoke out against the idea of Negro inferiority.

> I can with truth and sincerity declare that I have found amongst the Negroes as great a variety of talents as amongst a like number of whites; and I am bold to assert, that the notion entertained by some, that the blacks are inferior in their capacities, is a vulgar prejudice, founded on the pride or ignorance of their lordly masters, who have kept their slaves at such a distance, as to be unable to form a right judgment of them.[3]

Many other Quakers saw the need not only to give Christian instruction to Negroes, but to abolish slavery as well. In 1776, the Philadelphia Quakers decided to put an end to slaveholding. They founded the Pennsylvania Abolition Society, whose members included Benjamin Franklin, William Pitt, Noah Webster and Thomas Paine. This society aimed to establish schools for Negroes whenever possible, in addition to the abolition of slavery.

Prior to the Revolution there were a few other notable examples of attempts to educate the Negro. An early catechizing school was founded in New York City at Trinity Church in 1704, with instruction being given by Elia Neau. Reverend Thomas Bray in Maryland encouraged conversion and instruction, and, at times, white and Negro children were taught together.

Because of their concern for indoctrinating them with Christianity the French and Spanish settlers were more active in trying to educate slaves than the English. The Catholics in New Orleans, under the leadership of the Ursuline Nuns, attempted to teach Negroes and Indians in 1727, and established and conducted a school for Negroes in 1734.

The English were much slower to follow a similar policy until the provincial statutes and the declarations of the Bishop of London established the principles that conversion did not lead to manumission.[4]

FROM THE REVOLUTION TO THE CIVIL WAR [5]

The doctrine of the "natural rights" of man, which was a part of the philosophy of the American Revolution, helped the opponents of slavery espouse the right of the Negro education. Benjamin Franklin favored and encouraged the full education of the Negro. Thomas Jefferson thought that they should be given industrial and agricultural education but did not believe in the intellectual equality of Negroes and whites.

Education in the South

Despite legal restrictions and despite contentions of Southerners like John C. Calhoun that Negroes could not absorb educative experiences, Negro slaves did receive education in various parts of the South. According to

John H. Franklin,[6] some masters themselves taught their slaves. The case of Frederick Douglass having been taught by his mistress is perhaps the best known instance of an owner teaching a slave. One planter in northern Mississippi boasted that all twenty of his slaves could read and that they purchased their own books. In some cases, even where masters were opposed to their slaves receiving instruction, the children of masters would teach slaves to read and write.

The instruction of one or two slaves, though a violation of the law, was not regarded as serious, and there was hardly any danger of prosecution. However, the insurrection of 1800 so frightened Southern planters that further expansion of education for Negroes was discouraged. In the nineteenth century, Negroes in Southern states had to content themselves, for the most part, with clandestine schools and private teachers.

In some isolated instances, Negroes attended mixed schools in the South. In 1840, Negroes were permitted to attend schools with white children in Wilmington, Delaware. Julius Mebourn was sent to a white academy near Raleigh, North Carolina, by his mistress and remained there until it was discovered he was a Negro. Franklin [7] concludes that "There is no way of knowing the extent to which Negroes attended the schools of whites." Nor is there any way of ascertaining with any degree of accuracy the number of slaves who were literate before the Civil War. Amos Dresser believed that one out of every fifty slaves in the southwest could read and write. C. G. Parsons estimated that about five thousand of Georgia's 400 thousand slaves were literate.[8]

Education in the North

During the post-revolutionary period, Negroes in the North benefited from the general trend to establish and improve schools in the new nation. Whites in Boston taught Negro children both privately and in public institutions. In 1798, a separate school for Negro children was established by a white teacher in the home of Primus Hall, a prominent Negro. Two years later, Negroes asked the city of Boston for a separate school, but the request was refused. Negroes established a school anyway and employed two Harvard men as instructors. This school continued for many years; and finally, in 1820, the city of Boston opened an elementary school for Negroes.

One of the best known schools for Negroes during the period was the New York African Free School, established by the Manumission Society in 1787. It began with forty students and the number never exceeded sixty in its first decade of existence. At first, there was great opposition to the school, but in 1800 interest in it increased. New impetus for its continued growth came in 1810, when New York required masters to teach all slave children to read the Scriptures. By 1820, the institution had enrolled more than five hundred Negro children.

New Jersey began educating her Negro children in 1777. By 1801, there had been short-lived schools established in Burlington, Salem and Trenton. In addition, Quakers and other humanitarian groups were teaching Negro children privately. As early as 1774, the Quakers of Philadelphia established a school for Negro children, and after the war, thanks to funds provided by philanthropist Anthony Benezet, the program was enlarged. In 1787, a school was built in Philadelphia, and ten years later there were at least seven schools for Negroes in this city. This interest in the development of Negro education continued until the nineteenth century. In most places, however, separate schools were maintained. The separate schools established in Boston in 1820 was followed closely by other Massachusetts towns which organized schools for Negroes.

In 1849, Charles Sumner in the case *Roberts* vs. *The City of Boston*, appeared before the Massachusetts Supreme Court on behalf of a Negro girl who had been barred from a white school under the local ordinance providing for separate education of the races. The Massachusetts Supreme Court held against Sumner and the Negro plaintiff; however, by 1855, sufficient public opinion had been mobilized to persuade the Massachusetts legislature to repudiate the court. In that year, segregation in the public schools of the state was specifically prohibited by statute.[9]

Rhode Island and Connecticut maintained separate schools, and in the last decade before the Civil War larger funds were given to them. Not until 1824 did the New York Common Council begin to support African Free Schools. The city took them over altogether in 1834. Although some communities in the state permitted Negro children to attend white schools, the legislature made it clear in 1841 that any district could establish separate schools. New Jersey also maintained separate schools for Negro children. The citizens of Pennsylvania continued to give both public and private support to their Negro schools and they increased in number, particularly in the western part of the state.

As more and more Negroes migrated to the West, citizens were faced with the problem of education. Ohio excluded Negroes from public schools by law in 1829, and twenty years later provided separate schools, but never appropriated enough funds to set up anything creditable. Citizens of Indiana and Illinois were equally indifferent. Michigan and Wisconsin adopted more democratic policies, but most Negroes in the West had to wait until after the Civil War before they were able to be educated in considerable numbers at public expense.

It was during this period that Negroes began to attend some institutions of higher education. John Russwurm graduated from Bowdoin College in 1826. Before the Civil War a few Negroes were attending Oberlin, Franklin and Rutland Colleges and the Harvard Medical and other schools.

During the pre-Civil War period a few Negroes were appointed to the faculties of white colleges. Charles L. Reason, William G. Allen, and George B. Vashon each held for a time the professorship of Belle Lettres at Central College in McGrawville, New York. It was said that these teachers wore "the professor's mantle gracefully, giving proof of good scholarship and manly character." In this period also the American Missionary Association continued its work, administering the interesting experiment for the coeducaton of the races at Berea College in Kentucky.[10]

DEVELOPMENTS AFTER THE CIVIL WAR

Even after the Civil War efforts to educate the Negro were met with strong opposition. Public education was frequently denounced in Southern publications because it was identified with the idea of equality. Resentment against the Negro school and church sometimes flared into violence, with Negroes being forcibly stopped from attending schools and teachers being physically prevented from teaching. Churches which housed schools were often burned. In spite of these conditions, it was at this time that the first organized program of education was developed for the freedmen.

West Virginia, which became a separate political unit in 1863, was the first Southern state to make provision in its constitution for the "equal though separate" education of the Negro. In sections of Florida and Louisiana under the jurisdiction of the Union military forces, and in the border states, there were efforts to set up public schools for Negroes. In 1865, Missouri included Negroes in her school system.[11] In the border states, support for Negro public schools came from the taxes paid by Negroes. This was true even in the District of Columbia, where, in 1862, Congress passed a bill setting aside 10 percent of the taxes paid by Negroes to support Negro schools.[12]

During Reconstruction, the attitude of the South toward the education of the freedman was determined not only by the traditional attitudes toward the status of the Negro, but also by the outlook and interests of the various groups that emerged with the collapse of the Confederacy. Three elements in Southern society arose: (1) The Conservatives, who attempted (through the Black Codes) to reinstate as far as possible the servile status of the Negro. This class was opposed to any form of education of the Negro. (2) The moderates, who realized that slavery was dead and that the new status of the Negro should be recognized in creating a new society in the South. In this moderate group where many large plantation owners who were willing to provide some education for Negroes in order to secure a stable and reliable labor supply. (3) The radicals, comprised of the un-propertied whites and small farmers, who had no real interest in the slave system and who because of their cooperation with Negroes in establishing public schools were called "renegades and scalawags."

The chief contribution of the Reconstruction government was to set a precedent for the democratic right of all the people to public tax-supported education. However, education of whites and Negroes in the same school was not attempted on a large scale; and in Louisiana and South Carolina, where such attempts were made, there was violence or the whites generally boycotted the schools. At the time Negro leaders generally accepted separate schools as an inevitable consequence of the traditional attitudes of the whites toward the association of the races.

During the Civil War and immediately following, the War Department provided care and some instruction to Negroes who were either refugees or "contraband." The Freedman's Bureau (1865–72) acted as an agency of the department and expanded these early efforts under the leadership of General Oliver Otis Howard, Commissioner; Edwin M. Stanton, Secretary of War, and John W. Alvord, Superintendent of Instruction for the bureau. The Freedman's Bureau was influential in giving central organization, protection and financial support to the efforts of philanthropists, freedmen and the states. This framework was essential for the establishment of a system of education.

After the war, the Freedman's Bureau and various Freedman's aid societies helped to establish higher institutions as well as elementary and secondary schools for Negroes. But in addition to these efforts the churches also made a valuable contribution. Among the most important of these was the

American Missionary Association, which set up schools in Newport News, Portsmouth, Suffolk and Yorktown in Virginia and Washington, D.C., as well as in Columbus, Ohio, as early as 1863. Other important church groups which gave aid to the education of the recently emancipated Negroes were: The Friends Association for the Aid to Freedmen, the Board of Freedmen's Missions of the United Presbyterian Church, the Freedman's Aid Society of the Methodist Episcopal Church, the American Baptist Home Mission Society, the American Church Institute of the Episcopal Church, and the Conferences of the African Methodist Episcopal Church. Among the outstanding leaders associated with these organizations and religious movements were Levi Coffin, Salmon P. Chase, Henry Ward Beecher, John M. Walden, Richard S. Rust, Mathias W. Baldwin (locomotive industrialist), Edward T. Atkinson (textile manufacturer), and William Claflin (Governor of Massachusetts).

In the decade immediately following the close of the Civil War, leading church groups were active in the establishment of a number of schools which although in the beginning were hardly more than secondary schools, later became landmarks in the system of higher education in the South. The most important of these include Atlanta University (1865) in Atlanta, Georgia, Talladega, in Alabama, (1867), Fisk University (1866) in Nashville, Tennessee, and Tougaloo University (1869) in Mississippi—all established by the American Missionary Association. The Arkansas Agricultural, Mechanical, and Normal College began as Branch Normal in 1873 at Pine Bluff, Arkansas. Morehouse College of Atlanta, Georgia, was originally established in 1867 as the Augusta Institute in Augusta, Georgia. It was supported by the American Baptist Home Mission Society which was also instrumental in the founding and support of Virginia Union University in 1865, Shaw University in Raleigh, North Carolina, in 1865, and Benedict College in 1870 in South Carolina. The Methodist Episcopal Church established an institution at Holly Springs, Mississippi in 1867, a school which was later known as both Shaw University and Rust College. The Presbyterians in North Carolina established the Scotia Seminary, which today is known as Barber-Scotia College. Biddle University was founded the same year at Charlotte, North Carolina, and is known today as Johnson C. Smith University. The Methodist Episcopal Church founded the Centenary Biblical Institute in Baltimore in 1866, which later became Morgan College and is today Morgan State College. Howard University in Washington, D.C., was established in 1867. These represent a few of the institutions of higher education, significant in America today, which can trace their roots to the post Civil War period.

Philanthropy also aided materially in Negro education by providing buildings, endowments, scholarships, support for teacher training and industrial education. The Daniel Hand Fund and the Anna T. Jeanes Fund were established exclusively for Negroes.

Land-grant colleges for Negroes were established under the provisions of the Second Morrill Act (1890). This provided the framework for the state-supported institutions for higher education. The Second Morrill Act was one of the first means of assuring land-grant funds for Negro education where the dual system of education existed. On the other hand, it gave strength to the doctrine of "separate but equal," with the result that the seventeen Southern states maintained colleges which came to be known as the Negro land-grant colleges. It was at these institutions which received a minimum of Federal and state support that the public system of higher education for Negroes in the South was based.

Immediately following the end of the Reconstruction period, the South deprived the Negro not only of citizenship rights but also of educational privileges. During the period from 1876 to 1895, in the Southern states as a whole, the enrollment of whites increased markedly and that of the Negroes was moderate, the increase for whites being 106 percent as compared with 59 percent for Negroes. During the 1890's, Negroes were disfranchised by state constitutional provisions and their subordinate status was given legal basis in the South. As a result, education for Negroes became more segregated in those areas where mixed schools had existed, and inequalities developed in teachers' salaries and in other provisions for Negro education.

In 1890, the influence of Booker T. Washington had begun to be felt. His campaign to establish an educational program for Negroes that would be acceptable to the South was widely discussed. It was during this period also that philanthropy became an important factor in the support of Negro education in the South. Seizing upon these two factors, Southern states soon introduced inequality into their support of Negro and white education. Gains which had been made toward mixing the schools for the races were quickly stamped out.

A dictum from the famous case of *Plessy* vs. *Ferguson* (1896) was the basis of saddling the "separate but equal doctrine" on education in the South.[13] The United States Supreme Court actually went out of its way to recognize "that segregation in education was a general American practice, not an uniquely Southern one."

From 1896 to 1954, the dual system of education was developed and expanded in the South. Permissive segregation was maintained in the border states. Schools remained, in fact, *separate and unequal.*

DEVELOPMENTS DURING THE TWENTIETH CENTURY

In the early years of the twentieth century, public education for Negroes in the South received significant impetus from the outside through the contributions of such philanthropists as Rockefeller and Peabody. The Anna T. Jeanes Fund, in 1908, inaugurated the Jeanes Teacher program to improve the quality of instruction in rural Negro schools. Beginning in 1913, the Julius Rosenwald Fund provided grants for Negro school construction, and by 1932 more than 5,000 Negro school buildings in 883 counties of fifteen Southern and border states had been built with Rosenwald aid. Rosenwald grants provided an invaluable incentive and accounted for about 15 percent of the money spent on school construction for Negroes. In addition, 17 percent came from direct contributions made by Negroes themselves. At the end of the Rosenwald building program, the per-pupil value of Negro school property was still less than one-fifth as great as that of white schools. An even more telling index of the relative growth of the dual school system is provided by a comparison of teachers' salaries. Between 1900 and 1930, the average white teacher's salary rose from slightly less than two hundred dollars to nine hundred dollars, while the average Negro teacher's salary rose from one hundred dollars to four hundred dollars. And these figures reflect the peak of a national boom, both in national income and in school population.[14]

The effects of this disparate policy were evident in the concentration of Negro children in the lower grades during the first half of the twentieth century. As late as 1920, 85 percent of all Negro pupils in the South were enrolled in the first four grades. In 1916, there were only sixty-seven Negro public high schools with fewer than twenty thousand students.[15]

The two decades between World War I and World War II were marked by profound changes in Negro education. As noted by Low,[16] there was significant increase in public high schools for Negroes, North and South—especially in large urban areas. Capital outlays for schools increased in substantial amounts. The number of high school teachers employed, students enrolled and high school graduates grew markedly. And all of this growth was accompanied by programs of school consolidation, new curricula and other educational advances which reflected the general American patterns on elementary and secondary education.

Also during this period, Low points out, there was a large increase in the numbers of college graduates from Northern schools and Negro institutions in the South. Improvement in the quality of the Negro colleges led to more and more of them receiving accreditation from regional accrediting agencies.

The Negro land-grant colleges in this period surpassed the private colleges in financial support and in consequence attracted an enrollment larger than these privately financed institutions. One consequence of this was the establishment of the United Negro College Fund at the end of World War II to buttress the rising financial needs of the private colleges.

During this period Negro education came increasingly under the scrutiny of students of American education. The focus was on quality. Studies in Negro education appeared regularly in the *Journal of Negro Education,* first published in 1932. Federal, state and local research greatly augmented our knowledge of Negro education.

The more deeply scholars probed into Negro education and made comparisons with the education of white youth the more they became aware of the appalling gap between education for Negroes and whites. Many noted also the predominance of teacher training in Negro colleges and the lack of democracy in the administration of Negro schools and colleges. The toll of Negro education taken by the doctrine in the Plessy case became increasingly apparent.

LEGAL ATTACKS ON JIM CROW SCHOOLS

Between 1896, when the Plessy decision was handed down, and 1930, only three cases involving Negro education came before the Supreme Court. In none of these was school segregation directly challenged, nor did the Court find occasion to order relief of any kind for Negro plaintiffs. In 1899, the Supreme Court heard an appeal by a group of Negroes from Augusta, Georgia, who demanded an end to public support for two white high schools after the sole Negro high school had been discontinued. The majority opinion in *Cumming* vs. *Richmond County* held that the relief requested was improper. In 1908, the Court heard the case of *Berea College* vs. *Kentucky,* which involved the right of a privately chartered college to teach both races in defiance of the Kentucky law making segregation mandatory. The Court ruled against Berea on technical grounds. The case was generally accepted as a reflection of the Court's feeling that segregation was a matter better left to the states. *Gong Lum* vs. *Rice* came before the Court from Mississippi in 1927. The issue was whether Mississippi could properly classify a Chinese child as "colored" and therefore require her to attend a Negro school. The Court upheld the Mississippi law and Chief Justice Taft took the occasion to offer a reminder that the "separate but equal" doctrine was still in effect; "had the petition alleged specifically that there was no colored school in Martha Lum's neighborhood to which she could conveniently go, a different question would have been presented. . . ." None of these cases directly challenged the constitutionality of segregation in education.

In 1935, almost forty years after the Supreme Court handed down the Plessy decision permitting "separate but equal" public educational facilities, Donald Murray, a Negro, applied for admission to the law school of the University of Maryland at Baltimore and was refused in accordance with Maryland's segregation statutes. His complaint was that Maryland provided no law school for Negroes within its boundaries but had attempted to meet the Plessy doctrine by offering a limited number of scholarships for Negroes in institutions outside the state. The Maryland Court of Appeals upheld Murray's contention and accepted the argument that out of state scholarships, which covered only the cost of tuition, placed Negro students at an economic disadvantage.

The Gaines case in 1938 was the real forerunner of the decisions of the 1940's which opened graduate schools in the South to Negroes. Lloyd Gaines sued for admission to the law school of the University of Missouri on the grounds that no separate school of law for Negroes was provided in the state and that the out of state scholarships available to him did not satisfy the requirement of equal treatment. The Supreme Court reversed the courts of Missouri in an opinion which announced a new point of law.[17]

This set into motion in the South a feverish expansion of state-supported Negro graduate and professional schools, an expansion designed especially to deny Negroes admission to white state-supported colleges and universities.[18] The decade following the Murray and Gaines cases witnessed the most revolutionary change to take place in the whole history of education in the South: the entire South began to spend an unprecedented proportion of its income for the education of Negro children in public schools.

It came as a suprise to Southern state officials and legislators that Negroes were not impressed with the makeshift graduate schools, the increased expenditure on capital improvements, the attempts to equalize salaries and the general increase in expenditures for Negro education. Educational opportunities for Negroes were greatly improved, to be sure, but Negro citizens viewed this as irrelevant because they did not judge their conditions in comparison with, say, the impoverished millions in Asia. Instead, Negroes viewed their conditions by the standards of their white fellow citizens and by the guarantees the American system made for them. They were keenly aware that they were at the very crux of the Great American Experi-

Humble beginnings of Atlanta University.
Boxcars served as classrooms.
(United Negro College Fund Photo)

The Negro's path to a college degree is arduous and beset with many obstacles. Those who endure to graduation are *"likely to be men* [and women] *of the most indomitable purpose with a great capacity for hard work and tremendous self-sacrifice."*

(Howard University Photo)

ment and that their drive to secure full educational rights as human beings and citizens was the acid test of the American Way of Life.

Therefore, Negroes prepared to make an onslaught and frontal attack on the validity of segregation in higher education. In cases against the University of Oklahoma and the University of Texas [19] Negro plaintiffs carried to the United States Supreme Court between 1946 and 1949 issues sharply testing the right of the states to alter in any substantial particular the opportunities for graduate and professional study offered Negroes from that offered whites. Indeed in the Texas case (*Sweatt* vs. *The University of Texas*) the plaintiff's attorneys argued that no segregated Negro school actually could provide equal educational opportunities. They not only argued that the new Negro law school which had been established by Texas was materially inferior, but also offered the testimony of anthropologists, psychologists and educators to show that Negroes were as capable of learning as whites, that classification of students by race was arbitrary and unjust and that segregation was harmful to personality adjustment. The Court obviously gave weight to these contentions by ruling out segregation in specific instances and largely invalidating it in the field of graduate and professional training. Few if any state Negro colleges in the South could meet the requirements posed by the Court in its decision.

Meanwhile, the Southern states had pooled their resources to set up regional programs for higher education which would serve the students of both races from all participating states. This plan was denounced by Negro leaders as another device for preserving segregation at the university level. The Southern Regional Educational Board and the regional compact were immediately challenged in 1949 when a Negro applicant was denied admission to the University of Maryland School of Nursing on the grounds that she was entitled to out of state training at Meharry Medical School (Negro) under the regional plan. The Maryland Court of Appeals ordered her admitted to the state university. Beginning with this decision, more public institutions admitted Negroes. Enrollment of Negroes was restricted, however, primarily to graduate and professional schools.

The relentless legal assault upon the upper ramparts of the segregated educational structure had been planned and executed with great care. Negro leaders now reasoned that the anachronistic system of segregation in public elementary and secondary schools perpetuated segregation and discrimination in all other phases of public life of the nation. They maintained that segregation in the lower schools was a divisive and antidemocratic device perpetuating an obsolete caste system which flatly controverted the basic ethical concepts of the American Judeo-Christian tradition.

By this time the Negro masses were demanding that the National Association for the Advancement of Colored People press harder and with greater speed for equal rights in all fields. The masses, in the North and South, were making such great demands on Negro leaders that the leaders were actually being pressured into action in many instances where otherwise they would have been reluctant.

Therefore, in 1952, the long course of litigation over separate education in America brought before the Supreme Court five separate cases which challenged head-on the Plessy doctrine of "separate but equal." [20]

Each of these cases raised the basic issues of segregation in education in a somewhat different way. The implications reached the whole of the nation's segregated pattern as well as the basic division of authority between the Federal Government and the sovereign states. The moral overtones had practical repercussions on America's efforts in international politics to keep black, brown and yellow peoples of the world from swinging into the communist orbit.

On May 17, 1954, the United States Supreme Court ruled unanimously that segregation of the races in public education was unconstitutional. The Court made its position clear in the following unequivocal statement:

> In approaching this problem, we cannot turn the clock back to 1868 when the Amendment was adopted or even to 1896 when *Plessy* v. *Ferguson* was written. We must consider public education in the light of its full development and its present place in American life throughout the Nation. Only in this way can it be determined if segregation in public schools deprives these plaintiffs of the equal protection of the laws.
>
> . . . We come back to the question presented: Does segregation of children in public schools solely on the basis of race, even though the physical facilities and other "tangible" factors may be equal, deprive the children of the minority group of equal educational opportunities? We believe that it does.
>
> . . . Segregation of white and colored children in public schools has a detrimental effect upon the colored children. The impact is greater when it has the sanction of the law; for the policy of separating the races is usually interpreted as denoting the inferiority of the Negro group.

Desegregation was progressing slowly, even in the South, before this historic and far-reaching decision. In compliance with the decision, school desegregation began in the fall of 1954 in a few large cities, notably Wilmington, Delaware, Baltimore, Maryland, and Washington, D. C., and in some scattered counties in Missouri, Arkansas, and West Virginia. By the fourth anniversary of the Supreme Court's original decision, the desegregation process was at work in ten out of the seventeen states that previously had compulsory school segregation. In keeping with the Court-ordained "deliberate speed" clause, desegregation moved faster in Kentucky, Oklahoma and Texas than in Tennessee and North Carolina. But it did spread. Out of 2,889 Southern school districts with both white and colored pupils, desegregation had begun in 764 by the end of four years. Of these, fewer than forty were compelled to desegregate by specific court order.

Then, in the fall of 1958, desegregation appeared to have been brought almost to a standstill by deep Southern hostility. New desegregation moves were limited to thirteen school districts in the entire South; and in contrast to this modicum of progress toward compliance, schools were closed in Little Rock, Arkansas, and in sections of Virginia to avoid integration. Desegregation seemed to have been stopped short by seven states willing to dispense with public schools rather than to yield to racial mixing.

By the middle of the 1958–59 school year, the situation had taken a different turn. Negro pupils had entered white schools in Alexandria, Virginia, without incident, bringing a third new community into the desegregation column—and not in a border state but in Virginia, the former center of massive resistance. Desegregation was thus on the move again, having met the ultimate test of school closing and having proved, at least in Virginia, that parents placed sufficiently high value on public education for their children to endure a limited amount of integration. Georgia, Alabama and Mississippi seemed not to be ready to back away from the massive resistance. But the solid front had been broken, and desegregation was making some marked advances in its sixth year; once again it began slowly to approach inevitability.[21]

DESEGREGATION DEVELOPMENTS SINCE 1960

Public Schools in the South

During the fall term of 1963, a decade after the 1954 Supreme Court decision, only 9.2 percent of the Negro public school students in the Southern and border states were attending elementary and secondary schools with whites on a desegregated basis. According to a survey reported in *Southern School News* [22] (Table I), the region enrolled 10,918,793 white students and 3,403,925 Negro students, but only 314,571 of the Negroes were in school with whites. In the eleven former Confederate States (Alabama, Arkansas, Florida, Georgia, Louisiana, Mississippi, North Carolina, South Carolina, Tennessee, Texas and Virginia), 30,798 Negro children attend school in mixed classes, with 14,000 of these being in the state of Texas. The bulk of the desegregation had taken place in the border area (Delaware, District of Columbia, Kentucky, Maryland, Missouri, Oklahoma and West Virginia) where 283,773 Negro children were attending mixed classes. This, however, represented only 56.5 percent of the Negro children in this area.[23]

Alabama and South Carolina permitted a few students to attend white schools for the first time in 1963. Mississippi up to 1964 remained the only state with complete segregation in its public schools. The much publicized University of Mississippi, where James Meredith had managed to survive as the lone Negro student until graduation, had admitted another Negro and then expelled him for disciplinary reasons in the fall of 1963.

In 1961, there were 6,196 school districts in the seventeen Southern and border states. Of these, 3,052 had Negro and white students and 979 (32.1 percent) of these biracial districts had policies or practices permitting the admission of Negroes to formerly all-white schools.

In the fall of 1962, fifty-two districts desegregated by policy or practice for the first time, as compared with thirty-one the previous year. Thirteen of the newly desegregated districts acted under court order, although in many of the others legal action was pending or threatened.

A total of 114 school districts were reported to be desegregating for the first time in the fall of 1963, sixty-one more than September, 1962; and an additional eighty-three public school districts in eleven Southern states were desegregated in the 1964–65 school year. By fall of 1964 a total of 527 districts in these states were desegregated—about one-fourth of the 2,256 districts with students of both races enrolled.[24]

Thus, the number of school districts in the Southern states which claimed to be desegregating their schools was increasing. It should be noted, though, that the trend has been for a district to declare a policy of desegregation and then to permit only a very small number of Negro children to attend mixed classes. This was the policy followed in Atlanta in 1962 when only nine Negro students went to white schools. At the beginning of the same term, thirteen were admitted to mixed classes in Memphis and eighteen in Dallas. Thus the actual number of Negro children attending desegregated schools in the South remains exceedingly low.

The new resistance to desegregation, which amounts always to minimal compliance to the Supreme Court decision striking down compulsory school segregation, should properly be labeled *token desegregation*. This new strategy has several distinctive elements. First, desegregation plans are adopted which are as limited as possible. For example, the Nashville plan spreads the desegregation process out over a twelve-year period at the rate on one grade per year. Nashville began its plan with nineteen Negro students involved in the first-grade desegregation in 1957. Five years later it had 270 Negro children in the first five grades at formerly white schools.

Another example of tokenism is the pupil placement system which won court approval in North Carolina and Virginia. Under this plan only individual, "qualified" Negro students who actively seek admission may attend mixed classes. Negro children can and have been denied admission to white schools for academic, psychological, physical, geographic and other reasons. Applicants usually have been subjected to a series of special tests and personal interviews. Atlanta and New Orleans, as well as many other Southern communities, combined the grade-a-year plan with the pupil placement plan.

A final element of tokenism is the massive resistance and open defiance of the law by elected officials, including the governors of Arkansas, Mississippi and Alabama. Thus, defiantly in his inaugural address of January 14, 1963, Alabama's Governor George C. Wallace declared:

TABLE I—Public School Desegregation In Southern and Border States— 1963–1964

	School Districts With Negroes			Enrollment		In Desegregated Districts		Negroes In Schools With Whites	
	Total	& Whites	Deseg.	White	Negro	White	Negro	No.	% †
Alabama	114	114	4	539,996**	287,414*	106,199**	70,896**	21	.007
Arkansas	415	228	13	328,023**	112,012**	66,752	18,643	366	.327
Florida	67	67	16	964,241*	237,871*	669,375	130,667	3,650	1.53
Georgia	197	181	4	689,323	337,534	95,731	77,599	177	.052
Louisiana	67	67	2	460,589**	301,433**	68,700	79,077	1,814	.602
Mississippi	150	150	0	304,226**	291,971**	0	0	0	0
North Carolina	171	171	40	820,900*	347,063*	367,764*	133,164*	1,865	.537
South Carolina	108	108	1	368,496*	258,955*	3,108	9,539	10	.004
Tennessee	154	143	45	687,902*	164,940*	380,321	120,447	4,486	2.72
Texas	1,421	899	263	2,045,499	326,409*	1,300,000*	200,000*	18,000*	5.52
Virginia	130	128	55	710,176	228,961	486,231	145,658	3,721	1.63
SOUTH	**2,994**	**2,256**	**443**	**7,919,371**	**2,894,563**	**3,544,181**	**985,690**	**34,110**	**1.18**
Delaware	86	86	86	78,730	18,066	68,321	13,976	10,209	56.5
District of Columbia	1	1	1	19,803	117,915	19,803	117,915	98,813	83.8
Kentucky	204	165	163	611,126*	54,874*	492,701*	54,874*	29,855	54.4
Maryland	24	23	23	540,667	160,946	535,691	160,946	76,906	47.8
Missouri	1,597	212*	203*	793,000*	95,000*	NA	90,000*	40,000*	42.1
Oklahoma	1,160	241	197	541,125*	43,875*	324,023*	35,596*	12,289*	28.0
West Virginia	55	44	44	417,595*	23,449*	417,595*	23,449*	13,659*	58.2
BORDER	**3,127**	**772**	**717**	**3,002,046**	**514,125**	**1,858,134**††	**496,756**	**281,731**	**54.8**
REGION	**6,121**	**3,028**	**1,160**	**10,921,417**	**3,408,688**	**5,402,315**††	**1,482,446**	**315,841**	**9.3**

* Estimated. ** 1962–63. † No. of Negroes in schools with whites, compared to total Negro enrollment.
†† Missouri not included.

SOURCE: Table adapted by permission from *Southern School News*, Vol. 10, No. 11 (May 1, 1964), p. 1.

I draw the line in the dust and toss the gauntlet before the feet of tyranny; and I say segregation now, segregation tomorrow, segregation forever.

It should be noted, however, that when confronted by determined Federal law officers he receded from this position and permitted the enrollment of Negro students in Alabama's public collegiate institutions.

REGICNAL VARIATION IN DESEGREGATION

From a wide spectrum of rapid changes in the desegregation picture these developments compiled largely by the United States Commission on Civil Rights [25] are instructive:

The Border States (Delaware, Kentucky, Maryland, Missouri, Oklahoma, West Virginia)

While the principle of desegregation seems well established, actual practice is spotty. All school districts in Delaware which had made no plans to eliminate separate Negro schools were ordered by the Federal Court in 1959 to desegregate; but five years later in 1963–64 40 percent of the Negro children attended all-Negro schools. In Kentucky 137 out of 169 school districts have integrated schools attended by 54,000 Negro students, or one-half of the Negro school children in the state. The other half attend segregated schools. In Maryland twenty of its twenty-four school districts are desegregated, but Baltimore City and five western Maryland counties account for 97 percent of all the state's desegregation. In Missouri only 213 of the state's 1,597 school districts enrolled students in mixed schools. About 40,000 Negro youth were in schools with whites. Oklahoma, too, runs the gamut from wholly desegregated to wholly segregated school districts. All school districts in West Virginia had some integration and it was estimated in 1963 that 60 percent of the Negro children attended integrated school. West Virginia State College—once all-Negro—now actually has a slight majority of white students enrolled. As an investigator of the United States Commission on Civil Rights stated: "All in all, West Virginia has reached the point where it no longer fits the southern school mold."

In the early stages of the integration process a number of Negro teachers in all the border states were displaced, notably in Oklahoma where a survey by the State Department of Education in 1961 revealed that 394 Negro teachers had been released. Placement of Negro teachers in that state seems to be limited to all-Negro schools; in the other border states some Negro teachers work in integrated schools.

Generally, the developing climate in these schools is reflected by the following statement of the Kentucky State Department of Education:

There is very definite evidence that changing positive attitudes are taking place. Both races are growing in maturity, in education and in human development and relations.

The Deep South (Alabama, Georgia, Louisiana, Mississippi, South Carolina)

These states contain 636 school districts, but only fourteen of them were desegregated by the end of 1964. A hard core resistance to desegregation characterizes the educational climate in them.

Public high school desegregation had its first test in Alabama when thirteen Negro students were enrolled in Tuskeegee High School, Macon County, Alabama. Thereafter the school's 250 white students walked out. Then the school was closed. Immediately the Negro students were sent by the Federal court to enroll in another high school. This, too, was closed. At the end of the 1963–64 school term, the issue of the integration of public schools in Macon County, Alabama, was still undecided. Undecided also was the issue in the major cities of Birmingham and Mobile, where the Fifth Circuit Court of Appeals had issued desegregation orders. Pending was litigation in which Negro plaintiffs, supported by the United States Department of Justice, have contended that the governor of the state and the state board of education control education in Alabama and that, therefore, the Court should order the organization of the schools of the state into "a unitary, non-racial system." The court has not yet made so sweeping a ruling, but it had, by fall of 1964, ordered desegregation in four other Alabama counties, all of which agreed to comply.

In Georgia the only school system which actually had a desegregation program in operation by June, 1964, was the city of Atlanta, but only fifty-three of its 46,400 Negro children had by then been placed in biracial schools. Muskogee County School Board in the state, which has jurisdiction over the city of Columbus, agreed unanimously to the desegregation of its public schools and library. By fall, 1964, four additional counties had undertaken to desegregate their schools.

In Louisiana the school districts of East Baton Rouge and St. Helena have been under court order to desegregate since 1960, but not a single Negro child had been placed in a biracial school up to June of 1964. The parish of New Orleans was the only school district in the state where desegregation had commenced. Here, of the 59,000 Negro students enrolled in New Orleans public schools 107 were attending desegregated classes by mid-1964. Another 200 Negro children were attending biracial parochial schools.

The school systems of Mississippi and South Carolina remained completely segregated through 1963. All suits to force desegregation brought before the Federal District Judge in Mississippi had up to 1964 been dismissed and appeals were pending. By 1964 only ten of South Carolina's 235,000 Negro pupils were attending schools with whites.

For the school term 1963–64, desegregation accelerated in South Carolina, with six counties agreeing to admit Negroes to formerly white schools; and in Mississippi the first breach of lily-white policy was made when four counties complied with a court order to desegregate.

Other Southern States (Arkansas, Florida, North Carolina, Tennessee, Texas, Virginia)

Of 448,000 pupils enrolled in public schools in Arkansas in the 1962–63 school year 26.1 percent were Negro, but only 247 of the Negro pupils or two-tenths of one percent were then attending biracial schools. Despite the gigantic struggle for integration in Little Rock which brought Federal troops to the city to enforce Federal Court orders during the Eisenhower Administration [1957] there were by 1964 only seventy-eight Negro pupils in five grade levels in schools with whites. In the entire state 1,084 pupils were then attending biracial public schools.

Thirteen of Florida's sixty-seven county school systems had begun desegregation by 1964 and nearly four thousand Negro children were in biracial schools. In Dade County, the first school district to desegregate, a policy of nondiscrimination in the hiring and placement of teachers had been adopted. The Dade County school board declared:

> We do not believe we can teach democracy in our schools without demonstrating our belief in the way schools are operated. All employees are notified that they are expected to teach or work with other employees and to teach pupils and to supervise or to be supervised in their work by other employees without regard for the creed or color of any individual.[26]

North Carolina has a "pupil assignment law" which gives each of its 173 school districts the right to assign each pupil to a particular school. This device has been used effectively to slow down integration in the state to a snail's pace. Each Negro child complaining of discrimination in assignment has been compelled under rulings of the Federal District Court to exhaust every remedy of appeal in the state before coming into the Federal Court. The result is a long, drawn-out, expensive and cumbersome procedure which serves as a brake on the actual integration of Negro pupils.

Fewer than two of every one hundred Negro public school students in Tennessee were attending biracial classes. However, concurrent desegregation of big city and county school systems is more widespread in Tennessee than any other Southern state. In the state by 1964–65, forty-seven districts had been desegregated with more than 4,600 Negro children attending schools with whites. Nashville by the 1964–65 school year had reached the fifth grade in its grade-a-year desegregation plan.

By the 1964–65 school year 257 of Texas' 919 school districts had some form of desegregation plan and over 14,000 Negro pupils were attending biracial schools. This is an increase of thirteen school districts over the number which had desegregated in the previous year. However, more than 97 percent of Texas' Negro public school pupils still attend segregated schools.

Only 1,230 of Virginia's 229,105 Negro students were attending schools with white students in 1963—just over one-half of one percent. Of these more than eight hunderd were enrolled in the Washington, D.C., suburbs of northern Virginia and in the cities of Norfolk, Richmond and Roanoke. Only token desegregation existed in other school districts which had announced plans.

Ninety-six of the state's 128 school districts remained segregated in 1963. Most notorious of these had been the Prince Edward County School District, which abolished its public schools in 1960 rather than comply with a court desegregation order. By the 1964–65 school year, however, twenty-four new school districts in the state were desegregated.

HIGHER EDUCATION FOR NEGROES

The best available estimate of the number of Negro students attending American colleges and universities is about 225,000.[27] Although today substantial numbers of Negro students are attending both public and private

FIGURE 1—College Enrollment from 1953–1954 to 1963–1964 by Sex for 105 Predominantly Negro Institutions Contrasted with That of All Predominantly White Institutions in the United States

Note: This figure does not reflect enrollment of Negro students in other than predominantly Negro colleges and universities.

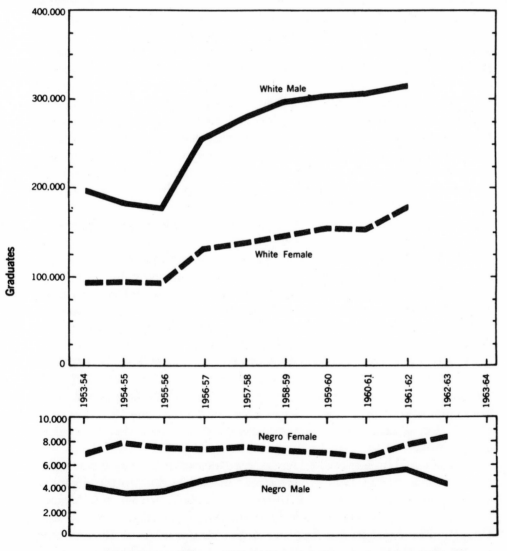

SOURCE: United States Office of Education, *Enrollment in Higher Education* (for years shown in the figure). Responses to questionnaire of the Phelps-Stokes Fund.

biracial institutions of higher education(mainly in the North and West), the main source of Negro college graduates was for many decades "the Negro College." The number of such institutions has changed very little since 1900. In 1900 there were 99, in 1950 there were 118, and in 1964 there were 116 four-year and two-year collegiate-rank institutions operated primarily for Negroes.[28]

Enrollment in institutions of higher education primarily for Negroes was 2,624 in 1900 and had increased to 74,526 by 1950. Figure 1 indicates the growth in enrollment over the last decade. Figure 2 shows the trend in the number of graduates produced by these schools. When it is realized that in 1900 only twenty-two women were graduated from these colleges, the increase in the number of women graduates is phenomenal.

Equally remarkable has been the increase of advanced degrees awarded by these colleges and universities. In 1920 the first record of the awarding of master's degrees by these schools showed that five had been granted. By 1950 the number had increased to 768, with women receiving about half of these. The growth has continued. Recently Howard University and Atlanta University has instituted programs leading to a doctoral degree in some fields, but these programs have not yet fully developed. Most doctoral degrees received by Negroes are granted by Northern white universities.

A study published in 1946 by Green [29] reported 381 Negroes known to have received Ph.D. degrees between 1876 and 1943. More than half of these had earned their first degree from a Negro college. A more recent study [30] records that between 1920 and 1962 there were awarded doctorates to 1,478 graduates of Negro colleges. There were 312 Ph.D. degrees awarded such graduates between 1960 and 1962 (about one percent of the total granted in the United States). If to this number we add degrees received by Negro graduates of white colleges for whom racial identification is impossible, it seems reasonable to estimate an annual production of Negro doctorates of between 160 and 175. By contrast the range in 1950 was between 30 and 50.

When one appraises the growth in enrollment, the increase in the number of graduates, the progress made in the number of its students seeking advanced degrees in graduate and professional schools which has been evidenced in Negro colleges, the conclusion is unmistakable that Negro institutions of higher education have played a unique role in advancing American democratic education. It is therefore important that some attention be given to the tremendous handicaps and disadvantages under which these institutions have been compelled to operate.

In 1950, there were 1,700 public and private colleges and universities in the United States. Of these, 118 were Negro institutions with 114 being located in the South and matriculating 85 percent of all the colored undergraduates from this section.[31] Approximately half of the Negro colleges of the United States were neither accredited nor approved by regional associations.[32]

Graduate and professional education for Negroes in the South was almost nonexistent as late as 1950. No work was offered leading to the doctorate. Two medical schools, Howard University Medical School and Meharry Medical School, supplied four-fifths of all Negro physicians and dentists. Opportunities for legal training and engineering were even more limited. By way of contrast, instruction was available for white students in medicine at thirty-one Southern institutions, in law at thirty-three, and in engineering at thirty-four.

In hearings before the Subcommittee of the Committee on Appropriations, 80th Congress, Mordecai W. Johnson, then president of Howard University, made the following summary on expenditures for education for Negroes in the seventeen Southern states:

> In states which maintain the segregated system of education there are about $137,000,000 annually spent on higher education. Of this sum $126,541,795 (including $86,000,000 of public funds) is spent on institutions for white youth only; from these institutions Negroes are rigidly excluded. Only $10,500,000 touches Negroes in any way; in fact, as far as state-supported schools are concerned, less than $5,000,000 touches Negroes. In these states there are about seventeen institutions undertaking to do higher education of college grade. . . .

FIGURE 2—College Graduates From 1953–1954 to 1963–1964, by Sex for 105 Predominantly Negro Institutions Contrasted with Those of All Predominantly White Institutions in the United States

Note: This figure does not reflect degrees granted Negroes in other than predominantly Negro colleges and universities.

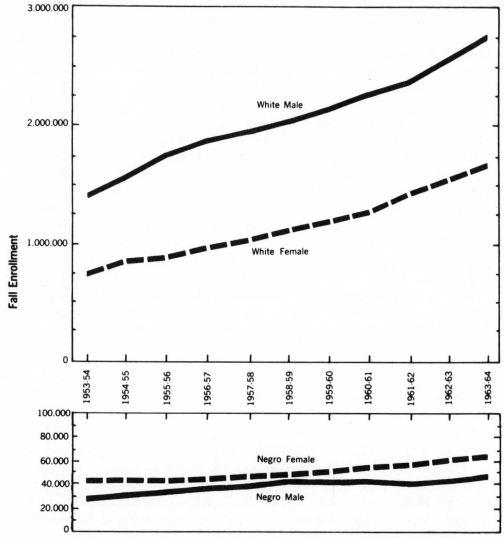

SOURCE: United States Office of Education, *Earned Degrees Conferred* (for years shown in the figure). Responses to questionnaire of the Phelps-Stokes Fund.

The amount of money spent on higher education by the states and Federal Government within these states is less than the budget of the University of Louisiana (in fact, only 65 per cent of the budget), which is maintained for a little over 1,000,000 in Louisiana. . . .

This is one index, but the most serious index is this: that this money is spread out over so wide an area and in such a way that in no one of these states is there anything approaching a first-class state university opportunity available to Negroes.[33]

Since the 1954 decision of the United States Supreme Court outlawing segregation in public schools, important changes have taken place in the higher education of the Negro in the South. Negro students are now admitted to formerly white institutions, especially to the graduate and professional schools. Since records are no longer kept on the basis of race, we have no statistics on the number of Negroes attending these institutions. Integration has become a two-way street. Approximately two hundred white students have enrolled in all-Negro colleges of the South since 1954 and the number is increasing.

In the border area, especially in West Virginia, Missouri and the District of Columbia, formerly Negro colleges have become truly integrated. West Virginia State College at Institute, W. Va., was all Negro in 1954. Immediately with the Supreme Court decision white students began enrolling, and the number has increased steadily until white students now make up over 50 percent of the enrollment. Bluefield State College at Bluefield, West Virginia, was also an all-Negro college in 1954 and now has an enrollment which is nearly 50 percent white. The faculties at both institutions are integrated.

Lincoln University in Jefferson City, Missouri, was the Negro Land Grant College in that state with an all-Negro enrollment in 1954. It also became integrated soon after that date and now has a 50 percent white enrollment.

Lincoln University in Oxford, Pennsylvania, the first higher institution established for Negroes in America, has always had an integrated faculty. The faculty is now about evenly divided between Negro and white and the student body, which is all male, is about 20 percent white.

Howard University has become a truly international institution, drawing faculty and student body from all races and many nationalities throughout the world.

Morgan State College in Baltimore, Maryland, enrolled an increasing number of white students in both the regular and evening sessions. Its faculty has always consisted of members of both races.

PROBLEMS OF NEGRO COLLEGES

Although the faculties and student bodies of many of the Negro colleges are becoming increasingly integrated, these institutions seem destined to remain, for some decades to come, a major factor in the college education of Negro youth in the United States. In view of this fact it is important to consider hindrances which prevent these schools from providing high quality education. The four most pressing problems facing these colleges are discussed below:

Adequate Financial Support   Financial support of the predominantly Negro state-supported college in the South still remains woefully inadequate. Historically, segregation in education has always been used as a weapon for discrimination. The doctrine of separate but unequal is deeply imbedded in the culture of the South. Consequently, the budget for almost any land-grant university with an enrollment of twenty thousand or more has an annual budget that far exceeds the combined budgets of all of the Negro state colleges and the additional thirty-two private Negro liberal arts colleges being supported by the United Negro College Fund.

An Adequately Trained Faculty Several forces operate in making it difficult to recruit and hold a highly competent faculty. Many other employment opportunities are now open to highly trained Negroes in industry and government. They therefore are attracted away from teaching. Formerly, teaching in a Negro college was almost the only employment open to them where they could use their advanced training. These new employment opportunities are more attractive than they might otherwise be because they are frequently more rewarding financially than the inadequately supported Negro college. Others leave teaching in these institutions because they prefer to bring their families to the North where they experience less hostility and discrimination because of race. Still others secure positions at "white" universities in the North because it is much easier to gain recognition and eminence as a scholar while attached to a "white" university.

A Student Body with an Academic Background for College Work The problem of an inadequately prepared student body can be attributed to two factors. In the first place most of the schools attended by Negroes below college level are themselves inferior because of the lack of financial support, teachers with little training and experience, old and barely adequate buildings and deprivation of the neighborhood where located. Thus, many Negro youth who enter college are not prepared up to the required level. The other factor is that the most capable students whose parents are economically able and are of a higher social class tend to send their youngsters to the "white" prestige colleges and state universities. This amounts to skimming off the cream of the academic crop that once attended in larger numbers the all-Negro college.

Consequences of an Inferior Status Assigned the Negro College by White Culture Another problem relating to the inferior status assigned to the Negro college is difficult to measure and assess in all its ramifications. The white majority seems never to hold the Negro college in as high esteem as institutions for whites. In the South, the Negro student is stigmatized as an individual because of the group to which he belongs. In reality he has a "double stigma" to overcome because the institution of higher education he attends, which is for the most part segregated, is also regarded as inferior. It has been subjected to a constant psychological attack in the press, on the screen and on the air. This "double stigma" has an adverse effect on personality, achievement, motivation and other factors contributing to success. This stigma of inferiority which is assigned to individuals and institutions in the segregated society was expressed in the Supreme Court's phrase, "separate educational facilities are inherently unequal."

FORCES FOR PROGRESS

One of the truly positive forces operating in the higher education of Negroes is the United Negro College Fund, which provides some of the

Teacher in New York preschool project introduces pupil
to the excitement of books.
(Ford Foundation Photo by Roy Stevens)

financial support for thirty-two private Negro liberal arts colleges. The aim of the fund is to strengthen the curriculum and faculty of these institutions. Their "cash capital fund campaign" was launched in 1964 with a goal of $50 million. The Ford Foundation contributed $15 million to this drive and by the end of 1964 over $30 million had been raised.

Other sectors in education give assistance of one type or another to the Negro colleges and universities. The American Council on Education has appointed an eight member Committee on Equality of Educational Opportunity headed by President Elvis Stahr of Indiana University. The aims of the committee are: to formulate plans to strengthen the quality of education at Negro institutions, to bring Negro colleges into closer contact with the rest of higher education in America and to broaden opportunities for Negro students and faculty members to become integrated into universities.

Another significant movement is the "Big Brother" program, which attempts to pair a large integrated university of the North with one of the the predominantly Negro colleges. The faculties are brought together, attempts are made to raise the educational sights of Negro students who have had inferior schooling prior to college admission, and it aims to provide aspiration and incentive to Negro students.

Many institutions in the North and West are trying to attract qualified Negro college students, at both graduate and undergraduate level. In January, 1964, Dr. Robert F. Goheen, President of Princeton University, said that the competition among colleges and universities for able Negro students was much more intense than the traditional competition for football players. He pointed out also that it was clear that the number of able colored students who had had adequate educational opportunities was very small. He also called for more money and a staff to develop and expand such a program. He thought that cooperative programs between a number of institutions would be helpful in reducing competition for the same students and in making the effort more effective.

The University of California took a much more positive step toward solving this problem early in 1964. A $100,000 scholarship fund was established to assist students who come from the disadvantaged segments of the country. Scholarships are to be provided during the 1964–65 school year for certain students of minority status whose grades might otherwise bar their admission to college. Dr. Jerzy Neyman, Professor of Statistics emeritus, University of California, is one of the prime movers in this project. He has indicated that professors from other universities, including Stanford, Harvard and the University of Illinois, had agreed previously that a regular channel, similar to the fund and program in California, should be provided to enable exceptionally talented people from slum areas to be incorporated into the intellectual life of the country.

COLLEGE MOTIVATION FOR AMERICAN NEGRO STUDENTS

The need for the kinds of programs as described above was highlighted in a study of Negro enrollment in the colleges and universities in Indiana. Early in 1964 a report on a survey of all thirty-one colleges and universities in Indiana showed that only 2.9 percent of the total enrollment for the current year was Negro. In the state 6 percent of the high school graduating classes of the previous spring were Negro. *In the Indiana colleges and universities there were actually more African Negro students enrolled than American Negro.* In addition, the survey found that 60 percent of the 2,595 Negro students in Indiana institutions of higher learning were enrolled only part time. By contrast, only 16 percent of the white students are enrolled part time.

Director Harold Hatcher of the Indiana Civil Rights Commission said that this survey found no evidence of discrimination because of race. Rather, he felt that the cause for the low percentage of Negro students could be attributed to the median income of all Negro families in Indiana, which was $1,500 below that of white families.[34]

The evidence seems to indicate that Negro students attending interracial colleges and universities are far less likely to drop out before graduation than are white students or Negro students attending segregated colleges. This was one of several very significant findings of a study entitled *The Negro Student at Integrated Colleges* by Kenneth B. Clark and Lawrence Plotkin under the sponsorship of the National Scholarship Service and Fund for Negro Students.[35] Some of the other important findings were: (1) The dropout rate was one-fourth the national one. Fewer than 10 percent of the Negro students studied failed to obtain a degree while approximately 40 percent of white students do not complete college. The authors advanced a motivational hypothesis to explain the very low dropout rate. These students feel motivated to complete college; "to drop out means that they will fall back into the ranks of the nonspecialized labor force where their race insures the permanence of low status." (2) Financial reasons for dropout lead all others. (3) The college grades received by these students were average with 31 percent earning an average "B" or better; less than 10 percent were graduated with honors; and a little more than one percent were elected to Phi Beta Kappa, the national scholastic honor society. (4) There was found no relationship between family income and academic success at college. (5) Academic success was found to be directly related to parents' occupational level. (6) The predictive value of intelligence tests administered in high school was not high.

PUBLIC SCHOOL EDUCATION FOR NEGROES IN THE NORTH

During the period since World War II, Negroes have migrated into the cities of the North at an unprecedented pace.[36] Housing is more segregated in the largest cities of the North than it was thirty years ago. Housing patterns have developed along social-class and caste lines and have therefore created *de facto* segregated neighborhoods and schools.

The first important fact about racial composition of public elementary schools in sixteen states in the North and West is that the percentage of nonwhite pupils greatly exceeds the proportion of nonwhites in the total population. Consider the nine largest cities. In Buffalo, Pittsburgh and St. Louis, the percentage of minority group children in the public elementary schools was more than double the proportion of the total population. In Chicago, New York and Philadelphia, it was almost exactly twice the total population percentage. Only in Baltimore, Detroit and Washington, D. C., was it proportionately less than twice the total population percentage. In the medium-sized cities, Camden, New Jersey, and Oakland, California, there were approximately more than twice as many Negroes in public elementary schools as in the general population. The small cities of Orange, New Jersey, had more than twice the proportion of Negroes in its elementary schools as in the total population.

The second important fact is that in five major cities, Baltimore, Newark, Philadelphia, St. Louis and Washington, the percentage of minority group children in the public elementary schools exceeded 50 percent of the total elementary school enrollment, the range being from 53 percent in Philadelphia to 86 percent in Washington. In six more the proportion was approaching 50 percent: 49.3 percent in Camden; 46 percent in Chicago; 46.2 percent in Detroit (that is, for all schools, high and elementary); 47.3 percent in Oakland, and 48.9 percent in Orange, New Jersey. In only four of the cities, Buffalo, Pittsburgh, Plainfield and Montclair, was the proportion below 40 percent, the range being from 32 percent in Montclair to 37 percent in Plainfield.

ACHIEVING RACIAL BALANCE IN SCHOOLS

It is well to note the significance of these concentrations of Negro population in terms of concepts of *de facto* segregation developed by social psychologists, educators and other experts.

School administrators have found Negro concentrations in schools in percentages ranging from 46 to 99 percent to be grounds for administrative action to reduce racial imbalance.

Pupil assignment to achieve desirable racial balance is not a simple process. Most Northern and Western cities have been operating public schools for seventy-five years or more. Many school buildings still in use were built fifty to seventy-five years ago. The size and location of these buildings were determined by the population density of the period in which they were built. New schools have been added and existing buildings enlarged to accommodate increased population. But change in population density has made many older schools in large cities inadequate for the present school population of the geographic area they serve.

St. Louis can be used as an example of this.[37] In the period between desegregation of the schools in September, 1955, and the school year 1961–62, the white elementary school population of St. Louis decreased from 44,779 to 37,669, and the Negro enrollment increased from 27,921 to 45,000.

The Negro-white inversion during this period was accompanied by an expanding of the Negro population from the central city line into the West End area in large numbers. The now crowded West End, a 98 percent white section in 1950, had become 64 percent Negro by 1960. Soldan High School, which serves this area as a general high school, was 74 percent white after desegregation in 1955 and 99 percent Negro in 1962. The eleven elementary schools in the West End district in 1955 ranged from 45 to 100 percent white in re-enrollment; six were over 90 percent or more white. In October, 1962, the school administration made a head count. At that date there was one more elementary school in the West End district than in 1955, making a total of twelve. All but two of the twelve schools were over 90 percent Negro.

Of greater importance, the enrollment in these schools had increased from 9,892 in 1955 to 19,527 in 1962. The classroom space which had been sufficient to accommodate the area's children in 1955 had become grossly inadequate because of the change in the density of the population. Enrollment in one elementary school in 1962 was almost three times its November, 1955, enrollment. Obviously, schools planned for some 10,000 pupils could not accommodate twice that number. St. Louis' partial answer has been to transfer about 5,000 of the pupils officially enrolled in these schools to distant and almost always predominantly white schools until the building program catches up with the increase in pupils.

New York City provides some interesting statistics and emerging patterns which are helpful in interpreting trends that are developing in other cities of the North. Three population trends stand out which have a direct bearing on what is happening to the public school system.

First, the population is more mobile; second, it is more segregated racially, and third, neighborhoods have become essentially of one social-class. Between 1950 and 1957, New York City lost a white population of about 750,000 and gained an ethnically identifiable Negro and Puerto Rican population of about 650,000.[38] During the period from 1956 to 1964 the number of predominantly Negro and Puerto Rican elementary and junior high schools in the city doubled.

In 1964, there were 264,616 Negro pupils in the New York City school system, an increase of 91,659, or 53 percent, over the 1957–58 total of 172,957. For 1964 there were 177,544 Puerto Rican children in the system, an increase of 48,564, or 37.6 percent. There were 596,356 "others" (a term used by the New York City school system to refer to students not Negro or Puerto Rican) in the system, a decrease of 54,323, or 8.3 percent.

As a result of these population changes the number of elementary and junior high schools with a Negro or Puerto Rican enrollment of 85 to 90 percent had increased. Such elementary schools had increased from 64 in 1957–58 to 134 in 1964 and the number of junior high schools had increased during this period from 13 to 31. This change took place during a period when the board of education was trying to improve the ethnic distribution of children in schools.

CULTURAL DEPRIVATION AND LOW ACADEMIC ACHIEVEMENT

Much of the current thinking about the problems of the culturally deprived child in our urban areas has been focused on the Negro. The authorities in the behavioral sciences are agreed that cultural deprivation is not race-related. The ego development of individuals in each subculture (including the subcultures in the Negro minority) is directly influenced by the special nature and quality of multidimensional cultural factors which are operating in the culture. Therefore, cultural deprivation is not specific to racial groups, but to cultural factors. Ausubel sums up the position thus:

> Many of the ecological features of the segregated Negro subculture impinge on personality development in early childhood are not specific to Negroes as such, but are characteristic of most lower-class populations. This fact is not widely appreciated by white Americans and hence contributes to much anti-Negro sentiment: many characteristic facets of the Negro's value system and behavior pattern are falsely attributed to his racial membership, whereas they really reflect his predominant membership in the lower social class.[39]

Some of the cultural factors which will be described below contribute to deprivation which manifests itself in low levels of motivation, low achievement on standardized tests, negative self-evaluation, low levels of aspiration and behavior which deviates from accepted middle-class norms.

The urban population has grown and is growing increasingly homogeneous. Both the inner city and the suburbs have become a series of "one social class" neighborhoods. People in these neighborhoods tend to be alike in income level, general employment classification, amount of schooling completed, racial identity and in ethnic background. The Negro migrant to the urban areas of the North must nearly always live in the worst and most crowded slum areas that are typically inhabited by his group. His economic resources, level of culture, sophistication and style of living all operate to force him to seek the "ghetto" as a place to live. Once in the "ghetto," he becomes even more isolated from the mainstream of American life than he was before moving to the city. His neighborhood, like other "one social class" neighborhoods, tends to be self-contained and an island unto itself. It is in this environment that children begin to take on a value system and patterns of behavior that are inconsistent with the demands and requirements for academic success in schools.

Typically, the neighborhood is more segregated racially than two or three decades ago; the school located there has ceased to represent a cross section of American life. The population in the neighborhood school is homogeneous. Therefore, the school no longer provides an opportunity for the cross-fertilization of ideas and cultures. It provides no opportunities for young people of different backgrounds to learn anything about each other. It provides no first-hand experiences which will help children to build understandings of and appreciations for people who are different.

The school has become the dominant institution in the control and socialization of youth because it is a major force in determining status transitions of youth. The child who is at the bottom of the socio-economic scale is isolated and completely apart from successful examples or models in the community and schools that can be emulated. Examples of success and of behavior that leads to high level attainment in the broader society are not a part of his environment at all. His world is void of abstract symbols, ideas, abstractions and a high level of verbal meanings. Therefore, it is not surprising that he has difficulty in making high scores on standardized intelligence and achievement tests.

The school tends to reflect the neighborhood in which it is located. Thus, schools in the higher social class neighborhoods tend to be of the "silk stocking" type with the better buildings and facilities, better and more enriched programs and better qualified teachers. At the bottom of this scale are typically found the all-Negro schools in the all-Negro residential areas of the inner city. These schools are nearly always inferior in quality. The larger society regards the people who attend these schools as being inferior and assigns to them a stigma and a negative evaluation. The teachers, the community, and the board in charge of operating the schools do not expect anything other than low-level performance. The curriculum is therefore accommodating and geared to a low level of ability and to shoddy academic performance. The consequence is that retardation begins for a large number of these children very soon after they enter school. By the time one-third of these children reach the fourth grade they are performing one grade behind their grade level. The longer they remain in school, the more retarded they become. It is a combination of these and other factors, thet most important of which is that of enforcing a negative self-evaluation on the Negro child that disarms him psychologically.

It is with these kinds of problems in our society that our educators are now working. Pioneer work of such scholars as Allison Davis [40] and Martin Jenkins [41] has provided us with a better understanding of the theoretical and practical significance of low scores that minority groups make on intelligence tests. As a result, psychologists now attribute the low average performance on intelligence tests of subcultures to cultural factors. Therefore, in the decade to come, the two most pressing and compelling factors related to the education of the Negro in America will be: (1) the desegregation of the schools, and (2) providing an adequate and meaningful education for the culturally deprived.

There now exist some notable examples of efforts to solve these problems in our major cities. The Higher Horizons Program in New York City, The Great Cities Project in fourteen major cities supported with Ford Foundation funds, the Banneker schools in St. Louis, and the Amidon School in Washington, all operate on the assumption that present problems of the culturally deprived youth in our schools can be solved by an expansion of services that have worked with middle-class white children. These are sometimes referred to as *saturation programs* which provide for more guidance, more remedial instruction, more emphasis on reading, more individual psychological testing, and more cultural programs. None of these programs has made extensive use of research in the behavioral sciences in designing programs and procedures. In the future more attention will have to be given to these areas for theoretical and empirical bases upon which to construct educational programs. Out of this search and effort may come answers which can be applied to the vital educational problems in America and in the emerging nations of the world.

NOTES

[1] John Hope Franklin, *From Slavery to Freedom* (New York: Alfred E. Knopf, 1947), p. 80.

[2] W. A. Low, "The Education of Negroes Viewed Historically," in V. A. Clift, *et al.* (eds.), *Negro Education in America* (New York: Harper & Row, 1962), p. 35.

[3] George S. Brookes, *Friend Anthony Benezet* (Philadelphia: University of Pennsylvania Press, 1937), pp. 46–47.

[4] E. Franklin Frazier, *The Negro in the United States* (New York: The Macmillan Co., 1957), p. 418.

[5] One of the best and most reliable references on the early education of the Negro is Carter G. Woodson, *The Education of the Negro Prior to 1861* (New York: G. P. Putnam's Sons, 1919). One of the best references for later years is Horace Mann Bond, *Education of the Negro in the American Social Order* (New York: Prentice-Hall, Inc., 1934.)

[6] Franklin, *op. cit.*, p. 200.

[7] Franklin, *ibid.*, p. 201.

[8] Woodson, *op. cit.*, p. 340.

[9] H. S. Ashmore, *The Negro and the Schools* (Chapel Hill: University of North Carolina Press, 1954), pp. 3–4.

[10] Franklin, *op. cit.*, pp. 383–84.

[11] Report of the U.S. Commission on Education, McKee's Report to the House Committee on Education and Labor, 1870, p. 187.

[12] W. E. B. Du Bois, *The Negro Common School* (Atlanta, Georgia: Atlanta University Press, 1901), p. 38.

[13] For full discussion of this case see Constance Baker Motley, "The Legal Status of the Negro," later in this volume, p. 484.

[14] Ashmore, *op. cit.*, pp. 17–18.

[15] For further information on the inequality of the segregated school system in the South, see Fourteenth U.S. Census, vol. 11, p. 1043; *The Negro Year Book, 1925–26* (Tuskeegee, Alabama, Negro Yearbook Publishing Co.); Bulletin No. 39, Department of Interior, Bureau of Education ("Negro Education"); N. C. Newbold, *Annals of the American Academy of Political and Social Sciences,* November, 1928, p. 209; and V. A. Clift, *School and Society,* 72 (October 7, 1952).

[16] W. A. Low, *op. cit.,* pp. 53–54.

[17] For fuller analysis of this and other education cases which came before the United States Supreme Court see Motley, *op. cit.* p. 484.

[18] For details on this new pattern of discrimination see V. A. Clift, *op. cit.,* p. 226.

[19] *Sipuel* vs. *The University of Oklahoma; McLaurin* vs. *The University of Oklahoma; Sweatt* vs. *The University of Texas.* See Motley, *op. cit.,* p. 484.

[20] These cases were from: Claredon, South Carolina (*Briggs* vs. *Elliot*); Prince Edward County, Va. (*Davis* vs. *County School Board*); Topeka, Kansas (*Brown* vs. *Board of Education*); Wilmington, Delaware (*Belton* vs. *Gebhart*), and Washington, D.C. (*Bolling* vs. *Sharpe*).

[21] Editorial, *Baltimore Sun,* March 8, 1959.

[22] *Southern School News* (Nashville, Tenn.), 10, No. 6 (December, 1963), p. 1.

[23] See Table I for detailed distribution and extent of desegregation.

[24] *Southern School News* [(II, No. 2 (August, 1964 p. 1)] The eleven Southern states in the fall of 1964 had desegregated 127 colleges and universities, leaving eighty-three still segregated; all eighty colleges in the border area have desegregated.

[25] From unpublished material of the commission.

[26] From unpublished material of the Commission.

[27] Reported 1963–64 enrollment from 105 colleges and universities attended predominantly by Negroes totalled 107,278. To these enrollees must be added Negro students attending colleges where white students predominate. Following an intensive study of the latter schools, Dr. Benjamin Fine has estimated an average enrollment of about 125,000 Negro students. See Benjamin Fine, "Reverse Integration Will Bring End of All-Colored Higher Learning." *North American Newspaper Alliance,* (November 3, 1963).

[28] This final number may not be absolutely accurate because of the rapid change in racial enrollment in some institutions in states where desegregation has taken place.

[29] Harry Washington Greene, *Holders of Doctorates Among American Negroes* (Boston: Meador Publishing Company, 1946), p. 74.

[30] Lindey R. Harmon and Herbert Soldz, compilers, *Doctorate Production of United States Universities, 1920–1962* (Washington, D.C., Publication No. 1142, National Research Council, National Academy of Science 1963), p. 963.

[31] G. Myrdal, *American Dilemma* (New York: Harper & Brothers, 1944), p. 947.

[32] Martin D. Jenkins, *Journal of Negro Education,* XVII (Spring, 1948), p. 207.

[33] Hearings before Subcommittee of the Committee on Appropriations, House of Representatives, 80th Congress, February, 1947, p. 245.

[34] Harold Hatcher, *Survey of Negro Enrollment at Indiana Colleges* (Indianapolis: Indiana Civil Rights Commission, 1964), pp. 10–61.

[35] Kenneth B. Clark and Lawrence Plotkin, *The Negro Student at Integrated Colleges* (New York: National Scholarship Service and Fund for Negro Students, 1963), pp. 7–9.

[36] Karl E. and Alma F. Taeuber, "The Negro Population in the United States," earlier in this volume, p. 36.

[37] The statistics presented here are taken from an unpublished report of the United States Commission on Civil Rights.

[38] Dan W. Dodson, *Interpreting the "Inner City,"* Human Relations Monograph No. 12 (New York: New York University, Center for Human Relations and Community Studies, 1961), p. 11.

[39] David P. Ausubel and Pearl Ausubel, "Ego Development Among Segregated Negro Children," in *Education in Depressed Areas,* A. Harry Passow (ed.). (New York: Bureau of Publications, Teachers College, Columbia University, 1963), p. 113. By permission.

[40] W. Allison Davis, with John Dollard, *Children of Bondage* (Washington, D.C.: American Council on Education, 1940); Kenneth W. Eells, under the chairmanship of Allison Davis, *Intelligence and Cultural Differences,* (Chicago: University of Chicago Press, 1951).

[41] Martin Jenkins, "Intelligence of Negro Children" in Paul A. Witty, ed. *Intelligence in a Changing Universe* (New York: Department of Supervisors and Directors of Instruction of the National Education Association of the United States, 1940).

chapter 8   *Harry V. Richardson*

The Negro
in American Religious Life

Harry V. Richardson. President of The Interdenominational Theological Center (Atlanta, Georgia; President of Georgia Council of Churches. Author of *Dark Glory*.

The great majority of Negro slaves imported into the Western Hemisphere came from the west coast of Central Africa. The region that is now the nation of Ghana was one of the focal points of the trade.

The natives of this region who were caught and sold into slavery came from tribes that had well-developed religions. Like most primitive peoples, religion played a large and fervent part in their lives. They were animistic, they believed in spirits, good and bad, and they practiced fetishism. In such religions with a multiplicity of spirits, there is usually one dominant or father spirit who is creator, ruler and protector. References to this dominant spirit, sometimes called Anyambe or Onyambe, are found in the language and practices of the people today, both Westernized and native.

Thus the fact that the African slaves already had a highly developed religious life when they arrived in America probably explains why many slaves, as they had the opportunity, took so readily to the Christian religion, and had so little trouble making the transition despite language and cultural barriers.

From the beginning, there was a serious effort to convert the slaves to Christianity. Indeed, this was one of the justifications for the slave trade. But for the first hundred years the question of converting slaves was highly controversial, and therefore was not as widespread or as effective as it might have been.

For example, at the time when the importation of Negro slaves began, it was commonly believed that one Christian should not hold another Christian in bondage. This meant that when a slave became a Christian he also should have been freed. This would have been ruinous to those who had invested in slaves, and it led to much of the opposition that missionaries faced in their efforts to convert the slaves.

To settle the issue in Virginia the legislature of that colony declared in 1667 that baptism did not alter the condition of a person as to his bondage or freedom. This started a process of enactments and rulings that removed the Christian religion as a legal barrier to slavery in the colonies. In 1729 the Crown Attorney and Solicitor General ruled that baptism in no way change a slave's legal status. Two years previously the Bishop of London had declared:

> . . . Christianity does not make the least alteration in civil property; that the freedom which Christianity gives, is a freedom from the bondage of sin and Satan, and from the dominion of their lusts and passions and inordinate desires; but as to their outward condition they remained as before, even after baptism.[1]

As the principle became established, that conversion did not alter slave status, ministers and missionaries were freer to work among the slaves. The religious body that most actively undertook this work in the seventeenth and early eighteenth centuries was the Church of England through its Society for the Propagation of the Gospel in Foreign Parts. Since the Anglican Church was the major religious body in the colonies, the responsibility of winning converts to Christianity fell mainly upon the ministers of this church. However, for many reasons they were not able to devote adequate effort to the task. To assist in evangelizing the growing colonial population the Society for the Propagation of the Gospel was organized in 1701. Its specific duties were: "the care and instruction of our people settled in the colonies; the conversion of the Indian savages, and the conversion of the Negroes."

Other bodies were active in the colonial period, but on a much smaller scale. Chief among them were the Moravian Brethren, the Presbyterians and the Society of Friends. The Friends took the most positive stand against slavery of any of the religious bodies during this period. They alone made the possession of slaves a cause for expulsion from the Society.

It is the opinion of Marcus W. Jernigan, a student of colonial history, that prior to the American Revolution, comparatively few slaves were converted to Christianity. His reasons as summarized from a published discussion of the subject are:

1. Masters feared that conversion would interfere with slave labor. Slaves were required to work on Sundays, which conflicted with Christian teaching, and further, when converted, slaves would be equal in one respect to their masters, which would make them harder to control.

2. The general interest in religion was low in colonial times. Masters were not much interested in their own spiritual welfare, and consequently were not deeply concerned about the welfare of their slaves.

3. Many slaves were unable to understand religious teachings, due in large part to their lack of knowledge of the English language.

4. The slave's environment was not conducive to the Christian life.

5. The sparsely settled country and the difficulties of travel made it hard for ministers to serve their members, to say nothing of evangelizing the unchurched.[2]

It was not until the latter half of the eighteenth century, around the time of the American Revolution, that a number of significant developments took place that did much to spread Christianity among the slaves and to shape the course of Negro religion in America.

The Influence of Cotton

First of these developments was the increased production of cotton in response to a rapidly rising world demand. A series of remarkable inventions, beginning with the spinning and weaving machines in England and culminating in Whitney's cotton gin in America, greatly increased the output of cotton goods. The soil of the Southern colonies was admirably suited to grow the necessary cotton if an adequate supply of labor could be obtained. This labor was found in African Negro slaves, who first were legally imported into the country, then illegally smuggled, and all the while bred to meet the great demand. In 1790 there were approximately 700,000 slaves in the United States. In 1860 there were 4 million. Over 3 million were in twelve Southern states, engaged for the most part in producing the cotton and other crops that were rapidly building up the fortunes of the wealthier group among the Southern planters.

This concentration of Negroes on the farms and plantations of the South gave the busy evangelists of the time excellent opportunities to reach the Negroes and to win large numbers of them to Christianity.

The Evangelicals and the Slave

The second great development in Negro religion was the coming of the evangelical Christian bodies, particularly the Methodists, Baptists, and

Presbyterians. These groups in their zeal to evangelize the young America, gave much attention to the growing body of slaves. In the early stage they were strongly abolitionist. They felt that slavery was wrong, and they openly preached against it. Freeborn Garretson said in 1776:

> It was God, not man, that taught me the impropriety of holding slaves; and I shall never be able to praise him enough for it. My very heart has bled since that for slaveholders, especially those who make a profession of religion; for I believe it to be a crying sin.[3]

Bishop Asbury records in his Journal in 1780: "This I know. God will plead the cause of the oppressed though it gives offense to say so here. . . . I am grieved for slavery and the manner of keeping these poor people." [4]

Many preachers followed their words by freeing slaves they already held and by refusing to become slaveholders. In 1780 the Methodists required all traveling preachers to set their slaves free. The Baptists, because of their policy of local church government, were not as uniform or as effective in their attack on slavery as the Methodists. Yet in 1789 a Baptist Convention declared:

> Slavery is a violent depredation of the rights of nature and inconsistent with a republican government, and therefore, [we] recommend it to our brethren, to make use of their local missions to extirpate this horrid evil from the land; and pray Almighty God that our honorable legislature may have in their power to proclaim the great jubilee consistent with the principles of good policy.[5]

Although the evangelicals found it necessary to retreat considerably from the high ground they first had taken against slavery, they continued their efforts to convert the slaves, and to plead in the name of Christianity for amelioration of the more brutal aspects of slavery.

In seeking converts, the evangelicals had one great advantage over the Anglicans and other early missionaries. The evangelical religion was simple, personal and only slightly ritualistic. It was ideally suited to the unlettered masses of the colonial frontier both white and black. In order to become an Anglican it was necessary to know the creed, the catechism and other articles of faith, as well as to be able to follow the ritual of the service. To become a Methodist or Baptist it was only necessary to repent and accept Christ as personal Savior. This was a religion even the field-hand slave could understand. In the early evangelistic drives such as the Great Awakening and the Great Revival, large numbers of Negroes were converted. But if the simplicity of the evangelical faith did much to determine the number of Negroes who became Christians, the emotionalism of the early evangelical faith did much to determine the nature of Negro worship. The religion that the Negro masses first received was characterized by such phenomena as laughing, weeping, shouting, dancing, barking, jerking, prostration and speaking in tongues. These were regarded as evidence of the Spirit at work in the heart of man, and they were also taken as evidence of the depth and sincerity of the conversion. It was inevitable, therefore, that early Negro worship should be filled with these emotional elements.

Although there is some tendency to regard high emotionalism as a phenomenon peculiar to the Negro church, in reality it is a hangover from

"The old time Negro preacher has not yet been given the niche in which he properly be-longs. . . . It was through him that the people of diverse languages and customs who were brought here from diverse parts of Africa and thrown into slavery were given their first sense of unity and solidarity."   James Weldon Johnson

(Standard Oil of N.J. Photo)

Interior of the First African Baptist Church in Savannah, Georgia. Organized in 1788, it is perhaps the oldest Negro church in the United States. (Photo by Roland Mitchell)

the days of frontier religion. It should also be said that emotionalism of this type is to be found today chiefly among the less cultured rural and urban churches.[6]

The Negro Preacher

The third development that did much to shape the course of Negro religion was the rise of Negro preachers. These leaders began to appear in the latter part of the eighteenth century, the time when large numbers of Negroes were being converted to Christianity. Prominent among them were Black Harry (c. 1782), who traveled with Bishop Asbury and was a great attraction; David George (c. 1775), preacher of the first Negro Baptist church at Silver Bluff, South Carolina; George Liele, of Burke County, Georgia, an eloquent preacher to blacks and whites; Andrew Bryan of Georgia (1737–1812), founder of the First African Baptist Church of Savannah; John Chavis (c. 1801), who was made a missionary to slaves by the Presbyterians, and Henry Evans, organizer of the white Methodist church at Fayetteville, North Carolina, in 1790.[7] Most unusual among these early preachers was Lemuel Haynes, 1753–1833, a mulatto of learning and eloquence who through all of his ministry pastored only white Congregational churches in New England. He was quite a theologian, and debated with power the theological issues of his time.

The Negro preacher played a significant part in the social and religious development of Negro life. First, preaching was an outlet for leadership ability. It was the one position of leadership permitted Negroes, and the office carried considerable prestige. It did much to keep aspiration alive among gifted Negro men. Secondly, the Negro preacher was able to communicate religion to the slave in a useful and intimate form. Being one of the people and suffering with them, he could make religion not only a discipline, but also a living ground of hope.

The preachers' task was hard, however. While preaching to slaves, they could not attack slavery, at least openly. The preacher himself was always suspected and closely watched as a potential source of rebellion. The controls over slave meetings even for worship were so rigid and severe that an attack on the slave system would have readily brought down terrible penalties upon both preacher and people.

Yet from the beginning the church served as the main outlet through which the slaves could express their sufferings and dissatisfaction. Although it was done covertly, the church rendered two great needed services to the slaves: first, it kept alive the consciousness that the slave system was wicked; and second, it kept alive the hope that in the plan of a good, just God, the wicked, brutal system under which they lived would have to pass away.

It should be said, however, that not all preachers were patient or unresisting. Nat Turner, for instance, who led the bloody revolt of 1831, was a Baptist exhorter.

In the time of slavery there were three distinct types of slave churches: the "mixed" church with slaves as members of the congregation; the separate church under white leadership; and the separate church under Negro leadership. All three types existed simultaneously, but the gradual tendency was toward the separate, all-Negro church.

THE EMANCIPATION AND AFTER

On September 22, 1862, President Lincoln issued the Emancipation Proclamation that was to become effective January 1, 1863. Although it was not immediately enforceable in many parts of the South since unoccupied sections were outside the control of the national government, freedom became a reality for all Negroes with the close of the Civil War. Thenceforth they were free to move and to organize as they wished.

The great mass of undeveloped, unchristianized freemen in the South presented opportunity for many kinds of humanitarian service. Along with philanthropic whites who came into the South to render educational as well as religious aid to the freedmen, Negro missionaries also came as representatives of independent Negro denominations, seeking to win members for their particular churches from among the former slaves.

Partly because of their racial appeal, partly because of their greater activity, the Negro workers won far more members than the representatives of the white church bodies. In fact, the early days of the Reconstruction were marked by a strong tendency toward independent, all-Negro religious organizations. In the decade between 1860 and 1870 the African Methodist Episcopal Zion Church, one of the two principal Negro Methodist bodies, grew from 26,746 members to 200,000. The African Methodist Episcopal Church, the leading Negro Methodist group, in 1880 claimed a membership of 400,000. For both churches most of their members were the freedmen in the rural South.

Baptists quickly became the most numerous group among Negroes in the South. In this church, as in the Methodist, the tendency was toward independent, all-Negro units. Even in cases where Negroes had been members of white churches on amicable terms, there still was a desire for the separate all-colored church.

THE PRESENT CHURCH

Major Negro Denominations

Denomination	Number of Members	Number of Churches	Number of Pastors	Sunday School Members
National Baptist Convention, U.S.A.	5,000,000	26,000	27,500	2,407,000
National Baptist Convention of America	2,668,000	11,398	7,598	2,500,000
AME Church	1,166,000	5,878	5,878	363,432
AME Zion Church	770,000	4,083	2,400	199,250
CME Church	444,493	2,523	1,792	115,424

The Baptists

Prior to the Civil War, the Baptist Church among Negroes consisted almost entirely of local congregations. Organization into district, state or national bodies was difficult both for slaves and free Negroes. With the coming of freedom, the organization of larger bodies rapidly took place. The first state Convention was organized in North Carolina in 1866, just one

St. Mark's Methodist Church in New York City sits in splendor on its own island.
(Photo by Roland Mitchell)

Ephesus Seventh Day Adventist Church lifts its spire high above Lenox Avenue. Westward is Morningside Heights dominated by the tower of Riverside Church.

(Photo by Roland Mitchell)

year after the close of the war. Alabama and Virginia followed in 1867, and by 1870 all the Southern states had state conventions.

On the national level, the Negro groups at first were affiliated with white national bodies. In 1867, however, the Consolidated American Baptist Convention was organized and continued until 1880, when the National Baptist Convention was established at Montgomery, Alabama. Three smaller conventions grew out of this body: the Foreign Mission Baptist Convention of the U.S.A., 1880; the American National Baptist Convention, 1880, and the American National Educational Baptist Convention, 1893. All of these were united in 1895 at Atlanta, Georgia, into the National Baptist Convention of the U.S.A., which was incorporated in 1915. This convention when formed had three million members, and thereby became the largest single denomination of Negro Christians in the world. Such tremendous growth in the fifty years from 1865 to 1915 reveals the rapidity with which the church grew among Negroes after Emancipation.

With the passing years the National Baptist Convention of the U.S.A. [Incorporated] has suffered a number of splits. The largest of these separating groups is the National Baptist Convention of America.

The tendency toward division, so characteristic of Baptists, continues to the present time. Today there are three national conventions: the National Baptist Convention of the U.S.A., the National Baptist Convention of America and the Progressive Baptist Convention.

Although divided, Baptists are by far the largest single group of Negro Christians in the world. They have approximately 7,668,000 members, 37,300 churches, and 4,900,000 children in church schools. There are 35,000 preachers in the Baptist ministry.

There are no distinctive doctrines or patterns of policy in the Negro Baptist Churches. They adhere in all basic essentials to the beliefs and practices of the major Baptist bodies of the nation. The Baptists have played a great part in the progress of the Negro group in education, in civic leadership and in other ways. They also have an extensive foreign mission program.

The Methodist Churches

Methodists were early active among Negroes both in colonial and post-Revolutionary times. They won large numbers to Methodism and took them readily into church membership. They organized a number of Negro congregations, usually presided over by white preachers, and took a number of Negroes into the ministry.

The Negro members, both slave and free, were usually restricted, however, in their participation in church life. They sat in segregated seats during services, and communed after the others or in special services. Dissatisfaction with such arrangements steadily increased, so that by 1785 in several Northern cities Negro members had organized themselves into separate congregations. In 1787 a company of Negroes in Philadelphia withdrew from the white church, and under the leadership of Richard Allen, a free and well-to-do Negro, built a chapel where they held separate services under an ordained Negro Episcopal priest.

Despite opposition from the white Methodists in Philadelphia, in 1793 Bishop Asbury dedicated the chapel as Bethel Church, and in 1799 he ordained Richard Allen a deacon.

In 1814, out of litigation brought by the white Methodists, the Supreme

Court of Pennsylvania ruled that Bethel Church was an independent body. In 1816 Richard Allen and others called together representatives of separate churches similar to Bethel that had been organized in Delaware, Maryland and New Jersey. This meeting resulted in the formation of the African Methodist Episcopal Church, the second separate Negro Methodist denomination. The first was the Union Church of Africans which had been incorporated in Wilmington, Delaware, in 1813. This church, however, has grown very little. About the same time a third separatist movement, much like the first, resulted in the formation of the African Methodist Episcopal Zion Church in 1820.

Prior to the Civil War, the Negro Methodist churches were not able to expand widely. The national pattern of church life characteristic of Methodism with its itinerant ministry and traveling officers, was not possible for Negroes, either slave or free. With the coming of freedom, permitting the movement and evangelism necessary for expansion, the Negro Methodist bodies grew very rapidly, but not as much as the Baptists. The Christian Methodist Episcopal Church, discussed below, illustrates the rise and growth of a church after the Emancipation.

The AME Church

The AME Church today is truly international in scope. It has churches in Africa, Canada and the Caribbean area. Figures on membership are only approximate because of the lack of reports. The last reported figure [1951] gave an inclusive membership of 1,166,301 and 5,878 churches. In the same year [1951] 6,472 Sunday Schools were reported, with 262,432 members. It seems that today this church has somewhere between a million and a million and a half members.

The AME Church is divided into eighteen episcopal districts. The governing bodies of the church are the General Conference, which meets quadrennially; the Council of Bishops and the General Board. The work of the church is under the supervision of ten Boards or Departments, such as the Board of Missions, the Board of Church Extension, the Department of Education and the Department of Evangelism. There are five publications, the *Christian Recorder*, *The AME Review*, the *Voice of Missions*, the *Southwestern Christian Recorder*, and the *Woman's Missionary Recorder*. The church maintains a publishing house in Nashville, Tennessee.

The AMEZ Church

The origin of the AMEZ Church is much like that of the AME. In 1796 a group of colored members, led by James Varick and others, withdrew from the John Street Methodist Church in New York City to escape the problems of segregation in church life. In 1800 they built a church which they named Zion. They at first maintained cooperative relationships with the white Methodist Church, but in 1820 this cooperation failed. Joining with separate Negro congregations in other cities, in 1821 they held an annual conference, and elected James Varick their first bishop. Several elders had been ordained by sympathetic white Methodist ministers. This gave them a ministry.

This church, like all the others, experienced its great growth after the

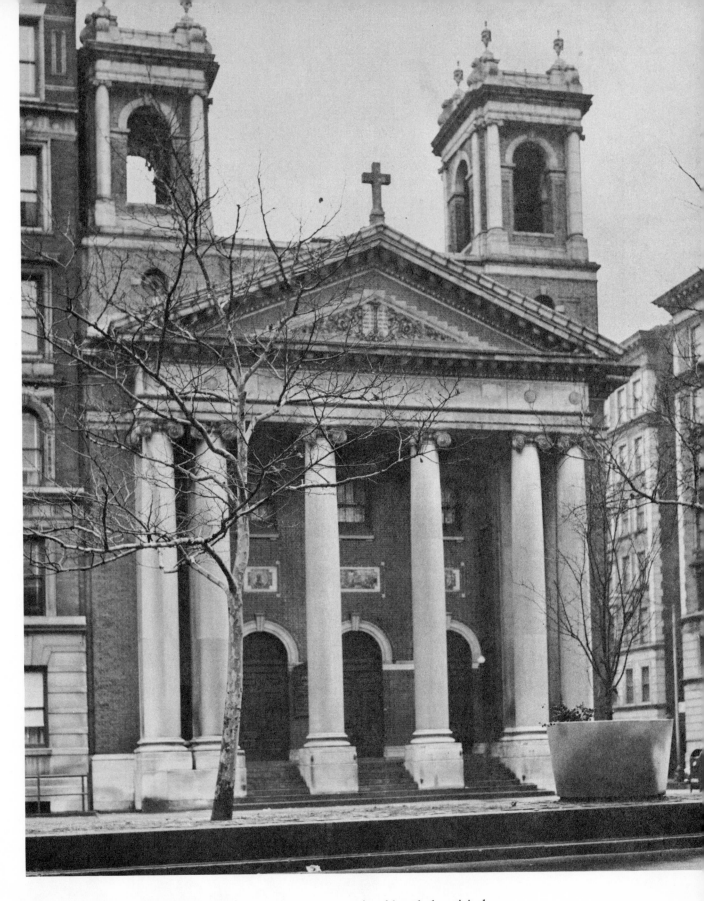

Harlem's Catholic churches have continued to serve the community although the original parishioners have left the area. (Photo by Roland Mitchell)

The parsonage of Salem Methodist Church
was the boyhood home of poet Countee Cullen.
(Photo by Roland Mitchell)

Dorothy Maynor, famed soprano, is the wife
of the pastor of St. James Presbyterian
Church and conducts the choir.
(Photo by Roland Mitchell)

Civil War. By 1880 fifteen annual conferences had been organized in the South. Today this church performs missionary work in West Africa, South America and the West Indies.

The CME Church

The third major Negro Methodist body is the Christian Methodist Episcopal Church. Originally it was called the Colored ME Church, but in 1956 the word *Colored* was changed to *Christian*.

At the close of the Civil War there were over 250,000 Negro members in the Methodist Episcopal Church, South. They had long been dissatisfied with the segregation and restrictions imposed upon the colored members. Immediately after the war, in 1866, they appealed to the General Conference of the ME Church, South, to be set apart in a church of their own. The conference ruled that wherever there were sufficient numbers, they be set aside in separate annual conferences. It further appointed a commission to study the request for a separate church and to report to the next general conference. In 1870 the commission recommended that the Negro members be organized into a church of their own. Later that year, in December, the first General Conference of the CME Church was held at Jackson, Tennessee. Two Negro bishops were elected, Henry Miles and Richard H. Vanderhorst.

In the years since the separation the ME Church, South, has kept its interest in the CME Church, and has assisted it in many ways, especially in organizing and operating the educational program.

This church, like the others, has had substantial growth. It now has 444,493 members and 2,523 churches.

Negro Membership in White Churches

The great majority of Negro Christians are in five separate and predominantly Negro denominations. All major church bodies, however, have some Negro members, and sometimes this membership is large. When these memberships are added together, they constitute a significant segment of Negro Christendom.

The Methodist Church has the largest number of Negro members, 370,315. This membership at present constitutes a separate, nationwide "Central Jurisdiction," organized on racial grounds. Efforts are now underway in this church to remove this segregated arrangement of the Negro constituency.

Examples of churches with sizeable Negro membership are the Protestant Episcopal Church with 78,375, the Congregational Church with 38,000, and the Seventh Day Adventists with 49,489. Other churches which also have large Negro memberships are the Presbyterians, the American Baptist Convention and the Churches of God. Some churches keep figures on members by race, and some do not. This makes it difficult if not impossible to get an accurate total. A reasonable estimate would seem to be about 800,000.

In all of these bodies the membership of Negroes varies from a few individuals in white congregations to separate local churches composed wholly or almost wholly of Negroes. Some of these Negro churches may be quite large, such as St. Mark's Methodist Church in New York City, one of the largest churches in the denomination, or the First Congregational

Church in Atlanta, the largest such church in the region.

In these denominations, Negroes often enjoy full participation in the life of the church, both as members and as officials. This is especially true of local congregations in Northern and Western regions, and in the regional and national boards of the churches. In the Methodist Church, for instance, the Negro bishops are equal in every respect to their white colleagues. Negroes serve on all national boards and agencies in the church. A Negro has served on the Judicial Council, one of the highest bodies in the church, and a Negro bishop has just been chosen president-elect of the Bishops' Council. Two Negro bishops have recently been appointed over predominantly white areas.

In addition to the established churches that have Negro members, there are also the sects, or smaller religious groups, some two hundred or more, nearly all of which have Negro members. Examples of such sects are various Churches of God, Holiness Churches, and Spiritualist Churches.

In the sects, as in the denominations, Negroes may be in separate congregations, or they may be full members of white congregations. Likewise, Negroes hold offices in the ministries and official life of these bodies. An estimate of this Negro membership is not possible.

Store Front Churches

For the past half-century an accelerating movement has been going on in America which is having a profound influence on Negro church life. That movement is the migration of Negroes from the rural areas of the South into the urban centers of the South, North and West. The movement began during the First World War, and it has grown continually ever since. It has been especially heavy in the past ten years because of the agricultural and technological changes in the South.

The present result of this migration is that large numbers of Negroes are crowded together in the decaying older sections of cities, living in poverty, without adequate employment or living necessities or hope. The more financially secure citizens, white and black, have fled to the suburbs, leaving the poorer masses piled in the inner city. The established church in many cases has followed its members, thus depriving the newly migrant masses in the city of effective service from the established church.

There are, however, certain churches that serve the inner city. These are the "store front" or "house front" churches. In depressed neighborhoods there are usually many vacant stores, which can easily be converted into meeting places. Or, where a store is not available, a residence may serve as well.

These churches are usually of the cult or sect type. Sometimes they are affiliated with national bodies, such as Holiness or Pentecostal groups. Sometimes they are single, separate churches arising out of the zeal of some interested evangelist. In most cases, these churches are marked by their emotionalism, by strict adherence to a biblical way of life and by severe injunctions to moral living. Their ministers are often poorly trained and have little concern with or ability to handle the social and economic conditions that depress the people.

There are four main reasons for the existence of the store front churches: (1) the lack of adequate follow-up by the established churches from which

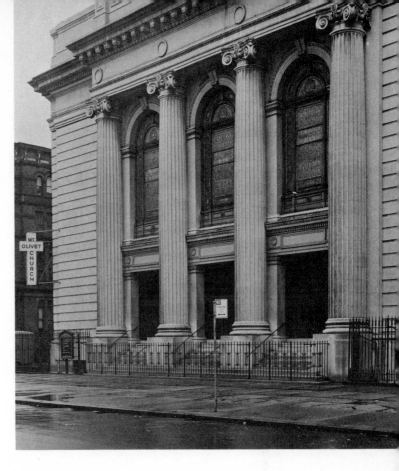

The present Mount Olivet Baptist Church building was previously a Jewish temple. (Photo by Roland Mitchell)

Many metropolitan churches formerly had other uses. The First Corinthian Baptist Church was once a theater. (Photo by Roland Mitchell)

This Catholic church is not Roman Catholic.

Some churches are small.

Even former bars have been converted to churches.

(Photos by Roland Mitchell)

the migrants come; (2) lack of concern or programs by the established churches in the areas; (3) the evangelistic zeal of preachers and Christian workers who want to save the people from the sins of their environment, and (4) the continuing and genuine interest of the depressed people in religion as a source of help in their troubles.

A discussion of these reasons is not possible here. It is known, however, that many of the migrants were church members in their home towns, but because their churches have been derelict in keeping membership records, or in following members who move, there is no continuity of church life for the migrant. Also, studies have shown that membership in the established church is too often a matter of status; that is, membership declines as the people lose economic and social standing.

Yet, despite its obvious faults, the store front church does serve a great purpose among the depressed people who have urgent religious needs: ". . . it provides a reason for existence, a feeling of belonging, and a temporary escape from the dreariness of their lot. It also provides for the large number of rural Southern migrants a means of facilitating urbanization by becoming part of a closely knit 'we group' with which they can identify and emulate."[8]

The Church and Education

The Emancipation Proclamation of 1863 gave the Negro freedom, but it left the freedmen with little means for their education and cultural development. To provide these essentials, men and women from the established churches rushed into the South—often at great personal sacrifice—to establish schools, to teach and to render other needed services to the freedmen. In doing this they wrote one of the brightest pages in the history of Christian missions. Among the most active of these churches were the Methodists, Congregationalists, Presbyterians and Baptists. They opened schools, sometimes called "colleges" or "universities," which in the beginning were little more than high schools or academies. However, as educational levels have risen, many of these schools have developed into first-rate, fully accredited institutions of higher learning. These schools taught not only academic subjects, but also the basic elements of American culture. They helped the Negro to bridge the gap between slavery and citizenship, and they have provided much of the Negro leadership of the past century.

The Negro Church and Education

The coming of freedom made it possible for the Negro church to work freely all over the nation, but especially in the South where most Negroes lived. The Negro churches were interested in gaining members, but they were also interested in the educational development of their people. They devoted a large share of their meager resources to setting up schools, colleges and seminaries. The AME Church, for instance, has seven colleges; the CME Church has three colleges plus several secondary schools, and a seminary.

The schools of the white and Negro denominations constitute the main source of private education among Negroes. At present these church schools train about 25,000 Negro students.

The Church and Civil Rights

It has already been seen that in the days of slavery the Negro's church was the main instrument for the expression of his sufferings on the one hand and of his hopes on the other. Similarly, in the contemporary struggle for civil rights the church is the main institution through which social dissatisfactions and civil aspirations can be expressed. In many communities, especially in the South, the Negro church is the only institution capable of working for civil rights at all. Because of its independent support and its relative freedom from governmental intimidation, the Negro church is often the center of protest meetings, voter registration projects and other mass efforts.

What is true of the church is also true of the Negro minister. He is playing a leading part in the struggle. In this social role he is perhaps best symbolized by Dr. Martin Luther King, Jr., a well-trained Negro pastor, who started with a revolt against segregated bus transportation in Montgomery, Alabama, and led that revolt into a great national demand for complete integration in the whole of American life. The Negro pastor and his church are still powerful influences in the social life and aspirations of Negroes in America.

The Catholic Church and the Negro

The Catholic Church has always been interested in the conversion of Negroes to that faith. In comparatively recent years, however, the work among Negroes has grown remarkably in scope and intensity. Negro membership has practically tripled in the past twenty-five years.

In 1963, the Catholic Church had 703,443 Negro members in 514 parishes, served by 775 priests. The church maintains 361 schools with an enrollment of 97,030 Catholic and non-Catholic students. In 1963 there were 12,638 adult baptisms (see Figure I).

In addition to these separate Negro churches, there are many Negroes who are members of "white" congregations, for whom separate figures are not kept. It thus can be seen that within a quarter-century the Catholic Church has grown to be one of the leading religious groups among Negroes, surpassing at least two, if not three of the major Negro denominations.

CHARACTERISTICS AND CONTRIBUTIONS

The question is often raised as to whether or not the Negro church possesses any distinct or unique features that would differentiate it from other church bodies. Does it differ significantly from other churches in theology or in polity or in patterns of church life?

The general conclusion is that the Negro church does not possess any significantly different features. In faith, in polity and in practice the Negro denominations all follow closely the parent white bodies from which they came. The Negro church was not born out of differences over theology or polity. It is simply a colored division of the general church.

Indeed, there is widespread objection to the very term "Negro church" on the ground that this is in itself a misnomer, and that there is no such thing as a "Negro" church. A more accurate term would seem to be the "Negro's church," or better still, "the church among Negroes."

But despite the lack of distinctive features, what we call the Negro church is well established as a separate institution or group of institutions, and bids well to remain so for a long time. The Negro church does participate fully, however, in cooperative activities with other churches. All major Negro

FIGURE 1—Growth of Catholicism among Negroes

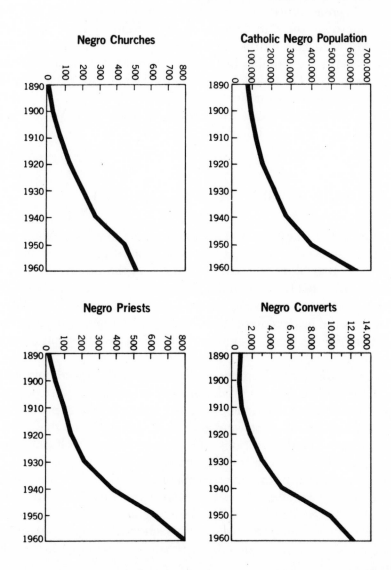

SOURCE: Rev. J. B. Tennelly, S.S. of the Commission for Catholic Missions among the Colored People and the Indians, Washington.

denominations are members of the National Council of the Churches of Christ. They also share fully in state and local councils of churches. In a number of instances Negro churchmen hold prominent places in these bodies, even in the South. In Georgia a Negro was recently elected (1965) President of the Georgia Council of Churches.

The beginnings of interchurch cooperation among the Negro denominations themselves may be seen in the Fraternal Council of Churches, an organization that embraces all of the major groups. It is perhaps best seen in the Interdenominational Theological Center in Atlanta, Georgia, a new, well-equipped, fully accredited seminary, formed through the cooperation the Methodist, AME, CME and Baptist Churches.

Perhaps the most distinguished contribution the Negro church has made to general Christendom has not been in theology but in music—the Negro "spirituals." These simple, rhythmic, harmonious songs, born in the hearts of slaves and freedmen, have spoken to the hearts of people everywhere. They have been accepted in established church music.

In their messages the spirituals reveal: (1) faith in God and in His ultimate justice ("My Lord Is A-writin' All The Time"); (2) patience and suffering ("Nobody Knows the Trouble I've Seen"); (3) the desire for freedom ("Go Down, Moses—Tell Ol' Pharaoh To Let My People Go"); (4) the passion for progress ("We Are Climbin' Jacob's Ladder"), and (5) the deep reverence of the Negro Christian ("Steal Away to Jesus" and "Were You There When They Crucified My Lord?").

THE CHURCH: PRESENT AND FUTURE

The church has traditionally been a formative and controlling influence in the life of the American Negro, not only in spiritual matters, but in other areas as well. It is by far the largest institution the group has had, having today better than twelve million members. It has served as an instrument of expression and action in civic, cultural and educational concerns. It has provided inspired leadership for the group in the struggle for fuller life. Will this position of preëminence continue? The answer will depend upon several facts.

First of all, life among Negroes is changing. From a predominantly rural people, they are becoming a predominantly urban people. At present most Negroes are a disadvantaged people, constituting pockets of poverty in inner cities, suffering serious social and economic privations in the midst of an affluent society. These conditions call for spiritual and cultural services of the most intensive kind. Can the church render these services?

Studies conducted in a number of major cities show that the established church is not serving the depressed urban masses as it should and as the people need. In the first place, the church tends to follow its members to the suburbs. It has not yet developed an effective program of serving the indigent masses in inner cities. Unfortunately, church service declines as economic status declines.

Secondly, the Negro church is handicapped by an inadequately trained ministry. Recent figures show that only one out of fifteen men entering the ministry has had seminary training. In other words, 92 percent of the men entering the Negro ministry each year are professionally unprepared. Can untrained leaders develop the intensive service programs necessary for the development of a handicapped people?

The answer, obviously, is that they cannot. As studies show, in Negro communities there are few church-sponsored programs for guidance of the young, for adult education, for health and cultural improvement or for help in occupational skills and placement. These are the kinds of services that will lead the people into a more abundant life.

At present the Negro church is a vast, influential, respected institution with between fifty and sixty thousand churches and forty to fifty thousand pastors. If this great body can develop the services that a growing and changing population needs, it will continue to grow and to hold its place in the life and esteem of the group. On the other hand, it is certain that people will not long respect or support an agency that plays no needed part in their lives.

NOTES

[1] W.E.B. Du Bois, *The Negro Church* (Atlanta, Georgia: The Atlanta University Press, 1903), p. 10.

[2] Summary of statement from "Slavery and Conversion in the American Colonies," by Marcus W. Jernigan, in *American Historical Review*, XXI, No. 3 (April 1916), pp 504–527. Used by permission.

[3] Carter G. Woodson, *History of the Negro Church* (Washington, D.C.: The Associated Publishers, 1921), p. 28. Used by permission.

[4] *Journal of Reverend Francis Asbury*, I (New York: Lane and Scott, 1852), p. 306.

[5] Woodson, *op. cit.*, p. 32.

[6] Gunnar Myrdal, *An American Dilemma*, II (New York: Harper and Brothers, 1944), pp. 937–38.

[7] Woodson, *op. cit.*, Chapter III.

[8] Patricia M. Pettiford, "Harlem's Ministry," unpublished master's thesis, College of the City of New York, 1963.

VOL. XI.—No. 568.]   NEW YORK, SATURDAY, NOVEMBER 16, 1867.   [SINGLE COPIES TEN CENTS.
$4.00 PER YEAR IN ADVANCE.

Entered according to Act of Congress, in the Year 1867, by Harper & Brothers, in the Clerk's Office of the District Court for the Southern District of New York.

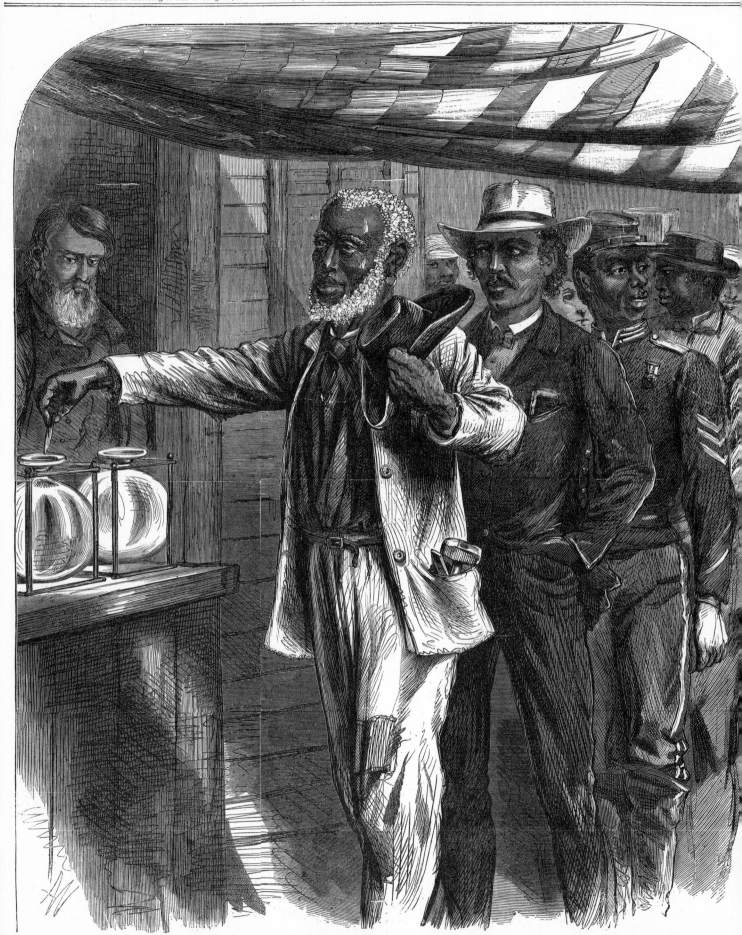

"THE FIRST VOTE."—Drawn by A. R. Waud.—[See next page.]   (Harper's Weekly)

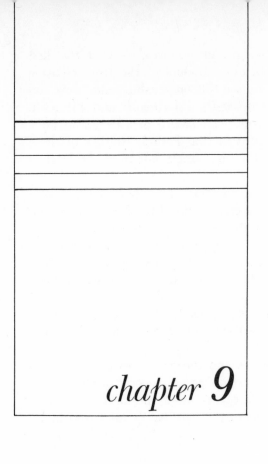

chapter 9

G. James Fleming

The Negro in American Politics:

The Past

G. James Fleming. Professor of Political Science and Director of Institute for Political Education, Morgan State College, Baltimore, Maryland. Author of *An All-Negro Ticket in Baltimore* and other studies of the Negro in politics.

It is a common belief that the Negro in America secured the first vestiges of citizenship only when Lincoln pronounced the Emancipation Proclamation. There are also those who see this citizenship made firm and universal with the passage of the Thirteenth, Fourteenth and Fifteenth Amendments. To these persons the American Negro first began to be a factor in politics only during the Reconstruction Period. Neither of these observations, however, is the fact, and neither singly nor together do they tell the whole story.

Negro Americans figured in political decisions long before they were citizens. Many laws and actions of the colonies and of the later Confederation governments were influenced by the presence of black men in the population. The Black Codes, the wording of the Articles of Confederation and of the Constitution, and court decisions, as in the Dred Scott Case, were all political acts and decisions which followed the patterns they did at least in part because of the presence of Negroes—although Negroes had no part in the making of any of these decisions. This was true for "free" Negroes and for slaves, for nowhere was the free Negro as free as the white man.

The exclusion of Negroes from politics and the privileges of citizenship was not monolithic and absolute. At least on paper, several of the constitutions of the new post-Revolution states extended the suffrage to free Negroes by not including any restrictions based on race. Accordingly, Negroes voted, but several states disfranchised them in later revisions of their constitutions.

Earliest Right to Vote

The New Jersey constitution of 1776 extended the suffrage to all residents of the colony, "of full age who were worth fifty pounds proclamation money." Not only were there no restrictions based on race or condition of servitude, but there was no restriction based on sex or place of birth; aliens could also vote. In 1807, however, New Jersey passed a "clarifying act" limiting the ballot to free, white, male citizens. There was protest, but this restrictive measure was reaffirmed in 1820.

In New York in the late 1700's, free Negroes could vote, if they owned land to the value of twenty pounds or showed financial substance in other ways. The first constitution, adopted in 1777, gave the right to vote for members of the State Assembly to "every male inhabitant of full age" who satisfied residence and property requirements, the latter being ownership of real property (a freehold) to the value of twenty pounds or the leasing of a tenement of forty shillings. To vote for the Senate the property requirement was a hundred pounds.[1] There was equality in the law as far as suffrage was concerned. These property requirements were nevertheless exorbitant for the rank and file of eighteenth-century Americans and more so for black men, who were the marginal workers.

Enough Negroes took to voting, however, to thereby irritate some politicians and their followers into devising ways and means of restricting or eliminating the Negro vote. This opposition first took the form of an act "to prevent frauds at elections." Section III of this act stated "that whenever any black person or person of color shall present himself to vote . . . , he shall produce to the inspectors or persons conducting such election a certificate of his freedom under the hand and seal of one of the clerks of the county of this state, or under the hand of any clerk with this state."[2]

Several objections were raised in the legislature to this bill, which set up prerequisites for voting that few Negroes could meet—prerequisites much more difficult of attainment than the property requirements. Wesley presents the objections that were sent to the Senate as follows:

> These were summarized as (1) the bill was "dangerous in precedent and against the public good"; (2) the description of a person of color was too vague; (3) many persons were born free and would find it difficult to secure freedom certificates; (4) the right to vote was subjected to the pleasure of others who in many cases would be interested in withholding the vote; (5) many Negroes lived and were far removed from their place of birth or manumission; (6) provisions necessary to qualify for the vote were impossible to secure before the election date of April 30, 1811; (7) there was no justification for the passing of an act which disfranchised a portion of the electors, even for a year; (8) there was no precedent for such a radical change in the election laws so close to an election.[3]

Nonetheless, this so-called antifraud act became law on April 9, 1811, shortly before a state election.

One of the reasons for the opposition to Negro voting was due to the contention that the Negroes tended to give their support to the Federalists, their aristocratic employers. This pro-Federalist alignment of Negroes is credited with providing the "balance of power" which kept the Federalists in power. The anti-Federalists and others were afraid that the growing Negro population would play an increasingly larger role in determining the outcome of New York's elections. Wesley notes that "In the election of 1800, it was extravagantly said that 'the political character of the national government was changed by the vote of a single Negro ward in the city of New York.'"[4] The opposition party to the Federalists, the Democratic-Republicans, also bellowed a campaign song whose theme was "Federalists with Blacks Unite."[5]

Despite the attempts to restrict Negro voting, black men could still vote if they met the stringent and discriminatory requirements of 1811. But they were to be restricted even more by the constitutional convention of 1821, in which Negro suffrage was a central argument. The convention was divided between those who urged equal suffrage for all citizens and those who were obsessed with the idea that the Negro vote was a bloc vote which could be manipulated against what these opponents considered the public good. In the legislature there were charges that the Negro was inferior, lacked intelligence and discretion, and was given to crime—and those who made these charges called on the Bible to help prove their points.

Negroes petitioned the New York legislature to protect their voting rights, and white men such as Peter Jay stressed that, although there were some 30,000 Negro voters in the state, they constituted only one-fortieth of the total vote and represented no threat to the body politic. Several other voices of non-Negroes were raised against restrictions on the Negro vote.

The proposal to limit the vote to white males only was lost, but a new plan was made into law which required of whites ownership of a 40-pound freehold, while setting a 250-pound freehold as the property requirement of Negroes. In addition, the law also set different residence requirements for whites and Negroes, with an unfavorable differential for Negroes. Whites could vote after a residence of only one year, while Negroes had to reside in the state three years. Furthermore, Negro voters had to have paid taxes, while whites could substitute highway or military service for money taxes.

In 1846 another constitutional convention retained all discriminatory differentials against Negroes, after most vituperative argument and after attempts both to strike out racial distinction and to deny the franchise to Negroes altogether were defeated.

While there were assertions that the Negro, voting as a bloc, could control New York City politics, Hirsch found that, according to the 1820 census, of 10,886 Negro voters registered in the city only 100 voted in 1819 and only 612 voted in 1820.[6] This was probably due to the restrictive law passed in 1811 and to the other obstacles raised by voting inspectors to keep Negroes from voting.

In addition to internal action by the state legislature, proposals to amend the New York constitution so as to strike down the discriminaion against Negro voters were also put before the people in referenda—in 1846, 1849, 1860 and 1869. In every instance the liberalizing proposal was lost. As late as 1869, the proposal was defeated, state-wide, by 249,802 to 282,403. The temper of the majority-group citizens (at least of their representatives) is also shown by the fact that the New York legislature, which had ratified the Fifteenth Amendment to the Federal constitution, rescinded its ratification in 1870, following the 1869 defeat of the local referendum. It took the ratification of the Fifteenth Amendment by three-fourths of the states to abolish racial discrimination in New York's suffrage laws.

New York furnishes the fullest example of the pattern of politics, especially to the right to vote, as far as Negroes were concerned, prior to the Emancipation Proclamation and the Reconstruction Period amendments to the U.S. Constitution. But there were other states in which Negroes enjoyed the suffrage, more or less, and for a shorter or longer period of time.

Vermont, Kentucky and Tennessee, in their constitutions of the 1790's, according to Wesley "made no provision in their constitutions concerning the exclusion of Negroes from the ballot." The Pennsylvania constitution of 1790 did not, on paper, exclude Negroes from the suffrage after the word "white" had been deleted in an earlier draft. The constitution adopted in Ohio in 1802 also granted the right of the ballot to Negroes, but intermittent objections to the inclusion of Negroes came to a head in the constitutional convention of 1850 and a resolution to limit the suffrage to white males was carried by a vote of 66 to 12.

In further reference to Pennsylvania, there is no evidence that Negroes voted in that state before 1790, although they could own property and were taxed. From different arguments in the state legislature over several years, there are also indications that the state constitution, as to whether Negroes could vote or not, was observed differently in different parts of the state and at different times. One interesting example of this occurred nearly twenty years before the Dred Scott Decision (1857), when the Pennsylvania Supreme Court held that the Negro was not a freeman and therefore not entitled to vote. The case came before the highest court when "a candidate for office in Bucks County, who was defeated, claimed his opponent's seat because Negroes had been permitted to vote for him [the opponent] . . . contrary to law." [7] This case aroused the pent-up ill will of Negro voters but the Pennsylvania constitution was amended in 1838 to make it clear that the suffrage was limited to whites.

Tennessee, Kentucky and North Carolina permitted Negroes to vote at

Hiram R. Revels, the first Negro Senator, and
early Negro Representatives in Congress.

Robert C. DeLarge   Jefferson H. Long

Hiram R. Revels   Benjamin S. Turner   Josiah T. Walls   Joseph H. Rainey   Robert B. Elliott

first, but after some years each amended its constitution to limit the suffrage to white males.

During the period between the Philadelphia conventions of 1787 and 1865, only Maine, New Hampshire, Vermont, Rhode Island and Massachusetts permitted Negroes to vote on equal terms with whites. All other states, at some time, have barred Negro Americans from the suffrage.[8]

Since citizen group activity is also political, it must be noted that free Negroes in New York, Ohio, Pennsylvania and the other states protested loudly against encroachment on their voting. They called *ad hoc* meetings, established numbers of organizations, filed petitions and made every effort to arouse sentiment favorable to the proposition that the ballot should be available to black men on the same terms as to whites. Some of the noted names of Negro history were in the forefront, including the Negro orator Joseph Sidney, of New York; Robert and James E. Forten, the inventors, of Philadelphia, and John M. Langston of Ohio, later member of Congress.

The Civil War and Reconstruction

Although Negroes enjoyed some right to vote before the Emancipation Proclamation and the related Fifteenth Amendment, no Negro was elected to any important office, although John M. Langston was elected a township clerk in Ohio. But with the Civil War over and the principal slave states brought under a Federal reconstruction plan, there was not only expansion of the suffrage, but Negroes also had an opportunity to fill both high elective and appointive office.

The Reconstruction, as designed by the "Radical Republicans" in Congress (the Reconstruction Act of 1867), divided the rebel states, except Tennessee, into five military districts, and called for new state constitutions, promulgated by constitutional conventions elected by loyal male citizens "of whatever race, color or previous condition." Black men now could vote; and they helped to select delegates to the conventions and later, to ratify the resulting constitutions and to elect the first post-war legislatures. Although all the constitutional conventions had Negro delegates, only one (South Carolina's) had a majority of Negroes. Louisiana's convention was equally divided between whites and Negroes. The other conventions had only a small token number of Negroes. The racial composition of these conventions was as follows: [9]

State	Whites	Negroes
Alabama	83	17
Arkansas	68	7
Florida	29	17
Georgia	133	33
Louisiana	52	40
Mississippi	68	17
North Carolina	107	13
South Carolina	34	63
Texas	81	9
Virginia	80	25
Total	735	241

The Reconstruction Act of 1867 came two years after the ratification of the Thirteenth Amendment and while the Fourteenth Amendment was waiting for ratification. It preceded the Fifteenth Amendment (legalizing the right to vote regardless of race, color or previous condition of servitude) by three years. While aimed at the South, the post-Civil War actions by Congress affected, or were to affect, the entire nation politically for, in 1867, there were several Northern states which denied Negroes the right to vote.

According to whom one reads, the Reconstruction conventions were (1) composed of, and dominated by, illiterate ex-slaves who scarcely knew how to conduct themselves; or (2) not dominated by Negroes but only included some Negroes (among them former "freemen"), many of whom had some schooling and much worldly experience, and several of whom had returned from the North when slavery had been outlawed. The most responsible commentators take the latter view. There is also much support for the position that the constitutions which were drafted by these conventions were "progressive," far-seeing, people-centered, aimed at improving the lot of whites as well as Negroes, and restrained in reference to former Confederates. Negroes, for instance, took the lead in giving constitutional authorization to publicly supported-education, perhaps because they knew so well the need for education.

By the time Reconstruction began, over 20 percent of the ex-slaves had had some schooling. At the Texas constitutional convention, it has been found that the delegates, "for the most part . . . were able to read and write. At least 30 percent of them had some college training.[10] North Carolina would make as good, or better, a showing in this area. Thus, the membership of the state conventions, the membership of the new state legislatures and the candidates for national office included Negroes of several levels of schooling and experience, the same as was the condition of white office-seekers. Woodson and Wesley note that, in some of the legislatures more than half of the Negro members could scarcely read or write," but the authors also hold that "the charge that all Negro officers were illiterate, ignorant of the science of government, cannot be sustained." [11]

Negroes filled many local elective and appointive offices during the Reconstruction years, but the total number of these offices and their incumbents are not as easy to ascertain as for the higher state and national offices. Two Negroes served for some time in the United States Senate: Hiram R. Revels, 1870–71 (an unexpired term), and B.K. Bruce, 1875–81 (a full term). Both were elected from Mississippi. Twenty-one Negroes served in the House of Representatives, from the 43rd through the 56th Congress, 1868–95. They were elected from eight states: Alabama, Florida, Georgia, Louisiana, Mississippi, North Carolina, South Carolina and Virginia. Eleven served a single full term (two years); six served two full terms each; two served three terms, and one, Joseph H. Rainey of South Carolina, served five terms. The largest number of Representatives, seven, came from South Carolina, followed by four from North Carolina; Georgia, Mississippi and Florida elected one each.

It should be noted that the Negroes elected to Congress were residents of states which were part of the military districts created by Congress in the Reconstruction Act of 1867. No Negro was elected from Tennessee, which was not subject to the Act and to post-war Federal "reconstruction." Similarly, during this same period no Negro was elected to the Congress from any northern congressional district. Prior to the establishment of Federal Reconstruction, the former Confederate states voted against extend-

Menard, First Negro to Take Floor in Congress: Although never seated, John Willis Menard of Louisiana was the first Negro elected to the U.S. House of Representatives and the first to speak on the floor when, in December 1868, he eloquently argued his case for being seated.   (Frank Leslie's Illustrated Newspaper, sketch by James E. Taylor)

THE AFRICAN RACE IN CONGRESS—HON. JOHN WILLIS MENARD ADDRESSING THE HOUSE OF REPRESENTATIVES, WASHINGTON, D. C., FEB. 27T.L.—FROM A SKETCH BY JAMES E. TAYLO

ing the suffrage to the emancipated Negroes; so also (during 1865–68) did the states of Michigan, New York, Connecticut, Wisconsin, Minnesota, Kansas and Ohio. In 1866, however, the suffrage was extended by Congress to Negroes in all the territories and the District of Columbia.

Negroes were also elected to the state legislatures during the Reconstruction period; but they did not control the former Confederacy. Except in South Carolina, Negro legislators were always a minority. For example, during 1870–71, the racial distribution in the lower houses was as follows (all the senates were heavily white): [12]

State	Whites	Negroes
Alabama	73	27
Arkansas	71	9
Georgia	149	26
Mississippi	77	30
North Carolina	101	1
South Carolina	49	75
Texas	82	8
Virginia	116	21

In a review entitled *Race and Conscience in America,* prepared by the American Friends Service Committee for its Quaker and Quaker-minded clientele, it is observed of the Reconstruction Period:

> Bills to establish or improve the public school system, to counteract political corruption and extravagance, to establish a homestead law, and to provide relief for the needy were introduced by Negroes. Some former slave states, while condemning political participation by Negroes in the state governments, have continued to function under constitutions which Negroes helped to write.[13]

There was another area in which the Negro members of Reconstruction legislatures made a contribution. They were of one mind in working for the ratification of the post-Civil War amendments that came before them (the Fourteenth and Fifteenth), making the Constitution, even until today, protective of rights which might never have come under the purview of constitutional authority if, for instance, the Fourteenth Amendment had not been ratified by the necessary three-fourths majority of the states.

The Negroes who went to Congress and those who filled high administrative office in the state and national governments acquitted themselves as men usually do in a world where there are relatively few mental giants. That is not to say, however, that Senators Bruce and Revels would not be several cuts above most national lawmakers even in the 1960's; so would John M. Langston (Virginia), H.M. Cheatham (North Carolina), John R. Lynch (Mississippi), Joseph H. Rainey and Robert Smalls (South Carolina), all of whom served in the United States House of Representatives. Men, such as Francis L. Cardozo, who served South Carolina as secretary of state and later as treasurer; P.B.S. Pinchback, one of three Negro lieutenant governors of Louisiana; T.W. Cardozo, Mississippi's superintendent of education—all would stand muster well. Francis Cardozo was educated at the University of Glasgow; Langston was graduated from Oberlin College; Senator Revels had studied at Knox College.

One proof of the ability of Reconstruction period Negro leaders and office-holders is that when the period came to an end or when they left their offices, they went on to show competence as teachers, church leaders, lawyers, administrators, diplomats and the like.

When white Southerners could permit themselves to do so, there were those who did not see everything in Reconstruction government as undeserving of praise. Some publicly lauded the "dignity" and "behavior" of the Negro state legislators; some, because of their knowledge of some Negroes, protested against the passage of the first jim crow laws following the assumption of home rule.

Reconstruction Ends

While Negroes were enjoying their new political opportunities, year by year the former Confederates were showing that they knew practical politics and respected the doctrine of (to use the vernacular) "if you can't lick 'em, join 'em." The Confederates submitted to the side in power just enough to be politically able to recapture their state governments. This they did gradually, as their leaders were pardoned individually or amnesties were declared. This led, first, to border states being able to return Democratic majorities in county elections and to the resurrection of the Southern wing of the Democratic Party. By the mid-1870's the Confederate Democrats, officially purged, were on the march, with the blessings of their former enemies-in-war. They were taking over their South to reconvert it to lily-whitism, both by right of law and outside the law. What ballots could not do, or would not do fast enough, was done with the aid of the Ku Klux Klan and other groups of its kind.

The final blow to Reconstruction was the withdrawal of Federal troops and other Federal supports from the Reconstruction states, on orders of President Rutherford B. Hayes with the backing of both parties in Congress.

By 1902, there was not a single Negro in a state legislature and not a single Negro in the national Congress. In addition, the Southern states adopted numerous devices to prevent Negroes from voting: intimidation, laws setting up property and poll tax requirements, the famous "grandfather clause" (which denied suffrage to anyone whose grandfather could not vote prior to 1876), and the "lily-white" primary. These political measures were followed by the resegregation of those institutions which had been desegregated during Reconstruction, including state universities and other public facilities. All this happened, despite the Civil Rights Act of 1875.[14] Of all that was done and would be done to destroy Reconstruction, preventing Negroes from voting was considered the most fatal.[15]

It has taken nearly ninety years; countless lawsuits, carried from lower courts to the United States Supreme Court; the passage of four Federal Civil Rights Acts (1957, 1960, 1964, 1965), and ratification of the Anti-Poll Tax Amendment (1963), to correct the imbalance somewhat and establish equal treatment under law. This imbalance began when "home rule" was returned to the former rebel states. In the mid-1960's there are still Negroes who are not permitted to register and vote. There is no Negro representing a Southern state in the Congress; but there are Negroes in the legislatures of two former Confederate states—Georgia, with two state senators and five members in its lower house and Tennessee with one member in its state assembly.

During the years that the defeated former Confederacy was represented by Negroes on the several levels of politics and government, there were almost no Negroes similarly situated in the North, with the exception of Massachusetts. In fact, Massachusetts was the first state to elect Negroes to its legislature. This it did in 1866; those elected were Edward G. Walker and Charles L. Mitchell.[16] Since that time the North has done better, but mostly in recent years.

When Oscar DePriest of Chicago entered the U.S. House of Representatives in 1929, it had been twenty-eight years since the last Negro sat as a member of Congress. Since then there have been seven other Negroes elected, all from the North. Together they are:

Oscar DePriest (R), Chicago, 1929–31
Arthur W. Mitchell (R), Chicago, 1934–43
William L. Dawson (D), Chicago, 1943–
A. Clayton Powell, Jr. (D), New York, 1945–
Charles C. Diggs, Jr. (D), Detroit, 1954–
Robert N. C. Nix (D), Philadelphia, 1958–
Augustus F. Hawkins (D), Los Angeles, 1962–
John L. Conyers (D), Detroit, 1964–

Some observers have said that the Negroes in Congress during Reconstruction made no notable contribution. This cannot be said of the more recent group. For instance, DePriest worked consistently to include in every bill possible a clause insuring no racial discrimination against Negroes. He held to this formula especially in reference to the emergency projects of the depression years. Representative Dawson, although not known as a "race fighter" in the open, has attained high office in his party, thus putting him in position to elevate the Negro because of his position as a vice president of the Democratic National Committee and chairman of the important House Committee on Government Operations. Representative Powell, a minister by profession, has been a racial protagonist, seldom being "polite" to those he suspects of doing or planning anything inimical to Negroes. He rubs many people the wrong way, but his constituents consider him "our man," and in the 88th Congress he demonstrated spectacular leadership in carrying President Johnson's welfare program through the House. He is chairman of the House Committee on Education and Labor. Representative Diggs has addressed himself especially to discrimination in the armed forces, at home and abroad. Representatives Nix and Hawkins are going through their learning years; Representative Conyers has just begun to serve.

Seniority has played an effective part in the kind of contribution present-day Congressmen are and will be able to make; in addition, Negro candidates for higher office have increasingly had rather wide previous experience in other public or private responsibilities. For instance, Representative Hawkins was a member of the California legislature for twenty-eight years and both Diggs and Dawson served, respectively, in the Michigan legislature and on the Chicago Board of Aldermen.

It is not as easy to keep track of the membership in state legislatures and city councils. The best count shows twenty-four states having ninety-two Negro members in their legislatures. Some states, including little Nebraska and Vermont, are in the list, Nebraska having boasted a Negro legislator for many years. Illinois, New York, Pennsylvania and Missouri have had Negro lawmakers for years; New York since shortly after World War I.

Los Angeles elected its first city councilman in 1962, but many other cities have had councilmen over a much longer period, going back again to World War I. George W. Harris and Fred R. Moore of New York were among the earliest, in the 1920's. Oscar DePriest and others were members of the Chicago Board of Aldermen before they were elected to Congress. Some smaller cities, such as Evanston, Illinois, have had city councilmen from time to time. Since World War II a number of cities in the South have also elected Negroes to their city councils. These include Durham, Winston-Salem, Fayetteville and Greensboro, in North Carolina; Oak Ridge, Tennessee, which has joined Nashville; Louisville, Kentucky, and some others, from time to time. St. Louis and the Kansas Cities have had councilmen for some time. At present there are 84 Negroes in city councils in nineteen states. George D. Carroll was elected mayor of Richmond, California, by his fellow councilmen in 1964. Perhaps the apex of municipal city positions which has been regularly held by a Negro, since the 1950's is that of President of the Borough of Manhattan (in New York City). Partly administrative, this position is most important as political "plum." The highest purely political decision-making position held by a Negro is that of "leader of Tammany Hall," more formally chairman of the Democratic County Committee of New York County. J. Raymond Jones, a practicing politician for nearly forty years, was elected in 1965.

The only statewide elective offices are held by Gerald Lamb, treasurer of Connecticut and Edward Brooke, attorney-general of Massachusetts.

One historic city, Tuskegee, Ala., for the first time, in 1964, elected two Negroes to the Macon County Board (officially the "Board of Revenue") and a third to the County Board of Education.

Negro members on school boards, North and South, are no longer unusual, although there are still countless school boards that have never had a Negro member. One of the important cities that recently elected such a board member was Houston, Texas, where both Negroes and whites joined in sponsoring and supporting the Negro candidate, Mrs. Hattie Mae White. Increasingly, also, Northern cities are appointing or electing Negroes to the judiciary above the justice of the peace level. The Federal Government and the large urban areas take the lead in this category, with New York, Chicago, Pennsylvania, Michigan and California having had several such judges regularly for some time. On the Federal level, William H. Hastie and Thurgood Marshall, on the Circuit Courts of Appeal, hold the highest Federal judgeships. Presently there are Negroes on the Customs and District Courts on the mainland. Another district judge serves in the U. S. Virgin Islands.

As Negroes have been more active in politics, more of them have received higher appointments, so much so that President John F. Kennedy openly said that he planned to name Robert C. Weaver to a Cabinet post, if a Department of Urban Affairs had been established during his presidency. Since then, President Lyndon B. Johnson has named Carl T. Rowan director of the United States Information Agency, with the right to sit on the National Security Council.

It is not the recognition that comes to the individual Negro that counts heavily anymore, however; it is what political involvement does or brings to the masses of Negroes, economically, socially and psychologically, which

PARTY REGULARITY SECURED: In the election of 1876, with the approval of President Ulysses S. Grant, Federal Marshals—supported by the military—watched polling places in the South lest Negroes stray from the Republican fold.

(Frank Leslie's Illustrated Newspaper, Sketch by J. Keppler)

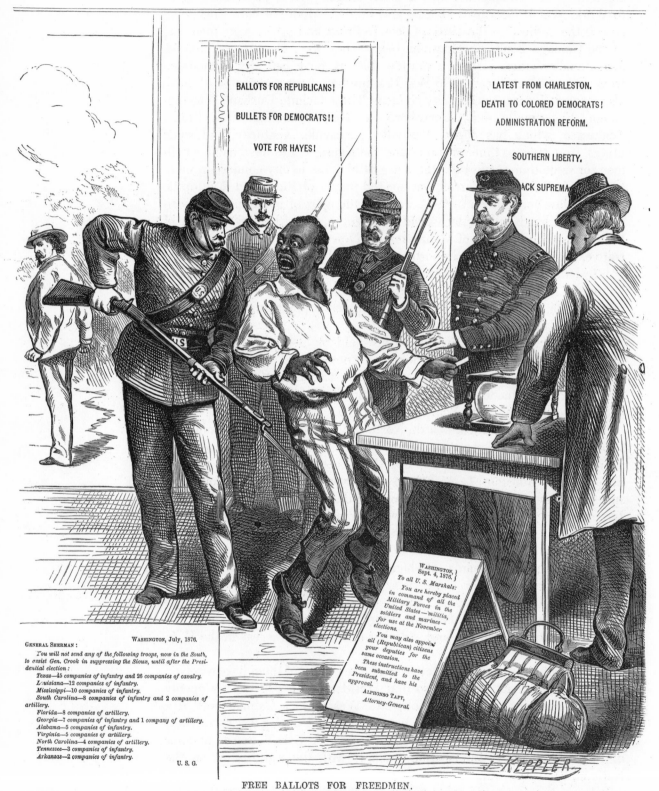

BALLOTS FOR REPUBLICANS!

BULLETS FOR DEMOCRATS!!

VOTE FOR HAYES!

LATEST FROM CHARLESTON.

DEATH TO COLORED DEMOCRATS!

ADMINISTRATION REFORM.

SOUTHERN LIBERTY.

ACK SUPREMA

WASHINGTON, July, 1876.

GENERAL SHERMAN :

You will not send any of the following troops, now in the South, to assist Gen. Crook in suppressing the Sioux, until after the Presidential election :

Texas—45 companies of infantry and 26 companies of cavalry.

Louisiana—12 companies of infantry.

Mississippi—10 companies of infantry.

South Carolina—8 companies of infantry and 2 companies of artillery.

Florida—8 companies of artillery.

Georgia—7 companies of infantry and 1 company of artillery.

Alabama—5 companies of infantry.

Virginia—5 companies of artillery.

North Carolina—4 companies of artillery.

Tennessee—3 companies of infantry.

Arkansas—2 companies of infantry.

U. S. G.

WASHINGTON,
Sept. 4, 1876.

To all U. S. Marshals:

You are hereby placed in command of all the Military Forces in the United States—militia, soldiers and marines—for use at the November elections.

You may also appoint all (Republican) citizens your deputies for the same occasion.

These instructions have been submitted to the President, and have his approval.

ALPHONSO TAFT,
Attorney-General.

FREE BALLOTS FOR FREEDMEN.

The Federal Army in the South will be, during the Fall elections, under the orders of the United States Marshals. Commanding officers will render what aid they can to the Republican ticket, and are recommended to personally inspect the Freedmen's votes, in order to prevent their being cast for Democratic candidates.

[Summary of Attorney-General Taft's instructions of September 4th.]

is held most important. This means not only prestige benefits, but also those benefits which millions of marginal, working, job-seeking, home-making men and women need most.

Patronage and Party Recognition

Outside the South and in nonelective and party organization politics, the Emancipation meant that thousands of free Negroes came North, especially into the nation's Capital. In Washington they could find steady, nonmenial or semimenial employment or enjoy the fruits of patronage. It did not matter that most of them received the lowest paying jobs. Washington meant being out of the South and under the protection of the Federal Government. One price paid for employment in the Government was the frequent turnover as administrations changed. *The Tuskegee Year Book* of 1912 listed "colored officers, clerks and other employees in the service of the U. S. Government." The number included members of the diplomatic corps, enlistees in the Army, laborers employed by the District of Columbia, post office personnel, and miscellaneous department employees. The list shows:

Diplomatic and consular corps	11
Enlistees in Army	2,948
District laborers	2,824
Post Office personnel	2,997
Miscellaneous	14,386
Total	**23,166**

In addition, some prestige positions were given Negroes, such as Secretary of the Treasury, Recorder of Deeds of the District of Columbia, and minister to all-Negro nations. Some Negro consuls served in non-Negro countries. John Mercer Langston became U.S. Minister to Haiti; Frederick Douglass, ex-slave, greatest of the abolitionist orators and frequent advisor to Lincoln, became Minister to Haiti and also served at different times as assistant secretary of the San Domingo Commission, marshal of the District of Columbia and Recorder of Deeds. Fred R. Moore, New York political leader and editor (the *New York Age*) was one of a long line of Negro ministers and ambassadors to the American-sponsored Republic of Liberia. Some Negroes became collectors of internal revenue, one serving in Honolulu; others were customs collectors, paymasters for the Army, and receivers of public monies. John C. Napier was Register of the Treasury; Henry Lincoln Johnson, a national committeeman of the Republican National Committee, once served as Recorder of Deeds of the District of Columbia, a position that has been filled by other Negroes down the years.

When Woodrow Wilson ascended to the Presidency, there were 5,836 Negroes in the Federal service in Washington, according to the *New York Age*. The paper goes on to complain that since Wilson came into office, twenty-nine of those Negroes holding the highest office had been "turned out" and their places "filled by white Democrats." [17] This periodic turnover was regular procedure for political appointees, but it struck Negroes hardest of all because of their limited employment opportunities.

Another area of political opportunity for Negroes after emancipation, and for many years after, came through being elected as delegates to the Republican National Convention and as members of the Republican National

Committee. But when the former Confederate states took over the state governments again and found ways to disfranchise Negroes, these national officers were leaders without an effective following. The last to serve was Perry W. Howard, a lawyer born in Ebeneezer, Mississippi, in 1877 and a graduate of Fisk University with an L.L.B. degree from DePauw University. He was once a special assistant to the Attorney General of the United States, and practiced law from 1905 to the late 1950's. Although national committeeman from Mississippi, he made Washington, D. C., his home for more than half of his adult years. But in his heyday he controlled the Federal patronage for Mississippi whenever the Republicans occupied the White House; he served on important committees at national conventions, and he led the Mississippi delegation (called "black and tan" by many in the state because it was racially mixed).

Howard and other Negro national committeemen were accused of representing "rotten boroughs," of preferring an all-Negro Republican Party in the South and, worst of all, of selling patronage. The latter accusation was made especially against Howard and became part of the U.S. Senate record when hearings were held in 1928 by the Presidental Special Committee Investigating Campaign Expenditures.[18]

Among other Republican national committeemen were Benjamin J. Davis and Henry L. Johnson, both from Georgia. Roscoe Conklin Simmons of Illinois, Robert R. Church of Tennessee, and William H. McDonald of Texas were also important Negro Republican leaders.

Benjamin Davis was the outspoken editor of the *Atlanta Independent*. He studied at Atlanta University and had been teacher and secretary of a national fraternal order, for which he arranged the building of a block of buildings. In addition to being a member of the Republican National Committee, he served as delegate-at-large to his party's convention for twenty-five years.

Simmons was journalist but became best known as a "silver-tongued" orator. Among Negroes he is remembered for standing under a White House window during the Hoover administration, when Negroes felt they had been forgotten by the Republican Party, and appealing: "Speak, Mr. President, speak. Tell us that Lincoln still lives." It is probably because Negroes felt they did not receive an answer that so many soon after turned to the Democratic party and Franklin Roosevelt. One writer says of Simmons that his "spell-binding oratory was the Negroes' answer to the fire-eating Vardaman, Bilbo and Heflin. . . ." [19]

Robert R. Church was a real estate operator and banker, born in Memphis in 1885 and educated at Oberlin College. He was a member of the Republican State Central Committee of Tennessee and Shelby County Executive and Congressional Committees. He was a delegate to the Republican National Conventions of 1912, 1916, 1920 and 1924. In 1922 he was appointed by Secretary of State Charles Evans Hughes on a special commission to study economic conditions in Haiti. Henry Lincoln Johnson was a noted fraternal leader, and William McDonald was reputedly a "Texas millionaire."

The foregoing is the typical experience of the Negro Republican leaders who figured largely as voices of the party and patronage dispensers between 1900 and 1932. They, like Frederick Douglass, believed "the Republican Party to be the ship, all else the sea." They were professionals.

There had been times when men such as Perry Howard have been called

RECONSTRUCTION BETRAYED: *"By the mid-1870's the Confederate Democrats . . . were on the march, with the blessings of their former enemies-in-war. They were taking over their South to reconvert it to lily-whitism, both by right of law and OUTSIDE THE LAW. What ballots could not do, or would not do fast enough, was done with the aid of the Ku Klux Klan and other groups of its kind."*

(Harper's Weekly, sketch by Thomas Nast)

712   HARPER'S WEEKLY.   [SEPTEMBER 2, 1876.

"IS *THIS* A REPUBLICAN FORM OF GOVERNMENT? IS *THIS* PROTECTING LIFE, LIBERTY, OR PROPERTY? IS *THIS* THE EQUAL PROTECTION OF THE LAWS?"

MR. LAMAR (*Democrat, Mississippi*). "In the words of the inspired Poet, 'Thy Gentleness has made thee Great.'" [Did Mr. LAMAR mean the Colored Race?]

THE NEGRO IN AMERICAN POLITICS: THE PAST   419

political bosses—bosses over certain groups of party followers in a given area; able to deliver promised or expected votes; having close relations with the greater powers that be in the party, and being in position to reward friends and punish enemies. But there have been other Negro bosses, both Republican and Democratic, not occupying offices as high as national committeemen. The bosses were usually allied with some white machine and were permitted to control certain territory, certain patronage or certain enterprises. Sometimes these enterprises were within the law, sometimes outside the law. The enterprises have included, at times, gambling or prostitution. Negro bossism has usually been a reflection of white bossism. At the present time, when old-fashioned bossism is no longer holding sway, Negro bosses as well as white have taken on a new image or disappeared.

Some Negro bosses, by supporting the "Big City" machines, have been able to increase their patronage and other gains for their districts. One reputed boss thereby secured Negro policemen in his Southern city decades before such employment was being made available to Negroes in the rest of the South. Other bosses were able to get new schools and other improvements for their people; still others controlled a share of the patronage jobs. Chicago, San Antonio, Baltimore, Memphis, New York, are cities often mentioned as having successful bosses. There have been many more subbosses and little bosses than top big bosses.

In Baltimore there were Marse Calloway, Republican, and Thomas Smith, Democrat, both of whom are credited with serving white overlords, sometimes even to the extent of "paying off" Negroes to prevent them from voting. Nevertheless, Marse Calloway is given credit for introducing one of the most popular and most highly esteemed men into politics—Theodore R. McKeldin, two-term Mayor of Baltimore and two-term Governor of Maryland.

Most Negroes in politics so far described have been Republicans because, over the long stretch of history and due to Reconstruction, most political activity by Negroes was in that party.

Since 1928, however, Negroes have increasingly supported the Democratic Party. Many Negroes were first attracted to the Democrats through New York's Governor Alfred E. Smith. Later, with the promise of the New Deal, they allied themselves to the Democratic Party and the majority have remained there since. Negroes are given credit—election after election—for helping the party carry the fifteen urban industrial centers of the country. In nearly every urban district, Negro registered Democrats outnumber Republicans by as much as 8 to 1. Some Republican candidates, in fact, have felt it is not worth the trouble to campaign in the Harlems of the country.

As a result of over thirty years of their support, the Democratic Party has rewarded Negroes with appointments to high-ranking responsible and prestige jobs. Under the Kennedy administration a Negro, Andrew Hatcher, was named associate White House press secretary, and President Johnson has named Hobart Taylor, a lawyer, an assistant special counsel on his White House staff.

In both the Kennedy and Johnson administrations, Presidential directives have called on departments and agencies to do special recruiting to bring more Negroes into nontraditional positions in the government. What has been done on the national level has also been done on state and local levels; in fact, local Democrats were first in recognizing Negroes as long ago as 1917 when Ferdinand Q. Morton was appointed to the Civil Service Commission of New York City.

In the earlier Republican administration of President Eisenhower pioneer recognition was given Negro Republicans. Thus J. Ernest Wilkins of Illinois was named Assistant Secretary of Labor and became the first Negro to sit in a White House Cabinet meeting, and E. Frederic Morrow of New Jersey was named an administrative aid to President Eisenhower. Mrs. Robert L. Vann of Pennsylvania was named a member of the International Development Advisory Board, and Archibald J. Carey, Jr. of Illinois was made chairman of the President's Committee on Government Employment Policy. Scovel Richardson was appointed a member of the Federal Parole Board (of which he became chairman), and was later named a Judge of the United States Customs Court. Scores of other appointments at lower levels were also made during the Eisenhower administration.

Thus, increasingly both major political parties at Federal, state and local levels have sought to improve their image with Negro voters through the use of significant patronage appointments. This trend is likely to continue, with the Republican party making a special effort as part of its post-Goldwater reconstruction.

NOTES

[1] After Leo H. Hirsch, "The Negro and New York, 1783–1865." *Journal of Negro Education*, XVI, No. 4 (October, 1931), 417.

[2] *Journal of the Senate of New York*, 1811, p. 143, as quoted by Charles H. Wesley in "Negro Suffrage in the Period of Constitution-Making, 1787–1865." *Journal of Negro History*, XXXII (April 1947, No. 2), 156.

[3] *Ibid.*, p. 156.

[4] *Ibid.*, p. 155. Soon to be published is a new examination of the extent to which the Negro vote in New York might have provided a "balance of power" in New York politics. The author is Dr. Elsie M. Lewis, associate professor of history at Howard University.

[5] *New York Spectator*, April 29, 1809, as quoted by Wesley.

[6] Hirsch, *op. cit.*, pp. 417–18.

[7] Wesley, p. 162.

[8] *Ibid.*, p. 166.

[9] *The Negro Year Book*, published by Tuskegee Institute, Tuskegee, Alabama (1921–22 edition), p. 176.

[10] John Mason Brewer, *Negro Legislators of Texas* (Dallas: Mathis Publishing Company, 1935), p. 217.

[11] Carter C. Woodson, and Charles H. Wesley, *Negro in Our History*, 10th ed. (Washington: Associated Publishers, 1962), p. 405.

[12] *Negro Year Book, op. cit.*, p. 176.

[13] By a "working party" of the American Friends Committee, including the present writer (Norman: University of Oklahoma Press, 1959), p. 13.

[14] This Act specifically provided to all citizens regardless of race, creed, color or previous condition of servitude "full and equal enjoyment of all accommodations at inns, conveyances on land or water, theaters, or other places of public amusement." It established a fine of up to $500 or imprisonment of from thirty days to one year for any persons excluding any one from these accommodations on account of race, etc. It further provided for equality in service on juries and set a penalty of up to a $5,000 fine levied against any person who excluded another from serving on a jury.

[15] V. O. Key, Jr., *Southern Politics* (New York: Alfred A. Knopf, 1950), p. 536; after an interpretation by S. S. Calhoun, president, the Mississippi Constitutional Convention of 1890.

[16] *The Negro Year Book*, published by Tuskegee Institute, Tuskegee, Alabama (1918–19 edition), p. 208.

[17] *New York Age*, October 26, 1916.

[18] See Report of the committee, pp. 718–35.

[19] Richard Bardolph, *The Negro Vanguard* (New York: Rinehart and Company, 1959), pp. 149–50.

VOTE FOR ~~ERT B.~~ ★

END RACIAL IN~~DIFFERENCE~~
AT HOME AND ABR~~OAD~~

REGISTER YOUR

PROTEST

VOTE
FOR
CLIFTON
DeBERRY
FOR
MAYOR

SOCIALIST WORKERS
PARTY

END the WA~~R~~
in VIETNAM

REGISTER YOUR

PROTEST

VOTE
FOR
CLIFTON
DeBERRY
FOR
MAYOR

SOCIALIST WORKERS
PARTY

ASSEMBLY~~MAN~~ MARK T. ★

~~DEMO~~CRATIC CANDIDATE ★

★ REGULAR DEMOCRAT~~IC~~ ~~CA~~NDIDAT~~E~~

END
in V~~IETNAM~~

~~RIC~~HARD

P. JONES RICHARD P.

~~LEGI~~SLATO~~R~~

~~4~~

~~DE~~MOCRATIC CANDIDATE

~~Tues~~ Sept. 14

Sworn-In as Asst. to Boro Pr~~es~~

Addressing a neigh~~bor~~

Sworn ~~In~~ as Asst. ~~to~~ Boro Boss Dudley

★

SOCI~~ALIST~~

Reading Negro History on P.S. ~~100~~

Inspecting Slum Housing

Reading Negro History at P.S. 100

★

FOR

Inspecting Slum

★ ASSEMBLY

79th A.D.

LAWYER · VETERAN · DIPLOMAT

★ ASSEMBL~~Y~~

79th A.D.

LAWYER · VETERAN · DIPLO~~MAT~~

~~VOTE EARLY~~ DEMOCRATIC PRIMARY DAY · TUES SEPT 1

chapter 10

James Q. Wilson

The Negro in American Politics:

The Present

James Q. Wilson. Associate Professor of Government, Harvard University, Cambridge, Massachusetts. Director of the Joint Center for Urban Studies of Massachusetts Institute of Technology and Harvard University. Author of *Negro Politics*. Coauthor (with E. C. Banfield) of *City Politics*.

In 1960, there were in the United States about 11 million nonwhites twenty-one years of age or over; the great majority of these were Negroes, slightly more than half of whom lived in the South and slightly less than half in the North and West. The total *potential* Negro vote is thus well over 10 million, but of course the actual vote is—and for the foreseeable future will continue to be—much less. The number of Negroes voting at any given election is almost impossible to estimate with any accuracy, but was probably less than 4 million in the 1960 Presidential contest and rose to nearly 6 million in the 1964 national elections. In the North and West, where Negroes may register and vote freely, sample surveys suggest that between 60 and 70 percent actually do vote.[1] Applied to a Northern adult Negro population of about 5.5 million, this would produce an active electorate of 3.3 million. In the South, discriminatory practices as well as other factors kept the number of Negroes registered to vote in 1960 down to about 1.4 million, or 28 percent of those of voting age.[2] By 1964 this figure had risen to 1.9 million voters, or 38 percent of those eligible.

The political participation of the Negro in the North is significantly higher than in the South but even so is lower than that of most other Northern population groups. In Philadelphia, for example, there were four wards where, in 1960, less than 45 percent of the total population was registered to vote; in three of these (Wards 28, 32 and 47) Negroes were over 90 percent of the population. Further, these three wards were among the five which had a turnout of less than 60 percent of the registered voters in the 1959 mayoralty election. In the 1960 Presidential election, Negro voting participation was much higher—over 80 percent of the registered voters in all wards—but still lower than that of almost all other wards.

The pattern varies from city to city, but the Philadelphia case—selected because it is one of the few Northern cities which keep registration figures by race—is a common one.[3] The reasons for relatively low participation are not hard to find. Social science surveys have repeatedly shown that persons who have little education, low incomes and blue-collar occupations vote less than persons with a higher socio-economic status.[4] Negroes, of course, rank low—in many cities, the lowest—in all these attributes, and thus their lower participation must be explained in part by considerations of class rather than race. In addition, persons who move a great deal are less likely to be able to meet residence requirements than those who stay in one home. On the average, almost one-fourth of all Negroes change residence each year, a proportion which is slightly higher than for whites.

The structure of government affects participation as well. In local elections where party labels do not appear on the ballot ("nonpartisan" elections), where the candidates for the city council run at large rather than from wards or districts, and where party organization is weak or nonexistent, the turnout of Negro voters (as well as of lower-income voters generally) is substantially lower than when the opposite of these conditions prevail.[5]

In sum, approximately one-third of adult Northern Negroes and five-sixths of adult Southern Negroes did not vote in recent Presidential elections;[6] a much larger—but unknown—proportion of these people did not vote in the most recent local elections.

The political strength of the Negro is affected by the political unit of which he is part as well as by his level of participation. The great internal migration of Negroes has not been simply from South to North but from farm to city and from small town to large. Seventy-five per cent of the Negro population in 1960 was "urban"—that is, living in communities with a population of 2,500 or more. In the North particularly, Negroes are not simply urban but "metropolitan"—that is, concentrated in the largest cities. In 1960 the twenty-one largest metropolitan areas (all but four of which were in the North) accounted for about one-third of all Negroes living in the United States. The electoral college method of choosing Presidents, by which the winner of a state's popular vote receives all the state's electoral votes, gives, of course, great importance to the big cities and thus to population groups (including Negroes) in the big cities.

In Congress, it is another matter. The very concentration of the Negro vote in the big cities—and in only certain sections of the big cities at that—means that, even if all Negroes could and did vote freely, they would be under-represented in the House of Representatives. In the 88th Congress, which was elected in 1962 and took office in 1963, there were only five Congressional districts with a population more than half Negro and only twenty-one which were more than 40 percent Negro.[7] Since in most cases a Negro is not elected to a Congressional seat in the North until the population is over half Negro, the residential concentration of Northern Negroes lessens their representation.

Negroes do not, of course, have to have one of their kind in office to be represented; their presence in large numbers even in a district represented by a white man will constitute an influence on him and thus on public policy, provided the Negroes can and do vote. In the North and West only 7.5 percent of all Congressional districts are one-fifth Negro or more. By contrast, *over half* the Southern Congressional districts are one-fifth Negro or more. In short, because the Negro population (but not the number of Congressional districts) is equally divided between North and South and because the geographic dispersion of Negroes is much greater in the South than in the North, the greatest *potential* Negro influence on Congress is in the South. Figure 1 illustrates this by giving, for each of three regions in the country, the number of Congressional districts with various proportions of Negroes.

The reapportionment of Congress which followed the 1960 census hurt Negroes in some ways and helped them in others. Before reapportionment, there were seven districts that were half Negro; by 1963, after reapportionment in eighteen states, there were only five (states where Negroes lost were Illinois and North Carolina). On the other hand, the number of districts that were 40 percent Negro or more went from nineteen in 1960 to twenty-one in 1963 (about half were in the South).

The factors which reduce Negro political participation in the South are well known. Administrative practices and community attitudes often make Negro registration impossible or so difficult and perilous as to be a meaningless opportunity. The United States Civil Rights Commission estimates that there are about one hundred counties in eight Southern states in which "there is reason to believe that Negro citizens are prevented—by outright discrimination or by fear of physical violence or economic reprisal—from exercising the right to vote."[8] In 1956, about 5 percent of the voting-age Negroes in these counties could vote. In 1963, after passage of two civil

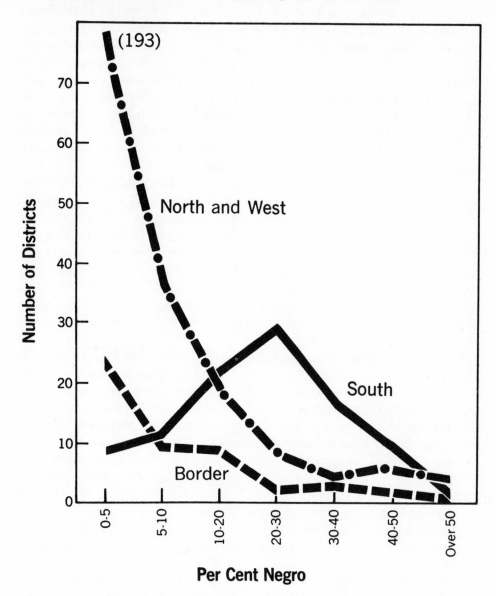

Per Cent Negro

rights laws (in 1957 and 1960), the institution of thirty-six voting rights
suits by the United States Department of Justice, the operation of several
privately sponsored registration drives (in 1962 there were an estimated 140
such drives in progress or in prospect), and the holding of hearings by the
United States Civil Rights Commission, Negro registration in those counties
had increased only to 8.3 percent of the adult Negroes.[9]

These one hundred problem counties are less than one-tenth of all the
counties in the South, but they contain one-third of all the region's voting-
age Negroes. Even if all discriminatory practices were ended, however, the
low socioeconomic status of the Negro would result in relatively low registration and voter turnout figures. In 1959, urban Southern Negroes had a
median income less than half that of urban Southern whites and less than
two-thirds that of Negroes living in Northern and Western cities.[10] Pro-

fessors Matthews and Prothro of the University of North Carolina, analyzing nearly one thousand Southern counties, estimate that socioeconomic factors are about as important as political ones in determining Negro registration levels; because of this, they caution that "reformers should not expect miracles in their efforts, through political and legal means, to increase the size and effectiveness of the Negro vote in the South. The Negro registration rate is low, in rather large part, because of the social and economic characteristics of southerners—both Negro and white. These factors are not easily and quickly changed by law or political actions." [11]

The two periods of greatest increase in Southern Negro voter registration were in the 1940's (registration rose from 5 percent of the voting-age Southern Negroes in 1940 to 28 percent in 1952) and again in 1963–64 (when registration rose to over 38 percent of the potential).[12] The first increase was the result, in great part, of the abolition by the Supreme Court in 1944 of the "white primary" laws and rules that had excluded Negroes from participation in Democratic party primaries.[13] The second increase was in part the result of intensive voter registration drives conducted, after the passage of the first two civil rights bills, by a variety of organizations, many under the auspices of the Voter Education Project of the Southern Regional Conference. These campaigns added more than half a million Negro voters to the rolls in eleven Southern states. Negro registration by state for the South is shown in Table 1. Many of the state figures are estimates only (some Southern states have no official registration figures) and should be used with caution.

In 1964, the Twenty-Fourth Amendment to the Constitution, abolishing the poll tax, was ratified by the states. It is not likely that this change will

TABLE I—Negro Voting Registration in Southern States, 1959 and 1964

State	Percentage of Voting-Age Negroes Registered		Estimated Number of Negroes Registered
	1959*	1964**	1964**
Alabama	13.7	21.6	104,000
Arkansas	37.7	43.5	80,000
Florida	39.0	51.1	240,616
Georgia	25.8	39.1	240,000
Louisiana	30.9	31.6	162,866
Mississippi	6.2	6.7	28,500
North Carolina	38.2	45.0	248,000
South Carolina	14.8	34.2	127,000
Tennessee	na	67.2	211,000
Texas	38.8	57.7	375,000
Virginia	23.0	27.7	121,000
Total	—	**38.6**	**1,937,982**

Note: These figures are estimates only and in many cases are subject to considerable error. Some states lack a formal registration procedure and as a result have no official registration figures for Negroes or whites. The data should be used with caution.

* SOURCE: 1959 *Report*, United States Civil Rights Commission, pp. 559–86, and 1961 *Report*, United States Civil Rights Commission, pp. 251–311.

** SOURCE: *Second Annual Report*, Voter Education Project of the Southern Regional Council, Inc., April 1, 1964.

have much effect on registration figures, as the poll tax requirement had long since been repealed or become a dead letter in most Southern states.[14]

The counties in which Negro registration is the lowest tend to be counties in which the Negro proportion of the total population is the largest: the more Negroes, the fewer are registered. Indeed, of all the socio-economic characteristics of Southern counties examined by Matthews and Prothro, a high Negro population percentage was most closely associated with a *low* Negro registration level.[15] Quite clearly, the larger the proportion of Negroes in a county, the greater the potential threat they represent to white voters and office holders and thus the greater the efforts made to prevent them from registering and voting. (There are some exceptions, of course; four of these exceptional counties will be discussed at the conclusion of this article.) There is some evidence that the size of the Negro population is even more important than the existence of restrictive suffrage laws in determining Negro voting participation. Professor Angus Campbell and associates present survey results suggesting—but not proving—that more Negroes vote in Southern counties with restrictive laws but a smaller proportion (under 30 percent) of Negroes than vote in counties with more liberal laws but a higher proportion of Negroes.[16] This indicates both the importance of informal as opposed to legal restrictions on voting and the possibility that, as Negroes continue to leave the South, their proportions in various counties may fall to the point where white fears—and hence white resistance—will begin to lessen.[17]

One apparent anomaly in the Southern Negro registration pattern is associated with religious differences. A careful study of registration by parish (*i.e.*, county) in Louisiana shows that, in general, the higher the proportion of Roman Catholics in a parish, the larger the proportion of adult Negroes who are registered to vote.[18] The twenty-five predominately French-Catholic parishes of southern Louisiana are also those in which Negro registration is highest (generally over 50 percent of the potential registration). In part this is no doubt the result of the economic structure of these areas. Unlike the Mississippi Delta region, most French-Catholic parishes have not had a plantation economy with its tenant farmers and tradition of master-slave relations. In part also these differences in registration are the consequence of differences in racial balance—on the whole, French-Catholic parishes have a lower proportion of Negroes than Protestant "Bible belt" areas. Nonetheless, cultural and religious factors are important even after allowance is made for the economy and the racial balance. In French-Catholic parishes which do have a plantation system, economic tenancy and high proportions of Negroes in the population, Negro registration is higher than in similar non-Catholic parishes.

Voting Behavior and Party Preference

Nationally, the Negro voter is a Democratic voter. He has not always been a Democrat and he has not invariably been a Democrat in all parts of the country, but since the 1940's his commitment to the Democratic Party, at least in the North, has been unswerving. There are no signs that this is about to change.

Table II shows the percentage of the two-party vote which was cast for the last four Democratic presidential candidates by voters in heavily Negro districts in the five largest Northern cities. The Negro in these big Northern

The concentration of the Negro vote in the big cities means that, even if all Negroes could and did vote freely, they would be under-represented in the House of Representatives.
(Haryou-Act Still Photography Workshop, Photo by Arthur Lobo)

cities has voted by large majorities for the Democratic presidential candidate; only President Eisenhower in 1956 was able to cause a significant drop in Democratic strength among Negroes, and even then not in all cities. President Kennedy more than recovered those temporary losses and President Johnson received an unparalleled majority.

Until the New Deal, the Negro voter was a Republican. He voted for the party of Abraham Lincoln when he could vote at all. It was not until Franklin Roosevelt persuaded Negroes that he was committed to welfare programs that would benefit low-income Negroes, and (at least in theory) to principles of equality that would benefit all Negroes that the massive shift from the Republican to the Democratic Party began. The speed of this shift varied from city to city and, within each city, from class to class. In 1932, Herbert Hoover captured a majority of Negro votes in Chicago, Baltimore, Philadelphia, Cleveland, New Haven, Wilmington (Delaware) and Columbus (Ohio). Indeed, in Chicago, the power of the Republican organization of William Hale ("Big Bill") Thompson was such that Negroes regularly gave him and his candidates over 80 percent of their votes. Where a Democratic machine was in power—as, for example, in Kansas City, Missouri—the Democrats did much better in the Negro precincts. (The heavily Negro Ward 4 in Kansas City voted over 70 percent for Roosevelt as early as 1932.)[19]

TABLE II—Democratic Vote as Percent of Two-Party Presidential Vote Nationally and for Heavily Negro Wards of the Five Largest Cities 1952–60

City and Ward (or District)	Percent Democratic			
	1952	1956	1960	1964
Chicago (Ward 2)	77	68	80	95
Detroit (Ward 3) *	90	84	90	
Los Angeles (62nd Assembly District) **	77	72	82	92 **
New York (11th Assembly District)	83	69	79	96
Philadelphia (Ward 32)	83	79	83	97
Nationally (estimate) ***	79	61	68	94

* Ward 3 abolished before 1964; no comparable figure available.
** Los Angeles redistricted; 1964 figure is for the new and comparable 53rd Assembly District.
*** Source of national estimate: Gallup Poll surveys as reported in *Congressional Quarterly*, Dec. 25, 1964.

By 1936, the swing to the Democrats had set in everywhere. In Cleveland, Philadelphia, Detroit, Kansas City, New Haven and Pittsburgh Negro voters gave Roosevelt large majorities (Chicago continued to lag behind this trend, the voters in Wards 2 and 3 giving a slight majority of their ballots to Landon.)[20] One study suggests that this transfer of allegiance began with the *least* disadvantaged Negroes; at first, it was a switch among middle-class Negroes who perhaps had greater information, were more sensitive to the ideological as distinguished from welfare aspects of the New Deal, and were less dependent upon the favors and friendships of precinct captains. Gosnell, for example, has shown for Chicago that the shift among Negroes in the 1930's occurred faster in those Negro areas with higher median rentals, lower unemployment rates and fewer relief cases.[21] Although somewhat slower to change originally (at least in Chicago), once committed to the Democratic party the lower-income Negroes have been the most steadfast. The defection to Eisenhower of some Negroes in 1956 was greater among middle-class than among lower-class Negroes.

In the South, some Negroes have been voting in a few large cities for many years. The Negro vote in Atlanta was important in the success of a school bond issue as early as 1921. Negro voters were a significant part of the political machines of Edward Crump of Memphis and the Bellinger family in San Antonio.[22] Even in the days of the "white primary" there were a few Negroes who voted in general elections and in at least the nonpartisan city elections. In recent years there has been a substantial—though unmeasured—increase in this vote. Of all the cities of the Deep South, Atlanta has perhaps registered the most conspicuous gains. More than twenty thousand Negroes (over one-fourth of the total electorate) were eligible to vote in Atlanta as early as 1946 (this figure did not increase significantly during the next ten years owing to weak organization and an absence of dramatic contests).[23] After a massive voter registration campaign in 1961 and 1962, the number of registered Negroes rose to about 52,000. The Negro vote was greater than the margin of victory of the winning candidate for mayor in 1949; in 1953, a Negro college president was elected to the Atlanta Board of Education largely, though not entirely, with Negro votes; in 1957, the Negro vote in the mayoralty primary was estimated to be over 18,000, more than 93 percent of which went to the winning candidate, Hartsfield. Negroes still are not registered proportionally to their population. In 1960 38.8 percent of Atlanta's population but only 29.5 percent of the registered voters were Negro.[24]

In the 1952 Presidential election, Negroes in most Southern cities voted overwhelmingly for the Democrat, Adlai Stevenson. In 1956, however, there occurred a massive shift to Eisenhower. The results are shown in Table III. (Eisenhower increased his vote among Northern Negroes as well, but not as much; in no major Northern city did he win a majority of Negro votes.) The reasons for the shift have not been documented—national opinion polls usually have so few Negroes in the sample that the surveys are virtually useless for any analysis that requires one to separate Negro voters by region, class and party affiliation. It seems likely, however, that the appeal was less that of Eisenhower's personality than the events following the May, 1954, Supreme Court school desegregation decision. Republicans could point to the fact that the decision was written by a "Republican" Chief Justice (Earl Warren), that it occurred during a Republican administration, and that it was being bitterly resisted by many Southern Democratic politicians at the national as well as the local level.

In 1960, of course, the Negro—North and South—was heavily Democratic. Again, no one can be certain of the reasons. Economic issues were probably important (there had been a serious recession); the Republican presidential candidate, Richard Nixon, seemed to be making a successful appeal for Southern white votes; Senator Kennedy placed a well-timed and well-publicized telephone call to the wife of Martin Luther King, Jr., then languishing in a Georgia jail.[25]

Whatever the reasons, the evidence of 1956 is strong enough to suggest that the Southern Negro voter is not as firmly committed as the Northern Negro voter to the Democratic Party. The former—perhaps because of his experience in nonpartisan local elections and Democratic Party primaries, where party labels are either absent or meaningless—is more sensitive to the positions of individuals and of factions and more susceptible to being organized by nonpartisan, all-Negro political associations.[26] The great importance of race issues in the South gives a racial sensitivity to the Southern Negro vote that has been absent from the party-oriented Northern Negro vote. (In Atlanta, over *99 percent* of the Negro voters are estimated to have voted for the winning mayoralty candidate in 1961.[27] It is inconceivable that such majorities could be obtained for a candidate in the North where *all* candidates profess to believe in equal rights and where party organization is much stronger.)

Negro voters are often described as holding the "balance of power." They are now 6 percent or more of the population of eight key states which have 210 electoral votes in presidential contests. In several of these states— California, Illinois, Michigan and New Jersey, among others—President Kennedy's margin among Negro voters in 1960 was greater than the margin by which he carried the state as a whole.[28] The same, however, could be said of any number of other groups—Catholics, for example, or Jews, or union members, or perhaps even college professors. Since all these groups— and more—could hold the "balance of power," then it is obviously incorrect to imply that any one of these groups holds it to the exclusion of the others. Furthermore, the Negro voter (particularly in the North) is *less* likely than other voters to change from one party to another (low-income voters are less likely than others to be "independent").[29] Negro votes are important, not because they are "swing" votes which reward friends and punish enemies, but because they are very numerous and strategically located; the object of a politician's strategy can only be to obtain a high turnout (if he is a Democrat) or a low turnout (if he is a Republican), not to change votes in wholesale numbers.

An illuminating case is that of Senator Jacob Javits of New York. A liberal Republican, Javits has been an outspoken proponent of vigorous civil rights measures. Nonetheless, he fared little better in the Negro areas of New York City when he ran, in 1962, against a conservative Democrat (James Donovan) whose position on civil rights was unclear than he did when he ran in 1956 against another outspoken liberal, Robert F. Wagner, Jr. Between 1956 and 1962, Javits' percentage of the two-party vote in certain Negro districts increased less than two percentage points—from 32.8 percent in 1956 to 34.5 percent in 1962.[30]

Negro Representation in Politics

There is an implicit tension between at least one conception of representation and the concept of integration. If all Negroes were fully assimilated into American society, distributed geographically and socially without regard to color, then Negroes might not occupy any elective offices —or they might occupy several, depending largely on chance. The greater the geographical concentration (*i.e.,* segregation, willing or unwilling) of Negroes, the greater the probability that Negroes will be elected to office,

"With the increased militancy of Negroes . . . many wholly nonpolitical voluntary associations in Negro communities are acquiring . . . political functions."
(Haryou-Act Still Photography Workshop, Photo by Randy Williams)

provided that elections are by districts.

Because of their dense concentration in relatively small political districts, Negroes in Chicago were able to elect an alderman as early as 1915, a ward committeeman (the key party official) in 1920, and a Congressman in 1928.[31] New York City, with somewhat larger districts, did not have a Negro district leader in the Democratic Party until 1935 or a Negro Congressman until 1944. Detroit, where council members are elected from the city at large rather than from districts, did not have a Negro council member until 1957. Los Angeles, with very large city council districts and relatively late Negro in-migration (mostly after World War II, rather than —as in the case of most Eastern cities—after World War I), did not have Negro council members until 1963.

The first Northern Negro Congressman—and the first Negro Congressman from any region since Reconstruction—was Oscar DePriest, a Chicago Republican who won office in 1928. The first Negro Congressman elected on the Democratic ticket was Arthur W. Mitchell, also of Chicago, who defeated DePriest in 1934. In each case, the Negro victory was made possible because the party's white nominee died before the election and had to be replaced; in each case, influential white politicians were persuaded to give the suddenly vacant nomination to a Negro.[32] Mitchell in turn was replaced by the present Negro Congressman from Chicago, William L. Dawson, in 1942.

In addition to Dawson, five other Negroes (all Democrats) serve in the United States House of Representatives: Adam Clayton Powell, Jr., of New York City (elected in 1944); Charles Diggs, Jr., of Detroit (elected in 1954); Robert N. C. Nix of Philadelphia (elected in 1958); Augustus F. Hawkins of Los Angeles (elected in 1962), and John L. Conyers of Detroit (elected in 1964).

In general, Negroes are elected to office when they constitute at least 50 percent of the electorate of the district or when a party organization seeks to offer the voters a "balanced ticket." Dawson, Powell and Nix were all elected from overwhelmingly Negro districts; all Negro city councilmen (or aldermen) in Chicago and New York are from Negro districts. In city-wide contests where a number of similar posts (such as county commissioner or municipal court judge) are to be filled, a strong party—as in Chicago or New York—will place one or more Negroes on the ticket in order to "recognize" that group within the party and, hopefully, secure a few additional votes from the group recognized without losing votes from other groups who are sufficiently loyal to the party label to refrain from "cutting" the ticket on the grounds that a Negro is on it. Hulan Jack was elected borough president of Manhattan even though Negroes were then only 21 percent of the population.

There are many exceptions, of course. Edward Brooke was elected attorney general of Massachusetts on the Republican ticket in 1962, even though Negroes are only about 2 percent of the population and party organization is particularly weak. Charles Diggs, Jr., became a Congressman in 1954 from a Detroit district which, as late as 1960, was less than half Negro.

There is no compilation of all the major elective offices held by Negroes. Table IV shows the number of Negroes on the legislative bodies of several large Northern cities. Negroes also sit in many state legislatures: as of 1962, Illinois and Michigan had nine each, Pennsylvania eleven, New York and Missouri six each, Maryland four and California three. For the first time in over ninety years, a Negro was elected in 1962 to the Georgia legislature as a state senator from Atlanta. Many other states have one or two Negro legislators.[33] After the 1964 elections, an estimated 280 Negroes held elective office.

The greatest formal political power held by Negroes is in the hands of two Congressmen, Dawson and Powell, each of whom has become—through the inexorable workings of the seniority system—chairman of an important committee in the House of Representatives (Dawson is chairman of the Government Operations Committee, Powell of the Education and Labor Committee).[34] At the local level, considerable influence—usually informal rather than formal—is wielded by Negroes who hold key party posts. Dawson is Democratic committeeman of Chicago's second ward, leader of the Negro bloc in the Cook County Democratic Committee, and vice chairman of the Democratic National Committee.

The prospects for increased Negro representation in Congress are fair in the North, slim in the South. There are (for the 88th Congress) twenty-

TABLE III—Percent Voting for Eisenhower in Negro Wards
and Precincts of Selected Southern Cities, 1952–56*

City	Percent for Eisenhower	
	1952	1956
Atlanta, Ga.	30.9%	85.3%
Charlotte, N.C.	16.3	38.5
Chattanooga, Tenn.	20.5	49.3
Houston, Texas	10.5	34.8
Jacksonville, Fla.	15.7	40.9
Knoxville, Tenn.	29.7	40.9
Memphis, Tenn.	34.4	54.0
New Orleans, La.	20.2	55.1
Richmond, Va.	21.9	73.0

* SOURCE: Henry Lee Moon, "The Negro Vote in the Presidential Election of 1956," *Journal of Negro Education*, XXVI (Summer, 1957), 224.

TABLE IV—Negro Representation on City Councils in Selected Non-Southern Cities

City	Total Council Seats	Seats Held by Negroes (March, 1965)	Percent of Seats Held by Negroes	Negroes as Percent of 1960 Population
Detroit	9	0	0	28.9
Cleveland	33	10	30.3	28.6
St. Louis	29	6	20.7	28.6
Philadelphia	17	2	11.8	26.4
Chicago	50	7	14.0	22.9
Cincinnati	9	1	11.1	21.6
New York City	35	2	5.7	14.0
Los Angeles	15	3	20.0	13.5
Boston	9	0	0	9.1

SOURCE: Updated from table in Edward C. Banfield and James Q. Wilson, *City Politics* (Cambridge: Harvard University Press, 1963), p. 293.

one congressional districts that are 40 percent or more Negro; of these, five are over half Negro. Six districts, all in the North, are now held by Negroes; of the remaining fifteen, ten are rural Southern districts and five are Northern urban districts. Assuming that no Negro will win an election in a rural Southern district for many years to come, additional Negro Congressmen will not for the immediate future exceed five and they will come from these Northern cities: Baltimore, Chicago, Cleveland, Detroit and Philadelphia.

The number and kind of political offices held by Negroes are not necessarily a reflection of Negro electoral strength. Negroes in Chicago, for example, are far better organized politically than Negroes in New York. In 1959, however, a count showed four Negro judges holding office in Chicago, seventeen in New York City.[35]

No comprehensive survey exists of the number of Negroes holding political appointive offices. Both major political parties claim they have made a substantial number of Negro appointments while holding power in Washington. Lists compiled by the Democratic and Republican National Committees showed between ninety and one hundred such appointments; it is unlikely that either list is complete or entirely accurate. The vast majority of Federal administrative appointments given to Negroes by both Democrats and Republicans have gone to Northerners rather than Southerners, despite the approximately equal division of the Negro population between North and South. Several factors are probably responsible: Northern Negroes are politically more active and they include a substantially larger percentage of the educated, professionally qualified segment of the race. The extent to which political participation by Northern Negroes has led to appointment should not be exaggerated, however. It is unlikely that many Negro appointees were able to "demand" a job because of the votes they controlled or the influence they wielded. Few Negroes occupy a position in the political system that would give them such power (Congressmen Dawson and Powell may be exceptions).

Furthermore, Negroes in most cases are appointed by white officials; this undoubtedly introduces a certain selectivity into the appointment process and places a few constraints on the appointee. White liberals who select Negroes for appointive positions are likely to be just as sensitive (perhaps more sensitive) to the views of the NAACP, the Urban League and white liberal organizations as to the views of Negro elective officials. (It is, after all, the protest organizations, and only rarely the politicians, which make the headlines.)

Negro appointments have grown in number and stature in recent years. For example, President Eisenhower appointed Negroes to be Assistant Secretary of Labor, Chairman of the President's Committee on Government Employment Policy, a Special Assistant to the President, and member of the Civil Rights Commission; President Kennedy selected Negroes to be members of the Federal Circuit Court of Appeals and Federal District Courts, Ambassador to Finland (and later director of the United States Information Agency) and to Norway, Administrator of the Housing and Home Finance Agency, Associate White House Press Secretary, and United States Attorney for San Francisco.

Negroes have, of course, long been beneficiaries of the Federal civil service system. In most cases, appointments to positions in the classified civil service have no direct connection with politics (although the recent effort to increase the number of Negroes working for the Government undoubtedly does in a general way). As of June, 1962, Negroes were slightly over-represented in the Federal service, holding about 13 percent of the jobs although they are only 10.3 percent of the work force.[36] Negro employment with the Federal Government has been growing faster than Federal employment generally (from June, 1962, to June, 1963, it increased 3 percent)[37] and the gains have most recently been greatest in the higher grades of the civil service where Negroes are still, absolutely and in proportion to whites, very few in number.

In finding Negroes for both political and merit appointments, a seller's market prevails. The desire of Federal officials to demonstrate that their agencies are integrated and the desire of Federal political leaders to prove that they are "doing something" for the Negro has led, in many departments, for massive talent hunts in which the absence of qualified Negroes more than the absence of job opportunities accounts for much of the limited progress so far made.[38]

Negro Political Organization

American politics, it is often noted, is local in orientation, decentralized in structure and divided in leadership. It is at the local level that political parties exist on a day-to-day basis; it is in the cities, counties, and states that most party personnel are to be found, most party funds raised and spent and most party business conducted. Negro political organizations, to the extent they are organizations at all, are part and parcel of this system, suffering from its weaknesses and enjoying its benefits.

Some Negro politicians are, of course, national rather than local figures. Adam Clayton Powell is a familiar personality, his role in Congress and in various protest movements depending as much or more on the national following he has among some Negroes as it does on his political organization. Indeed, judged by the standards of Chicago, Philadelphia or even Detroit, Representative Powell can hardly be said to have an organization at all. He is clearly the exception, however.

Not only are Negroes part of a fragmented political system, they usually find it necessary to be politicians first and Negroes second. There is nothing unusual or discreditable about this; any politician (or, for that matter, anyone acting in his professional capacity) must either act as the organization or profession expects him to act or have his effectiveness curtailed and perhaps his membership revoked.

This means that, in most cases, Negro politicians are not likely to be the vanguard of civil rights protest movements. This is particularly the case if they are part of a strong, city- or county-wide party organization that insists on maintaining unity and following the leadership. It is also the case if the Negro is elected from a constituency that includes white as well as Negro voters—for example, if the Negro is elected to the city council from the city at large. Some Negro politicians, of course, are elected from all-Negro districts and are "lone wolves" who, because the party organization in the city is weak, do not find it to their advantage to follow its leadership. The utterly different political styles of William Dawson of Chicago and Adam Clayton Powell of New York can be explained by the great differences in the political systems and organizations of which they are part as well as by personality factors.

CHARLES C. DIGGS (Photo by Roland Mitchell)

ADAM CLAYTON POWELL, JR. (Photo by Roland Mitchell)

WILLIAM L. DAWSON

The forms of Negro political organizations are almost infinitely various; in all cases, they are strongly influenced—not to say determined—by the form of the white political organization, if any, of which they are a part.[39] The classical political machine continues to function in Chicago generally and in the Negro wards particularly. Precinct captains, relying on the exchange of favors and friendship and information, induce voters to support the organization's candidates—Negro and white—for office. Party loyalty is the governing principle and a concern for concrete, individual, often material interests is the motive force. The causes of the more militant civil rights advocates interest the party leaders but are not at the center of their concern.

The weak and divided remnants of a political machine struggle on in New York City; the Negro elements of this organization struggle with the white elements and with each other. Alliances are made and broken, party loyalty is an oft-proclaimed but rarely attained goal, and either ideology or tactical maneuver (or both) have replaced allegiance to a party hierarchy as the dominant political style. In Detroit, at-large nonpartisan elections have prevented the emergence of either a strong local party organization (the local Democratic party and its affiliated labor unions are powerful in Michigan politics but comparatively weak in city affairs) or of a stable Negro political leadership structure. Elective Negro officials must appeal to whites as well as to Negroes and have a political style consistent with the "good government" ethos that prevails in the community.

In the South, where Negro elective officials are few, Negro politics—as far as Negroes can participate in politics at all—tends to be in the hands, not of professional politicians, but of part-time amateurs whose standing in the community depends as much or more on their role as minister, businessman, lawyer or educator as it does on their political leadership. In many Southern cities (such as Atlanta, Georgia, and Durham and Winston-Salem, North Carolina) the dominant Negro political organization is not an element of the regular party system but instead is a nonpartisan "voter's league" which endorses candidates, Negro and white, and mobilizes Negro votes for them.[40] The Atlanta Negro Voters' League, for example, was founded in 1949 to concentrate Negro voting strength behind those local candidates most advantageous (or least disadvantageous) to Negro interests while leaving members free to support candidates of their choice in national elections.[41] Since Atlanta has nonpartisan local elections, the endorsement of the Voters' League did not have to overcome traditional party loyalties in order to be effective. The Durham Committee on Negro Affairs has also proved to be an influential political force; like the Atlanta League, it has been able to muster large majorities in the Negro precincts (one observer estimates that 60 to 90 percent of the Negro voters will follow its endorsements).[42] Similar groups of varying effectiveness are found in other Southern cities. The polarization of public opinion on the race issue has made the Voters' League strategy far more effective in the South than the North: the policy of rewarding friends and punishing enemies is easier when one's enemies are openly and indisputably hostile.

Southern Negro political organizations differ in the extent to which they recruit and support, rather than simply endorse, candidates. Whatever the strategy, Negroes in the South as in the North tend to follow political patterns comparable to those of the whites. The weakness and factionalism of formal party organization in the one-party states of the South, coupled with widespread nonpartisan local elections (75 percent of all Southern cities over 25,000 population elect city council or commission members on ballots which do not reveal the party affiliation of candidates), has made it possible—even necessary—for white political leadership in many cities to be assumed by businessmen, civic associations, part-time political managers and a variety of individual political personalities and factions. Negro politics is often a mirror image of the white system with, in some cases, the additional advantage of a growing racial solidarity.

Not all Southern cities have organized Negro political movements. New Orleans, according to recent accounts, lacks—despite two decades of efforts —a city-wide Negro political organization; instead, a number of rival organizations and factions—numbering as many as eight—have contended with each other for supremacy. Their efforts have never been united behind a single Negro candidate.[43]

In the North, Negro politicians have rarely been influential at the state level because Negroes are concentrated in the big cities and it is in the big-city organizations that Negroes wield influence, if they wield it at all. In the South, however, Negroes were once important state figures in the Republican Party. After Reconstruction, when the South became a one-party region, Republicans lost all hope of winning votes or office. Yet some nominal Republican organization was necessary in order for the South to be represented every four years in the Republican national nominating convention. After the new Southern state constitutions of 1890–1910 succeeded in disfranchising the Negro almost entirely, the Republican Party—which at one time drew on a sizable block of Southern Negro voters and elected numerous Negroes to state and local offices—almost ceased to exist. By 1920 it had virtually abandoned electoral politics, not bothering to hold primaries and often failing even to offer candidates in the general elections.

Many Southern Republican leaders at this time were Negro. In Mississippi, for example, Perry Howard, a Mississippi-born Negro lawyer resident in Washington, D.C., was Republican national committeeman; Dr. S. D. Redmond (a Negro) was, until his death in 1948, chairman of the Republican state executive committee; the Republican national committeewoman was for a number of years also a Negro.[44] A Republican organization such as this was of course not a vote-winning but a patronage-dispensing organization. Its only real function was to send delegates to the national convention; Northern Republican factions courted these votes and, if a Republican were elected President, rewarded the local officials.

These "black-and-tan" Republican organizations were from time to time challenged by so-called "lily-white" Southern Republican movements. White Republicans were in many cases eager to supplant the Negroes, in part to end the identification of the Republican party with "scalawags" and "nigger-lovers" and in part to get access to the perquisites of office. Several national Republican figures gave support to this effort, which in most states was successful. With the emerging prospect of a genuine Republican Party in the South, the assertion of white leadership has of course become even more pronounced. Perry Howard of Mississippi was the last Negro Republican national committeeman in the South.

Negro politics is not always the province of Negro politicians. Traditionally, the Negro minister has played a crucial role in the community as virtually the only leader with a mass following. Indeed, the early efforts of Negro political participation typically occur under clerical auspices, the ministers forming the organization, recruiting the members, and dealing with the white community. If Negroes succeed in politics—particularly if they elect a member of their race to office or persuade a white official to appoint one to office—Negro politics begins to become professionalized, control falling into the hands of persons who make political leadership their special responsibility. A division of labor occurs, the ministers being replaced (for example) by lawyers who have politically valuable skills, who are free of the constraints imposed by the need to maintain a church congregation, and who often have careers in which politics can be personally rewarding. Finally, if a stable party apparatus is created, or if Negro elective officials acquire fulltime political positions on a long-term basis, the leaders cease being lawyers dabbling in politics and become instead politicians dabbling in law.

This, of course, is an oversimplified account of a very complex phenomenon that has, in general, been insufficiently studied. In many places the critical roles may be played, not by lawyers, but by teachers, students or other members of the growing professional middle class. But in general the pattern is a familiar one: political leadership moves institutionally from one mass base (usually a church or neighborhood association) to a different mass base (a party organization) via an intermediary stage of half-amateur, half-professional political managers.

With the increased militancy of Negroes and the greater involvement of the Negro masses that has occurred since 1963, many wholly nonpolitical voluntary associations in Negro communities are acquiring, wittingly or unwittingly, political functions. The NAACP, for example, has traditionally been a legal defense and lobbying organization; in many communities today, however, its branches have become involved in voter registration drives. These drives are, of course, nonpartisan (the NAACP could not afford to become wholly identified with one political party), but in fact the Negro voters added to the registration lists by such drives are overwhelmingly Democratic. It is not because they are Democrats, however, that they are registered, but rather because they are voters needed in local, nonpartisan contests (in elections, for example, of city school board members) where racial issues are less obscured by party labels and loyalties.

Other civic groups, permanent and *ad hoc,* play a political role. Some sentiment is expressed from time to time in favor of a "Negro political party," distinct from the major parties. In the context of the American political system, where third parties have rarely had a significant impact on policy and almost never influence the outcome of important elections, such a strategy seems unpromising. One leader of the Negro "Nation of Islam" (the so-called Black Muslim movement), Malcolm X, announced in early 1964 his intention of forming a Negro nationalist movement with direct and immediate political objectives (in contrast to the long-range, separatist goals of the Muslims); what those objectives might be or how they might be attained was not clear. Until the split in leadership, Negro Muslims—notably Elijah Muhammed, founder of the movement—renounced political or civic action, both because it implied cooperation with rather than separation from white society and because it could not succeed.[45]

TABLE V—Non-Southern States with "Open Occupancy" Laws Barring Discrimination in Private Housing Market

State and Year	Percent Negro (1960)
1959	
Colorado	2.3%
Connecticut	4.2
Massachusetts	2.2
Oregon	1.0
1961	
Minnesota	0.7
New Hampshire	0.3
New Jersey	8.5
New York	8.4
Pennsylvania	7.5
1962	
Alaska	3.0
1963	
California	5.6
Michigan	9.2
Washington	1.7

Effects of Negro Political Activity

The consequence of Negro participation in American politics are not as straightforward as they might at first seem. It is certainly true, of course, that the manner in which the President is chosen gives to him and his office almost regardless of party a particular sensitivity to the major population and interest groups—including the Negro which votes in the largest cities of the principal states. The first two civil rights bills were enacted under a Republican President; the third and fourth has been vigorously pressed by two Democratic Presidents, the last of whom—Johnson—is a Southerner.

The fact that American Presidents are proponents of civil rights should not lead us to assume that this response is solely the result of the strategic location of large numbers of voting Negroes. Presidents tend to be "liberal" on this and other matters because of the nature of their electorate as a whole and the key position in the national nominating conventions of liberal, urban forces (of which Negroes are only one part).

At the state level, the strengths and weaknesses of Negro political activity are clear. On the one hand, few governors of large Northern states would think of planning a campaign that did not include a reasonably clear defense of civil rights in general and Negro rights in particular. On the other hand, the Northern states with the earliest and strongest record of civil rights legislation are not necessarily the states with the most Negroes. For example (see Table V), the first four states to enact laws barring discrimination in the sale or rental of private housing (the so-called "open occupancy" laws) were Northern states with *few* Negroes (Colorado—2.3 percent Negro; Connecticut—4.2 percent Negro; Massachusetts—2.2 percent Negro; Oregon—1.0 percent Negro). By 1964, five years after these states had passed such laws, many of the Northern states with larger Negro populations had *not* acted. These included Delaware (13.6 percent Negro),

Illinois (10.3 percent Negro), Maryland (16.7 percent Negro), and Ohio (8.1 percent Negro).[46]

The explanation for this anomaly may be (no one knows) that a large Negro population is politically both an asset and a liability. A large Negro populace may not only expect to influence the commitments and behavior of a governor, but it also may expect to arouse the fears of many whites. The larger the Negro population, the greater the perceived threat (in the eyes of whites) and thus the greater the resistance to broad civil rights laws.[47]

In securing the passage of civil rights laws, state and local officials have probably been as alert to the demands of white liberal groups as to those of Negroes. It has been suggested, for example, that the extensive civil rights enactments in New York (city and state) are the result as much of white liberal (chiefly Jewish) pressure as of Negro pressure.[48] The reason for this is not hard to find. White liberals interested in civil rights tend, on the whole, to be at or above the median in income, education and occupation and thus to have precisely those characteristics which are associated with the so-called "independent" voter. Particularly in local contests, it is the white liberal vote, more than the Negro vote, which may shift and which thus must be courted.

The effect of Negro political activity is potentially greater in primary than in general elections. In primaries, all candidates have the same party label, and thus voting for racial interests is not blunted by traditional party loyalties. The difficulty, obviously, is that relatively few voters participate in primaries (between 1926 and 1952, almost three-fourths of all gubernatorial primaries held in fifteen Northern states had the participation of one-third or less of the potential electorate).[49] Not only do few voters participate, those that do—except in communities where there are strong party organizations—tend to be highly motivated voters or those with a strong sense of duty. Negroes are under-represented in this group and thus their voting strength is diluted.

Where the primary contest offers a clear choice between candidates who differ greatly in their attitude toward race relations, Negro participation (assuming they are free to participate at all) is likely to be considerable. In the South, where the Democratic party primary has usually been more important than the general election, Negro voter registration is higher—other things, such as socio-economic characteristics, being equal—in those states where the primary is a contest between two easily identifiable factions and where the candidates or factions differ in their attitude toward Negroes.[50] (Tennessee and North Carolina are examples of such states.)

The long-heralded advent of a two-party South may or may not increase Negro political effectiveness. Southern counties with a competitive two-party system have slightly higher Negro voter registration rates, but most of the difference is apparently the result, not of the two-party system, but of socio-economic factors.[51] One would think that as the two parties compete more evenly, each would bid for the vote of the major population groups and thereby bring more Negroes into the electorate for reasons of party advantage. This has not occurred to any significant extent, and the reason seems to be that the growth in party competitiveness is largely occurring in districts where relatively few Negroes live. Of the twenty-four Southern congressional districts in which the Republican candidate polled more than 35 percent of the vote in 1956, only two are more than one-fourth

Negro. Republicanism has long existed in a few Southern "mountain" counties where relatively few Negroes live; it is now making inroads in some middle-class urban districts where practically no Negroes live. In seventeen of the nineteen most Negro districts in the South, the Republicans did not even put up a congressional candidate in 1956.[52]

After all the qualifications have been made, however, it remains true that the presence of Negroes in a political unit affects the behavior of the politician who represents that unit. In the South, the presence of a large proportion of Negroes in the district makes the congressman from that district more hostile, not only to civil rights but to many other "liberal" issues. In the North, where the presence of Negroes means the presence of *voting* Negroes, the congressman is likely to be more sympathetic to liberal and civil rights issues. (These generalizations are all matters of degree, of course; no single factor—be it Negroes or anything else—can "explain" the whole of any congressman's behavior.)

One student has analyzed the Democratic votes on labor legislation in the United States House of Representatives since the Second World War in terms of the frequency with which congressmen supported the party leadership (*i.e.*, were "party regulars") and thus, generally, the more liberal position. Southern congressmen with the smallest proportion of Negroes in their district were most "regular" while those with the largest proportions of Negroes were "least regular." [53] On race-relations votes, another student has shown a similar general tendency for the Southern states with the smallest proportion of Negroes to have congressmen with a slightly higher level of support for civil rights legislation.[54]

In the North, it is hard to separate the influence of Negroes on congressmen from the influence of other factors. Northern congressmen from heavily urban districts are, in general, more "liberal" than ones from less urban areas; since Negroes are found most heavily in the big cities, the impact of the Negro voter is hard to distinguish from the impact of urban influences generally. However, there is some evidence that even among urban Northern Democratic congressmen, those with high proportions of Negroes in their districts are slightly more likely to follow the party leadership and thus, usually, the more "liberal" program.[55]

Viewed as a whole, Negro political activity must be judged as a strategy of limited objectives. Where Negroes can and do vote, they have it in their power to end the indifference or hostility of their elected representatives, but these representatives do not have it in their power to alter fundamentally the lot of the Negro. The vote is a legally important, morally essential weapon for the protection and advancement of individual and group interests but it cannot protect or advance *all* the relevant interests. It can force the passage of laws, the ending of obvious forms of state-sanctioned discrimination, and the removal from office of race-baiters and avowed segregationists. It can only marginally affect the income, housing, occupation, or life chances of Negro electorates.[56]

Even civil rights legislation is not simply the product of Negro voting. Although all five Negro congressmen voted for civil rights bills in 1964 none was prominently identified as a sponsor or legislative champion of these bills. Those who were such champions, like then Senator Hubert Humphrey, were not this simply (or even partly) because they had a "big Negro vote" at home to worry about (Minnesota in 1960 was less than one percent Negro). Between the casting of a Negro vote and the emergence of a civil

ROBERT N. C. NIX

AUGUSTUS F. HAWKINS

JOHN CONYERS

(Photos by Roland Mitchell)

rights bill, a vast and complicated institutional structure intervenes, including congressional committees, seniority system, party leadership, White House influence, the maneuvering of presidential candidates and the pressures of the mass media.

At the local level, political activity has a clear relationship to the incidence of at least certain kinds of abuses. The United States Commission on Civil Rights in its 1961 *Report*[57] examined twenty-one "black belt" counties (Southern counties in which the proportion of Negroes exceeded, in 1960, 50 percent), seventeen of which denied Negroes the right to vote almost entirely and four of which contained a substantial number (31 to 64 percent of the potential number) of registered Negroes.[58]

The commission compared these counties with respect to the civil rights status of Negroes in a variety of areas. Its conclusions were revealing. The principal differences between the two kinds of counties—the "nonvoting" and the "voting"—were in the administration of justice and education. In all the counties the schools were still firmly segregated, but those in the voting counties were of somewhat better quality (more were accredited by the state and fewer were in poor physical condition). In the voting counties, Negroes had served on juries and as justices of the peace (this was not true of most of the nonvoting counties); furthermore, the voting counties did not report any allegations of mob violence, police brutality or illegal police practices, while most of the nonvoting counties had a history of such abuses.[59]

In the other areas studied—housing, employment, public libraries, public accommodations and military establishments—"deprivations were found in all twenty-one counties, with little difference between the seventeen nonvoting and the four voting counties," according to the commission. "Negro housing in all counties was found invariably inferior to white housing and always segregated, with Negro quarters often lacking the public services, paved streets, street lighting, sewage disposal, and garbage collection that white neighborhoods were accorded."[60]

These findings were presaged twenty years earlier by Gunnar Myrdal who, writing a section entitled "What the Negro Gets Out of Politics" for his book, *An American Dilemma*, observed that "unquestionably the most important thing that Negroes get out of politics where they vote is legal justice—justice in the courts; police protection and protection against the persecution of the police. . . ."[61] To this ought to be added, perhaps, the role of politics as an avenue of upward social mobility for Negroes.

To be sure, in some places politics will have an even broader effect (Negro voting in Atlanta, for example, probably has produced more gains than would such activity in a rural or small-town area), but in general it is easier to overestimate than to underestimate the effects of political participation. This is not a counsel of despair but only a sobering reminder that political activity can only produce political gains and that other—and far more difficult—remedies must be sought for most of the problems of race relations in America.

NOTES

[1] Angus Campbell, et al., *The American Voter* (New York: John Wiley & Sons, 1960), p. 453.

[2] Donald R. Matthews and James W. Prothro, "Social and Economic Factors and Negro Voter Registration in the South," *American Political Science Review*, LVII (March, 1963), 27.

[3] See also comparable data in Oscar Glantz, "The Negro Voter in Northern Industrial Cities," *Western Political Quarterly*, XIII (December, 1960), 1004.

[4] Robert E. Lane, *Political Life* (Glencoe, Ill.: The Free Press, 1959) pp. 45–52.

[5] Edward C. Banfield and James Q. Wilson, *City Politics* (Cambridge: Harvard University Press, 1963), pp. 159–61.

[6] Campbell, et al., *op. cit.*, p. 453.

[7] United States Department of Commerce, Bureau of the Census, *Congressional District Data Book* (88th Congress).

[8] United States Commission on Civil Rights, *1961 Report*, "Voting," p. 5.

[9] United States Commission on Civil Rights, *1963 Report*, "Voting," pp. 14–15.

[10] United States Census of Population, 1960: General Social and Economic Characteristics, United States Summary: Final Report PC(1)–IC, Table 139.

[11] Matthews and Prothro, *op. cit.*, p. 43.

[12] *Ibid.*, p. 27.

[13] The early history of the white primary can be found in Paul Lewinson, *Race, Class and Party* (New York: Oxford University Press, 1932). It was declared unconstitutional in 1944 in *Smith vs. Allwright,* 321 U.S. 649 (1944).

[14] Only five Southern states—Alabama, Arkansas, Mississippi, Texas and Virginia—still had the poll tax in 1963. Even at the end of its constitutional history, it no doubt deterred voter registration among both whites and Negroes, but more so (how much more so no one can say) among the latter. See Donald R. Matthews and James W. Prothro, "Political Factors and Negro Voter Registration in the South," *American Political Science Review*, LVII (June, 1963), 357 ff.

[15] Matthews and Prothro, "Social and Economic Factors . . . ," *op. cit.*, p. 29. In some Southern communities, Negroes are allowed to vote in sizable numbers, despite the fact that they make up a large fraction of the population, because their vote can be manipulated by white politicians. See Alfred B. Clubok, et al., "The Manipulated Negro Vote: Some Pre-Conditions and Consequences," *Journal of Politics*, XXVI (1964), 112–29.

[16] Campbell, et al., *op. cit.*, p. 280.

[17] Matthews and Prothro, "Social and Economic Factors . . . ," *op. cit.*, p. 31.

[18] John H. Fenton and Kenneth H. Vines, "Negro Registration in Louisiana," *American Political Science Review*, LI (September, 1957), 704–713.

[19] Gunnar Myrdal, *An American Dilemma* (New York: Harper & Brothers, 1944), p. 496.

[20] *Ibid.*, and Henry Lee Moon, *Balance of Power: The Negro Vote* (Garden City, N.Y.: Doubleday & Co., 1948), pp. 18–19.

[21] Harold F. Gosnell, *Negro Politicians* (Chicago: University of Chicago Press, 1935), p. 34.

[22] Moon, *op. cit.*, p. 176, and Myrdal, *op. cit.*, pp. 488–500.

[23] Clarence A. Bacote, "The Negro Voter in Georgia Politics, Today," *Journal of Negro Education*, XXVI (Summer, 1957), 307–318; Jack Walker, "Negro Voting in Atlanta: 1953–1961," *Phylon*, XXIV (Winter, 1963), p. 380.

[24] Walker, *op. cit.*, p. 381.

[25] Harold F. Gosnell and Robert E. Martin, "The Negro as a Voter and Officeholder," *Journal of Negro Education*, XXXII (Fall, 1963), 420–21.

[26] Cf. H. Douglas Price, *The Negro and Southern Politics: A Chapter of Florida History* (New York: New York University Press, 1957); Douglas S. Gatlin, "A Case Study of a Negro Voters' League," Political Studies Program: *Research Reports*, No. 2, March, 1960 (University of North Carolina Department of Political Science); Henry Holloway, "The Negro and the Vote: The Case of Texas," *Journal of Politics*, XXIII (August, 1961), 526–56. These Negro voters' leagues are only effective if they operate within the consensual framework of the Negro community. Price (at page 72) notes that a "league endorsement of a wrong candidate in a contest where. a clear difference in attitude toward the Negro exists does not swing many Negro votes; rather it raises the question, 'who sold out?' " Holloway (at pages 539–40) observes that "Negro leaders don't have the power to deliver a bloc vote at will. . . . The Negro voter has his own fairly constant voting propensities which leaders disregard at risk to themselves."

[27] Walker, *op. cit.*, pp. 383–84.

[28] Richard H. Scammon, "How the Negroes Voted," *New Republic*, November 21, 1960, pp. 8–9.

[29] Bernard Berelson, Paul F. Lazarsfeld, and William N. McPhee, *Voting* (Chicago: University of Chicago Press, 1954) and Robert Agger, "Independents and Party

Identifiers: Characteristics and Behavior in 1952," in Eugene Burdick and Arthur G. Brodbeck, eds., *American Voting Behavior* (Glencoe, Ill.: The Free Press, 1959).

[30] Data courtesy of Professor Robert Peabody of Johns Hopkins University.

[31] James Q. Wilson, *Negro Politics: The Search for Leadership* (Glencoe, Ill.: The Free Press, 1959), pp. 22–33, 50–51.

[32] Gosnell, *op. cit.*, pp. 90–91, 180–84.

[33] Gosnell and Martin, *op. cit.*, pp. 423–24.

[34] Cf. James Q. Wilson, "Two Negro Politicians: An Interpretation," *Midwest Journal of Political Science* (November, 1960), 346–69.

[35] Wilson, *Negro Politics, op. cit.*, pp. 46, 320–21.

[36] John Hope II and Edward E. Shelton, "The Negro in the Federal Government," *Journal of Negro Education*, XXXII (Fall, 1963), 370.

[37] *The New York Times*, March 4, 1964, p. 27.

[38] The search for qualified Negroes to fill appointive political posts in a state government is discussed in Daniel Patrick Moynihan and James Q. Wilson, "Patronage in New York State: 1955–1959," *American Political Science Review* LVIII (June, 1964), pp. 286–301.

[39] Banfield and Wilson, *op. cit.*, pp. 303–08, discusses the general relationship between urban political systems and Negro political organization and leadership.

[40] Bradbury Seasholes and Frederic N. Cleveland, "Negro Political Participation in Two Piedmont Crescent Cities," in F. Stuart Chapin, Jr., and Shirley F. Weiss, eds., *Urban Growth Dynamics* (New York: John Wiley & Sons, 1962), pp. 265–70.

[41] Bacote, *op. cit.*, pp. 310–11.

[42] Seasholes and Cleveland, *op. cit.*, p. 266.

[43] Daniel C. Thompson, *The Negro Leadership Class* (Englewood Cliffs, N.J.: Prentice-Hall, Inc., 1963), pp. 112–14.

[44] V. O. Key, Jr., *Southern Politics in State and Nation* (New York: Alfred A. Knopf, 1950), pp. 286–91.

[45] On the Black Muslims generally, see E. U. Essien-Udom, *Black Nationalism* (Chicago: University of Chicago Press, 1962). Malcolm X was assassinated in 1965; the remnants of his organization have not shown any significant potential for political activity.

[46] Certain states with sizeable Negro populations were exceptions to this pattern. Michigan (9.2 percent Negro), New Jersey (8.5 percent Negro) and New York (8.4 percent Negro), have fairly strong civil rights laws and one of these—New York—was one of the first to act.

[47] White opinion is favorable to the granting of certain rights, hostile to the granting of others. The Louis Harris *Newsweek* poll, conducted in 1963, showed a majority (63 percent) of whites favoring the Kennedy civil rights bill but a majority (56 percent) opposing a Federal law forbidding discrimination in private housing. *Newsweek,* October 21, 1963, p. 45.

[48] Wilson, *Negro Politics, op. cit.*, pp. 150–55. In 1936 (the time of the last general religious census), the metropolitan portions of New York State were 28 percent Jewish.

[49] V. O. Key, Jr., *American State Politics* (New York: Alfred A. Knopf, 1956), p. 135.

[50] Matthews and Prothro, "Political Factors . . .", *op. cit.*, p. 362.

[51] *Ibid.*, pp. 360–61.

[52] Milton C. Cummings, "Congressman and the Electorate: A Study of House Elections in Presidential Years, 1920–1956," unpublished Ph.D. thesis, Department of Government, Harvard University (1960), pp. 406–15.

[53] David R. Mayhew, "Democrats and Republicans in the U. S. House of Representatives: A Study of Intra-Party Coalition Patterns in the Postwar Period," unpublished Ph. D. thesis, Department of Government, Harvard University (1964), pp. 161–71.

[54] Duncan MacRae, Jr., *Dimensions of Congressional Voting* (Berkeley and Los Angeles: University of California Press, 1958), pp. 269–71.

[55] Lewis A. Froman, Jr., *Congressmen and their Constituencies* (Chicago: Rand McNally, 1963), p. 93.

[56] James Q. Wilson, "The Changing Political Position of the Negro," in Arnold M. Rose, ed., *Assuring Freedom to the Free* (Detroit: Wayne State University Press, 1964), pp. 163–84.

[57] Book I, Part III. The Commission findings about these counties should be regarded as very tentative. It is not at all clear on what basis the counties were selected or how representative they are of all black belt counties.

[58] The four were Hancock and Liberty counties, Georgia; St. James parish, Louisiana, and Charles City, Virginia.

[59] U.S. Commission on Civil Rights, *1961 Report, op. cit.*, p. 187.

[60] *Ibid.*

[61] Myrdal, *op. cit.*, p. 497.